voices from criminal justice

This innovative text/reader for undergraduate criminal justice courses in the United States provides a companion or alternative to traditional texts. Instead of providing a "catalog of information" this book gives students rich insights into what it is like to work within the system (as practitioners) as well as from those who experience criminal justice as outsiders (as citizens, clients, jurors, probationers, or inmates). By providing qualitative and teachable articles from the perspective of those who experience the three components of the criminal justice system students will be better informed about the realities of the day-to-day job of criminal justice professionals. A second, but equally important, part of the readings asks that students look beyond the actual content of the articles and use a "critical thinking" perspective to develop their own thoughts about the functions of the criminal justice system on a broader societal level. The editors have used these articles and this approach very successfully in their large undergraduate criminal justice classes.

Heith Copes is an associate professor in the Department of Justice Sciences at the University of Alabama at Birmingham. His primary research uses qualitative methods to understand the decision to commit crime and deviance. His recent publications appear in *British Journal of Criminology, Crime and Justice: A Review of Research, Criminology and Public Policy*, and *Social Problems* and he has received funding from the National Institute of Justice.

Mark R. Pogrebin is a professor of criminal justice in the School of Public Affairs at the University of Colorado at Denver. He has authored and co-authored six books, the most recent, *Guns, Violence And Criminal Behavior*. He has published numerous journal articles and has thirty articles published in anthologies. He is a field researcher whose past studies have all used qualitative methods.

voices from criminal justice

thinking and reflecting on the system

edited by

heith copes
University of Alabama at Birmingham

mark r. pogrebin
University of Colorado, Denver

Routledge
Taylor & Francis Group

NEW YORK AND LONDON

First published 2012
by Routledge
711 Third Avenue, New York, NY 10017

Simultaneously published in the UK
by Routledge
2 Park Square, Milton Park, Abingdon, Oxon OX14 4RN

Routledge is an imprint of the Taylor & Francis Group, an informa business

Library of Congress Cataloging in Publication Data
Voices from criminal justice : thinking and reflecting on the system / edited by
Heith Copes, Mark R. Pogrebin.
 p. cm. — (Criminology and justice studies series)
 1. Criminal justice, Administration of—United States.   I. Copes, Heith.
 II. Pogrebin, Mark R.
 HV9950.V65 2011
 364.973—dc23

                                                              2011028568

ISBN: 978–0–415–88748–9 (hbk)
ISBN: 978–0–415–88749–6 (pbk)

Typeset in Minion
by RefineCatch Limited, Bungay, Suffolk, UK
Printed and bound in the United States of America on acid-free paper.
by Sheridan Books, Inc.

Heith Copes To Otha Lee Copes, my grandmother, who helped to keep me grounded.

Mark R. Pogrebin To my parents, Abraham and Esther Pogrebin, for teaching me about fairness and justice. You are greatly missed.

Contents

Conti documents the means by which police academy staff generated an interaction process that socializes recruits to the importance of obedience to authority before they can embrace the larger occupational culture.

Vera Sanchez and Rosenbaum examine how police officers socially construct race within Latino and African American neighborhoods.

Stenross and Kleinman analyze how detectives cope with the emotional labor of their jobs. They show that detectives had harder times dealing with the emotional displays of victims than they did with criminals.

Pogrebin and Poole explore the consequences of working undercover for police officers. They show that working undercover has a significant impact on how police interact with informants, criminals, other officers, and their families.

Bowen focuses on new types of plea-bargaining models as
compared to the more traditional.

Harris' study examines the court's organizational decision-making
process which determines the subsequent disposition that youth receive.
The criteria for keeping a case in the juvenile justice system or transferring
it to an adult criminal court are observed.

Frohman analyzes the prosecutorial discretion involved in preventing
a case from continuing beyond the arrest stage of the legal process,
focusing specifically on the district attorney's reasons for case
rejections.

McIntyre observes public defenders and the court setting in which they
practice their trade. She discusses the difficulties in practicing legal
defense work and the moral conflicts faced by public defenders who
represent guilty clients.

Rosecrance argues that probation presentence reports emphasize
some offender characteristics more than others. He explains how
a stereotyping process is used by officers who write these reports
and how current offense and prior criminal history determine a
scripted sentencing recommendation.

Christian explores family management of prison visitation with a
loved one and the collateral consequences of having a family
member serving time in prison.

Snyder's research examines incarcerated mothers' attempts at
maintaining relationships with their children through a visitation
program.

Preface

This book came about when the two us were discussing the value of ethnographic research for conveying the lived experiences of people. We recognized that many criminal justice students have never worked in the field and may have misguided notions of what it is like being a police officer, attorney, or correctional officer. The nature of most college courses dictates that students would not have the opportunity to learn what it is really like. This book fills this gap in the education of criminal justice students by presenting the perspectives of those who work within the criminal justice system (i.e., practitioners) and from those who experience it as outsiders (i.e., citizens, clients, jurors, probationers, or inmates).

In deciding which articles to include in the book, we evaluated them on their methodological rigor, ability to artfully portray the perspective of those being studied, and readability for students. By providing firsthand experiences of those who work in or are affected by the criminal justice system these articles will inform readers about what they should expect when selecting a career in criminal justice. In addition, these articles are precisely the types of scholarly work that students enjoy reading. It has been our experience that students are much more receptive and willing to consume research that provides firsthand accounts of those being studied than they are general textbooks or research involving complex statistical models. Thus, those who adopt the book can expect and assume that students will read the assigned text.

We also believe that these articles will allow professors to better develop students' abilities to think critically about criminal justice issues. To foster such critical thinking we have included questions after each article. These questions are designed to stimulate course discussion and to encourage students to make connections among the other articles and their own experiences. We recognize that sometimes it is necessary to test students to ensure that they have read the articles. Thus, we have also developed "fact based" questions to supplement the book. For those interested in copies of these questions please contact saleshss@taylorandfrancis.com.

Acknowledgements

We appreciate very much the support of Routledge in providing us the opportunity to put this book together. In particular, we thank Steve Rutter, our editor, for his patience, insights, and enthusiasm for the book. We also thank our research assistants Anastasia Brown at the University of Alabama at Birmingham and Alexander Dahl at the University of Colorado, Denver for putting up with a number of tedious, cryptic, and perhaps unreasonable requests. They have been patient, good natured, and diligent in their aid to us and we dare say that this book would have a publication date far in the future were it not for their efforts. We would also like to thank the reviewers of our manuscript prior to its publication: Brian Payne of Georgia State University, Shawna Cleary of University of Central Oklahoma, Jacinta Gau of University of Central Florida, San Bernardino, Joe Kuhns of University of North Carolina, Charlotte, and Catherine Marcum of Georgia Southern University. Their advice and recommendations on how to improve our manuscript for teaching were invaluable.

Introduction: Thinking and Reflecting on Criminal Justice Issues

Heith Copes and Mark R. Pogrebin

In the past several decades the size of the criminal justice system and the number of people interested in pursuing criminal justice careers has grown tremendously. Each year more and more students are majoring in criminal justice or enrolling in criminal justice classes. Introductory courses, once small and filled typically with majors, now seat large numbers of students from a variety of disciplines. In addition, the number of universities in the United States with doctoral programs in criminal justice and/or criminology has grown from 20 to 36 in the past 15 years. More people are graduating with doctorates in criminal justice/criminology than at any time in history. Correspondingly, the amount of research on criminal justice related topics has increased dramatically. We now know more about the function of criminal justice bureaucracies and those who work in them than ever before.

While this rise in attention to criminal justice has brought about many positive changes, there is also a downside. With more majors and more information to cover in criminal justice courses, the amount of in-depth, critical examinations of the system, which is vital for effective teaching, has been hampered. Those who teach introductory courses in criminal justice typically rely on large textbooks that cover a wide range of topics, but with little depth (Withrow, Weible and Bonnett 2004). Such textbooks eschew in-depth understanding of criminal justice occupations and issues and critical thinking for summary overviews. This trend is neither desired nor necessary.

In response to the changing nature of criminal justice courses we have put together this reader with two goals in mind. The first goal is to provide students with a richer, more realistic understanding of the lived experiences of those who work in the criminal justice system and those who find themselves in the system in roles (i.e., citizens, victims, or offenders). We think it is important that students of criminal justice know what it is really like to work in one of the three core components of the criminal justice system (policing, courts, and corrections). Traditional textbooks rarely provide insights into the day-to-day experiences of the people who make up the criminal justice system (as employees). The articles we have selected buck this trend by using ethnographic methods to understand the system from those within it.

The second goal is to encourage more critical thinking about criminal justice issues. Traditional textbooks are geared primarily to provide summary overviews of knowledge in a given field. Textbook writers are forced to forgo depth of coverage so that they can include the large amount of material for a subject. Such styles of textbooks lend themselves to multiple choice, true/false, and short answer questions. Thus, the ability to think critically and move beyond rote memorization is devalued. To overcome this limitation of most textbooks we place a stronger emphasis on making connections among the readings and on thinking about the root causes and unintended consequences of criminal justice issues and policies.

In selecting articles for this reader we sought to find those that could best help us reach our goals. With little doubt there are a number of methodologies that can offer insights into what it is like for police officers to arrest suspects, attorneys to defend clients they know are guilty, and for families of inmates to try and make sense of the confinement of their loved ones. We think, however, that the best suited methodology involves allowing study participants the opportunity to express their ideas, concerns, and thoughts in their own words. Instead of asking them to fill in boxes to predetermined categories on pen and paper questionnaires, we see greater value in letting individuals tell their own stories of their own volition. Thus, the articles we selected all focus on ethnographies. Additionally, all articles were trimmed for readability and to save space.

Providing Lived Experiences

Students majoring in criminal justice or criminology do so primarily to obtain an edge in landing a job as police officers, correctional officers, attorneys, probation officers, or some other criminal justice position. Except for those few who worked as interns during their college career most are unfamiliar with the day-to-day aspects of the job. Most educators would agree that it is important for students to understand what to expect when choosing or starting a new career. This compilation of articles includes information about what the day-to-day aspects of the job are like and how they are viewed by those outside their profession. While college textbooks provide some insights into what the job may be like, they seldom provide an insider's perspective. When they do it usually appears in small boxes separated from the text. Thus, professors are assigned the task of conveying what these jobs entail. A task that often proves difficult, given that many professors have not worked as a criminal justice professional in the field.

One of the primary goals of this reader is to fill this gap in the education of criminal justice students. Specifically, we have selected articles that provide insights into the three major aspects of criminal justice (policing, courts, and corrections) by presenting the perspectives of those who work within the system (i.e., practitioners) and from those who experience it as outsiders (i.e., citizens, clients, jurors, probationers, or inmates). All of the included articles use ethnographic and/or fieldwork methodologies because such methods are ideally suited to articulate how actors (in this case criminal justice practitioners and outsiders) make sense of and understand their worlds (Spradley 1979, 1980). That is, each article provides the words and lived experiences of those who work in or who are affected by the criminal justice system. We have selected each article for their methodological rigor, ability to artfully portray the perspective of those being studied, and readability for students.

By providing empirical research from the perspective of those who experience the three components of the criminal justice system, students (and possibly professors) will be better informed about the realities of the day-to-day job of criminal justice professionals. This includes discussing what it is "really" like to work as a police officer after going through formal training, how detectives handle the emotions of dealing with death, how probation officers determine if their clients are telling the truth, how prosecutors discredit witnesses to win decisions, and how women who work in jail deal with the stress and strains of doing so. In addition, these readings will provide insights into what it is "really" like for young minorities to interact with police, how victims of domestic violence interpret the actions and demeanor of responding officers, how jurors view various types of attorneys and how this influences their decisions, how women experience incarceration, how juveniles experience probation, and what sex offenders think about their sentencing.

Too often when studying the various components of the criminal justice system people focus solely on the experiences of those who work in such positions. While much can be gained from their perspective, it does not provide a full picture of what happens in each stage of the criminal justice system. As such, if we are to understand the role of police, courts, and corrections in society it is important to understand how practitioners in each are viewed by those they come in contact with. One may ask, why should we care what the public, especially the offending public, thinks about police, courts, or corrections? The answer is simple. By allowing these types of people to present their perspectives, police, judges, attorneys, and correctional officers (and others) can better evaluate the impact and efficacy of their policies and perspectives, a goal for which all criminal justice organizations should aspire. In addition, understanding the perspective of others will provide those working in the criminal justice system insights into how their actions will affect the people over which they have power. Knowing how bureaucratic policies are experienced by outsiders will likely go a long way in maintaining, or establishing, legitimacy of the criminal justice system.

Critical Thinking

A second, but equally important, part of the readings requests that the students look beyond the actual content of the articles and use a "critical thinking" perspective to develop their own thoughts about the functions of the criminal justice system on a broader societal level. Critical thinking is not an easily defined concept. We all "know" what it means, but have a hard time describing it when asked directly. To get some clarity on the issue we use the American Philosophical Association's (Facione 1990) conceptualization, which says:

> We understand critical thinking to be purposeful, self-regulatory judgment which results in interpretation, analysis, evaluation, and inference, as well as explanation of the evidential, conceptual, methodological, criteriological, or contextual considerations upon which that judgment is based. CT [Critical Thinking] is essential as a tool of inquiry. As such, CT is a liberating force in education and a powerful resource in one's personal and civic life. While not synonymous with good thinking, CT is a pervasive and self-rectifying human phenomenon.

In short, "The successful application of these core CT skills requires that one take into reasoned consideration the evidence, methods, contexts, theories, and criteria which, in effect, define specific disciplines, fields, and areas of human concern" (Facione 2000:65). Few of us have inherently developed these characteristics. Instead, they are learned and cultivated. This implies that anyone, and everyone, has the potential to think critically if encouraged and reinforced to do so.

One of our goals when constructing this reader was to encourage readers to develop and hone their critical thinking skills, especially when thinking about the criminal justice system. We think it is important for readers to analyze how all of the components of the criminal justice system affect the larger society they operate in. Thus, we encourage readers to think bigger and more abstractly about the readings. While much can be gained simply from reading each article on its own, we think greater pedagogical benefits come when people seek to make connections among the various articles and other issues raised in class.

Consider the following example. Two articles in the policing section (Stenross and Kleinman and Stephens and Sinden) give insights into police-victim interactions, but from different perspectives. Stephens and Sinden interviewed victims of domestic violence to determine their perceptions of police. They found that victims of domestic abuse became increasingly disillusioned by police officers with each interaction. Victims claimed that police were often detached and demeaning during the interactions. While these findings may paint a negative portrait of police, such attitudes are more easily understood when considering the findings of Stenross and Kleinman. They showed that police officers found the emotional labor of dealing with victims to be quite difficult. It was difficult because they could not easily dismiss the feelings and emotions of victims. Thus, upset victims often took an emotional toll on officers. So much so, that they often tried to shield themselves from the victims. This is but one example of how the various readings relate to one another and how readers should be looking for connections among them.

To encourage critical thinking, we offer brief comments after each article that will introduce readers to issues to think about and reflect on when using a critical eye. We do not mean for these passages to be exhaustive in their questioning. Instead, they are designed to whet the appetite for thinking critically and to stimulate discussion in class. Consistent with the dictates of critical thinking we expect that students and professors are bringing their own experiences and interpretations to the readings and, thus, will be able to provide their own unique insights and connections as they read the articles.

Using This Anthology

The size of introductory criminal justice classes should not prevent professors from incorporating a book of readings that will enhance the descriptive information found in the majority of introductory texts. The purpose of this anthology and the advantages for exposing students to the in-depth content for each component of the criminal justice system has been discussed in the preceding pages. However, before being found guilty of redundancy, we turn to recent thoughts on teaching lower-level criminal justice classes by Garcia (2011), who discusses her insightful goals for students:

Textbooks are adequate for a number of lower division courses, but they allow students to be lazy because they do much of what students should do for themselves—consume a wide variety of topics and synthesize the information in a meaningful way.

(23)

In short, Garcia desires her students to be critical thinkers, as most professors wish their students to become.

The issue of how to accomplish this lofty goal when using a text and a reader for a large introductory criminal justice class is often perplexing. We offer a brief explanation for accomplishing this task in order for lower-division students to become familiar with the realities of the justice system.

We have found it best to use a condensed version of the criminal justice text assigned to the class. Doing so allows for students to get a comprehensive overview of the three components of the system without the large number of pages. Additionally, and perhaps most importantly for students, it will also keep book costs down. After covering a particular subject section, we introduce the students to five readings about practitioners and five articles about those who experience the actions of the practitioners. This allows students to "experience" what it is like for practitioners and those they interact with when carrying out their duties.

To ensure that students read the articles, we either ask for volunteers or assign readings to students to present in class. In larger classes we often assign two students per article. We allot a certain amount of time to each presenter and ask them to highlight their article and be prepared to ask the class three in-depth questions or raise three major issues. This usually gets the rest of the class involved in the conversation. Of course, each instructor has to put time limits on each presentation and class discussion based on what they see most appropriate for their classes. Based on our experiences using this pedagogical technique, students' responses have indicated a much higher degree of class involvement and more inclusive participation for the class as a whole. We replicate this procedure for each section of the criminal justice system covered in the course. Inevitably our student class evaluations favor the anthology's real life subject analysis over our lecture format for covering the text material.

A great advantage we have found when using our anthology in this way is that it has allowed us to become observers of student input and it places them in the new position of facilitator, at least during the article discussion time. They often find this empowering. Further, exams have reflected an increased understanding of the complexities that exist within criminal justice agencies and external policies that are formulated by various governmental bodies that directly affect the operation of the three components of the criminal justice system. In sum, we have observed a raised awareness of the functions and dysfunctions of the system by our students, and an increased expectation for their commentary and analysis of the existing problems that our society faces in crime control. We believe these improvements in student understanding and engagement is due to the use of articles that present the "lived experiences" of those who work in the criminal justice system and those who go through it more than our inherent teaching ability. It is our hope that others who use this book will have similar success.

References

Facione, Peter. 1990. *Critical Thinking: A Statement of Expert Consensus for Purposes of Educational Assessment and Instruction*. Millbrae, CA: California Academic Press.

Facione, Peter. 2000. "The Disposition Toward Critical Thinking: Its Character, Measurement, and Relationship to Critical Thinking Skill." *Informal Logic* 20:61–84.

Garcia, C. A. 2011. "Teaching Tip: found! Teaching Treasure in ASC Meeting Registration Bags." *The Criminologist* 36 (3, May/June):22–24.

Spradley, James. 1979. *The Ethnographic Interview*. New York: Holt, Rinehart, & Winston.

Spradley, James. 1980. *Participant Observation*. New York: Holt, Rinehart, & Winston.

Withrow, Brian, Kerry Weible, and Jennifer Bonnett. 2004. "Aren't They All the Same? A Comparative Analysis of Introductory Criminal Justice Textbooks." *Journal of Criminal Justice Education* 15:1–18.

1 Police

The articles in this section are representative of qualitative studies that have been conducted on law enforcement officers and those they police. Because police are the most visible criminal justice agency, they are frequently in the public eye. Interest in their role within society has long been popularized by movies and television shows, which have enjoyed wide audiences on a national level. The popularity of police issues holds true for the news media, both print and television, and is reflective of the public fascination with this occupation. We believe that much of the curiosity about the world of law enforcement also has had an effect on social science research. We would venture to speculate that there has been more research and published journal articles, academic books, and journalistic accounts about the police profession than any other component of the criminal justice system.

The five articles that constitute the police practitioners section of this anthology offer insights into an array of subjects within the police occupation. The topics these articles address include police socialization (in the academy and on the job), the importance of emotional maintenance when interacting with the public, the influence of race and gender on the day-to-day life of officers, and the difficulties in being an undercover officer. While there are certainly numerous other topics that could have been addressed, we think that these topics exhibit the variation in how officers think about their roles as police and how they go about their day-to-day jobs. It should become clear that each of the issues raised in the articles (socialization, emotion work, hiring practices, and interacting with citizens) all are important aspects of policing. What is often less clear are the various unintended consequences of the actual behaviors and thoughts of police. As you read the articles you should think about these issues, even if not discussed directly in the article. Doing so will not only challenge prevailing notions of proper policing but may also allow you to seek solutions to emerging problems.

We also provide five articles that offer a glimpse into how citizens perceive police. These articles reflect the views of a range of individuals who have come in contact with police including those who sought help from police and those who were sought out by police for perceived wrongdoings. Needless to say, the reasons for interacting with police have a strong effect on perceptions about the quality of service police provide. Young males who see their interactions with police as oppressive and instigated by others, female victims of domestic violence who sought help and protection from police, secondary victims of homicide and their desire to get more from detectives, and domestic violence offenders who are being confronted (and arrested) all evaluate and understand police differently. By hearing the voices of citizens (victims and offenders alike) police officers can gain insights into how they are perceived by the public and, ideally, how they can be more effective at their jobs.

A Practitioners

1

A Visigoth System: Shame, Honor, and Police Socialization

Norman Conti

Abstract: *Conti documents the socialization process of new recruits. He shows that police academy staff members believe that recruits must possess a mentality of obedience to authority before they are ready to understand and embrace the larger police occupational culture. By attending a twenty-one week police academy, Conti was able to understand the moral career of the recruits as they learned to think like police officers by participating in a trying socialization process. He suggests that academy staff sought to demean recruits so that they could then build them back up in the image of "good" police officers.*

Skolnick (1964, 43) has argued that analysis of the cognitive propensities of police officers is "necessary to understand the practical dilemma ... [of] maintain[ing] order under the democratic rule of Jaw." In his discussion of the "working personality" of police officers, he noted that

> the police, as a result of combined features of their social situation, tend to develop ways of looking at the world distinctive to themselves, cognitive lenses through which to see situations and events. The strength of those lenses may be weaker or stronger depending upon certain conditions but they are grounded upon the same axis.
>
> (Skolnick 1964, 42)

Socialization begins during academy training, as a tremendously complicated rite of passage composed of a series of instructions, ceremonies, and tests through which the recruit is elevated from the status of ordinary civilian to that of police officer. Hopper (1977) explains that the technical skill and legal knowledge on which the formal curriculum is founded are not sufficient to prepare recruits for their upcoming role. Recruits must learn to play the part of police officer, anticipating what "others will expect of them and what they should expect of others" (Hopper 1977, 149). A key element of the training involves a moral socialization in the norms of copresence that accompany the police status.

This article develops Hopper's notions of a rite of passage and expectations in an ethnographic examination of an ongoing process of reintegrative shaming (Braithwaite 2007) that facilitates a moral career through which academy staff members seek to sensitize recruits to an interaction order of obedience to authority. Moreover, I am attempting to reconcile Skolnick's conception of the police officer's working personality with the more recent discourse on the diversity of police culture by documenting the interactive techniques through which a metropolitan police academy endeavors to generate some commonality in perspective through ritual and symbolism. The process of reintegrative shaming within the moral career is a dialectic in which mortifications of self in conjunction with the potential for status enhancement are, to use Skolnick's phrase, the axis on which the recruit's cognitive lenses are grounded.

Self-Defense

This research is both justified and inspired by what Alpert and Dunham (2004) call *authority maintenance theory*—an explanation for their findings on police–civilian encounters that culminate in violence. The theory explicates "the exaggerated role that authority plays in police–civilian interactions" (Alpert and Dunham 2004, 171) and is particularly interesting because it shifts the analysis away from psychological characteristics and personal attitudes of police in general and instead focuses on an interaction order of power (i.e., the officer's authority) and either deference (i.e., the civilian's submission) or resistance (i.e., the civilian's failure to submit) as a model for understanding police use of force. The authors contend that instances of police–civilian violence are the result of status threats whereby the officer's demeanor toward the civilian and its reciprocation are either generating or suppressing conflict. Their model fits with earlier research that documents the importance of "maintaining an edge" and being "one up" on civilians to ensure personal safety among police officers (Sykes and Brent 1980).

Van Maanen ([1978] 1999) explains that every civilian interaction opens police responsibility for public order to disgrace, embarrassment, and insult so they internalize a role that requires them to perpetually command their milieu. For police, civilian encounters are moral contests where the authority of the state is either recognized, rejected, or left uncertain. He argues that the ability to maintain command status during a civilian interaction is vital to officers because "the authority of the state is also his personal authority, and is, by necessity, a matter of some concern to him" (Van Maanen [1978] 1999, 353). Personal affronts challenge the police definition of the immediate situation, so a disrespectful civilian is a threat to the proper police drama as presented in everyday interactions. Any substantial status threat leads an officer to discredit the civilian with the label of "asshole" (Van Maanen [1978] 1999). Labeling a civilian an asshole describes and explains the individual has a set of motives contrary to the orderly function of society. Van Maanen notes,

> In this sense, the police function in street interaction is not unlike that of a psychiatrist diagnosing a patient. Both explain perceived deviancy in terms of a characterological genesis. Hence, the label implies that a different, inappropriate, and strange motivational scheme is used by the "type of person" known as an asshole. In this manner an act is made understandable by stripping away whatever meaning might be attributed to it by the actor. Thus, to make sense of the act is to assume that it does not make sense, that it is stupid, irrational, wrong, deranged, or dangerous. Any other assumption would be too dangerous.
>
> (Van Maanen [1978] 1999, 361)

Stigmatization dehumanizes the asshole and frames any behavior, or its motivation, as both senseless and threatening while the police officer is recognized as a force of order maintaining control over the ever present potential for chaos.

Goffman (1961b, 80) noted that even for civilians, encountering people who are awkward, unkempt, wrong moving, or talking is to be in the presence of "a dangerous giant, a destroyer of worlds." He recognized that deviants of this type posses the power to generate interpersonal and organizational chaos by contradicting our definition of the immediate situation (Goffman 1969). Orderly interaction is essential for everyone involved in an encounter because threats to the interaction order disrupt social life and undermine the selves of those involved (Gronfrien 1993); however, for police this circumstance takes on a professional significance. Disrespect toward the police is a situational impropriety taken as symptomatic of some moral failing on the part of the offender (Goffman 1983). It is also an attack on the professional self of the officer and in some cases can generate violence.

While it is unreasonable to assume that all police officers are the same and only recognize one way of doing things or possess a single working personality, there must still be a number of cultural elements that transcend difference and unite the whole. Moreover, the claim that officers are looking for signs that civilians are upholding their end of the interaction order and reacting when evidence is presented to the contrary does not necessitate a monolithic culture. Alpert and Dunham's theory excludes police who do not fully subscribe to an overly authoritarian conception of their role because they are probably not the officers responsible for the violence constituting the data. Authority maintenance theory allows room for intercultural variation because even though all properly socialized officers will recognize a breach of the interaction order, they will not all share the same threshold for tolerating disrespect or respond in the same manner in a given circumstance (i.e., one officer may be less prone to escalate minor conflict than another). However, authority maintenance theory is still effective in explaining encounters that result in violence, and this research describes one of the social mechanisms at its root.

Method

The context of this ethnography is a recruit class at the Rockport Police Department's training academy. The class consisted of seventy recruits and lasted for twenty-one weeks from late 1999 through early 2000. The data were collected through participant observation over the course of training. Access to the site was achieved through a written request to the chief of police that detailed a specific interest in police training and socialization. The department accommodated this request with the stipulation that the recruits' participation would have to be voluntary and anonymous. Recruit dossiers and other academy documentation were also made available.

I took an overt role and was identified to all present as a sociologist working on a research project and when questioned about topic and motive I claimed a general interest in communication patterns. Since it was mainly a classroom environment, detailed observations were recorded without much notice because with all of the recruits taking notes on the curriculum I was just one person, among seventy others, writing in a notebook. In addition to observing as much of the formal training as possible, I went to great lengths to frequently eat lunch with the recruits and maintain a presence during their periodic breaks. These experiences allowed me to observe and interact with the recruits at informal moments when they could be more candid in their discussions of the training.

This article is not necessarily about the moral career *as experienced* by police recruits. The analysis and conceptualization were not accomplished through detailed phenomenological interviews with the recruits. While an attempt to capture the essence of being a recruit in that fashion would be extremely valuable and is a logical direction for future research, this article explicates the moral career as a path laid out before recruits through the formal and informal elements of training. I am attempting to address ritual in the way that Waddington (1999, 295) analyzed bar room cop talk as "rhetoric that gives meaning to experience and sustains occupational self-esteem."

Police Training, the Moral Career, and Reintegrative Shaming

Moral career is defined as "the regular sequence of changes that career entails in the person's self and his framework of imagery for judging himself and others" (Goffman 1961a, 128). The consecutive alterations of self within the moral career are turning points in worldview marked by particular happenings (i.e., institutionalization or in this case admission to a police academy) that illustrate the link between self and society through which a public event, such as a shift in social category (i.e., from civilian to either mental patient or police recruit), has a very powerful effect on the self. Goffman identifies prepatient, inpatient, and expatient as the phases of the moral career of the mental patient. The academy staff attempts to channel recruits into a moral career path composed of three similar phases: candidate, recruit, and rookie. The recruit phase begins on entering the academy and entails the navigation of three distinct stages of self—noncivilian, paramilitary, and anticipatory police—each with specific potentials for degradation and elevation. Though inclusion in this process is voluntary and competitive, recruits might still only cynically follow the path, resisting elements of the indoctrination as they proceed.

Goffman's examples of transformations of self within the moral career are accomplished through largely negative means and do not include any discussion of potentials for status enhancement. He explains the onset of the moral career as follows:

> The recruit . . . begins a series of abasements, degradations, humiliations, and profanations of the self. His self is systematically, if often unintentionally, mortified. He begins some radical shifts in his moral career, a career composed of the progressive changes that occur in the beliefs that he has concerning himself and the significance of others.
>
> (Goffman 1961a, 14)

Since Goffman's discussion of the moral career is based more on his observations of the institutional environment rather than in-depth interviews with its inhabitants, his analysis, like this one, lacks the more immediate perspective of the recruit that other methods could provide. Still, many of Goffman's observations are echoed in recent police memoirs. Gallo (2001) discusses the change in conceptions of self and other metaphorically in terms of dreams, illusions, and conceptions of reality. She notes,

However quirky Chicago cops seem, they begin their career just like law-enforcement officers everywhere—with a grueling, intensive program at the Training Academy. It's a place designed to turn reasonably normal young men and women into cops, a place where dreams die and are born again, where illusions are trashed and replaced with a tenuous hold on reality, or what's real in the eyes of the Police Department.

(Gallo 2001, 16)

Defining the Situation

The noncivilian stage is framed by the argument that participation in the academy is a status enhancement because it offers an opportunity to achieve the idealized position of police officer. Instructors claimed that every seat in the classroom was a privilege and a blessing because close to twenty-five hundred people had taken the civil service examination and there were only seventy recruits in the cohort. Seats in this particular class were especially valuable because it was made up of the last batch of recruits to be taken off of the list of eligible applicants. Ironically, even in their elevation to the recruit status, this fact served to stigmatize the cohort with a "bottom of the barrel" label that would haunt them throughout the training and eventually be used to explain their greater than usual failure rate.

Any further elevation of self was contingent on submission to the training regime and acceptance of the subordination it entailed. The dialectical relationship between participation and subordination was apparent in the departmental identification cards issued for access to the building. Recruits were warned not to display the IDs outside of the academy because in the past, they had been flashed in attempts to convey police authority. However, since a police recruit in the city of Rockport has absolutely no police powers whatsoever, this was ill advised. Furthermore, the staff threatened that if they discovered such activity the recruit would be in some peril. They explained that the recruit ID was a temporary pass providing access to the police milieu and not a badge of honor.

A training officer told a horror story about a female recruit who refused to present the institutional guard posted at the entrance to police headquarters with her ID. It was the day of graduation and the recruit insisted that her official police uniform was all the identification she needed to get in. The commander of the academy discovered this and expelled her just hours before she was to be sworn in. The incident was presented as an ultimate degradation that resulted from assuming above one's position—literally for failing to present the correct self. In addition, it was a reminder that recruit status stands, absolute, until the moment of graduation when the academy comes to its official close. The recruits shuddered at the idea of completing all of the training that lay ahead just to be dismissed at the very last minute for a disciplinary violation.

As training began, the staff marked the onset of the noncivilian stage with the assertion that "You don't own your lives anymore" and "You are not normal anymore." The Deputy Chief of the department reinforced this in an interrogation of the recruits' motives for attending his ethics class. After listening to a number of recruits give accounts emphasizing service to the community and learning the craft of policing, he stopped them and explained,

> You're here because you have to be! You're basically prisoners. If you try to leave I'll shoot you in the back and I'll be justified.

Later he asked the class if any of them knew who the Visigoths were. When it was apparent that none of them did, he explained,

> The Visigoths were a Germanic tribe where leadership was determined by suffering. Whoever could take the most punishment got to be a leader. That's how this academy works.

In these two exchanges the Deputy Chief was both playfully mocking the degradation of the recruit status as well as noting the potential honor that their current trial would yield. Prisoner and Visigoth metaphors make it obvious that the recruit is in a rather unusual position, beyond the civilian experience but still not fully secure within the police organization.

Such sentiments were codified into deference rituals such as the practice of posting. Any time recruits were out of their classroom and an officer or civilian approached them they were to yell out "POST!" then jump up against the nearest wall and stand at attention until they were told to relax. The staff made it clear that, while outside of the classroom, the recruits should always be on the alert for "nonrecruits" because failure to post was a very serious violation of academy standards. Technically, with this stipulation, recruits could find themselves posting for criminal suspects on their way to or from interrogations. So, in these encounters, recruits are degraded to a status subordinate to even the most stigmatized of civilians.

Routine practices such as posting, a ritual adopted from military training, consist of specific prescriptions for movement and gesture employed while taking part in common interactions that perpetually illustrate the recruit's status. Every time they came into contact with a staff member, or for that matter anyone who was not a fellow recruit, they were forced to symbolically present a degraded self at the onset of the encounter. Even in casual interaction with other recruits the informality is solely the product of the common degraded status. Normally, after fifty minutes of class, instruction ceased and the recruits were granted some free time. These moments served as a much-needed breaks from the monotony of the average lecture while also being a chance for the group to informally discuss and evaluate the merit of what they were being taught. Breaks functioned as free or critical spaces (McCorkel 1998) during which the recruit moved from the position of being subject of discourse and attempted to pass judgment on his or her surroundings (i.e., expressing greater agency while still operating within the bounds of the academy).

Though less tense during breaks, there was still an anxiety about potential posting within the group. This anxiety was well illustrated by recruits cocking their heads toward the distant sound of an unseen officer's shoes, as they would come clicking in their general direction. The recruits seemed to grow ever more nervous as the foot-steps approached until an officer either rounded the corner and came into their field of vision or went in another direction. At the first sight of a nonrecruit the group would snap sharply out of their relaxation and post vigorously.

Scheff (2000, 254) notes that "shame is our moral gyroscope" and signals trouble in a relationship, and in terms of impression management the police academy is an environment of immediate consequences where situational improprieties (i.e., failure to show deference and present the proper recruit self) yield a shame that constitutes a deadly threat to the social bond (i.e., expulsion from training). Recruits are in a situation where they must constantly anticipate and avoid shame because the formal reaction to it is an extreme degradation of self (i.e., the loss of the recruit status or the failure to achieve police certification). Rituals such as the presentation of IDs and posting embody the formal core of the academy's structure.

For the first two months of the training, recruits wear indistinct black pants and white shirts that they were required to purchase from ordinary stores prior to the start of training. Though uniform in appearance, there was nothing reflective of the police status in these clothes. However, after a number of weeks in this ensemble, presenting a well-maintained noncivilian self, recruits were issued standard police uniforms. While these uniforms lacked any of the insignia of active officers (i.e., badges, patches, and etc.), the recruits were visibly excited at this milestone.

Ceremonial Degradation of the Police Recruit

Both Van Maanen (1973) and Fielding (1988) have observed that recruits with military or police experience enter the academy with the distinct advantage of knowing how to function under a training regime of strict discipline and deference. Among this subgroup of veteran recruits, about half of the class, there were a select few who had actually completed the full course of the Rockport academy in training for jobs with the housing or transit police. For these recruits, as well as some others who had been through an abbreviated version of the academy in training for institutional guard (i.e., jailor) or bailiff positions, the training was just an extension of what they had experienced only a few years earlier. The veteran recruits with both military and criminal justice experience were presented by the staff as a core of role models for the civilian recruits to emulate and elected to the various leadership positions within the class (i.e., class president, vice president, and squad leaders).

The gym staff constantly stressed the importance of upper body strength in police work and explained that behaviors such as smoking, arriving late for roll call, eating junk food, forgetting a piece of equipment, and wearing a misaligned uniform were all indicative of limited upper body strength. Since the staff was responsible for preparing recruits for "the streets," they would have to *help* any of the recruits witnessed exhibiting the civilian characteristics of a weak upper body by assigning them push-ups. To demonstrate the proper technique for doing push-ups, they called out the veteran recruits in groups. An instructor hollered, "Do we have any jarheads in here! Get over there and show them how you do push-ups Marines!" Recruits from one service branch were called out immediately after the previous group had finished in a rather intense exhibition of military discipline. Push-ups were counted out rhythmically and within the tension of the moment the veteran role models forged a standard.

To be effective within the training, reintegrative shaming must generate a process of role taking where recruits accept the perspective of the training staff and begin generating self sentiments of pride and shame based on how well, or ill, they measure up to the identity standards presented in the training. A dynamic variation of the looking glass self (Cooley 1922) is observed in the full-length mirror placed at the back of the main classroom with text at the top that read, "Before you can help others you must take care of yourself." At the bottom was another sign reading "P.R.I.D.E." (i.e., the official values of the Rockport Police Department: professionalism, respect, integrity, dedication, and excellence). Recruits were expected to stand in front of the mirror to take the role of the staff and anticipate a reaction to their presentation of self.

In confrontation with the gym staff, the cohort faced a most severe degradation of the civilian status. They would aggressively criticize recruits for their behavior, wardrobe, diet, and physique in the fashion of a Drill Sergeant at Boot Camp. The importance of a "squared away" appearance was said to be crucial because criminals are less likely to "try their luck" when faced with an officer wearing a properly maintained uniform and who looked to be in excellent physical condition. Once it was made clear that recruits should be continually cultivating a paramilitary presentation of self they began compulsively attending to their appearances, carrying shoe polish and lint brushes as surrogates for the guns and handcuffs they were yet to attain. This circumstance fits with Fielding's (1988, 61) observation that it is through "attitudes to physical standards of dress and deportment [that] the recruit learns the most basic aspect of the organization, its notion of compliance."

In response to the emphasis on dress and deportment, a system of informal peer socialization evolved where recruits would take the staff role and examine their colleagues' appearance in advance of the staff's arrival. Initially it was only the veteran recruits who offered these critiques, but over time as the others progressed beyond the noncivilian stage, they too began engaging more actively in the evaluations. These interactions were practice for negotiating the frequent encounters with staff in which they would receive immediate feedback on their effectiveness at maintaining the requisite police manners and standards. Late in the training, before an official inspection, two recruits were deeply scrutinizing each other to ensure the proper paramilitary presentation of self. During this informal ceremony the recruits were quoting lines from the classic boot camp scenes in *Full Metal Jacket*, a constant point of reference among the cohort. As the class president, a former Marine, and a juvenile detention officer straightened one of his friends uniforms, he joked, "You really look like shit today Leonard." Based on the ensuing laughter, the critique seemed to be a playful degradation of their former civilian statuses as well as a poke at the more degrading elements of the training structure, based on the scene between "Joker" and "Gomer Pyle/Leonard."

Initially, the gym staff conducted a baseline evaluation to determine how far the recruits were from the physical standards required for graduations. The overall standard was based on scoring in the fortieth percentile for fitness based on age. When many of the recruits failed this test, an instructor bellowed at them:

Your goal was to have 60 percent of the population be in better shape than you and you failed! How do you expect to go out there and arrest somebody? This is just a taste of what you are going to get over the next twenty-one weeks. If you don't want to work, take a hike now. If you need to do better we'll get you there, that's our job but you have to be willing to work.

In this admonition the instructor was pointing out that while the potential for violence in policing necessitates that officers should be physically superior to civilians, this group of recruits was not even on par with them. Throughout the training the staff discredits the civilian status in favor of the paramilitary discipline of the training regime in order to, as Paes-Machado and Albuquerque (2002, 71) explain "wash the soul of the remains of the old civilian condition."

Once the recruits accepted the basic requirements of the academy and began presenting the appropriate selves, they moved into this paramilitary stage of the training where the emphasis shifted from the taken for granted deference rituals to living up to meeting the requirements for graduation. The gym staff reemphasized the importance of living up to the training standards with the statement that "this is a family. It's an awesome family. You are not part of this family! Right now you are orphans and you are trying to get adopted." In highlighting the recruits' positions as outsiders seeking acceptance into the organization, the staff was making it evident that it would be the recruits themselves who would need to adopt the standards and live up to the requirements of the training environment.

The Nexus of Shame and Honor

While the three stages of self that constitute the recruit phase of the moral career are assumed to be sequential, the veteran recruit's situation demonstrates that it does not proceed in the same manner for all involved. As stated above, half of the class (i.e., the veterans) started training at the paramilitary stage, and within that group there is a subset with prior experience as police officers. These particular recruits were probably starting the process at the anticipatory police stage, and their time in the academy was almost a form of occupational captivity. For civilian recruits, this stage is presumed to start in the weeks before graduation when the real work of the training is complete and they are left feeling that they are just killing time before they hit the street. However, throughout the training, all of the recruits are provided with moments in which to anticipate the intense honor that accompanies the police status as well as the shame that can result from misconduct.

To justify the intensity of the training, instructors repeatedly made the point that police work is a very difficult occupation. In addition, they would point to the significant lack of veteran officers that resulted in rookies, just out of the academy, receiving their field training from officers with as little as three years of experience. As a result the academy was under a tremendous burden to turn out high-quality rookies who could get by with field training from relatively inexperienced officers. One instructor explained, "They are looking for the weak link. That's why they push you so hard. You see, there are no demerits on the street and that next call could be your last." In this statement the instructor was illustrating the severity of police work as well as the resulting need for the best possible training to manage the reality of that danger.

Aside from the physical danger inherent to the occupation, the instructors noted the legal entanglements in which police officers could find themselves ensnarled. Occasionally instructors would discuss recent examples of police corruption. One made the point that there were almost two thousand police officers in the Rockport Police Department and it was unlikely that every single one of them was completely without sin. He went on to add, "If I could choose from the angels, I would. But I can't. So the best I can do is reflect what society has to offer. I tell people that Christ only had twelve disciples and even one of them was bad." This instructor warned that "as a police officer there is always someone watching you." He claimed that "eyes" and "ears" are everywhere.

The idea of being subject to greater surveillance than civilians was stressed repeatedly throughout the training, and there were mechanisms in place designed to condition recruits to these circumstances. The staff informed the class that violations of the rules regarding conduct outside of the academy (i.e., bans on secondary employment and entering bars on the lunch break) would be reported to the department by civilian witnesses. The Sergeant running the training explained that "people know who you are and they know the rules." She warned that there would always be someone who knew them and knew that they were in the academy. She claimed that they would call her wanting to know what a recruit was doing working a part-time job. Her response to the concerned citizen would be, "And, I'll say 'Oh no, sir. Our recruits do not work at any other jobs while they're in the academy. There must be some kind of misunderstanding here.' And then I'll check into it and if you have made a liar out of me, I will not be happy."

Given the higher standards and greater visibility recruits were advised to look at their police career as a "new lease on life." The instructor above explained that whatever the recruits were doing prior to the start of their training, "legal or otherwise," this was the time to move on. It was his contention that being a police officer did not put anyone in a position where "you can get away with more than the average citizen." Quite the contrary, he argued that "police are under intense scrutiny and people are going to look at you differently once you are sworn in." Other instructors explained this as "higher standards and double standards." In such a situation, it would be ill advised to expect to escape detection when engaged in questionable behavior. He concluded his presentation by explaining,

> We got no problem locking up a cop. Once you're inside people are going to know you're a cop and then you're gonna have to scrap. You're either gonna fight or you're gonna give-it-up!

Above, all of the standard anxieties about prison life are amplified by the recruit's pending status as literally a sworn enemy of the prison population. The message in this was that the police officer is at greater risk and faces more severe penalties for criminal sanction than the average civilian.

A class titled "The Role of the American Police Officer," taught by the same instructor, included a discussion of a recent Ku Klux Klan rally that was held outside of police headquarters. Throughout the training the rally was a constant point of reference as an example of the ever-unflappable "thin blue line" and its value to the preservation of order. It was also frequently cited as an example of something that the police could be proud of since order was maintained throughout the event. Every available officer was called in to work security at the event. This meant that even a senior officer, like the instructor, had to stand the line between the Klan members and the anti-Klan protesters. He explained that being an African American man standing in front of the Klansmen and women, effectively protecting them from the angry mob that they were trying to further incite, while they shouted racial slurs directly at him was the hardest thing he ever had to do in his life. However, when it was over and he had done his job literally in the face of the adversity, he was proud of himself and proud to be a police officer. The story was an example of the honor that can result when a police officer does his or her job well and could serve as a metaphor for the whole of police work.

Discussion and Conclusion

Erikson (1976, 83) argues that "if one wants to understand how any given culture works, one should inquire into the characteristic counterpoints as well as its central values." This article has described the phase of police socialization in which recruits experience a sort of excommunication from the occupational subculture based entirely on their trainee status. Recruits are sequentially reintegrated through a process of shaming, during which they are expected to subscribe to an interaction order of obedience to authority. The analysis has illustrated the "meaningful contrast" between shame and honor as an identifying motif within the initial transmission of police culture. The interplay between degradation and elevation within the socialization process is representative of a larger theme in police culture. This dialectic mirrors the axis of variation (Erikson 1976) that cuts across the wider world of policing where officers are either envisioning themselves as "human garbage collectors" or "gods of the street." Conlon illustrates this well in the following:

> Whenever I hear denunciations of police power, in solemn editorials or in routine street static, I have to laugh a little. I think of the Transit cop's line, "You want to know what my job is like? Go to your garage, piss in the corner, and stand there for eight hours." Or I think about how when we are sick at home, we have to call in for permission to leave the house, and call again when we return.
>
> (Conlon 2004, 85)

Above, Conlon notes a powerful dialectic of degradation and elevation in policing that is encapsulate in the training.

For decades scholars have been discussing the various problems and failures of police training (Harris 1973; Lundman 1980; Fielding 1988; Buerger 1998; Chappell 2006). Recently, Birzer (2003) and Marenin (2004) have begun criticizing the role of pedagogy in police training. They have noted that a system utilizing a pedagogical structure (i.e., the transmission of information from expert to novice) implies that it is teaching to children. Each posits andragogy (i.e., the mutual involvement of expert and novice in the learning process) as an alternative training regime. An andragogical structure is expected to better orient officers toward problem solving, critical thinking, and the goals of policing in a democracy rather than the "robot, soldier-like mentality that has been perpetuated in the training classroom" under the pedagogical system (Birzer and Tannehill 2001, 236).

Moreover, Violanti (1993) has argued that training environments that apply pressure to recruits for the sole purpose of generating a response to that pressure (i.e., paramilitary stress academies) socialize recruits into maladaptive coping strategies. While this type of training is supposed to resocialize the recruit into a disciplined officer, its mechanisms have no educational value whatsoever (Shernock 1998). Lundman (1980) observes that paramilitary stress academies produce defensive and depersonalized officers, while collegiate nonstress training models, a small minority in American policing, have no such consequences. Furthermore, as McCreedy (1980) has noted, the stress model can result in unquestioning obedience to superiors, increased hostility, and low self-esteem. Albuquerque and Paes-Machado (2004) explain recruit degradation via hazing as a mechanism within Brazilian police training that puts forth a message opposed to the organizations formal position (i.e., authoritarian socialization vs. democratization).

The facilitation of a moral career based on shaming can be added to this list of criticisms since it is likely to generate the kind of ethos that is at the heart of Alpert and Dunham's (2004) theory of police violence. In the training, recruits are pushed to internalize an interaction order based on obedience to police authority. While all police will not subscribe to the use of violence against, or maintain the same threshold for tolerating, disrespectful civilians, those who do can find something equivalent to a subcultural justification for their behavior in their early socialization. Moreover, the fact that this interaction order fits with a number of the normative orders (i.e., morality, safety, competence, and machismo) that Herbert (1998) uses to explain the subculture as a whole makes it all the more powerful.

Critical Thinking

Conti's ethnography reveals many potentially negative aspects of the socialization process that take place in police academies. While such practices contribute to police officers being prepared for their day-to-day jobs, they may also bring with them unintended consequences. Think about how the process of demeaning police recruits may affect the way patrol officers interact with citizens. After reading the articles in the next section revisit the ideas in Conti's article to see if you can better understand why officers change the way they interact with repeat offenders and victims. Are there other methods of training recruits to be good officers that do not involve demeaning them?

References

Albuquerque, C. L., and Paes-Machado. 2004. The hazing machine: the shaping of Brazilian military police recruits. *Policing and Society* 14 (2): 75–92.

Alpert, G. P., and R. G. Dunham. 2004. *Understanding police use of force: Officers, suspects, and reciprocity*. Cambridge, UK: Cambridge University Press.

Birzer, M. L. 2003. The theory of andragogy applied to police training. *Policing: An International Journal of Strategies & Management* 26 (1): 29–42.

Birzer. M. L., and R. Tannehill. 2001. A more effective training approach for contemporary policing. *Police Quarterly* 4 (2): 233–52.

Braithwaite, J. 2007. *Crime, shame and reintegration*. New York: Cambridge University Press.

Buerger. M. E. 1998. Police training as Pentecost: Using tools significantly ill-suited to the purpose of reform. *Police Quarterly* 1:27–63.

Chappell, A. T. 2006. Learning in action: Training the community police officer. PhD diss., University of Florida.

Conlon, E. 2004. *Blue blood*. New York: Riverhead Books.

Cooley, C. H. 1922. *Human nature and the social order*. New York: Scribner's.

Erikson, K. T. 1976. *Everything in its path: Destruction of community in the Buffalo Creek flood*. New York: Simon & Schuster.

Fielding, N. G. 1988. *Joining forces: Police training, socialization and occupational competence*. London: Routledge.

Gallo, G. 2001. *Armed & dangerous: Memoirs of a Chicago police woman*. New York: Tom Doherty.

Goffman. E. 1961a. *Asylums: Essays on the social situation of mental patients and other inmates*. New York: Doubleday Anchor.

Goffman. E. 1961b. *Two studies in sociological interaction*. Indianapolis, IN: Bobbs-Merrill.

Goffman, E. 1969. The insanity of place. *Psychiatry: Journal for the Study of Interpersonal Process* 32 (4): 357–88.

Goffman, E. 1983. *Interaction ritual: Essays on face-to-face behavior*. New York: Pantheon.

Gronfrien, W. 1993. Sundered selves: Mental illness and the interaction order in the work of Erving Goffman. In *Goffman and social organization: Studies in a sociological legacy*, ed. G. Smith. 81–103. New York: Routledge.

Harris, R. 1973. *The police academy: An insiders view*. New York: John Wiley.

Herbert, S. 1998. The police subculture reconsidered. *Criminology* 36 (2): 343–69.

Hopper, M. 1977. Becoming a policeman: Socialization of cadets in a police academy. *Urban Life* 6 (2): 149–70.

Lundman, J. R. 1980. *Police and policing: An introduction*. New York: Holt, Rinehart & Winston.

Marenin, O. 2004. Police training for democracy. *Police Practice and Research* 5 (2): 102–23.

McCorkel. J. A. 1998. Going to the crackhouse: Critical space as a form of resistance in total institutions and everyday life. *Symbolic Interaction* 21 (3): 227–52.

McCreedy, K. R. 1980. The impact of a police academy on the socialization of new officers. PhD diss., University of Southern California.

Paes-Machado, E., and C. L. Albuquerque 2002. Jungle I.D.: Educational reform inside the Brazilian paramilitary police. *Policing & Society* 13 (1): 59–87.

Scheff, T. J. 2000. Shame in self and society. *Symbolic Interaction* 26 (2): 239–62.

Sherman, L. 1999. Learning police ethics. In *Policing perspectives: An anthology*, ed. Larry K. Gains and Gary W. Cordner, 301–10. Los Angeles: Roxbury.

Shernock. S. 1998. Police officer support for quasi-military stress training and orientation towards outsiders an non-law enforcement functions. *Journal of Police and Criminal Psychology* 13 (2): 87–99.

Skolnick, J. 1964. *Justice without trial: Law enforcement in a democratic society*. New York: John Wiley.

Sykes, R. E., and E. E. Brent. 1980. The regulation of interaction by police: A systems view of taking charge. *Criminology* 18 (2): 182–97.

Van Maanen, J. 1973. Observations on the making of policemen. *Human Organization* 32(4): 407–18.

Van Maanen, J. [1978] 1999. The asshole. In *The polite and society: Touchstone readings*, ed. V. E. Kappler, 304–25. Prospect Heights, IL: Waveland.

Violanti, J. M. 1993. What does high stress training teach recruits? An analysis of coping. *Journal of Criminal Justice* 21: 411–17.

Waddington, P. A. J. 1999. Police (canteen) sub-culture. An appreciation. *British Journal of Criminology* 39(2): 287–309.

2

Racialized Policing: Officers' Voices on Policing Latino and African American Neighborhoods

Claudio G. Vera Sanchez and Dennis P. Rosenbaum

Abstract: *Claudio Vera Sanchez and Dennis Rosenbaum argue that knowing how police perceive those they patrol is vital for understanding the complicated relationship between police and citizens. Thus, they interview patrol officers to learn how they socially construct race within African American or Latino neighborhoods. They show that police often spoke of African American communities as being morally deficient, while defining residents of Latino neighborhoods as being hard-working, good people. These perceptions of communities then affected the way police dealt with citizens residing in the communities.*

Since the 1960s, conflict between urban police forces and minority communities has been a staple topic for the media and researchers in the United States. The police have been accused of racially biased decision making that contributes to racial profiling, disrespectful encounters, excessive force, and, ultimately, disproportionate minority confinement. Unfortunately, much of what is known about the police is disseminated through media images and newspapers, often showcasing sensationalized cases of police use of excessive force; the experience of policing minority communities—from the viewpoint of police themselves—remains elusive. Researchers who study biased policing (Barlow & Hickman Barlow, 2000; Cohen, 1996; Platt et al., 1982) have introduced pioneering theoretical frameworks to the scientific community, yet fewer works incorporate a police perspective (Barlow & Hickman Barlow, 2002; Dowler, 2005; Ioimo, Tears, Meadows, Becton, & Charles, 2007; Moskos, 2008b). Because police officers are the primary gatekeepers to the criminal legal system and their power to arrest has considerable consequences for minority youth and adults, understanding their perspective about the communities they serve is of utmost importance. The objective of this study, therefore, is to explore the experiences of urban municipal officers who police predominately low-income, minority communities and how they perceive, or perhaps even racialize, Latinos and African Americans within those neighborhoods.

Focusing on populations of power, as a unit analysis, is long overdue because the trend in criminological and social research is to study downward, minorities or disadvantaged groups, with the objective of interpreting their experiences. In contrast, a careful study of police experiences may offer insight regarding the exercise of power and legal authority in our society. The police have been issued legitimate authority to initiate street and vehicular stops, make arrests, and employ deadly force (Fyfe, 1988).

Their behavior, then, may improve or worsen the plight of those with whom they interact. Exploring the attitudes, perspectives, and experiences of police officers vis-à-vis the minority communities they serve should help to advance our understanding and interpretation of police behavior in the field and ultimately provide guidance to improve police–minority relations. Issues about race and class biases in policing can be more fully understood and contextualized by hearing the voices of police officers who work in low-income minority neighborhoods.

Public Perceptions of the Police

Police–minority interactions and perceptions of each other are complex and multi-faceted. Much of what we know about this relationship stems from research on public attitudes toward the police, where minorities have expressed the most distrust and negative sentiment. African Americans, overall, report the most pessimistic attitudes toward the police followed by Latinos and then Whites (Schafer, Huebner, & Bynum, 2003; Skogan & Hartnett, 1997; Weitzer & Tuch, 2004). Further, attitudes vary by contextual and socioeconomic variables. Weitzer (2000) finds that middle class African Americans in Washington DC voice more positive views of the police than their low-income counterparts, although their attitudes remain less positive than those of Whites. Brown and Benedict's (2002) review of the literature concludes that higher status Whites report greater appreciation for, and confidence in, the police than higher status African Americans. In contrast, studies centered on low-income immigrant Latino communities, while few, highlight intense fear and apprehension toward the police by community residents (Carter, 1985; Skogan, 2006), fears occasionally attenuated through intensive community policing efforts (Torres & Vogel, 2001). All in all, minorities, both Latinos and African Americans, have consistently expressed more negative views of the police than Whites, and contextual and socio-economic factors contribute to skew these perceptions (Cao, Frank, & Cullen, 1996).

Attitudes toward the police may also vary by the type of contact minorities experience—either voluntary citizen-initiated (e.g., calling the police for assistance) or involuntary police-initiated (e.g., being stopped; Langan, Greenfield, Smith, Durose, & Levin, 2001). African Americans experience more involuntary encounters with the police in comparison to Whites (Lundman & Kaufman, 2003). Rusinko, Johnson, and Hornung (1978) indicate that voluntary police contact is a precursor to positive attitudes toward the police as opposed to involuntary contact. Although positive contact mitigates negative attitudes for African Americans, overall they continue to report more negative views of the police than Whites. Even though direct contact has been linked with negative attitudes toward the police (Jesilow, Meyer, & Namazzi, 1995; Scaglion & Condon, 1980), contact is not a prerequisite for negative perceptions (Hurst, Frank, & Browning, 2000). Rosenbaum, Schuck, Costello, Hawkins, and Ring (2005), for example, find that one recent contact alone is insufficient to fuel negative attitudes toward the police, and instead, vicarious experience (e.g., knowing someone with a negative experience) and possessing preconceived negative views about the police will accentuate negative perceptions of a recent encounter. Finally, in Skogan's (2006) review of the literature, what he describes as an "asymmetry" in police–citizen encounters reveals that negative contact overshadows positive experiences by 4 to 14 percentage points. That is, negative experience has a larger impact than positive experience on views of the police ("Bad news travels faster than good news."). Involuntary contacts, however, are not devoid of social context. Generally, low-income, high-crime contexts, due to high crime volumes and unique organization of the neighborhood, are susceptible to a style of policing that structures involuntary stops. If low-income, high-crime neighborhoods place minorities at risk for involuntary stops and searches, then displeasure with the police among minority residents is predictable.

Overall, past research indicates that minorities report more negative attitudes toward the police than Whites; unfortunately, the majority of studies reviewed rarely incorporate a police perspective or the effects of neighborhood context on police work. Serious attention to low-income and high-crime neighborhoods may also provide insight about police–community dynamics, police–minority conflicts, and the unique challenges police officers face. Neighborhood conditions, such as poverty and violent crime, may intensify aggressive policing and conflicts between the police and community residents (Kane, 2002, 2003). Hearing the voices of police officers who work in low-income minority neighborhoods, therefore, may improve our understanding of police–citizen encounters.

The extant literature reveals that Latinos and African Americans share negative images of the police and social scripts of what police do, but how do officers experience low-income minority neighborhoods and their residents? Aside from police surveys and official data, which capture general attitudes toward the community and community policing functions (see Lurigio & Rosenbaum, 1994; Skogan, 2005), researchers have given less attention to police officers' own perceptions of community residents in minority neighborhoods. There are frequent discussions of "police culture" in the policing literature, as well as early fieldwork on the subject (National Research Council, 2004), but race and ethnicity are not the central focus. Concepts such as danger, suspicion, group loyalty ("us vs. them"), and cynicism are commonplace in previous analyses (Skolnick, 1966). Race may be the "elephant in the room," but it is rarely examined in detail.

Policing and Neighborhood Context

A body of research suggests that racial disparities in policing are ubiquitous and attitudinal measures of minorities and official records corroborate with these data, yet an examination of neighborhood context can improve our understanding of the relationship between the police and the public (Schuck, Rosenbaum, & Hawkins, 2008). Few works have focused on how police officers negotiate or experience low-income minority neighborhoods. In addition to race, which is considered a possible source of biased policing, neighborhood context may be equally important in examining police harassment, profiling, and other types of police behavior.

Research shows that policing styles, including but not limited to harassment and excessive force, vary by neighborhood conditions (Klinger, 1997; Rosenbaum, 2007). Kane (2002) concludes that minorities residing in disadvantaged neighborhoods are recipients of over policing (Kane, 2002). Terrill and Reisig (2003) find that the police exercise excessive force in neighborhoods where serious offending (e.g. homicide rates) and concentrated disadvantage (e.g., percent of poverty, level of unemployment, and number of female-headed households) are endemic. The authors conclude, however, that race is a proxy for neighborhood disadvantage, because minorities are often segregated to high-crime and low-income areas. Terrill and Mastrofski (2002) find that police officers are more likely to apply excessive force toward males, minorities, youth, and those living in disadvantaged environments. However, Terrill (2005) shows that police officers often exercise less force than is legally permitted despite extreme situational exigencies; alternatively, when young minority males reside in high-crime communities, the continuum of force escalates even when suspects are not resistant. These results suggest that neighborhood context helps explain aggressive policing. Whether race plays a role during police–suspect encounters is difficult to determine without exploring police officers' experiences in minority neighborhoods.

Although excessive police force varies by neighborhood and suspect characteristics, other scholars contend that officer behaviors, although often read as mistreatment, may reflect not biased but proactive policing in low-income contexts. McCluskey and Terrill (2005) indicate that, "Officers who receive repeated complaints may not actually be so-called problem officers, but rather proactive officers" (p. 143). The authors suggest that "problem officers" score higher at proactive stops and interrogations in the field but score no differently in terms of physical force or discourtesy. Complaints against an officer, then, or being labeled as a problem officer may be interpreted by some as evidence of actually doing good police work. Quilian and Pager (2001) argue that the symbolic face of criminality in the public perception—the African American or minority male—has been shaped by neighborhood context; neighborhoods facing severe crime problems experience high volumes of calls for service that require an immediate police response. If the public routinely demands police presence in some neighborhoods, coupled with intense lobbying for arrest (Black & Reiss, 1970), then the public and the police may play a role in contributing to what appears to be biased policing. Also, the emergence of data-driven "hot spots policing" demands that greater police attention be given to high-crime minority neighborhoods (Rosenbaum, 2006). Past research reveals that police behavior is shaped by both suspect characteristics (e.g., race) and neighborhood context (e.g., calls for service and crime incidents); what remains unclear is how the police officer's mindset and interpretation of race and neighborhood context contribute to the outcome.

Overall, research indicates that police behavior and style vary by neighborhood conditions, yet few studies have explored how the police experience and perceive minority communities. What characteristics of low-income minority neighborhoods are salient to police officers? How do police officers describe low-income communities? A better understanding of how police perceive neighborhood conditions and local residents may shed light on their behavioral responses and the mediating processes involved.

Research Questions

The following research questions guided this qualitative inquiry:

1. Are police officers attuned to public dissatisfaction from residents in minority communities and how do they interpret or respond to it?
2. How do police officers perceive race, racialize, or socially construct race?
3. What aspects of Latinos and African Americans do police officers focus on when expressing their views about these groups?
4. What language do police officers use to describe low-income minority neighborhoods?

Methods

The data for this study were collected as part of a larger project on minority trust and confidence in the police consisting of self-reports from police officers, community adults, and community youth collected via focus groups, in-person interviews, and/or telephone interviews (Rosenbaum et al., 2005). This study is a qualitative inquiry that draws on the in-person interviews with police officers.

Interviews

Ten interviews were conducted with police officers in each of four racially distinct neighborhoods (i.e., Latino or African American) in a large Midwestern city, for a total of $N = 40$ Interviews. The interviews were conducted at police precincts, generally in vacant offices or roll call rooms. The watch commanders selected the police officers but participation was voluntary and informed consent procedures followed the institutional review board approved protocol. The interviews ranged from 30 min to 1 hr in length. Field notes were jotted down in notebooks and interviewers recorded the data into an electronic document shortly thereafter.

Once the actual interviews commenced, some of the officers appeared reluctant at times to discuss what they perceived as sensitive police practices. Secrecy within the police culture has been documented previously (Manning, 1977; Westley, 1970). Occasional single word answers and repetitive assurances were meant to suggest that "everything was perfect" in the communities that they policed. For example, many officers denied that racial profiling occurred in their beat, although many admitted that such practices were common in other parts of the city. Other police officers, however, were more candid about their feelings. They did not appear concerned with being politically correct and offered in-depth information to the interviewers.

Communities

The communities were selected based on their ethnic composition and quality of police–community relations. Data from telephone surveys were used to identify neighborhoods where police–community tensions were moderately strong. Census

2000 data were used to identify neighborhoods that were predominately African American, Latino, or White. Field observations from the research team were used to identify neighborhoods that were comparable on visible factors such as residential-commercial mix, housing quality, and levels of disorder. Approximately 10 communities were purposively selected and a narrowing process occurred through a combination of input from the research team, field notes about the various communities, and neighborhood profiles.

Researchers drove around and documented detailed neighborhood descriptions, including the physical structures, businesses, and the people, as well as an overall subjective feeling of the context. The researchers noted in a high-crime, low-income minority neighborhood, "Currency exchange, liquor stores, mechanic shop, empty lots, empty and boarded up rentals, church, abandoned industrial building . . . lots of people on the streets, lots of cars and foot traffic. Guys hanging out on the corner, all African American. A group of kids shouted at us." From this process, four communities in the city were selected for this study (two African American, two Latino). Police beats within the boundaries of the four communities were included in the study and used as the basis for selecting police officers.

Please see Table 2.1 for a description of the demographics of the neighborhoods studied in this large midwestern city, based on Census 2000 information. The percentage of households living below the poverty line for each of the neighborhoods exceeds the average for the city. The neighborhoods are also racially homogeneous, have lower median incomes, and have fewer homeowners than the typical neighborhood in the city. These communities can be considered low income and high crime, based on Census 2000 data, field accounts, and crime data.

Results

Six distinct themes emerged from the voices of the police officers. Each is described in the following with corresponding documentation.

Table 2.1 Neighborhood demographics

Neighborhood	Percent below Poverty	Percent of one Race	Median Income	Home Ownership	Percent below 9th Grade	Homicide per 100,000
African American A	27.1	97.04	33,081	45.78	5.2	33
African American B	24.1	89.70	33,663	39.54	9.6	29
Latino C	26.5	83.0	32,320	36.0	39.9	24
Latino D	31.1	43.4	36,667	33.6	23.3	22

Note: This table shows the demographic characteristics of the neighborhoods studied, such as percentage of individuals living below the poverty line, percentage of racial group of interest (Latino or African American), median income, percentage of residents who own their home, percent of individuals over 25 years of age with education levels below the 9th grade, and homicide in the neighborhood per 100,000.

Theme 1: Police Officers Feel Misunderstood and Unwelcome in Minority
Neighborhoods

Researchers have reported accounts of hostile and aggressive police personalities
(Chambliss, 1994; Skolnick, 1966), but in the current study, the police describe themselves as the victims of community abuse—they report feeling frustrated and angry
that they are unappreciated and even resented in minority neighborhoods. Police
officers were keen to offer verbal and behavioral indicators of community dissatisfaction with their presence.

> Everybody friendly downtown—they say hi. We don't get that here. We hear "F*** the police"
> and other stupid comments.
> (African American neighborhood A, Police Officer, White, Male)

> They see you as the enemy. The only time people deal with you is when they are in some kind
> of trouble or going through a crisis—a robbery or burglary for example. They don't stop police
> to say "Hi, how are you doing?" . . . not everybody is a bad person but when you go to some-
> body's house it's because there is something wrong. And when there is a potential to get hurt
> the first thing you will protect is yourself because you know you will get hurt from the people
> you are supposed to be serving. Then they become your enemy.
> (Latino neighborhood D, Police Officer, Latino, Male)

The behavioral displays such as "staring and spitting on the floor" or verbal statements such as "F*** the police" suggest to the police that they are unwelcome in the
neighborhood.

Officers are very aware of the tension between them and minority residents.
According to the respondents, statements such as being "at war" with segments of the
community or being perceived as "the enemy" highlight the conflict police officers
negotiate on a daily basis with the public. When officers feel unappreciated and
unwelcome, they find it more difficult to be good public servants to victims and others
who need their assistance. As one officer noted, "Most feel it is hard to help people in
the community."

Theme 2: The Police Contend that Their Views of the Community are Shaped
Largely by the Community's Attitudes and Actions toward Them

Often in a defensive tone, officers talked about citizens' complaints of unjustified
police harassment, intergenerational transmission of antipolice values, and police
interference with people's illegal activities.

We Harass Them for No Good Reason

According to police officers, minorities assume that they are being hassled unjustifi-
ably. Officers indicate that these reactions occur in the course of routine police work—
for instance, attending to traffic violations, clearing corners, and making arrests when
crimes are committed.

"Those bastards." [community people say] . . . they call us and don't like us when we get there. We're all racist and lock up their sons and daughters for no good reason.

(Latino neighborhood C, Police Officer, White, Female)

Community has this perception/thoughts that we are going to stop them, ask for the driving license, the insurance. They are not aware of the laws like drinking in public areas—they don't know the laws are to protect them. People drinking in the park cause problems but they think that we are harassing or bothering them.

(Latino neighborhood C, Police Officer, Latino, Male)

Intergenerational Transmission of Disrespect and Attitudes about the Police

Officers also reported that family upbringing encourages negative sentiments toward the police. The comments of police officers suggest that some individuals are socialized to respect the police and others have been raised to disrespect the police. According to some police officers, parents actively discourage their children from showing any positive regard toward the officers. Several officers described how family socialization contributes to dissatisfaction with the police.

They pass this hatred down to their children. If little kids try to wave to us they tell them, "don't say hi to the police."

(Latino neighborhood C, Police Officer, White, Male)

They [community residents] try to provoke the police and start fights. They're brought up thinking that the police are bad. I've seen little kids point their guns at the police. It's night and day when you look at how they respect the police.

(Latino neighborhood C, Police Officer, Latino, Male).

They are Doing Bad Things—Drug Dealers and Gangs—and Do Not Want Us to Interfere

Officers indicated that public disrespect for the police is due, in part, to police interrupting law-breaking behavior. The police reported stopping people from drinking in the park or putting drug dealers out of business as reasons why police are resented. But some officers expressed a more conditional, nuanced understanding of public sentiment that varies by type of citizen.

If they're drug dealers, they're going to be mad. We're putting them out of business. The majority of people are glad we're out there.

(African American neighborhood A, Police Officer, White, Male)

No one is afraid of the police unless they are doing wrong . . . most officers feel the people in the area are decent and realize a small segment causes most problems. Tensions do exist but the source can be narrowed down considerably (e.g., most tensions are with families at a specific address who have members that are in trouble with the police).

(Latino neighborhood D, Police Officer, White, Male)

In sum, officers' views of the community are shaped by their assessment of the community's negative assessment of police activity. Officers believe that in minority communities young people are taught by older generations to distrust the police, good abiding citizens perceive routine police work as harassment, and serious offenders do not appreciate police interference with their illegal activities.

Theme 3: A Person's Age Is a Stronger Determinant of Judgment by the Police than a Person's Race or Ethnicity

Police officers report a consistent apprehension toward young people in all communities. Not a single neighborhood was found, regardless of racial or ethnic composition, where the police failed to report tension with youth and alternatively felt more appreciated by older segments of the community. If the police were only racially motivated, one would not expect officers to consistently report positive images about older minority adults in these racially homogeneous minority neighborhoods. In contrast to the belief that police officers would express negative stereotypes across an entire neighborhood, they tended to emphasize their satisfaction with many law-abiding and "good" residents in high crime, economically disadvantaged, Latino and African American communities. Many statements made by police officers indicate that they felt appreciated by older residents and occasionally were flattered by young children who expressed positive regard.

> Older people love us. Others hanging on the corners will spit and eyeball you. Little kids will wave.
> (African American neighborhood A, Police Officer, White, Male)

> The male Black between 16 to 25 hate us and they are not going to like the police. Older Blacks are better . . . age plays a big role in attitudes about us.
> (African American neighborhood A, Police Officer, White, Male)

Police officers believe that older people's positive opinions of them stem from living in fear of offenders and youth gangs and that the police serve an important public safety function. Police officers indicate that older residents are occasionally too demanding of police services, but overall they are grateful for their service.

> Older people are glad when they see the police in the area, they feel safer. Younger people are disrespectful and don't care. If we try to get them off the corner they would either still stand there or just come back later.
> (African American neighborhood B, Police Officer, Latino, Male)

> Older adults are more comfortable but are upset that we can't do more. They have to set up "Gang Hot Spots" to stop loitering of juveniles. Older adults want police to do more.
> (African American neighborhood B, Police Officer, Latino, Male)

All in all, police officers report dissatisfaction with youth in every neighborhood. Police officers believe that young people make disrespectful comments while older people support police efforts to enhance public safety by removing youth from corners and cease their illegal activities. Police officers rarely spoke about race explicitly, in contrast to their many comments about "rowdy" or intractable youth. When profiling occurred, age was the dominant theme rather than race or ethnicity.

Theme 4: Police Officers Were More Likely to Moralize, rather than Racialize Homogenous African American Communities. But They Blamed Both Individuals and Society for the Observed Failures

To define morality, officers made references to the goodness or badness of individual's characters, rather than the racial makeup of the person. The comments made by officers suggest that they frown upon what they believe is a faulty socialization of children, disapprove of a perceived questionable work ethic, and are critical about what they understand to be a failure of neighborhood residents to perform informal social control and proactive community activities (e.g., keep the streets clean). In many cases, police officers view African American neighborhoods as "war-zones," individuals "without hope," where "no one seems to be working." In addition, it was uncommon for police officers to overtly use the words Black or African American when describing the negative attributes of African Americans and their neighborhoods. The extent to which race is interwoven in the subtext of these narratives is difficult to unveil given that many police officers today are sensitive to the importance of making politically correct statements in public. In any event, the words tend to focus on the moral character of the neighborhood as a whole.

> Neighborhood looks like a nuclear war zone—blighted, sad but true . . . high domestic abuse, high birth rate, high incidence of violent crime against persons.
> (African American neighborhood A, Police Officer, White, Male)

> I wouldn't know how to begin. It's filthy over here. All the structures are in disarray. From the look of the inside of their houses, they don't care how they live. Fences are in disrepair, garages falling apart, and there's garbage everywhere . . . they have no respect for anybody. They don't respect their moms, nobody.
> (African American neighborhood A, Police Officer, Latino, Female)

Other officers made moral statements yet were also empathetic to the issues faced by these communities, making external attributions, such as Section 8 housing and lack of opportunities, to explain the plight in these neighborhoods. Officers reported dissatisfaction with the social issues and conditions of the neighborhood but expressed a deeper appreciation and understanding for the individuals residing in these urban contexts.

> There's lots of garbage. The buildings are falling apart . . . the houses are pretty dirty. There's tons of narcotics. There's quite a bit of violence to solve, lots of problems. It's a population that needs help, and they're not able to solve their problems with words. Among this urban disaster, many people are just trying to live their lives. They go to work to make money.
> (African American neighborhood A, Police Officer, White, Male)

> It's drug infested and the worst beat in the district . . . people from the projects are moving into the neighborhood . . . they're bringing the same problems and lifestyle into an otherwise good neighborhood.
> (African American neighborhood B, Police Officer, African American, Male)

The comments of police officers, suggest that they focused on the moral aspects of African American neighborhoods. The social organization of the neighborhoods— what they believed was a poor work ethic, questionable transmission of prosocial values to children, and disinterest in improving the neighborhood were often mentioned. Other officers also highlighted the preceding neighborhood conditions but also expressed a deeper understanding for people's plight within these environments.

Theme 5: The Concept of Racial Profiling Is Illogical or Nonsensical to Police Officers Working in Racially Homogeneous Environments

Racial profiling is typically defined as police decisions that are influenced by the race of the citizens they encounter. From a police perspective, this concept is not meaningful when police officers are working in predominantly Latino or African American neighborhoods.

> The beat is all Black and so it would only be profiling if I stopped every White person on the block. So if a White person is stopped then one could say it is profiling but if a Black person is stopped it's hard to see how that could be profiling.
> (African American neighborhood A, Police officer, White. Male)

> Not in the minority neighborhood. There is no way you could be racial profiling in a minority neighborhood where there are only Hispanics and Blacks. Community don't really understand what racial profiling means. Mexicans say, "you stopped me because I am Mexican," when the neighborhood is Mexican.
> (Latino neighborhood C, Police Officer, Latino, Male)

Police officers also indicated that the race of the officer makes it difficult to participate in racial profiling. Minority officers, they argued, cannot be accused of profiling. Furthermore, they argued that working with minority officers makes racial bias by White officers unlikely. Hence, police officers used their own race or their partner's to rationalize the improbable nature of racial profiling.

> Personally, they think that I don't like them because I'm White. My partner is Hispanic and they think that he's sold out.
> (Latino neighborhood C, Police Officer, White, Female)

> Yes, if they see Hispanic or White officers stopping people they think they are messing with them. They don't have the same feelings if it is a Black officer stopping them.
> (African American neighborhood B, Police Officer, African American, Female)

But given that racial profiling is politically and organizationally disapproved, few individuals will admit racial bias or profiling. Nevertheless, officers were perplexed about the possibility of biased law enforcement within largely African American or Latino communities and urge the research community to develop alternative conceptualizations of racial profiling for these communities.

Theme 6: Police Officers Racialized African Americans in the Lowest Crime Latino Neighborhood

The Mexican neighborhood that had the lowest crime rate and lowest proportion of African Americans of the four neighborhoods studied is the only setting where police racialized or overtly expressed negative racial comments about African Americans and positive statements for Mexicans. Not even in the Puerto Rican community, where half of the population consists of African Americans, did the police officers report a negative image of race. Police officers described the North side (i.e., African American section) in negative terms and the South side (i.e., Mexican section) in positive terms. Some officers even characterized the Latino gang members as polite and friendly. Mexicans were racialized favorably. Although drug markets and gangs were mentioned, Mexicans were commended for their work ethic and internal social organization within the community and immigrants were characterized as coming to the United States to improve their life chances.

Latinos Positively Racialized

They care about their neighborhood, go to [police–community] meetings. The Hispanic section, and the Italian section . . . they are more cooperative.
(Latino neighborhood C, Police Officer, White, Female)

It's primarily Hispanic . . . working class people. There are gangs here. It is evident that they're here. Being on the beat, you see them. And when people get arrested you know who they are. My beat is very congested . . . there are some apartments where we go into basements and they are converted into six different units with one communal restroom and no kitchen. I mean they're like the size of this (gestures around the cubicle we are talking in).
(Latino neighborhood C, Police Officer, Latino, Male)

Difference Between Latinos and African Americans

The neighborhood is half Mexican and half Black and the two halves are night and day. The Black side is depressing. There's a lot of ignorance there. People get used to it, we get used to it. We get cynical. Most of the people on the Mexican side work and go through life to the best of their ability.
(Latino neighborhood C, Police Officer, White, Female)

You have to change your personality when you go to the north end [African American section]. You can't be cordial or polite. I know this from my experiences. All of the officers know this. The south end [Mexican side], there's no tension. There is a little gang trouble. But, the north end there's more violence and more tension. The housing is bad and people just stand on the street corner drinking.
(Latino neighborhood C, Police Officer, Latino, Male)

The officers described Mexicans and African Americans and their racial characteristics differently in the predominately Mexican community. Some officers stated that the differences were like "night and day." Community tensions, disrespect of the police, street drinking, and violence were some key differences noticed by police officers between the Latino and African American areas of the same neighborhood. The problems in the neighborhood, at least for the officers interviewed, originated from the different characteristics of racial and ethnic groups (Mexicans vs. African Americans) and police officers' interpretation of their law-abiding behavior.

Discussion and Conclusion

Police conceptions of minority communities are heavily influenced by the perceived quality of their encounters with the public and whether the officers feel respected by community residents. Consistent with prior research that identifies the "us versus them" mindset in the police culture (Chambliss, 1994), the narratives of police officers in our sample underscore the extent to which they feel misunderstood, disliked (even hated), and abused in minority communities. Officers feel that most of the negative sentiment originates from African American, instead of Latino residents, and particularly from young people. Whether older residents really have more positive regard for the police or have simply learned to suppress their feelings and interact with the police in less threatening ways is uncertain. In any event, these perceived responses from the community, in turn, seem to play some role in shaping officers' judgments and feelings about the communities they serve. Police officers do not hold undifferentiated views of minority communities. Rather, they seem to easily distinguish between Anderson's (1999) "decent families" and the "street families." Officers feel appreciated by the former and disrespected by the latter.

Police appear less able to make refined distinctions in their perceptions of neighborhood youth. Police have particularly harsh feelings about youth in minority neighborhoods, describing them with a wide range of negative attributes. And no particular subset of youth is immune from this criticism. In a nutshell, officers feel that youth and young adults have no respect for them and, therefore, the feelings and behaviors can be reciprocated. They cite a number of possible reasons for minority youth disliking them, particularly the dynamics of family and peers. Two "lay theories" are posited by the police regarding the intergenerational transmission of negative attitudes about the police: On the street, young adults (often gang members in their 20s) teach the younger teenagers to hate the police. In the family, the parents teach the preteen children to hate the police.

Intergenerational transmission of information about the police is a vicarious process (Rosenbaum et al., 2005) and such explanations by the police of negative community sentiment do not include direct experience as a factor in shaping the judgments of younger adults toward the police. Perhaps youths have their own experiences with the police to draw from as well. From the police narratives in the current study, only occasionally do the officers recognize their own role in these long-standing conflictual relationships with young minorities. The reality of urban policing is that young people are the primary targets of aggressive policing designed to control crime and disorder (Brunson & Weitzer, 2009; Jones-Brown, 2007). National and local data indicate that young minority males are stopped and searched at much higher rates than other segments of the population (Skogan & Steiner, 2004). Furthermore, in some cities, the new focus on hot spots policing results in substantially more police officers deployed to high-crime minority neighborhoods, primarily to make contact with young residents on the streets (Rosenbaum, 2006). Granted, many of these younger adults are not entirely innocent and no one knows that better than the officers on the street. Often they belong to gangs, deal drugs, use guns to resolve conflict, and exhibit considerable disrespect for the police and other authority figures. Research indicates that young adults also use their street authority to intimidate older members of the community (Wilkinson, 2007). Nevertheless, one theme from interviews with adults and youth in these same communities is that youth are "picked on" by the police and that police are unable to distinguish between the "good" and "bad" kids (Rosenbaum et al., 2005). Training, workshops, and supervision to address these concerns could go a long way toward improving the situation.

Although community-policing efforts have successfully motivated older adults within minority neighborhoods to attend police–citizen meetings (Skogan & Steiner, 2004), an alternative vision is for the police to actively build relationships with young people. Perhaps community-policing programs could give more thoughtful attention to strengthening police–youth relations and address the unique obstacles to achieving this goal (e.g., being considered a "snitch," differential power inherent in police–youth dynamics, and developmental factors such as a contempt for authority). Also, police officers who engage in foot or bicycle patrol (vs. motorized patrol) are more likely to get to know local youth and be able to distinguish between those who are "trouble makers" (e.g., gang members) and those who are not.

Police officers may not racialize but rather moralize African American neighborhoods. Manning (1977) suggests that police rhetoric emphasizes their crime control capabilities, but more often, they serve moral objectives—removing alcoholics, prostitutes, and noisy youth from the streets. Some police officers in our sample, consistent with the findings of Moskos (2008a), viewed African American communities as morally deficient. Officers reported a feeling that many community residents "did not care about anything." Although police officers acknowledged their distaste for crime, they also stressed family dysfunction, negative socialization of children, a faulty work ethic, and physically chaotic environments as salient descriptors, especially within African American neighborhoods. Broken windows theory suggests that police work is more about order maintenance than law enforcement (Kelling & Coles, 1996; Sousa & Kelling, 2006; Wilson & Kelling, 1982), and this may include the expectation that the police will maintain the moral order (e.g., by removing rowdy youth and prostitutes, extinguishing drug markets, and arresting gang members). Although policing disorder is often popular with local residents and is arguably responsive to community concerns, these activities are also controversial because of the political and cultural issues around defining disorder. In any event, the difference between racialization and moralization is theoretically precarious. Our definition of racialization, one of many, is "to impose racial character on or to perceive or experience in racial terms." The findings here suggest that officers infrequently imposed racial ascriptions by their words to residents in homogeneously African American neighborhoods.

Furthermore, officers often made reference to the "good" people in the neighborhood, empathizing with their plight of coping with a troubled environment. Hence, their moral sentiments were not directed at everyone in the community but, rather, individuals believed to possess characteristics that were precursors to crime and delinquency—being unemployed, having antipolice values, not caring about the community, and so forth. Muir (1977) found that the officers he interviewed had a strong sense of morality and immorality, and they equated deviance with immorality. Similarly, officers in our sample reported a clear and strict notion of morality and were unwilling to tolerate segments of the community they believed were responsible for creating community violence via maintaining drug markets, gang affiliation, and participation in other illicit activities—behaviors diametrically opposed to the mission of the police department.

The findings of this study, across four communities, suggest that urban police officers do not racialize or make racial characterizations of entire communities, except in situations where different racial and ethnic groups border each other in the same district and appear to have different levels of disadvantage. One community in our study, where African American and Latino neighborhoods were adjacent and shared the same police officers, provided a unique opportunity to examine racializations and social constuctions of race. This setting seemed to encourage invidious comparisons between the groups, with Latinos being positively racialized and African Americans being negatively racialized by the police.

The mechanisms underlying this racialization process are unclear, but several sources of variation deserve mentioning. These two minority neighborhoods within the same police district were described by the police as different in several ways. The African American neighborhood, in comparison to the Latino community, was characterized as having (a) more serious street-level problems with violence, gangs, and drug markets; (b) more serious physical and social disorder problems such as drinking in public (although this is debatable); and (c) more noncriminal behavior in the community that is negatively valued by the police. Two types of noncriminal behavior are noted: more negative demeanor toward the police and a poor work ethic. Certainly, these variables may interact in complex ways. For example, the police are forced to intervene more often when violence and disorder problems occur and, in turn, these encounters are often negative, thus introducing potentially more problems with civilian (and police) demeanor. In any event, this study suggests that when police officers are given the opportunity to make comparisons between racial and ethnic groups within their beats, racialization is more likely to occur and the comparisons are more likely to favor Latinos than African Americans for a host of reasons. And these comparisons are not always based in fact. For example, officers implied that Latinos were more inclined to attend local community meetings, but these types of statements are inconsistent with the facts (Skogan, 2002).

The police acknowledge that racial profiling is a popular concern, but they are totally befuddled by the concept and feel it does not apply in police beats that are racially homogeneous. How can a police officer profile someone when everyone in the neighborhood is African American or Latino? While this argument is logical, in these narratives we also find subtle indications that racial homogeneity gives police officers license to stop anyone, anywhere, for anything, without concern about racial bias. Furthermore, officers felt that if they, themselves, were a minority or if they had a minority partner, they were completely protected from complaints about racial profiling.

The primary purpose of this article was to understand how the police experience minority communities and, specifically, whether race plays a role in how officers perceive and interpret events and people in African American and Latino neighborhoods. The findings suggest that police are attuned to race in heterogeneous neighborhoods where different racial and ethnic groups live side by side. But for homogenous minority neighborhoods, a new conceptualization of racialization or biased policing may be needed to understand police interpretations of the environment. For example, officers claim that racial profiling is not possible where working in all-minority neighborhoods. Organizational (rather than individual) decisions may explain why some neighborhoods receive more aggressive policing than others. Police organizations that measure performance by the numbers (e.g., arrests, gun seizures, drugs, money) and that deploy large numbers of police officers to minority communities to combat "hot spots" of crime, could be accused of "racially profiling communities" (rather than individuals) and contributing to disproportionate minority mistreatment, arrests, and confinement (Rosenbaum, 2006).

Finally, we need to acknowledge that the absence of police talk about race does not imply that race is not an underlying driver of judgments, especially given cultural sensitivities about racism. More subtle methods of inquiry may be required in future research on this topic.

Critical Thinking

The authors show that race affects the way officers perceive and interpret events and people in African American and Latino neighborhoods. How much do you think that these labels affect the way that police use discretion in these neighborhoods? Do you think that the unequal use of discretion plays a role in how African American and Latino citizens respond to police? Could this be at least a partial explanation for varying crime rates in the neighborhoods?

References

Anderson, E. (1999). *Code of the streets.* New York: Norton.

Barlow, D. E., & Hickman Barlow, M. (2000). *Police in a multicultural society: An American story.* Prospect Heights, IL: Waveland Press.

Barlow, D. E., & Hickman Barlow, M. (2002). Racial profiling: A survey of African American police officers. *Police Quarterly, 5*, 334–358.

Black. D. J, & Reiss, A. J. (1970). Police control of juveniles. *American Sociological Review, 35*(1), 63–77.

Brown, B., & Benedict, W. (2002). Perceptions of the police: Past findings, methodological issues, conceptual issues and policy implications. *Policing: An International Journal of Police Strategies & Management, 25*, 543–580.

Brunson, R. K., & Weitzer, R. (2009). Police relations with White and Black youths in different urban neighborhoods. *Urban Affairs Review, 44*, 858–885.

Cao, L., Frank, J., & Cullen, F. T. (1996). Race, community context, and confidence in the police. *American Journal of Police, 25*(1), 3–22.

Carter, D. L. (1985). Hispanic perceptions of police performance: An empirical assessment. *Journal of Criminal Justice, 13*, 487–500.

Chambliss, W. J. (1994). Policing the ghetto underclass: The politics of law and enforcement. *Social Problems, 41*(2), 177–194.

Cohen, D. S. (1996). Official oppression: A historical analysis of low-level police abuse and modern attempt at reform. *Columbia Human Rights Law Review, 165*(28), 165–199.

Dowler, K. (2005). Jobs satisfaction, burnout, and perception of unfair treatment: The relationship between race and police work. *Police Quarterly, 8*, 476–489.

Fyfe, J. J. (1988). Police use of deadly force: Research and reform. *Justice Quarterly, 5*, 165–205.

Hurst, Y. G., Frank, J., & Browning, S. L. (2000). The attitudes of juveniles toward the police: A comparison of black and white youth. *Policing: An International Journal of Police Strategies & Management, 23*(1), 37–53.

Ioimo, R., Tears, R. S., Meadows, L. A., Becton, B. J., & Charles, M. T. (2007). The police view of bias-based policing. *Police Quarterly, 10*, 270–287.

Jesilow, P., Meyer, J. O., & Namazzi, N. (1995). Public attitudes toward the police. *American Journal of Police, 14*(2), 67–88.

Jones-Brown, D. D. (2007). Forever the symbolic assailant: The more things change, the more they stay the same. *Criminology & Public Policy*, 6(1), 103–122.

Kane, R. J. (2002). The social ecology of police misconduct. *Criminology*, 40, 867–896.

Kane, R. J. (2003). Social control in the metropolis: A community-level examination of the minority group-threat hypothesis. *Justice Quarterly*, 20, 265–295.

Kelling, G. L., & Coles, C. M. (1996). *Fixing broken windows: Restoring order and reducing crime in our communities*. New York, NY: Martin Kessler Books.

Klinger, D. A. (1997). Negotiating order in patrol work: An ecological theory of police response to deviance. *Criminology, 35*, 277–306.

Langan, P., Greenfield, L., Smith, S., Durose, M., & Levin, D. (2001). *Contacts between police & the public: Findings from the 1999 national survey*. Washington, DC: Bureau of Justice Statistics, U.S. Department of Justice.

Lundman, R. J., & Kaufman, R. L. (2003). Driving while black: Effects of race, ethnicity, and gender on citizen self-reports of traffic stops and police actions. *Criminology*, 41, 195–201.

Lurigio, A. J., & Rosenbaum, D. P. (1994). The impact of community policing on police personnel: A review of the literature. In D. P. Rosenbaum (Ed.), *The challenge of community policing*. Thousand Oaks. CA: Sage.

Manning, P. K. (1977). *Police work: The social organization of policing*. Cambridge, MA: The Massachusetts Institute of Technology.

McCluskey, J. D., & Terrill, W. (2005). Departmental and citizen complaints as predictors of police coercion. *Policing: An International Journal of Police Strategies & Management, 28*, 513–529.

Moskos, P. (2008a). Two shades of blue: Black and white in the blue brotherhood. *Law Enforcement Executive Forum*, 8(5), 57–86.

Moskos, P. (2008b). *Cop in the hood: My year policing Baltimore's eastern district*. Princeton, NJ: Princeton University Press.

Muir, W. K. (1977). *Police: Streetcorner politicians*. Chicago, IL: University of Chicago Press.

National Research Council. (2004). *Fairness and effectiveness in policing: The evidence*. Washington, DC: National Academies Press.

Pickett, J. (2000). *The American heritage dictionary of the English language, 4th edition*. Boston, MA: Houghton Mifflin Company.

Platt, T., Frappier, J., Ray, G., Schauffler, R., Trujillo, L., & Cooper, L. (1982). *The iron fist and the velvet glove: An analysis of the U.S. police* (3rd ed.). San Francisco, CA: Synthex Press.

Quilian, L., & Pager, D. (2001). Black neighbors, high crime? The role of racial stereotypes in evaluations of neighborhood crime. *The American Journal of Sociology, 3*, 717–767.

Rosenbaum, D. P. (2006). The limits of hot spots policing. In D. Weisburd & A. A. Braga (Eds.), *Police innovation: Contrasting perspectives* (pp. 245–266). New York, NY: Cambridge University Press.

Rosenbaum, D. P. (2007). Police innovation post 1980: Assessing effectiveness and equity concerns in the information technology era. *Institute for the Prevention of Crime Review, 1*, 11–44.

Rosenbaum, D. P., Schuck, A. M., Costello, S. K., Hawkins, D. F., & Ring, M. K. (2005). Attitudes toward the police: The effects of direct and vicarious experience. *Police Quarterly, 8*, 343–365.

Rusinko, W. T., Johnson, K. W., & Hornung, C. A. (1978). The importance of police contact in the formulation of youths' attitudes toward police. *Journal of Criminal Justice, 6*, 53–67.

Scaglion. R., & Condon, R. G. (1980). Determinants of attitudes toward city police. *Criminology, 17*, 485–494.

Schafer, J. A., Huebner, B. M., & Bynum, T. S. (2003). Citizen perceptions of police services: Race, neighborhood context and community policing. *Police Quarterly, 6*, 440–468.

Schuck, A., Rosenbaum, D., & Hawkins, D. (2008). Influence of race/ethnicity, social class, and neighborhood context on residents' attitudes toward the police. *Police Quarterly, 11*, 496–520.

Skogan, W. G. (2002). *Community policing and "the new immigrant": Latinos in Chicago*. Washington, DC: U.S. Department of Justice.

Skogan, W. G. (2005). Citizen satisfaction with police encounters. *Police Quarterly, 8*, 298–321.

Skogan, W. G. (2006). Asymmetry in the impact of encounters with police. *Policing & Society, 16*(2), 99–126.

Skogan, W. G., & Hartnett, S. M. (1997). *Community policing, Chicago style*. New York, NY: Oxford University Press.

Skogan, W. G., & Steiner, L. (2004). *Community policing in Chicago, year ten: An evaluation of Chicago's alternative policing strategy*. Chicago, IL: Illinois Criminal Justice Information Authority.

Skolnick, J. H. (1966). *Justice without trial: Law enforcement in a democratic society*. New York, NY: Wiley.

Smith, D. A., Visher, C. A., & Davidson, L A. (1984). Equity and discretionary justice: The influence of race on police arrest decisions. *Journal of Criminal Law & Criminology, 75*(1), 234–246.

Sousa, W. H., & Kelling, G. L. (2006). Of 'broken windows', criminology, and criminal justice. In D. Weisburd & A. A. Braga (eds.), *Police innovation: Contrasting perspectives* (pp. 77–97). New York, NY: Cambridge University Press.

Terrill, W. (2005). Police use of force: A transactional approach. *Justice Quarterly, 22*, 107–138.

Terrill, W., & Matrofski, S. D. (2002). Situational and officer-based determinants of police coercion. *Justice Quarterly*, *19*, 215–248.

Terrill, W., & Reisig, M. D. (2003). Neighborhood context and police use of force. *Journal of Research in Crime and Delinquency*, *40*, 291–321.

Torres, S., & Vogel, R. (2001). Pre and post-test differences between Vietnamese and Latino residents involved in a community policing experiment: Reducing fear of crime and improving attitudes towards the police. *Policing: An International Journal of Police Strategies & Management*, *24*, 40–55.

U.S. Census. (2000). *State and county housing unit estimates*. Retrieved from http://www.census.gov/

Weitzer, R. (2000). Racialized policing: Residents' perceptions in three neighborhoods. *Law and Society Review*, *34*(1), 129–155.

Weitzer, R., & Tuch, S. A. (2004). Race and perceptions of police misconduct. *Social Problems*, *51*, 305–325.

Westley, W. A. (1970). *Violence and the police: A sociological study of law, custom, and morality*. Cambridge, MA: The Massachusetts Institute of Technology.

Wilkinson, D. L. (2007). Local social ties and willingness to intervene: Textured views among violent urban youth of neighborhood social control dynamics and situations. *Justice Quarterly*, *24*, 185–220.

Wilson, J. Q., & Kelling, G. L. (1982). The police and neighborhood safety. *Atlantic Monthly*, *249*(3), 29–38.

3

The Highs and Lows of Emotional Labor: Detectives' Encounters with Criminals and Victims

Barbara Stenross and Sherryl Kleinman

Abstract: *Like other occupations that require employees to interact with citizens, police detectives must find ways to manage their own and others' emotions. This can be a difficult task and often leads to burnout. Detectives must interact with offenders and victims, both bring about different types of emotional labor. Stenross and Kleinman show that detectives disliked their encounters with victims, but enjoyed their interactions with offenders. Detectives found interacting with criminals a game, one that they could win. However, detectives could not use the same strategies with victims. Therefore, they found their interactions with victims to be emotionally trying.*

With the shift from a production to a service economy, increasing numbers of Americans have jobs that require them to manage their own and others' feelings. Workers who do "emotional labor" often experience burnout and become estranged from their feelings (Hochschild, 1983). Those called upon to make clients feel good (e.g., flight attendants) must suppress their own feelings of anger; those called upon to make others feel bad (e.g., bill collectors) must suppress their own feelings of compassion. Emotional labor, Hochschild argues, may alienate workers more than the oppressive manual labor of the factory worker. Manual laborers must bend their body to the task, but emotional laborers must surrender their heart.

Some workers find their emotional labor bearable because they have "status shields" (Hochschild, 1983) that protect them from others' emotional onslaughts. For example, the high status of career diplomats, doctors, and judges makes others less likely to challenge them.

What happens to lower-status emotional laborers, those who lack a status shield? The detectives we interviewed considered their "core task" (Hughes, 1958) to be solving crimes and arresting criminals (see also Sanders, 1977; Skolnick, 1966; Waegel, 1981). Yet emotional labor became a part of their work as they faced the outbursts of criminals and victims. Since victims and detectives are on the same side, we expected the detectives to get along well with victims. Perhaps victims would even look up to those who are in a position to help them. And we expected the detectives to find their interactions with criminals a trying experience. Instead, we found the opposite: The detectives felt burdened by victims and energized by criminals. Why?

The detectives lacked a status shield, but they protected themselves from criminals' abusive language and scornful gestures by denying the authenticity of these expressive displays. In addition, criminals gave the detectives opportunities to do "real detective work," to redefine their emotional labor as higher status mental work, and to derive an emotional high from it. Detectives viewed victims' emotional displays as genuine and thus they could not discount them. In addition, victims vented their feelings of frustration on the detectives and expected them to do the kind of emotional labor the detectives could not transform into anything better.

We will examine differences in detectives' emotional labor with criminals and with victims, outlining the strategies that those without status shields may use to transform emotional labor into engaging work. Our study suggests that emotional labor need not be alienating. Even within the same occupation workers may find some emotional labor alienating but other emotional labor bearable or even satisfying.

Research Setting and Methods

We interviewed the investigative staffs of a police and a sheriff's department located in adjacent counties in the southeast. The departments served similar jurisdictions of about 40,000 people. The sheriff's department employed seven investigators and a department head who worked mainly as an administrator. The police department employed six investigators and a department head who also investigated crimes. The detectives, all men, came from both working and middle class backgrounds. Most were born and raised in the South. Five of the detectives were black; about half had attended college.

The detectives began their days by reporting for duty and receiving their new case assignments. When assigned a case, the detectives received the investigative report form that had been filed by the officer on duty when the crime was reported. Those forms included the complainant's (usually the victim's) statement, as well as other details about the crime. The detective's job was to do the follow-up investigation on the cases for which a suspect was not already apprehended. (In violent crimes the dispatcher notified the detective division immediately, and a detective usually joined the patrol officer at the crime scene.) Property crimes, including breaking and enterings, larcenies, and vandalism, made up 89% of the incoming cases in the sheriff's department and 87% in the police department. The average case load per detective was approximately 25 to 30 cases per month.

We conducted semistructured, in-depth interviews to study detectives' interpretations of their work. The interviews took place in the detectives' offices or in interrogation or briefing rooms at the department. Questions included how many cases detectives worked, how they spent their days, how they solved crimes, how their job varied by shift and type of crime, and how they felt about their encounters with criminals, victims, witnesses, and informants. We also asked the detectives to tell us about any matters we overlooked. Each interview ranged from 45 minutes to two and one-half hours.

Since the police are open to public scrutiny and criticism, we expected them to hold back information during interviews. But we found that the detectives' statements were candid and not particularly flattering to themselves or their occupation. For example, the detectives admitted that they did little or no work on many reported crimes, and they were also critical of programs popular among the public, such as community watch and routine dusting for prints. The detectives may have felt comfortable with the interviewer because they knew her husband was a sheriff's deputy. Manning (1967) has suggested that respondents will participate more fully in an interview when they feel they don't have to ingratiate themselves to the interviewer.

Detectives interact with many members of the public. We will limit our discussion to detectives' relations with criminals and victims because these are the audiences the detectives talked about the most and regarded as most important in making them feel good or bad about their work.

Detectives and Criminals

Doing Real Detective Work

The detectives considered themselves crime-solvers and thief-takers (Klockars, 1985). Yet most of the leads the detectives followed led nowhere, and the detectives spent much of their time writing reports and sitting in court (see also Greenwood et al., 1977). Against this background of boredom and bureaucratic routine, their encounters with criminals felt like a breath of fresh air. Criminals gave the detectives opportunities to learn many things street cops and bureaucrats do not know: how criminals commit crimes, how the "criminal mind" works, what criminals do with stolen property, and how they enter the "world of crime." The detectives felt that handling criminals was "real detective work" (see also Van Maanen, 1974: 97), and looked forward to their encounters with them.

All of the detectives believed that burglars and other criminals have particular methods of operation, often specializing in certain kinds of crime. During interviews and interrogations, the detectives tried to get inside information about criminal methods from the criminals themselves. Most criminals did not readily volunteer information about their own or others' crime techniques. But in return for an actual or expected favor (e.g., a lower bond), or by getting the criminal to boast about the crime, the detectives often finagled such information out of them. A novice detective revealed his excitement at learning the ins and outs of how a burglary was committed:

> So he [the burglar] looked in and saw all this [alarm system], so he just took something and popped the glass and knocked it out, reached in and pulled himself in, never set the alarm off! [laugh] He broke into five houses right there in that neighborhood.

The detectives used their familiarity with criminals and criminal techniques to develop notions of "normal crimes" (Sudnow, 1965; Waegel, 1981) and to build suspect pools for future crime-solving. As a veteran detective in the sheriff's department explained,

> You look for patterns of previous break-ins to try to tie them into the same people.

The detectives especially liked to deal with "seasoned" criminals. These criminals were often recalcitrant, but the detectives thought of them as a knowledgeable audience who could evaluate their growing expertise and insights. The detectives believed that seasoned criminals "knew the law" and would only confess to a crime or plead guilty if the detective had built a solid case:

> People that've been through the system won't tell you much unless you got something on them. If you got them *dead right*, got enough on them, they'll do a little talking. They don't want to go back to prison again.

Criminals, then, not only gave the detectives insights into the world of crime, but also served as an audience that could put the stamp of approval on the work they did.

Shielding Themselves

The detectives wanted to solve crimes and put criminals away, so it made sense that they enjoyed arresting suspects and bringing them in for interviews or interrogations. Arrests and interrogations were occasions when the detectives' work finally came to a head. Success was now assured or at least within reach. But criminals did not make things easy for detectives. Brought in for arrest, criminal suspects often yelled at the detectives, cursed them, or refused to talk. At times they cried or became hysterical.

Yet the detectives found a way to let the criminals' emotional outbursts or stubborn silences roll off their backs. They discounted criminals' expressive displays by interpreting them as feigned rather than genuine. The detectives believed that criminals would fake almost any emotion to shake the detective's composure. An older detective who now heads a detective division explained:

> A lot of times they [criminal suspects] are trying to get you angry so that you make a mistake, and that becomes one of the hardest parts of the job.

The detectives dismissed the criminals' emotional displays by conceiving of them as "strategic interaction" (Goffman, 1969), or part of a game. They considered criminals' expressive displays moves, not real emotions. Hence, the criminals' barbs did not go deep. Workers will only take others' emotional displays to heart when they view the emotions as genuine.

The Fun of Mental Work

By regarding criminals as gamesmen, the detectives also set the frame for reinterpreting the emotional labor they did with criminals as mental work. The detectives clearly performed emotional labor with criminals, but their redefinition of it as higher status mental work enabled them to *enjoy* it, thinking of their encounters with criminals as challenging intellectual games.

The detectives liked interrogating suspects because it was their chance to match wits with, and win out over, their archrivals in crime. Until detectives have enough evidence to make an arrest, one young detective explained, "the criminal has the upper hand." But during interrogation, he added with a smile, "the tables are turned." The detectives used information and evidence to "show up" the criminal and control him. The detectives found it exciting to con those whose business is conning:

> You're giving him [the suspect] something he's going to get anyway [a reduced charge], but he doesn't know that yet, and he thinks he's got it because of your, ah, being benevolent, or your influence with other officers. So you use him, you're conning him at the same time they're going to try to con you. And they're going to con you every chance they get.

In face-to-face encounters with criminals the detectives played their hands with cunning and care. For example, when the detectives did not have all the evidence they wanted, they often bluffed, making the suspect believe they had more evidence than they did:

> It depends on how much information you have on the suspect as to which way you would go. You can bluff 'em, of course, make them think you have more than you *do*. Sometimes then they'll reveal a lot more information.

Or, they got the suspect to tell a lie and used the suspect's mistake to "catch him." For example, one detective said he often asked suspects the same questions over and over until they tripped up:

> You ask a lot of questions and you bring this guy in *for* interrogation. And then you start checking him, checking him, and you can pass him the same questions over and over and over until he just makes some mistakes. Then you know you've got him!

The detectives believed that "psyching out" their opponent was crucial for successful interrogation. Before they brought a suspect in for questioning, the detectives tried to find out as much as possible about him so they could "plan what [they're] going to do as far as the suspect." For example, one older black detective said he often tried to talk with the suspect's mother, his high school teacher, or people in the neighborhood before he brought the suspect in for interrogation. But sometimes detectives had to size up suspects they had never met. They found this work challenging:

> You have to *learn* the person that you are dealing with, even though you may have just picked him up on the street. . . . But right then and there begin formulating a picture of this person so you can interview him more intelligently and approach him in a way that he will be more willing to tell you things.

The detectives believed that each suspect required a different style of interrogation (as suggested in textbooks on the interrogation process, e.g., Inbau and Reid, 1953). For example, a veteran detective said he varied his style with suspects. He claimed that some suspects responded well to a "straightforward approach," but others required "playing John Wayne":

> For instance, a 16-year-old boy who has had no experience with the law and has perceived the law in a certain light, if you approach him like a teacher—very honest, straightforward—he may respond. But he'll be more likely to respond if he perceives you as Kojak or John Wayne.

Detectives and Victims Hand-Holding Victims:

The detectives said that victims were often distraught, upset, or angry. Some victims cried or became too upset to endure the interview; others complained endlessly about the crime. A young black detective who had worked for years with the state bureau of investigation complained about an encounter he had just had:

> I went to the house and the man talked two hours. I just couldn't turn him off. He wanted to show me where this happened. He wanted me to talk to this individual.

Another detective said he disliked working the "first part" of rape cases because of the uncomfortable feelings the crime evoked in himself and others:

> I don't like to see anybody beat, or well, maybe she don't have to be beat—crying, you know. You gotta go home and tell her husband, or you gotta tell her mother, and you gotta sit up with her. It's just, I don't like that part.

Even workers who are trained as counselors find it difficult to deal with clients who flood out and lose control (Joffe, 1978). The detectives often felt powerless before victims' emotional outbursts.

The detectives dismissed criminals' emotional displays by viewing them as moves in a game. But the detectives could not use the same strategy with victims. They felt that most victims' emotional displays were authentic, not phony, and even justified. Hence, the detectives thought they *should* feel sympathy for crime victims. Although crime was a routine event for the detectives, they knew it was traumatic for the victim.

In addition, the detective said their superiors *expected* them to cool victims out as a matter of public relations. Police and sheriffs departments are political organizations. Top officials can get ahead only if they maintain good relations with the public (Reiss and Bordua, 1967; Wilson, 1968: 69–70). Consequently, detectives and other subordinates receive pressure from the top to take citizens' complaints seriously. The detectives said they worried that they would get into trouble with the sheriff or police chief if a crime victim complained about lack of attention:

> You really try to go out here and do a job, but you forgot about this one guy over here. I mean, you're really doing a good job for 90% of the people, but this one guy calls the sheriff, "I ain't seen him out here but one time, and blah, blah, blah, blah, blah." And then you got to catch it.

Several detectives talked about pacifying victims as a department policy:

> You can't do anything [on the case], you *know* you can't do anything, you got other things you *can do*, but you go talk to this man [the victim], pacify him, tell him you're going to do something.

The detectives often had a hard time acting sympathetic when people had their microwaves or stereos stolen (a common crime they regarded as not very serious). But they knew that if they did not seem upset, victims might accuse them of indifference and complain to their superiors. This added to the anxiety they felt in encountering victims. A middle-aged detective complained bitterly:

if they're [victims] excited and they're upset, some people resent the fact that the officer doesn't seem to be as bent out of shape as they are about it. People just accuse us of being hard-hearted or say we just don't give a damn.

The detectives found their interactions with victims emotionally trying. They had empathy for victims, but they still resented having to "hold their hands." Moreover, they were supported in their view by the masculine—even macho—ethic of the police culture. Within that occupational culture (Manning, 1969), nurturing others is regarded as low-status women's work (Hunt, 1984). Yet the police are not alone in regarding sympathetic emotional labor as low status. Within the helping professions (such as medicine and law), the highest prestige goes to those who do the *least* nurturing (Abbot, 1974). For example, surgery has the highest prestige in medicine, while psychiatry has the lowest. And corporate tax law has high status, while family law has low status. Although victims were often high-status clients, the detectives disliked dealing with them because they still had to do low-status emotional labor.

Fighting for Autonomy

Many victims usurped the detectives' investigative role, telling them how to solve the case. The detectives felt that their supervisors had the right to direct them. But they resented victims—people without authority or expertise—who told them what to do (see also Mennerick, 1974).

The detectives complained that victims often "played detective." Burglary victims believed they knew who committed the crime, claiming that someone who had recently been to their house (e.g., an electrician or exterminator) had "cased the place" and then returned to steal their property. The detectives were reluctant to follow these suggestions, but knew that many victims would check on whether they had. Also, since following *any* lead is central to solving crimes, the detectives halfheartedly thought of ways to approach those accused by victims. A detective explained:

> A lot of times we have people who are trying to do investigation, they'll give us suspects, and you know, the suspects, their reasons for being suspects are, "He was here, ah, the other day with my son," or something like that. But that's the only reason they got for him being a suspect and they want you to watch him, talk to him, and all this stuff.

The detectives said that victims often demanded that they dust for fingerprints (see also Sanders, 1977: 98). The detectives knew that fingerprints could not be lifted off all surfaces, and that even good prints rarely helped them solve cases that have no suspect leads. As one detective put it, "If you don't have any idea of who that person is to compare those fingerprints with, fingerprints aren't worth a dime to you." When the detectives believed prints would help them make an arrest or pacify a victim they tried to get an identifications expert or patrol officer to do it. Because this was not always possible and victims often demanded prints, the detectives sometimes ended up dusting for prints themselves—a task they regarded as dirty and unpleasant. For example, one detective described his efforts to lift prints in a house trailer:

> It's a real messy job. A lot of us don't like it because that dust goes everywhere. It gets up in
> your nose, in your face. I did it with a white shirt on not too long ago, and it's sort of
> greasy. . . . There was a trailer broken into and the man had a window open on one side and the
> door on the other and I was spreading the stuff and someone says, "It's all over your back"
> [laugh].

The detectives felt even more insulted by victims who suggested that they take
suspects aside and beat them up. The detectives disliked this perception of them as
"heavies" in the war on crime, and resented having to explain that such behavior was
in fact illegal:

> [Victims] think that you can just run out there and kick doors in, arrest people for no reason,
> grab a suspect and smash him up, beat him up and make him tell you that he's been in your
> house. I mean, you know, "I think if you *lean* on him a little, he'll tell you what you want to
> know"—I've had people *say* that!

The detectives believed that victims got their ideas about detective work from television. Since TV crimes are solved within the hour, detectives complained that victims
often expected quick results. As one detective put it, "Victims feel that we can do a lot
more than we can right off the bat, and it's not that simple." Yet the detectives could
not easily put victims off. Some victims called the police station if they did not get
results soon enough or felt the detective was ignoring their case. The detectives felt
hounded by victims:

> Some people, when you've done all you can really do, and you're getting nowhere and you don't
> have any suspects, you're not going to get their property back, uh, you just can't *do* any more,
> and they still keep on saying: [in a whisper] "Whatcha gonna do? Whatcha gonna do?" I tell
> them I've done all I can, but they don't want to hear that. They won't let you rest with that.

Ingratitude

The detectives might have felt more charitable toward victims if they believed that
victims did *their* part. But the detectives said that many victims let them down and
were ungrateful. For example, theft cases require a lot of legwork: Detectives must enter
property descriptors into the state computer system, visit pawnshops in search of the
stolen items, ask their informants about the crime, and go through case files looking for
similar methods of operation or similar thefts. Yet few victims had information about
their property that would make the detectives' efforts worthwhile. Detectives said that
few people mark their property or keep a record of serial numbers for such frequently
stolen items as televisions and stereos. Some victims even give the wrong information
about their property, reporting the theft of a Magnavox TV when they actually
owned a Panasonic. Without good property descriptions, detectives complained, they
could not identify and locate victims' property. One disgruntled detective said:

> People don't understand that if you can't identify your property, there's nothing I can do about it.

When the detectives did recover stolen property, their work was often futile, because
victims could not conclusively identify the item as theirs. Pointing in the direction of

the room where the department stored recovered property, one detective said in frustration:

> A lot of people can't identify their property. Our property room can be loaded with a hundred thousand dollars, but we can't do anything with it.

The detectives also learned that they could not rely on victims to appear in court. Once victims got their property back or received their insurance money, many no longer cared about catching the criminal. One detective mimicked an ungrateful victim:

> I got my stuff back, I don't care what you all do with him, don't call me no more. I'm not coming to court.

The detectives had sympathy for victims' plight, but felt that victims became an emotional burden. Victims took out their anger and frustration on the detectives, misinterpreted the detectives' role as "heavies" or counselors, and abandoned them in their hour of need. The detectives knew the department could not ignore crime victims. But they wished that they weren't the ones who had to keep seeing them. As one detective put it, "Hopefully, someday, we'll have someone right here in the bureau that can sit at a desk and call these people." Other detectives agreed. They thought the department should hire *other* workers to visit or call victims, to free them to do real detective work:

> I think it would take a lot off the investigator if we had someone contact the victim. So the investigator could go out and make the contacts he needs to make in order to solve some of the crimes.

Ironically, they would then be free to spend time with the very people one would expect them to abhor: criminals.

Discussion and Conclusion

The case of the detectives suggests that emotional labor need not be alienating. Even in the same occupation, some emotional labor will be satisfying or at least bearable, while other emotional labor will be alienating.

The detectives' encounters with victims suggest (by their absence) two conditions that may make emotional labor bearable for *other* workers: organizational shields provided by the organization, and status shields provided by prestige.

First, some organizations provided workers with an organizational status shield. For example, bosses can rely on secretaries to field requests and complaints, screen callers and visitors, and serve as the "human face" (Kanter, 1977) of the corporation. The detectives longed for their organization to provide a buffer between themselves and victims. In fact, police and sheriff's organizations do send patrol officers out to take victims' initial complaints. Yet the detectives wanted their departments to hire workers to do all the public relations work the departments expected of them.

Second, prestigious positions offer status shields for workers. For example, doctors, lawyers, and other professionals have acquired the license and mandate (Becker, 1970;

Hughes, 1958) to answer to themselves rather than to others. In addition, students in professional schools learn to distance themselves emotionally from their clients (e.g., Haas and Shaffir, 1977; Kleinman, 1984; Smith and Kleinman, 1988). This "affectively neutral" stance (Parsons, 1951) keeps professionals from feeling put upon by clients' threats or emotional displays. Also, by cultivating a demeanor that people associate with authority, clients often feel too intimidated by professionals to complain to them face-to-face. Affective neutrality sets up an emotional distance in the relationship that clients, having less power and feeling vulnerable, are likely to go along with. This "professional demeanor" may well cut down on the amount of emotional labor a professional will have to do.

Despite these shields, clients may on occasion challenge professionals. Yet the case of the detectives suggests that workers who lack status shields (and those who temporarily find themselves without one) may discover ways to make their work bearable or even enjoyable.

Workers will make work bearable if they can convince themselves that clients' emotions are phony. The detectives felt that criminals feigned emotions in order to protect themselves. Similarly, teachers psych out students, judging between those whose tears are genuine and those whose are ploys to get their grades raised.

Workers will make emotional labor enjoyable if they redefine that work as relevant to the task they value the most. The detectives wanted to solve crimes. Since they defined their encounters with criminals as a way to catch more criminals, the detectives turned an emotionally trying experience into a valuable learning experience. Such a positive redefinition enabled the detectives to regard their encounters with criminals as a challenging and exciting intellectual game. They enjoyed delving into the "criminal mind" and figuring out which interactional style would best elicit information from particular suspects. By reframing their emotional labor as mental work, they transformed these encounters into fun.

Critical Thinking

Stenross and Kleinman discuss the highs and lows of emotional labor for detectives, but all police must engage in emotional labor of some sorts. Think about some of the "highs" and "lows" of emotional labor for patrol officers, dispatchers, crime scene investigators, and parking authorities. In what ways would these various positions bring about different types of emotional labor based on who and how they interact with citizens? Additionally, think about the emotional labor required to successfully get through college. How have you engaged in emotional labor with fellow students, faculty, and administration?

References

Abbott, A. (1974) "Status and status strain in the professions." *American Journal of Sociology* 86: 819–835.

Becker, H. S. (1970) "The nature of a profession," pp. 87–103 in H. S. Becker (ed.) *Sociological Work: Method and Substance*. Chicago: Aldine.

Goffman, E. (1969) *Strategic Interaction*. Philadelphia: Univ. of Pennsylvania Press.

Greenwood, P. J., J. M. Chaiken, and J. Petersilia (1977) *The Criminal Investigation Process*. Lexington, MA: D. C. Heath.

Haas, J. and W. Shaffir (1977) "The professionalization of medical students: developing competence and a cloak of competence." *Symbolic Interaction* 1: 71–88.

Hochschild, A. R. (1983) *The Managed Heart: Commercialization of Human Feeling*. Berkeley: Univ. of California Press.

Hughes, E. C. (1958) *Men and Their Work*. Glencoe, IL: Free Press.

Hunt, J. (1984) "The development of rapport through the negotiation of gender in field work among police." *Human Organization* 43: 283–296.

Inbau, F. E. and J. E. Reid (1953) *Lie Detection and Criminal Investigation* (3rd ed.). Baltimore: Williams and Watkins.

Joffe, C. (1978) "What abortion counselors want from their clients." *Social Problems* 26: 112–121.

Kanter, R. M. (1977) *Men and Women of the Corporation*. New York: Basic Books.

Kleinman, S. (1984) *Equals Before God: Seminarians as Humanistic Professionals*. Chicago: Univ. of Chicago Press.

Klockars, C. B. (1985) *The Idea of Police*. Beverly Hills, CA: Sage.

Manning, P. K. (1967) "Problems in interpreting interview data." *Sociology and Social Research* 51: 302–316.

Manning, P. K. (1969) "Organization and environment: influences on police work," pp. 98–123 in R. V. G. Clark and J. M. Hough (eds.) *The Effectiveness of Policing*. Westmead, England: Gower.

Mennerick, L. A. (1974) "Client typologies: a method of coping with conflict in the service worker-client relationship." *Soc. of Work and Occupations* 1: 396–418.

Parsons, T. (1951) *The Social System*. Glencoe, IL: Free Press.

Reiss, A. J., Jr., and D. J. Bordua (1967) "Environment and organization: a perspective on the police," pp. 25–55 in D. J. Bordua (ed.) *The Police: Six Sociological Essays*. New York: John Wiley.

Sanders, W. B. (1977) *Detective Work: A Study of Criminal Investigation*. New York: Free Press.

Skolnick, J. H. (1966) *Justice Without Trial*. New York: John Wiley.

Smith, A. C. and S. Kleinman (1988) "Managing emotions in medical school: students' contacts with the living and the dead," Presented at the annual meeting of the American Sociological Association, Atlanta, Georgia.

Sudnow, D. (1965) "Normal crimes: sociological features of the penal code." *Social Problems* 12: 255–270.

Van Maanen, J. (1974) "Working the street: a developmental view of police behavior," pp. 83–130 in H. Jacob (ed.) *The Potential for Reform of Criminal Justice*. Beverly Hills, CA: Sage.

Waegel, W. B. (1981) "Case routinization in investigative police work." *Social Problems* 28: 263–275.

Wilson, J. Q. (1968) *Varieties of Police Work*. New York: Atheneum.

4

Vice Isn't Nice: A Look at the Effects of Working Undercover

Mark R. Pogrebin and Eric D. Poole

Abstract: *Undercover work is important for proactive policing, but it can create a number of negative consequences for those who do. Using interviews with undercover officers from federal and municipal agencies, Pogrebin and Poole examine the consequences of working undercover for police officers. Specifically, they discuss the impact of working undercover on officers' interactions with informants, suspects, interpersonal relationships with family, and readjustment to routine police duties.*

Undercover police operations have increased greatly since the 1970s (Marx, 1988). An extensive body of work has addressed a variety of issues involving covert police activities, such as deceptive tactics (Skolnick, 1982), criminal inducements and entrapment (Marx, 1988; Stitt and James, 1985), corruption (Pogrebin and Atkins, 1979), and moral dilemmas and ethical decisionmaking (Schoeman, 1986). These studies generally have dealt with criminal justice policy implications of undercover operations; little attention has focused on the effects of undercover work on the officers themselves (Girodo, 1984; 1985).

In this study undercover work was defined as assignments of police officers to investigative roles in which they adopt fictitious civilian identities for a sustained period of time in order to discover criminal activities that are not usually reported to police or to infiltrate criminal groups that are normally difficult to access (see Miller, 1992). This study examined the consequences of working undercover for police officers. Focusing on role dynamics and situated identity in undercover assignments, it explored the impact of work experiences on officers with respect to their interaction with informants and suspects, interpersonal relations with family and friends, and readjustment to routine police activities.

The Nature of Undercover Work

Assignments to undercover units are avidly sought and highly valued. The selection process typically is intense and very competitive. Most undercover police units require interested officers to make application in the form of a request to transfer, which is followed by a series of rigorous interviews and assessments to screen out all but the best qualified for the specialized unit. Since an elite few are actually selected for undercover assignments, these officers enjoy a professional mystique associated with the unique nature of their work.

Undercover assignments allow officers wide discretionary and procedural latitude in their covert roles. This latitude, coupled with minimal departmental supervision, allows the undercover agent to operate with fewer constraints, exercise more personal initiative, and enjoy greater professional autonomy than regular patrol officers. Manning (1980) cautioned that such conditions may lessen officer accountability, lower adherence to procedural due process, and undermine normative subscription to the rule of law.

Marx (1988) further argued that police subcultural norms of suspicion and solidarity may take a conspiratorial turn as undercover agents adopt a protective code of silence not unlike that characteristic of organized crime. Covert intelligence gathering procedures and processes become highly insular, almost peripheral to routine police operations. There develops a need-to-know doctrine in which information is strictly guarded and selectively shared. The secrecy required for clandestine police work offers rich opportunities for self-aggrandizement, with many agents developing an exaggerated sense of power. As Marx (1988:161) concluded, "the work has an addictive quality as [officers] come to enjoy the power, intrigue, excitement and their protected contact with illegality."

The undercover agent typically must operate alone; moreover, the deeper the level of cover required in the investigation, the more isolated the officer becomes (Williams and Guess, 1981). Direct and sustained management of covert activities is practically impossible because of the solitary nature of the work. When supervision is lax or nonexistent, undercover officers are prone to cut corners, which may lead to an end-justifies-the-means type of attitude (Manning, 1980). In addition to the inadequate supervision, often there are no written departmental policy guidelines covering undercover operations for officers to rely on in lieu of direct supervisory control. Even when policies are explicated in departmental operations manuals, typically they are neither known nor followed by officers (Farkas, 1986).

Lack of supervision and effective policy guidelines diminish operational accountability and responsibility at the department level, leaving officers in the field to fend for themselves. Consequently, undercover agents often devise their own operational procedures in order to accomplish unit objectives. These officers develop individualized styles of working, relying on personal expertise and judgment (Marx, 1985; 1988).

Methods

Three federal law enforcement agencies and eight municipal police departments located in the greater Denver metropolitan area participated in the present study. The researchers approached each agency with a request to obtain the names of officers who were presently or formerly assigned to undercover operations and who would be available for personal interviews with the researchers. Utilizing the lists of study volunteers provided by the respective agencies, the researchers contacted each officer initially to determine his or her length of undercover experience and present assignment. The officers were then stratified according to these two variables so that a wide range of work experiences, from entry to termination of undercover work, would be tapped. Next, 20 officers who currently were working undercover were selected—ten having less than three years and ten having three or more years of undercover experience, and 20 officers who were not presently assigned to undercover operations also were selected—ten having less than three years and ten having three or more years of prior undercover experience. The sample of 40 officers was comprised of 35 men and 5 women. Their ages ranged from 28 to 45 (mean = 37), and their undercover experience ranged from one to seven years (mean = 4).

All interviews were conducted at the respective agencies in either subject offices, private conference rooms, or interrogation rooms. Each interview lasted approximately two hours and was tape-recorded with the subject's consent. An unstructured in-depth interview format was used, which relied on sequential probes to pursue leads provided by subjects.

The Impact of Undercover Work

Informant Relations

Since officers must learn to operate on their own much of the time and since undercover work is proactive, one of the most critical requirements is the ability to cultivate informants for information on illegal activities and for contacts with active criminals. The relationship between an officer and an informant is to a great extent symbiotic, for they come to rely upon one another for services they can obtain only from each other. The cooperation of informants in supplying information is fundamental in most police intelligence-gathering operations. Deals and bargains must be struck and honored for cases to be made. Informant relations are really exchange relations. For example, Skolnick (1975) noted that at each link in the chain of a narcotics investigation officers must make arrangements with suspects in order to move to the next higher level in the criminal organization responsible for the purchase, manufacture, and distribution of the narcotics. According to one federal agent,

> An informant is the easiest, quickest way to do police work. . . . [He] can walk you in the front door and take you directly to the crook and introduce you face-to-face.

Officers must develop and maintain stable relations with informants who can provide reliable information over time. The incentives that officers can offer informants to secure their cooperation or compliance often involve a carrot-and-stick approach. One officer provided several examples of the tactics he has used with his informants:

> Getting cases dropped . . . or dealing with probation officers for not going hard on them. Lobbying district attorneys or city attorneys about the cases, or getting bonds reduced so that they can bond out of jail. . . . Getting their cars released from the pound so they can get their wheels back. I have even loaned them money out of my own pocket.

Left to their own personal devices in working with informants, however, some officers may resort to questionable practices:

We would have the person arrested by other officers, not knowing why they were involved. They usually were arrested for misdemeanor warrants. We would then get them out of jail in return for information. It would appear to the informant that we were doing him a favor.

A related problem involves officers' discretion to overlook illegal activities of informants in order to preserve access to information. This practice may cause agents to lose their sense of perspective regarding the relative importance of their operations in crime control; that is, these officers may come to believe that the types of crimes they are fighting pose a greater public safety concern than the offenses committed by their informants. The immediate justice meted out through arrests of informants for their crimes seems to be far outweighed by the long-term crime control benefits that may be realized only through the use of information these individuals provide. This utilitarian view may be advanced even by police administrators, who emphasize the larger public safety view of crime control; that is, these administrators convey the view that the activities of street criminals may be ignored for the purpose of getting at the "heavy hitters" who run criminal organizations. As one officer observed,

> You see captains and lieutenants using people and not putting them in jail for certain warrants so that they can get more information. . . . You see there is no problem doing it even though it was a violation of the operations manual. We feel if the captain can do it, and do it in front of us like that, then we can do it.

This reliance on active criminals for information about other active and ostensibly more serious criminals creates a variety of challenges to the integrity of police work. For example, informants are not bound by procedural due process constraints. Moreover, the tolerance of informant lawlessness by law enforcement officials in the interest of securing information may blur the line between legal and illegal police practices.

> [Informants] . . . are going to screw up, so you've got to cover their ass. I've had to do things on several occasions, like setting up some guy, just to clear an informant. . . . You just know that when they screw up . . . they're always able to turn around and offer something that makes up for that.

On the other hand, many officers are sensitive to the risks involved in depending on informants for information to do their jobs. Informant information may be faulty and, if acted upon, could jeopardize, compromise, or embarrass the officer. One federal agent illustrated the problem:

> The main basis for our intelligence and what we go by in initiating investigations usually is a confidential informant, who are criminals themselves, which makes their motives suspect. I have seen cases where we were sure as we could be about a suspect, and we have been wrong. Our information came from an informant who had been corroborated in the past and had been pretty trustworthy, and you still get burned.

The officer–informant relationship is driven by reciprocity but grounded in deceit. Both the agent and the informant must create illusions in the dual roles they play— both pretend to be people they are not. Credibility and reliability are tenuous commodities where misrepresentation of self is the key to continued relations.

Informants, as active participants in illicit enterprises, are part of the cover that affords police access to criminals (Manning, 1980); however, the illegal activities informants engage in while working for the police pose a problem of control. Police undercover operations must not disrupt routine criminal processes, which include illegal behavior by informants. Thus, it is not uncommon for informants to take advantage of their protected status by pursuing more criminal opportunities. For police, it is imperative that informants' motivations for cooperation be judged and their roles in undercover operations be monitored. Assessing informant motivation and directing informant participation are critical in managing undercover operations. The observations of officers typify this perspective:

> A guy that is motivated by money is pretty easy to control. The ones that are into revenge are also easy to control, because if they think they are getting back at someone, or as long as you keep them thinking that you are doing this to get back at so-and-so, they are okay. . . . The hard ones to control are the ones who are doing it because it's fun or a game to them. They think they are smarter than you. . . . You control snitches by strength of personality—letting them know your rules and . . . knowing their motivation.

> You never take anything they [informants] do for granted. I put myseif in their position and ask, "What's in it for me?" You then get a feeling for what they're doing and why. What you don't want is surprises.

As Levine (1990:45) noted, " 'Never trust a snitch' . . . is one of the most important proverbs in the unwritten bible of a narc." Many undercover officers have echoed this sentiment, often adding that informants do not deserve to be treated well. After all, informants typically commit a range of criminal acts, and they may be perceived as no different than the offenders who are being targeted. Two agents sized up their informants as follows:

> [Y]ou can't turn your back on them for a second or they will bite you. They lie to you all the time. They are untrustworthy. They have the morals of an alley cat.

> [I]nformants are some of the sorriest excuses for human beings imaginable—like sociopaths, no conscience. They're just looking out for themselves. . . . I have dealt with some real scum bags, and you can feel awfully dirty later on . . . .

From such sentiments arise purely utilitarian justifications for the manipulation of informants and their treatment as disposable byproducts of undercover operations. For example, several officers noted that it would be counterproductive to become too concerned about the personal well-being of an informant simply because informants are expendable; that is, once a police operation concludes, an informant may be cut off from the department or, in some cases, arrested and prosecuted. For many veteran officers, informants become almost invisible, blending into the background of the criminal environment. There is no affect associated with their dealings with informants; personal relations are feigned for instrumental purposes. One officer summed up this approach:

> Informants can appear to be our friends and we can appear to be theirs; however, they are a necessary tool of our trade and must be treated that way. . . .

In contrast, some officers experience genuine feelings of concern for informants as individuals. They point out that they frequently must establish and nurture relationships with key informants over extended periods of time. Such relations inevitably lead to a mutual exchange of personal information. It is not surprising that these relationships may foster conflicting emotions among officers:

> I have sympathy for some of my informants. . . . You spend a great deal of time working with them and listening to their problems. Basically, you are their keeper while they are working for you. You start to feel responsible for what they do. You wonder why their life is such a mess. I try to keep that separate, but you really can't . . . .

While relations with informants pose significant problems for officers, close association with targeted criminals heightens the challenges of the undercover role considerably. As the next section shows, the stakes are higher and the costs of deception are greater.

Identification with Criminals

As noted previously in this article, undercover infiltration into criminal networks requires the use of techniques that include presenting a false identity in interaction with offenders in their environment. However, the agent is not feigning his or her entire presentation of self. Much of his or her genuine self is actually incorporated into the false identity created. After all, he or she is playing a role, and, like a method actor, the officer actually strives to identify personally with the part:

> You have to learn to be an actor because you're pretending to be somebody you're not. . . . [Y]ou're pretending to be a crook, and the crook thinks you're a crook, so you must rely on personal experience.

The officer's job is actually made easier through incorporating much of himself or herself into the performance. As one undercover agent observed.

> It's best to tell as few lies as possible. The fewer lies you tell, the easier the lies are to remember and keep straight. And your lies should be related to your personal life experiences. This makes recall easier. . . . You should not attempt to change your life history . . . because you are likely to confuse what you said to each crook.

In a Federal Bureau of Investigation study of its special agents who were involved in deep undercover operations, many operatives were found to experience profound changes in their value systems, often resulting in overidentification with criminals and a questioning of certain criminal statutes they were sworn to enforce (U.S. Department of Justice, Federal Bureau of Investigation, 1978). Two federal agents in the present study reported these types of problems in their long-term undercover assignments:

> I identified very strongly with the bad guys. . . . Even though these people were breaking the law, they had some fairly good reasons for doing it. . . . I realized everything wasn't black and white. Everything became kind of gray. . . .

> It didn't take me long to get into the way of thinking like the crooks I was running with. I started identifying with these people very quickly. . . . [P]art of it was identifying with them and part of it was trying to fit in with them.

The deep undercover operative who lives under false pretenses for months or years necessarily forms close relationships with those under investigation, as well as with their associates, friends, or families. There are subtle assimilation processes involved in undercover work since officers must adjust and adapt to an unfamiliar criminal subculture; consequently, officers may take on, in greater or lesser degree, the folkways, mores, and customs of that criminal subculture. For some, the net result is having their conventional outlook undermined and conventional bonds of social control weakened. Such processes free the officer to engage in nonconventional activities characteristic of the criminal primary group with which he or she affiliates, as illustrated in the following report:

> You get into a case where you are undercover for a very long period of time, where you are acting like a puke-ball for a year or more in order to make a huge case. I mean, you start hanging around these guys and start picking up their bad habits . . ., doing things that are not really related to the case and hanging out with people you shouldn't be with.

Undercover operatives come to share many experiences with those under investigation in order to be perceived as authentic. While this sharing heightens officer credibility, it also promotes bonding, which in turn fosters understanding of and sympathy for the targeted individuals.

> You are only human and you get to know and like a lot of people. When you're a year with these people, they become your friends. You share your problems with them . . . [and] they make sacrifices for you . . . .

Prolonged and intense interaction within a criminal network leads to emotional conflicts. Since deception requires a dual self-identity for the agent, there is constant tension between loyalty and betrayal in performing an undercover role and an uneasy moral ambiguity, as revealed in the following remarks of [a] narcotics officer:

> There are cases that you don't want to see come to an end because you don't want to arrest them. You like the people. You hate to see their lives ruined. You hate to think about what they are going to think about you. . . . You would like to just slide out of the picture and never be seen again.

The observations of the next two officers indicate that they felt morally tainted by the undercover experience.

> It is something that you have to live with that just doesn't go away. It nags and eats at you. You feel really bad about it—all the people that got caught up . . . [in the operation], and their lives were ruined and their kids' lives.

> Knowing what I know now, I don't think I could ever work narcotics again . . . . I know I've changed. Certainly more cynical about what we're doing . . . . And for what? To dirty ourselves like the crooks?

The work orientations and habits developed by undercover officers often have spillover effects on their interpersonal relations with family and friends. These problems are described in the next section.

Relations with Family and Friends

Undercover assignments may disrupt or interfere with an officer's family relationships and activities. As Marx (1988:166–67) observed, undercover work exerts pressure on interpersonal relations because of "the odd hours, days, weeks away from home, unpredictability of work schedules, concern over safety, late night temptations and partying that the role may bring, and personality and life style changes that the agent may undergo."

Some undercover officers have difficulty separating the traits and attributes associated with their deceptive criminal roles from their normal demeanor in conventional social roles. They experience role strain in shifting between the criminal identity at work and the conventional identity at home.

> Trying to be what the crooks were caused me some real problems with my wife right off the bat. We would go to a social gathering and I would end up off in some corner staring into the back yard and probably drinking too much, because I didn't like the pressure. People would come up and ask me what I did for a living and I had some cockamamie story I would give . . .; it was always some lie.

For some officers, adopting a deceptive criminal identity for an undercover assignment essentially precludes their assuming their conventional identity while off-duty. As a veteran agent observed,

> There are a lot of guys who I don't think have been able to put their undercover role aside when they go home. When they work undercover, they are always undercover.

In Farkas's (1986) study of former and current undercover police officers in Honolulu, 41 percent reported adverse changes in interpersonal relations with family and friends, 37 percent experienced stress in associating with family and friends in public, and 33 percent expressed anxiety over not being able to discuss their assignments with family and friends. In the following observations, officers in the present study have provided first-hand accounts of the types of problems revealed in the research by Farkas (1986). First, an officer described some of the disruptive effects of his work on family relationships:

> [A] lot of times I was involved in undercover operations where I would spend so much time away from home . . . . Then you go home grumpy. You don't feel like doing anything with the family. They want to go out for a burger. I just got through eating fifty burgers in the last two weeks . . . . The last thing I want to do is go out and get in the car. So, undercover work messes up your family life a lot.

Second, being in an active undercover role often can cause officers to worry about the safety of their families when they are with them in public; there is concern about the possibility of chance encounters with suspects or criminal associates who know the officers by undercover identities:

> [W]e may have gone to a shopping mall or somewhere with my family and see somebody who may be involved in a case or may know who you are, so you wouldn't want your family to be part of it. So, I found myself limiting my activities . . . to pretty much just staying at home with

> the family. Or when I did go out, not taking them with me. This isolation was definitely stressful for all of us.

Third, the need to maintain secrecy in covert operations restricts communication with family and friends, heightening feelings of uncertainty and danger associated with the work:

> I was totally isolated from my family and friends. I couldn't tell them where I was . . ., how [I was] doing or what [I was] working on . . . . [It] was extremely painful and upsetting [and frightening] to them . . . . My whole family really took a beating over that period of time.

Law enforcement organizations rarely prepare officers or their families for the kinds of interpersonal problems they are likely to face as a result of an undercover assignment. Two former narcotics officers in the present study lamented the negative effects in hindsight:

> I would give anything if prior to working undercover I would have known some of the pitfalls and some of the pressures that were going to be put on my family situation.

> Things got kind of crazy . . ., out of control, really. I lost perspective on a lot of things, including my wife and kids, and she ended up divorcing me . . . . I should have seen it coming, but I was so into my work that it didn't matter at the time. Nothing mattered at the time.

A common theme of undercover work that runs through the dramatic life-style changes revealed above is a "separation of self." Undercover work typically requires officers to adopt a criminal persona, distancing themselves from a conventional life style. This transformation involves isolation from police peers, family members, and friends, as well as from conventional places where activities with these individuals normally occur. These people and places provide the emotional, psychological, social, and moral bearings for conventional living. To a great extent, these bearings reflect and reinforce one's personality, a part of the self; thus, the separation of that part of the self is akin to a loss of identity. Officers working undercover are expected to seem to be people they are not through role-playing; however, their isolation in those roles actually may foster real changes in attitudes, values, beliefs, manner, habits, demeanor, character, and identity (Strauss, 1988). Operatives may begin to think and feel like the criminals they are impersonating. Who they are, or are becoming, may be confusing to family, friends, and colleagues. These individuals are perceived as different. The relational landscapes are altered, and the situations are disorienting.

Return to Routine Police Work

Ending an undercover assignment and returning to patrol duty can be awkward for many officers. These former operatives often experience difficulty in adjusting to the everyday routine of traditional police work. Farkas (1986) reported that former undercover agents frequently suffer from such emotional problems as anxiety, loneliness, and suspiciousness; moreover, they experience disruptions in marital relations. Similarly, Girodo (1984) noted that the return to regular police duties after a lengthy assignment as an undercover operative is analogous to coming down from an emotional high. Officers in this situation often report feeling lethargic and depressed as well as experiencing self-estrangement in their new assignments. After six years in an undercover unit, this former narcotics agent described his adjustment problems:

> I was well trained for something else. What am I doing here? At times it hits you hard. For three months on graves I didn't want to hear about vice and narcotics. I didn't want to see them, hear about them, or know anything about them. I just didn't want any contact because it was painful. . . . I don't blame anybody. I knew I was going to be rotated out . . ., but yet I feel cheated somehow.

Two former undercover officers commented on the psychological impact of being transferred back to patrol:

> I was really pissed off. I had a short fuse and would go off for no reason at all. I guess I was even trying to provoke some sort of response. . . .

> I was bored and restless and resented what I was doing. I just didn't feel good about myself and was mad at everybody. I didn't feel anybody understood what I was going through because they hadn't done the things I had.

Many of the problems associated with reassignment to patrol duties can be attributed to decreased autonomy and diminished personal initiative in job performance. For example, working a certain geographic area of the community, responding primarily to radio-dispatched calls for service, handling noncriminal cases, and being subject to closer supervisory monitoring of activities all make for less exciting work experiences than those enjoyed in undercover assignments (Marx, 1988). A veteran officer reflected upon what he missed the most following his transfer to patrol after five years in an undercover unit:

> The excitement in undercover work is, to me, the ultimate. An officer is actually doing something and creating things that are happening. He comes back on the street and back to a daily routine . . . . I still miss the close-knit unit and having the kind of freedom and control we did.

Former undercover agents generally see themselves as having developed and honed special skills as a result of their undercover experiences; consequently, they feel that their talents and abilities are wasted in routine assignments. As the following comments show, officers view their return to patrol as the functional equivalent of a demotion:

> It's like stepping backwards. I mean, you have accomplished a lot of things . . . [in] seven years in undercover. You get better and better over time and suddenly you're sent back to where you were seven years ago—right back at the bottom.

> Narcotics is not a glamorous job. You got to be tough mentally. You get that only from experience. . . . Narcotics officers should be assigned on a permanent basis and not rotated out after a set number of years. . . . I'll never be able to adjust to patrol; my career is ruined.

For several former narcotics officers, the return to routine police duties was even more devastating; they expressed deeply held personal beliefs and commitment concerning the societal importance of their undercover work. As undercover narcotics agents, they saw themselves not just on the "front lines" fighting the war on drugs;

they felt they had assumed even greater risks by going undercover "behind enemy lines" to infiltrate and destroy criminal networks. Their experiences were intense, inherently dangerous, and exciting. Some of these officers actually perceived themselves as engaged in a perverse form of trench warfare, as soldiers whose mission was to win the war on drugs one dealer at a time. The following comment is representative of this sentiment:

> Highly committed members of an elite narcotics unit want no part of ordinary police duties . . ., handling DUIs, domestics, and noise complaints. . . . Drugs are our number one problem, and I got tremendous satisfaction getting drug traffickers off the street . . . . There is a drug war going on out there, and it bothers me a lot I'm no longer . . . doing my part.

Finally, Girodo (1985) noted that some attributes thought to be beneficial in an undercover assignment (e.g., deceptive, manipulative, inclined toward risk taking) may have adverse consequences in routine police work. For example, ex-undercover officers tend to adopt a more proactive approach to policing, with an emphasis on the "strategic management" of suspects. As one former undercover investigator explained;

> I talk to arrestees differently. I am always looking for what information they can give me as opposed to throwing them in jail and forgetting about them like I did before I was in undercover. Now all I think about is, "Can I get something out of them?"

Undercover officers are likely to have developed a different working style and demeanor—often characterized by heightened suspicion, cynicism, and caution—that may escalate conflict in interaction with suspects or undermine citizen satisfaction and confidence in service calls. Such consequences have led several officers to stress the need for a decompression period; that is, former operatives need time off for gradual reentry into their new assignments:

> I think it's extremely dangerous to go back on the street in uniform and deal with citizen complaints just off a long undercover assignment. You're just not ready to handle those types of problems. . . . I mean, you're not comfortable or as confident as you should be. And I guess you try to make up for that with a lot of bravado. . . . You really need some time away to get things straight again.

For many officers, an understanding of the dramatic changes they have undergone as a result of their undercover experiences arises only in retrospect, after they have had time to appreciate the stark contrast between the demands of their former and present work assignments fully.

Conclusions

Unlike police officers with conventional assignments, undercover agents tend to operate primarily within criminal networks. The agent's ability to blend in—to resemble and be accepted by criminals—is critical for any undercover operation. Deception is continuous and must be adhered to consistently for the illusion to be maintained; that is, the officer's appearance and demeanor must seem natural and genuine.

An operative is required to adopt an alternate identity. The undercover officer must be a good improviser in order to perform convincingly in accordance with the role demands of a false identity. When a person's identity is changed, even for the temporary purpose of acting a part, the individual comes to view himself or herself differently; he or she is not the same person as before. This identity transformation helps the officer to fit in with those of the criminal world in which he or she now operates. It is not unexpected, then, that prolonged participation in a criminal subculture may create role conflicts for the officer.

In addition, the officer must manage a split between conventional and non-conventional identities. Typically, undercover work requires the officer to obtain new identification documents, to change appearance (e.g., clothes, hair style, beard, make-up, etc.), and to alter demeanor, speech, and life-style in order to fit in with suspects. Over an extended period of time, undercover pursuits tend to isolate the officer from contact with friends and relatives, thus limiting or precluding participation in conventional activities. The undercover officer is often far removed, both physically and emotionally, from support systems and institutional symbols that serve to define his or her conventional self. Without such relational ties to reinforce his or her normal identity, sustained interaction with law violators threatens to undermine the maintenance of a conventional self concept. The line separating the self concept associated with the role of an undercover cop and the self concept tied to the responses of deviant others who reinforce the role performances becomes increasingly blurred. The norms of police ethics may thus be turned upside down in undercover work.

Critical Thinking

One of the major findings from this study is that working undercover can exact a heavy toll on detectives. Consider the article by Stenross and Kleinman about emotional labor. How do you think working undercover affects the emotional labor of being a detective? In what ways do you think working undercover exacerbates the difficulties detectives have when interacting with innocents, victims, offenders, and their families?

References

Farkas, G. (1986). Stress in undercover policing. In *Psychological services for law enforcement*, ed. J. T. Reese and H. A. Goldstein. Washington, DC: U.S. Government Printing Office.

Girodo, M. (1984). Entry and re-entry strain in undercover agents. In *Role transitions: Explorations and explanations*, ed. V. L. Allen and E. van de Vliert. New York: Plenum Press.

—— (1985). Health and legal issues in narcotics investigations: Misrepresented evidence. *Behavioral Sciences & the Law* 3:299–308.

Levine, M. (1990). *Deep cover*. New York: Delacorte Press.

Manning, P. K. (1980). *The narc's game: Organizational and informational limits on drug enforcement*. Cambridge, MA: MIT Press.

Marx, G. T. (1985). Who really gets stung? Some issues raised by the new police undercover work. In *Moral issues in police work*, ed. F. A. Elliston and M. Feldberg. Totowa, NJ: Rowman and Allanheld.

Marx, G. T. (1988). *Undercover: Police surveillance in America*. Berkeley, CA: University of California Press.

Miller, G. I. (1992). Observations on police undercover work. In *Order under law* (4th ed.), ed. R. G. Culbertson and R. Weisheit. Prospect Heights, IL: Waveland Press.

Pogrebin, M. R., and Atkins, B. (1979). Some perspectives on police corruption. In *Legality, morality and ethics in criminal justice*, ed. N. N. Kittrie and J. Susman. New York: Praeger Publishers.

Schoeman, F. (1986). Undercover operations: Some moral questions about S. 804. *Crim Just Ethics* 5:16–22.

Skolnick. J. H. (1975). *Justice without trial: Law enforcement in democratic society*, 2nd ed. New York: John Wiley and Sons.

—— (1982). Deception by police. *Crim Just Ethics* 1:40–54.

Stitt, B. G., and James, G. (1985). Entrapment: An ethical analysis. In *Moral issues in police work*, ed. F. A. Elliston and M. Feldberg. Totowa. NJ: Rowman and Allanheld.

Strauss, A. L. (1988). Turning points in identity. In *Social Interaction*, ed., C. Clark and H. Robbey. New York: St. Martin's Press.

U.S. Department of Justice, Federal Bureau of Investigation (1978). *The special agent in undercover investigations*. Washington, DC: U.S. Department of Justice.

Williams, J., and Guess. L. (1981). The informant: A narcotics enforcement dilemma. *Journal of Psychoactive Research* 13:235–45.

5

Reflections of African-American Women on their Careers in Urban Policing: Their Experiences of Racial and Sexual Discrimination

Mark R. Pogrebin, Mary Dodge, and Harold Chatman

Abstract: *Pogrebin, Dodge, and Chatman examine the social organizational relationships and interactions that position African-American police women as outsiders within their own department. Their exclusion arises not only from dominant white males but also from subordinate groups, such as white female and black male officers. They find that persistent and pervasive patterns of perceived sexual and racial discrimination permeate the work environment for African-American police women. Black women often experience gender discrimination related to professional abilities, job performance, and supervisory responsibilities. They also experience racism in the form of derogatory remarks, and in the areas of hiring and promotion. Their marginal status based on gender and race is also readily apparent in their relationships with other officers.*

Introduction

The experience of African-American women in a largely white male-dominated occupation is almost entirely lacking from the research literature. Overall, research on the experiences of minority women has been limited in number and restricted in scope (Gilkes 1981). Studies of black women have been regarded as deviant cases or incorporated into studies of women in general with the primary focus on white women's universal experiences (Collins 1986; Gilkes 1981). Few systematic studies have focused on discrimination against minority women (Nkomo 1988; Schroedel 1985). This research explores gender and race discrimination as experienced by black female police officers.

Historically, occupational norms have been linked to work segregation by sex (Jacobs 1989; Laws 1979; Stockard & Johnson 1980). Sex typing by specific jobs, though arbitrary, follows one basic rule: men and women are different and should be doing different things. Such stereotypical thinking has long sustained the stigmatization of those who violate norms of occupational segregation, thus reinforcing sex-role typing in the work place. Sex-role stereotypes function to keep women in ancillary and supportive roles, rather than in positions of independence, authority, and leadership (Safilos-Rothschild 1979).

Early studies and contemporary literature reveal that women who have entered a variety of traditional male occupations have faced discriminatory hiring assignments and practices, opposition from co-workers, and inadequate on-the-job training (Gray

1984; Gruber & Bjorn 1982; Kanter 1977; Meyer & Lee 1978; O'Farrell & Harlan 1982; Swerdlow 1989; Walshok 1981). Policewomen remain a marginalized, unaccepted minority, not only in the United States but also in other countries, despite a long history of involvement in policing (Brown 1997, 2000; Dene 1992; Heidensohn 1992; Reiner 1992). Women officers may be labeled by their male counterparts as interlopers, who have invaded male territory. By entering an occupation that is perceived as masculine in nature, women may be seen as intruders into the male police officers' self-defined role of brave, strong, and courageous protectors of the community (Yoder 1991). Women who enter the profession and hold their own as good police officers often present a threat to the masculine self-perception and image that male police wish to maintain. The cop culture, described by Reiner (1992:124) is one of "old-fashioned machismo" (for a discussion of this problem in the UK see Brown 2000).

The marginalization of policewomen is well documented, but generally ignored within law enforcement agencies. The informal "canteen" cop culture is entrenched in offensive humor, sexual stereotypes, and harassment (Balkin 1988; Brown 1997; Fielding 1994; Heidensohn 1992; Hunt 1990; Martin 1990; Reiner 1992; Young 1991). Reiner (1992) suggests that internal solidarity among police officers coupled with social isolation masks conflicts within the organization. Consequently, the divisions between male and female officers are rarely addressed by administrators and are exacerbated by informal rules embedded in the masculine subculture. The "cult of masculinity" continues to denigrate, condescend, and deny full access to women who seek policing careers (Young 1991).

The problems of acceptance for African-Americans in police work appear to be particularly acute. Alex (1969) argued that African-American males often experience "double marginality" as a result of the expectations held by the dominant majority for their dual roles as minority group members and as police officers. Belknap and Shelley (1992) concluded from their study of policewomen that race played a role in how minority females were perceived within their departments. Further, they suggest that black women were less likely than white policewomen to believe that male police recognized them for good police work. Belknap and Shelley also found that black female police officers experience double marginality as a result of being a woman and a member of a racial minority. Black female police officers, who face the additional obstacles associated with gender discrimination, seem to suffer from marginality to a much greater degree than their male minority counterparts.

Black women's occupational experiences in the police world point to the existence of racism and sexism that Collins (1990) believes are an integral part of male domination over women in occupations that are defined as male-oriented. When sexism and racism are two dominating factors that are prevalent in an organization it remains unclear which attribute, race or gender, is the principal cause of the differential treatment (Martin 1994; West & Fenstermaker 1995; Yoder & Aniakudo 1997). Lewis (1977), however, noted that many black women perceive race as a more important factor for their subordinate positions than gender. For black policewomen it may be unclear whether discriminatory behavior toward them is the result of gender or of racial bias. Martin (1994) concluded from her study that 77 percent of white policewomen reported facing sex discrimination from male officers while 61 percent of black females reported racial discrimination and 55 percent reported sex discrimination as the more frequent experience. Clearly, there is evidence to suggest that both sexual and racial discriminatory practices may be widespread throughout police departments in the United States.

Minority police and women also are subject to special stressors such as exclusion from the informal channels of support and information, as well as ostracism and overt racial or sexist comments by white officers (Ellison & Genz 1983; Morash & Haarr 1995). Martin (1994), who studied the social and work relations of black policewomen, found that the forms of exclusion black females experienced were poor instruction communication; peer hostility and ostracism through the silent treatment; over-supervision; exposure to dangerous situations; and inadequate back-up by male officers. Strained relationships among officers cause additional stress for many female policewomen (Pogrebin & Poole 1998; Yoder, et al. 1983). Additionally, black women often experience degrading stereotyping (Dill 1979). According to Doerner (1995) in a study of police officer retention patterns, black females leave the job at a much higher rate compared to all other police—on average leaving during their fourth year. One important reason for early termination may be the direct result of exclusionary practices that black women experience in a white male environment.

Methods

This research focused on African-American policewomen who work in an urban police department. The department has approximately 1400 sworn law enforcement officers of which only 21 are black females—all of whom served as respondents in this study. The median age of the women was 37 years old (range = 21 – 51). Their police employment ranged from 1 to 22 years. Their educational background varied from high school to post-graduate degrees, with more than half having attended or graduated from college.

Interviews were conducted at the respondent's homes, in restaurants, on ride-alongs, and at off-duty jobs. Each interview lasted approximately 90 minutes and was tape-recorded with the subject's consent. A semi-structured interview format was used, which relied on sequential probes to pursue leads provided by the women, allowing the officers to identify and elaborate on important domains they perceived to characterize their experiences in police work. The interview tapes were transcribed for qualitative data analysis, employing grounded theory techniques advanced by Glaser and Strauss (1967).

Findings

Gender Discrimination

The majority of officers in this study experienced a wide variety of discrimination. The respondents indicated mixed feelings concerning which discriminatory practice—gender or race—was most prevalent. Sexual and racial discrimination can be subtle.

Often the recipient is unaware of the discrimination, as demonstrated by one respondent who stated: "I think a lot of times we don't realize we are just being discriminated against, and we put it off on something else. So sometimes it's hard to identify". In contrast, another officer described being a black woman in a predominantly white male organization as "just being a double minority, black female, you are going to have it, you know, three times as hard". Rhode (1989) differentiates between sexual and racial discrimination—the latter often is motivated by the intent to degrade and disempower, while the former is motivated by paternalism. The results show that gender appears to take precedence over race in terms of sexist behavior in three areas: professional abilities, job performance, and supervisory duties.

Discrimination based on gender was seen as a common problem among the women interviewed. One woman stated: "I find it more directed at the fact that I'm a woman as opposed to I'm black. If there is any kind of negative feelings ever, it's always the woman thing". When reflecting on what she would tell her daughter about being a minority policewoman, this officer related the following thoughts concerning race and gender:

> Hopefully by the time she [is] old enough, some things [will] have changed. But I would have to tell her that there is prejudice among the police in the department, not only because she's black, but because she is a woman. In my personal experience, I've faced a lot more prejudice or negative remarks because I was a woman, more so than because I was black.

Another respondent described her view of the discrimination she experienced during her struggle to enter the Homicide Bureau: "I had more trouble getting there because of being a woman than I did because I was black". Similarly, one officer claimed that gender discrimination is more relevant to the status of minority women in the department than race. She explained that white males are less likely to perceive black women as a threat compared to black males. Consequently, she believes that "black females tend to suffer more from gender related issues than racial issues".

In instances where sexism is overt and rather easy to identify, we found that black woman experience similar treatment from both black and white males. Male officers of both races share some of the same gender attitudes when judging female police. In an incident at the training academy, a young black recruit commented: "Why's those bitches here? You guys, you should be cooking, fixing dinner for your husband".

In another example, a lesbian policewoman related her treatment by white male peers in the gang unit:

> The guys really resented the fact that I don't sleep around with anybody. They put things on my locker, nasty notes, anti-gay material, anti-woman material, pornographic pictures. The toilet I would go in on the weekends, and I'd be the only female there, would be overflowing with excretion. It was just unbelievable.

The issue of potentially threatening situations and the male officer's desire for masculine backup by fellow officers may make gender a more important factor than race to male officers in certain circumstances. This is expressed pointedly by a female minority officer. Here, gender rather than race, appears to be the important variable:

They [white males] don't know if in a fight they can count on you. I think that this is their main concern. Will you be there in the end? Will you be there side-by-side fighting with me? I think that's more of a concern for them. They know a black guy's going to fight and be there for them. You know what I'm saying? A white male police officer doesn't, in my opinion, have to worry in his mind whether or not the black male is going to be there as his partner fighting and protecting him or what needs to be done. However, the white male is definitely wondering about what a female is going to do, not what this black female is going to do, but what is this female going to do?

Police Subculture Exclusion

Male police officers in the Vice Squad displayed a paternalistic attitude toward one of the interviewees when she was temporarily assigned to the unit. The minority female officer was required to visit a topless bar with some of her male peers. The males working with her felt she shouldn't be exposed to this environment. The respondent expressed her views on this behavior:

Then the night guys, they were like embarrassed. They were embarrassed to take me to a topless bar where women were dancing. We were supposed to be there, I mean this is our job. I mean they can go out there and watch women shake their pussy in their face and everything, but if they go with a female officer, then they are embarrassed that I'm there.

A few women described blatant incidents when they were excluded from mainstream communication. One respondent, for example, received the clear message that she was not a valued member of the team and that she would never be accepted as part of the unit no matter what she did in the way of accomplishments on the job. She noted:

I was being left out of the information loop, therefore, I didn't have the information when I'd go on calls. I was being completely left out. If I did not come in and research an incident on my own, I would not know. The guys in my unit would get together and have coffee and lunch. They would make sure they'd get on the air and call out that they were going to coffee. They would specifically name names, this is who is invited to coffee, and I would be the only one on the east side left out. It got really bad. I knew that this was becoming a real bad situation when I had three armed suspects at the shopping center at gunpoint, and I'm calling for help. All the people in my unit were sitting at Denny's, and they never gave me backup.

Failing to provide backup when a peer is calling for help on the radio is probably the most flagrant act of malfeasance for police officers. Yet, according to this respondent, she often encountered this type of behavior. Few examples of exclusion can be more unambiguous than your peers knowing you are in a dangerous situation and ignoring your calls for assistance.

Specialized assignments in various areas of police departments are looked upon as earned rewards for good police work. Women have a difficult time obtaining these assignments and often higher-ranking police, who select officers for these positions, feel that women are incapable of performing adequately. In one instance, a black woman discussed her struggle to get into the elite Homicide Bureau:

I knew from past experience with the captain there that he didn't think that Homicide was an appropriate job for a woman. Then because of a female captain, I got the job in Homicide. You never know what new battle you've got to fight. You don't know if it will be a battle because of sexism or it will be because of racism.

Paternalistic behavior toward female officers may be problematic in the areas of supervision and evaluation. A female line patrol officer found herself in a frustrating situation that she believed resulted from stereotypical attributes ascribed to women. This woman explained how her sergeant's patronizing attitudes toward women resulted in an unfair evaluation. According to the interviewee, the sergeant said: "I don't think you're going to make a very good officer. You're too nice. You actually talk to people".

The acceptance of women in police work remains problematic for many male officers, and supervision by a woman is even more difficult to accept. Perhaps men view women who have more experience, expertise, and knowledge as threatening. One officer described the difficulty with men who refused to accept her knowledge of various aspects of police work:

> No, they don't look at me as a senior officer because I am female and don't any male officer want a female to teach them anything or think they can be taught anything by a female officer who happens to be black.

Women at the supervisory rank experience difficulties with male police officers working under their direction. Even in these instances, where the authority comes with the rank, male police often are unco-operative. A black female sergeant explained her problems with men whose attitudes about working for a woman caused real problems in her unit:

> You have got to be prepared to face a lot of discrimination because there are a lot of men that point blank refuse to work for you, not only because you're a female, but because you are a person of color and they will not hide that. They do not care what kind of alleged discipline might happen to them because of it.

Racial Discrimination

The officers interviewed were exposed to racist as well as sexist attitudes within the organization. For these respondents, race also cast them as outsiders. This point was made in a somewhat different way by one woman, who said: "believe it or not, I think that racism is more open. Sexism is more subtle". The racism experienced by participants was most apparent in the derogatory racial remarks made by fellow officers in their presence. Racism also was a predominant theme in hiring and promotion.

In their study of minority policewomen on the Los Angeles Police Department, Felknes and Schroedal (1993) found that minority female officers reported receiving racial slurs from their supervisors and peers. Approximately 40 percent of black women officers and 36 percent of Hispanic women police claimed that they had experienced such verbal abuse. They also report that nonwhite females in the department are the recipients of a greater degree of discrimination than their white female peers or male minority police. This research indicates that derogatory racial remarks were common for women in this study. The following sums up a respondent's feelings about white officers who made derogatory racial remarks in front of her:

> Young white cops discriminate against minorities openly. The thing that scares me is that the older officers maybe know how to hide it better, but the newer officers, it's real blatant. You can go to a call with them, they will call someone a nigger in front of you and not think twice.

When racial remarks are made openly by police officers, one would expect that their superiors would take action against such utterances and that punitive sanctions would be forthcoming. Unfortunately, superiors often ignore such remarks. One of the most disturbing aspects of their Los Angeles study, noted Felknes and Schroedal (1993), was management's obvious tolerance for racial remarks. When complaints were made about particular racist and sexist groups to the organization, complainants were told that the remarks and discriminatory behavior were only jokes and pranks. Those interviewed experienced similar reactions by their superiors:

> If you make those command officers or anybody else of rank above you accountable for the actions of the people who work for them and follow the police manual, then maybe we could get some people for discrimination. The diversity training we went through is just documented bullshit; there is no one to enforce it.

Police officers often know that racial remarks are overlooked by their department. The lack of punishment for those police who continually disparage minorities may encourage openly racial remarks. Overt sexist remarks, however, are taboo because police managers appear to be more willing to enforce sex discrimination policies. One woman explained that blatantly sexist acts were prohibited, but "it's okay to make racist comments openly because nobody is beating anyone across the head and getting disciplined for that". One officer explained that "it's serious when your administrators are not aware of certain words and terms that are sensitive to black people. Because they are not aware of it they perpetuate the problem".

The fact that both black male and female police officers are such a small percentage of the overall organization may explain why some white policemen feel free to openly verbalize racial slurs about minority citizens without fear of reprisals. Obviously, such derogatory statements do little to help improve relations between black and white police officers. One woman stated:

> You hear it all the time in the way they describe suspects. For people that are supposed to be trained, intelligent people, who feel that blacks can't do the job and aren't educated enough, they themselves are blatantly ignorant when they try to describe different ethnic groups or when they use a lot of ethnic slang when they are on the radio or off the radio or just out on a call out of the ear shot of the commanders. They figure, what the hell, what are they going to do? Fire me? They really don't give a shit.

Black police officers may discover that being culturally different is seldom tolerated within the organization. Griffin (1997) notes that black police officers are segregated by culture in their own organizations. According to the black policewomen we interviewed, the non-acceptance of black culture by the majority of white police tends to isolate minority officers. One respondent questioned how black individuals can be expected to leave their race behind when it is repeatedly thrown back in their face: "I don't make an issue of my race, it's just who I am. I walk in, I'm black. That's just the way it is. I have heard them call me 'bitch', 'fucking bitch', and 'black bitch' ".

Yamoto (1995) argues that racial prejudice shapes minority self-perception. According to Yamoto, racism results in the acceptance of mistreatment by some people by leading them to believe that being treated with little or no respect is to be expected because of their race. Others may respond differently, choosing to fight racial disrespect whenever they encounter it, as one respondent suggested:

> When we hear someone calling someone a "spic", we can't just sit there and say, "O.K., dang, I'm glad he didn't call me a 'nigger' ". We have to react to that, too. It's not just on us, it's not just a black thing. Prejudice is prejudice. You have to react to it. You have to take a stand and let them know that it's not going to be tolerated whether they're calling someone "nigger" or "spic" or whatever.

Hiring and Promotion Issues

Some white officers may believe that police departments hire blacks because of their minority status. A simultaneous perception by dominant white males is that minorities who are hired under affirmative action guidelines are unqualified for the positions they attain. The following excerpt exemplifies a respondent's perception that white officers believe people of color who are on the police force were hired as a result of rigged selection schemes:

> You come on the department, and you're told you're only hired because you're black. They had a hiring quota. They had a different list for blacks and a different list for whites. We are told that the tests are fixed for you to pass and all this other garbage.

The black policewomen in this study commonly were told that they were unqualified or that they would be unable to measure up adequately once they began street patrol. The following response indicates that, from the interviewee's perspective, white male officers perceive minorities as a threat to the status quo: "I mean there is still racism and prejudice, and they still think black people don't belong on this job anyway".

The attitude on the part of many white officers toward black women, as expressed by the women, leads one to conclude that white males see black females as unqualified to be police officers. One respondent stated: "The whites' attitude was that they lowered standards for us to get in, which is a lie. Then they would say that it doesn't mean just because they hired you that we're going to keep you".

Once on the job for a period of time, some black women actually attained advancement in the department. White males reacted negatively in those rare instances when this occurred. One black woman made detective after only three a half years on the force. She commented on the "heartaches" and "jealousy" that accompanied her promotion. She explained that fellow officers believed that her accomplishments were because "she's a black female". The same officer was told the following concerning her promotion to the Detective Bureau: "I heard a detective say, 'It's strange to me that they would promote you at this time. They only did it because you are black' ".

White male police seem to have a difficult time distinguishing between merit and preferential treatment for minorities when they are promoted. Such a pervasive attitude on the part of white male police was expressed by another woman, who stated:

"Since I've been here, all I have seen is gripes, and I hear complaints about blacks who only get promoted cause they are black". She explained, "If a white person winds up lower on the list than a black person, and that black person gets promoted, it's only because he's black". Clearly, the women perceive that their white male peers believe that both black women and men receive preferential treatment as a result of race. In reality, few blacks have been promoted above the rank of sergeant in this department. A reaction to these allegations concerning the promotion of minorities being based on race is exemplified by the following statement of one respondent:

> I can't explain it, except that it makes no sense to me that every time a person of color, or a black person is up for promotion, it always seems like, they can't quietly get promoted and go on with their lives. There's always gotta be some issue surrounding either who they are or how they got to where they were. It's not like that with white officers. White officers make rank everyday, and you never hear all of the other issues like you do with black officers.

One participant explained that many black officers feel that not standing out improves their chances for advancement:

> I think with black officers it plays a part in how they make decisions. That's why I always think for blacks in order to get where you want to, you have to try to be as neutral as possible without compromising yourself or without demeaning yourself. You have to be as neutral as possible in their world because it makes them [white police] feel uncomfortable.

Remaining neutral and not making waves, while simultaneously not demeaning oneself, places a minority police officer in a compromised position. To gain a promotion requires the presentation of a non-controversial and conforming image to white police supervisors. Paradoxically, members of a minority who need to stand up against racism must submerge their self-image to exhibit the characteristics required for promotion.

One woman provided an additional reason for the problematic nature of minority promotion. She raised the issue of the comfort level whites require: "I think they are afraid to put black people in charge. It doesn't have anything to do with our qualifications, it has to do with if we make them comfortable". According to the majority of respondents, conditions for black officers are unlikely to improve. One woman, for example, stated: "They are never going to allow blacks on this job to constitute more than the quota for the population. And now that mandatory hiring for minorities no longer exists, I think I see it going backwards". In the areas of hiring and promotion of minority police, the majority of black women officers believe conditions are not improving fast enough in the department to make notable differences during their working lives.

A Shared Pride

Black policewomen appear to be excluded from the police subculture both internally and externally. Martin (1994) claims that black women have limited expectations of climbing onto the pedestal as many white women do or of becoming one of the boys. Black women, Martin notes, have been able to distance themselves from the police culture and adopt a more critical view of it as well as find a place in which they feel comfortable. This may be one reason black women avoid off-duty social contact with both white and black male officers. A respondent explained:

> So as a rule, I would say black women don't have time to socialize with other cops. The black women that I know already feel under siege for being black, for being female, so I don't have time to be playing hanky panky with anybody.

Black female respondents said that often they view their white female peers as needing protection from male officers when involved in threatening street encounters. The women we interviewed prided themselves in not having to be as dependent on male officers to rescue them in similar situations. A shared pride in their ability to handle tough circumstances as a result of their lifelong experiences exists among these officers and is exemplified by the following remark: "It's like black women since they have been on the bottom for so long, are a lot stronger than white women. Just internally stronger". The respondents also felt that white women were overly concerned with being accepted by higher status white males, often at the expense of other women, as noted by the following statement: "I've seen some women really go at it. I mean not physically, but I'm talking about back stabbing, the rumors, the cut throatness".

The perception of support by black male officers for black female officers varied widely by respondent. Some of the women officers believe that their presence on the police department actually improved black males' status position among the white male officers of the department. From the perspective of some black policewomen, many black male officers are deliberately not supportive of black women as a result of their own minority status in the department. One woman explained her viewpoint of the situation: "The black men, even on this job, are just a little bitty cut of society, and they don't support black women". Another woman offered a functional explanation for the lack of support black females receive from their black male counterparts. She said: "I found them non-supportive, self-interested. I don't know if they were conscious about it, they had gone into a protective stance, and that's where they stayed. So it was to protect themselves and you had to deal with looking after yourself". Protecting one's self-interest may be linked to conscious perceptions that black male police have concerning their desire for inclusion within the police organization. In short, being overtly and enthusiastically supportive of black women police may not be beneficial to a minority male's occupational status due to prejudices on the part of many white males who control the politics of the department.

Black female officers in this study also experienced alienation from white male officers. A woman commented that "the majority of white officers are kind of afraid of black women. They don't know what to do with us. How to categorize us. Where to put us. They don't understand us". Many of the women seemed to feel that white policemen stereotype women to keep them subordinate. A respondent discussed one stereotype that she believed was prevalent: "Unless you are a little blonde headed, beautiful looking floozy with a nice ass and good boobs; you know they don't want anything to do with you for showing that you are a Tarzan and you can pick up a stolen car or shoot 20 rounds". Overall, the women indicated that they perceive white officers with skepticism and usually appear to distrust their intentions. Being accepted into the police subculture is difficult for black women who are cognizant of the separation that color makes within the department. One respondent stated: "On this job, they really want you to believe we're all one. But once you take your uniform off and you're driving home, boom! You're black again. You're not blue".

Conclusions

The experiences of African-American police officers in this research show a pervasive pattern of racial and sexual discrimination. It appears that black policewomen suffer from a three-fold dilemma occupationally. They are female members of a minority group in a white male dominated organization. Formal and informal organizational norms contribute to the continuing marginalization of minorities and women. Research on the social organization of policing shows that officers adjust their working relationships and interactions with their own perceptions of the social and political departmental environment as well as their own interests and experiences in the organization (Fielding 1988; Haarr 1997). Tolerance of sexist and racial behavior, along with discriminatory hiring and promotional practices, perpetuates discrimination, exclusive subcultures, and stereotyping among police officers.

Though many of the policewomen were able to contextualize and separate problems related to either sexist or racist behaviors, they also acknowledge the combined effect of being a woman and a minority as a unique problem. Historically, the treatment of race and gender as mutually exclusive categories has resulted in isolating black women from feminist theory and anti-racist policy discourse based on a discrete set of experiences that ignores multi-dimensionality (Crenshaw 1991). Denial of the intersection of race and gender forces women to devalue the part of the self that does not fit or is not accepted with a particular category (Williams 1991). The problem is exacerbated for African-American policewomen because of their dual marginality in a predominately male organization.

Occupational obstacles that African-American policewomen face may diminish as an increasing number of women enter the workforce, though support of their peers both off and on the job is a crucial element for reducing discrimination. Few people, however, are willing to align themselves with those at the bottom. Martin (1994) asserts that white and minority women see acceptance by male officers of the same race as more important than the support of other women, for both work-related and social reasons. The respondents overwhelmingly focused on the need for racial solidarity. One woman believed, for example, that "there is an understanding that we need to look out for each other; that we need to take care of each other". The women we interviewed understand the importance of a cohesive and supportive group, but many feel that they are unable to come together to discuss their problems. The women also recognize that this lack of unification perpetuate their problematic experiences. Some officers, however, noted positive change and increased support among minority members of the department.

Despite affirmative action mandates and research that shows women make satisfactory police officers (Martin 1992), females comprise only ten percent of all municipal police officers in America (Polisar & Milgram 1998; Reaves 1989). Female police often experience hostility and resentment from their male peers (Balkin 1988; Belknap & Shelley 1992; Brown 1997; Herrington 1993; Townsey 1982). Discrimination against women officers is prevalent and continuous (Coffey *et al.* 1992; Erez & Tontodonato 1992). This negative treatment is thought to be an important stress factor for women officers (Anderson *et al.* 1993; Balkin 1988; Poole & Pogrebin 1988; Wexler & Logan 1983). It is unlikely that the opportunities for black female officers will improve unless police departments hire more black women. The organizational subculture must change from within before minority groups will gain acceptance, fair treatment, and job satisfaction. Women will continue to be viewed as outsiders as long as sexist and racist behaviors are tolerated.

Critical Thinking

The authors find that discrimination in the work place has had a lengthy history for racial minorities and women. Although there have been gains made in hiring and promotion, these groups are still under-represented in police departments today despite equal opportunity laws passed some years ago. Why do you think this is? Are women and minorities not attracted to such positions or are they blocked from gaining entry into them? How do you think community perceptions of police affect the decisions of women and minorities to choose policing as an occupation?

References

Alex, H. (1969) *Black and Blue.* New York: Appleton, Century, Crofts.

Anderson, R., Brown, J. & Campbell, E. (1993) *Aspects of Sex Discrimination Within the Police Service in England and Wales.* London: Home Office Police Research Group.

Balkin, J. (1988) Why policemen don't like policewomen. *Journal of Police Science and Administration* **16**, 24–38.

Belknap, J. & Shelley, J. (1992) The new lone ranger: policewomen on patrol. *American Journal of Police* **12**, 47–75.

Brown, J. (1997) European policewomen: a comparative research perspective. *International Journal of the Sociology of Law* **25**, 1–19.

Brown, J. (2000) Discriminatory experiences of women police. A comparison of officers serving in England and Wales, Scotland, Northern Ireland and the Republic of Ireland. *International Journal of the Sociology of Law* **28**, 91–111.

Coffey, S., Brown, J. & Savage, S. (1992) Policewomen's career aspirations: some reflections on the role and capabilities of women in policing in Britain. *Police Studies* **15**, 13–19.

Collins, P. (1986) Learning from the outsider within: the sociological significance of black feminist thought. *Social Problems* **33**, 14–30.

Collins, P. (1990) *Black Feminist Thought: Knowledge, Consciousness, and the Politics of Empowerment.* New York: Routledge.

Crenshaw, K. (1991) Demarginalizing the intersection of race and sex: a Black feminist critique of antidiscrimination doctrine, feminist theory, and antiracist politics. In *Feminist Legal Theory* (Bartlett, K.T. & Kennedy, R., Eds). Boulder, CO: Westview: pp. 57–80.

Dene, E. (1992) A comparison of the history of entry of women into policing in France and England and Wales. *Police Journal* **65**, 236–242.

Dill, B. (1979) The dialectics of Black womanhood. *Signs* **4**, 543–555.

Doerner, W. (1995) Officer retention patterns: an affirmative action concern for police agencies. *American Journal of Police* **14**, 197–210.

Ellison, K. & Genz, J. (1983) *Stress and the Police Officer.* Springfield, IL: Charles Thomas.

Erez, E. & Tontodonato, P. (1992) Sexual harassment in the criminal justice system. In *The Changing Roles of Women in the Criminal Justice System* (Moyer, I., Ed.). Prospect Heights, IL: Waveland, pp. 227–252.

Felknes, G. & Schroedal, J. (1993) A case study of minority women in policing. *Women and Criminal Justice* 4, 65–89.

Fielding, N. (1988) *Joining Forces: Police Training, Socialization, and Occupational Competence.* New York: Routledge.

Fielding, N. (1994) Cop canteen culture. In *Just Boys Doing the Business: Men, Masculinity and Crime* (Newburn, T. & Stanko, E., Eds). London: Routledge, pp. 46–63.

Gilkes, C. (1981) From slavery to social welfare: racism and the control of Black women. In *Class, Race and Sex* (Swerdlow, A. & Lessing, H., Eds). Boston: G.K. Hall, pp. 288–300.

Glaser, B. & Strauss, A. (1967) *The Discovery of Grounded Theory: Strategies for Qualitative Research.* Chicago: Aldine.

Gray, S. (1984) Sharing the shop floor: women and men on the assembly line. *Radical America* 18, 69–88.

Griffin, J. (1997) African Americans in policing. In *Policing America: Methods, Issues, Challenges* (Peak, K. Ed.). Uppersaddle River: Prentice-Hall, p. 357.

Gruber, J. & Bjorn, L. (1982) Blue-collar blues: the sexual harassment of women auto-workers. *Work and Occupation* 4, 271–198.

Haarr, R. (1997) Patterns of interaction in a police patrol bureau: race and gender barriers to integration. *Justice Quarterly* 14, 53–85.

Heidensohn, F. (1992) *Women in Control? The Role of Women in Law Enforcement.* Oxford: Clarendon Press.

Herrington, N. (1993) Female cops. In *Critical Issues in Policing* (Dunham, R. & Aldert, G, Eds). Prospect Heights, IL: Waveland, pp. 361–366.

Hunt, J. (1990) The logic of sexism among police. *Women and Criminal Justice* 2, 3–30.

Jacobs, J. (1989) *Revolving Doors: Sex Segregation and Women's Careers.* Stanford, CA: Stanford University.

Kanter, R. (1977) *Men and Women of the Corporation.* New York: Basic Books.

Laws, J. (1979) *The Second X: Sex Role and Social Role.* New York: Elsevicr.

Lewis, D. (1977) A response to inequality: Black women, racism and sexism. *Signs* 3, 339–361.

Martin, S. (1990) *On the Move: The Status of Women in Policing.* Washington: Police Foundation.

Martin, S. (1992) The interactive effects of race and sex on women police officers. *The Justice Professional* 6, 155–172.

Martin, S. (1994) Outsider within the station house: the impact of race and gender on Black women police. *Social Problems* 41, 383–400.

Meyer, H. & Lee, M. (1978) *Women in Traditionally Male Jobs: The Experiences of Ten Public Utility Companies.* U.S. Department of Labor, Employment, and Training Administration. U.S. Government Printing Office: Washington, D.C.

Morash, M. & Haarr, R. (1995) Gender, workplace problems and stress in policing. *Justice Quarterly* 12, 113–135.

Nkomo, S. (1988) Race and sex: the forgotten case of the Black female manager. In *Women's Careers: Pathways and Pitfalls* (Rose, S. & Larwood, L., Eds). New York: Praeger.

O'Farrell, B. & Harlan, S. (1982) Craftworkers and clerks: the effect of Male coworker hostility on women's satisfaction with nontraditional jobs. *Social Problems* 29, 252–265.

Pogrebin, M. & Poole, E. (1998) Sex, gender, and work: the case of women jail officers. In *The Sociology of Crime, Law, and Deviance* (Ulmer, J., Ed.). Greenwich, CT: JAI Press, pp. 105–124.

Polisar, J. & Milgram, D. (1998) Strategies that work. *Police Chief*, October, 42.

Poole, E. & Pogrebin, M. (1988) Factors affecting the decision to remain in policing: a study of women officers. *Journal of Police Science and Administration* 16, 49–55.

Reaves, B. (1989) *Police Departments in Large Cities, 1987.* Washington, D.C: U.S. Department of Justice, Bureau of Justice Statistics.

Reiner, R. (1992) *The Politics of the Police* (2nd edition). Toronto: University of Toronto.

Rhode, D. (1989) *Justice and Gender: Sex Discrimination and the Law.* Cambridge, MA: Harvard University.

Safilos-Rothschild, C. (1979). *Sex Role Stereotypes and Sex Discrimination: A Synthesis and Critique of the Literature.* U.S. Department of Health, Education, and Welfare, National Institute of Education. Washington, D.C.: U.S. Government Printing Office.

Schroedal, J. (1985) *Alone in a Crowd: Women in the Trades Tell Their Stories.* Philadelphia, PA: Temple University.

Stockard, J. & Johnson, M. (1980) *Sex Roles.* Englewood Cliffs, NJ: Prentice-Hall.

Swerdlow, M. (1989) Men's accommodations to women entering a nontraditional occupation: a case of rapid transit operatives. *Gender and Society* 3, 373–387.

Townsey, R. (1982) Black women in American policing: an advancement display. *Journal of Criminal Justice* 10, 455–468.

Walshok, M. (1981) *Blue-Collar Women: Pioneers on the Male Frontier.* New York: Anchor.

West, C. & Fenstermaker, S. (1995) Doing difference. *Gender and Society* 5, 178–192.

Wexler, J. & Logan, D. (1983) Sources of stress among women police officers. *Journal of Police Science and Administration* 11, 46–53.

Williams, P.J. (1991). On being the object of property. In *Feminist Legal Theory* (Bartlett, K.T. & Kennedy, R., Eds). Boulder CO: Westview Press, pp. 165–180.

Yamoto, G. (1995) Race and racism. In *Race, Class, and Gender* (Anderson, M. & Collins, P., Eds). Belmont, CA: Wadsworth Publishing, pp. 71–75.

Yoder, J. (1991) Rethinking tokenism: looking beyond numbers. *Gender and Society* **55**, 178–192.

Yoder, J. & Aniakudo, P. (1997) Outsiders within the firehouse: subordination and difference in the social interactions of African American women firefighters. *Gender and Society* **11**, 324–341.

Yoder, J., Adams, J. & Prince, H. (1983) The price of a token. *Journal of Political and Military Sociology* **11**, 327–337.

Young, M. (1991) *An Inside Job*. Oxford: Clarendon Press.

B Outsiders

6

Procedural Justice and Order Maintenance Policing: A Study of Inner-City Young Men's Perceptions of Police Legitimacy

Jacinta M. Gau and Rod K. Brunson

Abstract: *Jacinta Gau and Rod Brunson examine young men's self-described experiences with order maintenance policing. They interviewed 45 male adolescents who resided in disadvantaged neighborhoods in St. Louis, Missouri, about their experiences with involuntary interactions with police. They find that young men perceive much bias in interactions with police. For them police stops are simply harassment for being young and black. The authors conclude that order maintenance policing strategies have negative implications for police legitimacy and crime control efforts via their potential to damage citizens' views of procedural justice.*

Police and citizens often hold vastly different views of law enforcement practices. Where order maintenance policing efforts are concerned, this discrepancy may be especially pronounced. Many police administrators and politicians assert that aggressive enforcement of low-level criminal activity sends a strong message to potential offenders that officers will not tolerate even the slightest transgressions. By altering the social meaning of disorder, zero tolerance initiatives are intended to create an environment of perceived constant surveillance (Bratton & Knobler, 1998; Kelling & Coles, 1996; Wilson & Kelling, 1982; see Greene, 1999).

Citizens' perceptions of such tactics, however, may be quite different from those of police and city leaders. Proactive policing initiatives directed at minor offenses exemplify the state's exertion of a level of power disproportionate to the severity of the crimes being committed (Harcourt, 2001); that is, the state brings its law enforcement power down forcefully against offenses that some might consider non-serious or even downright trivial. There is not consensus as to whether the state is justified in employing such extraordinary measures. In addition, evidence suggests that some order maintenance strategies may disparately affect disenfranchised persons such as minorities and the poor (Roberts, 1999; see also Duneier, 1999), as these efforts are not always distributed evenly throughout social strata.

Standing in juxtaposition to the concept of order maintenance policing are the notions of procedural justice and police legitimacy. Procedural justice is the process-based criterion by which individuals evaluate whether they were treated fairly (Tyler & Wakslak, 2004) and it can mean the difference between satisfied and disaffected citizens. The policing literature contains ample evidence attesting to the importance of procedural justice in police–citizen encounters (e.g., Tyler, 1990; Tyler & Folger,

1980), even when such interactions result in arrest (Bouffard & Piquero, 2010; Paternoster, Brame, Bachman, & Sherman, 1997; see also Sherman, 1993).

Uniting the concepts of order maintenance policing and procedural justice makes clear the potential for conflict. On the one hand, order maintenance supporters tout the strategy as an indispensable crime-fighting tool (e.g., Dilulio, 1995; Kelling & Bratton, 1998; Kelling & Coles, 1996). On the other hand, aggressive policing can leave citizens feeling humiliated, violated, or even victimized (e.g., Brunson, 2007; Duneier, 1999; see also Sherman, 1993). The popularity of aggressive order maintenance policing among police executives and politicians has, unfortunately, outpaced academic research regarding the strategy's capacity to reduce crime (Worrall, 2006) and scholars' efforts to better understand its impact on police-community relations (see Roberts, 1999). The need for more research concerning the effects—both direct and collateral—of aggressive order maintenance policing is clear.

Some researchers have examined the effects of order maintenance policing on crime and/or fear. Most have relied upon survey research or official crime data and have typically focused on adult citizens' general perceptions of disorder, crime, and fear (Bennett, 1991; Braga et al., 1999; Hawdon, Ryan, & Griffin, 2003; Katz, Webb, & Schaefer, 2001; Novak, Harman, Holsinger, & Turner, 1999; Sampson & Cohen, 1988). Quantitative data derived from adult samples, however, capture only a thin cross-section of society and overlook those who may be the very ones who have the most to say about the effectiveness and collateral consequences of order maintenance policing.

In-depth interviews offer a unique opportunity to focus on the experiences of people who have been subjects of involuntary police contacts. Order maintenance policing strategies are supposed to send a particular message to active and potential law-breakers, but it is not at all clear whether or how that message is being received by its intended recipients. Some researchers have undertaken qualitative examinations of these issues in order to gain more in-depth, nuanced understandings of individuals' experiences (Carr, Napolitano, & Keating, 2007; Carvalho & Lewis, 2003; Chesluk, 2004; Duneier, 1999; Golub, Johnson, & Taylor, 2003) and some have interviewed offenders to investigate their perceptions about crime, disorder (St. Jean, 2007), and aggressive policing (Golub et al., 2003). Again, these studies have revolved primarily around adults' accounts, with little attention paid to juveniles' experiences (for an exception, see Carr et al., 2007). This is an unfortunate oversight, as youth are disproportionately involved in violent crime, both as perpetrators and victims (Blumstein, 2000), a fact that supports in-depth examination of their views on order maintenance policing.

The present study contributes to the literature on aggressive policing initiatives in two ways. First, we examine the experiences and perceptions of those who often bear the brunt of proactive policing efforts: urban, adolescent males. This group is disproportionately targeted for street stops, pat-downs, and arrests (Fagan & Davies, 2000; Hemmens & Levin, 2000; Spitzer, 1999). By considering young men's accounts, we have the potential to better understand whether order maintenance policing accomplishes its goal or if the consequences outweigh any possible benefits. Second, we are able to compare the involuntary police experiences of law-abiding young men with those of active offenders. This allows us to examine whether perceptions of and experiences with mistreatment by police are unique to those youth who are involved in serious delinquency, or if, conversely, these negative experiences transcend delinquency status.

Procedural Justice, Police Legitimacy, and Aggressive Order Maintenance

While movies, news reports, and other media sources affect people's perceptions of the police, personal experience with officers also ranks high on the list of influential factors (Cheurprakobkit, 2000; Skogan, 2005; Weitzer & Tuch, 2002). Citizens value police professionalism (Cheurprakobkit & Bartsch, 2001) and tend to feel better about brushes with the criminal justice system, in general, when they believe that they were treated fairly (Thibaut & Walker, 1978; see also Casper, Tyler, & Fisher, 1988; McEwen & Maiman, 1984; Tyler, 1984). It is, therefore, not enough for police to plow headlong into their law enforcement mission—they must also consider the evenhandedness with which they execute their duties (Skogan & Frydl, 2004; Tyler & Folger, 1980). Failure to do so has the potential to reduce their legitimacy and ultimately undermine their capacity to influence citizens' behavior and effectively control crime.

Procedural justice fosters a belief in the legitimacy of police (Sunshine & Tyler, 2003) and inspires greater compliance with the law (Lind & Tyler, 1988; McCluskey, Mastrofski, & Parks, 1999). Put simply, believing in the legitimacy of the police and of the criminal law leads people to internalize a moral obligation to obey the law. This framework stands in opposition to a purely instrumental, deterrence-based system of compulsory compliance predicated upon the threat of punishment for misconduct (Tyler, 1990). Compliance with the law is greater when people follow it because they believe in it rather than because they are afraid of being caught and punished. It is, therefore, not just *what* police do that is important but, also, *how* they do it. Failure to adhere to principles of procedural justice can reduce public support for police and, in the long run, may even increase crime (Bouffard & Piquero, 2010; Paternoster et al., 1997; Sherman, 1993; see also Braithwaite, 1989; Hay, 2001).

The legitimacy that procedural justice engenders is a necessary component of any policing paradigm, including order maintenance. Aggressive policing tactics carry the potential to undermine police legitimacy for at least two reasons. First, the focus of order maintenance policing—so-called "disorderly" behavior—eludes precise articulation of the specific behaviors that should be considered unacceptable and of the reasons why these behaviors are deleterious to community well-being. Disorder-related infractions generally do not have obvious victims but are, rather, violations of the general public order and standards of conduct (see, e.g., Wilson & Kelling, 1982). The idea of "public (dis)order" is far more definitionally fluid than are criminal codes delineating particular prohibited behaviors. Symptomatic of this underlying conceptual ambiguity is a lack of clarity in disorder-related laws and codes, which allows for subjective and potentially arbitrary law enforcement (Roberts, 1999).

Vague or overly broad statutes provide little guidance to individual officers working the streets (Hemmens & Levin, 2000; Roberts, 1999; see also *Chicago v. Morales*, 1998). Officers face many situations wherein there is no apparent "right" way to proceed. Under these circumstances, police may turn to suspect characteristics or the socio-structural environment for help in deciding the best course of action. The likelihood of these extralegal factors seeping into criminal justice agents' decision-making is greatest when legal factors (e.g., offense seriousness, evidence of criminal activity) are murkiest (Kalven & Zeisel, 1966; Reskin & Visher, 1986; Spohn & Cederblom, 1991). An abundant body of knowledge has established that police decisions can be affected by a suspect's race and/or social standing (Alpert, Dunham, & MacDonald, 2004; Mastrofski, Reisig, & McCluskey, 2002; Skogan, 2005), gender (Brunson & Miller, 2006a), demeanor (Engel, Sobol, & Worden, 2000; Klinger, 1996; Lundman, 1996; Worden & Shepard, 1996), and the environment wherein a given police-citizen encounter transpires (Fagan & Davies, 2000; Klinger, 1997; Meehan & Ponder, 2002; Terrill & Reisig, 2003). This gives rise to decision-making that citizens may perceive as arbitrary even when officers have no intention to discriminate and are unaware that they are conveying such an impression.

Seemingly capricious decisions can undermine the public's trust in police because fairness is one of the attributes that individuals desire most from officers (Skogan & Frydl, 2004). When citizens trust the police to exercise their powers fairly and to distribute justice equitably, they are more supportive of officers having a wide range of discretion (Sunshine & Tyler, 2003). Even citizens who have involuntary police contacts express greater satisfaction afterward if they believe the officer treated them fairly (Tyler & Folger, 1980). Conversely, people who believe that the police engage in unfair practices, such as racially discriminatory policing, express much lower support for and trust in the police (Tyler & Wakslak, 2004).

The second reason that aggressive order maintenance policing may run counter to procedural justice and police legitimacy is that the linchpin of some order maintenance policing strategies—stop-and-frisks—can harm police–citizen relations. Stop-and-frisks are commonly used by police departments that seek to reduce social disorder. Officers may be directed to watch for disorderly behaviors in progress, such as loitering or aggressive panhandling, or for behaviors that are about to take place, such as youths preparing to paint graffiti. Stops can be of pedestrians or vehicles, though in the present study most respondents experienced the former. Stops are not confined to order maintenance activities and also take place when officers suspect persons of being about to commit serious crimes, so any police department using stops and frisks for order maintenance purposes will see stops for serious crimes mixed in.

In theory, order maintenance policing efforts—even those with a stop-and-frisk emphasis—do not have to conflict with procedural justice or police legitimacy. The desire for police protection and effective law enforcement transcends racial and economic lines, and even groups who have historically suffered injustices at the hands of police want something done about local crime and disorder (Brooks, 2000; see also Bobo & Johnson, 2004). The concern, though, is not what order maintenance looks like in theory but, rather, how it plays out in practice. Even Wilson and Kelling (1982), the original architects of broken windows and order maintenance policing, recognized the potential for this strategy to go sour. The fact that order maintenance deals in relatively low-level, non-serious offenses means that there is a lot of room for police discretion and this discretion, in turn, means there is considerable latitude for order maintenance tactics to be applied in a discriminatory fashion. In the present study, the focus is on the practical aspects of order maintenance policing.

A heavy reliance on stop-and-frisks can reduce individuals' respect for and desire to comply with police because those on the receiving end may view these tactics as unfair and/or heavy-handed. Aggressive stop-and-frisks are a staple of many order maintenance policing efforts (see Braga et al., 1999; Fagan & Davies, 2000; Spitzer, 1999). Vehicle and pedestrian stops require only reasonable suspicion that "criminal activity may be afoot" Terry v. Ohio, 1968, p. 30), as opposed to the higher standard of probable cause necessary to make an arrest. Investigatory stops are, therefore, key to allowing police to legally interfere with the voluntary movement of "suspicious persons" even when police do not have legal standing to arrest these individuals.

Stop-and-frisks are an important tool for police to have at their disposal, but they do carry risks for both actual and perceived misuse. Proactive policing strategies that revolve around widespread use of field interrogations can lead to the frequent stopping of "troublemakers" even when these people are not committing crimes or behaving suspiciously (Brunson & Miller, 2006b). Instances of frequent, unwelcome police contact have the potential to lead certain segments of the population to believe that police openly dislike them (Brunson, 2007).

It has also been documented that police often conduct stop-and-frisks illegally. Determining how often unlawful searches and seizures take place is difficult because officers will likely avoid documenting activities they know to be prohibited (Skogan & Frydl, 2004). Evidence from field observations suggests that a substantial portion of stops and pat-downs would not pass constitutional muster should they be challenged in court. Most people who are subjected to unconstitutional searches, however, are not formally arrested and therefore have no opportunity to vindicate the violation of their rights (Gould & Mastrofski, 2004). Any system of law or government that wishes to be seen by its masses as legitimate must obey its own laws (Lind & Tyler, 1988), and the police, therefore, must adhere to the law if they expect citizens to do likewise. Unfortunately, studies of officer compliance with search and seizure laws paint a disturbing picture. Though most police follow constitutional guidelines much of the time, a substantial minority of stops and frisks are conducted unlawfully (Skogan & Frydl, 2004; Skogan & Meares, 2004).

There are other problems associated with the widespread use of stop-and-frisks that threaten citizens' sense of fairness and procedural justice. Evidence suggests that police stop different racial groups at disparate rates. In particular, African Americans are subjected to pedestrian and vehicle stops at rates disproportionate to their representation in the population, a phenomenon that stems more from area rates of poverty (Fagan & Davies, 2000) and racial composition (Meehan & Ponder, 2002; Spitzer, 1999) than from differential offending patterns across race. Blacks, moreover, may be stopped without cause more often than whites are, as evidenced by whites' greater likelihood of being arrested after a stop-and-frisk (Spitzer, 1999).

Individuals' perceptions of racially biased policing have important implications for procedural justice and police legitimacy (Wilson, Dunham, & Alpert, 2004). Specifically, research concerning citizens' attitudes toward police has consistently found that black adults and adolescents report more dissatisfaction and distrust than their counterparts from other racial groups (Hurst & Frank, 2000; Hurst, Frank, & Browning, 2000; Leiber, Nalla, & Farnworth, 1998; Taylor, Turner, Finn-Aage, &

Winfree, 2001). In addition, police can unwittingly contribute to impressions that they harbor personal animosity toward certain groups (Brunson, 2007).

In sum, an over-reliance on stop-and-frisks to carry out order maintenance policing can have implications for police legitimacy because it can damage citizens' perceptions of the fairness with which police utilize their law enforcement authority. The current study pits the procedural justice and police legitimacy framework against aggressive order maintenance policing to examine the interactions of these perspectives in practice.

Methodology and Study Setting

Data for this study come from a larger study investigating the lived experiences of black and white mate adolescents residing in disadvantaged St. Louis neighborhoods. The present investigation is based on information obtained from surveys and in-depth interviews with 45 male adolescents who were interviewed between the fall of 2005 and the spring of 2006. The data collection focused exclusively on young males because research has identified them as a group for whom unwelcome police attention is commonplace in the USA (Hurst et al., 2000). Only a handful of studies, however, have offered an in-depth investigation of young men's perceptions of and experiences with the police.

Respondents ranged in age from 13 to 19, with a mean age of 16. Participation in the study was voluntary and respondents were assured confidentiality. They were paid $25 for participating. Sampling was purposive in nature. Respondents were recruited with the assistance of community-based organizations working with at-risk adolescents. Staff members were asked to identify and approach young men who were known to live in distressed neighborhoods in the city, interviews lasted approximately one hour and all except one were conducted in private offices at each location.

The goal was to interview young males who were either currently involved in or who were at risk for involvement in delinquent activities, as these youths would likely have more involuntary contacts with police. In other words, purposive sampling was designed to compile a sample of young men who likely had experiences with police and whose experiences may have been unfavorable. We did not, however, seek out persons known to have had negative encounters or who had overtly expressed hostility toward the police. The sampling was not intended to be representative of all young people living in distressed St. Louis neighborhoods. The interview team consisted of four graduate students. Two were African American and two were white; each student primarily interviewed same-race respondents. The black interviewers and one of the white researchers were from the same communities as many of the research participants.

Data collection began with the administration of a survey and followed with a taped interview. The survey supplied baseline information about young men's perceptions of police in their neighborhoods. Respondents were asked how often they believed the police: do a good job enforcing laws; respond quickly to calls; work hard to solve crimes in the neighborhood; are easy to talk to; are polite to people in the neighborhood; do a good job preventing crime; and harass or mistreat people in the neighborhood. Youths were then asked whether they had been personally mistreated by the police and whether they knew someone who had been mistreated. These surveys functioned as the basis for some quantitative analyses to complement the qualitative findings. The qualitative data were gathered using a series of open-ended questions that explored youths' experiences with and observations of the police, including detailed renderings of their encounters. Reliability was strengthened by cross-checking participants' responses to the survey and in-depth interview questions and by probing for detailed accounts during the interviews.

The data are restricted to young men's accounts and perceptions of their encounters with St. Louis police officers. In the following discussion of respondents' experiences with officers, we do not take for granted that the youths' descriptions of incidents are necessarily correct or that they have provided full accounts in all instances. We are mindful that citizens may misinterpret police officers' behaviors and motives. Nonetheless, what matters for the present study is precisely how youths described their experiences, observations, and attitudes toward the police. The interviewers attempted to enhance the validity and reliability of the data by asking youths about their experiences at multiple points across the two interviews, by inquiring about their observations of police actions as well as personal experiences, and by probing for detailed, concrete descriptions of events.

Study Findings

Several respondents reported having had both personal and vicarious experiences with police harassment. Nearly half reported having experienced direct harassment and 6 out of 10 claimed that someone they knew had been harassed or otherwise treated poorly by the police. The qualitative data revealed that respondents were especially resentful of aggressive police tactics when they were in what they considered law-abiding contexts. Further, they believed that "doing nothing wrong" should have been enough to insulate them from involuntary stops and physically intrusive searches.

Respondents' unfavorable views on police courtesy stemmed in part from their perceptions of widespread police harassment in their neighborhoods. Study participants' detailed accounts of what they viewed as heavy-handed policing tactics seemingly undermined police legitimacy by weakening officers' moral authority in the eyes of community residents.

Aggressive Order Maintenance Policing: Widespread use of Stop-and-Frisks

Respondents felt that their neighborhoods had been besieged by police and they reported that law enforcement efforts on their streets consisted primarily of widespread stop-and-frisks. Many study participants came to view this style of policing as overly aggressive and they characterized their involuntary contacts with the police as demeaning and of inordinate frequency.

Nearly 78% reported having been stopped by police at least once in their lives and the number of times they reported having been stopped ranged from 1 to 100 times (mean = 15.84). It is clear from this that the youths in this sample had extensive personal experience with police in stop-based situations. Over 45% of respondents also said that they had been arrested at least once in their lifetime and 22% reported having been arrested in the past six months. Again, this demonstrates that many of these youths were no strangers to direct experiences with police.

Young men reported that police frequently stopped and questioned them for "no reason." Study participants believed that the poor treatment they received from the police was multi-faceted and was intimately tied to their status as poor, urban males. For example, Maurice said, "[The police] assume you run the streets, steal cars or smoke weed because you dress a certain way, like baggy pants or a long t-shirt and Nike brand shoes. They consider you as a gang member just because of what you were wearing or how you talk." In agreement, Nate explained, "It's the way we dress and talk. [Police] pretty much stereotype people. . . . They think if kids do saggin' pants and grills, gold [teeth] in they mouth, [that] we punks or we ain't no good." Likewise, Kyle commented, "We look thuggish, so [the police] treat us like thugs. . . . But if you grew up in a perfect neighborhood, the [police] treat you like you're a human being."

There was a slight racial difference among respondents in terms of their likelihood of receiving such treatment. White study participants had less troubled relationships with and more positive views of the police than black respondents did. Whereas black and white youths alike reported experiencing unwelcome police encounters, the frequency was less for whites, who primarily risked being stopped in a more narrow set of situations.

Study participants also specifically mentioned the aggressiveness of officers' actions. For instance, James noted, "[Police officers] ride around and see what's going on, but some be harassing. They just jump out on you, tell you to put your hands up." Similarly, Derek observed, "[The police always] harass us, constantly think we stealing and robbing." And David reported, "Me and my friends was walkin' and I guess [the police] thought we was hangin' on the corner. [The police] rode up and pulled us over. First thing they said was, 'Get on the hood [of the patrol car].' . . . They told us to spread our arms and legs and then searched us." These types of police behaviors directly contravene the concept of procedural justice. For people to believe that the police are fair and that the force they wield is legitimate, they must see officers' actions as reasonable and equitable (see Sunshine & Tyler, 2003; Tyler & Wakslak, 2004). Officers who appear to act on caprice or malice can threaten citizens' notions of justice.

Young men regarded officers' proactive policing practices as insidious and believed that officers attempted to restrict their movement within the neighborhood by threatening to arrest them for minor ordinance violations (i.e., demonstrating, loitering, trespassing, and peace disturbance). Many respondents attributed officers' poor treatment of them to the types of neighborhoods they lived in. For example, Darius observed, "[The police] will lock you up for anything." Further, several young men said that friends and relatives were reluctant to visit because of the pervasiveness of aggressive policing in their communities. Mike explained, "[My neighborhood] is hot, real hot. [The police] lockin' you up for anything, just for trespassin'. . . . You gotta meet people down the street, or out on the corner to get picked up." A handful of young men also expressed concern about visitors' well-being. For instance, Raynard noted, "I was talking to [some] of my friends, and they was just getting ready to leave my house and had started walking down the street. The police pulled up and started patting them down for no reason." Respondents' determinations that officers' actions were guided, in part, by the characteristics of the neighborhood offers further confirmation of previous researchers' findings that neighborhood context can shape police behavior (Fagan & Davies, 2000; Klinger, 1997; Meehan & Ponder, 2002; Terrill & Reisig, 2003).

Respondents appeared to understand the need for crime-control efforts in their neighborhoods. They also acknowledged that as part of the law enforcement mission, it was sometimes necessary for officers to detain and question "suspicious looking people." The majority of our study participants could not understand, however, why police would target them when they were engaged in clearly lawful activities. For instance, Todd and his friends were detained by officers as they walked home from school: "The police got out of the car and were like, 'What ya'll doing?' I said, 'We're coming home from school.' [The officer] was like, 'What's in the book bags?' He came over and started checking but couldn't find nothing but books." Similarly, Martez described how he and his friends were subjected to a series of physically intrusive searches while in what they considered an unquestionably law-abiding context:

> We was playin' basketball and [my friend] put a wristband in his gym bag. . . . The police thought it was some crack so they stopped him and was harassing him, like, "where its at?" He was like, "I ain't got nothin'." After they checked him, they checked all of us. Only thing they found was wristbands, white wristbands. . . . [The police officers] took all six of us in [to the station] and was checkin' our mouth[s] and [other body parts] . . . to see if we have drugs and they found out [that] we didn't.

As Martez' account points out, police interactions with respondents and their associates were not just experienced as invasive, but also were physically intrusive. Further, young men seldom considered avoidance of arrest following involuntary police contact to be appropriate conciliation. For example, Jamal described an encounter with police. He noted, "The [police] stopped me and they ran my name and said I needed an [identification card] 'cause I wasn't in the system. [The officer] was like, 'I'm not arresting you [but] can I put you in handcuffs though and run your name?' " Jamal's, Martez's, and Todd's accounts illustrate what many young men considered the arbitrariness of officers' decisions to stop, question, and search them. Further, even though Jamal realized that he was not under arrest, he took exception to the public humiliation of being placed in handcuffs like "a common criminal" while the officer called in his personal information.

Some respondents spoke directly to the effects that these seemingly groundless police actions had on the respondents' ensuing behavior toward the police. Respondents who believed they had done nothing wrong were more likely to defy police commands and were more likely to adopt an outwardly hostile demeanor toward the officers. Maurice recounted a time when officers suddenly surrounded him as he sat on the front porch of his home. Maurice recalled that, "This one policeman said, '[Do] you live here?' I said, 'Yeah.' He said, 'Come down here.' I said, 'No.' He said 'Why you refuse to come down here?' I said 'Cause this my front [and] I can sit on it. Why you messin' wit me?' He said 'Well, you shouldn't be on the front porch. Come down here, sir.' I walked into the house."

Young men's accounts thus provide strong support for prior researchers' notions of procedural justice and the consequences of police actions that run afoul of fairness (e.g., Mastrofski et al., 2002; Tyler, 1990). We next analyze what happens when stop-and-frisks (justified or not) turn ugly. We investigate in detail study participants' encounters with discourteous officers and how their perceptions of these situations helped to undermine police legitimacy.

Officer Discourtesy: Eroding Police Legitimacy

It was not simply that study participants took issue with being stopped, questioned, and searched on a frequent basis—most young men were especially troubled by the way officers spoke to them during these unwelcome interactions (see also, Mastrofski et al., 2002; Tyler & Wakslak, 2004). Specifically, they reported that officers were routinely discourteous and that they used inflammatory language, racial slurs, and name-calling. For example, Kyle said, "[The] police will drive by and yell, 'You get off the corner or we're gonna . . . whoop your asses'." Similarly, Antwan noted that the police shouted at him and his friends to "get ya'll asses off this corner. What the fuck are ya'll big, stupid motherfuckers doing?" And Lorenz said:

> We was [sitting] in the car; we was just sittin' in there. [Police] got us out the car, check[ed] us and said he found some drugs in the car. And [the officers] said, "One of ya'll goin' with us." [To decide] they said, "Eeny, meeny, miny, moe, catch a nigga by his throat," and locked up my friend because he was the oldest.

While most of our respondents said that police occasionally spoke harshly to them, they reported that officers were more apt to direct demeaning and offensive language toward blacks. For example, black study participants said that officers frequently used racial slurs. Bob explained, "[Police] like to curse at people for no apparent reason. They shout bitches, hoes, niggers." Other young men linked officers' crude language to racist attitudes. For example, Martez offered, "I think cops [are] racists. That's what I think because they call us niggas." In addition to undermining police legitimacy, discourteous language was viewed by several respondents as dehumanizing. For instance, Antwan complained that, "I'm a citizen and a human being just like [the police]. I deserve respect." There was no apparent relationship between officer race and the use of derogatory language toward respondents; in fact, most respondents did not mention the race of the police officers at all and, when asked, said they believed that officers' race is not a factor in the way they treat citizens. One exception to this trend was black study participants who reported that African American officers were more likely to show concern for their well-being.

Prior research has shown that citizens' demeanor is often influenced by police officers' behavior toward them (Wiley & Hudik, 1974); thus, aggressive or demoralizing police actions have the potential to inflame a situation and expose citizens to more serious kinds of malfeasance. For example, Tommie noted, "There was a fight in the neighborhood and a bunch of people was standing around. [The police] was like, 'Ya'll gotta go home,' and somebody said, 'We ain't gotta go nowhere.' They thought it was me and the officer said, 'I'll have you missing [cause your disappearance].'" Officers also took exception to being questioned about the appropriateness of their conduct. For instance, Jamal observed, "I guess [the police] thought we were fina run. He was like, 'Why you guys walkin' away?' My friend kept asking, 'What did we do?' The police was like, 'I should punch you in the mouth.'" Respondents argued that officers routinely provoked youths in order to have a reason to physically assault them. James explained:

> It was the Fourth of July, and the police thought I had been shooting off fireworks. When they jumped out I didn't have no fireworks, but I did have a lighter. [One of the officers] was like, "We should beat your ass [just] for having this." I just looked at him. . . . I wasn't gonna respond to him like, "Yeah right," [because] he would have just hit me.

Young men's accounts provide evidence of the potential for serious ramifications when those charged with enforcing the law do so in a manner that is unjust or even illegal.

The Experiences of Law-Abiding vs. Law-Violating Young Men

In all, more than one-third of the young men reported participating in serious delinquency within the last six months. On the other hand, almost all of the youths reported having engaged in minor forms of delinquency or status offenses, including: skipping classes; being loud or rowdy in public; avoiding paying for things; drinking beer or liquor; stealing $5 or less; lying about their age to get into someplace or buy something; or running away. Thus, our sample captured variations in delinquent involvement. It is, of course, worthy of note that all 45 of the teens interviewed did come from disadvantaged areas and were considered to be at risk for delinquency even if they had never actually committed any criminal acts. A sample of low-risk youths from a wealthier area of the city might have produced different findings. We see this not as a validity issue but as an indication that care should be taken when generalizing these results to youths of other backgrounds.

While one might expect that individuals involved in crime or serious forms of delinquency would report having more negative police contacts relative to law-abiding respondents, young men's accounts revealed few systematic differences in the nature and extent of their experiences with aggressive policing. Specifically, both serious delinquents and non-delinquents complained of what they considered frequent, routine harassment by police. Our research suggests that young men came to understand that no matter how hard they tried, they were not able to convincingly present themselves to officers as law-abiding, even when they were just that.

Discussion

This study was an effort to better understand the intersection of procedural justice and aggressive order maintenance policing. Interview data from 45 young men in a socioeconomically disadvantaged urban area revealed that these citizens harbored ambivalent feelings about the police. While study participants recognized that the police had a difficult job to do, they questioned the wisdom and utility of relying heavily on stops, frisks, and field interviews. In particular, respondents resented what they considered unfair, aggressive targeting by police. They believed their socioeconomic status and/or race made them *de facto* "suspicious persons" in the eyes of officers and that as a result, they were subjected to heightened and unwarranted-levels of police scrutiny. Study participants perceived officers' widespread use of stop-and-frisks for suspected disorderly behavior as a form of harassment because they sometimes felt that they had done nothing that merited such treatment. Several respondents expressed the view that police judged them based on their clothing, accessories, friends, and/or the neighborhoods in which they resided. They felt that police would use the inferences they drew from these surface characteristics as justification for stopping, questioning, and/or frisking them even when they were not engaging in crime. Overall, young men reported feeling that they were perpetually under officers' gaze.

Several respondents believed that police treated citizens differently depending on where they encountered them. These findings are especially troublesome. In particular, using neighborhood-level characteristics as heuristic devices for decisions regarding how to treat residents could further exacerbate one's perception that the police act unfairly toward them. Citizens of disadvantaged neighborhoods run the risk of feeling that they are being judged on the basis of the neighborhoods they live in (Jones-Brown, 2007). Such a perception could strain the already tense relationship between police and poor, minority citizens.

Another theme that emerged from the analyses was respondents' feeling that officers were frequently discourteous and even verbally abusive. In addition to the potentially deleterious effects that such disrespectful treatment of citizens may have on police legitimacy, this kind of behavior also increases the likelihood that police-citizen encounters will be rife with animosity emanating from both parties. Prior research shows that citizen demeanor can influence police actions and, therefore, help determine whether an encounter is civil or confrontational (Engel et al., 2000; Klinger, 1996; Lundman, 1996; Worden & Shepard, 1996). This finding indicates that people, such as the young men under study here, who are subjected to routine maltreatment at the hands of police may begin approaching police encounters with an uncooperative demeanor. Outward displays of hostility toward police could put police on edge in anticipation of possible verbal or physical attack. Whether or not the encounter turns violent, the mutual suspicion and distrust exuded by police and citizens could leave both with negative feelings about one another.

The broad conclusion is that aggressive order maintenance manifesting in the form of widespread stop-and-frisks can compromise procedural justice and, therefore, undermine police legitimacy. This has a wide range of implications for police policy, both at the level of the patrol officer who interacts with the public daily and at the administrative level where departmental missions and philosophies are forged. Prior research has documented that tattered faith in officers' ability to carry out their duties fairly and equitably can spark a decline in public support for police organizations (Sunshine & Tyler, 2003; Tyler & Wakslak, 2004) and in the public's compliance with the criminal law in general (Bouffard & Piquero, 2010; Lind & Tyler, 1988; Paternoster et al., 1997; Sherman, 1993; Tyler, 1990). Police agencies that embrace order maintenance, therefore, need to be aware of the possible ramifications of this strategy; specifically, they need to cast a keen eye toward the collateral consequences of waging a battle against social disorder. Police–community relations are already strained in many cities and neighborhoods, especially those that are socially and economically distressed (Renauer, 2007; see also Klinger, 1997; Sampson & Bartusch, 1998), and aggressive order maintenance could hit these shaky alliances particularly hard.

Study participants' accounts underscore the need for police agencies to ensure that officers engaging in order maintenance and other aggressive policing activities carry out their duties fairly and equitably and that they adhere to strict standards of professionalism. The fact that many of the youths' experiences analyzed in the present study involved stops, frisks, and other activities that fell short of formal arrest is no reason to take these young men's accounts less seriously. Stops and frisks that do not result in arrest may seem harmless because the citizen is not subjected to formal sanctions. Formal sanctions, however, are but one potential consequence of stops and frisks—there also are a host of informal outcomes such as shame, embarrassment, anger, and feelings that one's personal integrity has been violated. For these reasons, stop-and-frisk policies should not be taken lightly and police departments should be cognizant of the profound effects that even these relatively informal police procedures can have for police–citizen relations.

As described earlier, order maintenance policing entails a large amount of officer discretion and abuse of this decision-making power can discredit police in the eyes of community members. The establishment of boundaries for the exercise of discretion could help ensure that officers are allowed enough discretion to do their jobs but are not granted unbridled decision-making authority. Clear guidelines should be in place so that officers know when it is (and is not) appropriate to stop citizens and how intrusive frisks may (or may not) be under different circumstances. Academy and in-service trainings should educate officers on the laws of search and seizure and on the importance of upholding citizens' rights for both the legal purpose of evidence suppression and for social reasons, such as the need to promote healthy relationships with the community. Police administrators and supervisors should promote a culture of respect within the department and make it clear that mistreatment of citizens will not be tolerated within the organization.

Public awareness campaigns and the solicitation of feedback from citizens could help police ensure that the crime-reduction strategy they have chosen has not compromised perceptions of fairness and justice. One vital component of a strategy such as order maintenance is notifying the community of the types of behaviors that police will be cracking down on so that citizens know in advance what actions are likely to draw the attention of police. A notification policy such as this could also serve as a check on police behavior, as a public statement declaring that police will be watching for certain activities obligates officers to limit their enforcement efforts to only those persons whose behavior clearly falls within the prohibited realm. As demonstrated in the current study, a constant source of frustration among the vast majority of respondents was that the police routinely stopped them for what they perceived to be no valid reason.

Efforts are also necessary to force into the open a dialogue about sensitive issues such as the long-standing tension between police and some of society's traditionally marginalized groups. Officers may believe in good faith that what they are doing is a legitimate and effective effort at crime control and that their actions (e.g., stops, frisks, and/or field investigations) are justifiable even when premised more on gut-level suspicion than on observations of unlawful activity. It is important for officers to understand the damage that such factually groundless stop-and-frisks can do over time. A two-way exchange of information between police and the local community could elucidate to each group the other's reasons for responding the way they do sometimes. Police departments have a tendency to shy away from candid discussions with the public concerning uncomfortable or potentially volatile topics such as citizens' perceptions of racial discrimination. Many departments that have confronted these issues head-on have improved police-community relationships (Harris, 2007), an example that should help dispel the lingering fear that continues to hold other departments back.

In a similar vein, allowing community members to express their opinions about local problems and police performance can help assure citizens that the police department is attentive and genuinely concerned about working with the community. Feeling that one's voice has been heard and taken seriously is, as discussed earlier, integral to procedural justice and police legitimacy (Paternoster et al., 1997; see also Thibaut & Walker, 1978). Respectfulness, moreover, is very important to citizens and something that many residents of poor, urban areas feel they do not typically receive (Stoutland, 2001). Police executives and supervisors can make it clear to patrol officers and others who deal with the public regularly that professionalism and respectful treatment toward all citizens is non-negotiable. Internal guidelines that require officers to be courteous and professional in all their dealings with the public can reduce citizen complaints against officers without hindering officers' law enforcement capabilities (Davis, Mateu-Gelabert, & Miller, 2005; Greene, 1999). After all, fairness and effectiveness are complementary—not competing—principles of policing (Skogan & Frydl, 2004).

Critical Thinking

The words of these young males suggest that they and the police have differing perceptions of what constitutes disorder, which clearly leads to conflict between the two groups. Why would most assume that the perspective of disorder presented by police is in fact accurate? Should police and policymakers take the perception of those they police (including those who may violate the law) into account when developing and instituting policy? Is it possible that police can enforce the law and protect citizens while also maintaining respect with youth in these areas?

References

Alpert, G. P., Dunham, R. G., & MacDonald, J. M. (2004). Interactive police-citizen encounters that result in force. *Police Quarterly*, *7*, 475–488.

Bennett, T. (1991). The effectiveness of a police-initiated fear-reducing strategy. *British Journal of Criminology*, *31*(1), 1–14.

Blumstein, A. (2000). Disaggregating the violence trends. In A. Blumstein & J. Wallman (Eds.), *The crime drop in America*, pp. 13–44. Cambridge: Cambridge University Press.

Bobo, L. D., & Johnson, D. (2004). A taste for punishment: Black and white Americans' views on the death penalty and the War on Drugs. *Du Bois Review*, *1*, 151–180.

Bouffard, L. A., & Piquero, N. L. (2010). Defiance theory and life course explanations of persistent offending. *Crime & Delinqency*, *56*, 227–252.

Braga, A. A., Weisburd, D. L., Waring, E. J., Mazerolle, L. G., Spelman, W., & Gajewski, F. (1999), Problem-oriented policing in violent crime places: A randomized controlled experiment. *Criminology*, *37*(3), 541–580.

Braithwaite, J. (1989). *Crime, shame, and reintegration*. Cambridge: Cambridge University Press.

Bratton, W. J., & Knobler, P. (1998). *Turnaround: How America's top cop reversed the crime epidemic*. New York: Random House.

Brooks, R. R. W. (2000). Fear and fairness in the city: Criminal enforcement and perceptions of fairness in minority communities. *Southern California Law Review*, *73*, 1219–1270.

Brunson, R. K. (2007). "Police don't like black people:" African-American young men's accumulated police experiences. *Criminology & Public Policy*, *6*(1), 71–102.

Brunson, R. K., & Miller, J. (2006a). Gender, race, and urban policing: The experience of African American youths. *Gender & Society*, *20*, 531–552.

Brunson, R. K., & Miller, J. (2006b), Young black men and urban policing in the United States. *British Journal of Criminology*, *46*, 613–640.

Carr, P. J., Napolitano, L., & Keating, J. (2007). We never call the cops and here is why: A qualitative examination of legal cynicism in three Philadelphia neighborhoods. *Criminology*, *45*, 445–480.

Carvalho, I., & Lewis, D. A. (2003). Beyond community: Reactions to crime and disorder among inner-city residents. *Criminology*, *41*(3), 779–811.

Casper, J. D., Tyler, T., & Fisher, B. (1988). Procedural justice in felony cases. *Law & Society Review*, *22*(3), 483–508.

Chesluk, B. (2004). "Visible signs of a community out of control:" Community policing in New York City. *Cultural Anthropology*, *19*(2), 250–275.

Cheurprakobkit, S. (2000). Police-citizen contact and police performance: Attitudinal differences between Hispanics and non-Hispanics. *Journal of Criminal Justice*, *28*, 325–336.

Cheurprakobkit, S., & Bartsch, R. A. (2001). Police performance: A model for assessing citizens' satisfaction and the importance of police attributes. *Police Quarterly*, *4*(4), 449–468.

Chicago v. Morales, 527 U.S. 41 (1998).

Davis, R. C., Mateu-Gelabert, P., & Miller, J. (2005). Can effective policing also be respectful? Two examples in the South Bronx. *Police Quarterly*, *8*(2), 229–247.

Dilulio, J., Jr. (1995). Arresting ideas [electronic version]. *Policy Review*, *74*, 12–17.

Duneier, M. (1999). *Sidewalk*. New York: Farrar, Straus and Giroux.

Engel, R. S., Sobol, J. J., & Worden, R. E. (2000). Further exploration of the demeanor hypothesis: The interaction effects of suspects' characteristics and demeanor on police behavior. *Justice Quarterly*, *17*, 235–258.

Fagan, J., & Davies, G. (2000). Street cops and broken windows: Terry, race, and disorder in New York City. *Fordham Urban Law Journal*, *28*, 457–504.

Golub, A., Johnson, B. D., & Taylor, A. (2003). Quality-of-life policing: Do offenders get the message? *Policing: An International Journal of Police Strategies and Management*, *26*(4), 690–707.

Gould, J. B., & Mastrofski, S. D. (2004). Suspect searches: Assessing police behavior under the U.S. constitution. *Criminology & Public Policy*, *3*, 315–361.

Greene, J. A. (1999). Zero tolerance: A case study of police policies and practices in New York City. *Crime & Delinquency*, *45*(2), 171–187.

Harcourt, B. E. (2001). *Illusion of order: The false promise of broken windows policing*. Cambridge: Harvard University Press.

Harris, D. A. (2007). The importance of research on race and policing: Making race salient to individuals and institutions within criminal justice. *Criminology & Public Policy*, *6*, 5–24.

Hawdon, J. E., Ryan, J., & Griffin, S. P. (2003). Policing tactics and perceptions of police legitimacy. *Police Quarterly*, *6*(4), 469–491.

Hay, C. (2001). An exploratory test of Braithwaite's reintegrative shaming theory. *Journal of Research in Crime and Delinquency*, *38*(2), 132–153.

Hemmens, C., & Levin, D. (2000). Resistance is futile: The right to resist unlawful arrest in an era of aggressive policing. *Crime & Delinquency*, *46*(4), 472–496.

Hurst, Y. G., & Frank, J. (2000). How kids view cops: The nature of juvenile attitudes toward police. *Journal of Criminal Justice*, *28*, 189–202.

Hurst, Y. G., Frank, J., & Browning, S. L. (2000). The attitudes of juveniles toward the police: A comparison of black and white youth. *Policing*, *23*, 37–53.

Jones-Brown, D. (2007). Forever the symbolic assailant: The more things change, the more they remain the same. *Criminology & Public Policy*, *6*, 103–122.

Kalven, H., & Zeisel, H. (1966). *The American jury*. Boston, MA: Little, Brown.

Katz, C. M., Webb, V. J., & Schaefer, D. R. (2001). An assessment of the impact of quality-of-life policing on crime and disorder. *Justice Quarterly, 18*(4), 825–876.

Kelling, G. L., & Bratton, W. J. (1998). Declining crime rates: Insiders' views of the New York City story. *Journal of Criminal Law & Criminology, 88*(4), 1217–1231.

Kelling, G. L., & Coles, C. M. (1996). *Fixing broken windows.* New York: Simon & Schuster.

Klinger, D. A. (1996). More on demeanor and arrest in Dade County. *Criminology, 34,* 61–79.

Klinger, D. A. (1997). Negotiating order in patrol work: An ecological theory of police response to deviance. *Criminology, 35,* 277–306.

Leiber, M. J., Nalla, M. K., & Farnworth, M. (1998). Explaining juveniles' attitudes toward the police. *Justice Quarterly, 15,* 151–174.

Lind, E. A., & Tyler, T. R. (1988). *The social psychology of procedural justice.* New York: Plenum Press.

Lundman, R. J. (1996). Demeanor and arrest: Additional evidence from previously unpublished data. *Journal of Research in Crime and Delinquency, 33,* 306–323.

Mastrofski, S. D., Reisig, M. D., & McCluskey, J. D. (2002). Police disrespect toward the public: An encounter-based analysis. *Criminology, 40,* 515–551.

McCluskey, J. D., Mastrofski, S. D., & Parks, R. B. (1999). To acquiesce or rebel: Predicting citizen compliance with police requests. *Police Quarterly, 2,* 389–416.

McEwen, C. A., & Maiman, R. J. (1984). Mediation in small claims court: Achieving compliance through consent. *Law & Society Review, 18*(1), 11–49.

Meehan, A. J., & Ponder, M. C. (2002). Race and place: The ecology of racial profiling African American motorists. *Justice Quarterly, 19*(3), 399–430.

Novak, K. J., Harman, J. L., Holsinger, A. M., & Turner, M. G. (1999). The effects of aggressive policing of disorder on serious crime. *Policing: An International Journal of Police Strategies & Management, 22*(2), 171–190.

Paternoster, R., Brame, R., Bachman, R., & Sherman, L. W. (1997). Do fair procedures matter? The effect of procedural justice on spouse assault. *Law & Society Review, 31*(1), 163–204.

Renauer, B. C. (2007). Is neighborhood policing related to informal social control? *Policing: An International Journal of Police Strategies & Management, 30*(1), 61–81.

Reskin, B. F., & Visher, C. A. (1986). The impacts of evidence and extralegal factors in jurors' decisions. *Law & Society Review, 20*(3), 423–438.

Roberts, D. E. (1999). Race, vagueness, and the social meaning of order-maintenance policing. *Journal of Criminal Law & Criminology, 89*(3), 775–836.

Sampson, R. J., & Bartusch, D. J. (1998). Legal cynicism and (subcultural?) tolerance of deviance: The neighborhood context of racial differences. *Law & Society Review, 32*(4), 777–804.

Sampson, R. J., & Cohen, J. (1988). Deterrent effects of the police on crime: A replication and theoretical extension. *Law & Society Review, 22*(1), 163–189.

Sherman, L. W. (1993). Defiance, deterrence, and irrelevance: A theory of the criminal sanction. *Journal of Research in Crime and Delinquency, 30*(4), 445–473.

Skogan, W. G. (2005). Citizen satisfaction with police encounters. *Police Quarterly, 8*(3), 298–321.

Skogan, W. G., & Frydl, K. (2004). *Fairness and effectiveness in policing: The evidence.* Washington, DC: The National Academies Press.

Skogan, W. G., & Meares, T. L. (2004). Lawful policing. *Annals of the American Academy, of Political and Social Science, 593,* 66–83.

Spitzer, E. (1999). *The New York City police department's "stop & frisk" practices: A report to the people of the State of New York from the Office of the Attorney General.* New York: Office of the Attorney General of the State of New York.

Spohn, C., & Cederblom, J. (1991). Race and disparities in sentencing: A test of the liberation hypothesis. *Justice Quarterly, 8,* 305–327.

St. Jean, P. K. B. (2007). *Pockets of crime.* Chicago: The University of Chicago Press.

Stoutland, S. (2001). The multiple dimensions of trust in resident/police relations in Boston. *Journal of Research in Crime and Delinquency, 38,* 226–256.

Sunshine, J., & Tyler, T. R. (2003). The role of procedural justice and legitimacy in shaping public support for policing. *Law & Society Review, 37*(3), 513–547.

Taylor, T. J., Turner, K. B., Finn-Aage, E., & Winfree, L. T., Jr. (2001). Coppin' an attitude: Attitudinal differences among juveniles toward the police. *Journal of Criminal Justice, 29,* 295–305.

Terrill, W., & Reisig, M. D. (2003). Neighborhood context and police use of force. *Journal of Research in Crime and Delinquency, 40,* 291–321.

Terry v. Ohio, 392 U.S. 1 (1968).

Thibaut, J., & Walker, L. (1978). A theory of procedure. *California Law Review, 66,* 541–566.

Tyler, T. R. (1984). The role of perceived injustice in defendants' evaluations of their courtroom experience. *Law & Society Review, 18*(1), 51–74.

Tyler, T. R. (1990). *Why people obey the Law.* New Haven, CT: Yale University Press.

Tyler, T. R., & Folger, R. (1980). Distributional and procedural aspects of satisfaction with citizen-police encounters. *Basic and Applied Social Psychology, 1*(4), 281–292.

Tyler, T. R., & Wakslak, C. J. (2004). Profiling and police legitimacy: Procedural justice, attributions of motive, and acceptance of police authority. *Criminology, 42*(2), 253–281.

Weitzer, R., & Tuch, S. A. (2002). Perceptions of racial profiling: Race, class, and personal experience. *Criminology, 40*(2), 435–456.

Wiley, M., & Hudik, T. (1974). Police-citizen encounters: A field test of exchange theory. *Social Problems, 22,* 119–127.

Wilson, G., Dunham, R., & Alpert, G. (2004). Prejudice in police profiling: Assessing an overlooked aspect in prior research. *American Behavioral Scientist, 47,* 896–909.

Wilson, J. Q., & Kelling, G. L. (1982). The police and neighborhood safety: Broken windows. *Atlantic Monthly, March,* 29–38.

Worden, R. E., & Shepard, R. L. (1996). Demeanor, crime, and police behavior: A reexamination of the police services study data. *Criminology, 34,* 83–105.

Worrall, J. L. (2006). Does targeting minor offenses reduce serious crime? A provisional, affirmative answer based on an analysis of county-level data. *Police Quarterly, 9*(1), 47–72.

7

Urban Youth Encounters with Legitimately Oppressive Gang Enforcement

Robert Durán

Abstract: *Robert Durán explores how police assigned to suppress gangs interact with inner-city Mexican Americans. Using ethnographic measures and insights from prior membership in a gang, the author suggests that stereotyping Mexican American communities as gang "infested" and equating gangs as synonymous with crime allows for differential policing that no longer emphasizes criminal acts, but rather perpetually criminal people. He concludes by arguing that gang enforcement is over-inclusive and embedded with practices that create opportunities for abuse of authority.*

Policing of urban youth of color has changed greatly since the 1980s when the concept of gangs began to legitimize and open the door to more aggressive forms of law enforcement. Violating an individual's civil rights became less of a concern as barrios and ghettos began to be equated with breeding grounds for gangs and criminality: the terms being used interchangeably. Gang members have been primarily characterized in large cities as male (97 percent), poor (85 percent) and of the following racial and ethnic groups: Latino (47 percent), black (38 percent), and very rarely as white (8 percent) (National Youth Gang Survey, 2009). Both Latinos and blacks are three times overrepresented on gang lists compared to their proportion of the population in the United States, whereas whites are 12 times underrepresented. Additionally, involvement in gangs has been found to increase self-reported involvement in delinquency and crime than non-gang members (Battin, Karl, Abott, Catalano, & Hawkins, 1998; Bjerregaard & Smith, 1993; Curry, Ball, & Decker, 1996; Esbensen & Huizinga, 1993; Miller, 1992; Thornberry, 1998). Thus, two profiles merge into a social created reality: 1) gang members are primarily black and Latino; and 2) gang members' self-report more criminal activity than non-gang members.

In response to this image of a new "urban predator," a large number of cities since the mid-1980s have created specialized gang units to support a "war on gangs" that will eliminate this alleged threat. As a society we are bombarded with a "law and order" view of gangs and their communities. The History Channel's "Gangland" has commercialized this criminal image with the help of law enforcement and gang member bravado. Police officers routinely recognize how such a war on gangs is hindered by traditional constitutional protections, but have developed support to create methods and tactics to sidestep disapproval; in essence gang suppression/ oppression has become legitimated.

Police officers and those involved in gangs often occupy different social worlds. Nationwide, law enforcement continues to be white (80 percent) and male (90 percent) (Reaves and Hickman, 2004). Differences in age, class, race and ethnicity, and living location do not support an equal relationship between those who enforce the law and the individuals considered outlaws (i.e., gang members). Officer behavior and the reasons for the stop will shape urban youth demeanor, as will the historical relationship between police and minority communities. The key strategy for urban youth is to decrease interactions with law enforcement. Avoidance is important because both legal (majority of the time) and illegal behavior can result in a stop. In this chapter, I will provide an "urban youth of color" point of view when describing interactions between police and individuals considered gang members. I will explore how these interactions are oppressively unequal, yet legitimized and encouraged by dominant society.

Gangs and Their Policing

Gangs have taken an almost mythical status through news media, movies, music, and portrayals from law enforcement. Yet, empirical evidence suggests that much of these portrayals may amount to nothing more than a moral panic. Klein (2004, 2007), who has studied gangs for over 40 years, found that most gang crime is minor; most gang activity is noncriminal; street gangs were social groups; street life becomes a part of gang culture; and the community context in which gangs arise was often ignored. He argued most gang activity is boring and far from the excitement described by gang members or law enforcement (Klein, 1995). Vigil (2002, 2007) reported most youth, even in the poorest neighborhoods, do not join gangs. Estimates are that approximately 4–14 percent of all urban youth join a gang and the duration of membership is often short. Moore (1978, 1991) who has conducted the longest ongoing field research with gangs, more than fifteen years, described how barrio youth are cut-off from the American dream including equality, justice, and economic betterment. Most Americans will never experience this minority experience of failure with public institutions and thus gangs, drugs, and prison have become normal in these segregated settings. Less than 20 percent of her interviewees reported coming from "gang families" despite these gangs existing for more than 45 years at the time of the study. Moreover, the main activities of these gangs included hanging around and partying rather than chronic offending and violence. Sánchez-Jankowski's (1991, 2008) ten years of ethnographic research of gangs in three cities found that gangs do not represent a menace, but rather serve as a legitimate means to maximize security in poor neighborhoods. Brotherton and Barrios (2004) argue that urban youth struggle to create their own communities in a society that shows little inclination to meaningfully include them and instead the dominant framework focuses upon repressive techniques.

Contrary to ethnographic research data finding normal behavior for gang members and less prevalent involvement in criminal activity, the increased involvement of law enforcement into urban barrios and ghettos highlights a post-civil rights form of racism where myths are more important than reality. Justification of gang enforcement simply calls for a "kernel of truth" that some violent incident occurred and now *all* gang members are the problem. Such panics have occurred, to some degree, in day care centers (de Young, 1998), with the legislation of drugs (Reinarman, 2003), and with marginalized groups in society (Cohen, 1980; McCorkle & Miethe, 2002; Zatz, 1987). Mainstream, white society offers support by encouraging more aggressive tactics disregarding how the segregated communities of color will be targeted. These repressive and oppressive strategies have been found by gang researchers to enhance the marginalization of poor minority communities. Werthman and Piliavin (1967, p. 57) described this as "ecological contamination." These researchers found gang members and police occupy separate cultural and structural conditions. A mere perception of a gang neighborhood could infect many suspicious persons who lived there and subject these residents to police officers' discretion and to their power to investigate, which creates problems of law.

Researchers have tracked the growth of gang enforcement and specialized units targeting gangs (Huff & McBride, 1993; Katz, 2003; Katz & Webb, 2006; Klein, 1995, 2004; Needle & Stapleton, 1983, Spergel, 1995). Through a survey of 261 police departments, Klein (1995) found that intelligence gathering, crime investigation, and suppression were the most common police actions against gangs, and that many states had instituted increased consequences for gang-related crimes. Spergel (1995) agreed that a vigorous "lock-em-up" approach remained the key action of police departments, particularly in large cities with acknowledged gang problems. Since the 1980s, more than 360 gang units began operating nationwide to respond to the perceived and actual threat caused by gangs (Katz, 2001). Katz and Webb (2006), who studied gang units in four cities (Albuquerque, Inglewood, Las Vegas, and Phoenix) by interviewing police officers and participating in ride-alongs, found many units lacking in governing policies, procedures, rules, and training. The gang units' insufficient knowledge of gangs often led to officers engaging in prohibited street enforcement tactics and falsifying official reports. Most gang unit problems originated from a decoupled organizational style, where they operated separately from the police department. Operating autonomously from the police department is thought to have played a role in facilitating the illegal activities of the Los Angeles CRASH unit and Chicago gang unit. The two researchers encouraged efforts to control gangs but advised that such efforts will require adjusting current forms of gang enforcement to be more effective.

Analyzing the impact of policing and communities of color by using gang labels is enhanced by the incorporation of the work of Erving Goffman and Elijah Anderson. Goffman (1959, 1963, 1982) analyzed interactions as a type of performance. He described how first impressions shape subsequent treatment. Maintaining face is deemed highly important for each actor and thus the best way to prevent role threats is to avoid contact. Impression management can provide structure to social encounters. There are individuals who are treated as stigmatized in society due to their race and/or behavior. This differential impact on an identity can reduce the life chances of stigmatized groups and such negative labeling can be concentrated within certain neighborhoods. Anderson (1990) reported how black men in public are perceived and treated as predators. Individuals within the community are unable to determine law abiding black males and others. According to Anderson, urban youth use images of dangerousness to prevent others from threatening their safety. This aggressive presentation of self receives peer approval and reduces victimization. Goffman provides a guide for analyzing interactions and Anderson offers a framework for exploring these interactions with urban youth of color.

My study of urban youth interactions with police due to gang enforcement is developed from two different cities: Ogden, Utah and Denver, Colorado. Both cities have similar levels of poverty and levels of economic, ethnic, and racial segregation. The urban sections of the city, barrios and ghettos, have higher levels of socio-economic inequality and higher concentrations of blacks and Latinos. In this chapter I examine how young people in Latino neighborhoods perceive of the legitimacy of police. In doing so I discuss how the use of violence by police maintains a hostile relationship between communities of color and law enforcement and compare current police practices designed to control space (i.e., urban barrios and ghettos) and racial and ethnic groups with previous historical attempts to eliminate marginalized groups.

Methods

The research reported in this chapter is based upon my life experiences with gangs as both a member and ex-gang member (1992–2010), my research of gangs in Ogden, Utah (1997–2006) and Denver, Colorado (2000–2006). Ethnographic methods allowed me the opportunity to associate with gang members, associates, and urban youth in the community and directly observe police stops. I used ethnographic research methods such as direct observation, casual interaction, semi-structured interviews, introspection, photography, and videotaping to collect these data.

I observed over 200 police stops, 47 of these stops included gang units, in all areas of these two cities for three years. Most of my time involved patrolling nightlife areas such as cruising boulevards and minority communities because this is where most police activity was concentrated. The use of police scanners helped me travel to the segregated white suburbs when an infrequent stop was made. Observation of stops along cruising boulevards allowed me to witness a wide variety of racial and ethnic group encounters with the police. Overwhelmingly, these areas were adjacent to communities of color which aided my ability to patrol both areas. All of the observed gang unit stops included Latinos followed by blacks and Asians. I used this information to compare urban youth experiences with police officers and the media. Observing the inequality of policing was enhanced by my ethnographic walks and study of the five highest concentrated black, Latino, and white census tracts.

My participant observation was supplemented with 123 interviews: 64 gang members, 12 ex-gang members, 38 gang associates, and 9 youth who had no affiliation with gangs. My interviewees included 102 males and 21 females who were primarily Latino (78 percent) or black (11 percent). Ninety-seven percent of my interviews were members of racial and ethnic minority groups. These interviews reflect associations with 20 different gangs in 2 different cities. All of these individuals have at one time or another lived or continued to live in the barrio or ghetto areas of these cities. Ogden is a small city of 77,226 residents located within a mid-size metropolitan area of slightly more than a million people. Denver is a mid-size city of 554,636 residents located within a large-size metropolitan area of more than two million people. Twenty-nine to 34 percent of residents are Latino.

Targeting Minority Neighborhoods with the Gang Label

Regular patrol officers often did not know how to distinguish gang members from non-gang members and thus primarily considered the entire urban youth of color population as possible suspects for membership. Gang units utilized the "duck" profile for determining gang membership: "If it looks like a duck, quacks like a duck, then it's probably a duck." This unsophisticated form of profiling differentiated urban youth based upon appearances, but because many youth dressed in a similar way it made it difficult to separate members from non-members. Discerning gang membership is not always easy for urban youth either. Individuals appearing (i.e., clothing, tattoos, vehicles) to belong to a rival gang, along with their family members and friends can often enhance perceptions of danger. Many urban youth appear to enjoy this dangerous image until confronted by a rival gang when quickly denying membership can hopefully de-escalate a potential violent encounter.

Before joining a gang, I associated with a total of four gangs, of which three groups were allies and one was a rival. One evening, I was hanging out with two individuals who were associates of the rival gang. As I drove my car into a fast-food parking lot, my friends and I were quickly approached by 11 young men excited to physically attack us. Quickly and pleadingly we announced that we were not gang members and after several minutes of questioning one of the individuals who confronted us was about to verify the accuracy of these claims. Thus rival gangs often mirror the police in providing a blanket level of suspicion towards the entire group of individuals until information is obtained proving or disproving membership. There is however a difference for members who belong to a particular gang, and then it is clearly known who has been jumped-in and who still maintains an associate or outside role to the gang. Associates are potential candidates for inclusion into the gang but for various reasons have not been formally initiated.

Gang members and urban youth often shared a similar background and living situation, on the contrary the police and urban youth are often direct opposites. Structural issues of race and ethnicity were more than likely replicated in such unequal interactions. In Ogden, Utah, the entire police department of 140 sworn officers is almost all white whereas two-thirds of the listed gang members are Latino. In Denver, Colorado, one-third of the 1,550 sworn personnel but more than 90 percent of the listed gang members are considered non-white. Such differential numbers in regards to racial and ethnic diversity has played a role in enhancing divisions between the police and minority communities. In addition, as reported in Denver, several police officers of color are often accused of being more racist and violent than their white counterparts by many community members. Thus reducing the historical division will more than likely also require structural changes that go beyond diversity initiatives. Not all police officers were the same in attitude, demeanor, or use of discretion. The variable types of officers was clearly reported during interviews and while observing police interactions with urban youth. Some officers were considered friendly, professional, and attempting to do a good job of enforcing the law. Indeed, several interviewees considered police important in the community to stop criminal activity. On the other hand, participants saw another segment of the policing population as perceiving themselves superior to urban youth of color and did everything possible to reinforce this dominating and controlling personality. These officers were despised and hated.

Interacting with Suspected Gang Members

Urban youth claimed that if you are black or brown you will always be treated as a crime suspect or gang member. Some behaviors can enhance this profiling such as style of dress and associating with more than one individual in public. Denying gang membership often carried little support when an officer's "duck" profile was met, which made interactions between police and urban minority youth tense because the origin of the stop was often vague. Urban youth believed that the police will often attempt to incite or provoke an incident in order to justify increased harassment, searches, and arrests. The overall goal for urban youth is to avoid the police. When this is not possible they try to be respectful and to remain silent.

Intelligence gathering was a key component of police suppression tactics. Donner (1980) reported surveillance conducted on people and groups was justified on preventive grounds against violence. However, police intelligence gathering has allowed the labeling of entire racial and ethnic groups, especially men, as gang members (Durán, 2009a, 2009b; Johnson, 1993; Lopez, 1993). Once people land on such lists, it becomes more likely that their future acts will be discovered, prosecuted, and dealt with punitively (Anderson, 1990). Gang lists in Denver and Ogden do not require criminal activity for admission and they remain in the file for at least five years. For police officers to create these lists, urban youth were repeatedly asked to what gang they belonged. According to the police department gang protocol, people who admitted gang membership satisfied the first and primary requirement for being placed on a gang list, yet most people denied membership. The police used different tactics to discover gang involvement ranging from talking nonchalantly to coercion. Most respondents interviewed who were not involved with gangs believed that officers suspected them of lying in denying membership. Officers would search for clues by asking individuals to pull up their shirts, looking for tattoos, or asking what high school they attended, to denote possible gang membership. Tone, a 28-year-old "convict" who chose to stay away from a gang lifestyle, said:

> They [police] would throw a couple different gang names at me and ask me which one I belonged to and I would say none. But they would always look like they didn't believe me if you didn't tell them what they wanted to hear.

Anne, a 24-year-old gang associate from Ogden, said:

> I was pregnant and me and my friend were cruising and we were just sitting there parked and the cops came over and a couple other people were parked there and they were in a gang but they said we couldn't be loitering around there. And right away they were yelling at us what gang were we in. I said, "I'm not in a gang," and he said, "Don't lie," like yelling at me, "don't lie." I was like, "I'm not in a gang." And then he asked, "Why you around all of these gang members if you're not in a gang?" I was pregnant and a girl hanging out with another girl and so it made me pretty mad. And frustrated too because I kept telling him but he wouldn't let it go. He kept saying, "You're in a gang! Tell me!"

Although Anne was associating with gang members, she was not a member. A large number of people in the barrio know someone in a gang, but this does not make them a member. Individual gang membership created a stereotype that spread to everyone living in the barrio of this particular racial or ethnic background. Police officers could then use the gang label to legitimate all interactions with the urban minority community. These labels were then maintained by the presumption of clear and precise policies and guidelines that countered all forms of legal challenges and the negation of complaints, yet no one outside the gang unit had access to the police files to verify its accuracy.

Others whose family members were involved in gangs were often treated as members of the gang. Monique, a 22-year-old from Ogden who had two brothers involved in gangs, mentioned how the police automatically assumed she was a member and treated her poorly. Lucita, a 25-year-old associate with a traditional gang who had two brothers who were previously involved in gangs, concurred with this negative treatment when she said:

> For a while there I was getting pulled over a lot. They assumed I was affiliated with so and so, they see you one time with this one person, therefore you have information that you are withholding from them or they think you know the whereabouts of an individual. Stuff like that. You get harassed and you get them on your back you can't get them off. They are on you constantly and they will pull you over for anything. I think they put the word out, look for this vehicle with this person driving.

Lucita, in fact wished the police were friendlier with her and the Latino community. A higher level of trust and mutual support could foster the belief that the police were actually here to protect and serve.

Frequent disrespect from the police was unanimously reported by more than 97 percent of the urban youth interviewed, and they took little time to recall instances of verbal and body language abuse. Although Mastrofski, Reisig, and McCluskey (2002) reported that police disrespect was very rare (4 percent of all police stops) almost half of these incidents were unprovoked. The police attempted to dominate these interactions with the power of the law, authority, and entrusted discretion. Mack-one, a twenty-four-year-old ex-gang associate from Denver, said:

> They treated me bad. They thought I was a gang member. They didn't really do any physical harm to me but, verbally they definitely thought of me as a lower human being.

Although acting civil and cordial may not be a requirement for policing, these stops produced feelings of anger, distrust, and hopelessness particularly when police could do whatever they wished and get away with it. Everyone interviewed could cite examples of being treated disrespectfully and then simply told to go on their way once officers found no reason to take the stop further (the majority of the time). Police officers' "fishing expeditions" would not always pay off. Anne, the 24-year-old gang associate from Ogden, said:

> They're dicks; they don't care, and they don't care if you're a girl. I had one of the gang cops search me, and I know that is against the law. Not search me but pat me down, like really pat me down! I know they are not supposed to do that, and I told him, "You can't pat me down." I'm like, "You're supposed to have a female officer." He was all, "You don't tell me what to do." You know, just their little attitude, they'll put you down to your face. You're nothing, you're a piece of shit, they totally don't have any respect for anybody who is a gang member or who they think is a gang member. I don't know how they choose the gang task force but they don't seem to understand anything about gangs. All they focus on is getting them off the street and into jail. It's awful.

Smiley, a 23-year-old ex-gang associate, said:

> They treat you like you are lower than everybody you know, like you are a bad person, like you are always committing felonies or that you are involved in crime. They just treat you with no respect. They just treat you like you are scum or something, like you are a bad person.

These two interactions between Mexican American community members and the police highlight the perception that the police are attempting to gather intelligence to bring individuals down and disrespect them during the process. Police officials primarily applied the gang label to Latinos and blacks thus increasing the likelihood that the only people who could be perceived as non-gang members were whites. Gang intelligence gathering was blatantly discriminatory when gang unit officers would stop countless Latinos and blacks and leave groups of whites alone. Conducting sweeps on groups of white youth and justifying it with gang reasoning had the potential to put gang unit funding and continued operations in jeopardy. Police officers repeated profiling based on stereotypical perceptions and coercive intelligence on urban youth justified increased funding, increased gang legislation, and the movement to relocate greater numbers of this population to the penitentiary.

Interacting with Confirmed Gang Members

Gang-labeled urban youth, those who were on the gang list or completely meeting the duck profile, were approached differently because they were seen and treated as constant criminals even when following the law. Police perceptions shaped gang membership as a "master status" that combines ascribed and achieved statuses with the belief of lifelong gang involvement (Hughes, 1945). Changing this image was very difficult for gang members, particularly those attempting to leave the gang lifestyle. D-loc thought gang members were treated three times worse than non-gang members by the police. Based upon my research and experiences, D-loc's claim was supported by my observations of gang members encountering a greater frequency of stops and increased levels of scrutiny. Many police stops of gang members would begin with ordering these urban youth out of their vehicle and telling them to put their hands up in the air or lie face down on the ground. The officers more frequently drew their guns on gang confirmed individuals than others and attempted to investigate assumed gang involvement and planned activities. Law enforcement stops of gang members held a greater potential for abusive conduct because they often took the continuum of force to occasionally require fighting violence with violence. To reduce the potential danger to officers, a gang stop was more than likely to proceed in the following order: 1) Stop; 2) Order suspect out of the vehicle at gun point. Tell suspect to raise both hands in the air and walk backward; 3) Frisk upper body and lower body: this can be done with the suspect standing up or being told to kneel or lie face down on the ground. Possibly place in handcuffs and have sit on the curb. This will often be done for each individual in the car; 4) Question each suspect about guilt and participation in gang and crime; 5) Run background check for warrants on each individual. Take photographs of tattoos and ask suspects to take pictures throwing gang signs. Such type of stops are frustrating and annoying to encounter. For gang members, it becomes part of life and you simply "suck-it-up," but let some middle or upper class youth go through this routine and they will quickly counter with formal complaints that get acknowledged. In the barrios and ghettos, such complaints get ignored.

Cyclone, a 25-year-old ex-gang member and ex-prison inmate, said:

> I got labeled as a known violent gang member and never been caught of a gang crime with anybody and it's odd because they label you as that and it's not a good label because it sticks with you for life. When I get pulled over it doesn't matter who I am with they pull me out of the car and pat me down. Every time. I mean they run my name, the NCI report comes up that says I am a violent person and they wait for three or four more cops to show up and then they get me out of the car just to check me. While I am with my family, my kids, I am getting discriminated. They've embarrass me in huge way with the people I'm with. They will tell the people I'm with I'm a bad influence or I'm trouble.

Cyclone was adamant that the police have consistently tried to hurt him and also not provide personal protection to prevent his victimization from rival gangs. Raul, an 18-year-old ex-gang member from Denver, said:

> They [police] mess with you all of the time. Like if you are a gang member they be stopping you all of the time. Checking to see if you have any weapons, some of these police officers are racist, they think we are all violent and do bad crimes but I think we are different. One time they stopped us and they were taking off our shirts and checking if we had any gang tattoos. Writing things on their computer, about when they stopped you, what gang tattoos you have. They even took pictures of me one time, and I don't know why.

Raul adamantly denied the police viewpoint when describing his friends and how it differed greatly from the violent and criminal projection given by law enforcement.

Respondents interviewed claimed that both Denver's and Ogden's police departments often used excessive physical force. Although researchers for the Bureau of Justice Statistics (Greenfeld, Langan, & Smith, 1999) reported that the use of force occurred in less than 1 percent of all encounters with citizens during the year of their survey, at least 34 percent of my respondents had experienced physical abuse one or more times. Sixty-five percent of this misconduct occurred during an arrest and in an isolated area during evening hours. Individuals were more likely to be victimized by police in impoverished black and Latino neighborhoods. The full level of abuse and misconduct in these cities has not been exposed in the same way as the infamous Rampart CRASH division case with detailed investigations and hearings. Nevertheless, several of my respondents were adamant that officers similar to the character played by Denzel Washington in the movie *Training Day* exist in the Denver and Ogden police departments.

Problematic urban conditions and minority presence has resulted in police violence being used proactively rather than simply reacting a criminal threat (Jacobs & O'Brien, 1998; Terrill & Resig, 2003). The Latino and black communities recognized that a simple stop or interaction with the police had a variety of outcomes that were seen as legally permissible, but that law enforcement officers were not going to treat whites living in their racially segregated suburbs with the same type of aggression. Holmes (2000) reported that there is reliable data to conclude that Southwestern Latinos are targets of police brutality based on his study of civil rights complaints filed with the

U.S. Department of Justice. Furthermore, Kane (2002) reported that an increase in the percent of the Latino population increased police misconduct.

The captain of the Denver Gang Unit assured me that many policies and protections were instituted to prevent misconduct from happening within his city. Nevertheless, two Denver gang officers were charged for not logging at least 80 pieces of drug evidence into the police department property bureau after making numerous arrests and tickets for marijuana possession and paraphernalia (Vaughan, 2000). One of these officers was accused of harassing and brutalizing gang members within the Denver area, and this may be the reason he was shot by a suspected gang member during a questionable traffic stop (Ritter, 2003; 2004 Interviews). The alleged gang member was also shot to death during this incident. Denver had a high rate of police shootings, from 1980 to 2008 there were 231 people shot and 103 people killed, by the Denver Police Department.

In another Denver case, an off-duty gang officer was driving home late at night after getting off work and became involved in an incident in which he fired six shots at a Salvadorian immigrant, who died at the scene. Forensic evidence contradicted the officer's testimony about whether the immigrant was holding a gun (Lowe, 2001). An ex-military and highly decorated African American man filed a racial profiling complaint against the Gang Unit. He described how several gang officers stopped him without cause, crashed into his wife's car, and held him down at gunpoint while making lewd remarks towards his wife (Lindsay, 2004). Nevertheless, the Gang Unit claimed they had few complaints. Rodney, an African American and Latino resident who was a gang associate from Denver, told me:

> I wish every gang member would actually report the abuse that they would go through by the Denver Police Department. Then we would have a better picture of what the role is that unit plays. But the gang members don't feel like they have a right to report when they have been beat up. If they actually took the time to document this stuff we would actually see the Denver Police is putting in more work than anybody. They function as a gang. (They said they had low amounts of complaints that come from that unit?) They said they have a low amount of complaints; yeah they do, because the people they are attacking are scared to complain. A lot of times, I don't even want to say scared, they don't feel empowered to complain. They feel like they are a gang member so they just have to deal with what they got.

The Ogden Gang Unit was the least prepared for dealing with "harassment" practices by their officers because their white officers were rarely formally challenged or questioned about how they operated. Therefore, the Ogden Gang Unit practiced a higher number of profile stops than Denver. Jay, a 27-year-old ex-Ogden-gang member, said:

> I think that some of their methods and tactics are a little on the borderline of police brutality, or excessive force. One of my friends who works at the police department is in close contact with the Gang Unit, told me that this one officer hates little gang members. He is one of the head guys and has been in there for like 27 years or so, and he specifically hates little gang bangers you know. He calls them on whether it be a fist fight, a weapons fight, whatever. He will physically challenge them, you know, you bring your stick and I'll bring mine. I guess they figure they got to do what they got to do.

Jay saw the need in the community for better policing. This drove him to continue pursuing the possibility of one day becoming a police officer himself.

Several community members challenged Ogden Gang Unit officers for their role in inciting a riot with about 75 urban youth of color at a hip hop concert. The officers had received a call that alcohol was present and when they attempted to enter the building security officials denied them entrance. As a result, several people were beaten with police batons and charged with felony rioting (Gurrister, 2003). After this case was turned over to the FBI for investigation, one of the key officers suspected of brutality began to target the individual who filed the complaint (Gurrister, 2004, 2004a, 2004b). Several individuals in Ogden have attempted to take their complaints against the Ogden Police Department to court. Such actions, they believe, have resulted in retaliation. In 2010, the city of Ogden recently passed the first gang injunction in the state of Utah against 485 individuals listed as a member of one gang. The injunction makes it a class B misdemeanor to associate with members listed as part of the gang, sets a curfew of 11 p.m., and denies possession of alcohol or guns. The injunction was not set to a particular neighborhood as other injunctions but rather the entire 27 square miles of the city. These increased law enforcement powers have only further encouraged police officers to continue their level of racial profiling and harassment. The American Civil Liberties Union has been attempting to legally challenge these actions in Utah's Supreme Court.

Human Rights Watch (1998, p. 2) argued that "race continues to play a central role in police brutality in the United States. Indeed, despite gains in many areas since the civil rights movement of the 1950s and 1960s, one area that has been stubbornly resistant to change has been the treatment afforded racial minorities by the police." Their research involving 14 cities reported that habitually brutal officers, usually a small percentage on the force, might receive repeated complaints but were usually protected by other officers and poor internal police investigations. These data mirrored the city of Denver, where it was discovered that a small number of officers accounted for the largest proportion of shootings. Cyclone, the 25-year-old ex-gang member and ex-prison inmate, said:

> I've been beaten by cops before. I was running from the police and I was drunk. I wrecked a car and I got out and started to run and I noticed there were five different counties of cops. There were cops from every district surrounding me. I laid down on the ground and the cop that jumped on me started punching me on the back of the head. I went into County [Jail] and let them know that I was having serious migraines and I showed them the bumps on my head. They took a report and that's all that was ever said. They didn't do anything to the officer that whupped my ass. I got charged with resisting arrest and was tied to the bumper of a car. (How many times do you think he hit you in the back of the head?) Probably about four of five. (What were you doing?) I was in handcuffs on my stomach while his knee was in my back, and the other cops were watching. They know something happened. If I wasn't in cuffs when he was hitting me I would have defended myself. They have the reports on the bumps on my head, severe handcuff marks on my arms; I couldn't feel my left hand for nearly an hour after they took the cuffs off.

Cyclone did his best to stay employed and help raise his children in a setting where he believed the police preferred that he was dead or incarcerated.

Several of the interviewees also believed that undocumented immigrants were treated worse by police. Mirandé (1987) suggested that immigrants were especially vulnerable because they lacked resources and familiarity with the justice system. Immigrants also reported fewer instances of abuse because they feared deportation. Nite Owl, an undocumented 17-year-old gang member, said:

> One time I was walking, and they [police] told me stop, and I stopped, and they didn't tell me to turn around or anything they just came up and tackled me. They hit me two times with their stick and put the cuffs on my hands. Maybe they could say I'm sorry we messed up or something, but they didn't say nothing like that. They just sorry, it wasn't you. I said it wasn't me and they said shut up, so I didn't say anything.

Nite Owl viewed his situation as being in the wrong place at the wrong time, but there was nothing he could have done to prevent his receiving a severe beating. Nationwide and in both Denver and Ogden, U.S. Immigration and Customs Enforcement have worked with gang units to launch raids against undocumented immigrants who are allegedly involved with gangs. As of September 7, 2010, Immigration and Customs Enforcement claims to have removed 176,736 "criminal aliens" from the United States with this program that began in 2006 (http://www.ice.gov/pi/nr/1009/100928denver. htm). Despite the reason given for the raid being for criminality and gang membership, never was a separate court hearing instituted to determine the accuracy of either claim.

Conclusion

In an ideal world, gangs are the bad guys and the cops are the good guys. But in this social world of urban neighborhoods of color, the roles are often reversed. Gangs often serve as the social and protective group in the neighborhood whereas the police are seen as acting as a gang. Such contradictory roles do not do not make for better community and police relationships. My previous publications have focused on how this labeling occurs (Durán, 2009a) and how the community responds to these abuses (Durán, 2009b). This chapter concentrated on the interactions between police and gangs. I did not find that Gang Unit officers or law enforcement officials were incorrect in all criminal stops, but rather the majority of gang enforcement stops were predicated on non-criminal activity and included more non-gang members. The barrio residents were not anti-police. They *were* against the profiling and demeaning treatment. The end result of aggressive differential policing was greater division between the barrio and law enforcement.

Bonilla-Silva (2001) and Feagin (2010) have argued that whites have developed powerful explanations to justify racial and ethnic inequality. One of these explanations involves the ability to use agency (choice) to supersede the power of structure. Many individuals may argue that these urban youth get what they deserve for "choosing" to dress like, associate, or belong to gangs. Although this chapter did not focus on the activities of gangs or the structural reasons that have shaped their creation, such viewpoints are the dominant propaganda disseminated and accepted for mainstream suburban residents who live outside of barrio and ghetto. Yes, some individual gang members do atrocious acts and deserve to be held accountable as do rogue officers who remain protected by departments operating under a code of silence. The explanation of choices, however, does not get to the root of this inequality and the repeated patterns of friction that maintain forms of polarization.

Other individuals may argue that the individuals interviewed in my study are lying, upstanding police officers do not harass or mistreat youth and responses of law enforcement are controlled by legal guidelines of reasonable suspicion and probable cause, urban youth are more than likely acting suspiciously to bring such legal oversight in their direction. These mainstream arguments have in fact encouraged such targeted law enforcement practices to continue unabated. "Truth" from members of minority groups is regularly dismissed in police departments where claims of misconduct are rarely substantiated. As long as an officer can demonstrate that at least 10 percent of those they stop are gang members, then they can claim they have done good police work to prevent future criminality. It doesn't really matter if standards of reasonable suspicion or probable cause become stretched to include legal behavior. Most of these urban youths will never file a complaint or plead not guilty. Most will take a plea bargain or simply accept their treatment as routine. Those lowest in social power rarely possess the legal recourse or the professional networks to stop such treatment. I was continually amazed from my interviews and observations of police how legitimized such aggressive law enforcement has become. I've wondered where the lawyers or advocacy groups were to change this structural inequality.

Despite mainstream white racial frames of "choice" and "untruthfulness," there were a significant number of observed patterns of unequal treatment from police towards racial and ethnic minority group members living in segregated urban environments. The most powerful and relevant critique I have seen on ghetto neighborhoods and oppressive treatment was not explored in the United States but rather in Germany where ghettos were created to segregate Jews from the rest of the population. In the long run these ghettos were replaced with concentration camps. In the United States, prisons are the result of segregated neighborhoods and the aggressive law enforcement and under-protection from victimization makes this a reality. There is no doubt that the issue of context plays a significant role in Denver and Ogden. Urban barrios and ghettos across the United States most likely exist on a continuum of worst to slightly worse than average. The community in southern New Mexico, where I live now has negative conflicts with the police but at a rate much lower than Denver and Ogden. Durkheim described the coming together of individuals as *sui generis:* A creation unique unto its own. There is no doubt a structural conflict exists between police and urban youth of color. As long as these structural inequalities exist in society, racial and ethnic minorities will continue to experience differential treatment from law enforcement and their voices of opposition will be ignored. And the gang label will continue to serve its purpose.

Critical Thinking

Without a doubt Duran's study and his interpretation of what his participants revealed is affected by his race and his former participation as a gang member; however, we should not take this to mean that his findings are wrong. When reading this article think about how the level of rapport and understanding with gang members allowed Duran to get them to open up to him. How do you think the social and cultural distance between police and citizens contributes to problems? Do you think it would help if police departments made concerted efforts to hire police from the communities they patrol? In short, is diversity among police a good thing for improving community relations?

References

Anderson, E. (1990). *Streetwise: Race, class, and change in an urban community*. Chicago: University of Chicago Press.

Battin, S. R., Karl, G. H., Abott, R. D., Catalano, R. C., & Hawkins, D. J. (1988). The contribution of gang membership to delinquency beyond delinquent friends. *Criminology*, 36, 93–115.

Bjerregaard, B., & Smith, C. (1993). Gender differences in gang participation, delinquency, and substance use. *Journal of Quantitative Criminology*, 9, 329–355.

Bonilla-Silva, E. (2001). *White supremacy and racism in the post-civil rights era*. Boulder, CO: Lynn Rienner.

Brotherton, D. C., & Barrios, L. (2004). *The almighty Latin king and queen nation: Street politics and the transformation of a New York City gang*. New York: Columbia University Press.

Cohen, S. (1980). *Folk devils and moral panics: The creation of the mods and rockers*. New York: St. Martin's.

Curry, G. D., Ball, R. A., & Decker, S. H. (1996). *Estimating the national scope of gang crime from law enforcement data*. Research in Brief. Washington, DC: U.S. Department of Justice, Office of Justice Programs, National Institute of Justice. NCJ 161477.

de Young, M. (1998). Another look at moral panics: The case of satanic day care centers. *Deviant Behavior*, 19, 257–278.

Donner, F. J. (1980). *The age of surveillance: The aims and methods of Americas political intelligence system*. New York: Alfred A. Knopf.

Durán, R. J. (2009a). Legitimated oppression: Inner-city Mexican American experiences with police gang enforcement. *Journal of Contemporary Ethnography*, 38, 143–168.

Durán, R. J. (2009b). Over-inclusive gang enforcement and urban resistance: A comparison between two cities. *Social Justice: A Journal of Crime, Conflict and World Order*, 36, 82–101.

Esbensen, F., & Huizinga, D. (1993). Gangs, drugs, and delinquency in a survey of urban youth. *Criminology*, 31, 565–589.

Feagin, J. R. (2010). *The white racial frame: Centuries of racial framing and counterframing*. New York, NY: Routledge.

Goffman, E. (1959). *The presentation of self in everyday life*. Garden City, NY: Anchor.

Goffman, E. (1963). *Stigma: Notes on the management of spoiled identity*. New York: Simon & Schuster.

Goffman, E. (1982). *Interaction ritual: Essays on face-to-face behavior*. New York: Pantheon.

Greenfeld, L. A., Langan, P. A., & Smith, S. K. (1999), November. *Police use of force: Collection of national data*. Washington, DC: U.S. Department of Justice, Bureau of Justice Statistics and National Institute of Justice. NCJ 165040.

Gurrister, T. (2003), October 23. Police tactics queried: Union station case builds. *Standard Examiner*.

Gurrister, T. (2004a), February 22. FBI probing Ogden incident. *Standard Examiner*.

Gurrister, T. (2004b), April 1. Officer accused of payback arrest. *Standard Examiner*.

Holmes, M. D. (2000). Minority threat and police brutality: Determinants of civil rights criminal complaints in U.S. municipalities. *Criminology*, 38, 343–367.

Huff, C. R., & McBride, W. (1993). Gangs and the police. In A. P. Goldstein, & C. R. Huff (Eds.), *Gang intervention handbook* (pp. 401–415). Champaign, IL: Research Press.

Hughes, E. C. (1945). Dilemmas and contradictions of status. *American Journal of Sociology*, 50, 353–359.

Human Rights Watch. (1998). *Shielded from justice: Police brutality and accountability in the United States*. New York: Human Rights Watch.

Jacobs, D., & O'Brien, R. M. (1998). The determinants of deadly force: A structural analysis of police violence. *American Journal of Sociology*, 103, 837–862.

Johnson, D. (1993), December 11. 2 out of 3 young black men in Denver are on gang suspect list. *New York Times*.

Kane, R. J. (2002). The social ecology of police misconduct. *Criminology*, 40, 867–896.

Katz, C. M. (2001). The establishment of a police gang unit: Organizational and environmental factors. *Criminology*, 39, 37–73.

Katz, C. M. (2003). Issues in the production and dissemination of gang statistics: An ethnographic study of a large midwestern police gang unit. *Crime and Delinquency*, 49, 485–516.

Katz, C. M., & Webb, V. J. (2006). *Policing gangs in America*. New York, NY: Cambridge University Press.

Klein, M. W. (1995). *The American street gang: Its nature, prevalence, and control*. New York: Oxford University Press.

Klein, M. W. (2004). *Gang cop: The words and ways of officer Paco Domingo*. Walnut Creek, CA: AltaMira.

Klein, M. W. (2007). *Chasing after street gangs: A forty-year journey*. Upper Saddle River, NJ: Pearson Prentice Hall.

Lindsay, S. (2004), April 21. Police acted 'inappropriately.' *Rocky Mountain News*.

Lopez, C. (1993), December 5. List brands 2 of 3 young black men. *Denver Post*.

Lowe, P. (2001), November 24. Panel, police see different theories in glass shards: Glass, gun and blood focus 'forensic battle.' *Rocky Mountain News*.

Mastrofski, S. D., Resig, M. D., & McCluskey, J. D. (2002). Police disrespect toward the public: An encounter-based analysis. *Criminology*, 40, 515–551.

McCorkle, R. C., & Miethe, T. D. (2002). *Panic: The social construction of the street gang problem.* Upper Saddle River, N J: Prentice Hall.

Miller, W. B. (1992). Revised from 1982. *Crime by youth gangs and groups in the United States.* Washington, DC: U.S. Department of Justice, Office of Justice Programs, Office of Juvenile Justice and Delinquency Prevention. NCJ 156221.

Mirandé, A. (1987). *Gringo justice.* Notre Dame, IND: University of Notre Dame.

Moore, J. W. (1978). *Homeboys: Gangs, drugs, and prison in the barrios of Los Angeles.* Philadelphia, PA: Temple University Press.

Moore, J.W. (1991) *Going down to the barrio: Homeboys and homegirls in change.* Philadelphia, PA: Temple University Press.

National Youth Gang Survey. (2009). National Youth Gang Survey Analysis. Retrieved [September 30, 2010] from http://www.nationalgangcenter.gov/Survey-Analysis

Needle, J. A., & Stapleton, W. V. (1983). *Police handling of youth gangs.* Reports of the National Juvenile Justice Assessment Centers. Washington, DC. U.S. Department of Justice.

Reaves, B. A., & Hickman, M. J. (2004). *Law enforcement management and administrative statistics, 2000: Data for individual state and local agencies with 100 or more officers.* Wahington, DC: Bureau of Justice Statistics.

Reinarman, C. (2003). The social construction of drug scares. In P. A. Adler and P. Adler *Constructions of deviance: Social power, context, and interaction* (pp. 137–148). Belmont, CA: Wadsworth/Thomson Learning.

Ritter, B. (2003). Investigation of the shooting death of Anthony Ray Jefferson. [On-line]. Retrieved [March 7, 2008] from http://www.denverda.org/Decision_Letters/02Jefferson.htm

Sánchez-Jankowski, M. (1991). *Islands in the street: Gangs and American urban society.* Berkeley, CA: University of California Press.

Sánchez-Jankowski, M. (2008). *Cracks in the pavement: Social change and resilience in poor neighborhoods.* Berkeley, CA: University of California Press.

Spergel, I. A. (1995). *The youth gang problem: A community approach.* New York, NY: Oxford University Press.

Terrill, W. & Resig, M. D. (2003). Neighborhood context and police use of force. *Journal of Research in Crime and Delinquency,* 40, 291–321.

Thornberry, T. P. (1998). Membership in youth gangs and involvement in serious and violent offending. In R. Loeber and D. P. Farrington (Eds.), *Serious and violent offenders: Risk factors and successful interventions.* Thousand Oaks, CA: Sage Publications.

Vaughan, K. (2000), July 20. Charges filed against two cops veteran gang officers accused of destroying evidence in "at least" 80 criminal cases. *Rocky Mountain News,* Section Local, 20.

Vigil, J. D. (2002). *A rainbow of gangs: Street cultures in the mega-city.* Austin, TX: University of Texas Press.

Vigil, J. D. (2007). The projects: Gang and non-gang families in East Los Angeles. Austin, TX: University of Texas Press.

Werthman, C., & Piliavin, I. (1967). Gang members and the police. In D. Bordua (Ed.), *The police: Six sociological essays.* New York: John Wiley and Sons.

Zatz, M. S. (1987). Chicano youth gangs and crime: The creation of a moral panic. *Contemporary Crisis,* 11, 129–158.

8

The Role of Law Enforcement in Making Sense of the Unimaginable

Paul Stretesky, Tara O'Connor-Shelley, Michael J. Hogan, and N. Prabha Unnithan

Abstract: *Paul Stretesky and colleagues sought to understand how the families of murder victims whose case has turned cold make sense of the crime and view the detectives assigned to the case. Using interviews with family members of murder victims (e.g., parents, siblings, spouses, children, aunts, uncles, grandparents, and friends of the victims) the authors discover that family members consider frequent and productive communication with law enforcement personnel to be important in their quest to make sense of the events, but such communication seldom occurs. The majority of participants think that communication is sporadic, information is inadequate or erroneous, and that police have given up on the investigation. Participants interpret the decrease in communication as a symbol for the way police trivialize the murder and the well-being of family members. Many participants assume that police think that the case does not warrant a proper investigation because of officers' prejudices against characteristics of the victims. These participants claim that because of the victim's race, religion, sexual orientation, profession, prior behavior, affiliations, or habits, officers are unwilling to launch an adequate investigation.*

Every day I do hurt. I hurt every day. Every day I do. My whole life has changed. I'm just existing. I am not living. I think once they find out who hurt my son, maybe I can start living again. I just get up and I just go. I'm not living right now. I'm just goin' through the motions, really, to be honest with you. You know, once they find who hurt my son, maybe I can start living again.

Mother of an unsolved murder

Colorado law enforcement recorded 151 murders in 2008. National data suggest that approximately one-third of these homicides will remain unsolved or unresolved for more than a year. According to the Families of Homicide Victims and Missing Persons inc., there are more than 1,500 "cold-case" murders in Colorado that date back to 1970. Our research draws upon the perceptions of the families and friends of cold-case homicide victims to determine how they see their interactions with law enforcement to better understand how those interactions may assist or hinder bereavement. Throughout this research we define the family and friends of unresolved and unsolved homicides as "co-victims" (Hertz, Prothrow-Smith, & Chery, 2005).

While grieving is always a difficult process, homicide co-victims often suffer from what mental health specialists refer to as complicated grief—grief made even more difficult by the traumatic nature of the loss. The ability of co-victims to make sense of what has happened to their loved one can determine how they grieve, how they see themselves, and how they see others in a post-loss world. We argue that the grieving process can be compromised in cases where murders go unsolved for an extended period. This is true because unsolved murder cases are characterized by ongoing uncertainty, fear, and intense anger, leaving co-victims with little information and, eventually, little hope about ever making sense of the murder. This study examines the role that law enforcement plays in that process by drawing upon interviews with 37 family members and friends of unsolved murder victims to better understand if and how communications with the criminal justice system affected their ability to make sense of their loss. The co-victims we interviewed held mostly negative views of police and prosecutors because those criminal justice officials failed to locate information about the murder. These negative feelings toward law enforcement intensified over time. In some cases, co-victims viewed the failure of the criminal justice system to resolve the murder to be based on discrimination against the victim or the victim's behavior. We conclude with some modest suggestions to law enforcement about what they can do to attenuate the problem of secondary victimization and promote bereavement.

Sensemaking

An extensive amount of research has focused on the concept of sensemaking, or the notion that victims create a subjective understanding of their loss (Currier, Holland, & Neimeyer, 2006, 2008; Frankl, 1963; Pakenham, 2008; Updegraff, Silver, & Holman, 2009). For the purposes of this research we define sensemaking as a form of meaning-making that focuses on understanding the murder, and thus contributes to post-loss identity reconstruction. The ability to make sense of a loss is thought to play a central role in bereavement therapy because it aids in the re-creation of the self post-loss (Armour, 2006). Thus, sensemaking may alleviate some of the anguish associated with death of a loved one (Park & Folkman, 1997). People suffering from the loss of a significant other find themselves asking questions about the circumstances surrounding their loss as well as questions about who they are in a post-loss world. While the process of sensemaking is thought to be restorative, the most difficult losses fail to make sense. While studies of sensemaking have expanded to include many types of trauma (cancer, suicide, accidents, homicide), the concept has not been studied in the context of unsolved homicide co-victims. Sensemaking among these particular co-victims seems particularly relevant because it is likely to be extremely difficult to construct any type of post-loss meaning when the circumstances surrounding a murder are unknown, uncertain, and ongoing (Armour, 2006; Bucholz, 2002). Uncertainty surrounding murders creates significant fear of the unknown that may extend to fear of living without a loved one to fear that the killer will return.

Grief

The idea that grief progresses through normal stages is widely accepted in the bereavement literature, and recent empirical evidence suggests a sequence through the following stages: disbelief, separation distress, depression-mourning, and recovery (Maciejewski et al., 2007). However, grief stage theory largely focuses on depressive symptoms, and therefore does not account for more complicated patterns of grief that can often be attributed to traumatic loss (Meciejewski et al., 2007). Traumatic loss is typically defined in terms of a sudden violent death characterized by fatal accident, suicide, or homicide (Norris, 1990). Malone (2007:384) also notes that when a loved one is murdered, the emotional and psychological processes of grieving may not follow the traditional stages of grief. In addition, Weiner (2007:2962) has recently argued that it may be counterproductive and dangerous to apply normal patterns of grief to traumatic loss (see also Silver & Wortman, 2007).

As a result, researchers have developed the notion of complicated grief (or "traumatic grief," see Prigerson et al., 1999) to better characterize the typical bereavement associated with horrific events such as murder (Armour, 2007; Bucholz 2002). Complicated grief is thought to be a reaction to stress response syndrome and associated with long-lasting painful emotions that are severe (Prigerson et al., 1995). Individuals suffering from complicated grief have trouble accepting death and resuming life. Prigerson et al. (1995:22), for example, report that symptoms of traumatic grief include "searching, yearning, preoccupation with thoughts of the deceased, crying, disbelief regarding the death, feeling stunned by the death, and lack of acceptance of the death." In addition to complicated grief, homicide co-victims may also suffer from post-traumatic stress disorder (PTSD). Amick-McMullan et al. (1991:545) discovered that 23.3 percent of homicide co-victims developed PTSD. The American Psychiatric Association (2000) also reports that homicide co-victims exhibit clinical symptoms that include PTSD and acute post-traumatic stress. PTSD is thought to be associated with feelings of "disbelief, anger, shock, avoidance, numbness, a sense of futility about the future, a fragmented sense of security, trust, and control" (Prigerson et al., 1999:67). Stress among homicide co-victims may also be related to physical illness (see Baliko & Tuck, 2008). In short, individual grief as a response to stress is often complicated and can vary tremendously in "duration, intensity, and complexity" (Malone, 2007:384).

The Criminal Justice System and Bereavement

Unsolved homicide co-victims often turn to the criminal justice system for answers to aid their bereavement (Bucholz, 2002); however, research suggests that interactions with the criminal justice system can also intensify victimization (see Bucholz, 2002 for homicide co-victims; see Karmen 2007 for review). Unfortunately, individuals who report a violent loss such as murder are also likely to be the least successful at making sense of that loss (Armour, 2006). Recently, Updegraff et al. (2008) have suggested that in the case of severe trauma people are less likely to find meaning but also more likely to search for meaning. The study of the role that others, such as criminal justice actors, can have on the process of sensemaking among unsolved homicide co-victims is largely neglected. By showing disapproval and distancing themselves from victims and co-victims, criminal justice personnel can cause additional harm (Ryan, 1971). This occurs because interactions (or a lack of interactions) between police, prosecutors, and co-victims can themselves be traumatic and therefore complicate grief by causing additional stress among co-victims (Bucholz, 2002). This phenomenon, known as secondary victimization, is often reported by homicide co-victims (Rock, 1998). Unfortunately, few studies have linked sensemaking to secondary victimization by examining co-victims' perceptions of their interactions with law enforcement.

Co victims report facing many challenges with respect to the criminal justice system and often describe their interactions with the system as extremely frustrating (Bucholz, 2002, Baliko & Tuck, 2008). Bucholz (2002) argues that for these co-victims, justice can be perceived as being "minimized, delayed, or denied," leading to feelings of outrage and powerlessness. Rock (1998:76) argues that a co-victim's alienation from the justice process "constitutes one of the most potent symbolic assaults suffered by families in the wake of murder."

Recently, Baliko and Tuck (2008) reported that homicide co-victims reported feelings of anger and dissatisfaction due to the criminal justice process. These feelings may impede sensemaking by co-victims, especially unsolved homicide co-victims. Updegraff et al. (2008:710) suggest that "in the context of negative events, having an explanation [of the event] should lessen the emotional impact and facilitate long-term adaptation." In the case of unsolved homicides, then, there is considerable reason to suspect that sensemaking is especially difficult because many aspects of the crime are not known and because the offender is still at large. Thus, interactions with criminal justice officials about the murder and possible events leading up to the crime may be critical to the sensemaking process because these agencies have access to information and are responsible for gaining information about their loved one's murder. It is for this reason that we examine unsolved homicide co-victims' experiences with the criminal justice system as it relates to their perceptions of sensemaking.

Methods

Thirty-seven co-victims were interviewed for this study and represent 29 separate cold-case murders that occurred in 10 law enforcement jurisdictions throughout Colorado, including rural, urban, and suburban jurisdictions. Sixty percent of the co-victims in this study were white, and 76 percent were female. The mean age of co-victims interviewed was 57. The cold-case murders covered in this research occurred, on average, 15 years prior to the study. The oldest murder took place 40 years prior to the interview and the most recent murder occurred one year prior to the interview. Twenty co-victims were the parents and nine co-victims were the siblings of the murder victim. The remaining co-victims represent spouses, children, aunts, uncles, grandparents, and friends of murder victim. Interview questions were designed to focus on the level, quality, and intensity of the co-victims' communications and interactions with the criminal justice system, rather than on the features of the unsolved case. The interviews lasted from one to four hours and were conducted in the co-victim's home, office, or other private place. Interview responses were coded to identify general themes and statements about relationships among categories of observations. The ensuing analysis revealed sensemaking as a major issue, and thus the observations and perceptions of co-victims' experiences with the criminal justice system as impacting sensemaking directed the empirical generalizations and themes described below.

Findings

Findings are organized according to four major themes that emerged from our interviews and relate to sensemaking. These themes focused on: (1) perceptions about the lack of communication in the investigation; (2) perceptions about law enforcement's reaction to the victim's status; (3) perceptions about prosecutors' unwillingness to charge strongly suspected murderers with a crime; and (4) co-victims' responses to perceptions of police inactivity. The first three themes demonstrate how law enforcement inhibits sensemaking among unsolved homicide co-victims and the last theme addresses the victim's response to this perceived inactivity. Names of co-victims used in this paper are pseudonyms.

Lack of Communication

The nature and frequency of communication with co-victims was important to sensemaking among co-victims. All but one of the co-victims reported that they were dissatisfied with the current level of communication with law enforcement. Thirty-four of those co-victims believed that the police were no longer actively investigating their unsolved homicide. Over time all co-victims reported a decrease in communication. This decrease is symbolic to co-victims and suggests that their loved ones' murders, and their lives by extension, are not important. Thus, co-victims' negative perceptions about police communication and competence increase over time. Once communication with law enforcement stopped, most co-victims lost hope in the criminal justice system, which impacted sensemaking by: (1) complicating their post-loss understanding of justice; and (2) limiting information about the case. This lack of communication, then, appears to prevent sensemaking and may lead to secondary victimization through the promotion of complicated grief.

Hallie, whose son was murdered approximately one year prior to the interview, emphasizes the importance of police communication with her family. She believes that the police were taking the murder seriously because they kept in constant contact and she had a favorable impression of the detective assigned to her son's case.

> HALLIE: *He was a very good investigator. He kept in communication very well. [Detective] would return my phone call, if not the same day, the next day or so.*
> INTERVIEWER: *So when you called, he called back and gave you an update?*
> HALLIE: *Yeah, I think he did a good job, actually, knowing and finding out things. I have no problem with [Detective]. He's really good. He communicated with me and he's working hard.*

Hallie underscores the importance between communication and information. She held out hope that her son's murder could be solved because the detective was still responsive to her requests for information. She also emphasized that finding out what happened and who killed her son will help with post-loss resolution:

> *Every day I do hurt. I hurt every day. Every day I do. My whole life has changed. I'm just existing. I am not living. I think once they find out who hurt my son, maybe I can start living again. I just get up and I just go. I'm not living right now. I'm just goin' through the motions, really, to be honest with you. You know, once they find who hurt my son, maybe I can start living again.*

For Hallie, and many other co-victims, catching the killer may aid in sensemaking because it implies that justice does exist and that information about the case will help with resolution. Unlike nearly all other homicide co-victims, however, Hallie felt that the detective was forthcoming about the murder and potential killer. Thus, the attention to communication by law enforcement appears to send a critical and symbolic signal so that she may eventually be able to live again because the murder is important and information is forthcoming.

Mark and Molly's comments are more reflective of co-victims whose cases remain unsolved. Their teenage daughter was murdered nearly 20 years prior to the interview and, like Hallie, they agree the police did a good job communicating during the initial investigative stages. Mark and Molly both felt that subsequent communication with the police dropped off significantly. Thus, they suggest they will never make sense of the murder or receive justice. They suggest that police no longer communicate or worry about solving their daughter's murder:

> *It just started to get cold, so they didn't—they used to call us up, but now, they don't seem to have anything new. . . . There's no updates. It's kind of like the same thing over and over: no money, no time.*

These feelings of despair about the lack of information led Mark and Molly to the police department to examine their daughter's case file. Both Mark and Molly indicated that it was important for them to look at the file, but without any additional information their ability to discover why this happened is clearly diminished. The couple continues to ask the same questions they did right after the murder.

> *Now, after all these years, I've mellowed out a lot and I don't feel that much hate. It's still there. I don't think I'll ever lose it. . . . I don't know, it's like that until you find the person who did it. Maybe you'll have some closure after that, but until then, everybody you look at, the same thing crosses your mind. Is that the person? . . . Who would want her dead?*

Thus, for Mark, the uncertainty about the murder was clearly associated with a lack of information about who may be responsible. It could be anybody. Mark and Molly also believe that law enforcement has given up on the case and views the family's inquiries concerning the status of the murder investigation as bothersome. This perception of law enforcement has intensified Mark's sense of injustice and his feelings of hate and fear.

Co-victims report that the lack of communication by the police department was especially apparent and harmful when detective reassignments occurred without notification. Seventeen co-victims told the interviewer that a change in the primary detective assigned to their murder case signaled that the case was no longer a police priority.

Thus, reassignments were painful because they signaled that law enforcement had given up the quest for justice. These co-victims believed they would never have the important details they needed to understand the world post-loss. Seventeen homicide co-victims reported that they had endured several of these "reassignments." Most co-victims could not identify the detective currently assigned to their cold case. Such admissions to the interviewer were emotionally distressful to the co-victim and signaled potential secondary victimization. This was clearly the case with Quinton, who was a teenager at the time his father was murdered.

> The families are not notified when the detective changes. I mean, I even asked [the Department], "Is he [the detective who initially investigated my father's murder] still here?" "Yeah, he still works here." So that part I think is more hurtful than anything else, to feel like, OK, this person has literally taken control of a murder investigation that has impacted our family in more ways than most people can ever comprehend, and then for us to just kind of become a project that goes by the wayside.

The fact that the detective was reassigned led Quinton to question the veracity of the detective's commitment. For Quinton, the detectives assigned to the case played a central role in helping the family make sense of the crime. In short, most co-victims believed that a change in the primary detective assigned to the case signaled a decrease in departmental commitment to their investigation because, they argued, the detectives probably believed that the cases were not solvable. This left co-victims with a feeling of hopelessness that they would never discover what had actually happened.

While perceptions about changes in detectives were common, they were not universal. Two co-victims noted that the initial interactions with the primary detective in charge of their cases were so negative and the detectives so unresponsive that they welcomed the change. In both cases the new detectives assigned to the case appeared more willing to share more information, which appeared to be associated with sensemaking and notions of justice. Gwen, whose son was murdered 12 years prior to the study interview, notes that information increased with the reassignment of the first lead detective:

> About three years after my son was murdered [detective] started workin' on the case. And he gave me more information than I've ever had in the years that it happened. He brought other people in and started interviewing them again. He talked to both my twin boys and myself, and he was trying to get in touch with the girl that he was livin' with at the time, but she would never go down there. And the person that was with him when he got shot, he would never go. It's just like, I think they know who did it, but they won't tell who did it, it's a situation like that. All the years that this case has been here, [detective] was the one that gave me more information than anybody.

Notions of post-loss sense of justice also emerged alongside the lack of information. For example, 11 co-victims believed that the police perceived their calls as bothersome and problematic. In these 11 instances, co-victims reported that the police were trying to cover up the fact that they had no leads or did not (at the time) believe the case was a murder. For example, Winnie's daughter was murdered nearly 15 years ago and she still calls the police department every year for an update. Winnie reports that the police are not willing to talk to her because they believe the case is unsolvable. Winnie notes that she may never get resolution and justice:

INTERVIEWER: *So you've had no update over the past few years?*

WINNIE: *None. Because whenever you call, you get the same thing. "We just had a forest fire or whatever, don't you know? And you're worried about your dead daughter? We've got a forest fire." So unless I have the mental fortitude to deal with it, it just backlashes too much into my current existence now, just tryin' to meet everyday needs and stuff like that. So I try not to deal with that too much for right now.*

Winnie was able to get some information about her daughter's murder from another source and noted the importance of that information to the interviewer. She clearly believes that God played a role in bringing her the information about her daughter so she could make sense of life post-loss and become a better Christian.

The feeling that co-victims were bothering law enforcement when they asked for information to help make sense of the unsolved crime, then, is not uncommon. Many co-victims called the police to find out that even the detective assigned to their unsolved homicide reported that they had very little (if any) knowledge about the circumstances of the murder. These feelings about law enforcement leave co-victims angry and pessimistic about coming to resolution about the case. Most co-victims reported that these experiences left them feeling like they had been victimized a second time and they reported that this intensified their struggle to make sense of justice and the police role in that process during pre- and post-loss while at the same time dealing with their stress of their traumatic and ongoing loss (e.g., the unsolved murder of their loved one).

The Role of Race, Ethnicity, and Gender

Sixteen co-victims reported that they thought the murder of their loved one was not being adequately investigated because the police believed the case was less worthy of investigative resources because the victim was somehow "unconventional" (i.e., the victim was black, Hispanic, poor, and/or was involved in drugs or prostitution). A total of four homicide co-victims in this sample perceived that their family member's case was not adequately investigated because of their race. These co-victims appear to have made sense of the fact that the case was unsolved by drawing on larger prejudices in society to help explain the perceived police response. Several co-victims even argued that the case was solvable and information about the murderer and murder exists.

Unlike black co-victims, Hispanic co-victims argued that factors such as drug use, domestic violence, or gang membership also affected the investigation into their family member's murder because it is the perception of most police that Hispanics engage in these illegal activities. Orlando emphasizes that his murdered brother was not in a gang, but that the police treated the case as a gangland murder and thus did not investigate the case vigorously. Orlando and his mother Olivia report that the police told them that the victim's gang activity and membership caused his death. They became extremely angry at the police because they were presented with an account of the murder that was not compatible with their sensemaking.

There's nobody working on the case right now. We know they're very, very busy. It's not like my brother is the only murder case. There are a lot of other cases. It's not like somebody else's case is more important or my brother's case is more important than somebody else's. It doesn't matter who the person is or what they've done, they've still been murdered. It's not like, "This person's a very bad guy so we're just gonna push his case over here." That should be a priority, but not put anybody's case to the side just because they feel that it's gang-related or this person's a drug dealer or anything like that. Anybody should have the right for their case to be solved and worked on.

Victor also talks about the importance of race in his daughter's three-year-old murder investigation. He argues that race is the reason his daughter's murderer was still at large. He expressed anguish that the murder would never be solved and that he had no information about the case, and also reported feeling both helpless and depressed. Victor's lack of agency caused him to view the police as an obstacle to catching his daughter's killer(s).

Here's a black child . . . probably used drugs. You know she did some prostitution. And that's just the way it is. I don't think that's gonna change for a while. I do not believe the police department's gonna change. Why won't the police department change? Because the power that be is not gonna do anything to institute change within the police department. They will always be able to tell me, "Well, we just don't know," and there won't be a thing that I can do about it. I really can't put pressure on these people.

Thus, Victor believes that the police will not give him information to help him make sense of the case because his daughter is black. Moreover, Victor has given up hope that the police will find the killer and has come to the conclusion that the case is unsolved because of his daughter's race. Police and prosecutors may unintentionally send signals to co-victims that their deceased loved one was at least partially responsible for being murdered and may suggest to co-victims that some cases may be more deserving of investigation than others (Karmen, 2007). It is not possible to know what signals law enforcement sent Victor in this case, but it is clear that he believes that racism has played a direct role in the way his case was handled by law enforcement, and that has prevented him from ever seeing the killer brought to justice or gaining some insight into the mysterious circumstances surrounding the murder of his daughter.

Past deviant or illegal behavior on the part of the murder victim can also impact a co-victim's ability to make sense of the murder and cause them to question the effort police put into an investigation. Sometimes this feeling is perpetuated by the media, who spread what co-victims consider to be lies about the murder victim (Armour, 2002), and that further prevents sensemaking and complicates grief. Thus, at the same time that co-victims seek to convey a conventional image of the murder victim to the public, and to stop any negative public judgments, they also worry about the impact such perceptions may have on the murder investigation and their notion of what happened in the case.

Karla, for instance, felt that her husband's murder was not being investigated because his bad reputation was emphasized in local newspapers when describing his death. As Karla was fighting the newspaper, law enforcement began asking questions about her husband's untoward past. Even though the information about Karla's husband later turned out to be false, and the newspaper retracted the story, she continues to believe that the police are still influenced by those reports and her husband's delinquent past. Thus, even when she was in the initial stages of making some sense of the unsolved murder she perceived the police were undermining her belief in her husband as a good person:

I believe that they aren't doing anything. I feel that my husband had a lot of run-ins as a juvenile, as a young adult, with law enforcement, a lot of city police knew him and his brother by name. And I believe that it's felt there's one less troublemaker on the streets. If I looked at his past, he was still human. He still deserves the same effort that they would put into anyone else's murder. He's got family. He had two kids. They ask me all the time, "How come So-and-so's in jail for this murder, but nobody's in jail for killing my dad?" He's human. He does have family regardless of what kind of past he had. No one deserves to be shot and killed.

Paula's perceptions are similar to Karla's. While Paula explains that her brother was an alcoholic and needed help, she also argues that he often went out drinking late at night and was known to carry around a large sum of money. She believes that the police did not take her brother's case seriously because of his risky behavior. She could not make sense of her brother's murder with the accounts that the police had given and was still trying to identify the killer, get justice, and come to some resolution about the murder. The inability of the police to accept or even acknowledge, her account of her brother's murder caused Paula great anger and distress:

In fact, when my son and sister-in-law and I went and kind of walked that whole area after [my brother's] death, I found some items that might have been kicked out of a car that was parked there, and that's where those people said that car was parked. I picked those items up, and I've still got them. It's like, packets of crackers and stuff like that. But the [department] didn't want to hear anything like that. It was like, No, this was a drunk [that] got hit, and that's the end of the story.

Moreover, Paula, like other co-victims in this study, is upset that the police refuse to take seriously the evidence she has collected. Such reports appear to be consistent with yet an additional secondary victimization on the part of unsolved homicide co-victims who reported high levels of stress over their perceptions of what evidence may be important to the case.

Self-Investigation

An inability to make sense of the murder and to bring the killer to justice appears to complicate co-victims' grief. Most families longed for communication from law enforcement that indicated that the case was still active and that new information about the case would be forthcoming as their questions about the case developed through the process of trying to make sense of the murder. Co-victims' perceptions that police were not investigating the case and providing appropriate levels of information, however, delayed the restorative process. This lack of information pushed many co-victims into action. Sixteen co-victims indicated some sort of self-initiated effort in trying to solve their loved one's murder. Thus, they tried to make sense of the case by solving it themselves. Molly explained that she often wanted to investigate her own case given the response she sometimes gets from law enforcement when she asks if they have any leads on her daughter's killer.

That's another thing I pick up on when we go over there, they say, "Do you have anything new for us?" It's like, are we doing the investigating now? I know some people do if they have something like this in their family. They go out and investigate. But that's a special kind of person, I think. Not everybody can do that. You have to give up your life. Follow all the leads you can, whatever. Not everybody can do that. But I kind of feel like they throw it back on us, like they feel like we're accusing them of not doing anything. "Do you have anything for us?"

This reported reaction is similar to Goffman's (1952) notion of betrayal in "cooling out the mark" where co-victims report that they have come to realize that the police who are supposed to be on their side throughout the process have really been trying to distance themselves from the murder case because (co-victims believe) it cannot be solved. Co-victims report that these feelings challenged their sense of justice and caused them considerable additional anger and stress—feelings that are counter-productive to the notion of sensemaking and represent yet another victimization by the criminal justice system.

In other instances, co-victims actually conducted their own investigations to make sense of the case. Debra, for example, reports that she consulted with her detective prior to conducting an interview for fear of jeopardizing her daughter's case. However, she wanted to know why and how her daughter was murdered. She believed that she could gain information about the reason for her daughter's murder and that would ultimately help the prosecutors gain a conviction:

Let me tell you right now, I went out on my own and interviewed people I thought I wanted to talk to. I always told [detective] "I'm going to do this." And he would say, "Back off," or like he did with [witness] he'd say, "Wait till after the trial because I don't think he should talk to you before the trial."

Several co-victims in this sample were working vigorously to solve their loved one's murders. However, these co-victims perceived that the detectives working their cases thought that this investigation was unnecessary and potentially harmful. Self-initiated detective work caused a number of hardships for co-victims, ranging from financial strain to mental instability to threats of harm and violence. However, co-victims persisted in these investigative efforts in order to gain information that would help them identify the murderer and make sense of the murder. For example, Xandria, who believed she had identified her daughter's killer, reports that the police initially did not take her investigation seriously. She was convinced, despite all the resistance from the police, that her daughter's boyfriend had killed her. In the end, and only after the suspect was convicted of another murder, Xandria reports that the police did use the evidence she collected to build a case against her daughter's murderer. Xandria's investigation consisted of videotapes obtained from the convenience store where her daughter was last seen and interviews of potential witnesses and informants. She spent a large portion of her time searching for her daughter's body and looking for physical evidence. She believed that she had made sense of the case through her investigation of events. In a matter of a few years, her intense investigation into her daughter's case interfered with nearly every aspect of her life, caused her to lose her business, and she nearly died from poor health exacerbated by extreme stress.

If you look in the police evidence box, 98 percent of the evidence is from [me]. And they are lucky they even have a case. And you know, people just—I still have family members that I—it's very strained because they say, "You should let the police do their job." And [my ex- husband] and I say, you know, we hope they never know. We hope they never have our experience—they never need to know, if you don't do it, nothing happens.

In the end Xandria's ability to make sense of the case helped her to find resolution despite the fact that the killer had not yet been brought to justice. The fact that the murderer was still free did present Xandria with some anxiety, but she was again healthy, working, and going about her life.

Caroline also spent years collecting evidence resulting in extreme financial hardship and periods of homelessness. She invested considerable time reconstructing her mother's murder and interviewing people involved in the case and its investigation in order to make sense of her mother's murder and see resolution in her case. Caroline invested an immense amount of time and money into her investigation:

> I had to pay. I've got thousands of dollars, which is horrible, because I don't make thousands of dollars, in paperwork. But I had to have it in order to first understand and second of all, to make anybody else listen. I had to bring their own paper to them and prove it. . . . I went and I read page for page for page. And then I broke it down into investigators, witnesses, and I got online and I started finding people and people would give me numbers to people and I would contact them and—it wasn't like it was an all-day, every-day thing, but it was consuming, and I wanted to know what happened. And the more questions I had, the more I would get a run-around or the more answers I got, it would lead me to different branches. Some people would open the door and welcome me, and some people [told me to leave].

After years of investigation Caroline was able to make sense of the murder, and her mother's killer was eventually convicted of the crime. Caroline reported that her investigation provided her with a sense of what happened to her mother and the prosecution provided her with affirmation of that sensemaking in a public forum. Importantly, she notes that when she talked with the judge she received affirmation:

> He [the judge] apologized to me because he was on bench when it originally happened. He said, "We let you down, we let your mother down, we let your folks down, and I feel terrible about that. I am very proud of you for all that you've accomplished." It is what it is. I went for the truth and not out here for brownie buttons or anything other than to keep it out there, to get the law enacted, and to hopefully prevent somebody else. I don't think it would prevent somebody else from doing it, although it makes people aware of who he is, he can't fly through life any more.

Thus, Caroline was able to make sense of her mother's murder and have that resolution affirmed in a public forum. While she reports that she is still suffering because of her mother's murder, she is in the unique position of finding resolution in her case.

Unfortunately most family members did not get as much information about their case as Caroline and Xandria. While most unsolved homicide co-victims worked their loved one's cases with determination, they often report having little understanding of investigative techniques and lacked adequate resources, protection, and support. Paula worked on her brother's unsolved murder case for several years before coming to the conclusion that it would remain unsolved.

PAULA: *Like I said, after working so hard all those years, I just decided, okay, patience. Let [my brother's case] cool down. Let it take its own course and maybe something will come out of it.*

INTERVIEWER: *That must have been hard, to just let it die down. It sounds like those first two years you were working and trying to work on your brother's case. I assume when you say kids . . .*

PAULA: *I have one, but I had just hurt myself, and I was working in pain every day and trying to work on my brother's case, and everything, and I wasn't getting much rest and everything between the nightmares and pain and everything else, just after a few years, I couldn't do it anymore. So I thought, OK, this is it. I'm not getting anywhere. I'm just going around in circles and pounding my head against the wall. Let it cool down and have patience. Get back into it later.*

Paula was unable to make sense of her brother's murder and, after years of investigation, had to step back because of the toll it was taking on her family and her health. She was forced to choose between trying to make sense of her traumatic loss and losing her husband, job, and health.

In the end, the fact that many co-victims could not get information about their unsolved murder led them to see the criminal justice system as an under-resourced bureaucratic organization incapable of solving many crimes. As noted, this realization intensified co-victims' feelings of despair and suspicion.

Implications for Bereavement and Criminal Justice

The Federal Bureau of Investigation (FBI, 2008) reports that 38.2 percent (or 6,568) of the 16,929 murders and non-negligent manslaughters that occur in the United States will not be immediately solved. Hawkins (2008) recently noted that the clearance rate for homicides dropped from 91 percent in 1963 to 61 percent in 2007. These data suggest many co-victims are faced with conditions that may lead them to complicated and prolonged forms of grief, and that the circumstances of their interactions with law enforcement may cause them to be especially prone to forms of secondary victimization at the hands of the criminal justice system. Co-victims of unsolved homicides report that they are in a position where they are unable to find meaning or to make sense of the murder because of the enormous amount of uncertainty that surrounds the unsolved homicide combined with the fact that their notions of justice are undermined in their interactions with law enforcement. In short, without resolution to a case, sensemaking on the part of co-victims is difficult at best. It is clear that co-victims believe that the criminal justice system is often at odds with their capacity to develop a sense of understanding about their loss. Without critical information about the case, many co-victims are never able to construct such an understanding.

With respect to a lack of information, crime victims often turn to the criminal justice system to get information about the murder (Bucholz, 2002). In that respect, cold-case co-victims are no different than most crime victims in wanting information about the crime. Specifically, co-victims clearly asserted that they wanted more information about the murder to help them understand what happened. This notion is compatible with the process of sensemaking and suggests that it may be hard to construct post-loss meaning when circumstances surrounding the death are unknown and uncertain. Consistent with the notion of sensemaking, co-victims reported that information about the case would help them formulate some type of resolution. Thus, many co-victims became extremely frustrated when the system served to limit or even intentionally block their access to information. Co-victims reported that this lack of information extended their bereavement and many were still grieving despite the passage of time.

The co-victims interviewed for this study were nearly universal in their belief that police stopped actively instigating their case when it turned cold (i.e., after one year). These perceptions are based on co-victims' observations that law enforcement failed to provide regular case updates, return phone calls, or notify co-victims of personnel changes. Co-victims believed that better communication by law enforcement would lead to additional information to help them understand what happened and give them hope that the case was still being investigated. Instead, they lived with large amounts of uncertainty about the facts of the case and what, if anything, the police were doing to catch the killer. The lack of information implied to co-victims that the criminal justice system did not take the murder seriously.

We also discovered that several co-victims believed that the lack of contact that signaled the end of the investigation was the result of race, ethnicity, economic status, or deviant behavior. In short, the co-victims interviewed for this study indicate that the lack of communication made grieving more difficult because it increased uncertainly about what was being done in the case and because it signaled that victim characteristics might prevent the case from being solved.

A post-loss understanding of criminal justice may also be problematic because several co-victims could not understand why their case was not prosecuted when the system could identify the murderer. As noted, co-victims reported that law enforcement told them they know who did it, "but could not prove it." It is clear that these co-victims have little faith in notions of justice and fairness. Again, these co-victims report that they are frustrated by the system and believe that the criminals have more rights than the victims. The sensemaking literature indicates that it is difficult to construct a post-loss identity under such conditions (Armour, 2006). Frustration with the criminal justice system and a need to find the murderer led several co-victims to actively investigate their own cases. These investigations were usually not successful and sometimes dangerous.

Co-victims continually report that above all, and as one would expect, they would like their cases resolved. For example, a co-victim in Baliko and Tuck's (2008:31) study of the interaction between co-victims and homicide offenders points out, "I don't hold it as a grudge . . . no need to live bitter . . . as long as you got him in custody, and he's going to be somewhere."

While solving cases is clearly the priority, there are policies that police and prosecutors can adopt to reduce uncertainty and facilitate notions of justice. These policies should aid in the promotion of sensemaking among co-victims. First, this research suggests that police departments should adopt a policy to contact co-victims when the detectives investigating the cold-case change. Only one Colorado jurisdiction claimed to have such a policy in place at the time of our interviews. Thus, two co-victims in this study reported that the police did contact them when there was a change in the lead detective. We believe a department policy to notify co-victims of detective changes could be easily implemented within jurisdictions. Ideally, detectives handling the cases would make the contact with the co-victims.

An alternative could be to amend a state's victims' rights act to include such contact as mandatory. As with other mandatory victims' rights notifications, co-victims who wished to be notified could simply ask the department to alert them of a change. For example, in some states victims can provide a written request under the state's victims' rights acts if they would like to be notified of cold-case updates.

Co-victims suggest that updates about who is working on the case would signal that the case is active and important. The policy of notifying cold-case co-victims of detective changes may also reduce the belief by many co-victims that cases are not pursued because of victim characteristics (i.e., race, ethnicity, or deviance). This is because co-victims appear to be likely to draw upon notions of race, ethnicity and victim status when there is a lack of communication between co-victims and law enforcement. As noted, many cold-case co-victims did not know who was working the case and, by extension, believed that nothing was being done because the victim was black, Hispanic, or lived an unconventional lifestyle.

Second, this research suggests that departments should adopt a policy of allowing co-victims to examine their cold-case files when possible. Dannemiller (2002:7) suggests that "deaths are upsetting in proportion to uncertainty that surrounds them." Thus, law enforcement agencies can also adopt policies that reduce case uncertainty by promoting better communication about the investigation. This is because co-victims of unsolved homicides report that they are unable to find meaning or to make sense of the murder because of the enormous amount of uncertainty that surrounds the unsolved homicide. Co-victims in this study suggested that sharing information, and when possible case files, is helpful. If co-victims' perceptions about communication with law enforcement were more positive than negative (see for example, follow up with bereaved next of kin of critical care patients in Cuthbertson et al., 2000), this may help attenuate this potential form of secondary victimization by removing impediments to sensemaking. Despite law enforcement arguments to the contrary, the few co-victims interviewed in this research that were allowed to look over police and prosecutor case files report that the information they gained from the process was helpful in bereavement. Thus, this strategy should become standard, when feasible, among law enforcement agencies when charges cannot be filed as it may provide a sense of understanding about what information the police and prose-cutors have regarding the murder.

This proposed policy is likely to be controversial because law enforcement culture is not one where information is readily shared with outsiders and because sharing some types of information may jeopardize a case. However, it is important to note here that several co-victims did believe that looking over evidence might also benefit the case because it may help co-victims provide information that is useful to law enforcement. Thus, some co-victims asserted that if they were more involved in the investigation, for example, that might improve the likelihood that a case would be solved. Such a policy of sharing information might also reduce the motivation for some co-victims to engage in their own murder investigations due to a perception that nothing was being done by police.

Third, states should consider revising victim's rights acts to *retroactively* provide for various types of victim's support services to unsolved homicide co-victims. Because the bereavement process is delayed there may be many co-victims that were not eligible or did not receive information about victim's assistance when their loved ones were murdered.

Fourth, law enforcement personnel who interact with unsolved homicide co-victims should be trained in recognizing complicated grief. While we have found that some departments have pursued such training, it is not likely to occur in rural areas where agencies operate on limited budgets. Agencies must have a policy to engage in regular, empathic communication with families and loved ones of unsolved homicides, including contacting the families and loved ones when law enforcement personnel assigned to the case are changed. We believe that the families and loved ones of murder victims, when possible, should be able to review case files and discuss possible theories with law enforcement personnel and prosecutors.

In the end we hope that the information obtained from this study is also useful because it encourages future research on sensemaking among cold-case co-victims. Especially important in terms of future research are issues of race, ethnicity, and class as indicators of secondary victimization among cold-case co-victims. Our finding that the status of the victim may inhibit sensemaking has important consequences for social inequality. Thus, any additional research in this area should focus some attention on what can be done to better promote sensemaking among traditionally disadvantaged and marginalized populations.

Critical Thinking

The results of the present study bring to mind several larger issues. At what point should detectives give up on a case that has gone cold? Is it possible that characteristics of the victim do affect the way police pursue the case? One would hope that race, gender, and class would not influence the way police handle a murder investigation, so we must ask ourselves, are the perceptions of these family members accurate or is their grief clouding their perceptions?

References

American Psychiatric Association. 2000. *Diagnostic and Statistical Manual of Mental Disorders* (4th edition). Washington, DC: APA.

Amick-McMullan, A. D. Kilpatrick, and H. Resnick. 1991. Homicide as a risk factor for PTSD among surviving family members. *Behavior Modification* 15:545–559.

Armour, M. (2002). Journey of family members of homicide victims: A qualitative study of their posthomicide experience. *American Journal of Orthopsychiatry* 72:372–382.

Armour, M. 2006. Meaning making for survivors of violent death. Pages 101–121 in *Violent Death*, edited by Edward Rynearson. New York, NY: Routledge.

Baliko, B. and I. Tuck. 2008. Perceptions of survivors of loss by homicide: Opportunities for nursing practice. *Journal of Psychosocial Nursing and Mental Health Services* 46:26.

Bucholz, J. A. 2002. *Homicide Survivors: Misunderstood Grievers*. Amityville, N Y: Baywood Publishing Company.

Currier, J. M., J. M. Holland, R. A. Coleman, and R. A. Neimeyer. 2008. Bereavement following violent death: An assault on life and meaning. Pages 177–202 in *Perspectives on Violence and Violent Death*, edited by R. Stevenson and G. Cox. Amityville, NY: Baywood.

Currier, J. M., J. M. Holland, and R. A. Neimeyer. 2006. Sensemaking, grief, and the experience of violent loss: Toward a mediated model. *Death Studies* 30:403–428.

Currier, J. M., J. M, Holland, and R. A. Neimeyer. 2008. Making sense of loss: A content analysis of end-of-life practitioners' therapeutic approaches. *OMEGA – Journal of Death and Dying* 57:121–141.

Cuthbertson, S. J., M. A. Margetts, and S. J. Street. 2000. Bereavement follow-up after critical illness. *Critical Care Medicine* 28:1196–1201.

Dannemiller, C.H. 2002. The parents' response to a child's murder. *OMEGA – Journal of Death and Dying* 45:1–21.

Federal Bureau of Investigation. 2008. *Crime in the United States, 2007*. Washington, DC: U.S. Department of Justice, Federal Bureau of Investigation. Retrieved May 28, 2009 (http://www.fbi.gov/ucr/ucr.htm).

Frankl, V. 1963. *Man's Search for Meaning*. New York, NY: Washington Square Press.

Goffman, E. 1952. On cooling the mark out: Some aspects of adaptation to failure. *Psychiatry* 15:451–463.

Hawkins, K. 2008. More people are getting away with murder in the U.S. *Associated Press*. Released Monday, December 8 at 4:06p.m. EST.

Hertz, M. F., R.C. Prothrow-Smith, & C. Chery. 2005. Homicide survivors: Research and practice implications. *American Journal of Preventive Medicine* 29(552):288–295.

Karmen, A. 2007. *Crime Victims: An Introduction to Victimology*. Belmont, CA: Wadsworth.

Maciejewski, P. K., H. Z. Baohui, S. D. Block, and H. G. Prigerson. 2007. An empirical examination of the stage theory of grief. *JAMA–Journal of the American Medical Association* 297:716–723.

Malone, L. 2007. In the aftermath: Listening to people bereaved by homicide. *Probation Journal* 54:383–393.

Norris, F. 1990. Screening for traumatic stress: A scale for use in the general population. *Journal of Applied Social Psychology* 20:1704–1718.

Pakenham, K. 2008. Making sense of caregiving for persons with multiple sclerosis: The dimensional structure of sense making and relations with positive and negative adjustment. *International Journal of Behavioral Medicine* 15:241–252.

Park, C. and S. Folkman. 1997. Meaning in the context of stress and coping. *Review of General Psychology* 1:115–144.

Prigerson, H. G., E. Frank, S. V. Kasl, C. F. Reynolds 3rd, B. Anderson, G. S. Zubenko, P. R. Houck, C. J. George, and D. J. Kupfer. 1995. Complicated grief and bereavement-related depression as distinct disorders: Preliminary empirical validation in elderly bereaved spouses. *American Journal of Psychiatry* 152:22.

Prigerson, H. G., M. K. Shear, S. C. Jacobs, C. F. Reynolds 3rd, P. K. Maciejewski, J. R. Davidson, R. Rosenheck, P. A. Pilkonis, C. B. Wortman, and J. B. Williams. 1999. Consensus criteria for traumatic grief. A preliminary empirical test. *The British Journal of Psychiatry* 174:67–73.

Rock, P. 1998. *After Homicide: Practical and Political Responses to Bereavement*. Oxford, UK: Oxford University Press.

Ryan, W. 1971. *Blaming the Victim*. New York, NY: Vintage.

Silver, R.C. and C.B. Wortman. 2007. The stage theory of grief. *JAMA – Journal of the American Medical Association* 297:2692.

Updegraff, J. A., R. C. Silver, and A. Holman. 2008. Searching for and finding meaning in collective trauma: Results from a national longitudinal study of 9/11 terrorist attacks. *Journal of Personality and Social Psychology* 95: 709–722.

Updegraff, J. A., R. C. Silver, and A. Holman. 2009. Searching for and finding meaning in collective trauma: Results from a national longitudinal study of 9/11 terrorist attacks. *Journal of Personality and Social Psychology* 95:709–722.

Weiner, J. S. 2007. The stage theory of grief. *JAMA – Journal of the American Medical Association* 297:2692–2693.

9

Victims' Voices: Domestic Assault Victims' Perceptions of Police Demeanor

B. Joyce Stephens and Peter G. Sinden

Abstract: *Joyce Stephens and Peter Sinden interviewed domestic violence victims whose assailants had been arrested under mandatory arrest policies to determine how these victims perceived police. Interestingly, but perhaps not surprising, the number of interactions for domestic violence had a strong impact on how victims perceived the responding officers. Onetime victims thought that police understood what they were experiencing and genuinely cared about their well-being. Whereas first time victims saw police as caring and warm, it appears that successive encounters led to increasing dissatisfaction with the way police handled the situation. These victims began to interpret police responses to them as antagonistic, unsympathetic, and unconcerned. This is in stark contrast to those who had fewer interactions with police.*

More than a decade has passed since the findings of the Minneapolis Experiment were reported. The Minneapolis Police Department was the testing site for an investigation of the deterrent effect of three different law enforcement responses to domestic violence situations. Of the three responses—arrest of perpetrator, separation of the parties for a cooling off period, and counseling/referral to social services—the arrest option was associated with the lowest rate of recidivism after a 6-month follow-up. Widely disseminated by researchers and policy makers and given maximum exposure by the media, this study was a major catalyst for changes in how the justice system responds to the problem of intimate violence. Quickly following the release of this report, police departments nationwide began to institute reforms, chief among them was the adoption of proarrest policies with regard to perpetrators of domestic violence. In some states, legislatures passed mandatory arrest statutes, sparking a contentious policy debate that continues to divide groups concerned with the formulation of domestic violence policies.

Various interest groups, including victims' rights advocates, feminists, academics, and criminal justice officials, have contributed to the ongoing dialogue about mandatory arrest laws for domestic assault. Mandatory arrest continues to receive strong endorsement from legislators and criminal justice spokespersons, although confidence in the strongly deterrent consequences of proarrest laws was dealt a severe blow when replication studies failed to confirm the Minneapolis results. Supporters argue that not only will such reforms lower victim risk, but in addition they will result in improved police response and an increase in victims' confidence in the criminal justice system. Underrepresented in this policy debate have been the perspectives and experiences of the victims themselves.

Arguably, it is the victims who have the most to gain (or lose) from the current trend toward a more aggressive law enforcement treatment of family violence, but we know little about victims' experiences with the new laws and their interactions with law enforcement officers. Their voices are needed to inform and guide efforts to evaluate the changes in law enforcement practices.

Review of the Literature

Legislative reforms and changes in law enforcement practices reflect an increased societal intolerance of violent crimes committed against family members. Victims of violent acts by intimate partners have been the objects of much concern, but the subjects of only limited research that explores their perceptions and experiences with police interventions. This paucity stands in contrast with the relatively large number of published studies of police attitudes and responses to domestic violence.

Existing research on victims' points of view can be categorized into two periods, roughly corresponding to the time before and the time after the wide-spread enactment of laws that authorized or mandated warrantless, probable cause arrests for misdemeanor assault. In the early 1980s, two studies addressed issues relevant to victims' perceptions of police officers' victim-related attitudes.

In a self-administered questionnaire, Pagelow (1981) asked a sample of 143 domestic violence victims to respond to the item, "What was the attitude and the behavior of the police toward you?" Of the participants, 53 reported favorable attitudes, 78 reported unfavorable attitudes, and 12 reported neutral attitudes. Bowker's (1982) survey of victims found that they had a number of concerns, including the demeanor the police displayed. Reluctance to arrest, failure to listen or provide encouragement, reassurance, or material aid were mentioned as examples of police insensitivity to the needs of victims. More recent research in Canada (Radford, 1987) and Holland (Zoomer, 1989) reported similar patterns of police insensitivities.

Victim-centered research during the second period remains sparse. Kennedy and Homant (1984) and Brown (1984) recorded favorable evaluations of police conduct in their surveys of victims. In Kennedy and Homant's sample of residents of shelters for battered women, 63% characterized the police as very or a little helpful. Brown also found a favorable evaluation of the police in his survey of victims; 71% thought that the police were concerned and helpful, whereas only 21% thought the police were rude, angry, or blaming.

Buzawa, Austin, Bannon, and Jackson (1992) and Buzawa and Austin (1993) concluded that victims' approval ratings of the police increased when victim preferences with regard to arrest were followed and when victims perceived that they were not trivialized or belittled by the police. Muraoka's (1996) survey of 61 residents of a shelter in Omaha had the respondents rate their experiences with the police. Respondents rated recent experiences as slightly more satisfactory than past experiences, and a majority cited interpersonal reasons for their approval. Prominent among the reasons they gave were that police treated them with respect, police listened and understood, and police did not blame victim.

It probably is not surprising that much of the current research is system oriented in that it involves issues of concern to law enforcement and the criminal justice system generally. Deterrence and recidivism are priority matters for those formulating system responses to domestic violence; however, as the policy debate about appropriate institutional responses moves forward, it is critical to understand the dynamic between police and victim. It is essential to explore the perspectives and experiences of victims in detail and in depth, including those who have encountered intervention by officers acting under the requirements of a mandatory arrest law. As of yet, such a study has not been done.

Method

In January 1996, the state of New York began implementation of the mandatory arrest provision of the Family Protection and Domestic Violence Intervention Act (*Criminal Procedure Law of the State of New York*, 1996/7). This legislation requires police to make arrests when a family offense misdemeanor has been committed against a member of the same family or household. To study victims' experiences and perspectives, we conducted interviews with 25 victims whose assailants had been arrested under the provisions of the new law.

The participants were referred to the researchers by the director of a victim witness assistance program located in a semi-rural county in western New York state. Taped interviews that averaged 1½ to 2 hours provided the data for our study.

Of the interviewees, 24 were female and 1 was male. The youngest was aged 21 and the oldest was aged 51, with a median age of 33 years. All but 1 were Caucasian (1 participant was Native American). The ethnic and racial homogeneity of the sample was reflective of the small town and village populations in the rural county in which they lived. A majority ($n = 13$) were divorced from their assailants at the time of the study, 3 had divorces pending, 7 were single, and only 2 remained married. They had an average of two children. Eleven participants completed high school, 12 had some college, 1 had a bachelor's degree, and 1 had some graduate-level courses. Most of the interviewees were employed ($n = 19$) and 2 were students. Incomes ranged from less than $10,000 ($n = 5$) to $42,000 ($n = 1$). Most of the interviewees ($n = 21$) reported annual incomes less than $20,000.

Findings and Discussion

We were especially interested in two aspects of the participants' experiences: their perceptions of police demeanor toward them and their assessment of the officers' handling of the arrest event. This article is a report on our findings with regard to the first issue. By *demeanor* we are referring to the participants' perceptions of the attitudes of the police as expressed in their behavior toward the victims and assailants. Thus, from the point of view of the victims, the manner in which the officers conducted themselves was reflective of the officers' beliefs and assumptions about the victim, the perpetrator, the nature of their relationship, and the type of relationship the officer should establish with the participants. As perceived by the victim, an officer's actions (or inactions) could convey a wide spectrum of attitudes—concern, sympathy, seriousness, boredom, frustration, anger, contempt, indifference, and so forth. A hostile officer who makes it clear by his demeanor that domestic disputes are not his idea of real police work confirms a victim's feelings of worthlessness and fears that nothing will be done to change her situation. That she deserves a nonviolent life and will be safe can be affirmed by the presence of an officer whose manner expresses concern and seriousness of purpose.

Participants with a Single Police Encounter

Nearly three quarters ($n = 18$) of the participants had had multiple encounters with the police prior to the arrest event. Of the 7 whose single experience with law enforcement culminated in their assailant's arrest, 3 described the officers' demeanors in positive terms. Their comments depicted the officers as "great," "genuinely concerned," "very attentive," and "very caring." For these victims, the actions of officers were not simply objective events but reflected officers' assessments of the moral worth of the victims. Verbal reassurances that the victim had done the right thing by notifying the police, listening to the victim's account without showing impatience or trying to rush it, offering to transport her to the hospital and other forms of assistance had conveyed the message that the victim's situation was being taken seriously and merited police intervention.

One participant was surprised at the police response, stating that she had not thought that they would pay that much attention or care that much about what happened to her. Another individual, who had gone to the police department after being assaulted by her ex-husband, described her interaction with a lieutenant in glowing terms. As important to her as explaining her rights and showing her how to apply for an order of protection was his willingness to spend a considerable amount of time with her, allowing her to "work up" to telling the humiliating details of the assault. Furthermore, the officer gave her his office phone number, advising her to call him directly if she had further questions. The most unexceptional acts—making the person feel comfortable, asking about her children, offering her coffee or a tissue—took on a weightier meaning in that, for the victims, these acts signified that they deserved to be treated well.

Of the victims who described a negative encounter with the police, 1 reported that she "got the third degree" from state troopers who gave every indication of discrediting her account. From their first remark, "so what did you do?" these officers made it clear that they were neither interested nor concerned about the victim and her children. When the victim asked to be allowed to leave (her hand was bleeding), the trooper insisted that she wait with her children in a truck and then left, returning a half hour later to grill her about the situation. The victim was especially upset that they did not offer her the use of their first-aid kit to treat her injured hand. The troopers continued to express doubt as to her credibility by suggesting that she "must have done something," although eventually they did arrest her assailant. Another dissenter expressed strong dissatisfaction with the deputies who did not "give a crap" about which one they arrested and whose "attitude" made things worse for her and her children.

Participants with Multiple Encounters with Police

For the majority of participants with previous and multiple encounters with law enforcement, nearly all ($n = 16$) described negative and psychologically bruising experiences with the police that had occurred prior to the arrest event. We identified four common types of police demeanor that had been corrosive in their effects on victim confidence and satisfaction with law enforcement.

Minimizing the Situation

A common experience of the participants was to be confronted with officers whose demeanor conveyed the message that they doubted the seriousness of the victim's situation. The ways in which officers appeared to the victims to downplay the gravity of what had occurred were legion. In some cases, the discounting of the victim's appeal for help was pointed and explicit. When one victim showed the officer her finger broken by her boyfriend, his reply was "that's no big thing." Another officer, presumably tired of dealing with the same violent husband, told his victim, "Hey, husbands kill wives all the time." A majority of the participants in this study had encountered law enforcement officials who "just brushed it off" or "treated it like a joke." In the words of these women, officers "acted like it was just a domestic, no big deal, just a part of life." Not atypical were the remarks made to one victim by a responding trooper that "Well, what do you want me to do about it? He'll just be back tomorrow."

Victims felt particularly humiliated when their violent relationships were a source of humor to officers. During the interviews, in their words and body language, the participants expressed bitterness toward officers who laughed and "giggled" at their predicament. Usually, such moments of levity occurred when the officer took the perpetrator aside to speak privately.

Victims drew their own conclusions when the events prompting them to notify the police were downplayed and treated as not serious. They drew conclusions about the unreliability of law enforcement and by extension, the justice system. They also drew conclusions about the meaning of intimate violence to the police: It is not important and you are not important.

Disbelieving the Victim

Also undermining victim–police interactions were the participants' beliefs that officers did not believe their version of events. Disbelief was expressed in several ways:

verbal challenges to the victim's explanations, accusations that both parties were culpable, statements that the victim had provoked (and thus, was responsible) for the altercation, and so forth. Victims were less likely to be believed if they had been drinking and if they were not married to their abusers. Some victims were not believed when they asserted that they had restraining orders. In one case, the officer ignored the victim's document, insisting that it was irrelevant unless the police department also had a copy. Several hours later the department found its copy.

Discrediting the victim's accounts was also accomplished by threatening to arrest both parties and take the children into custody. The latter threat sent a chilling message to victims that their own physical safety might be gained at too high a price. Most of the participants doubted that the police were genuinely ignorant of what had happened; rather, they suspected that the officers were reluctant to credit their stories for other reasons. Such reasons included frustration with having to make repeated calls, disgust with emotional victims, sympathy with the male ("The Brotherhood," as one participant put it) as a consequence of having been manipulated by the perpetrator.

We Don't Care

Destructive to victim–police interactions was a police manner that conveyed attitudes of unconcern and indifference. Even when they were believed, victims' trust in officers was undermined when they perceived the police as being unmoved by their situation. Participants felt belittled by a police style that focused solely on getting the facts. Participants were critical of officers who did not show concern for them or compassion or sympathy. Although they appreciated efficiency (especially with regard to the time it took for police to arrive) and professionalism, they were alienated when confronted with police reserve and flat affect.

One participant, contrasting the demeanor of the two officers who arrived together, described one as "nonchalant, cold . . . he just didn't care," whereas the other "listened to me . . . was very, very sympathetic . . . made me feel good about myself . . . never made me feel small." All of the individuals we interviewed judged the police not only on their behavioral responsiveness (i.e., quick arrival, taking charge, ensuring the victim's safety) but also their emotional responsiveness (i.e., concern and compassion for the victim).

Macho Cop

According to the participants, they often encountered arrogant police officers whose rude and even contemptuous treatment of them was especially demoralizing. With considerable passion, they offered example after example of insolent police conduct toward them. Many of these victims were convinced that the police viewed them and their problems as undeserving of police time or effort. Such convictions had been reinforced over time and after repeated abrasive experiences with law enforcement officials.

When one victim, in tears, asked the responding sheriff's deputy, "What can I do?" his retort, "I have no idea and I wasn't the one who married him," conveyed a clear message of scornful dismissal. Another participant was stunned when an officer suggested that she must be "awfully good in bed" for her ex-husband to continue his stalking and harassment of her. One woman who, after waiting more than an hour for the police to arrive asked what had taken so long, described the officers' response: "He was cocky, really kind of macho acting and said, 'Oh, you're going to complain about the service. I'll just turn around and leave.' I didn't dare say more because he got nasty."

Some of the participants wondered if the officers they had dealt with might be abusers themselves. An example of this was the woman who, before going to the emergency room, overheard her abusive boyfriend joking around with the state trooper, who said, "Oh boy, you must have really pissed her off. She'll be back, they never leave for long. You should keep your woman in line." The participants made it clear to the interviewer that experiences such as these engendered feelings of futility and shame and reinforced their suspicions that the police viewed them with contempt.

Police Demeanor and the Arrest Event

Thus far, we have considered the victims' perceptions of police demeanor during previous situations that did not result in an arrest. Now we shall present findings that pertain to those victim–police encounters that culminated in their partner being arrested.

Police demeanor toward the assailants was also of interest to us, as presumably, it implicitly carries meaning with regard to their attitudes toward the victims. However, we were unable to obtain these data for most of the cases as only 4 of the participants were present at the assailants' arrests. Three described the police as allowing the assailants to verbally abuse them (the victims) before making the arrest. The lone male in our sample was convinced that the officers' reluctance to arrest his abusive spouse was due to their incredulity, indeed discomfort, when dealing with a male victim of abuse.

For the 21 participants not present at the actual arrest, we obtained data on their assessments of police demeanor toward them based on the interactions that led directly to the arrests. Of the participants, 15 (71%) depicted police attitudes and behaviors toward them in positive terms, free of demeaning or negative qualities. As these participants explained, the officers listened to them, believed them, showed concern, were sympathetic and helpful, explained their rights and available services, and treated them with respect.

Representative of this group was the woman who recounted with gratitude how the deputy "calmed me down and listened to my problems. He treated me really good, actually. The last thing he said, 'You don't have to be treated like this. Not even for him,' and he pointed at my kid, and I just remembered that." Another participant felt reassured by the thorough manner with which the officer addressed her complaint, attributing this to genuine concern on his part. "Detective [name] encouraged me to think about my options—arrest, an order of protection. He is excellent. I'm going to write a letter of recommendation for him because he is very, very, very good. He really cares."

Participants who described police demeanor in positive terms emphasized the following: listening to the victim (this is not merely getting the facts of the crime, but permitting the victim to talk about related problems in the relationship), believing the victim, taking the victim's situation seriously, informing the victim of options and services (explaining them and answering questions), reassuring the victim that he or she (and their children) will be protected, and showing understanding and concern for the victim.

This last aspect of police demeanor—empathy with the victim—was of paramount significance. Whatever else they did or failed to do, said or did not say, the officers' willingness to show a human face overlay other considerations. From the victims' viewpoint, the nature of their relationship with the police was to a larger degree contingent on whether the officers seemed to understand and were emotionally moved by their plight. Victim attribution of meaning to all components of the police presence (asserting authority, establishing order, implementing legal procedures, etc.) was filtered through this primary aspect of police demeanor.

Three of the participants' evaluations of police demeanor were conflicted. For 2 of these individuals, their experiences with several officers during events resulting in the arrest produced divergent impressions of police attitudes. An example of this is the woman who sat, weeping and ignored, for 3 hours in the troopers' barracks, during which she overheard officers in an adjacent room laughing and talking about her. Then, "I just went to pieces. My God, I've been here three hours. Nobody has talked to me. What is wrong with these people?" Eventually, a "very, very nice, sympathetic sergeant" wrote up the report.

> I was just so thankful for him. He made me feel safe. He constantly asked did I need some water. He handed me tissues. Those other officers did absolutely nothing for me, nothing. But he was incredible. He listened to my problems. He really made me feel good.

A third ($n = 7$) of the participants were very critical of the police officers' attitudes and conduct toward them. Chief among the sources of dissatisfaction were victims' beliefs that the officers had been dismissive of the gravity of their situation and their failure to show concern for victims. A repeating theme in this study, victim trust is undermined in interactions with officers who, by their manner, seem indifferent to the victim's suffering and dismissive of the seriousness of victim's concerns. The potential for victim alienation is magnified as officers, adhering to their own procedures, are perceived by victims as hiding behind protocol and dealing with victims only reluctantly and without any real interest in them.

The participants drew conclusions about the attitudes of the police based on virtually any and every aspect of the officers' behaviors. A brusque, nononsense style was likely to be experienced by victims as rudeness and arrogance. Officers who did not immediately stop the abusers' verbal attacks were assumed to be hostile to the victims. Similar to other crime victims, these individuals wanted the police to instantly accept their version of events, bitterly resenting any indication that the police doubted their story. Shared by many of the respondents, one type of explanation of police motives and attitudes alleges pervasive police skepticism and victim-blaming in domestic violence situations. As one participant stated,

> The police make you look like you're probably wanting the relationship and you're not telling all the truth. It's like, she's half nuts or something. They think, oh no, she's on an emotional run. And they discredit you. They think women are too emotional. They think he didn't mean to, we'll give him another chance.

In addition to lack of compassion, another recurring motif was the complaint that the police were unwilling to spend enough time listening to participants, but instead limited the interaction to a narrow focus on legal aspects of the participants' acts. To the participants, not listening to their problems clearly reflects an overall disinterest in their condition.

> They don't want to, really. They want facts and I understand. But, if you talk to someone long enough, you'll see the real person. You'll see the pain and hurt and [how] they're caught and don't know how to get out.

For victims, listening and talking constitutes a necessary first step to helping them; when the police are unwilling or unable to do this, it is easy for victims to attribute hostile attitudes to the police.

In five of the cases, trust in the police reached a nadir when they made specific threats to the victim—3 victims were told they might be arrested, and 2 victims were told that their children could be taken from them. Whether intended by the police as a strategy to achieve a truce between fractious spouses or to reprove victims whose seemingly intractable problems engender frustration, even disgust, the victims imbued these threats with two meanings. First, police actually know who has broken the law, but because of their denigration of victims of domestic crimes want to dispense with them as quickly as possible. As one participant recounted her reaction to this threat, "It's got to be like common sense. The sheriff knew that he [ex-husband] was full of poo poo. I think he knew exactly what had happened. They said, 'well, that's what he says and we don't know what happened.'" The second meaning for victims is that these threats are real—if they are not careful, the police will arrest them and their children will be taken from them.

The legacy of distrust was especially marked for the 5 participants who had generalized their assessments of specific individuals to all law enforcement. These women viewed the police as a kind of male club, loyal to each other, sympathetic to male abusers, and either indifferent or actively hostile to women. Two alleged that their abusers had personal connections with the police that enabled them to act with impunity. In their words,

> There's a lot of men police officers like a club and everybody knows it. There's a brotherhood between policemen. I represented an ex-wife trying to screw over her husband. I represented what can or maybe has happened to them. If I was a man, I'd'a been arrested and gone for life. But, "when you're dead, give us a call." They told me in different ways than words that he is going to do what he is going to do and, "oh yeah, we'll be investigating it."
>
> The police are chauvinist. They aren't fair to women still. They aren't fair. I never got concern, I don't feel, as a woman. And that officer I dealt with previously, I believe he's an abuser himself. I tried to be calm. They don't like it when you're nerved up and talking a lot. And the police cover up for each other. And I'm tired of it. The state police lost everything I

filled out. They said, "We're dismissing it." So, I thought the law isn't on my side. If the law isn't on your side, what are you going to do?

Conclusion

This study focused on aspects of police demeanor that are of great concern to victims of intimate violence. We described the following four categories of police demeanor of which most victims were critical: (a) minimizing the situation, (b) disbelieving the victim, (c) we don't care, and (d) macho cop. From the victims' perspectives, listening and believing are the first steps that police must take to begin the process of helping them, but this is not enough to guarantee police credibility in the eyes of victims: Victims want the police to show empathy for them and their situation. Victims expect the police to act effectively on their behalf, but equally important they want the police to treat them as worthy of police concern and intervention.

A provocative finding was that, when compared with earlier (nonarrest) encounters with law enforcement, the tendency was for participants to have more positive assessments of police demeanor during the arrest event. Optimistically, it may be that police attitudes are changing as a consequence of new training and reforms in police policy. On the other hand, it is possible that by this point victims are so relieved at the arrest of their tormentors that they tend to remember only the positive aspects of their encounters with the police. It could even be that one consequence of involvement with a victim witness program is more positive victim perceptions of criminal justice officials, including the police. However, existing research does not support this explanation.

Whatever the reasons for this change, it is clear that the experiences and preferences of victims must in some measure be represented in the criminal justice system's reform agenda. Feminists, academic, and advocacy groups have purported to speak for the victims of intimate violence. Legislators and police administrators have moved rapidly to criminalize acts that historically were of little interest to the state. The new harshness has been driven by system needs, in particular, concern over the public's lack of confidence in its justice institutions. The danger is that the most important group of all may be sidelined during the national debate about the future of our society's response to domestic violence. Lacking victim input, the formulation of policies may continue to be shaped by ideology and pragmatic politics. Yet, if these policies are to be credible and effective, they must be informed by the voices of victims.

Critical Thinking

These findings suggest that police change the way they interact with repeat victims and imply that police think that those who stay with abusers do not deserve continued respect and concern. If this is the case, how will such attitudes affect the reporting of domestic violence? At what point do victims think the lack of concern, and possible ridicule, from police is not worth calling them? If women do stop calling police for help in these situations are they truly getting equal protection under the law?

References

Bowker, L. H. (1982). Police services to battered women: Bad or not so bad? *Criminal Justice and Behavior, 9*, 475–496.

Brown, S.E. (1984). Police responses to wife beating: Neglect of a crime of violence. *Journal of Criminal Justice, 12*(3), 277–288.

Buzawa, E. S., & Austin, T. (1993). Determining police response to domestic violence victims. *American Behavioral Scientist, 36,* 610–623.

Buzawa, E. S., Austin, T. L., Bannon, J., & Jackson, J. (1992). Rule of victim preference in determining police response to victims of domestic violence. In E. S. Buzawa & C. G. Buzawa (Eds.), *Domestic violence: The changing criminal justice response* (pp. 256–269). Westwood, CT: Auburn House.

Criminal procedure law of the State of New York. (1996/7). Section 140.10/4. Flushing, New York: Looseleaf Law Publication.

Kennedy, D. B., & Homant, R. J. (1984). Battered women's evaluation of police response. *Victimology: An International Journal, 9,* 174–179.

Muraoka, S. M. (1996). *Use of police services by victims of domestic violence.* Unpublished doctoral dissertation, University of Nebraska.

Pagelow, M. D. (1981). *Woman-battering: Victims and their experiences.* Beverly Hills, CA: Sage.

Radford, J. (1987). Policing male violence—policing women. In J. Hammer & M. Maynard (Eds.), *Women, violence and social control* (pp. 30–45). London: MacMillan.

Zoomer, O. J. (1989). Policing women battering in the Netherlands. In J. Hammer, J. Radford, & B. Stanko (Eds.), *Women, policing and male violence* (pp. 125–154). London: Routledge.

10

Between Normality and Deviance: The Breakdown of Batterers' Identity Following Police Intervention

Eli Buchbinder and Zvi Eisikovits

Abstract: *Eli Buchbinder and Zvi Eisikovits examine how those accused of domestic violence view their interactions with responding police. They show that the number of interactions with police has a strong impact on how they view police and how police respond to them. Initial feelings of surprise gave way to hurt and betrayal with subsequent interactions with police. Despite being arrested for domestic violence these men are able to maintain a positive sense of self, as they believe that officers took their sides in the dispute. Additionally, the accused think that the actions of police did not necessarily indicate the beliefs of responding officers. This evaluation of events places the participant in a victim position as an "oppressed gender class" victimized by power-hungry women who have learned to exploit their positions in society by playing on societal beliefs and the requirements of police officers.*

The purpose of this study was to examine how men who batter their intimate partners perceive, interpret, and reconstruct their experiences with police over time, how they are affected on the personal and interpersonal levels, and how they evaluate these police interventions.

The police are widely recognized as having a pivotal role in changing or preserving social attitudes toward domestic violence (Carlson, 1984; Heise, 1998). They are the gatekeeper for the entire criminal justice system and provide important legal and personal services for victims, referring them to social, medical, and legal services (e.g., Bowker, 1983; Smith, 1989). In a review of 12 studies addressing community services for battered women, Gordon (1996) found that police were the most frequently used service by survivors of intimate violence.

With the transformation of intimate violence from a personal to a social problem, there has been increased public and professional scrutiny of police activities and pressure toward increased police effectiveness in working with battered women and perpetrators of violence (Buzawa & Buzawa, 1996). This is particularly so in light of previous allegations maintaining that police perpetuate patriarchal attitudes toward women (Dobash & Dobash, 1992) and are lenient with the perpetrators (Avakame & Fyfe, 2001; Buzawa & Buzawa, 1993). Consequently, efforts have been made to induce systemic change in police organizations (Edleson & Tolman, 1992; Gelles, 1993). During the first wave of changes, two important interrelated areas were identified as being in need of change: One relates to defining intimate violence as a crime, and the other refers to the use of mandatory arrest of perpetrators as an expression of the former (e.g., Stark, 1993). It was assumed that such changes would be enough to deter batterers (Jaffe, Hastings, Reitzel, & Austin, 1993).

At the present time, it appears that police handle most complaints on intimate violence as misdemeanors, making mandatory arrest policies difficult to implement (Hutchison, Hirschel, & Pesackis, 1994). Passing new laws is no guarantee of their implementation through changes in the modus operandi of law enforcement organizations (Jacobson & Gottman, 1998) Although some initial research suggested that mandatory arrest has a deterrent effect on perpetrators (e.g., the initial Minneapolis experiment) (Garner & Maxwell, 2000; Sherman & Berk, 1984), researchers and advocates became gradually disenchanted with this procedure and stopped viewing it as a universal panacea. It appears that the effectiveness of arrest is mediated by such variables as social class, race, employment status, and recidivism (e.g., Schmidt & Sherman, 1993; Tolman & Weisz, 1995). Research and experience in the field increasingly show that when arrest is performed, it seldom lowers violence and often has adverse effects on the victim. More recent evidence points to the fact that the criminalization of intimate violence increases the allegations of mutual violence and dual arrests (e.g., Hamberger & Potente, 1994; Martin, 1997) and as such, may lead to further victimization of the victims, usually the women.

Battered women's satisfaction with police intervention was often identified as a measure of improved police work in domestic violence cases. Despite the increased scope and intensity of police services for battered women, studies have repeatedly shown that satisfaction with these is lower as compared with other community services (Bowker, 1983; Gordon, 1996; Saunders & Size, 1986). For instance, Hamilton and Coates (1993) found that in a community sample of 270 women who had contact with 124 helping agencies, police had the lowest scores of satisfaction in comparison with social and medical services. Similarly, Shoham (2000) found that in Israel, women called police when feeling fear and humiliation, expecting in vain support and protection from their batterers. Police were perceived as insensitive, did not understand the victim's situation, and were suspicious of women's motives.

In sharp contrast to the available knowledge about battered women's perceptions of police interventions, the perspective of the batterer is virtually nonexistent in the literature (Hearn, 1998). This is particularly significant in light of some findings hinting to the fact that men tend to feel misunderstood and alienated in their relationship with the various helping systems for domestic violence (Eisikovits & Buchbinder, 2000). Such findings seem to substantiate the notion that most battering men feel disempowered, both within and outside their dyadic relationship, describing their use of force with their partners as a desperate and futile attempt to regain power. Batterers often perceive themselves as victims, whether by lacking control over their lives, being manipulated by their partners, or being trapped psychologically and socially, insisting that violence is their last resource (Eisikovits & Buchbinder, 1997; Holtzworth-Munroe & Hutchison, 1993; Reitz, 1999). Such male perceptions have been mostly categorized as accounts, attributions, excuses, justifications, rationalizations, and neutralizing techniques (e.g., Bograd, 1988; Dutton, 1986; Eisikovits, Goldblatt, & Winstok, 1999; Holtzworth-Munroe & Hutchison, 1993; Ptacek, 1988; Stamp & Sabourin, 1995).

However, effective clinical and institutional interventions with batterers need to take into account their perspectives, their perceptions, their range of choices, and limitations on choice as experienced by them. Although we are aware of the fact that men often restructure their stories of violence in a manner that relieves them from responsibility, we still believe that capturing the subjective nature of their experiences with police may have important value in finding better ways to handle them.

Method

This study is based on in-depth interviews conducted with violent men concerning their experiences with police intervention. Data were collected as part of a nationwide study performed in Israel evaluating various aspects of police intervention in domestic violence during 1996 and 1997. The study had quantitative and qualitative components. The quantitative component included (a) evaluating a representative random sample of 1,000 domestic violence police files regarding various police interventions and (b) admimstering a questionnaire assessing police attitudes among a stratified representative sample of 400 police officers at various ranks and levels of seniority.

The qualitative component included (a) 35 in-depth interviews with key respondents within the police force and the social welfare system working with police and (b) 60 interviews with a sample of clients, namely, women and men who were involved with police as victims and perpetrators of abuse. The present study is based on the interviews with the male clients. Participants were identified from a sample of police stations in a large metropolitan area in northern Israel. Police asked for informed consent from perpetrators and survivors of intimate violence who were on their records during a time period of 3 months. After written consent was granted, trained interviewers contacted the participants at their place of residence.

The present study was based on a purposive sample of 20 men between the ages of 31 and 50 who were cohabiting with their partners for periods ranging from 3 to 27 years and who had from two to four children. They were mostly middle class and low-middle class. Only 3 had criminal records for offenses other than intimate violence. All of the men were working at the time of the study; none were known to have criminal careers, mental illness, or mental retardation. Their involvement with police ranged from one complaint to those who did not remember how many contacts they had had with the police regarding intimate violence.

The interview guide covered several content categories, including description of the violent event for which police intervention was sought, expectations from police intervention, actual police intervention, perception and evaluation of police activities, previous intervention history, the impact of police intervention on the dyadic relationship, overall satisfaction with police intervention, and suggestions for change. The interviews lasted about 2 hours, were tape-recorded, and transcribed literally.

Findings

The analysis of interviews with batterers concerning their experience with police yielded a continuum of self-management, ranging from attempts to validate their normative identity in the first encounter, through struggling against the threat of being transformed into criminals in the second encounter, and finally adopting a relatively stable victim identity in the third encounter. In subsequent encounters, the men tended to become reified in their beliefs, perceptions, emotions, and behaviors, which combined victimhood and increased hostility. This management and reorganization of self, vis-à-vis the police, has far-reaching effects on men's self-perceptions and perceptions of their partner, the dyadic unit, and the police.

The First Encounter with Police

The "beginners" described themselves as invariably surprised by their partner's contact with the police. One man describes the argument that led to the initial police intervention as follows:

> I said I need the car and if I don't get it to go out, she shouldn't either. This was the trigger. Ruth called the police and said that I threatened her and that I wouldn't let her leave the house. . . . There was no trace of physical violence nor any specific verbal violence, except the argument about the car which we have all the time. Oh! I almost forgot. I was accused that I threatened her with a gun. And then I said, "My God, that's impossible. I don't even have the gun for 6 months now." At some point, Ruth hid the gun from me. And this was the only thing I could say.

The man describes the context of his wife's call to the police as a specific and isolated argument between equals about the family car. By so doing, he frames the phenomenological context of the act of calling the police in a manner that makes it sound to the listener/interviewer as identical to his own interpretation: not understandable, unnecessary, and somewhat absurd. The man's narrative guides us to interpret his wife's act as an irrational overreaction arising from a distortion of his intentions. His version is presented as factual and confirmed by logic, compared to his partner's as emotional and aimed to illustrate its own absurdity. The validity and inner logic of his partner's version is denied, and there is little sensitivity to her contextual understanding. He attempts to construct for the audience the additional related "facts" as marginal. To achieve this effect, he fragments the narrative and the emerging reality. We as researchers, and as such part of his audience, are led through the man's attempts to decontextualize the event and thus find ourselves reconstructing his reconstruction and trying to correct his selective inattention to the details of the occurrences: for instance, the fact that his partner hid the gun and the causes of this act are mentioned only in passing. We can assume from the subtext that such actions were not performed in a vacuum but in the context of the woman's fear for her life. Calling the police is presented as unexpected and thus leading to disorientation and discontinuity. The proper police action, as expected by the man, would be to clear up the inaccuracies, reiterate the factual nature of his version, and find no basis to her allegations of violence. Such a course of action would help reestablish continuity and support a smooth return to the normal course of life.

The element of surprise and manipulation of the quality and intent of their actions are important factors in the meaning assigned by men to the violence and subsequent police intervention.

It all started by an argument we had. At some point during the argument. I grabbed her throat, not to choke her or anything, just to shake her up. She went to the room and locked herself in. I heard she was calling the police and said, "My husband is threatening me." I can't remember if she said that I threatened to murder her or not, but she said she wanted them to come right away and then there was silence.

Question: What did you think at the time?

Answer: Nothing. I said they should come to me and I was clear that they know there are two sides to the story. I was waiting for them downstairs, I was watering the lawn. . . . I couldn't see anything deadly in what I did, since I wasn't going to harm her. . . . I understood they would come, ask some questions: Who are you? What happened? How did it happen? And that's all.

This man describes the sequence of events leading to violence in "jumps" leaping from an argument to the point of grabbing the partner's throat. However, the intent is clarified immediately: the choking was directed to "shake her up" rather than to actually harm her. The man expects the police to validate his version by using a "rational" model of thinking and acting, which may include asking routine questions, investigating, probing, and finally concluding that the call was not what it seemed when performed by an emotionally driven wife. To emphasize the triviality of the event in his own eyes, the man continues to water the garden while waiting for the police. This also helps him to distance himself from the event, normalize the situation, and calm down by assuming that it will soon be over. His expectation is for the police to balance the two versions, leading them to the final conclusion that the power struggle was momentary, the violence accidental and mutually induced.

Following their first encounter with police, men not only reframe their violent acts as routine and marginal conflicts but also attempt to trivialize the police encounter and reconstruct it as gamelike. The following quote is a case in point:

I can't remember too many details. I think someone made a stupid mistake calling the police, and the police made the stupid mistake of keeping up the game. . . . All in all, I expected that this whole thing would go nowhere.

Question: Did you talk to your wife and ask her why she called the police?

Answer: I did, but there was no answer. And to tell you the truth, I didn't really look into this any further. We made up in a funny way. I really never understood this scene with the police and I left it alone.

In the first encounter with police, violent men attempt to redefine themselves as rational, reasoned, balanced, circumspect, objective, and especially nondangerous. The police's involvement is part of a chain of mistakes, which is perpetuated in the form of a "game" with a preset and well-known ritual, leading nowhere. Once the man perceives police intervention as a game, he locates himself outside and above it all, defines it as alien to his life and presents it in degrading terms, as a "stupid mistake" perpetuated by all those involved. He need not experience the process but only its outcome: "something that needs to get done, so let's get it over with." The entire encounter comes to be viewed as technical, routine, ceremonial, and meaningless.

There was a police investigator who wanted to hear my version and my wife's. I explained my side, I explained what I know that took place at the time of this argument. . . . He [the police officer] never told me anything bad regarding what I said, and actually we had it wrapped up in general terms. I can't remember him telling me something specific. Just sign here, sign there. . . . I didn't see in the signing anything specific. What they made me sign is that I wouldn't

threaten her. Since I never threaten anyway, I had no problems with signing. I can't remember
all the details. It looked pretty meaningless to me.

This quote is significant both in terms of its content and its underlying tone and
atmosphere. On the content level, the encounter is perceived as balanced and noncon-
frontational. The message conveyed by the batterer and supported by the police investigator in his perception is that they have reached a joint perspective on the events
and that there is no need for any in-depth investigation but only some formal agreement concerning the future that needs to be sanctioned by his signature. The atmosphere described by the interviewee is emotionally flat, with no particular personal
investment on either side. With nothing specific to remember, the event is registered
in the perpetrator's mind in the most general terms. This predictable sequence of
events, associated with the perfunctory and technical nature of the police investigation, reinforces the man's belief that the entire scene is unreal. No one means serious
business, the police perform a series of formal actions in keeping with their role, and
the man can preserve a normative self-image.

Men evaluate police personnel in light of their attitude toward the violent incident.
A "really OK policeman who wasn't just doing the dry bureaucratic stuff" is credited
by a batterer with the following message:

Listen, I don't think it pays off to get to these things . . . think twice. It's better to get up and
leave rather than get entangled. . . . You saw you are getting pissed, get up and leave. Just go.
Return in two hours. Every single touch, even a minor one or even if you don't touch her, just
verbal violence can get you in trouble. And to write you up and fill in all these forms and have
a record, it doesn't fit you. So go home, get some clothes, and leave for a couple of days.

In the man's perception, the "good policeman" is focused on keeping the batterer
out of trouble rather than on confronting him about the allegations of violence. The
interaction with police is focused on cautioning him about the potential consequences
of violence through the use of extreme and absurd conditions ("a single touch . . . or
word"). This creates a subtext of danger for the man: He is at risk, not his partner. He
comes to understand police procedures according to which he is an assumed suspect.
As such, anything he does can be interpreted as violence. This perceived status solidi-
fies his emerging sense of injustice, and his use of dramatic language emphasizes his
claim that the violence and the actual institutional response to it are grossly exaggerated. By so doing, he responds to his status as a suspect rather than to the allegations
concerning his behavior.

From the batterer's perspective, the first encounter with police bounds the parties
in a difficult situation: The police need to act under strict orders and to create trouble
for the man, even when they do not believe that such actions are warranted in cases in
which their client is not a "real criminal." The way in which they bridge the gap
between the organizational constraints and their own beliefs is to adopt the role of
"consultant." The man, in turn, is reinforced by what he interprets as a mild reaction
to his redefinition of the encounter, which is focused on counseling the client about
staying out of trouble rather than on investigating the violent act. He may conclude
that he successfully reframed the reality of his intimate relationship with the tacit
collaboration of the police, through which his normative identity remains intact. He

may further conclude that the police are neither capable of, nor interested in, unveiling the truth but are more concerned with legitimizing the man's normative self-image.

> The first time they came here they wanted to arrest me. The policeman persuaded her [his wife] to cancel the complaint. 'Cause if I would have had a police record, I would have lost my job. He [the policeman] understood and identified with me, especially when he saw that I am not some sort of criminal and have no criminal record, that I look like a nice guy and that I have a job. . . . So he suggested, "Why don't you two make up and let's get this thing over with."

The quote reflects the man's belief that he joins the police in an effort to reinforce his normative identity by avoiding a complaint for domestic violence. Once such a joint alliance is established in his mind, the man becomes "one of us" rather than "one of them" and successfully dissociates himself from the regular police clientele. His behavior is examined in light of his normative identity rather than his violent behavior.

A parallel dynamic in the man's interpretation is that his partner develops an illusion of "empowerment" stemming from being placed in the position of decision maker. However, such an apparent change in the power relationship is illusory because if she decides to have him arrested, she will be blamed for his possible criminal record and subsequent consequences, such as possible job loss. Thus, she is left with only one option that rule out the choices constituting the source of her empowerment. This further reinforces the "unreal" nature of the entire situation and enables the man to create a split between his violent actions and their consequences in terms of outside intervention.

To sum up, battering men perceive the first encounter with police as ritualistic, following a well-rehearsed script in which police personnel go through the motions of hearing and validating both stories equally. They aim to warn and advise the men to keep out of trouble by avoiding this potentially dangerous thing: "the woman." Men evaluate the first experience with police as a positive one, concluding that the police understand them and usually validate their side of the story. They create a successful split from the situation, which they define as unreal. This may explain the fact that this encounter has only marginal negative effects on their personal identity and their intimate relationships.

The Second Encounter

The men's second encounter with the police constitutes a qualitative turning point in their perception of police attitudes and behavior. This is illustrated by the following quote:

> In this case, no one really talked to me at all. They told me simply, "You come with us to the station." I was really angry. The first time they were really nice to me, they told me to come to the station in my own car. The second time around, they did it all public, ugly, and ordered me around: "No, you won't drive your car, you'll come with us." You get in the car like someone who is arrested. It's really shameful.

The experience of batterers during the second encounter clashes with their expectations formed during the first one. In this encounter, police action replaces talking and ordering replaces negotiation. The interpersonal "touch" that governed the first encounter is over, and the relationship is not only impersonal and adversarial, but the man's role is transformed into that of a suspect. He feels publicly degraded, inferior, deprived of his power, and betrayed by police. The man clings to his previously formulated assumptions and focuses on the inappropriateness of the police's behavior, which intensifies his anger toward them. He continuously rejects the idea of being an offender and uses the metaphor of "as if" (like someone . . .) when attempting to split between his personal and public identity. The gradual realization of decline in their status is reflected in the following quote:

> The first time they listened to me and understood me. I wasn't offended and I was satisfied. The second time they were unwilling to listen, they only heard my wife. . . . They are not interested in helping me. I didn't like it and felt helpless. I felt there is a powerful system, which works against me. . . . I felt they did injustice to me. . . . I felt the police are looking for ways to get people. The minute she went to the police, they believed her. The case is sealed: She speaks the truth and I am a liar.

The man views his partner's second complaint as successfully achieving a split between the past (i.e., the first encounter) and the present, thus blocking the possibility of any effective dialogue with the police. Whereas during the first encounter the police's attitude showed willingness to listen and understand, in the second one they are hostile in their denial of his version and therefore his "truth." He perceives that they have already accused him, judged him, and established his guilt. He feels alone as he confronts the hostile forces of the "system" that are acting against him. Given that his partner has the capacity to activate this system, he believes that it is necessary to be constantly on alert.

> This policeman took me down to the station and told me, "That's how women are, don't get into trouble. They are out to get you. Just like men are looking to catch women and cheat on them, the woman is out to get you on this one. She'll prepare your case for court."

The batterer interprets police activity at this point as conveying a double message: one says now the rules have changed and he is in trouble and the other is conveyed as friendly advice about what women really want: to destroy men, including him. His belief that from now on, he should always expect the worst from his wife is reinforced, and in order to survive, he must acquire a sense of paranoia. Such construction perpetuates the batterer's belief that the police continue forging the alliance with him. Thus they feel equally helpless and dominated by forces larger than they can handle.

Between these conflicting messages, the man ends his second encounter with the police constructing a bewildering picture that the number of complaints against him is more significant than the violent event itself and that from now on, police intervention is serious business despite their perceived sympathetic attitude toward him. He believes in a parallel double message conveyed to the man's partner.

> When my wife sat with the investigating officer, he was telling her that since this is the second time he'd arrest me and put me in jail. Actually, this scared her. . . . He suggested to her to let the whole thing go and let it be . . . they tried to persuade Sarah to drop the story since it is not worth it; I may get hurt and my job may be affected. I also think he explained to her that she doesn't have a good case and all she can get out of this is to scare me.

In the batterer's interpretation, his partner receives a double message from police that is both empowering and disempowering: Empowering because the police give her the power to decide and disempowering because they spell out to her that they expect her to come forward with a complaint. They try simultaneously to deter the man by showing him what the woman can do to him and the woman by pointing out what will happen if she does it. They both frame the woman as the enemy and act as advocates in pleading with her to cancel her complaint.

The man summarizes the emerging dilemma in which everyone is involved: The police are estimating the optimal severity of their reaction, the woman is considering the price that she and her family will have to pay for complaining, and the man is attempting to outguess the police's thinking as a way to survive and predict their reaction. One man explains the process as follows:

> I know how they think. They think she wants to hurt me with these complaints, but on the other hand, they know that ultimately we'll make up and she'll come home and the result will be that she's hurt me with all these legal procedures.

One of the core issues that men face following the second encounter with police is a profound and haunting question regarding their own identity, as reflected in the police encounter: Are they criminals or not? In the first interaction with police, their normative identity remains stable and the encounter reinforces their self-perception as nonviolent men. In the second encounter, they learn that their normative identity is questionable, as described by one interviewee.

> When we walked into the station, the officer asked the other policemen whether I was violent against them. I was shocked! Where did he get the idea that I am a violent man? And he said immediately, "Book him."

The quote reflects a gap between the social identity of a criminal and the self-perceived normative identity of a nonviolent man. At this point in the process of coping with police intervention, his focus shifts from the violent event to the need to keep his self-perception intact. Although an actual arrest was not the police's preferred option, the threat of arrest during the second encounter led to a substantive change in the intensity and quality of the process. As one interviewee indicates, the sense of injustice experienced is both personal and social.

> The man's got a problem, too. He's got feelings, he is human, he's got respect, and he's in a crisis. The police are just making it worse. . . . Instead of helping him to change his violent style, they make it worse. To relate to a man like he's a drug addict or a criminal humiliates him most. . . . It would be better not to arrest the man, not to reprimand him and humiliate him, but send him right away to treatment.

In constructing the police's attitude as indifference to his problem, this man opts for the "patient" role. He feels vulnerable and is even willing to acknowledge his violence in exchange for portraying the police as brutal and ruthless. By shifting his narrative to the third person, he becomes the representative of an oppressed group, locked in a desperate situation, in need of help rather than retribution. This approach enables him to maintain his self-perception of the law-abiding citizen while attempting a release from responsibility for his present situation. He blames the police for falsely accusing him and casting him in the criminal role, and he sees this as further evidence of the circumstantial nature of his "crime."

Arrest will lead to further entrapment because the batterer is likely to return to his family defeated and more vulnerable. As one man relates, the sense of injustice becomes his sole source of energy: "The experience [of arrest] was very difficult. But it also broke my fear of police and jail. Today I am willing to do time 10 more times. I overcame this barrier. It doesn't deter me anymore." This man successfully redefined the meaning of the experience of arrest as overcoming the humiliation and attempts by the police to force on him a deviant identity. As such, this is a double victory for him: He overcomes fear and transforms himself in the process.

The negative effect of the second encounter spills over into the dyadic relationship, particularly given the damaging nature of the woman's testimony.

> She said I am endangering the children's lives and other horrible stuff about me as a father and a husband. I felt really humiliated. As a consequence, I was handed a protection order and was ordered to stay away from my place of residence. This initiates a thousand thoughts of vengeance.

The man feels demonized by his wife as the result of her cumulative negative experience over time, rather than the result of any specific event. In contrast to the previous complaints, he perceives her now as moving from specific allegations to global all-encompassing accusations. This heightens his sense of threat insofar as it attacks his core self-image. At this point, any specific defense or account would not be effective because it would be viewed as partial. Thus, to defend his self-image, the man must turn to further widening the gap between himself and his partner. The police behavior, as well as the woman's formal complaints, is interpreted by the man as betrayal and casts doubt on the endurance of the relationship. Although following the first encounter the man still feels in control, subsequent encounters change the balance of power between the partners and place the man in a position of inferiority.

> I really got hurt from this. Perhaps because I can't forgive her for what she did. At times we have misunderstandings. I would throw in words such as "shut up" . . . but today I have no trust in her, and perhaps she'll put me in jail again and do me injustice. I feel deprived.

The man perceives himself as being in danger and must therefore be constantly on guard. The complaint serves as a control mechanism over what he can say and do. He attributes to his partner the power to control his freedom, generalizing from specific daily life situations to his entire life. By focusing on his fear and loss of trust, he alludes to his growing anger. Even when police intervention forces him to reflect on his violent behavior, there is still much ambivalence concerning the entire intervention.

> It [the police intervention] had a bad effect, both the process and the way they handled me and related to me. On the other hand, I asked myself: Why did I let myself degenerate to this point? And I was thinking that even though she made a mistake, even if she was wrong, I have to control the situation and not get to the point of the police being involved . . . I don't accept it, but I put up with it. I closed this thing and I don't want to look back, a clean start. I am not angry with her, but it is an open wound. I also blame myself because I brought it on myself.

The contradictions in this experience are reflected in the metaphor of the "open wound" resulting from the second encounter. His narrative includes a reflective element that leads him to reassess his behavior and take responsibility for controlling himself. Yet he continues to argue that calling the police was his partner's mistake. Despite his attempt to develop some measure of wisdom from the events, it is the "open wound" that ultimately overshadows the relationship. The best he can do is to force himself to live with the construction of "a clean start," which is never fully realized because of the ever-present pain and the blame directed toward himself and his partner.

In sum, the men perceive the second encounter with the police as disempowering. The rules of the game have changed: They are now in an adversarial position against forces that they have no ability to control. They feel betrayed by their partner, regarded as criminals by the police, and caught in an identity crisis between their own normative self-perception and the deviant evaluation attributed to them by both their: partner and social control agents. As a result, their animosity toward both increases.

Repeated Encounters with Police

The analysis of men's subsequent encounters with police reveals a pattern of escalation in their perception of the police. They feel increasingly isolated and perceive an emerging alliance between their partners and police against them.

> The problem I've got is that my wife has backing from the police. And the backing is often used to break my will . . . to show me that she is stronger than I am. That's the issue. Not that she actually needs them for anything.

Men construct a firm belief that their partners and the police have joined forces in an antagonistic coalition against them. The alliance with him in the first encounter is replaced with a metaphoric view of the relationship with police as a power struggle.

The perception of the partner also changes throughout the encounters. Initially, she is perceived as making a mistake by calling the police, leading to anger and hurt following the second encounter, and finally to the strong conviction that she is deliberately trying to acquire power through the use of police intervention. As illustrated above, sustained interaction with the police brings the man to the conclusion that his partner has learned how to use police protection for her own purposes: to achieve control over him. This control is not viewed in behavioral terms alone but rather as a total action system aimed to overtake his basic self ("willpower") and eventually to break him. Once the situation is reduced to a metaphoric view by which he is isolated in an unnecessary hostile power struggle, the man tends to focus on the urgent need to defend himself rather than his partner's pain. Feeling alone against powers that are stronger than him widens the gap between the batterer and his surrounding world. He is under the growing threat of becoming weaker and lonelier vis-à-vis the cooperation between his partner and the police. His life seems increasingly restricted and determined by extraneous rules and forces. Because the police are perceived as less and less understanding, there is no exit from the escalating situation. Such isolation leads to a sense of injustice and legitimizes the need to fight it, but it also helps the men to save face. Their struggle now involves a broader coalition of legal/bureaucratic forces, which their partners skillfully orchestrate against them in repeated encounters with police.

> The law defends the woman. In this country, everything is carried to an extreme. The law has to defend the woman since she is weak, and this leads to a situation of discrimination against us [the men]. I guess, reverse discrimination makes us men as discriminated against, and you now have a situation in which you have two things to fix instead of one. . . . It's a dictatorship. Where is the democracy here? They (the police) say, "We have no authority to change it, we have no responsibility, and we cannot jeopardize ourselves. If something will happen to her, we would have to pay with our heads."

This interviewee makes a distinction between the social and private reality in a paradoxical way. Although he shows understanding of the social situation of women, whom he perceives as weaker and in need of protection, he presents his own private situation as being a victim of women's position in society. Given this, he comes to the conclusion that the system is defective and that the mazes of organizational and legal constraints ultimately work against him.

Implicit in this man's account is a double message conveyed by police: One is that they are bound by regulations and by the need to cover themselves in cases of violence, and the other is that their accounts of what they do are not necessarily in line with what they think and feel. Under different social arrangements, they would have a better relationship with them, much the same as during the first encounter.

Following repeated experiences with the police, men construct a script according to which the police investigation takes a path that diverges from the "facts" and has nothing in common with the "truth." By portraying this experience as totalitarian and anti-democratic, they place themselves in an oppressed gender class, thus achieving symmetry with their partners. Furthermore, the interaction with police, which is depicted as being governed by rigid enforcement of rules, leaves the men feeling powerless and coerced into sacrificing their families.

> I am simply helpless. Even if I decide to rehabilitate the relationship, and I am trying hard, no one is willing to give me a chance. Rather, they [the police] tell you to do it the other way around. They would say just go, leave the family, leave everything. That's the best solution for them. . . . But I said to myself, "I will not give in, I have children" and they kept saying, "You are stupid, leave it all, why would you need all this?" The whole system is geared today to destroy the marriage. . . . It's weird.

In this way, the man attempts to redefine the meaning of his dyadic relationship following repeated police intervention, transforming the police involvement into the cause rather than the consequence of the deterioration in his relationship. Now he fights against all odds to save a family life ravaged by his wife's breach of trust and the police's brutal intervention. By adding the element of the children, he becomes not only a savior of the dyadic unit but of the family unit as well. He is sacrificing what he believes in for the benefit of his children and becomes a martyr in his own eyes. In the process, his victim identity is reinforced once again.

> We men live in fear. It's impossible to live this way. When a woman gets into this "trance" of craziness, she can make the man into a rag. She is using this dry legal police stuff and she puts

pressure on me, keeps me in an unbelievable fear. I live in fear. I am insecure, weak. I never used to be like that. I feel defeated, I am nervous at work and it makes me crazy.

The above description has both personal and universal elements. The man exposes his private emotions while also speaking as the representative of an entire class ("we men live in fear"). Portraying his partner as being in a "trance" and making him into "a rag" with the help of inhuman police intervention, completes the role reversal in his perception. His entrapment intensifies with every police encounter. He is alone, misunderstood, betrayed, unable to communicate with his partner, and caught up institutionally in legalistic and dehumanized definitions of the situation. When the next encounter with police comes, his victimization rather than his violence will be the focus of the interaction.

In sum, repeated (more than two) encounters with police lead battering men to the conclusion that exposure of the family to outside agents has powerful negative effects on the self and the dyadic unit and shatters their personal, interpersonal, and social reality. The men come to view police intervention as a means by which society fosters women's egotistic goals over the truth, his good intentions, and dyadic and family needs. The repeated encounters bring the conflict to a new and qualitatively different level of escalation, which in retrospect adds justification to its everlasting presence.

Discussion

During the first encounter with police, battering men's initial attitude is that violence is part of everyday normal life and that calling the police is therefore a departure from unspoken and taken-for-granted family rules. Thus, turning to police is labeled as a lamentable mistake that needs to be rectified. Initial police actions are perceived as reinforcing the man's perception of reality, carried out in a noncriminalizing way intended to keep them out of trouble. Men view such actions as discontinuous and "unreal" and frame them as unnecessary, ritualistic, and technical in light of the marginality and triviality of violence as they see it. The men's normative identity and self-perception are strengthened, whereas the couple's identity is not fundamentally affected. Thus, men come to the second encounter with the police from a power position, expecting a repeat performance of the first interaction. Much to their surprise, the police perceive the situation as recidivism in spite of their previously manifested good will. They proceed to define the men within the constraints of their institutionalized legal categories as violent criminals. Men's expectations are not met, and they feel disenchanted with the police, believing that they switched sides. As a consequence, they develop a sense of betrayal and injustice toward their partners and the police alike. Subsequently, the police's reaction is now viewed as conveying double messages, which trigger vacillation between normative and criminal identity as well as strong emotional reactions ranging from bewilderment to shock. The major task of the battering men during the third encounter is to adjust to the qualitative transformation of police attitudes since the second encounter. In an attempt to avoid surprise, they take the position of expecting the worst and prepare themselves to be in a vulnerable position. At this point, the relationship with the police is associated with generalized emotions of anger toward the partners, the police, and society at large, which are all viewed as entering into a hostile coalition aimed to destroy them. They now feel trapped in a no-win situation and cope by assuming a victim identity.

The different stages in the encounters between battering men and police need to be interpreted in the context of men's expectations whereby the interactions should proceed according to an assumed gender script that will dictate a known set of power relations. When men's attempts to maintain their domination are contrasted with a sense of powerlessness and failed machismo, violence may be a likely consequence (Gondolf & Hanneken, 1987; Yllo, 1993). Whereas during the first encounter with the police, these gender scripts are validated, the second encounter reveals a crisis of control. The victim identity resulting from this process may be regarded as a manifestation of the gap between assumptions regarding existing social arrangements and the actual realities resulting from police intervention. The above-described process illustrates the changes in the men's selves as an outcome of how they are portrayed in other people and institution's "minds." In a socially constructed identity, there is an ongoing dynamic reconstruction that mediates between an individual's social behavior and the meanings assigned to it (Hogg, Terry, & White, 1995). Within such conceptualization, the man comes to his initial encounter with police with a normative social identity and he enters an escalatory conflict concerning his social self. Because "the self is multifaceted, made up of interdependent and independent, mutually reinforcing and conflicting parts" (Stryker & Burke, 2000, p. 286), the men need to cope with the conflict between the way they define themselves and the way others define them. In the tension between the various contradictory selves and other meanings, the batterers need to settle competing identities. They attempt to maneuver and define situations, which helps reinforce the most salient identity as perceived by them. However, such identity negotiations depend on how others respond to their claims (Stryker & Burke, 2000). The men gradually come to realize that their preferred identity as normative persons is rejected and the alternative identity suggested is unbearable to them. To fill in the painful gap, they need a causal explanation to their predicament. From an attribution perspective, the causes of police action are not situational but emerge as characteristics of the system ("dispositional attribution") (Monson, 1983; Weiner, 1990). These attributions become increasingly stable with every additional police contact and become reified over time (Hewstone, 1989; Ross & Nisbett, 1991; Weiner, 1986). When this happens, the element of control is diminished and thus the men increasingly perceive the causes to their situation as beyond their control. Such explanations may account for recent findings in intimate violence research suggesting that battering men use extensively negative global attribution toward their partners (Moore, Eisler, & Franchina, 2000; Tonizzo, Howells, Day, Reidpath, & Froyland, 2000). Their solution of choice was to attribute themselves a victim identity.

Although initially they may experience themselves as weak and frightened in interpersonal relationships, they continuously sustain their public image as fierce, strong, and domineering (Brooks, 1998). Repeated encounters with police tear off the mask of strength from the men's face and force them to confront the limitations of their social-existential position, thus exposing their pain, isolation, and sense of inadequacy and powerlessness. This painful awakening has both personal and social dimensions.

Once the patriarchal dominance as a social resource is blocked, men need to reconstruct their identity as angry "gender victims."

Loss is threatening to the self and impairs the ability to attach new meanings (Marris, 1974). The loss of patriarchal power triggered by interactions with the police attacks the sense of future meaning, and all defenses are directed at keeping continuity in the meaning system. When men are accused of trying to dominate and control their relationships, they invariably fail to connect to painful emotions (Eisikovits & Buchbinder, 1997; Harway & Evans, 1999). In addition, as Hearn (1998) pointed out, battering men appear to maintain double self-narratives: one of a violent self from the distant past and the other of a nonviolent self in the present. We meet the "nonviolent" self in the first encounter through the "help" of police. However, confronting police in the second encounter leads to a collision of the two selves, with the nonviolent self now assuming the role of an angry victim.

This identity reflects the men's experience of loss when their machismo is substituted by shame as the core emotion underlying their social existence. As Sartre (1956) wrote, "Shame is by nature recognition. I recognize that I am as the other sees me" (pp. 221–222). In the coming encounters, there is no escape from the shame revealed by police, which in turn forces them to confront their own version of reality. By struggling for their version to prevail over that of their partner's, the men transform their shame into anger and direct it toward their partners and the authorities. This conflict enhances their sense of anger, betrayal, helplessness, and loneliness. The presentation of self as victim is an attempt to steady a shaken identity, compensating for the ongoing loss of self and a sense of chaos.

As stated before, battering men are portrayed in the literature as skillful manipulators of their narratives. In their interactions with the police, they often use accounts such as denials, excuses, and justifications, which ultimately deny the reality of their intentions or the effects of their actions on their partners (Harway & Evans, 1999; Hearn, 1998). Their accounts may be fostered by the seemingly contradictory messages perceived in police behavior and attitudes. Our findings show that during the encounters with police, two parallel processes emerge: The first is related to men's awareness that police have many doubts about whether to use vigorous modes of intervention in domestic violence cases, such as arrest, or to confine themselves to verbal condemnation and avoidance by casting doubt on the woman's version (Shoham, 2000). Such lenient police approaches toward battering men, as compared with other violent offenders, have been documented in previous studies (e.g., Avakame & Fyfe, 2001). The second is a process of escalation in the relationship and assumptions of a siege mentality. This mentality is reinforced by men's inner conviction that the dominant social and legal institutions construct wife abuse in a manner that de-emphasizes violence and uses it for the broader purpose of degrading their social position of power. These two sets of meanings attributed by battering men may help explain the existing findings that police intervention designed to achieve a deterrent effect may often lead to recidivism (e.g., Schmidt & Sherman, 1993). In addition, previous findings have documented that battering men were found to have lower levels of moral reasoning than nonbatterers (Buttell, 1999). Repeated encounters with police may generate hostility from both police and partners, leading in turn to a need for revenge that is likely to be channeled toward the partner.

Critical Thinking

Like the victims of domestic violence studied by Stephens and Sinden, the domestic violence perpetrators' subsequent encounters with police were perceived quite differently than initial ones. Consider the differences in how repeat victims interpret their interactions with police. How is it that both the abusers and the victims become increasingly disillusioned with police?

References

Avakame, E. F., & Fyfe, J. J. (2001). Differential police treatment of male-on-female spousal violence: Additional evidence on the leniency thesis. *Violence Against Women, 7*, 22–45.

Bograd, M. (1988). How battered women and abusive men account for domestic violence: Excuses, justifications, or explanations? In G. T. Hotaling. D. Finkelhor, J. T. Kirkpatrick, & M. A. Straus (Eds.), *Coping with family violence: Research & policy perspectives* (pp. 60–77). Newbury Park, CA: Sage.

Bowker, L. H. (1983). *Beating wife-beating*. Lexington, MA: D. C. Heath.

Brooks, G. R. (1998). *A new psychotherapy for traditional men*. San Francisco: Jossey-Bass.

Buttell, F. P. (1999). Moral development among court-ordered domestic violence offenders: A descriptive analysis. *Journal of Social Service Research, 26*(2), 37–52.

Buzawa, E. S., & Buzawa, C. G. (1993). The scientific evidence is not conclusive: Arrest is no panacea. In R. J. Gelles & D. R. Loseke (Eds.), *Current controversies on family violence* (pp. 337–356). Newbury Park, CA: Sage.

Buzawa, E. S., & Buzawa, C. G. (1996). *Domestic violence: The criminal justice response* (2nd ed.). Thousand Oaks, CA: Sage.

Carlson, B. E. (1984). Causes and maintenance of domestic violence: An ecological analysis. *Social Service Review, 58*, 569–587.

Dobash, R. E., & Dobash, R. P. (1992). *Women, violence and social change*. London: Routledge Kegan Paul.

Dutton, D. G. (1986). Wife assaulters' explanations for assault: The neutralization of self-punishment. *Canadian Journal of Behavioral Science, 18*, 381–390.

Edleson, J., & Tolman, R. (1992). *Intervention for men who batter: An ecological approach*. Newbury Park, CA: Sage.

Eisikovits, Z., & Buchbinder, E. (1997). Talking violent: A phenomenological study of metaphors battering men use. *Violence Against Women, 3*, 482–498.

Eisikovits, Z., & Buchbinder, E. (2000). *Locked in a violent embrace: Understanding and intervening in domestic violence*. Thousand Oaks, CA: Sage.

Eisikovits, Z., Goldblatt, H., & Winstok, Z. (1999). Partner accounts of intimate violence: Towards a theoretical model. *Families in Society, 80*, 606–619.

Garner, J. H., & Maxwell, C. D. (2000). What are the lessons of the police arrests studies? *Journal of Aggression, Maltreatment & Trauma, 4*, 83–114.

Gelles, R. J. (1993). Constraints against family violence: How well do they work? *American Behavioral Scientist, 36*, 575–586.

Gondolf, E. W., & Hanneken, J. (1987). The gender warrior: Reformed batterers on abuse, treatment, and change. *Journal of Family Violence, 2*, 177–191.

Gordon, J. S. (1996). Community services for abused women: A review of perceived usefulness and efficacy. *Journal of Family Violence, 11*, 315–329.

Hamberger, L. K., & Potente, T. (1994). Counseling heterosexual women arrested for domestic violence: Implications for theory and practice. *Violence and Victims, 9*, 125–137.

Hamilton, B., & Coates, J. (1993). Perceived helpfulness and the use of professional services by abused women. *Journal of Family Violence, 8*, 313–324.

Harway, M., & Evans, K. (1999). Working in groups with men who batter. In M. P. Andronico (Ed.), *Men in groups: Insights, interventions, and psychoeducational work* (pp. 357–375). Washington, DC: American Psychological Association.

Hearn, J. (1998). *The violences of men: How men talk about and how agencies respond to men's violence to women*. London: Sage.

Heise, L. L. (1998). Violence against women: An integrated, ecological framework. *Violence Against Women, 4*, 262–290.

Hewstone, M. (1989). *Casual attribution from cognitive processes to collective beliefs.* Oxford, UK: Basil Blackwell.

Hogg, M. A., Terry, D. J., & White, K. M. (1995). A tale of two theories: A critical comparison of identity theory with social identity theory. *Social Psychology Quarterly, 58,* 255–269.

Holtzworth-Munroe, A., & Hutchison, G. (1993). Attributing negative intent to wife behavior: The attribution of maritally violent versus non-violent men. *Journal of Abnormal Psychology, 102,* 206–211.

Hutchison, I. W., Hirschel, J. D., & Pesackis, C. E. (1994). Family violence and police utilization. *Violence and Victims, 9,* 299–313.

Jacobson, N. S., & Gottman, J. M. (1998). *When men batter women: New insights into ending abusive relationships.* New York: Simon & Schuster.

Jaffe, P. G., Hastings, E., Reitzel, D., & Austin, G. W. (1993). The impact of police lying charges. In N. Z. Hilton (Ed.), *Legal responses to wife assault: Current trends and evaluation* (pp. 62–95). Newbury Park, CA: Sage.

Marris, P. (1974). *Loss and change.* London: Routledge Kegan Paul.

Martin. M. E. (1997). Double your trouble: Duel arrests in the family violence. *Journal of Family Violence, 12,* 139–157.

Monson, T. C. (1983). Implications of the traits vs. situations controversy for differences in the attributions of actors and observers. In J. Jaspars, F. D. Fincham, & M. Hewstone (Eds.), *Attribution theory and research: Conceptual, developmental and social dimensions* (pp. 293–314). London: Academic Press.

Moore, T. M., Eisler, R. M., & Franchina, J. J. (2000). Casual attributions and affective responses to provocative female partner behavior by abusive and nonabusive males. *Journal of Family Violence, 15,* 69–80.

Ptacek, J. (1988). Why do men batter their wives? In K. Yllo & M. Bograd (Eds.), *Feminist perspectives on wife abuse* (pp. 133–157). Newbury Park. CA: Sage.

Reitz, R. R. (1999). Batterers' experiences of being violent: A phenomenological study. *Psychology of Women Quarterly, 23,* 143–165.

Ross, L., & Nisbett, R. E. (1991). *The person and the situation: Perspectives of social psychology.* New York: McGraw-Hill.

Sartre, J. P. (1956). *Being and nothingness.* New York: Washington Square Press.

Saunders. D. G., & Size, P. B. (1986). Attitudes about woman abuse among police officers, victims, and victim advocates. *Journal of Interpersonal Violence, 1,* 25–42.

Schmidt, J. D., & Sherman, L. W. (1993). Does arrest deter domestic violence? *American Behavioral Scientist, 36,* 601–609.

Schofield, J. W. (1993). Increasing the generalizability of qualitative research. In M. Hammersley (Ed.), *Social research: Philosophy, politics and practice* (pp. 200–225). London: Sage.

Sherman, L. W., & Berk, R. A. (1984). The specific deterrent effects of arrests for domestic assault. *American Sociological Review, 49,* 261–272.

Shoham, E. (2000). The battered wife's perception of the characteristics of her encounter with the police. *International Journal of Offender Therapy and Comparative Criminology, 44,* 242–257.

Smith, L. J. F. (1989). *Domestic violence: An overview of the literature.* London: Her Majesty's Stationery Office.

Stamp, G. H., & Sabourin. T. C. (1995). Accounting for violence: An analysis of male spousal abuse narratives. *Journal of Applied Communication Research, 23,* 284–307.

Stark, E. (1993). Mandatory arrest of batterers: A reply to its critics. *American Behavioral Scientist, 36,* 651–680.

Stryker, S., & Burke, P. J. (2000). The past, present, and the future of an identity theory. *Social Psychology Quarterly, 63,* 284–297.

Tolman, R. M., & Weisz, A. (1995). Coordinated community intervention for domestic violence: The effects of arrest and prosecution on recidivism of woman abuse perpetrators. *Crime and Delinquency, 41,* 481–495.

Tonizzo, S., Howells, K., Day, A., Reidpath, D., & Froyland, I. (2000). Attributions of negative partner behavior by men who physically abuse their partners. *Journal of Family Violence, 15,* 155–167.

Weiner, B. (1986). *An attribution theory of motivation and emotion.* New York: Springer.

Weiner, B. (1990). Searching for the roots of applied attribution theory. In S. Graham & V. S. Folkes (Eds.), *Attribution theory: Applications to achievement, mental health, and interpersonal conflict* (pp. 1–16). Hillsdale, NJ: Lawrence Erlbaum.

Yllo, K. A. (1993). Through a feminist lens: Gender, power, and violence. In R. J. Gelles & D. R. Loseke (Eds.), *Current controversies on family violence* (pp. 47–62). Newbury Park, CA: Sage.

II Judicial

Whereas the police are highly visible in the community, the opposite is true for the criminal courts. The media image of actors in the judicial arena is one characterized by frequent criminal trials, with each side battling for truth within an adversarial environment. Although this image may be true on occasion, it is not the way the adjudicative process operates in reality. Over 90 percent of criminal cases are officially disposed of by plea bargaining agreements that take place between the prosecutor's office and defense attorneys. Often these behind-the-scenes deliberations take place over a very short period, although not always, as one of the authors in this section points out.

Conducting qualitative research in courthouses, attorneys' offices, and judge's chambers is no easy task. But studies conducted through painstaking observation and interviewing have lifted the hidden operational process of courtroom decision-making that have seldom been well understood, especially for outsiders and those going through the system. Ingratiating one's self with the courthouse work group and developing rapport for purposes of gaining entrée over a sustained time is an absolute necessity if one is to attain some degree of insider status. It is only by being there and witnessing firsthand the way criminal cases are handled that researchers can formulate theoretical propositions to explain the informal judicial decision-making process that affects all cases.

The articles selected for the first part of this section represent qualitative approaches that analyze some of the most important issues facing the criminal courts today. Although they may overlap somewhat, these articles provide an opportunity for the reader to see and understand why the judicial system works the way it does. Social class and its effects on adjudication, the judges' role, and probation recommendations are represented in the qualitative approaches presented here.

The articles included in the second part of this section analyze the perspective of those who are involved in the court system for short terms and are, for the most part, outsiders to the goings on of the judicial bureaucracy. They do not make their living by being attorneys or judges. Instead, they were either brought to the court out of civic duty (e.g., jurors or witnesses) or they are there because they were either the victim or culprit of a crime. Although not comprehensive, we have chosen research studies in both sections that cover most of the important issues addressing due process questions and the court systems' treatment of criminal defendants. It is through these field study efforts that we have come to better comprehend the practices of actors in our criminal courts.

A Practitioners

11

Calling Your Bluff: How Prosecutors and Defense Attorneys Adapt Plea Bargaining Strategies to Increased Formalization

Deirdre M. Bowen

Abstract: *Deidre Bowen examines the functioning of plea-bargaining in an urban district attorney's office. Specifically, she focuses on the balance of power between the prosecutor and defense attorney and on how legal actors adapt to long established institutional rules to attain efficiency and justice. She observed the process whereby defense lawyers find ways to equalize the balance of power when particular criminal cases do not fall under the "normal crimes" model. Her observations of the negotiation strategies between both sides of the plea-bargaining process provide insight into whether prosecutors and defense lawyers behave differently under a rationalized system of plea negotiation as compared with a more traditional model that has historically been used.*

Introduction

Social scientists and legal scholars have long debated the suitability of plea-bargaining as the dominant method for disposing of cases in the criminal justice system.

Bibas (2004c) suggests that the nature of plea bargaining reform should not focus on creating alternative systems, or eliminating plea bargaining, or reducing prosecutorial power in plea negotiations, but should instead create a balance of power by enhancing the power of other legal actors. Bibas (2004c) agrees with Uviller's (2000) suggestion that setting the criminal charges and negotiating pleas should be handled dispassionately and institutionally separately from the trying of cases. However, Bibas (2004c) also adds that limits should be placed on the types of plea offers made available.

In this ethnographic work, I concentrate on a rationalized approach to plea-bargaining that the Superior Court in Seattle, Washington adopted, a system which happens to incorporate some of the ideas Bibas (2004c) and Uviller (2000) discuss. I examine the organizational structure and background of the Early Plea Unit (EPU) where non-drug felony plea negotiations take place and explore the rules, the actors, and their perceptions of this model. I specifically focus on two questions: (1) whether and how attorneys create a balance of power in the pursuit of justice; and (2) whether attorneys behave differently under a new, highly rationalized model of plea bargaining compared to the models studied thirty years ago.

Literature Review

The legal and policy debate over plea bargaining has narrowed its focus to prosecutorial power within the criminal justice system. This shift in focus occurred both in the Supreme Court's observation in *Bordenkircher v. Hayes* (1978) as well as in the literature. The Court became increasingly concerned about the prosecutor's power to threaten more severe punishment or charges in retaliation for a defendant's rejection of a plea in favor of a trial. Specifically, as legislatures have responded to the public's call to get tough on crime measures by increasing prosecutorial powers, legal scholars have increased their criticisms over the use of these prosecutorial tools (Barkow, 2006; Bibas, 2004a; Stunts, 2004).

A division exists on how to respond to these plea bargaining criticisms. One camp advocates an outright ban on plea bargaining while the other suggests reform of a system that it is here to stay. One such reform idea calls for a restructuring of the prosecutorial office from within. Uviller (2000) advocates for a three tiered prosecutorial approach to case disposition. This approach would address the concerns for achieving justice in an adversarial model of unbalanced power. He suggests that a case should be processed in a bifurcated manner. The investigation, where the appropriate charge is identified, and adjudication, where the appropriate punishment in exchange for a guilty plea is meted out, should occur in a neutral fashion with a dispassionate prosecutor who is not responsible for trying the case. Only if and when the negotiations fall apart should a prosecutor take on a zealous advocacy role.

Wright and Miller (2002) propose a model akin to Uviller's (2000) approach, but place more emphasis on case screening resources as opposed to neutrality. The intended effect is to reduce the need for plea bargaining. Indeed, the results of their analysis demonstrated that plea bargains by charge or sentence reduction decreased substantially when prosecutors screened cases more effectively. Bibas (2004a) builds on these ideas by arguing that the best reforms will come from building a system of checks and balances that constrain prosecutorial power and have the effect of increasing defense attorneys' power (Bibas, 2004b). Prosecutors should focus on filing only the most serious and provable charges, stop charge bargaining, write down all plea offers, and get approval for them from a supervisor. And more generally, Ma (2002) advocates that the United States follow a continental model of plea bargaining as found in France, Germany, and Italy. Again the emphasis is on restricting prosecutorial power by increasing control and supervision.

All of these writers stress that plea bargaining under an imbalanced system does not achieve justice, much less arrive at something akin to empirical or legal truth. While the criticisms and suggested reforms of plea bargaining have remained relatively consistent, the nature of the plea bargaining process in the current criminal justice system has not. Specifically, institutionalized plea bargaining embodies the criminal justice system's desire to create efficiency, calculability, predictability, and control in the processing of defendants (Ritzer, 1993).

Wright and Miller (2002) observe that empirical studies have ignored the inner workings of justice agencies and what values emerge in the production of justice. Yet, understanding the culture of these agencies within the context of these new approaches to plea bargaining is essential to developing policies around case processing reforms. As Mather (1979) observed almost 30 years ago, to understand the process of "sorting cases" that legal actors engage in, it is essential to describe the court behavior.

In this work, I examine an approach to plea bargaining that adopts some of the ideas suggested by Bibas (2004c) and Uviller (2000) at the King County Prosecutor's Office in Seattle Washington. The King County Prosecutor's Office created the Early Plea Unit (EPU) originally in 1990 to increase efficiency in processing cases. The Prosecutor's Office revised the EPU again in 1999 to incorporate a highly rationalized process of negotiation that exists independently from the Trial Unit. This particular organizational approach happens to follow a lot of the recommendations of Uviller (2000) and Bibas (2004c): the charging and plea negotiating are handled institutionally separately from the trying of cases; the prosecutor charges conservatively, a supervising attorney reviews each action; and all plea agreements are written down.

While in King County all of the cases are being processed in the same institution, the charging attorney and plea negotiating attorney exist in independent units from the trial attorney and are not invested in trying the case. Therefore, according to Uviller (2000), these prosecutors are more likely to be dispassionate about the case. Only when it reaches the trial team should zealous advocacy appear. However, a key prosecutorial tool, the trial penalty, is available in King County, which tips the balance of power Bibas (2004c) and Uviller (2000) advocate for. If the defendant declines to accept the offer given at the EPU, she or he not only faces the possibility of no plea negotiations with the trial prosecutor, or at least no better offer than the EPU offer, the defendant also faces the threat of additional charges, enhancements, or a recommendation of the high end of the sentencing range if convicted at trial.

Methods

This study came out of a larger research project examining new systems of plea bargaining and comparing them to the traditional model of plea negotiations at the King County Superior Courthouse in Seattle, Washington. I collected data from three sources in the King County Prosecutor's Office from February through December 2000. I chose this location for my research because it is one of only a handful of jurisdictions that is employing more rationalized and institutionalized systems of plea bargaining.

The population consisted of the prosecutors and their superiors who were part of the felony trial team, and the Early Plea Unit (EPU). In addition, private attorneys and the public defenders from the four corporations that are under contract with the Public Defender's Office were included in the study. Every attorney was Caucasian, almost evenly split between male and female and in the 30–50 years-of-age range.

Three approaches were used to gather data for this research. First, direct observation was used to watch attorneys negotiate and process pleas of 42 cases in the Early Plea Unit. Second, I interviewed a number of times, both formally and informally, over 25 attorneys involved in the plea system, and finally, I collected data on the characteristics and disposition of each case I observed from court documents, and created a database to both qualitatively and quantitatively analyze them. These observations occurred over a five-month period.

Results

Bureaucratic Organization of the King County Prosecutor's Office

The King County Prosecutor's Office ("KCPO") is located in the financial district of downtown Seattle. The Office occupies a number of floors in the King County Superior Court Building, it is the largest prosecutor's office in Washington State. Over 500 people are employed there, 240 of whom are prosecuting attorneys.

An executive group manages the four divisions that make up the Prosecutor's Office: Civil Division, Fraud Prevention, Family Support Division and Criminal Division. The Criminal Division, the largest of the four divisions, has 156 attorneys. It comprises ten highly specialized units, one of which is the EPU.

After an arrest is made and the investigation is complete, the charge is filed by the King County (KC) Prosecutor's Office. The prosecutor's office has a specific set of internal guidelines on the rules used in filing charges and disposing of cases. These guidelines are used by the junior deputy prosecuting attorneys to assist them in filing the appropriate charges. In general, the guidelines advise that the defendant should be charged only for what can be reasonably proven and that the prosecutor should charge conservatively.

The KC Prosecutor's Office only files charges on the offenses that it is quite confident it can win at trial. It does not add additional charges just because the facts may allow for it, and it does not add enhancements. As part of its carrot and stick approach, the Prosecutor's Office encourages defendants to plead guilty early in the process of disposing of the case because it offers the best chance of receiving the lowest sentence for the fewest and least serious offenses. If the defendant decides not to plead guilty, and the case is assigned to trial, the KC Prosecutor's Office reserves the right to file additional charges and enhancements based on the facts of the case. Thus, the "stick" part of the process emerges as the trial penalty.

Under the conservative charging approach, the Prosecutor's Office asserts that the defense attorney knows exactly what to expect. If their client pleads guilty, then the low range of the appropriate sentence will be recommended. The defense attorney can advise their client as such, and the case can move forward without any continuances. Thus, defense attorneys are forced to accept the offer as-is unless they have truly identified legal challenges or evidentiary issues that require further attention. If the defendant chooses to not to plead earlier on, the State will apply the "stick." Additional charges and enhancements are filed in preparation for trial, where both prosecutor and defense attorney have more time to investigate their legal worthiness.

After the arrest, the charges are set first by less experienced prosecutors in the Charging Unit. They investigate the case for the purpose of conservatively identifying only those charges that can be easily proven at trial. An experienced supervising prosecutor reviews each charge, if the case is a non-drug, nonviolent class B or C felony, it is then transferred to the Early Plea Unit. The prosecutor's sole task in EPU is to negotiate a plea for these cases. The pleas are written down and reviewed by a supervisor. If the case is not successfully negotiated at the EPU, the case is transferred to a third unit, the Trial Unit. There, it's assigned to the trial team to prepare for litigation, with clearly defined limitations on plea offers. Each stage is organizationally separate from the other.

Background and Purpose of the EPU

On its face, the charging guidelines as well as the purpose of the EPU seem to follow Uviller's (2000) proposal of dispassionate assessment of a case's worthiness for trial. According to the prosecutor, who negotiates within the EPU, it is to act as a checkpoint. Again, the language mirrors the goals articulated by both Bibas (2004c) and Uviller (2000): "To protect the process. The objective is to make sure we've got the right stuff for trial. If the case does not negotiate at EPU, then I give a heads up to the trial team about a potential issue" (EPU Prosecutor).

The defense community believes the real goal is efficiency. While their understanding is that the KCPO created the unit to increase efficiency in the processing of cases, one defense attorney observed: 'They could devote more resources if they really wanted to negotiate, but I think they are just as happy to go to trial" (Public Defender).

The Criminal Division Supervising Prosecutor stated in an interview that the KCPO established the EPU in 1990, indeed, as an efficiency measure. He observed that a review of cases showed that plenty of negotiations were occurring between prosecutors and defense attorneys, but the cases were staying in the system too long. The goal was to get cases processed in 30–45 days instead of 8–10 weeks. The KCPO developed internal standards to improve consistency, increase fair results, and to create greater access to the prosecutors for negotiations. The EPU, in its current form, emerged in 1999.

EPU Case Characteristics

In its present form, the EPU consists of one prosecutor who negotiates all non-drug, non-preassigned (to the trial team), nonviolent felony cases. These cases are known as mainstream cases. They largely consist of Class C and some Class B felonies. The supervising prosecutor of the EPU and the Trial Team makes decisions on an ad hoc basis as to whether a case should be preassigned to the trial team or sent to the EPU. The decision-making process seems to follow the supervisor's initial assessment as to whether they can be quickly negotiated based on the legal characteristics of the case, and the personal characteristics of the individuals involved in the case.

Institutional Rules, Process, and Norms of the EPU

The word "unit" is a bit of a misnomer as only one prosecutor negotiates with all the defense attorneys handling EPU cases. After the arraignment, in theory, the case is supposed to be plea bargained or set for trial at the case setting hearing within two weeks. This schedule is rarely followed. Defense attorneys as well as the EPU prosecutor requested an average of two continuances with each one lasting two weeks. Sixty percent of the cases seem to take a minimum of six weeks to process.

When the defense attorney is assigned the case, they goes to the records department to request the case file for the EPU. In general, most defense attorneys don't go to the EPU until a day or two before the case setting hearing. The defense attorney waits outside the EPU prosecutor's office until she's available to discuss the case. Negotiations with the EPU prosecutor can occur over several weeks. Continuances are used to allow time to examine any issues raised by the parties. The general issues raised tend to surround the offender score, whether the charge is supported by the facts, a clarification of the facts from witnesses or victims, consultation with the victim, or search and seizure issues.

The EPU process, as arranged by the institution in its present form, seems relatively straightforward to the newcomer. The organizational structure of the system, however, is teeming with frustration for the defense community. It creates what Utz describes as, "an atmosphere of cooperation under conditions of organizational conflict" (Utz, 1978, p. 4.)

From the defense attorneys' perspectives, three factors prevent them from doing their job effectively. First, only one prosecutor is assigned to negotiate with approximately 50 attorneys who do business with the EPU on a regular basis. This increases the wait time significantly. In addition, when other defense attorneys are waiting outside the EPU office, the defense attorneys feel that the EPU prosecutor shortens their negotiation time and is quick to suggest a continuance for any issues raised. When defense attorneys are trying to assess whether a deal is likely, a continuance just creates a delay that must now be factored into the assessment of whether to pursue a plea. If a deal can't be made, defense attorneys would like to quickly move on to the trial team. Continuances come at the expense of their clients, particularly those that are in pretrial detention. On occasion, the time taken to dispose of their case is longer than the sentence given. Finally, it is sometimes the case that no one is available to negotiate at all when the EPU prosecutor is absent. Just as likely, the defense attorneys don't wish to negotiate with the substitute prosecutor because of the unpredictability it brings.

In an interview with a supervising prosecuting attorney, I raised these issues with him. He responded that the prosecutor's office has limited resources to work with and that the defense attorneys "all follow a cattle trail. They need to be more inventive about their practice. Change the way they spend their time." This interview offers the first hint of organizational tension that exists between defense attorneys and prosecutors.

Content and Sequence of Bargaining Discourse

Similar to Maynard's (1984) observations, the attorneys in this study engaged in a bargaining sequence that involved a "proposal" and "position report." In these negotiations, most defense attorneys enter the bargaining session silently, waiting to see what the prosecutor will propose. The offer will reveal some level of information about the prosecutor's view of the case, or as Mather (1979) and Eisenstein and Jacob (1976) pointed out, the prosecutor's assessed "value" of the case. The defense attorney views it as an important strategy, similar to Maynard's (1984) "framing strategy," particularly in cases where they believe no factual or legal points exist to argue on behalf of the defendant. Furthermore, the reply techniques Maynard (1984) identified in his analysis are used by these attorneys too, specifically, the uses of utterances to delay a position report.

DEFENSE ATTORNEY: Last time we talked I think it was about scoring. [Defendant's offender score.]

PROSECUTOR: Yes. We were looking at a 7 or an 8.

DEFENSE ATTORNEY: Um.

PROSECUTOR: We need check on these felonies in California. . . . To see if the crimes are comparable felonies here.

DEFENSE ATTORNEY: Huh?

PROSECUTOR: We need to check the California code on the conspiracy to commit a crime.

DEFENSE ATTORNEY: What crime?

PROSECUTOR: Theft. I don't think the theft is comparable, but the conspiracy is.

DEFENSE ATTORNEY: What happens when the DOC [Department of Corrections] doesn't agree with our scoring?

PROSECUTOR: We would be willing to drop the theft, but not the conspiracy. Why don't we get a continuance and you bring me a copy of the California code next time you come in?

DEFENSE ATTORNEY: If we go to trial, they'll split into two trials as one will be a misdemeanor.

PROSECUTOR: If you set for trial, it will give us more time to figure out the circumstances of the California crimes and increase the offender score.

In this exchange, the defense attorney uses a number of indirect utterances to get the prosecutor to define her proposal without giving a clear position report until the end of the conversation. When the defense attorney does give a position report that threatens to reject the offer, the prosecutor reminds him to whose advantage a trial would be. As Maynard (1984) observed, the attorneys will move to explicit bargaining and use formal justice if "convergence" does not occur between counsel. In addition, the defense attorney strategically uses the phrase "our scoring," suggesting the teamwork that should be involved in solving this issue.

Maynard (1984) also observed that facts and characteristics were not essential to case disposition, but rather charging and sentencing were the key to case disposition. Indeed, much of the content in the negotiations revolved around those ideas. However, both prosecutor and defense attorneys acknowledged that character could be an important part of the content. As Mather (1979) observed, defense attorneys use character to add "value" to a case when other factors cannot be argued. The defense attorneys and the prosecutor both agreed it could be used effectively, only if done strategically. In this exchange, I asked the EPU prosecutor under what circumstances she would consider character.

PROSECUTOR: Mental Health issues. Juveniles. Overall, I can't think about character because where is the dividing line? I let them say their piece, but I don't care, is that awful?

INTERVIEWER: Can they make their case in the sentencing hearing?

PROSECUTOR: Well, yes. Exactly. They can argue it there.

From the defense attorneys' perspective, this was unfair. A key component in meting out justice was allowing for second chances. Character was a key determinant of that. According to defense counsel, the sentencing hearing seemed to be an ineffective, if not unpredictable, place to argue character because judges are so prone to follow the prosecutor's sentencing recommendation. However, the defense attorneys did use character strategically in their negotiating and effectively added "value" to their case.

A significant theme observed in Maynard's (1984) discourse analysis, as well as in Feeley's (1979) and Mather's (1979) work is that most of the negotiating involves implicit bargaining. The parties quickly come to an alignment of the shared value of the case. In this exchange the attorneys view the offense as a "normal crime" and agree on the "going rate."

DEFENSE ATTORNEY: Do you have an offer for me on this?

PROSECUTOR: A misdemeanor with restitution. Criminal Trespass?

DEFENSE ATTORNEY: This mother is driving me nuts. I'd never make it in Juvy [Juvenile Court] because of all the whiney mothers. I'd tell them it's their fault and get fired. So are we thinking along the same lines? Deferred Sentence? 12 month rec?

PROSECUTOR: Okay, but 20 days in custody and credit for time served. He'll be out at sentencing.

DEFENSE ATTORNEY: But you're not doing it out of the goodness of your heart. Hey, we're going to the game on Friday?

PROSECUTOR: Yeah, but he is still getting the benefit of it.

There is no discussion about the facts of the case. Instead, the end result is agreed upon in the midst of non-legal discussion. What's also being communicated here is an acknowledgment by the prosecutor that some incarceration period is included in the offer to justify the time the defendant has already spent in pretrial detention. When asked about this type of exchange the prosecutor said, "A lot of times, when I know the attorney well, we just look at each other and agree on what needs to happen here. I feel like we work together on it. They know I'm reasonable and going for broke is not a good idea" (EPU Prosecutor).

This implicit bargaining was consistent with Feeley's (1979) and Mather's (1979) observations that in these less serious cases substantive justice was more appealing than formal justice. The challenge was balancing the costs of pretrial detention. On the one hand, the sentencing range is so small for less serious felonies that it would have been low risk to go to trial, or at least investigate potential issues, but the time it would take to investigate and/or get to trial would mean the defendant often spent more time in detention waiting through continuances than his sentence would be. Therefore, pretrial detention became a strong motivator to plea bargain in less serious felony cases. In those cases where the defendant had spent more time in detention than the sentence agreed to in the plea bargain, the prosecutor made adjustments to the sentence offer, as noted in the previous negotiation exchange.

Cooperation within the Workgroup

Despite the increasing tension around the organizational structure of the EPU, evidence of cooperation within the workgroup revealed itself in a number of ways. Overwhelmingly, attorneys took the view that they should work together to settle on the appropriate charge and punishment. When they did not agree, they respected each other's position to go to trial, but it often belied defense attorney resentment at "wasting time with the EPU." Overall though, the attorneys' approaches in interacting with each other suggested a sense of familiarity and ease that comes from working together regularly over a long period of time.

Cooperation in the workgroup originates from an understanding of what the two parties are trying to achieve. Both sides know that the court and prosecutor's office endorse plea negotiations to increase the efficiency of case processing. The defense attorneys acknowledged the seemingly objective approach the EPU prosecutor takes. If the case has problems, it should be investigated. The EPU prosecutor explained her philosophy this way:

> It's a credibility issue. We tend to agree because I see my job as being objective. I advocate for the state, but I must make sure we can make our case. At the same time, I'm not going to tell them all the issues or hide them all either because that would mean ineffective assistance of counsel.
>
> (EPU Prosecutor)

When defense attorneys questioned the facts, the charge, evidentiary or scoring issues, the EPU prosecutor always agreed to a continuance to investigate the case further. She willingly shared resources with the defense counsel and went so far as to point out potential issues that the defense counsel appeared to have not picked up on. In addition, when the defense attorney determined that trying the case was a better strategy, or that a request denied by the prosecutor would be raised at the sentencing hearing, the EPU prosecutor respected that position. This example illustrates this behavior.

A defense attorney began negotiations on an assault case questioning whether the charge of Assault in the third degree was appropriate given the facts of the case. The victim was the landlord who shared a house with the defendant. The victim confronted the defendant about not paying rent as well as his messy room. A fight ensued in which both parties were arrested, but only the defendant was charged. When the defense attorney did not elaborate on why Assault in the fourth degree would have been more appropriate, the EPU prosecutor handed him the charging standards to review. The defense attorney asked for help in looking them up. The prosecutor read them aloud. Together, they listened to the 911 tape and examined the pictures of the injuries in light of the charging standards. The prosecutor then conceded:

PROSECUTOR:	It's an assault 4 [then jokes] with the stipulation that the defendant keep his room clean!
DEFENSE ATTORNEY:	Agreed! I do have to check with my client though.
PROSECUTOR:	If the defendant won't agree, just set it for trial.

In this exchange, the parties clearly worked together in the dispassionate manner Uviller (2000) recommends to find the appropriate charge. The prosecutor agrees to reduce the charge and wants a guilty plea in exchange for the low end of the sentence range recommendation. All of this is implicit bargaining. However, the defense attorney does not readily agree because there is an unspoken character issue of which both parties are aware. The defense attorney knows, however, it would be bad strategy to articulate it explicitly. The victim is gay and the defendant is straight. The attorneys know socially sensitive characteristics can be problematic for a jury. The defense attorney is testing to see if there is room for further negotiation by leaving himself room to check with his client. The prosecutor makes her position clear with the last statement. The tone of the exchange is pleasant and even includes a joke, but ultimately the prosecutor has made clear she will not negotiate further.

Reasonableness seemed to have its limits, and similar to Heumann's (1979) observations about "ungentlemanly" behavior, attorneys who raise frivolous legal issues that they cannot support are perceived as wasting the prosecutor's time. In one case, the defense attorney came in for the initial negotiations and asked for a misdemeanor on an eluding police case. The defense attorney suggested there was an identification issue, but did not elaborate. The prosecutor disagreed and offered that perhaps there is a search issue instead. She advised the defense attorney to read the case law, and then they'd ask for a continuance. The prosecutor even read him the cite to the case. When he returns with the case law in hand, but does not actually argue the case, defense counsel's request for a misdemeanor is met with silence. The prosecutor explained her reaction: "I think we'll lose on the search issue, but it doesn't kill the case. Yeah, sure, I could have given him reckless endangerment, but I did not want to do it. Sometimes I'm surprised how unprepared they are. Why not argue why the case applies?" (EPU Prosecutor).

On the other hand, some defense attorneys asserted that the prosecutor was not always prepared either, but the defense attorneys claimed that this could be to their advantage. The defense attorneys entered these types of negotiations simply waiting for an offer, rather than arguing the case. On occasion, the prosecutor would underestimate the value of the case, and the defense counsel perceived that the EPU prosecutor gave a better offer than the "going rate." Defense counsel particularly relished these moments because they could go back to their clients and legitimately argue that the defendant got a discount off their "theoretical exposure." In other situations, when the offer was too good, defense counsel took it as a signal that something was wrong with the case and a better offer could be had if they waited and set it for trial.

Overall, defense attorneys felt that they operated in a subculture of cooperation, in which most cases were readily negotiated because of the shared knowledge and easy alignment in terms of "normal crimes" and "going rates." Most defense attorneys thought that the EPU had a place in the judicial system and that certain types of "no brainer" cases belonged there—victimless crimes in particular. The defense attorneys found they could work with the EPU prosecutor in a cooperative manner, but certainly under tense circumstances. They believed that the lack of resources made available suggested that the prosecutor's office did not care about efficiency and fairness. Consistently, the defense attorneys voiced concern about the time it took to negotiate cases in EPU because only one prosecutor was assigned to the Unit. Every request to investigate a case further meant a delay in resolving the case.

Decision Making and Adaptation to the Institutional Rules and Process

Despite the perceived impediments of the EPU's organizational system, the actors within the workgroup almost approached a sense of camaraderie as they completed their daily tasks. While the defense attorneys tolerated the structural arrangement of the EPU (less so as the study wore on) 80 percent expressed deep frustration about two institutional rules of the bargaining process. The first rule stated that once negotiations failed at the EPU, no negotiations *should* occur at the trial level, and if the case absolutely required them, the trial team could not offer a deal better than what was offered at the EPU. The second rule declared that negotiations were *not* available at all if a case bypassed the EPU and was immediately set for trial. These rules were viewed as another form of a trial penalty.

With regard to the first rule, every defense attorney had a story to tell about the deputy trial team offering a better deal than the EPU, only to have it withdrawn when the trial team discovered that the EPU had made a less attractive offer. One defense attorney explained it this way:

> There's almost an incentive not to submit the case to EPU and set it for trial. Because sometimes a deal is offered by the trial team and they can't make the offer because the EPU set a tougher deal, I had a defendant where three cases were involved. I said, "My guy will plead if two are dismissed." EPU said "one" and the trial deputy said "two" and then looked in the file and said, "I can't because of the policy on EPU offers. It's almost better not to open the can of worms [at EPU]."
>
> (Public Defender)

The defense attorney's comment suggests that he is more confident in the second rule being broken: the trial team's willingness to negotiate even if the defense attorneys bypass EPU because the trial prosecutor is facing the pressure of whether they can win at trial.

The rule that the trial team cannot offer a deal better than the EPU causes additional angst particularly when the defendant has been in pretrial detention. While the attorneys negotiate the case at EPU, the defendant spends weeks or even months in jail only to have the process start all over again with the trial team. The additional time incarcerated may afford the defendant a better deal on paper only; overcoming the risks of trial and a more severe sentence could, in the end lead to a better offer, but the amount of time he spends in jail waiting for two different prosecutors and his defense attorney to resolve the case may surpass his actual sentence.

A defense attorney described the problem of the EPU in the following manner:

> The problem is that this is a traffic jam. You have to have continuances. I average three or four a case because you need the time to determine if there's a good defense. You're just shooting from the hip; both of us [prosecutor and defense attorney] need to get up to speed. Maybe one out of 30–40 cases do I get a deal on the first try.
>
> (Public Defender)

Defense attorneys chose one of two ways to adapt to this situation. Typically, if the deputy trial attorney refused to negotiate or revised an offer to remain consistent with the EPU's offer, the defense attorneys approached the supervising trial attorneys.

The defense attorneys who tried this method were usually more senior than the deputy trial attorneys with whom they were negotiating. Public defenders, in particular, perceived that they had more success with the supervising prosecutors because of one key factor—history. According to one defense attorney:

> I go to the supervisor because I usually have a history with the supervisor. There is no substitute for history with a person. I'd love to work with someone I've bonded with in trial. We've bonded through the stress and we know how the disagreements will fall out.
>
> (Public Defender)

The other adaptation employed by about 20 percent of the defense attorneys was to bypass the EPU and set the case for trial. Although the defense attorneys ran the risk of having the trial prosecutor enforce the second rule—no negotiating, they knew that if the case fell apart or the trial attorney had a full calendar, a deal could be made. The majority of defense attorneys informed me that they monitor the deputy trial attorneys' calendars. They deemed it good strategy to set the case for trial and have a "highly stressed prosecutor call for a deal."

Over 90 percent of the trial team prosecutors interviewed said that they would initially enforce the no negotiation rule unless it was a private attorney unfamiliar with the process. However, every trial team prosecutor thought that each case should be negotiated, if possible, but some noted that defense attorneys who bypassed EPU should not receive as good a deal as those that followed the process. This prosecutor's opinion summarizes most of the trial team's view:

> Even if it's gone through EPU, I basically think the negotiating has to happen. Every case needs the opportunity to be resolved. I'm not trying to jumpstart a case, but every case can unravel, witnesses go missing or evidentiary issues come up. It's a mistake not to listen to the defense attorney. In my last eight or nine cases, I've given better deals in two or three cases [than EPU].
>
> (Deputy Trial Attorney)

The defense attorney's engaged in a two-part decision-making analysis, similar to the approach taken by the attorneys in Emmelman's (1996) work. First, the defense attorneys assess the value of the case based on the seriousness of the case, the strength of the evidence, and the background characteristics. The more serious the case, the more inclined defense counsel was to take it directly to the trial team and try negotiations there; particularly after engaging in part two of the analysis-the potential costs of delay by setting the case for trial after going to EPU. The defense attorneys felt that the possibility of lost witnesses, better defense evidence emerging, and a clogged prosecutor calendar could all be used in their favor regardless of the risk of a trial penalty. In the end, the defense attorneys know that these rules are flexible. A plea bargain is possible with either the EPU or the trial team. Thus, the defense attorneys felt that they used this knowledge to create a balance of power.

Organizational Challenges of Having Separate Units Process the Same Case

Notwithstanding, the defense attorneys found the negotiating process challenging whether it was with the EPU prosecutor or the trial team deputy prosecutors. They felt a truly effective negotiation could not occur if both parties were not approaching the bargaining with the same level of investment in the case. The defense attorneys thought that the EPU prosecutor was too removed from the case because she would not actually be trying the case. She was not really eyeing the case for trial in the same way a defense attorney was because the EPU prosecutor was not facing the same consequences of *trying* the case if the plea fell through. Consequently, she had less at stake than the trial attorney.

The following example illustrates this point. In two burglary cases, the defendants had substantial offender scores that significantly increased the lengths of their sentences. The EPU offers in both of these cases were at the higher end of the sentencing range because:

> There is nothing to lose by going to trial. I offered midrange because I was appalled by the offender scores. They're off the charts. Sure I could have gone lower, but I didn't want to. Let trial team deal with it, if they have too.
>
> (EPU Prosecutor)

In this case, there was a shared understanding as to the crime, but no convergence around the sentence length. The defense attorney was frustrated because he had to begin the negotiation process again with the trial team, under the guise that the trial team could not offer anything better; yet EPU knew the defense counsel would try to get a better deal.

In fact, the trial prosecutor offered the minimum range in one of the cases, as he was unable to get any response from the victim. In the other case, the trial prosecutor kept the EPU offer open. The defense attorney advised her client to plead guilty. Ultimately, defense counsel obtained a significantly lower punishment at the sentencing hearing after describing in detail that the defendant had mental health issues for which he desperately wished to seek treatment. This shows how the defense attorney used the manipulation of his knowledge of the rules to his advantage at every stage. The trial attorney, having greater investment in the case, saw the need to plead out the cases. While discussing characteristics would not influence the EPU prosecutor, or perhaps even the trial prosecutor, it did impact the judge's sentencing. Only if both the prosecutor and the defense attorney sign an "agreed" plea, will the defense attorney not attempt to get a lower sentence at the sentencing hearing. Regardless, the defense attorney felt the case could have been processed more efficiently if the EPU prosecutor actually had an investment in the case going to trial.

While Bibas (2004c) advocated greater supervision of plea agreements, defense attorneys thought there was too much supervision. Defense counsel felt that deputy trial prosecutors did not have adequate ownership over their cases. In comparing the organization of trial prosecutors in another county, one defense attorney observed: "In Thurston [county], the attorney has ownership over the case and they'll review it as if going to trial. They feel better about the job because they're independent thinkers. Deputy prosecutors here need approval for everything" (Private Defense Counsel).

In fact, the single biggest improvement that the defense attorneys wanted was for the deputy prosecutors to have more power over their cases. While the trial prosecutors examined the case as if going to trial, they did not have the ultimate say in whether a deal could be accepted. Again, the final decision went to a supervisor who would not be trying the case.

Furthermore, 75 percent of defense attorneys bitterly expressed resentment towards the Prosecutor's Office in general. They could not understand why the institution was so unwilling to devote resources to increase the efficiency of both defense and prosecutorial tasks in the pursuit for justice. They felt that too much time was wasted on continuances because the EPU prosecutor was overwhelmed with cases that needed further investigation. The defense attorneys in this study were continually under pressure to avoid delays not only for themselves, but also for their clients in pretrial detention. While the EPU prosecutor certainly wanted to process cases, she was not facing a trial calendar pressure point like defense counsel. In that sense, for non-"no brainer" cases, the defense attorneys felt that there was always an unequal balance of power at the EPU that could not be overcome without bypassing it, which came with risks.

At the end of the study, one defense attorney was so frustrated by this situation that he was conducting an experiment of his own. He was immediately setting all of his cases for trial to see if he could obtain better outcomes faster than in the EPU alone or in an EPU/Trial Team combination because of his confidence in manipulating the rules to his advantage.

Discussion

This article has examined the internal machinations of a highly rationalized model of plea bargaining from the legal actors' perspectives. It has sought to answer three questions under this so-called reform model: (1) Do the behaviors, norms, and language of the attorneys differ from the more traditional models studied? (2) Does this institutionally separate model of case processing lead to the balance of power sought by Bibas (2004c) and Uviller (2000)? (3) If not, what adaptations, if any, are made by defense counsel to achieve some balance of power?

On one level, this model demonstrates an efficient and cooperative model of plea bargaining for those cases that fit Sudnow's (1965) "normal crimes" definition. While the structural organization and resource allocation of the EPU led to tension, the legal actors were able to come to an agreed upon plea in over 70 percent of the cases that were processed through the EPU. Essentially, both defenders and prosecutors engage in routinization to efficiently process these cases. While cooperation abounds in the "no brainer" cases, the adversarial nature of the trial emerges in the EPU when cases don't fit this model.

Norms, Language, and Behavior

The attorneys sort cases in the same way, relying on shared understandings of "normal crimes" and "going rates." While the name of the "normal" crimes has changed to "no-brainers," these attorneys work under a largely congenial work-group setting, where a shared history appears to assist in the bargaining process. The bargaining sequence and content is remarkably similar to Maynard's (1984) descriptions. The attorneys engage in the same proposal and position report, with strategic uses of utterances and silences to delay responses. They use implicit bargaining for "no brainer" cases and explicit bargaining for more complex cases. The attorneys also engaged in information control. They discuss mostly offender scores and sentencing more so than charging, but strategically mention character to add value to their cases when possible to do so. Finally, as Emmelman (1996) and others before her noted, case pressure does not appear to be a key motivator for defense attorneys in negotiating their pleas.

Balance of Power

While the norms, behavior, and discourse can appear to be significantly analogous, some key distinctions do emerge in this new setting and serve to decrease the balance of power in the prosecutor's favor. The EPU model appears to follow Bibas' (2004c) and Uviller's (2000) recommendations: separate charging, negotiating and trial units with differing levels of advocacy and investment in the case; high level prosecutorial review of charges and pleas; charges conservatively filed and readily provable, with less charge bargaining; and all plea offers written down. However, this structural model does not create the general power balance Bibas (2004c) supports. Moreover, despite this structural organization, the EPU does not follow the ideological frame-work of neutrality as advocated by Uviller (2000). It engages in institutional retali-ation through its threat of trial penalties, its no trial team negotiation if the EPU is bypassed rule, and its no better offer than the EPU offer rule.

For the majority of cases, defined as no-brainer cases that can be easily aligned, this model seems to be highly effective, according to prosecutors and defense attorneys alike. For the remaining 30 percent of more complex cases, this model can be trou-bling. It appears to create even less efficiency, more strain, and less power for defense attorneys for a number of reasons.

First, the institutional rules around trial penalties and limited negotiation opportu-nities with the trial team are quite different from traditional models, and thus, signifi-cantly impact prosecutorial power. The attorneys' behavior in this study more closely mirrored the attorneys' motivations in Feeley's (1979) work. The attorneys in this study felt compelled to plea bargain cases not because of resource conservation, but because of the threat of a trial penalty.

Second, while delay was a significant tactic employed by defense attorneys in earlier studies, it seemed to benefit the EPU in this study. The organizational structure and limited EPU resources in this study, however, meant that defense attorneys could not use delay as effectively. Because the EPU attorney was not taking the case to trial, she was not as concerned about a case going stale. Furthermore, the EPU prosecutor knew that even if the case did go to trial and get stale, the trial prosecutor was under significant pressure to offer no better deal than what she had offered.

The defense attorneys are put in a less powerful position when they have to consider the EPU prosecutor's case pressure against their client's pretrial detention. Defense counsel worried about the ability to properly examine the legal issues in the case at EPU, frustration from the EPU prosecutor if she felt the continuances and investigation were unwarranted, and then further delays if they felt the case needed to be set for trial.

Third, differences in negotiation content also restrict defense counsel's bargaining power. Instead, more conversations were around sentencing or offender scores, which directly impact the sentencing range, rather than charges. In addition, character seemed to be used much more sparingly in this setting than in prior studies, where it was a key negotiating tactic. Under this organization structure, defense counsel experienced significant pressure to delay any character discussion until the sentencing hearing. However, defense attorneys often felt that arguing character at the sentencing hearing was futile because the judges deferred overwhelmingly to the prosecutors' recommendations. They asserted that the judge's deference to the prosecutors' recommendations meant that prosecutors held too much power in the system. Unlike in Mather's (1979) work prosecutors in this study were not passive about sentencing.

Finally, an exchange relationship is essential to any negotiation. Both parties must feel that they are gaining from the bargain. However, in the EPU structural model, it did not feel like an exchange was taking place. The defense attorneys could negotiate with only one EPU attorney who may have been too dispassionate in that she had little at stake if the deal fell through. Either way, the case would leave her desk without her taking it to trial. The defense attorneys had more at stake and more to gain from the deal. Defense attorneys exhibited an undercurrent of distrust towards the EPU prosecutor. When the prosecutor offered a deal lower than expected, the defense attorneys were just as likely to take the case to the trial team as when the deal offered was too high. They suspected that the prosecutor had reduced the case value because it was a weak case. Again, the perceived uneven investment in the case actually increased the adversarial tone at the EPU. The defense attorneys did not trust that the EPU prosecutor could be acting in a reasonable manner for non "no brainer" cases. Thus, by taking the case to the trial team, the defense attorneys were decreasing efficiency and increasing risks for their client.

Under the EPU model, the rules and penalties on plea bargaining attempted to remove the human element to increase predictability, efficiency, and fairness. Instead, they appeared to alienate the prosecutor and disempower the defense community. However, as will be seen in the next section, defense counsel used relationships and personalities to subvert these rules and achieve some modicum of justice.

Adaptations

Despite the frustrations articulated about EPU, and in fact, most attorneys lamented not being able to go straight to trial counsel in the non- "no brainer" cases, the defense attorneys knew that the rules could be breached. Meaning, some defense attorneys could equalize the power in the bargain. Specifically, the use of supervisors cut both ways for the attorneys. On the one hand, the supervisor may have appeared too dispassionate, even a hindrance, in disallowing the subordinate trial prosecutor's offer, while experienced defense attorneys used supervisors to their advantage. If they had a trial history with the supervisor, they could often get a better deal than what the less experienced trial prosecutor was offering them. Relationships, personality, and reputation were seen as key to their success in this maneuver.

The defense attorneys were also quite adept at acquiring bargaining power by sidestepping the EPU entirely. They were confident that in certain more serious, complex cases, the closer one got to trial, evidence and loss of witnesses could be turned to their advantage. In fact, defense counsel and prosecutors both agreed that they gave better "going rates" the closer the case came to trial in spite of rules to the contrary. In addition, defense counsel used trial prosecutors' case pressure to their benefit in exacting deals that weren't available at EPU or supposed to be available from the trial team. Ultimately, defense counsel also found highly effective ways to call the prosecutor office's bluff. However, much of this power was achieved because of the trial experience, history and relationships that existed between defense counsel and trial prosecutors.

Conclusion

Despite the presence of structural changes advocated for by Bibas (2004c), the neutrality Uviller (2000) suggests did not materialize in this reformed model of plea bargaining. Under the current organization of "reformed" plea bargaining in this study, efficiency was achieved at the EPU in 70 percent of the cases, but it's unclear whether justice was. The structure, resources, and rules lent considerable more power to the prosecutors than under the traditional model. While the attorneys in this study behaved remarkably similar to the attorneys in traditional models when it came to processing "normal crimes," this imbalance in power led to tension and distrust in resolving more complex cases.

The defense attorneys were under significant pressure to screen cases in the midst of negotiating and minimizing continuances, particularly for clients in pretrial detention. In some cases, this may have caused them to treat certain cases as "no brainer" cases that might have deserved further legal attention. Under these circumstances, the defense attorneys tended towards substantive justice over formal justice. In addition, working under the threat of the trial penalty, no trial team negotiation rules, and further time delays, defense counsel experienced significant pressure to accept the EPU plea offers. This study suggests recommendations are not enough, more should be done.

First, more resources, should be allocated to Early Plea Units so that both prosecutor and defense counsel can carefully examine the case for triable issues without the burden of excessive time delays.

Second, neutrality is more likely to emerge if both parties have the same level of dispassion around the case. Defense counsel should be assigned to EPU cases in a similar model to the prosecutor's office. Certain defense counsel should work only on EPU cases. When both dispassionate parties agree that the case has a triable issue that can't be pled out, then the case should be assigned to a new trial team, including a new trial defense counsel and a new trial prosecutor.

Third, the trial penalty should be removed. While there may be a sentence discount to provide an incentive in taking a plea, the state should act in good faith and charge only what it intends to prove at trial and remain consistent with that charge. If a triable issue emerges, defendants should not be punished for asserting their Constitutional rights to trial.

The rules prohibiting plea bargaining between trial counsel should be eliminated. As has been shown, these rules can be subverted if a case starts to fall apart for either party. Furthermore, defense counsel will not bypass the EPU, nor have the incentive to do so, if they have confidence that counsel on both sides is dispassionately and efficiently reviewing the case.

Finally, the judges should take an active role in reviewing the sentence. If character is not an appropriate subject for the plea bargain, it is appropriate at the sentencing hearing. Judges should take careful note of the recommendation, but also review the presentence report and the evidence presented at the hearing to ensure the defendant is receiving a fair sentence given all aspects of the case. At this stage in this process, the judge is in the best position to ensure a balance of power in the disposition of the case.

At a minimum, the prosecutor's office should examine its screening procedures for the 30 percent of cases that do not get resolved in the EPU. Perhaps those types of cases should be immediately assigned to the trial team, where a more traditional model can be followed. As it stands now, this study suggests that we have not yet found a reform model of plea bargaining that addresses the concerns of legal scholars, social scientists, or practitioners.

Critical Thinking

The issues of case disposition and the court's demands for efficiency directly influence a defendant's actual sentence. Fairness needs to be taken into consideration when analyzing plea negotiations as we have learned from Bowen's study. The balance of power lies with the prosecutor in the vast majority of criminal cases, which places defense attorneys at a real disadvantage in representing their clients' best interests. How does the uneven balance of power favoring prosecutors result in a defendant's opportunity to attain a just plea negotiation? What changes to the system do you think would lead to a more equal balance of power?

References

Barkow, R.E. (2006). Separation of powers and the criminal law. *Stanford Law Review*, *58*, 989.

Bibas, S. (2004a). The Feeney amendment and the continuing rise of prosecutorial power to plea bargain. *Journal of Criminal Law & Criminology*, *94*, 295–309.

Bibas, S. (2004b). Plea's progress. *Michigan Law Review, 6,* 1024.

Bibas, S. (2004c). Plea bargaining outside the shadow of trial. *Harvard Law Review, 117,* 2463.

Eisenstein, J., & Jacob, J. (1976). *Felony justice: an organizational analysis of criminal courts.* Boston: Little Brown.

Emmelman, D. (1996). Trial by plea bargain: case settlement as a product of recursive decisionmaking. *Law and Society Review, 30,* 335–360.

Feeley, M. (1979). Perspectives on plea bargaining. *Law and Society Review, 13,* 199–249.

Heumann, M. (1978). *Plea bargaining: the experience of prosecutors, judges, and defense attorneys.* Chicago: University of Chicago Press.

Lee, S-H. (2005). The scales of justice: balancing neutrality and efficiency in plea-bargaining encounters. *Discourse & Society, 16,* 33–44.

Ma, Y. (2002). Prosecutorial discretion and plea bargaining in the United States, France, Germany, and Italy: A comparative perspective. *International Criminal Justice Review, 12,* 22–52.

Mather, L. (1979). *Plea bargaining or trial? The process of criminal case disposition.* Lexington, MA: Lexington Books.

Maynard, D. (1984). *Inside plea bargaining: the language of negotiation.* New York: Plenum Press.

Ritzer, G. (1993). *The McDonaldization of society.* Newbury Park, CA. Pine Forge.

Stunts, W. J. (2004). Plea bargaining and criminal law's disappearing shadow. *Harvard Law Review, 117,* 2548.

Sudnow, D. (1965). Normal crimes: sociological features of the penal code in the public defender's office. *Social Problems, 12,* 255–276.

Utz, P. (1978). *Settling the facts.* Lexington, MA: Lexington Books

Uviller, R. (2000). The neutral prosecutor: the obligation of dispassion in a passion pursuit. *Fordham Law Review, 68,* 1695.

Wright, R., & Miller, M. (2002). The screening/bargaining tradeoff. *Stanford Law Review, 55,* 29.

Case Cited

Bordenkircher v. Hayes 434 US 357 (1978).

12

The Social Construction of "Sophisticated" Adolescents: How Judges Integrate Juvenile and Criminal Justice Decision-Making Models

Alexes Harris

<u>Abstract</u>: *Alexes Harris examines the decision-making process of judges when determining the disposition of youth who appear in juvenile courts. Her research focuses on how judges selectively use parts of a juvenile's case histories to formulate justifications for the decision to keep a kid in the juvenile justice system or to transfer the case to adult criminal court for adjudication. By analyzing the juvenile court's waiver hearings, Harris develops several decision-making models that explain processing decisions that are made for juveniles.*

People-processing institutions shape individuals' lives by sorting them and conferring a public status (Hasenfeld 1972). Officials employed at institutions such as hospitals, welfare agencies, and university admissions offices are challenged with sets of cases they must assess, categorize, and label for further processing. Similarly, juvenile courts can be analyzed as people-processing institutions because they sort individuals into categories to determine appropriate treatment and sentencing options (Hasenfeld and Cheung 1985). These sorting decisions result in different outcomes and fates for young people, fundamentally changing their legal status.

An interesting example of these institutional sorting processes is the juvenile court waiver hearing. Increasingly sociological and criminological research has investigated the judicial waiver process: the juvenile court practice of transferring young people from the juvenile justice system to the criminal justice system for prosecution and punishment (Fagan and Zimring 2000; Feld 1987). This processing point, which is performed by a juvenile court judge, determines whether youth will be labeled as minors, who will be adjudicated and sentenced in the juvenile justice system, or as adults, who will be adjudicated and sentenced in the (adult) criminal justice system. The legal aim of the hearing is to identify "chronic" and "serious" offenders who are a threat to society and viewed as no longer rehabilitatable. During the waiver hearing juvenile court judges' assessments are guided by formalized legal criteria that emphasize accountability and give primacy to offense characteristics.

The traditional decision-making model commonly associated with the juvenile justice system is one that emphasizes individualized assessments and the rehabilitation of young people (Feld 1999; Sutton 1998). The waiver hearing could be viewed as antithetical to the traditional juvenile justice model, in that the goals of the hearing are to assess and identify youth who are no longer amenable to the care and treatment of the juvenile court services (CA WIC 707). In 1966 the United States Supreme Court formalized the judicial waiver process by establishing a set of legal criteria to guide the waiver hearing (*Kent v the United States*). These criteria focus on an array of social and legal factors including; the seriousness, nature, and extent of the offense, the "sophistication" and maturity of the youth, the record and previous history of the youth, the prospects of the protection of the public, and the reasonable rehabilitation of the youth. While these criteria leave room for individualized assessments of youth, they could possibly change the nature of juvenile justice decision-making by refocusing the emphasis of evaluation away from the offender to the offense.

The aim of the present study is to investigate how people-processing decisions are made within an institutional setting. I investigate how decision makers engage in practical reasoning by exploring the methods they use to organize information about youth and accomplish their judicial duties (Garfinkel 1967, 2002; Garfinkel and Sacks 1970). An analysis of judicial waiver hearing proceedings is used as an example of institutional processing and will build on previous theoretical explanations for how decisions are made in justice settings. Two research questions are investigated. First, what ideological perspectives about youth and delinquency are judges using to guide their assessments and processing of these adolescents? Second, does the decision-making process used in the judicial waiver hearing suggest a change in the way that juvenile justice is being performed today? The study uses observational and interview data from a case study of three juvenile courthouses in a California county to investigate official case processing and illustrates the type of frameworks and types of information judges use to construct their assessments of youth during judicial waiver hearings.

This analysis contributes to current sociological and criminological research on institutional processing in general and judicial waiver hearings in particular for two reasons. First, I investigate how judges use legal criteria to create characterizations of young people to determine whether to label them as amenable ("fit" for the juvenile court) or unamenable ("unfit" for the juvenile court) to the juvenile justice system. Second, with an understanding of the approaches judges use to arrive at their legal assessments and characterizations of youth, I show how judges negotiate between the ideal-typical models of juvenile and criminal justice frameworks to arrive at a seemingly logical and individualized assessment while prioritizing offense details over youths' rehabilitative potential. Overall this study identifies how justice is performed for a segment of young people in the juvenile justice system by uncovering the effects that increasingly punitive juvenile justice statutes have on judicial processing decisions within the juvenile justice system. The findings help juvenile as well as criminal justice researchers, practitioners, and law makers conceptualize the changing nature of juvenile justice processing by illustrating the factors and mechanisms used by decision makers to assess and label young people.

Literature Review

Juvenile Waiver

Over the past fifteen years, states have been revamping juvenile statutes to broaden criteria making young people eligible for prosecution in the criminal justice system

(Torbet et al. 1996). There are three types of statutes that guide the waiver process: judicial waiver (where a juvenile court judge determines which you are appropriate for transfer), prosecutorial waiver (where juvenile prosecutors and criminal prosecutors determine which jurisdiction should prosecute youth), and automatic/exclusionary waiver (where certain youth are "automatically" excluded from juvenile court as a result of the type of offenses charged by prosecutors, and age criteria).

A key question then is how are these youth being assessed and labeled by juvenile bench officers? More specifically, how are youths' offenses characterized and understood by court officials? How do court officials evaluate youths' potential for future success, and how much does this rehabilitative promise matter in judicial assessments? Except for a few important studies on the waiver process (Podkopacz and Feld 1995; Singer 1995) we know little about how court officials make their assessments of the social and legal factors during waiver hearings. And thus we know little about how the labels of "serious" and "chronic" offenders are applied.

Juvenile Justice Decision-Making

Previous ethnographic research in the juvenile justice system illustrates this traditional framework and has found that when processing cases court officials explore, interpret, and assess social, legal, and organizational aspects about youth and offenses to arrive at characterizations (Bortner 1986). These characterizations of youth are then used by court officials to logically justify one of several available treatment (punishment) options (Emerson 1969). Both Emerson (1969) and Cicourel (1968) provide substantive insights about how social control decisions are constructed, and the processes by which decisions are made.

For example, Cicourel's discussion of the process by which officials create case histories is a useful concept to understand how decision makers approach cases (1968, 328–9). Cicourel suggests that social control agents (police, probation officers, prosecutors, judges) construct young peoples' legal histories using background expectancies as a framework to understand information (legal "facts," young peoples' actions and statements). These legal histories are used to inform subsequent social control decisions. Key to this process are decision makers' working theories about "how background expectancies render everyday activities recognizable and intelligible" (Cicourel 1968, 329). That is, how social control agents understand social structure and the context of the institution in which they are working matters for how cases are processed. This understanding allows decision makers to make sense of their social world and construct coherent stories about cases and subsequent processing decisions.

Cicourel illustrates that when creating these case histories court officials rely on their background experiences and use previously constructed frameworks to organize the information about offenders into socially and legally relevant categories:

> The officer's tacit knowledge combines with information he has received, and his own observations of the action scene, to provide him with a preliminary mapping, but he invariably asks fairly standardized questions about "what happened" and who were the principal actors involved.
>
> (Cicourel 1968, 113)

Cicourel found that frequently probation officers focus on details of the offense in attempt to construct a story to determine the next course of action. Along similar lines, Emerson finds that to construct legal histories processing agents commonly focus on building their evaluations around not "what happened" but rather, "what is the *problem* here?" (Emerson 1969, 87). Emerson finds that decision makers focus on the *problem* to label the behavior and character of the young person. That characterization of the youth is then used to reinterpret the details of the offense and shapes staff's decisions.

In making distinctions among the categories of delinquents, similarly to Cicourel, Emerson finds court officers rely on notions of youths' moral character to guide processing decisions. Initially decision makers make a distinction between troubled and untroubled cases; this categorization helps officials determine whether cases need "special handling" or could be "let go" (Emerson 1969, 90). The assessment of moral character is used by decision makers to determine a second stage of processing, the determination of the *kind* of handling that is required. If youth are labeled as not having trouble than they are assumed to have normal character. If a case is flagged as one involving trouble, youth are described as "hard-core" or "criminal-like" delinquents who are "maliciously or hostilely motivated" (p. 91). A third category of delinquents are labeled as "disturbed" when court officials describe the problem as senseless or irrational. According to previous ethnographies, juvenile justice decision making has relied on substantive rational practices to determine which "type" of youth is before the court and consequently assigns the most "appropriate" disposition. This work suggests that assessments during judicial waiver processes will focus on the social characteristics of the youth.

The above literature review has outlined two decision-making models; one from the criminal justice system and one from juvenile justice system. The following analysis will investigate the extent to which these frameworks are applicable to judicial waiver processing decisions. Focal concerns theory predicts that judges will focus on the culpability and dangerousness of the offender, the seriousness of the offense, and the implications of decisions. Research theorizing juvenile justice decision-making practices outlines the process by which decision makers come to arrive at their characterizations of youth: moving from constructing legal histories about youth, to evaluations of "what happened" during the present offense, to finally arriving at a label of "typical" or "trouble." Driving these juvenile justice assessments is the notion of rehabilitation. These conceptual frameworks will be used to investigate how processing decisions are made and presented in juvenile waiver hearings—is the decision-making process during judicial waiver consistent with either of the models?

Method and Sample Characteristics

The present study is based on observations, interviews, and relevant court documents in three juvenile courthouses in Hughes County, California. To provide a demographic context, the total population of this county was 3.7 million in the year 2000 with 46.9 percent being White, 11.2 percent African American, and 10 percent Asian American. In addition, the Latino population (of any race) in this county was 46.5 percent.

The field research was conducted between January 2000 and lasted through September 2001.

Three field sites were selected primarily based on access to informants and information as well as the geographic location of the courthouse within the county. The primary field site, "Hughes Juvenile Justice Center" (HJJC), stands in the middle of an impoverished minority community, historically African American, but because of rapid demographic shifts has become increasingly Latino. The two commissioners at this courthouse are African American males in their sixties. The second field site, "Garfield Juvenile Hall" (GJH), was selected because it is the "Flagship" operations—as one prosecutor describes the courthouse—it is the central juvenile hall for the county. The majority of the fitness hearings within the county are held here. This courthouse is located in a predominantly Latino community where many immigrants and poor families live.

I observed twenty-nine waiver hearings at these three courthouses. The charges for these crimes ranged from molestation, armed robbery, assault, attempted murder, and murder. All of the youth I observed during these fitness hearings, except four, were waived to adult court. The youth were of color, primarily Latino and African American. They ranged from fourteen to twenty-one years of age. Only two of the youth observed during the waiver hearings were female. During the observations, I recorded field notes of attorneys' presentations of youths' cases, judges' concluding remarks, and final decisions, as well as informal comments made before, during, and after the hearings.

I conducted forty-one formal interviews with judges (sixteen), prosecutors (fifteen), probation officers (three), defense attorneys (six), and a social worker (one). The interviews lasted between forty-five to ninety minutes. The selection of the interviewees was purposive and also occurred through snowballing. All but one person contacted and asked to be interviewed agreed to participate—one prosecutor refused. The interviews consisted of a set of open-ended questions that were designed to begin a dialogue about court officials' roles during the fitness process. For example, I asked, "What is your position in the courtroom? What are your responsibilities and daily duties? What kinds of things do you consider when making an assessment about a youth before the court?" I made an effort to elicit how the court officials assess the legal criteria for transfer through discussion of past and recent cases. I attempted to read any documents that pertained to the waiver hearings of the youth observed including probation reports, prior records, psychiatric evaluations, and police reports of the alleged incidents.

California Judicial Waiver Hearing

The Fitness Hearing

Over the past ten years, states have been revamping juvenile statutes to broaden criteria making young people eligible for prosecution in the criminal justice system (Torbet et al. 1996). California's juvenile court judicial waiver system will be used as an example of a setting where court actors process cases based on legal criteria and present arguments to justify their decisions. The developing criminalization policies in California are representative of changes occurring nationwide in juvenile justice policy (Torbet et al. 1996). Such criminalization policies include blended sentencing, extended jurisdiction, "strike-able" offenses, lack of confidentiality during healings and in reporting of sustained charges, and expanding waiver eligibility to younger offenders and less serious offenses. The waiver process is a further example of juvenile legislation that criminalizes youthful offenders treating them more as traditional adults than children under the law.

More specifically, under California's judicial waiver process, juvenile prosecutors have the option to petition for waiver hearings if they believe the youth "is not a 'fit' and proper subject to be dealt with under the juvenile court law" (CA WIC 707 b). During the hearing, judges determine whether youth are either "fit" to remain in the juvenile justice system, or are "unfit" to the juvenile system, and will be transferred to the criminal system for adult prosecution. When Deputy District Attorneys (DDAs) file juvenile court charges against youth that include acts labeled as violent felony offenses, they have the discretion to also file an accompanying petition for a waiver hearing. Once a DDA files a waiver petition the fitness hearing is held.

Legal Criteria

During this amenability hearing court officials evaluate offenses according to five legal criteria. The legal term of amenability "refers to the likelihood of an individual desisting from crime and/or being rehabilitated when treated with some sort of intervention" (Steinberg and Cauffman 2000, 399). In the context of waiver hearings, judges determine whether youth are amenable to treatment, and if they are found not to be, then the youth will be transferred to the criminal court system. The legal criteria are number: (1) the degree of criminal sophistication; (2) whether the youth can be rehabilitated prior to the expiration of the juvenile courts' jurisdiction (twenty-five years of age); (3) previous delinquent history; (4) success of previous attempts by the juvenile court to rehabilitate the youth; and (5) the circumstances and gravity of the offense (see the appendix). In practice these criteria were measured by (1) the apparent amount of planning used to commit the offense, a youth's level of participation in the offense, any evident remorse; (2) the youth's assessed level of maturity as an individual and as a criminal; (3) any formal and informal petitions brought against the youth, and also any sort of contact he/she had with the juvenile justice system; (4) the youth's previous delinquent history after contact had been made with the juvenile system and performance while on probation; (5) the type of offense and circumstances alleged and the context within which it was committed.

At the beginning of waiver hearings judges "read in" to the record information from past minute orders, previous probation reports regarding youths' behavior while under court supervision, psychiatric recommendations and the district attorney's complaint. Defense attorneys present arguments pertaining to the five criteria explaining why youth are "fit" to remain in the juvenile system. Prosecutors offer counterarguments as to why the youth are "unfit" to remain in the juvenile system. Both sides have the opportunity to rebut the others' arguments before the judge makes the final decision of fitness. Legally, judges must state the reasoning for their findings on each of the five criteria.

Findings

Focal Concerns during Judicial Waiver

The key focus of judicial attention during waiver hearings was on the legal criterion of "sophistication." Factors used by judges to create assessments of "sophistication" were partially consistent with focal concerns theory; judges relied on perceptions of youths' culpability and dangerousness, as well as the severity of the offense to inform processing decisions. However, inconsistent with the third focal concern, judges were not overly concerned with either practical limitations or with the future implications of their decisions (in terms of what would happen to the youth). The following subsection illustrates judges' focal concerns during judicial waiver hearings. These concerns include; the "sophistication" of the youth and the offense, the circumstances of the offense, and the "lifestyle" of the youth.

Sophistication

During waiver hearings bench officers, prosecuting attorneys, and defense attorneys primarily focused on criterion number one, the degree of criminal "sophistication." Assessments of the "sophistication" criterion involved evaluations of youths' level of participation in offenses, their amount of planning, remorse, intent, and assessments of their social characteristics (school performance, family, and social lifestyle). Practically bench officers defined "sophistication" in terms of youths' motives for committing offenses. The "sophistication" of the offense and the youth were assessed at the same time. For example, in the following waiver hearing the judge found three Latino male youth aged fourteen, sixteen, and seventeen years, as "unfit" to remain in the juvenile court because of their perceived level of "sophistication" and the "sophistication" of the offense. The three cousins were charged with the murder and conspiracy to commit murder of the mother of the sixteen-year-old and the aunt of the fourteen- and fifteen-year-olds. Granted this is an extreme case involving a violent murder. The point is to demonstrate how judges focused and assessed the legal criterion of "sophistication" when little or no prior delinquency existed. All three of the youth had minimal previous contact with the juvenile justice system. The prosecuting attorney argued that the murder was planned in order for the youth to obtain money to purchase materials to replicate scenes from a popular teen murder movie. The judge concluded:

> Therefore, I find that each minor, because of their involvement in the planning and strategic organization involving the surrounding of the circumstances, and how they were going to equate the circumstances of the movie to the actual carrying out of the homicide, makes all three of them not amenable to juvenile court under criteria [sic] one and I find each of them unfit.

During the summation of the waiver hearing, this judge concluded the youths' planning prior to the offense indicated a high level of criminal "sophistication." As others have found, when a crime appeals to be planned or is accompanied by the use of professional or sophisticated techniques, judges will often view such circumstances as indicators of youths' "exposure to criminal ways of doing things and criminal purposes" (Emerson 1969, 116). This information is used as evidence of "sophistication" and when coupled with the gravity of the offense, was used by the judge to overshadow the youths' lack of previous delinquent involvement, and also served to indicate their lack of amenability to the court.

To contrast this example with a less extreme case, the following fitness hearing illustrates how two youth charged with armed robbery, which resulted in no injury to the victim, was assessed. Both youth were sixteen years of age and Asian American; one was male and one was female. The judge relied on evidence indicating the offense was planned, that the youth had obtained tools to hide their identity, and the youth had associated with an adult criminal street gang member to arrive at his decision:

> I've analyzed each case [minor] individually, but I have come to the same conclusion, each is unfit [for the juvenile court] at 16 years old. With [criterion] number one [sophistication], some points in time these three people sat down and planned this crime. Both were active participants. They planned it with each other and a member of a notorious Asian gang. Gloves were used. AH of this goes to the criminal sophistication. A weapon was used—not by these individuals—but at this robbery [by the adult defendant]. It is not the type of callous sophisticated crime that we would see with other minors [who are unfit], but it is sophisticated.

In this example the judge acknowledged differing levels of seriousness in the notion of "sophistication." He stated that while these youth may not be as callous as some other youth, the case still can be labeled as sophisticated. The judge inferred information from the way the offense appeared to be conducted to assess the type of youth and level of "sophistication" and used this "legal" information to justify why the youth should not be processed in the juvenile justice system.

The Circumstances of the Offense

Clearly related to the criterion of "sophistication" is criterion five, the circumstances and gravity of the offense. At times judges would explore the context of the offense in attempts to shape an understanding about individuals' motives, thus shaping images about the level of "sophistication." In the following example, details of the offense were actually shaped by the judge to create a positive image of the individual. In this case a judge determined that Erin, a seventeen-year-old Latino male, was "fit" to remain in juvenile court. Erin was charged with assault with a deadly weapon: the police report stated that Erin was spray painting on the side of a building when a resident holding a beer can came out and challenged him to stop. In response, Erin asked the man for the beer. When the man denied his request and began moving toward Erin, Erin threw the paint can and hit the man on his forehead. The judge concluded:

> I find the minor fit [for the juvenile court] under [the] criteria as indicated by criminal sophistication. It would appear that this is a crime of opportunity, the crime was committed on

impulse … [continues to explain why he finds Erin fit on criteria 2–4] … [In terms of the] circumstances and gravity, clearly, this is an unprovoked attempt, it could have caused significant harm. This instance the court has to decide was the minor in a position to willfully and wantonly to perform this crime … the minor who by his admission had been sniffing paint was high and appeared so, and demanded beer. When that was declined, the minor reacted violently and the minor hit the victim in the eye. Clearly, the gravity of the offense is a serious offense. The circumstances when viewed in totality, I find the minor has borne the burden [presumption of unfitness]; he is fit to be dealt with by the juvenile court law.

The judge claimed that Erin was not criminally sophisticated because it did not appear to the judge that Erin had planned to assault the victim. To support this judgment, the bench officer used information about Erin's state of mind to inform his evaluation of criterion five. The judge relied on evidence that Erin was high on paint fumes at the time of the offense as an indication of the presence of mitigating factors— suggesting that Erin was unable to form intent to hurt the individual. Because he was intoxicated, Erin was assessed as not "willfully or wantonly" able to carryout this offense. Furthermore, the judge labeled Erin's previous delinquent history as one that was successful; he had gone through a probationary run camp program and was released, apparently indicating that he had no further behavioral problems. The judge could have just as easily assessed the evidence that Erin had been high on paint fumes as aggravating the gravity of the offense. Similarly, his prior record could have been seen as escalating in severity; processed as evidence indicating his lack of control and regard for his probation. However, information about the offense—particularly the weapon usage—coupled with offender information was used by the judge to construct a positive assessment, or at least one where criminal culpability and "sophistication" were lacking.

Lifestyle

In addition to investigating the apparent circumstances and motives for youth having committed offenses, bench officers also relied on information about youths' lifestyles to construct arguments about amenability. Indicators used to create assessments about youths' lifestyles included school involvement and performance, family interactions, and gang membership. In an exploration of these lifestyle dimensions, bench officers established images that led to judgments of the quality of the youth before the court; essentially asking, is this a "good" or "bad" kid? During an interview a judge told me he begins evaluating cases by asking himself the following questions:

I look to see if the minor is himself sophisticated. Is he emancipated, living on his own. Does he have his own address? Is he on his own with his own source of shadow income? Is he under the supervision of an adult, or just living in their house?

As illustrated in this excerpt, bench officers would often treat the absence of adult guardianship as negative qualities of adolescents. Youth who were living on their own, taking care of their own finances and not attending school were viewed by judges as qualitatively different from youth living with their parents. In a discussion with a judge following a fitness hearing for a youth who was charged with arson and murder, the judge justified how she came to the conclusion that the youth was sophisticated.

> He went out to the adult world, he worked, he didn't go to school. He has been acting in our emancipated way. [To me] You are an adult right? [Yes.] And, you have to pay rent? [Yes.] And you have to do your laundry and things like that? People will hold you responsible.

The youth this judge was referring to was an immigrant and was working to help financially support his mother and younger brother. He and his brother had been playing with matches near an abandoned mattress in their apartment building. When the mattress accidentally caught on fire the older brother told his younger brother to run and tell their mother that the building was on fire while the older brother ran throughout the building to warn people. A woman died as a result from being trapped in the burning building. This judge chose to focus her assessment on evidence that the youth was working to support his family as evidence that he was criminally sophisticated—"unfit" for the juvenile justice system.

Even when youth appear to be successfully managing their lives with or without adult supervision, judges inferred a tainted image of their lives. Judges concluded that because adolescents were employed and paying rent, they were living in "adult worlds." Youth who lived on their own, for whatever reasons, were characterized by the court as no longer having childlike dispositions, and therefore are no longer deserving of treatment by the juvenile court.

Another important lifestyle aspect that bench officers weighed heavily was the extent of youths' gang involvement. Individuals who were identified as gang members were viewed by most judges as street wise, criminal-like, and inherently of bad moral character. A basic assumption many court officials held about street gangs is that they were crime-involved and a violent threat to society. Cases that involved youth labeled as gang members were viewed as quick and simple assessments of criminal-like behavior. During an interview, the following judge candidly described an effortless waiver hearing decision.

> There was a bar-b-que that some gang bangers weren't invited to but they crashed it. They were told to get out. They came back with a gun and shot two or three people. They already had an assault. That was a slam-dunk. Very easy.

Based on the label of "gang," judges quickly made determinations of youths' characters. Thus, fitness hearings involving youth labeled as gang members were discussed by judges as being relatively "easy" or "slam-dunks." In fact, many of the public defenders interviewed stated that defending youth who were associated with gangs was almost useless: "anytime you have something cloaked in anything that looks like gang, you can forget about" trying to defend the client.

It is important to note that while the primary focus of judges during waiver hearings centered on the degree of criminal "sophistication" and the circumstances and gravity of the offense, bench officers did at times spend time discussing the other three criteria; whether the youth could be rehabilitated prior to the expiration of juvenile court jurisdiction (age twenty-five), the extent of the youth's previous delinquent history, and the success of previous attempts by the juvenile justice system to rehabilitate the youth. Many times these three criteria were irrelevant to youths' amenability evaluations because of a lack of prior contact with the juvenile justice system (thus no previous attempts to rehabilitate), and because their ages (all youth were under seventeen years of age which left a minimum of seven years for treatment within the juvenile justice system). The defense attorneys would often cite youths' lack of previous delinquent histories and either minimal or no contacts with juvenile court services as evidence of their potential for rehabilitation. Yet, I never observed a waiver hearing where a positive assessment of the middle three criteria—a youth was evaluated as having high rehabilitative potential—was used to outweigh, or mitigate, a negative assessment of criteria one ("sophistication") or five (circumstances and gravity).

This section illustrates how bench officers applied the five legal criteria outlined in the juvenile law to arrive at their assessments of youths' amenability during the judicial fitness hearings. Judges would primarily focus on criteria numbers one and five, the "sophistication" of the offense and the youth, and the circumstances and gravity of the offense. However, bench officers relied on a combination of information about youths' lives and offense circumstances to justify their findings of "sophistication" or lack of "sophistication." Assessments overtly prioritized issues of dangerousness, culpability, and harm done to the victim, over rehabilitation or perceptions of what might happen to the case if/when sent to the criminal justice system. The following section illustrates how bench officers merged traditional models of juvenile justice decision making—one focused on individualized rehabilitative-oriented evaluations, with a criminal justice decision-making model—one focused on the offense and punishment.

Constructing What Happened

Similarly to Cicourel (1968) and Emerson's (1969) descriptions of juvenile court officials, judges during waiver hearings relied on their perceptions of "the problem" or "what happened" to arrive at a fitness finding. Judges created a legal history, in a sense a story, about who the youth was, and the type of life he/she was living, to bolster either a "fit" or "unfit" finding. In the following analysis, constructions of youths' legal histories are highlighted during court officials' exploration of "what happened" during the offense, which is used subsequently to construct characterizations of normalcy or seriousness.

The "Typical" Delinquent Youth

Frequently during waiver hearings judges would construct images of ideal delinquents (ones who made bad decisions, but ultimately were viewed as "good" kids) with a discredited image of youth who were criminally sophisticated. Typical waiver-eligible cases were assessed as "fit" for the juvenile court, and troubled cases are labeled as "unfit" for the juvenile courts. The legal criteria making youth waiver-eligible, and the legal assumptions that presume such youth as unamenable, pre-assign all of these cases as trouble, however, judges relied on substantive offender and offense factors during their required assessments to sort through the youth, and to support and finalize their legal assessments.

Past research in the juvenile justice system has found a similar shorthand method that officials use to sort and process cases. Cicourel defines "normal" delinquency as actions typical to young people's behavior on a weekend at a party or school gathering where drinking, sexual activity, curfew violations, or fighting might occur; actions often times expected of adolescents. These actions, as translated into offenses, would include "petty theft, malicious mischief, joyriding, shooting in the city limits, battery" (Cicourel 1968, 119). Cicourel finds that probation officers are less concerned with the actions, but more with their regularity and frequency. "Serious" offenses are any type of offenses but are committed by young people labeled as "hard core" or "gangster" (p. 120). These characterizations are based on the family structure, youth demeanor, or official past record, and are used to indicate the need for serious dispositions, such as placement in the Youth Authority.

Within the courts observed crimes of the typical offenders would often times be described by judges as occurring by happenstance or on the spur of the moment. Bench officers often described youth who were found "fit" to remain in the juvenile court as participating in offenses that occurred by happenstance. This explanation would often be coupled with information describing the youth as having "good [family] backgrounds," having "so much going for them," and having "potential" for the future. Amenable youth were often labeled by court officers as not being too far gone from the rehabilitative arm of the juvenile court or the control of their parents. These types of youth were seen as "typical"—ones deserving of treatment within the juvenile justice system.

Unamenable or atypical offenders would be described as having planned their offenses: having outlined their tactics for achieving success (gaining access to money or jewelry and successfully evading detection). A youth's deliberation prior to engaging in illegal activity was viewed by judges as very different from the normal kid-like behavior seen in juvenile court. For example, judges often compared a youth snatching a bike from another kid at the park to a robbery with a handgun as a kid-like versus adult-like offense. Through the use of this typical-kid framework judges moved back and forth between information about the offense and the offender to construct images of either child-like youth—deserving of treatment in the juvenile justice system—or criminal-like youth—deserving of adult punishment.

Assigning Moral Character

The dialectic judges used to frame their analyses of typical and criminal offenders surrounded the notion of moral character. What is interesting about the waiver hearings is the focus of judicial assessments on the *type* of the youth before the court. Essentially, judges searched to construct the character of the youth. At all other points in judicial processes (juvenile and adult), while the character of the individual may be an underlying issue, the past and prior record and severity of the offense are taken into discussion and are the center of open court deliberation. However, during fitness hearings the offense is legally presumed to have occurred as illustrated by police and probation officers in their reports, and as a result, the character of the youth is at the forefront of discussion and analysis, not the determination of guilt.

In their concluding remarks at fitness hearings judges would present stories about youths' character and use these images as justifications for either "fit" or "unfit" decisions. While direct comments about "character" or "nature" of young people were not stated, implicitly in the summation of their evaluations of the legal criteria judges indicated the "type" of youth. For example, the following waiver hearing was for two Latino males, both sixteen years old, who were labeled as gang members and charged with attempted murder. During the delivery of her evaluation the judge concluded that both youth were "unfit" to the juvenile court because of their predatory behavior.

> The court [the judge] finds both minors 16 years of age or older; the minors are not amenable. Criteria [sic] number one [sophistication]: I find this a situation where two youth, Cherry Street Gang members, already under injunction of the Superior Court [informing them that their gang membership was illegal], went out looking for the rival gang member. They choose to go there. I am diminished as a person to speak these words that human beings would go out to a neighborhood to seek out other human beings. If the police weren't there, Miguel would have been dead. The neighbors were so scared they wouldn't have helped him. They attacked an innocent person. I don't care if he [the victim] is a gang member. They were willful acts. [A] car club [was used to] bludgeoned him almost to death. The fact that Miguel did not die does not matter [in terms of the gravity of the offense]. They are fit [on criteria] 2, 3, 4. Criteria [sic] number five: the circumstances and gravity are so severe that they do not belong in juvenile court.

Judicial analyses of the "sophistication" and gravity of the offense were commonly used to shape a story about offenders—who they are as members of society. In this case, the judge understood the youth as having purposefully chosen the location of the offense and victim. The judge characterized the youth as violent predators who "attacked" people during "willful acts." This information was used by the judge to construct a vision of criminally responsible offenders. The two youth in this fitness hearing had minimal involvement with the juvenile justice system prior to this offense, making them "fit" on criteria two, three, and four. Despite this finding, the judge meshed the concept of "sophistication"—the characterizations of who these youth were inherently—with notions about the circumstances and gravity of the offense to support a finding of unfitness to the juvenile court.

As the above example illustrates, during their assessments judges created an understanding about the case through a combination of information about the offender and the offense. The decision makers' emphasis on "sophistication" was a judgment about both the nature of the youth and how their related offense was understood and labeled. Young people were assessed in light of the offenses they were charged. Similarly, offense type and gravity were assessed in light of the type of youth viewed to be before the judge.

While judges often had initial reactions to offenses and used these reactions to create assessments of the youth, judges also at times had initial reactions about the nature of the youth, and then used this understanding to assess the offenses. The following example is a further illustration of how judicial assessments of youths' moral character were used to assess whether or not youth were typical or criminal. In the following example the judge described a case of an adolescent who was originally charged with murder. He and his friend had been jumping on a bed, horsing around, when the youth at one point picked up a loaded shotgun in the corner of the room and shot and killed his friend. The judge had found the youth "fit" to remain in juvenile court and in an interview described her impression of him as she conducted the adjudication of his case:

> It was a young boy, 17 years old, that killed his best friend at gunpoint range. He was a good student, church going . . . This was reckless and wanton, [but] not like driving down the street drunk and hitting someone inside a crosswalk. It wasn't like that. It was an accident. The problem [in finding him fit] was he was an intelligent young boy; he had fired the gun and knew that it was defective.

Despite characterizing the offense as "reckless and wanton," and indicating that she believed the youth knew and understood that he was playing with a volatile weapon (the judge said that the youth had been warned by his father not to play with the gun because it was loaded), the judge characterized the youth as lacking "sophistication" and was essentially amenable to the juvenile system. The dilemma for this judge was that in the face of a grave crime, she viewed the youth as intelligent; someone who should have known not to play with the gun. However, this judge decided to rely on information about the youth's positive behavior in school and community to characterize him as a "typical" youth who was amenable to the juvenile justice system; one who had made a horrible decision, but was reachable.

This judge used reports from family members and the probation officer to generate facts about the youth's life which in turn were used to create a case history about the youth, an understanding about the character and aptitude of the youth. This case history was then used by the judge as evidence that the youth was a typical kid who made a bad decision. This bench officer could have framed her decision in a dramatically different way had she chosen to do so. One could have argued that the youth knew the gun was loaded and because he picked it up and shot at his friend he meant to kill him. The gravity and circumstances of the offense—the death of a young man—could have easily been used to justify finding the youth "unfit" to remain in the juvenile system. This example demonstrates how subjective the characterizations of youths' amenability are and how case information is shaped to support a judge's characterization of youth.

Context Specific Typicality

As evident from the above examples, an important point to make is that the notion of a typical delinquent was not consistent across the courtrooms observed. The following remarks by a judge during a fitness hearing illustrates how the same type of offense and offender information that have been used in previous examples to justify an "unfit" finding are used by a different judge to support a decision to retain two youth in juvenile court. In the following example two friends, who were both African

American males and seventeen years old, had been living in a neighborhood with heavy gang activity. The youth, who had been labeled by probation and police officers as being gang members, were charged with attempted murder. They had been walking down the street and a car full of rival gang members slowed down and drove past them. One of the youth walking down the street yelled out his gang name and the other youth pulled out a gun and shot at the car. The judge concluded in the fitness hearing that the youth were amenable to remain in the juvenile system.

> [Criteria] number one, there is no criminal sophistication. None. Guys are walking down the street; one says Neighborhood Crips the other pulls out a gun. What is sophisticated about that? It doesn't seem to me that there is anything inherently sophisticated about this act. It is stupid, lacks judgment . . . So, the offense itself I don't find it to be criminally sophisticated. And the youth is not criminally sophisticated.

In contrast to the Cherry Street Gang case, the circumstances of this offense and the context of the youths' lives were characterized by the judge as being unsophisticated. In this case, the youth where charged with attempted murder (no one was physically injured)—shooting a gun at a car loaded with rival gang members. The judge relied on the criterion of "sophistication" and determined that none existed. Essentially, the youth were viewed as not criminally culpable because they were characterized as having "lacked judgment." The individuals were also found "fit" on criteria two through five, consequently, the judge found the youth amenable to the juvenile system. The same law and criteria were applied to this case as in the Cherry Street case, yet the judge found no criminal "sophistication," and as a result allowed the youth to remain in the juvenile court system.

This is an important similarity with Cicourel's (1968) work. With these two gang examples we see how "legal histories" are applied to cases differently. In the examples illustrating judicial characterizations of the Cherry Street and the Neighborhood Crips, none of the youth involved had prior legal contacts with the juvenile court. Yet, in the first instance, involving the Cherry Street youth, their prior legal history was not presented by the judge as important information to the presentation of their character. However, in the second example, a different judge relied on the legal history, the lack of legal priors, to support his evaluation of these being "typical" youth who made stupid decisions. In addition, this judge used information obtained from a letter one of the youth had written to the judge to further develop a characterization about the youth. The following excerpt from the judge's statement during the fitness hearing illustrates how he chose to represent these youth:

> On behalf of Karl, perhaps under [the criterion of the] circumstances and gravity [of the offense] we had testimony [a letter] of his feelings about someone who died. His letter—and Ms. Washington [district attorney] you have his letter—again whether you believe it or not to be self serving—it shows mitigation. He talks about the neighborhood he has been living [in], fear of streets, people he knows who have been killed. [Quoting from letter] "Sir, I had the weapon because I felt I needed to protect myself." Whether you agree or not, I'm certain it was mitigation.

The judge cited one of the youth's statements of being fearful to live in his neighborhood as evidence of mitigation. The youth wrote in the letter that he was fearful of rival gang members: a fear recently reinforced by the loss of a cousin who had been killed. To this judge, within the context of the community the courthouse was located, these offenders were typical, and their actions, while "stupid" and "lacking judgment," were not sophisticated, but rather a reasonable response to a perceived threat (a car slowing down when it drove past them).

In other instances, youth labeled as gang members, or who used weapons, were assessed within the context of a broader, maybe more idealistic society, where "normal" youth do not engage in such behavior. Under these latter conditions the youth were assessed as atypical; more criminal-like and sophisticated. Thus, while the same gang-like characteristics were used to construct a characterization of youth who were non-typical and in need of criminal punishment in earlier examples, here a judge used the very same information to construct a characterization of youth who carry and use weapons out of fear and self-defense.

One may argue the circumstances of the offense varied: in one case a victim was beaten and in the other the victims were not harmed. These differences could have influenced the judges' assessment of the youth. However in the Neighborhood Crips example the judge did not rely on the lack of injury as a mitigating factor to support his evaluation. These youth, at least in the Neighborhood Crips case, were labeled as typical youth in this court jurisdiction, and as a result were found "fit" to remain in the juvenile justice system. In all of the examples, the primary focus of judges' evaluations is on the offense and how information about the youth can be used to justify the overall evaluation.

Discussion and Conclusion

Partially consistent with the criminal justice framework outlined above, judges' focal concerns during judicial waiver hearings centered on perceptions of youths' culpability, dangerousness, and the severity of the offense. However, there were no discussions of what might happen to the case once transferred to criminal court or if the case was retained in juvenile court. Instead, there was an implicit assumption that transfer to the criminal justice system meant accountability and punishment for the youth, and safety for society.

What is distinctive about the waiver hearing in terms of other processing points in both juvenile and criminal justice systems is that judges have to decide at one point in time many issues that they normally have a longer period of time to formulate; moral character, youths' amenability to rehabilitation, and remorse. In addition, they assume youths' guilt in the process as outlined in the waiver statute. What culminates is a ceremony of legitimacy where the subject under evaluation, the youth, "becomes in the eyes of his condemners literally a different and *new* person. . . . He is not changed, he is reconstituted" (Garfinkel 1956, 421). The above analysis demonstrates how these assessments represent a legal formulation of non-legal characteristics that primarily focus on the notion of "sophistication," producing a new legal label for many young people. Judges relied on local notions of rationality to achieve a sense of justice.

Models of Justice: Not Juvenile or Criminal, but Sophisticated

This analysis found that similar juvenile court decision-making patterns that have been identified in past juvenile and criminal justice systems are being used in current courts. The traditional juvenile justice model emphasizing individualized assessments and focusing on the character of the youth was employed. Judges determine whether youth are salvageable by the juvenile court system based on characterizations of youths' lives coupled with an understanding of the offense and context.

As a result of criminalization policies like the judicial waiver hearing, what we see is a blend between the "principle of individualized justice" and the "principle of the offense" (Matza 1964). At least among the cases observed, there was not a clear line between the traditional rehabilitative model of the juvenile court relying on informal processing, offender-based evaluations, rehabilitative treatment, and lower standards of culpability (Emerson 1969; Feld 1999; Platt 1977), and the criminal justice model for adult offenders, involving formal processing, offense-based evaluations, and punishment-oriented sentencing (Hagan 1974; Mears and Field 2000). Rather, a simultaneous combination of assessments driven by offense information, but coupled with offender information, guided judgments of waiver-eligible youth. Judges created a short hand, or rule of thumb, account of the typical amenable youth to bring order to the various pieces of information about the case to guide the waiver hearing process.

Substantive Rationality in the Performance of "Justice"

Through a socially constructed process, one that involved judgments, morals, and stereotypes, judges realized the law. The outcome of this accomplishment was that judges acted in a way that demonstrated rationality and objectivity. It is important to note the importance of the notion of youths' lifestyles in judicial creation of youths' case histories. Judges applied legal categories of "sophistication" and gravity not only to offenses, but also to the social categories of school, family, and lifestyle, to guide their assessments of youths' amenability to the court. This analysis illustrates that the legal criterion of "sophistication" is amorphous and ill defined. Court actors were granted the discretion to apply the criteria relying on their norms, morals, assumptions, and stereotypes about the youth before them. In a circular reasoning pattern, judges' assessments of youths' life circumstances went hand in hand with their evaluation of the details of the acts committed.

While relying on characterizations of youths' life circumstances to inform notions of "sophistication" offenders living nontraditional lifestyles are assessed as being sophisticated, when in actuality many show no indication of lacking control over their lives. The waiver hearings become contradictory in that the behavior of youth used to identity them as sophisticated are these very actions of which mark them as "immature" youth: for example, such youth often are teen parents, do not listen to the direction of adults, seek out the security of gang ties and fall under their persuasion, and are failing in school. Judges, nevertheless, deem these offenders sophisticated. Consequently, youth who are raised in nontraditional life circumstances are viewed in an unfavorable light and are very likely to be transferred to criminal court. As previous research has found, and as witnessed, these youth will typically be of color and from lower socioeconomic backgrounds (Bishop and Frazier 1996; Leiber 2002; Leiber and Mack 2003; Podkopacz and Feld 1995).

Organizationally Situated Justice

It is important to note that the processing of young people in the courts observed was dependent on the local courthouse norms, values, and types of cases observed. This is a similar process that others have found in the study of justice decision making (Maynard and Manzo 1993). The above analysis shows the local rationality of judges' accounting procedures. In certain settings judges offered accounts that justified their findings of amenability, however, in other court settings such analyses might be unacceptable. Some judges would be labeled as abusing their discretion for making such "fit" decisions and have their decisions legally challenged (Harris 2007). Thus, these people-processing assessments were situationally dependent. This finding raises important questions about justice and fairness. Should youth be assessed within the context of the communities they come from? Should considerations be made to the level of acceptable violence, or at least acceptable weapons presence, in certain communities? Who should be able to create and judge such standards? Future studies should investigate how the cultures of court communities might vary in terms of attitudes toward different categories of offenses and offenders.

Conclusion

This study is about organizational decision making; how decision makers "historicize" legal cases, which in turn determine the course of action regarding social control, the label attached to the youth, and the subsequent rights, punishment, and/or treatment youth will receive (Cicourel 1968, 328–9). The focus of this study is not about the outcomes of cases, but instead how judges selectively take parts of case histories to construct their justifications for deciding if a youth is "fit" or "unfit" for the juvenile justice system. The decision-making process outlined in this study reveals how youth are processed within certain frames of reference and provides an illustration of the mechanisms through which elite actors in judicial institutions incorporate social factors into judicial decision making. Once legal and social concepts are unpacked, examining members' meanings and applications of the law, a dynamic and multi-faceted decision-making process involving members' evaluation of structural, value-based, and legal factors associated with characterizations of offenders' lifestyles is revealed.

The study offers three important theoretical insights; a revised theoretical frame-work for understanding juvenile justice decision making that incorporates criminal justice frameworks, an analysis of how substantive factors (e.g., values, stereotypes, assumptions) can enter into decision making, and an illustration of how decision making is organizationally situated. This analysis adds to existing sociological and crimino-logical research by demonstrating the applicability of criminal justice theorizing to juvenile justice by illustrating a complex processing framework that prioritizes focal concerns about offense-related details.

Critical Thinking

As Harris has shown, the move to more punitive models in criminal courts has led to an increase in the power of district attorneys to use the legal action of direct filing and avoid the juvenile court's decision-making waiver process. Can you explain why the criminal court model, which uses a more punitive approach toward juveniles accused of committing serious offenses, has moved further away from the juvenile court's philosophy of maintaining the welfare of children who come before it? Further, do you think that juvenile judges have become judicial bystanders as a result of the increased prosecutorial power to charge juveniles as adults?

References

Bishop, D., and C. Frazier. 1996. Race effects in juvenile justice decision making: Findings from a statewide analysis. *Journal of Criminology and Criminal Law* 86 (3): 392–414.

Bortner, M. A. 1986. Traditional rhetoric, organizational realities: Remand of juveniles to adult court. *Crime and Delinquency* 32 (1): 53–73.

Cicourel, A. 1968. *The social organization of juvenile justice*. New Brunswick: Transaction.

Emerson, R. 1969. *Judging delinquents: Context and process in juvenile court*. Chicago: Aldine.

Fagan, J., and F. Zimring. 2000. *The Changing borders of juvenile justice: Transfer of adolescents to the criminal court*. Chicago: The University of Chicago Press.

Feld, B. 1987. The juvenile court meets the principle of the offense: Legislative changes in juvenile waiver statutes. *The Journal of Criminal Law and Criminology* 78 (3): 471–533.

———. 1999. *Bad kids: Race and the transformation of the juvenile court*. New York, Oxford Press.

Garfinkel, H. 1956. Conditions of successful degradation ceremonies. *American Journal of Sociology* 61 (5): 420–24.

———. 1967. *Studies in ethnomethodology*. Englewood Cliffs, NJ: Prentice-Hall.

———. 2002. *Ethnomethodology's program*. Englewood Cliffs, NJ: Prentice-Hall.

Garfinkel, H., and H. Sacks. 1970. On formal structures of practical action. In *Theoretical sociology: Perspectives and developments*, edited by J. C. Tiryakian and E. A. McKinney, 337–66. New York: Appleton-Century-Crofts.

Hagan, J. 1974. Extra legal attributes and criminal sentencing: An assessment of a sociological viewpoint. *Law and Society Review* 8:357–83.

Harris, A. 2007. Diverting and abdicating judicial discretion: Cultural, political, and procedural changes in California juvenile justice. *Law & Society Review* 41 (2): 387–428.

Hasenfeld, Y. 1972. People processing organizations: An exchange approach. *American Sociological Review* 37: 256–63.

Hasenfeld, Y., and P. Cheung. 1985. The juvenile court as a people-processing organization: A political economy perspective. *American Journal of Sociology* 90 (4): 801–24.

Kupchik, A. 2003. Prosecuting adolescents in criminal courts: Criminal or juvenile justice? *Social Problems* 50 (3): 439–60.

Leiber, M. 2002. Disproportionate Minority Confinement (DMC) of youth: An analysis of state and federal efforts to address the issue. *Crime and Delinquency* 48 (1): 3–45.

Leiber, M., and K. Y. Mack. 2003. The individual and joint effects of race, gender, and family status on juvenile justice decision-making. *Journal of Research in Crime and Delinquency* 40 (1): 34–70.

Maynard, D., and J. Manzo. 1993. On the sociology of justice: Theoretical notes from an actual jury deliberation. *Sociological Theory* 11 (2): 171–93.

Matza, D. 1964. *Delinquency and drift*. New York: Wiley.

Mears, D., and S. Field. 2000. Theorizing sanctioning in a criminalized juvenile court. *Criminology* 38 (4): 983–1019.

Platt, A. M. 1977. *The child savers: The invention of delinquency*. Chicago: University of Chicago Press.

Podkopacz, M., and B. Feld. 1995. Judicial waiver policy and practice: Persistence, seriousness and race. *Law and Inequality* December (1): 73–178.

Singer, S. 1995. *Recriminalizing delinquency: violent juvenile crime and juvenile justice reform*. Cambridge, MA: Cambridge University Press.

Steinberg, L., and E. Cauffman. 2000. Developmental perspectives on jurisdictional boundary. In *The changing borders of juvenile justice: Transfer of adolescents to the criminal court*, edited by Jeffrey Fagan and Franklin Zimring, 379–406. Chicago: University of Chicago Press.

Sutton, J. 1998. *Stubborn children: Controlling delinquency in the United States, 1640–1981*. Berkeley, CA: University of California Press.

Torbet, P., R. Gable, H. Hurst, I. Montgomery, L. Szymanski. and D. Thomas. 1996. *State responses to, serious and violent juvenile crime*. Washington, DC: Office of Juvenile Justice and Delinquency Prevention.

Case Cited

Kent v. United States, 383 U.S. 5419 (1966).

13

Discrediting Victims' Allegations of Sexual Assault: Prosecutorial Accounts of Case Rejections

Lisa Frohmann

Abstract: *Complaint filing is an extremely important stage in the prosecution of a case, for it is at this stage that the district attorney decides which cases will be filed for adjudication by the courts. Frohman describes and analyzes the organizational dynamics of the prosecutor's office, researching the ways in which sexual assault victims are made to feel devalued if their case did not fall into a stereotypical norm and was rejected for prosecution. She finds that prosecutors attempt to discredit the victim's allegations by unearthing discrepancies in the victim's stories. To do this prosecutors rely on official reports, typification of rapes, and knowledge of the victim's personal life.*

Case screening is the gateway to the criminal court system. Prosecutors, acting as gatekeepers, decide which instances of alleged victimization will be passed on for adjudication by the courts. A recent study by the Department of Justice (Boland et al. 1990) suggests that a significant percentage of felony cases never get beyond this point, with only cases characterized as "solid" or "convictable" being filed (Stanko 1981, 1982; Mather 1979). This paper will examine how prosecutors account for the decision to reject sexual assault cases for prosecution and looks at the centrality of discrediting victims' rape allegations in this justification.

A number of studies on sexual assault have found that victim credibility is important in police decisions to investigate and make arrests in sexual assault cases (LaFree 1981; Rose and Randall 1982; Kerstetter 1990; Kerstetter and Van Winkle 1990). Similarly, victim credibility has been shown to influence prosecutors' decisions at a number of stages in the handling of sexual assault cases (LaFree 1980, 1989; Chandler and Torney 1981; Kerstetter 1990).

Much of this prior research has assumed, to varying degrees, that victim credibility is a phenomenon that exists independently of prosecutors' interpretations and assessments of such credibility. Particularly when operationalized in terms of quantitative variables, victim credibility is treated statistically as a series of fixed, objective features of cases. Such approaches neglect the processes whereby prosecutors actively assess and negotiate victim credibility in actual, ongoing case processing.

An alternative view examines victim credibility as a phenomenon constructed and maintained through interaction (Stanko 1980). Several qualitative studies have begun to identify and analyze these processes. For example, Holmstrom and Burgess's (1983) analysis of a victim's experience with the institutional handling of sexual assault cases discusses the importance of victim credibility through the prosecutor's evaluation of a complainant as a "good witness." A "good witness" is someone who, through her appearance and demeanor, can convince a jury to accept her account of "what happened." Her testimony is "consistent" her behavior "sincere," and she cooperates in case preparation. Stanko's (1981, 1982) study of felony case filing decisions similarly emphasizes prosecutors' reliance on the notion of the "stand-up" witness— someone who can appear to the judge and jury as articulate and credible. Her work emphasizes the centrality of victim credibility in complaint-filing decisions.

In this article I extend these approaches by systematically analyzing the kinds of accounts prosecutors offer in sexual assault cases to support their complaint-filing decisions. Examining the justifications for decisions provides an understanding of how these decisions appear rational, necessary, and appropriate to decision-makers as they do the work of case screening. It allows us to uncover the inner, indigenous logic of prosecutors' decisions and the organizational structures in which those decisions are embedded (Garfinkel 1984).

I focus on prosecutorial accounting for case rejection for three reasons. First, since a significant percentage of cases are not filed, an important component of the case-screening process involves case rejection. Second, the organization of case filing requires prosecutors to justify case rejection, not case acceptance, to superiors and fellow deputies. By examining deputy district attorneys' (DDAs') reasons for case rejection, we can gain access to what they consider "solid" cases, providing further insight into the case-filing process. Third, in case screening, prosecutors orient to the rule—when in doubt, reject. Their behavior is organized more to avoiding the error of filing cases that are not likely to result in conviction than to avoiding the error of rejecting cases that will probably end in conviction (Scheff 1966). Thus, I suggest that prosecutors are actively looking for "holes" or problems that will make the victim's version of "what happened" unbelievable or not convincing beyond a reasonable doubt, hence unconvictable (see Miller [1970], Neubauer [1974], and Stanko [1980, 1981] for the importance of conviction in prosecutors' decisions to file cases). This bias is grounded within the organizational context of complaint filing.

Data and Methods

The research was part of an ethnographic field study of the prosecution of sexual assault crimes by deputy district attorneys in the sexual assault units of two branch offices of the district attorney's offices in a metropolitan area on the West Coast. Research was conducted on a full-time basis in 1989 for nine months in Bay City and on a full-time basis in 1990 for eight months in Center Heights. Three prosecutors were assigned to the unit in Bay City, and four prosecutors to the unit in Center Heights. The data came from 17 months of observation of more than three hundred case screenings. These screenings involved the presentation and assessment of a police report by a sexual assault detective to a prosecutor, conversations between detectives and deputies regarding the "filability"/reject status of a police report, interviews of victims by deputies about the alleged sexual assault, and discussions between deputies regarding the file/reject status of a report. Since tape recordings were prohibited, I took extensive field notes and tried to record as accurately as possible conversation between the parties. In addition, I also conducted open-ended interviews with prosecutors in the sexual assault units and with investigating officers who handled these cases. The accounts presented in the data below include both those offered in the course of negotiating a decision to reject or file a case (usually to the investigating officer [IO] but sometimes with other prosecutors or to me as an insider), and the more or less fixed accounts offered for a decision already made (usually to me). Although I will indicate the context in which the account occurs, I will not emphasize the differences between accounts in the analysis.

The two branches of the district attorney's office I studied cover two communities differing in socioeconomic and racial composition. Bay City is primarily a white middle-to-upper-class community, and Center Heights is primarily a black and Latino lower-class community. Center Heights has heavy gang-drug activity, and most of the cases brought to the district attorney were assumed to involve gang members (both the complainant and the assailant) or a sex-drug or sex-money transaction. Because of the activities that occur in this community, the prior relationships between the parties are often the result of gang affiliation. This tendency, in connection with the sex-drug and sex-money transactions, gives a twist to the "consent defense" in "acquaintance" rapes. In Bay City, in contrast, the gang activity is much more limited and the majority of acquaintance situations that came to the prosecutors' attention could be categorized as "date rape."

The Organizational Context of Complaint Filing

Several features of the court setting that I studied provided the context for prosecutors' decisions. These features are prosecutorial concern with maintaining a high conviction rate to promote an image of the "community's legal protector," and prosecutorial and court procedures for processing sexual assault cases.

The promotion policy of the county district attorney's (DA) office encourages prosecutors to accept only "strong" or "winnable" cases for prosecution by using conviction rates as a measure of prosecutorial performance. In the DA's office, guilty verdicts carry more weight than a conviction by case settlement. The stronger the case, the greater likelihood of a guilty verdict, the better the "stats" for promotion considerations. The inducement to take risks—to take cases to court that might not result in conviction—is tempered in three ways; First a pattern of not-guilty verdicts is used by the DA's office as an indicator of prosecutorial incompetency. Second, prosecutors are given credit for the number of cases they reject as a recognition of their commitment to the organizational concern of reducing the case load of an already overcrowded court system. Third, to continually pursue cases that should have been rejected outright may lead judges to question the prosecutor's competence as a member of the court.

Sexual assault cases are among those crimes that have been deemed by the state legislature to be priority prosecution cases. That is, in instances where both "sex" and "nonsex" cases are trailing (waiting for a court date to open), sexual assault cases are given priority for court time. Judges become annoyed when they feel that court time is being "wasted" with cases that "should" have been negotiated or rejected in the first place, especially when those cases have been given priority over other cases. Procedurally, the prosecutor's office handles sexual assault crimes differently from other felony crimes. Other felonies are handled by a referral system; they are handed from one DDA to another at each stage in the prosecution of the case. But sexual assault cases are vertically prosecuted; the deputy who files the case remains with it until its disposition, and therefore is closely connected with the case outcome.

Accounting for Rejection because of "Discrepancies"

Within this organizational context, a central feature of prosecutorial accounts of case rejection is the discrediting of victims' allegations of sexual assault. Below I examine two techniques used by prosecutors to discredit victim's complaints: discrepant accounts and ulterior motives.

Using Official Reports and Records to Detect Discrepancies

In the course of reporting a rape, victims recount their story to several criminal justice officials. Prosecutors treat consistent accounts of the incident over time as an indicator of a victim's credibility. In the first example two prosecutors are discussing a case brought in for filing the previous day.

> DDA Tamara Jacobs: In the police report she said all three men were kissing the victim. Later in the interview she said that was wrong. It seems strange because there are things wrong on major events like oral copulation and intercourse . . . for example whether she had John's penis in her mouth. Another thing wrong is whether he forced her into the bedroom immediately after they got to his room or, as the police report said, they all sat on the couch and watched TV. This is something a cop isn't going to get wrong, how the report started.
>
> (Bay City)

The prosecutor questions the credibility of the victim's allegation by finding "inconsistencies" between the complainant's account given to the police and the account given to the prosecutor. The prosecutor formulates differences in these accounts as "discrepancies" by noting that they involve "major events"—events so significant no one would confuse them, forget them, or get them wrong. This is in contrast to some differences that may involve acceptable, "normal inconsistencies" in victims' accounts of sexual assault. By "normal inconsistencies," I mean those that are expected and explainable because the victim is confused, upset, or shaken after the assault.

The DDA also discredited the victim's account by referring to a typification of police work. She assumes that the inconsistencies in the accounts could not be attributed to the incorrect writing of the report by the police officer on the grounds that they "wouldn't get wrong how the report started." Similarly, in the following example, a typification of police work is invoked to discredit the victim's account. Below the DDA and IO are discussing the case immediately after the victim interview.

DDA Sabrina Johnson: [T]he police report doesn't say anything about her face being swollen, only her hand. If they took pictures of her hand, wouldn't the police have taken a picture of her face if it was swollen?

(Bay City)

The prosecutor calls the credibility of the victim's complaint into question by pointing to a discrepancy between her subsequent account of injuries received during the incident and the notation of injuries on the police reports taken at the time the incident was reported. Suspicion of the complainant's account is also expressed in the prosecutor's inference that if the police went to the trouble of photographing the victim's injured hand they would have taken pictures of her face had it also shown signs of injury.

In the next case the prosecutor cites two types of inconsistencies between accounts. The first set of inconsistencies is the victim's accounts to the prosecutor and to the police. The second set is between the account the victim gave to the prosecutor and the statements the defendants gave to the police. This excerpt was obtained during an interview.

DDA Tracy Timmerton: The reason I did not believe her [the victim] was, I get the police report first and I'll read that, so I have read the police report which recounts her version of the facts but it also has the statement of both defendants. Both defendants were arrested at separate times and give[n] separate independent statements that were virtually the same. Her story when I had her recount it to me in the DA's office, the number of acts changed, the chronological order of how they happened has changed.

(Bay City)

When the prosecutor compared the suspects' accounts with the victim's account, she interpreted the suspects' accounts as credible because both of their accounts, given separately to police, were similar. This rests on the assumption that if suspects give similar accounts when arrested together, they are presumed to have colluded on the story, but if they give similar accounts independent of the knowledge of the other's arrest, there is presumed to be a degree of truth to the story. This stands in contrast to the discrepant accounts the complainant gave to law enforcement officials and the prosecutor.

Using Official Typifications of Rape-Relevant Behavior

In the routine handling of sexual assault cases prosecutors develop a repertoire of knowledge about the features of these crimes. This knowledge includes how particular kinds of rape are committed, post-incident interaction between the parties in an acquaintance situation, and victims' emotional and psychological reactions to rape and their effects on victims' behavior. The typifications of rape-relevant behavior are another resource for discrediting a victim's account of "what happened."

Typifications of rape scenarios

Prosecutors distinguish between different types of sexual assault. They characterize these types by the sex acts that occur, the situation in which the incident occurred, and the relationship between the parties. In the following excerpt the prosecutor discredits the victim's version of events by focusing on incongruities between the victim's description of the sex acts and the prosecutor's knowledge of the typical features of kidnap-rape. During an interview a DDA described the following:

> DDA Tracy Timmerton: [T]he only act she complained of was intercourse, and my experience has been that when a rapist has a victim cornered for a long period of time, they engage in multiple acts and different types of sexual acts and very rarely do just intercourse.
>
> (Bay City)

The victim's account is questioned by noting that she did not complain about or describe other sex acts considered "typical" of kidnap-rape situations. She only complained of intercourse. In the next example the DDA and IO are talking about a case involving the molestation of a teenage girl.

> DDA William Nelson: Something bothers me, all three acts are the same. She's on her stomach and has her clothes on and he has a "hard and long penis." All three times he is grinding his penis into her butt. It seems to me he should be trying to do more than that by the third time.
>
> (Center Heights)

Here the prosecutor is challenging the credibility of the victim's account by comparing her version of "what happened" with his typification of the way these crimes usually occur. His experience suggests there should be an escalation of sex acts over time, not repetition of the same act.

Often the typification invoked by the prosecutor is highly situational and local. In discussing a drug-sex-related rape in Center Heights, for example, the prosecutor draws on his knowledge of street activity in that community and the types of rapes that occur there to question whether the victim's version of events is what "really" happened. The prosecutor is describing a case he received the day before to an investigating officer there on another matter.

> DDA Kent Fernome: I really feel guilty about this case I got yesterday. The girl is 20 going on 65. She is real skinny and gangly. Looks like a cluckhead [crack addict]—they cut off her hair. She went to her uncle's house, left her clothes there, drinks some beers and said she was going to visit a friend in Center Heights who she said she met at a drug rehab program. She is not sure where this friend Cathy lives. Why she went to Center Heights after midnight, God knows? It isn't clear what she was doing between 12 and 4 a.m. Some gang bangers came by and offered her a ride. They picked her up on the corner of Main and Lincoln. I think she was turning a trick, or looking for a rock, but she wouldn't budge from her story. . . . There are lots of conflicts between what she told the police and what she told me. The sequence of events, the sex acts performed, who ejaculates. She doesn't say who is who. . . . She's beat up, bruises on face and a laceration on her neck. The cop and doctor say there is no trauma—she's done by six guys. That concerns me. There is no semen that they see. It looks like this to me—maybe she is a strawberry, she's hooking or looking for a rock, but somewhere along the line it is not consensual. . . . She is [a] real street-worn woman. She's not leveling with me—visiting a woman with an unknown address on a bus in Center Heights—I don't buy it . . .
>
> (Center Heights)

The prosecutor questioned the complainant's reason for being in Center Heights because, based on his knowledge of the area, he found it unlikely that a woman would come to this community at midnight to visit a friend at an unknown address. The deputy proposed an alternative account of the victim's action based on his knowledge of activities in the community—specifically, prostitution and drug dealing—and questioned elements of the victim's account, particularly her insufficiently accounted for activity between 12 and 4 a.m., coming to Center Heights late at night to visit a friend at an unknown address, and "hanging out" on the corner.

The DDA uses "person-descriptions" (Maynard 1984) to construct part of the account, describing the complainant's appearance as a "cluckhead" and "street-worn." These descriptions suggested she was a drug user, did not have a "stable" residence or employment, and was probably in Center Heights in search of drugs. This description is filled in by her previous "participation in a drug rehab program," the description of her activity as "hanging out" and being "picked up" by gang bangers, and a medical report which states that no trauma or semen was found when she was "done by six guys." Each of these features of the account suggests that the complainant is a prostitute or "strawberry" who came to Center Heights to trade sex or money for drugs. This alternative scenario combined with "conflicts between what she told the police and what she told me" justify case rejection because it is unlikely that the prosecutor could get a conviction.

The prosecutor acknowledges the distinction between the violation of women's sexual/physical integrity—"somewhere along the line it wasn't consensual"—and prosecutable actions. The organizational concern with "downstream consequences" (Emerson and Paley, forthcoming) mitigate against the case being filed.

Typifications of Post-Incident Interaction

In an acquaintance rape, the interaction between the parties after the incident is a critical element in assessing the validity of a rape complaint. As implied below by the prosecutors, the typical interaction pattern between victim and suspect after a rape incident is not to see one another. In the following cases the prosecutor challenges the validity of the victims' allegations by suggesting that the complainants' behavior runs counter to a typical rape victim's behavior. In the first instance the parties involved in the incident had a previous relationship and were planning to live together. The DDA is talking to me about the case prior to her decision to reject.

> DDA Sabrina Johnson: I am going to reject the case. She is making it very difficult to try the case. She told me she let him into her apartment last night because she is easily influenced. The week before this happened [the alleged rape] she agreed to have sex with him. Also, first she says "he raped me" and then she lets him into her apartment.
>
> (Bay City)

Here the prosecutor raises doubt about the veracity of the victim's rape allegation by contrasting it to her willingness to allow the suspect into her apartment after the incident. This "atypical" behavior is used to discredit the complainant's allegation.

In the next excerpt the prosecutor was talking about two cases. In both instances the parties knew each other prior to the rape incident as well as having had sexual relations after the incident. As in the previous instance, the victims' allegations are discredited by referring to their atypical behavior.

> DDA Sabrina Johnson: I can't take either case because of the women's behavior after the fact. By seeing these guys again and having sex with them they are absolving them of their guilt.
>
> (Bay City)

In each instance the "downstream" concern with convictability is indicated in the prosecutor's talk—"She is making it very difficult to try the case" and "By seeing these guys again and having sex with them they are absolving them of their guilt." This concern is informed by a series of common-sense assumptions about normal hetero-sexual relations that the prosecutors assume judges and juries use to assess the believ-ability of the victim: First, appropriate behavior within ongoing relationships is noncoercive and nonviolent. Second, sex that occurs within the context of ongoing relationships is consensual. Third, if coercion or violence occurs, the appropriate response is to sever the relationship, at least for a time. When complainants allege they have been raped by their partner within a continuing relationship, they challenge the taken-for-granted assumptions of normal heterosexual relationships. The prosecu-tors anticipate that this challenge will create problems for the successful prosecution of a case because they think that judges and jurors will use this typification to ques-tion the credibility of the victim's allegation. They assume that the triers of fact will assume that if there is "evidence" of ongoing normal heterosexual relations—she didn't leave and the sexual relationship continued—then there was no coercive sex. Thus the certitude that a crime originally occurred can be retrospectively undermined by the interaction between complainant and suspect after the alleged incident. Implicit in this is the assumed primacy of the normal heterosexual relations typification as the standard on which to assess the victim's credibility even though an allegation of rape has been made.

Typifications of Rape Reporting

An important feature of sexual assault cases is the timeliness in which they are reported to the police (see Torrey, forthcoming). Prosecutors expect rape victims to report the incident relatively promptly: "She didn't call the police until four hours later. That isn't consistent with someone who has been raped." If a woman reports "late," her motives for reporting and the sincerity of her allegation are questioned if they fall outside the typification of officially recognizable/explainable reasons for late reporting. The typification is characterized by the features that can be explained by Rape Trauma Syndrome (RTS). In the first excerpt the victim's credibility is not challenged as a result of her delayed reporting. The prosecutor describes her behavior and motives as characteristic of RTS. The DDA is describing a case to me that came in that morning.

> DDA Tamara Jacobs: Charlene was in the car with her three assailants after the rape. John [the driver] was pulled over by the CHP [California Highway Patrol] for erratic driving behavior. The victim did not tell the officers that she had just been raped by these three men. When she arrived home, she didn't tell anyone what happened for approximately 24 hours. When her best friend found out from the assailants [who were mutual friends] and confronted the victim, Charlene told her what happened. She then reported it to the police. When asked why she didn't report the crime earlier, she said that she was embarrassed and afraid they would

hurt her more if she reported it to the police. The DDA went on to say that the victim's behavior and reasons for delayed reporting were symptomatic of RTS. During the trial an expert in Rape Trauma Syndrome was called by the prosecution to explain the "normality" and commonness of the victim's reaction.

(Bay City)

Other typical motives include "wanting to return home first and get family support" or "wanting to talk the decision to report over with family and friends." In all these examples, the victims sustained injuries of varying degrees in addition to the trauma of the rape itself, and they reported the crime within 24 hours. At the time the victims reported the incident, their injuries were still visible, providing corroboration for their accounts of what happened.

In the next excerpt we see the connection between atypical motives for delayed reporting and ulterior motives for reporting a rape allegation. At this point I focus on the prosecutors' use of typification as a resource for discrediting the victim's account. I will examine ulterior motives as a technique of discrediting in a later section. The deputy is telling me about a case she recently rejected.

> DDA Sabrina Johnson: She doesn't tell anyone after the rape. Soon after this happened she met him in a public place to talk business. Her car doesn't start, he drives her home and starts to attack her. She jumps from the car and runs home. Again she doesn't tell anyone. She said she didn't tell anyone because she didn't want to lose his business. Then the check bounces, and she ends up with VD. She has to tell her fiancé so he can be treated. He insists she tell the police. It is three weeks after the incident I have to look at what the defense would say about the cases. Looks like she consented, and told only when she had to because of the infection and because he made a fool out of her by having the check bounce.
>
> (Bay City)

The victim's account is discredited because her motives for delayed reporting—not wanting to jeopardize a business deal—fall outside those considered officially recognizable and explicable.

Typifications of Victim's Demeanor

In the course of interviewing hundreds of victims, prosecutors develop a notion of a victim's comportment when she tells what happened. They distinguish between behavior that signifies "lying" versus "discomfort." In the first two exchanges the DDA and IO cite the victim's behavior as an indication of lying. Below, the deputy and IO are discussing the case immediately after the intake interview.

IO NANCY FAUTECK:	I think something happened. There was an exchange of body language that makes me question what she was doing. She was yawning, hedging, fudging something.
DDA SABRINA JOHNSON:	Yawning is a sign of stress and nervousness.
IO NANCY FAUTECK:	She started yawning when I talked to her about her record earlier, and she stopped when we finished talking about it.

(Bay City)

The prosecutor and the investigating officer collaboratively draw on their common-sense knowledge and practical work experience to interpret the yawns, nervousness, and demeanor of the complainant as running counter to behavior they expect from one who is "telling the whole truth." They interpret the victim's behavior as a continuum of interaction first with the investigating officer and then with the district attorney. The investigating officer refers to the victim's recurrent behavior (yawning) as an indication that something other than what the victim is reporting actually occurred.

In the next excerpt the prosecutor and IO discredit the victim's account by referencing two typifications—demeanor and appropriate rape-victim behavior. The IO and prosecutor are telling me about the case immediately after they finished the screening interview.

IO DINA ALVAREZ:	One on one, no corroboration.
DDA WILLIAM NELSON:	She's a poor witness, though that doesn't means she wasn't raped. I won't file a one-on-one case.
IO DINA ALVAREZ:	I don't like her body language.
DDA WILLIAM NELSON:	She's timid, shy, naive, virginal, and she didn't do all the right things. I'm not convinced she is even telling the truth. She's not even angry about what happened to her. . . .
DDA WILLIAM NELSON:	Before a jury if we have a one on one, he denies it, no witnesses, no physical evidence or medical corroboration they won't vote guilty.
IO DINA ALVAREZ:	I agree, and I didn't believe her because of her body language. She looks down, mumbles, crosses her arms, and twists her hands.
DDA WILLIAM NELSON:	. . . She has the same mannerisms and demeanor as a person who is lying. A jury just won't believe her. She has low self-esteem and self-confidence. . . .

(Center Heights)

The prosecutor and IO account for case rejection by characterizing the victim as unbelievable and the case as unconvictable. They establish their disbelief in the victim's account by citing the victim's actions that fall outside the typified notions of believable and expected behavior—"she has the same mannerisms and demeanor as a person who is lying," and "I'm not convinced she is even telling the truth. She isn't even angry about what happened." They assume that potential jurors will also find the victim's demeanor and post-incident behavior problematic. They demonstrate the unconvictability of the case by citing the "holes" in the case—a combination of a "poor witness" whom "the jury just won't believe" and "one on one, [with] no corroboration" and a defense in which the defendant denies anything happened or denies it was nonconsensual sex.

Prosecutors and investigating officers do not routinely provide explicit accounts of "expected/honest" demeanor. Explicit accounts of victim demeanor tend to occur when DDAs are providing grounds for discrediting a rape allegation. When as a researcher I pushed for an account of expected behavior, the following exchange occurred. The DDA had just concluded the interview and asked the victim to wait in the lobby.

IO NANCY FAUTECK:	Don't you think he's credible?
DDA SABRINA JOHNSON:	Yes.
LF:	What seems funny to me is that someone who said he was so unwilling to do this talked about it pretty easily.
IO NANCY FAUTECK:	Didn't you see his eyes, they were like saucers.
[DID]DDA SABRINA JOHNSON:	And [he] was shaking too.

(Bay City)

This provides evidence that DDAs and IOs are orienting to victims' comportment and could provide accounts of "expected/honest" demeanor if necessary. Other behavior that might be included in this typification are the switch from looking at to looking away from the prosecutor when the victim begins to discuss the specific details of the rape itself; a stiffening of the body and tightening of the face as though to hold in tears when the victim begins to tell about the particulars of the incident; shaking of the body and crying when describing the details of the incident; and a lowering of the voice and long pauses when the victim tells the specifics of the sexual assault incident.

Prosecutors have a number of resources they call on to develop typification related to rape scenarios and reporting. These include how sexual assaults are committed, community residents and activities, interactions between suspect and defendants after a rape incident, and the way victims' emotional and psychological responses to rape influence their behavior. These typifications highlight discrepancies between prosecutors' knowledge and victims' accounts. They are used to discredit the victims' allegation of events, justifying case rejection.

As we have seen, one technique used by prosecutors to discredit a victim's allegations of rape as a justification of case rejection is the detection of discrepancies. The resources for this are official documents and records and typifications of rape scenarios and rape reporting. A second technique prosecutors use is the identification of ulterior motives for the victim's rape allegation.

Accounting for Rejection by "Ulterior Motive"

Ulterior motives rest on the assumption that a woman consented to sexual activity and for some reason needed to deny it afterwards. These motives are drawn from the prosecutor's knowledge of the victim's personal history and the community in which the incident occurred. They are elaborated and supported by other techniques and knowledge prosecutors use in the accounting process.

I identify two types of ulterior motives prosecutors use to justify rejection: The first type suggests the victim has a reason to file a false rape complaint. The second type acknowledges the legitimacy of the rape allegation, framing the motives as an organizational concern with convictability.

Knowledge of Victims' Current Circumstances

Prosecutors accumulate the details of victims' lives from police interviews, official documents, and filing interviews. They may identify ulterior motives by drawing on this information. Note that unlike the court trial itself, where the rape incident is often taken out of the context of the victim's life, here the DDAs call on the texture of a victim's life to justify case rejection. In an excerpt previously discussed, the DDA uses her knowledge of the victim's personal relationship and business transactions as a resource for formulating ulterior motives. Drawing on the victim's current circumstances, the prosecutor suggests two ulterior motives for the rape allegation—disclosure to her fiancé about the need to treat a sexually transmitted disease, and anger and embarrassment about the bounced check. Both of these are motives for making a false complaint. The ulterior motives are supported by the typification for case reporting. Twice unreported sexual assault incidents with the same suspect, a three-week delay in reporting, and reporting only after the fiancé insisted she do so are not within the typified behavior and reasons for late reporting. Her atypical behavior provides plausibility to the alternative version of the events—the interaction was consensual and only reported as a rape because the victim needed to explain a potentially explosive matter (how she contracted venereal disease) to her fiancé. In addition she felt duped on a business deal.

Resources for imputing ulterior motives also come from the specifics of the rape incident. Below, the prosecutor's knowledge of the residents and activities in Center Heights supply the reason: the type of activity the victim wanted to cover up from her boyfriend. The justification for rejection is strengthened by conflicting accounts between the victim and witness on the purpose for being in Center Heights. The DDA and IO are talking about the case before they interview the complainant.

DDA WILLIAM NELSON:	A white girl from Addison comes to buy dope. She gets kidnapped and raped.
IO BRANDON PALMER:	She tells her boyfriend and he beats her up for being so stupid for going to Center Heights. . . . The drug dealer positively ID'd the two suspects, but she's got a credibility problem because she said she wasn't selling dope, but the other two witnesses say they bought dope from her. . . .
LF:	I see you have a blue sheet [a sheet used to write up case rejections] already written up.
IO BRANDON PALMER:	Oh yes. But there was no doubt in my mind that she was raped. But do you see the problems?
DDA WILLIAM NELSON:	Too bad because these guys really messed her up. . . . She has a credibility problem. I don't think she is telling the truth about the drugs. It would be better if she said she did come to buy drugs. The defense is going to rip her up because of the drugs. He is going to say, isn't it true you had sex with these guys but didn't want to tell your boyfriend, so you lied about the rape like you did about the drugs, or that she had sex for drugs. . . .

(Center Heights)

The prosecutor expresses doubt about the victim's account because it conflicts with his knowledge of the community. He uses this knowledge to formulate the ulterior motive for the victim's complaint—to hide from her boyfriend the "fact" that she trading sex for drugs. The victim, "a white woman from Addison," alleges she drove to Center Heights "in the middle of the night" as a favor to a friend. She asserted that she did not come to purchase drugs. The DDA "knows" that white people don't live in Center Heights. He assumes that whites who come to Center Heights, especially in the middle of the night, are there to buy drugs or trade sex for drugs. The prosecutor's scenario is strengthened by the statements of the victim's two friends who accompanied her to Center Heights, were present at the scene, and admitted buying drugs. The prosecutor frames the ulterior motives as an organizational concern with defense arguments and convictability. This concern is reinforced by citing conflicting accounts between witnesses and the victim. He does not suggest that the victim's allegation was false—"there is no doubt in my mind she was raped": rather, the case isn't convictable—"she has a credibility problem" and "the defense is going to rip her up."

Criminal Connections

The presence of criminal connections can also be used as a resource for identifying ulterior motives. Knowledge of a victim's criminal activity enables prosecutors to "find" ulterior motives for her allegation. In the first excerpt the complainant's presence in an area known by police as "where prostitutes bring their clients" is used to formulate an ulterior motive for her rape complaint. This excerpt is from an exchange in which the DDA was telling me about a case he had just rejected.

> DDA William Nelson: Young female is raped under questionable circumstances. One on one. The guy states it is consensual sex. There is no corroboration, no medicals. We ran the woman's rap sheet, and she has a series of prostitution arrests. She's with this guy in the car in a dark alley having sex. The police know this is where prostitutes bring their customers, so she knew she had better do something fast unless she is going to be busted for prostitution, so, lo and behold, she comes running out of the car yelling "he's raped me." He says no. He picked her up on Long Beach Boulevard, paid her $25 and this is "where she brought me." He's real scared, he has no record.
>
> (Center Heights)

Above, the prosecutor, relying on police knowledge of a particular location, assumes the woman is a prostitute. Her presence in the location places her in a "suspicious" category, triggering a check on her criminal history. Her record of prostitution arrests is used as the resource for developing an ulterior motive for her complaint: To avoid being busted for prostitution again, she made a false allegation of rape. Here the woman's record of prostitution and the imminent possibility of arrest are used to provide the ulterior motive to discredit her account. The woman's account is further discredited by comparing her criminal history—"a series of prostitution arrests" with that of the suspect, who "has no record," thus suggesting that he is the more credible of the two parties.

Prosecutors and investigating officers often decide to run a rap sheet (a chronicle of a person's arrests and convictions) on a rape victim. These decisions are triggered when a victim falls into certain "suspicious" categories, categories that have a class/race bias. Rap sheets are not run on women who live in the wealthier parts of town (the majority of whom are white) or have professional careers. They are run on women who live in Center Heights (who are black and Latina), who are homeless, or who are involved in illegal activities that could be related to the incident.

Prosecutors develop the basis for ulterior motives from the knowledge they have of the victim's personal life and criminal connections. They create two types of ulterior motives, those that suggest the victim made a false rape complaint and those that acknowledge the legitimacy of the complaint but discredit the account because of its unconvictability. In the accounts prosecutors give, ulterior motives for case rejection are supported with discrepancies in victims' accounts and other practitioners' knowledge.

Conclusion

Case filing is a critical stage in the prosecutorial process. It is here that prosecutors decide which instances of alleged victimization will be forwarded for adjudication by the courts. A significant percentage of sexual assault cases are rejected at this stage. This research has examined prosecutorial accounts for case rejection and the centrality of victim discreditability in those accounts. I have elucidated the techniques of case rejection (discrepant accounts and ulterior motives), the resources prosecutors use to develop these techniques (official reports and records, typifications of rape-relevant behavior, criminal connections, and knowledge of a victim's personal life), and how these resources are used to discredit victims' allegations of sexual assault.

This examination has also provided the beginnings of an investigation into the logic and organization of prosecutors' decisions to reject/accept cases for prosecution. The research suggests that prosecutors are orienting to a "downstream" concern with convictability. They are constantly "in dialogue with" anticipated defense arguments and anticipated judge and juror responses to case testimony. These dialogues illustrate the intricacy of prosecutorial decision-making. They make visible how prosecutors rely on assumptions about relationships, gender, and sexuality (implicit in this analysis, but critical and requiring of specific and explicit attention) in complaint filing of sexual assault cases. They also make evident how the processes of distinguishing truths from untruths and the practical concerns of trying cases are central to these decisions. Each of these issues, in all its complexity, needs to be examined if we are to understand the logic and organization of filing sexual assault cases.

The organizational logic unveiled by these accounts has political implications for the prosecution of sexual assault crimes. These implications are particularly acute for acquaintance rape situations. As I have shown, the typification of normal heterosexual relations plays an important role in assessing these cases, and case conviction is key to filing cases. As noted by DDA William Nelson: "There is a difference between believing a woman was assaulted and being able to get a conviction in court." Unless we are able to challenge the assumptions on which these typifications are based, many cases of rape will never get beyond the filing process because of unconvictability.

Critical Thinking

An important issue discussed in this article has to do with the victim's socio-economic status and the ability to have a jury deliver a guilty verdict for the defendant. Such factors were found to be important in the prosecutor's decision to forward the case for adjudication by the courts. Social class, educational level, and past history with the suspect all seem to be overriding factors in determining the worth of a sexual assault case. Do such practices imply that certain types of women cannot be the victims of rape? How do you think such behaviors affect victims' decisions to report their victimization and testify in court? In short, do you think such practices prevent certain rape victims from equal protection under the law?

References

Boland, Barbara, Catherine H. Conly, Paul Mahanna, Lynn Warner, and Ronald Sones. (1990). *The Prosecution of Felony Arrests, 1987*. Washington, D.C.: Bureau of Justice Statistics, U.S. Department of Justice.

Chandler, Susan M., and Martha Torney. (1981). "The decision and the processing of rape victims through the criminal justice system." *California Sociologist* 4:155–69.

Emerson, Robert M. (1969). *Judging Delinquents: Context and Process in Juvenile Court.* C Publishing Co.

Emerson, Robert M., and Blair Paley (forthcoming). "Organizational horizons and complaint-fili *Discretion*, ed. Keith Hawkins. Oxford: Oxford University Press.

Garfinkel, Harold (1984). *Studies in Ethnomethodology.* Cambridge, Eng.: Polity Press.

Holmstrom, Lynda Lytle, and Ann Wolbert Burgess. (1983) *The Victim of Rape: Institutional Reactions.* New Brunswick, N.J.: Transaction Books.

Kerstetter, Wayne A. (1990) "Gateway to justice: Police and prosecutorial response to sexual assaults against women." *Journal of Criminal Law and Criminology* 81:267–313.

Kerstetter, Wayne A., and Barrik Van Winkle. (1990). "Who decides? A study of the complainant's decision to prosecute in rape cases." *Criminal Justice and Behavior* 17:266–83.

LaFree, Gary D. (1980). "Variables affecting guilty pleas and convictions in rape cases: Toward a social theory of rape processing." *Social Forces* 58:833–50.

——. (1981). "Official reactions to social problems: Police decisions in sexual assault cases." *Social Problems* 28:582–94.

——. (1989). *Rape and Criminal Justice: The Social Construction of Sexual Assault Belmont,* Calif.: Wadsworth Publishing Co.

Mather, Lynn M. (1979). *Plea Bargaining or Trial? The Process of Criminal-Case Disposition.* Lexington, Mass.: Lexington Books.

Maynard, Douglas W. (1984). *Inside Plea Bargaining: The Language of Negotiation.* New York: Plenum Press.

Miller, Frank. (1970). *Prosecution: The Decision to Charge a Suspect with a Crime.* Boston: Little, Brown.

Neubauer, David. (1974). *Criminal Justice in Middle America.* Morristown, N.J.: General Learning Press.

Rose, Vicki M., and Susan C. Randall. (1982) "The impact of investigator perceptions of victim legitimacy on the processing of rape/sexual assault cases." *Symbolic Interaction* 5:23–36.

Rubinstein, Jonathan. (1973). *City Police.* New York: Farrar, Straus & Giroux.

Scheff, Thomas. (1966). *Being Mentally Ill: A Sociological Theory.* Chicago: Aldine Publishing Co.

Stanko, Elizabeth A. (1980) "These are the cases that try themselves: An examination of the extra-legal criteria in felony case processing." Presented at the Annual Meetings of the North Central Sociological Association, December. Buffalo, N.Y.

——. (1981). "The impact of victim assessment on prosecutor's screening decisions: The case of the New York District Attorney's Office." *Law and Society Review* 16:225–39.

——. (1982). "Would you believe this woman? Prosecutorial screening for 'credible' witnesses and a problem of justice," In *Judge, Lawyer, Victim, Thief,* ed. Nicole Hahn Rafter and Elizabeth A. Stanko, 63–82. Boston: Northeastern University Press.

Sudnow, David. (1965). "Normal crimes: Sociological features of the penal code in a public defenders office." *Social Problems* 12:255–76.

Torrey, Morrison. (forthcoming). "When will we be believed? Rape myths and the idea of a fair trial in rape prosecutions." U.C. Davis Law Review.

14

But How Can You Sleep Nights?

Lisa J. McIntyre

Abstract: *Lisa McIntyre examines public defenders and the court setting in which they practice their trade. This classic article provides a realistic view of the ups and downs of practicing legal defense work as well as the moral conflicts that public defenders face when they represent indigent clients whom they know are guilty. McIntyre illustrates these moral dilemmas for public defenders by revealing how they are perceived and addressed by the courtroom work group. She then offers insightful descriptions of criminal defense lawyers' justifications for representing such clients. She shows that defense lawyers often claim that defending such persons serves the important purpose of upholding the constitutional guarantee to provide all indigent defendants with legal counsel.*

Hardly anyone will take issue with the idea that everyone, guilty or innocent, is entitled to a fair trial. But beyond this, the views of lawyers and nonlawyers diverge. To the nonlawyer, a fair trial is one that results in convicting the defendant who is factually guilty and acquitting the defendant who is not. But it is the lawyer's job to do every possible thing that can be done for the defendant, even when that means getting a criminal off scot-free, Loopholes and technicalities are defense attorneys' major weapons. Lay people are inclined to feel that using legal tricks to gain acquittals for the guilty is at least morally objectionable, if not reprehensible. What many people want to know is how defense attorneys can live with themselves after they help a guilty person escape punishment.

It might be supposed that lawyers are unimpressed by what, to the rest of us, is the core dilemma of their profession—that is, how to justify defending a guilty person. It might be reasoned that lawyers escape this quandary because their legal training has taught them that it does not exist. In law school everyone learns that a defendant is innocent until proved guilty. Lawyers believe this—and can act on it—because they have been taught to "think like lawyers." Legal reasoning, "although not synonymous with formal reasoning and logic . . . is closely tied to them. Promotion of these skills encourages abstracting legal issues out of their social contexts to see issues narrowly and with precision" (Zemans and Rosenblum 1981, 205).

Simply put, legal reasoning depends on a closed set of premises; some propositions are legal, others are not. The nonlawyer can scarcely be expected to appreciate or understand the difference, for it takes "trained men" to "winnow one from the other" (Friedman 1973, 245). But lawyers, by virtue of this training, are expected to cope with complex issues, to detach themselves from difficult moral questions and focus on legal ones, to take any side of an argument while remaining personally uninvolved, and to avoid making judgments about their clients or their clients' cases. Thus—and this is a surprise to nonlawyers—the factual guilt or innocence of the client is *supposed* to be irrelevant. A lawyer is expected take a point of view and argue it; a criminal defense lawyer is expected to put on a vigorous defense even when the client is known to be guilty.

On the other hand, however much their training sets them apart, there are some attorneys who cannot detach themselves, cannot overlook the social and moral meanings and consequences of their jobs. There are lawyers who in fact see the issues very much as nonlawyers do. Ohio attorney Ronald L. Burdge explained to columnist Bob Greene why he had given up defending criminal cases:

> "If your client is guilty and you defend him successfully, then you have a criminal walking the streets because of your expertise. I have a couple of children. I just didn't like the idea of going home at night knowing that I was doing something so—unpalatable. I found it difficult to look at my kids knowing that this was how I was making a living" (Greene 1982, 1).

Wishman (1981) remembered how he had humiliated a woman when she testified against his client, how by cross-examination he had undone her claim that she had been raped and had made her seem to be little more than a prostitute. Seeing her rage started him thinking that society—and, more specifically, the victims of those whom he had defended—were "casualties" of his skill as a defense lawyer. After years spent preparing for and practicing criminal law, Wishman believed that he had to change: "I had never turned down a case because the crime or the criminal was despicable—but now that would change. I could no longer cope with the ugliness and brutality that had for so long, too long, been part of my life."

Encounters between defense lawyers and those who question the ethics of their work are seldom as dramatic as the one experienced by Wishman. But it is certain that such encounters occur with great frequency in the lives of defense attorneys. All of the current public defenders with whom I spoke and nearly all (93 percent) of the former assistants interviewed in my research agreed that people "constantly" ask public defenders, "How can you defend those people?" But the disenchanted public defender quoted above seems to speak for only a minority of lawyers. The overwhelming majority (97 percent) of former public defenders interviewed agreed that they had believed that they were putting their legal skills to good use by working as public defenders. Only five (8 percent) said that they would not join the office if they had it to do over again.

Given that the public defender's goal is to zealously defend and to work toward acquittal for his or her clients (even clients whom they themselves believe are guilty of heinous crimes), how do these lawyers justify their work? As I explain below, it is not as if public defenders harbor any illusions about the factual innocence of the usual client; on the contrary, most will openly admit that the majority of their clients are factually guilty. If conventional morality has it that defending guilty people is tantamount to an obstruction of justice, how do public defenders justify their rebellion? How *do* they defend those people?

How can you defend people whom you know are guilty? Public defenders say that question is incredibly naive, that for the most part they have little patience with that question and little time for anyone who asks it. One suspects that they would like to answer with shock and outrage when asked how they do what they do—and sometimes they do answer like that. But usually they respond in a manner that is more weary than indignant:

> Oh God, *that* question! How do you represent someone you know is guilty? So you go through all the things. You know, "he's not guilty until he's proven guilty, until a judge or a jury say he's guilty, until he's been proved guilty beyond a reasonable doubt." I think everyone deserves the best possible defense, the most fair trial he can get. It's a guarantee of the Constitution, no more, no less.
>   I tell them it's easy, and I give them a whole list of reasons why it's easy. . . . Everyone has a right to a trial, and with that right to a trial you have a right to a lawyer. I'm that lawyer. That's the American way.

Without exception the public defenders whom I interviewed all had spiels prepared for that question—another testimony to the fact that answering it is part of their routine. As a reporter who interviewed Public Defender James Doherty in 1983 observed, "If you don't ask him soon enough, he'll preempt you" (Spencer 1984, 1). Some lawyers even had two spiels, one for people who phrased it *as* a question and another for those who made it an accusation: "I have developed a patter that depends on how aggressively I am asked. When asked aggressively, I respond aggresively— 'How can you possibly ask me such a question? Have you never read the Constitution?' It gets meaner. When I am asked, well, you know, in a relatively dispassionate way, a neutral sort of way, basically the response is, 'It makes no difference to me whether they are guilty or not, whether they have committed the offense or not, the person is entitled to have representation to protect his Constitutional rights.'" Simply put, public defenders believe that they come not to destroy the law but to fulfill it.

The sincerity of the public defenders' beliefs is compelling, but the persuasiveness of their arguments is less so. The litany of constitutional ideals rarely convinces the hearer any more (as I will suggest) than it emotionally empowers public defense lawyers to act zealously in the defense of their clients. Attorney Burdge, for example, states unequivocally that *he* still *believed* in the constitutional rights of defendants, that all he was abandoning was his personal protection of these rights: "I just think I'll let other lawyers defend them" (Greene 1982, 1).

Making a Case Defensible

Public defenders who daily "flout" conventional morality by defending guilty people are perhaps no more focused only on the narrow legal issues than are those who are troubled by what public defenders do. In fact, if pursued (tactfully) beyond the obvious constitutional justifications, the question How can you defend someone you know is guilty? uncovers the fact that other sorts of rationales are used. Although none of the lawyers went so far as to say, "Yes, I like putting guilty people back on the streets, and I am proud of myself each time I do it," they find justification for doing defense work precisely where Burdge and Wishman found justification for abandoning it—that is, in its social and moral (rather than simply legal) context. Of course, as one might expect, most public defenders stress a different kind of moral and social context than Burdge and Wishman emphasized.

Under some circumstances, mere empathy with the client's situation permits lawyers to feel justified when defending someone whom they know is factually guilty:

> Especially when I was in misdemeanor courts, I could see myself as a defendant. Sometimes you get angry enough at somebody to take a swing at them—if you had a gun, to take a shot at them, I could see myself doing that. . . . Just because somebody was arrested and charged with a crime doesn't mean they are some kind of evil person.

> Look, kids get into trouble, some kids get into serious trouble. I can understand that. In juvenile court our job isn't to punish, the result is supposed to be in the best interests of the minor. Here you've got to keep them with their family and give them all the services you can so they don't do this again.

Not unexpectedly, at some point the ability to empathize breaks down. This is especially true for public defenders who have passed through juvenile or misdemeanor assignments and into felony trial courts, where they are less able—or maybe less willing—to see themselves as being like their clients:

> They [the clients] are seedy and they tend to be, compared to the general population, they are seedier, dirtier, less intelligent, have less conscience, are more sociopathic, more inconsiderate of others, more violent, more poverty stricken and more schizophrenic.
> They don't make their appointments; they aren't articulate enough to take the stand. All those things make it hard.

While the differences between attorney and client mean that the attorney sometimes has a hard time understanding his or her client (and especially the client's motive), *it does not mean* that the client cannot be defended:

> A guy hits somebody over the head and takes a wallet—no problem. A guy that gets into a drunken brawl—no problem. I understand that. Somebody that goes out in the street and commits a rape—I still don't know what goes on his mind. No, it doesn't make it harder to defend. There is *never* any excuse for a rape, but you don't have to understand what makes a rapist tick to defend him effectively.
> Sometimes I would question their motives—if it [the crime] seemed senseless, if it seemed particularly brutal or something like that. Then I realized that those were really, for me, irrelevant questions. I still wonder, of course, but I don't ask anymore.

But the alien character especially of the crimes that their clients are alleged to have committed—and the sorts of attributions that they make about their clients because of their crimes—often mean that "you have to care more about your clients' rights than you can usually care about your clients."

A. The Moral Context of Public Defending

> Why do I do it? I do it because the day that I start laying down and not doing my job is the day that people who aren't guilty are going to be found guilty, and that person might be you because the whole system will have degenerated to the point where they can arrest and convict you on very little evidence. So I am protecting you, I am protecting the middle-class.

On the surface, what a defense lawyer does is simply protect the client's rights. But many lawyers transform the nature of the battle. They are not fighting for the freedom of their client per se but to keep the system honest: "It doesn't mean that I want to get everybody off. It means that I try to make sure the state's attorneys meet up to their obligations, which means that the only way they can prove someone guilty is beyond reasonable doubt, with competent evidence, and overcoming the presumption of innocence. If they can do that, then they get a guilty. If they can't do that, then my client deserves to go home."

The lawyers' way of "bracketing" their role (Weick 1979), of focusing not on the guilt or innocence of their client but on the culpability of the state, transforms circumstances of low or questionable morality into something for which they can legitimately fight. They do not defend simply because their clients have rights but because they believe that those rights have been, are, or will be ignored by others in the criminal justice system. That their adversaries often cheat is taken for granted by public defenders. As one put it, "I expected a fairly corrupt system, and I found one. Here I am representing people who cheat, lie, and steal, and I find the same intellect represented in the police who arrest them, in some of the prosecutors and some of the judges as well." Even when not asked to provide examples, every public defender with whom I spoke offered examples of cheating. There was cheating by the police:

> When I was [working] in the state's attorney's office, I would have cops walking up to me as I was preparing a case and I would say, "Officer, tell me what happened." And they would say, "Well, how do *you* want it to have happened?"
> The biggest form of police dishonesty was this street files thing. They were hiding evidence that would get people off—or get the correct person. But they had decided in their own minds, "This guy is the guy I'm going after," instead of letting the court system decide who was right.

And there was cheating by state's attorneys:

> Sometimes you know it; sometimes you just suspect that they are kinking the case. One guy, fairly high up in the state's attorney's office, described one of their lawyers as naive because he'd been shocked to find a state's attorney had kinked the case. He said of the lawyer, "He thinks this is for real?"

> Q: Kinked the case?
> R: You might call it suborning perjury; you might call it jogging the memory.
> Q: Are you saying that state's attorneys are sometimes a little unprofessional?
> R: Yes, yes, yes! Lying, having witnesses lie; they lie themselves on the record, they make inferences that I'm lying. It's just a basic matter of cheating, of not being professional. Because they feel they must win the case and will do anything to win the case.... Their obligation is not to win; it is to make sure the law is upheld—and to make sure that my client gets a fair trial. And to them, that is a fallacy.

> I remember in that case the prosecutor basically pulled every trick she could: she argued things that were outside the record; she told the jury that [my client] had a record, that he had put a contract out on the witness. She would stop at nothing to win.

This is not to say that one can walk into a Cook County courtroom and expect to see public defenders and state's attorneys at each others' throats. That does happen (at least verbally) on occasion (as I illustrate below), but most public defenders say that they try to maintain a good rapport with their opponents—if only because it helps them do their jobs. And I was cautioned by some lawyers not to listen to those who would condemn state's attorneys universally. As one lawyer told me, "Most of them are not unreasonable; most of them are not [pause] dirty. Most of them are just doing their jobs as best they can."

Actually, public defenders in Cook County seem to be of two minds about their judges. On the one hand, they seem willing to trust the judges to do the right thing.

> If the facts are on your side then you usually take a bench trial. Because you know if you take it before a decent judge, he'll give you a not guilty.
> I think if you stand up there and talk like you know what you are talking about, judges who don't know the law tend to listen to you. If you can present it in a fair-minded way and not ranting and raving and saying, "You idiot, you can't do that and you can't do that!" Sometimes it doesn't work, but, for the most part, it is better if you rationally and calmly explain why you are right.

On the other hand, one gets a definite impression that what public defenders trust about judges is not their fair-mindedness and good-will, but rather, in many cases, the judges' desire not to get into trouble by being overturned by a higher court. In any case, many public defenders told me that they just do not trust the judges' "instincts":

> Knowing legal theory is important, I guess, but it doesn't do any good in Cook County courts, because the question is not Does the law apply? but Can you get the judge to obey it, even though his instincts are to fuck you?
> Oh, I wised up real quick and found that judges don't care about the law; they don't always follow the law.
> q: Do they know the law?
> r: Sometimes . . .
> q: But there's always a public defender there to teach them?
> r: Yea [laugh], but they don't usually care.
>   I view judges as another state's attorney. I see judges as essentially enemies I have to deal with . . . most of them are just bangers.
> q: Bangers?
> r: Someone who gives heavy sentences—oftentimes regardless of the facts of the case.

The sort of cheating to which public defenders attribute their hostility toward police, prosecutors, and judges is something that public defenders say they see a lot. And though such cheating may be expected, public defenders find it unacceptable—and are not afraid to say so. It is ironic, but listening to public defenders talk about their cases and why they do what they do is like listening to someone who has just been mugged, Public defenders do feel as if they are often mugged—by the legal system. There is a lot of real and passionate anger:

> Some people said I'd become cynical after a while. Well, I might be more cynical about some things, but I don't think I have really changed my attitude. If anything, I might have become a little more gung ho. You see that there really is an awful lot of injustice. It becomes very real and it's scary. I find myself becoming very angry in this job, all the time.

Whether or not public defenders are correct in their assumptions that police lie, that prosecutors will often do anything to win, and that judges do not really care or know enough to be fair, it is quite clear that the way in which the public defenders see the world not only excuses their work but makes it seem important. Their rationales are enabling mechanisms for the public defenders. But what ultimately pushes the lawyer to do the job is, I believe, something even more personal—the desire to win.

B. "Adversariness"

Perspectives on the criminal justice system sometimes make use of two ideal type models: the classic adversarial model, which is "couched in constitutional-ideological terms of due process" (Blumberg 1979, 291), and the "dispositional" or "bureaucratic" model, which serves only "bland obeisance to constitutional principles. It is characterized by the superficial ceremonies and formal niceties of traditional due process, but not its substance" (*Ibid.*, 145). (See also Eisenstein and Jacob 1977; Packer 1964.) The difference between the two models is the difference between the presumption of innocence and the presumption of guilt.

It is significant that social scientists who study public defenders tend to discuss their findings only in terms of the second model—the bureaucratic or bargaining model. Never is the matter of how public defenders measure up as trial attorneys studied. The stereotype of the public defender as plea bargainer is, to put it mildly, firmly entrenched in the literature (see, e.g., Blumberg 1967, 1979; Eisenstein and Jacob 1977; Heumann 1978; Jackson 1983; Nardulli 1978; Sudnow 1965).

It is a fact that most cases that come into the, criminal trial courts are disposed of through pleas of guilty; many of these are negotiated—that is, based on a reduction of charges or sentences. Kalven and Zeisel's (1966) estimate that 75 percent of total criminal prosecutions are disposed of through pleas is now seen as conservative; more often the estimate is between 85 percent and 95 percent (depending on whether misdemeanor cases are included in the count) (see Blumberg 1979, 168). The National Advisory Commission on Criminal Justice Standards and Goals (1974, 42) has estimated that in many courts the rate of guilty pleas is 90 percent.

Public defenders do not deny the importance of plea bargaining in their work; they openly and easily acknowledge that the greatest majority of their cases are ultimately disposed of through pleas of guilty. But, they stress, plea bargaining is not their reason for being there but is just a tool:

> Q: Now here you are telling me that you are a "trial attorney." How can you say that? To be fair, isn't most of your work really plea bargaining?
>
> R: Plea bargaining is just part of procedure. Just like I wouldn't say, "I'm a procedural attorney." . . . It's part of what you go through, and it's one of the options available to my clients. You know, "If you in fact did this, and you want this deal, and you understand what you are offered, here is the deal."

In some cases, I was told, the structure that ostensibly exists to handle plea bargaining is used in the lawyer's trial strategy:

> In most courtrooms you have a conference before the trial and lay out your case and say what you are going to do. This happens before the judge. Part of this is a function of State's Attorney Daley's office. The state's attorneys are very rarely giving very reasonable offers. They are putting it all on the judges; they make the judge make the decision.
>
> So, in general what you do is ask for a plea conference. You go back with the state to the judge's chambers.

Supposedly, you are there for the state to say their side, for you to say your side, and for the state to make an offer.

What I'm finding though, is that you are trying your case that way—for the judge. We [public defenders] are stronger, better prepared. Even if I'm not getting an offer that my man is going to plead guilty to, I'm taking the case in front of the judge. It gives me an advantage in the trial.

The Role of Trials in Local Justice

The majority of their clients do plead guilty, but trials are not unimportant in the world of the public defender. They are important, on the one hand, because what happens during trials helps determine the outcome of cases that are plea bargained. For example, prosecutors wish to maintain a strong record of conviction at trial or else defendants who might otherwise opt for a plea bargain will seek acquittal at a trial. Rulings on evidence made by judges during trials also have an impact on the negotiating process. Attorneys from both sides will evaluate the strength of their positions by the standards evolved through trial court and appellate hearings; these rulings made by trial judges, as well as the sentences given to defendants found guilty, help parties in a plea bargain to determine what their respective cases are "worth" (Jacob 1980, 80).

But more fundamentally, trials are important in the public defender's world (and hence are stressed here) because, at least in Cook County, public defenders first and last define themselves as trial lawyers. Lawyers become public defenders primarily to gain trial experience; once they have become public defenders, performance at trial is much more crucial to attributions that they make about themselves and each other than one could ever guess given the relative frequency of these performances.

Public defenders often said that they like the trial work more than any other part of their job. Each one will admit, however, that there are some who do not feel that way. These were pointed out to me as examples of bad public defenders or "kickers." "Sometimes we get a public defender that does not work. He'll force his guy to take a plea, finally on the last day before trial: 'Listen guy, you can take a plea which is the best thing you could do or you can go to trial. But I'm not prepared for trial and you're going to lose because you are *supposed* to lose this case—you know that too.'" Some public defenders are labeled as bad lawyers because they cannot hack it in the courtroom; the reason that they cannot hack it (it is said) is that they are afraid. As many pointed out, being "on trial" is scary. One veteran lawyer told me: "We lose a lot of public defenders because they can't handle being on trial."

But all of them, even the lawyers who love trial work, are ambivalent about it. Trial work, or so most of them acknowledge (in words, if not by deed), is as terrifying as it is exhilarating.

You know [a lawyer who is now in private practice]? Now he is one of the better trial lawyers. But he used to throw up before final arguments. Once he did it right in front of the jury; he just went over to the wastebasket and threw up.

Trials? *That's* when I can't sleep well at night; I'm too busy thinking. A trial is not one issue, it's many. It's win or lose; it's deadlines, organizing things, making sore your witnesses are ready, looking good in front of the jury, looking confident in front of the judge, watching everything you are doing, being alert, keeping a lot of things in your mind at once. And remembering that your client's freedom depends on your polish, how well you can bring it off.

Doing Trials

On television a defense lawyer confronts his clients with demands for the truth: "Okay, I'm your lawyer and you gotta trust me. If I'm going to do a good job I need to know exactly what happened. Don't be afraid to tell me, I can't defend you unless you are perfectly straight with me." The client is thus persuaded to tell all to his lawyer.

This sort of dialogue may appeal to the viewer's common sense—that is, of course the lawyer needs to know what happened and whether the client is guilty. But in real life, things do not happen that way—at least they do not happen that way when the lawyer is a public defender. Public defenders are quick to admit that they usually *do not* ask their clients whether they are guilty or innocent. Why not ask? The lawyers claimed that it was simply not relevant, that it was something that they did not need to know.

> I don't ask "Did you do it?" anymore. I realized it was irrelevant.
> I say to them first thing: "I don't care if you did it or not"
> I say: "I don't give a damn whether you did it or not. I'm not your judge, I'm not your priest, I'm not your father. My job is to defend you, and I don't care whether you did it."

It might be that public defenders do not ask because they know that their client is probably guilty and because, as one said, "they will all lie anyway." But there seems to be more to it, than that. Many said that, when it comes down to it, they do not ask because they are afraid that the client will tell them the truth!

> Q: Don't you ever ask your clients if they are guilty or innocent?
> R: Never!
> Q: Why is that?
> R: Because, in the first place, it is irrelevant. It's not my role to decide whether they are guilty—in our sense of the term guilt.
> Q: What about the "second place?"
> R: Well, it is my role to fashion a defense and to be creative. If the person says to me "this is how I did it," it's pretty hard for me to come around and try to do something for them. In general, I fence around with some of my questions. I ask them about an alibi or something like that. But the more I think they are guilty, the less I will ask.

Public defenders do not begin their relationship with a client by asking awkward questions (e.g., Did you do it?) because once the client admits guilt, it limits what the public defender can ethically do:

> I don't ask them because you put them at a disadvantage if you ask them and they say they did it.
> I had a client once who was charged with battery, and he said, "Yea, I hit him, and I've been meaning to hit him for a long time. But it's just his word against mine, and I'm gonna say I didn't do it."
> And I said: "*not* with me as your lawyer you're not! You are not going to say anything like that."
> So it's important to get the transcript [from the preliminary hearing] and look at the police reports and say "Look, this is the evidence against us" and then let him make up his own story. It's the only way to do it.

Being honest, ethical, and "scrupled" in a system that many of them believe is corrupt is very important to the lawyers with whom I spoke. Although some (naive observers) may wonder at the fragility of this honesty, it is something in which the public defenders take pride:

> There aren't many public defenders—if any—that I can point to and say: "that man is dishonest. He lied and distorted everything, just to get a client off." That just doesn't happen. The same cannot be said for lawyers in the state's attorney's office.
>
> You test the state's evidence, you doubt it, you put it into its worst light. But that is not dishonest. Quite the contrary, that is how you get at the truth!

Public defenders learn quickly that the tell-me-the-truth approach will only help defend an innocent person—the exceptional client. Public defenders argue that it is not their job to decide who is guilty and who is not. Instead, it is the public defender's job to judge the quality of the case that the state has against the defendant. If the lawyer does decide that the state has a case that cannot be called into reasonable doubt, then the lawyer will probably try to get the defendant to admit guilt so that pleading is more palatable—but usually *only* then.

Bad Cases and Good Lawyers

> There is a saying in the office: "Good facts make good lawyers." A good lawyer, I think, is one who doesn't screw up a case. Someone who takes a case that's a winner—one that should be won—and wins it; gets a not guilty. A bad lawyer is a person who takes a case that should be won and loses it. A good lawyer isn't necessarily one that wins a loser case. You get lucky; you get a good jury and win a case that no one could possibly win. That doesn't prove anything; that is very often luck, and it doesn't mean anything.

In practice, a more diffuse yardstick is used: "competency is taking the right cases to trial and winning them." As I show below, the lawyers following this logic are in peril of succumbing to a painful tautological trap.

Public defenders try not to go into a trial with cases that cannot be won. Unfortunately, most of their cases are of this type—loser (or "dead-bang loser") cases, cut-and-dried situations in which the client was caught red-handed and "the state has everything but a video tape of the crime." In the face of overwhelming evidence, the lawyers will try to talk the client into taking a plea or "copping out." One reason for this is the knowledge that taking a loser case to trial will hurt the client:

> My philosophy is that if you are going down and you know it, you should get the best deal for your client that you can. And you should try and make your client see the wisdom of that. It's better for your client. I could say "Sure, I'll take this to trial, sure I can use the experience," but that doesn't do your client any good if he's going down for more time.
>
> I have a client who I have been dealing with just recently who, ah, I was his attorney and I told him he ought to plead guilty. I told him I got this *great* deal for him: I had packed up several cases he had pending in several courtrooms and got him two years. And he had been convicted before!
>
> But he didn't like it. He got himself a private attorney who gave him a guarantee of probation or something. He calls me up add said the private attorney had come back to him with an offer of *six* years. He said to me: "You were right!"

In large part, being competent is being able to convince a client that it is not in his or her best interests to insist on a trial that cannot be won. One lawyer explained how he had learned this lesson back when he was assigned to a preliminary hearing court:

Well, pal, listen. They caught you inside this guy's home, this guy held you down while his wife called the police. You are not going to get a chance to beat this case. You say you were drunk, but being drunk just isn't a good excuse anymore. It's up to you. The state is making you an offer and if you take it, you'll be better off than if you go upstairs [to the trial court].

Everybody told you to say things like that and sure enough, when I got up to the trial courts, I realized it was true. The offers *are* much better in preliminary hearing courts.

But to confront those guys with that decision. It was incredible, it was so hard. Now I can do it fairly routinely because I have been doing it long enough to have confidence in what I'm saying, I know it is true. And I learned that you aren't doing anyone a favor when you bring a loser case upstairs—it's no good for the client, it's no good for the lawyer. But then I felt incredibly guilty.

Once it is decided that they have a loser case, different attorneys have different ways of trying to "cool out" clients who want to go to trial. However, all of the attorneys with whom I spoke and all of the public defenders that I observed with clients seemed uncomfortable with the idea of forcing anyone to take a plea. Most emphasized that they always tried to reason with their clients:

Most of our clients do feel that if you are a public defender you are not going to give it your all, because you have so many cases, or you just don't care, or whatever. They feel that you are just there to cop them out.

But my partner and I sit down with a guy and say: "Look, we are lawyers, and we are paid to analyze facts. After we have analyzed the facts we might say to you, 'we don't think you have a good case and we think you should cop out.' If you don't feel that way, it's up to you."

We let *them* make the decision.

I always leave it up to the defendant. I lay it out for him what the risks are, and if he asks me I'll tell him what his chances of winning are. But just like I can't play God and say if he's guilty or not, I can't play God and tell a guy "You go to trial," or "You don't go to trial."

But, public defenders admitted, reasoning with a client does not always produce the desired result. One lawyer, now a supervisor, admitted that occasionally he would resort to a little "bullying." What did he mean by that? "I would come in, and I would say things like, 'You know, you are a damn fool if you don't take this deal, because this is the best you are going to get. If you go on trial, in my opinion, you are going to be found guilty and you are going to get more time.' And then people would say—not often, but occasionally, the person would say—'I don't care; I didn't do it, and I want a trial!' And I would say, 'Okay, okay. If *that's* your attitude, let's go to trial!' "

If public defenders resist taking loser cases to trial because it will hurt the client, they resist too because it will be painful for the lawyer. One of the worst things about being a public defender, said one former assistant, was "not the realization that most of your clients were in fact guilty" but the fact that "there was very little you could do to get the system to give them a not guilty" or that, as another said, "your clients never had any real obvious defense and you [the attorney] were just stuck."

Ask any public defender "What was your worst case?" and you may or may not hear about some horrible crime; you may or may not hear about the case that lasted the longest or took the most preparation. Chances are, however, you will hear about a case that was a loser. Understanding the nature of a loser case is crucial, for embedded in the concept—and in the distinctions that lawyers make between losers and other sorts of cases—is the clue to what makes public defenders tick.

The worst case is where the state has an overwhelming amount of evidence and there is nothing you can do with it. . . . It's a case where you are just overwhelmed by the state's evidence. It's a case where you get beat up in court. And that is just *no fun*.

You are so relieved when a guy pleads out on a case that you know you can't win, and you are going to get your head beaten on, and the jury is probably going to throw rocks at you when you make the closing argument.

My worst case was a very hopeless case, a rape and armed robbery, and the persons were captured by the police and they were contending that they were the wrong guys.

The opposite of a loser case is not necessarily a winner. It is a fun case, which in turn must be distinguished from a boring case.

I don't like armed robberies because they are boring. There are only one or two issues—either the guy did it or he didn't—and that doesn't make for very interesting work.

The case I am trying with _____ right now is a murder that is really a lot of fun.

Listen to me! "A murder is a lot of fun." How can I say that? [Laugh] It's a murder of a baby, and here I am with my two little kids and you would think that I would feel terrible about that, wouldn't you?

But it's an interesting case because the facts are such that they [the state] don't really have much evidence in the case—a lot of other people could have done it. It's all circumstantial evidence. That's fun. It's something for me to get excited about and get into, whereas a lot of cases—there are just no issues and that makes them boring.

I don't know if I have a favorite kind of case, there are some that are a lot more fun to do—if you just think of it in terms. I may sound horrible, but, just because of the circumstances, usually murder cases are kind of fun.

Usually what kills you in a case is somebody is on the witness stand pointing a finger at your client, saying "that guy robbed me with his gun." Whereas in a murder case you don't have a victim.

Q: What you mean is that you don't have a victim who can come to testify in court, right?

R: Right, he's not there in court. And all the evidence—well, oftentimes you have a totally circumstantial case which gives you a lot to do.

And rape cases. I hate to say it, but there's a lot to play with in a rape case: identification, consent, much more so than in your average armed robbery. You never, for example, you never have the issue of consent in armed robbery.

It is shocking to hear the lawyers talk about their favorite cases, and they are not unmindful of this. But the point is important: a favorite case is the opposite of a loser—a loser is not a loser just because it is a case that will be lost. A case is a loser when it leaves the lawyer nothing to do for the client.

The lawyers are possessed by the very human desire, as they put it, not to make "assholes" of themselves or be perceived as "jerks" in court. The jury may not really throw rocks at them but, what is worse (or so the lawyers think), will think that they are naive or stupid for "falling for what the defendant told them." A case is fun to the degree that it allows the lawyers to act in the way in which they think that lawyers ought to act; a case is interesting when it gives them an opportunity to "comport yourself in a professional manner, to be an advocate for your client without looking *ridiculous* in the process, when you can get across to the jury that there is, at least, a *respectable* difference of opinion here."

Loser cases put the lawyer-as-a-professional at a terrible disadvantage:

I had one case where the, one of the defendants shot the leg off a ten-year-old girl with a shotgun. You know, that's kind of rough.

What are you supposed to say in defense of that? But because the state wasn't offering us anything decent in the plea bargain and we offered some pretrial motions that we could only preserve by going to trial, we had to go to trial.

> The worst case is one where you just don't have anything. And you know you are just going to go out there and lose, and there is *nothing* you can do.
>
> Like, they will have two counts and one will be for aggravated battery and one will be for robbery and [the state] will toss the agg. batt., drop it down to plain battery, if you plead. But If you don't, and If you go to trial, you get a finding of agg. batt.
>
> Well, I had to go to trial on this case because the kid swears up and down that he didn't do it. But I haven't got *anything*! They've got two eyeball witnesses, and all I have is the kid saying, "But I didn't do it!" *And what am I going to do with that?*
>
> And it's a sure loser, but I am going to trial because the kid won't admit.

The lawyers feel that, with a loser case, it is hard—if not impossible—to look respectable. With a loser case it is often difficult to look as if you are doing *anything*.

Losing

In his look at the legal profession, sociologist Talcott Parsons (1954) commented that adherence to procedure (i.e., doing everything that can be done when it ought to be done and as it ought to be done) protects lawyers from being devastated when they lose: "The fact that the case can be tried by a standard procedure relieves [the attorney] of some pressure of commitment to the case of his client. He can feel that, if he does his best then having assured his client's case of a fair trial, he is relieved of the responsibility for an unfavorable verdict" (1954, 380).

One of the attorneys with whom I spoke seemed to confirm Parsons's hypothesis, at least with respect to loser cases: "There is a certain consolation of going to trial with a loser case. If I lose, what the hell. I gave it my best shot. If I lose, *it was a loser*. If I win, it's amazing."

Most of the attorneys, however, were not so sanguine and could not detach themselves from the outcomes of their cases so easily. Even losing a loser case, most of them said, is incredibly hard on the attorney.

> It's hard, you know? You can tell someone the facts of the case, and they say, "What did you expect? It was a loser." But that doesn't make me feel any better when I lose a loser. I want to win.
>
> Ah, idealistically I've talked about why I'm a public defender, about how I want to keep the state on the straight and narrow. And I *could* go home and say, "Well, I forced the state to prove their case beyond a reasonable doubt," but, ah, I still that isn't what I *really* feel when I lose. What I *really* feel is just that I lost this case and I wanted to win this case.

The attorneys are not much comforted by the fact that the client was guilty—or probably guilty, anyway.

> Q: When you feel bad about losing a case, doesn't it help to know that the client was probably guilty anyway?
> R: Yea [pause], maybe. But in the middle of the trial, it's you, you know? You are trying to make them believe what you are trying to sell them, and, if you don't win, it means that they don't believe *you*. That's probably one of the reasons that it doesn't help.

> There was a case, not too long ago, that I really came to believe that they had no evidence on my man, and I fought very hard for him. We lost, and I felt very bad about that.
>
> Afterward, he just fell apart, started screaming at me back in the lock-up. We had this big fight. And I yelled at him: "You know, I really put myself on the line too, and I did everything I could for you, and what are you doing yelling at me? Cause I really believed, and I worked hard."

And then I misspoke myself, because I said, "And I really believed that you didn't do this." And he said, "Would it make you feel any better if I told you that I *did* do it?" [Laugh].

Q: How did you answer him?
R: [Laugh] I said, "I don't want to know: don't tell me!" I still don't want to know, and that's how it is.

Most telling is how these lawyers talk about doing trial work. They do not say, "I'm doing a trial now"; they do not ask, "Are you doing a trial this week?" They say, "*I'm on trial*"; they ask, "Are *you* on trial?"

Lawyers hate to lose because, although reason tells them a case is a loser, sentiment says that justice favors not the stronger case but the better lawyer. What makes losing any case, even a loser, so bad is their belief that, in the hands of a *good* attorney, there is really no such thing as a dead-bang loser case. One attorney told me: "Fewer and fewer of my cases are losers. . . . Because I am a better and better lawyer."

Most of the attorneys seemed to feel the same way:

> One of the maxims I've learned is that the evidence is always better than the way it looks on paper. There is always some goof-up of a witness, something that comes up in fee trial, so that you always have something to work with. Invariably that is so.
>
> By the time I walk into the courtroom, even if rationally I sat down when I first heard the case and said "Well, there is no way I can win," by the time I walk into the courtroom I will figure out some way to argue to the judge or the jury that I think I can convince them. By that time, I believe I can win the case.
>
> You start out thinking "I can't win this, no one can win this." Then you start to get a glimmer, a way out of it being a loser case. Then you think that, if only you can make the jury understand things the way you understand things, they will go along with you and give you a not guilty. Part of you knows—or at least that is what you tell yourself later—part of you knows you *can't* win, that you aren't going to win, but that gets lost in the part of you that wants so much to win this case for your guy—and to win this case for you.

Of course, you have to be good to take advantage of those goof-ups, those things that invariably come your way in the trial. Because of the suspicion that there is always something, when it cannot be found or when it does not work, the lawyer is apt to feel at fault. Even when they know that their client was factually guilty, public defenders are likely to feel, "I let my client down."

> The most stressful time is on a difficult case and you realize that, well, some *other* lawyer could win this, why the hell can't I? I will do everything I can, but there will still be something I miss. And yet, maybe nobody in the courtroom, not even my client, knows about it. But it can destroy our case. Then, when you lose, you feel the weight of your client's sentence on your shoulders. When my client gets sentenced, part of me is going with him.
>
> You go home and you have those "ah, shit! God damn, why didn't I? If I only would have, if I only would have spent ten more minutes, if I only would have asked him this, if I would have gone out and asked, or done more investigations". . . . Your mistakes? Your mistakes go to jail.

The stress of being on trial and the pain of losing are compounded on those rare occasions when the lawyer believes the defendant is innocent. For this reason, although the lawyers will say, "I don't care if he's guilty or innocent," their claim to neutrality is often a lie. When they say, "I don't care if my client is guilty," what they usually mean is, "I *prefer* my clients to be guilty."

> Most defense attorneys would rather not have a client they think is innocent, because it's just irrelevant. Because it's your job to fight the state's case no matter what. You *hate* to lose, and you are worried about losing just because it's your job to win. And if you think he's innocent, you worry more. And that is just aggravation, which is really irrelevant to your job.

None of the current public defenders with whom I spoke said they preferred innocent clients, and all but two said they actually preferred representing defendants whom they believed were guilty. Many of the attorneys did not want to talk about such cases, even hypothetically. Most of them just said something like, "In my own gut I know I have a harder time defending people I know are innocent than people I suspect are guilty—the pressure to win is so much greater then," or "it is just harder to defend an innocent person because there is so much pressure." Although no public defender said as much, given what they did say, I suspect that what makes defending an innocent client so stressful is the fact that if one should fail to win an acquittal, it would be difficult to avoid the conclusion that it was the lawyer's fault (although in theory, this may not be true). In such cases, the weight of the client's sentence really hangs on the defender. One lawyer told me how he protected himself from the possibility of that kind of "incredible stress." He explained that he "tried not to think about having innocent clients [pause], but it's academic since they are all guilty anyway."

Coping with Losing

Losing is one of the costs of being an attorney; losing a lot (I was told) is one of the costs of being a public defender:

> You must try to convince the judge or the jury that what you are saying must be followed. But as a public defender, you get the realization that no matter how hard you do this, no matter how well you do this, you are probably not going to get it across. Or, even if you do, the judge or the jury is going to say no. You cannot be afraid to lose, because mostly it's a lost cause. You cannot have a personality where you must win or it's going to screw you.
>
> Sometimes it's just that you get rotten case after rotten case. It drives you crazy. What it does is it makes you think you can't win.
>
> When you lose a few in a row, you question yourself. And then it becomes real hard to go back into court and try again.

Public defenders do not like to lose—but said that one must just learn to accept it. Nevertheless, watching them try their cases and listening to them talk about their cases made it clear to me that the attorneys do not just accept losing. In many instances, the attorneys seemed to try to outwit defeat.

However it looks to the spectator—or, for that matter, to the defendant—public defenders can show you how a trial is not a zero-sum situation. Even when the lawyer does not win freedom for his or her client, *something* may have been won: "I don't feel defeatist. There is a lot you can do, even if you lose—like mitigate a person's involvement or partly win by getting a guilty on one charge and not on another."

Even when there is no way to mitigate the client's guilt or to partly win, there is such a thing as an almost win. Those count too—at least they are counted by the attorneys, especially if the case had seemed to be open and shut. There is a certain measure of satisfaction that can be drawn, for example, from keeping the jury out longer than could have been expected.

> It was a terrible case, a terrible case. It was a brutal, cold-blooded slaying of a ma-and-pa grocer. They had a witness, a flipper. The guy who drove the car flipped against them both. They found the guns in my guy's house; they had a dead-bang loser case against them.
>
> We tried to discredit the flipper and minimize the effect of the gun being found, saying that they couldn't absolutely prove that it was the same gun that had been used.
>
> We lost. We kept the jury out for about ten hours or so, and that was something. But we ended up losing.
>
> We did a jury trial a few weeks ago—the case was a rape, a 14-year-old. Both my partner and I felt he would be found guilty and that he probably did it. But we tried that case *so* hard, then we lost it.
>
> But we kept the jury out almost three hours, and we thought it was going to be like 15-minute guilty verdict.

Moreover, the lawyers are helped some by their ability to distinguish a loss from a defeat. Even when they lose, public defenders search for evidence that they did a better job, that they "out-tried" the state's attorneys. Out-trying one's adversaries can mean anything from simply acting more professional to forcing your opponent to commit reversible error. Sometimes it just means making him or her look silly in court.

During long or tough cases the level of exchange between defense and prosecuting attorneys can destroy all ideals that one might have about noble adversaries. Attorneys (as they themselves admit) will sometimes bait each other, trying to force their opponents to do something regrettable. The following are snatches of dialogue from a death-penalty case. All these exchanges took place on the record (I have, however, changed the lawyers' names). Mr. Buford and Mr. Petrone speak for the prosecution; attorneys Carney, Stone, and Richert appeared for the defense:

[Time One]

RICHERT: [To the court] During Mr. Carney's remarks, Mr. Buford came to me personally and pointed to Mr. Stone and said, "Do you realize your partner looks like Lenin?" I would appreciate if the prosecutor would avoid interfering with my participation in proceedings such as these.

THE COURT: Which prosecutor? Who is he talking about? Who looks like Lenin?

[Later that day]

CARNEY: [To Buford] Oh, put your foot down [off the table]. Act like an attorney. What is wrong with you?

BUFORD: Come on.

CARNEY: Take your foot off the table!

BUFORD: You don't tell me what to do!

CARNEY: It insults me as an attorney.

BUFORD: I may do that, but you don't tell me what to do!

THE COURT: We will take a recess.

[Time Two]

PETRONE: Let's go. We have been waiting seven months for it.

STONE: That's unprofessional.

PETRONE: That's as unprofessional as you, Mr. Stone.

STONE: Wasn't it enough that we showed you how to pick a jury?

PETRONE: You showed us how to pick a jury? You pleaded him right into the electric chair!

[Time Three]

BUFORD: [in chambers] I am at this time requesting that we go out in the court and requesting that—I just did—that we go on fee record, because once again, I am

	not going to put up with any more of this state's attorney baiting or this other bullshit that's gone on here in chambers.
CARNEY:	*That's on the record!*
BUFORD:	Right: exactly, That has gone on here for eight weeks. I request that we go out in open court. Let the record reflect [pause]. [To judge] Look at Mr. Carney!
CARNEY:	And I am looking at Mr. Buford, Judge. And I have never heard *that* word said in a court of law in eight years, Judge, by a state's attorney or any defense lawyer, and I am *really* shocked!
BUFORD:	Look at these faces that they are making. I am asking that you hold them in direct contempt!
THE COURT:	All right, but I just wanted to know what witnesses are you calling?

The defense lost the case. They had hoped to "win" by getting a life sentence, but their client was sentenced to death. To any observer; it was a total loss. After listening to testimony for several weeks, the jury took less than an hour and only one vote to make the decision unanimous. Still, the attorneys (Mr. Carney, in particular) appeared to derive a great deal of satisfaction from their belief that they had not been "defeated," that they had caused their opponents (Mr. Buford, in particular) to "lose it" several times during the case. The night before the case ended, Mr. Carney recalled what for him had been a major highlight of the case. "Lisa, you know what Buford said to me that first day? He said, 'Carney, I heard you were a choker; I *collect* chokers, Carney.' When Buford said 'bullshit' in chambers, I leaned over and whispered to him: 'C-H-O-K-E.'" After the end of the last day in court, after hearing that their client would be sentenced to death, at a dinner that could more properly be called a wake, a deeply depressed Carney repeated several times: "We sure got that bastard Buford; we sure beat their asses, didn't we?" "Yes," he was assured again and again, "we *sure* did."

In retrospect the attorneys seemed a bit childish, their bickering like juvenile acting-out. Yet when one is trying to salvage something that is a lost cause, anyway, every little bit seems to help.

It should be noted too that the above exchanges are unusual, a result of the fact that, in the attorneys' minds, baiting the state's attorneys could not make things any worse for their client than it was inevitably going to be—and might, if they could push the prosecutor far enough, win him a mistrial. Normally, the attorneys are mindful of the fact that acting out will probably hurt one's client. Even in this case, the lawyers (the defense lawyers, anyway) never got totally out of control. It should be noted that while all of these exchanges (and others like them) took place on the record, they took place out of the hearing of the jury.

But even if the public defenders do not usually feel free to really mix it up with the prosecutor in court, there is still an important kind of anticipatory satisfaction that emerges from knowing that oftentimes the "only reason the state wins is because the facts are on their side." The satisfaction comes from knowing that *someday* most of those prosecutors are going to leave the state's attorney's office, and many of them are going to turn their hands to criminal defense work. That day, believe many public defenders, will be the day when these prosecutors will get what is coming to them. Public defenders sometimes sound almost smug when they talk about what is in store for prosecutors: "One of the ways I deal with [losing], with when I have to look over at the state's attorneys as they gleefully congratulate each other on their records of victory, when I know I have out-tried them on a case, well, you just say, 'chalk it up.' They are going to leave the office some day; they are going to find out that they are not such hot shit. That's a *big* satisfaction, a very big satisfaction."

Perhaps the most important way in which they cope with losing is knowing that they do not always lose. When I asked one attorney "How do you keep going when you lose?" he said: "Always remembering that there is a flip side of that—you feel great when you win. There is no feeling like it. And *that* wouldn't feel as good if it weren't so hard to win." In fact, the lawyers seem to go into each trial with great expectations of winning. The knowledge that the next case may be the one you win seems to keep them going.

Coping with Winning

> I do not apologize for (or feel guilty about) helping to let a murderer go free—even though I realize that someday one of my clients may go out and kill again. Since nothing like that has ever happened, I cannot know for sure how I would react. I know that I would feel terrible for the victim. But I hope that I would not regret what I had done—any more than a surgeon should regret saving the life of a patient who recovers and later kills an innocent victim.
> (Dershowitz 1983, xiv)

Doctors lose patients; lawyers lose cases. Failure is something with which every professional must cope. But implicit in the question, How can you defend those people? is the idea that public defenders ought to have trouble coping with winning.

The possibility of getting a guilty person off is not a specter that haunts public defenders, at least not to the extent that you would notice it. In misdemeanor and juvenile courts, the majority of defendants represented by public defenders are relatively innocent and/or harmless criminals accused of relatively innocent or harmless crimes. The lawyers are protected by the fact that they rarely win cases for clients who are horrible criminals: winning an acquittal for a burglar or even an armed robber is, for a public defender, hardly cause for intense introspective examinations of one's morality or personal guilt. It is not that they have lost all sense of proportion, but that they have gained a new one—by the time that they get to felony courtrooms, the lawyers are, most of them, convinced that what they see happen to their clients in the jails or in the courts is as bad as or worse than most of what happens to victims out on the streets. There is, moreover, often a sense that the injustices perpetrated by the system are worse because they are committed by people who really ought to know better.

However rarely it occurs, the possibility of winning big someday and then having your client kill again exists in the future of every defense lawyer. It is not something that they seem to talk about very often. It is difficult to talk about it perhaps because there is so much emphasis on the importance of the defendant's right to a lawyer who will do everything possible to win a case. Moreover, in the tough, heroic world of the trial lawyer, it is perhaps difficult to conceive of feeling bad about winning.

A few years ago, an episode of the television show "Hill Street Blues" featured the story of a public defender who got a murderer freed on a "technicality." Some time later, the client murdered again. This time, the victim was a friend of the public defender, who, unable to deal with the guilt, quit the office.

At the time, many public defenders were avid fans of this television show, in large part (I thought) because the writers had created a very competent, tough, and sympathetic role for a public defender on the show. A few days after this particular episode aired, a group of lawyers in the office discussed the story-line and decided that it was unrealistic. I later asked one of them why. "Because the lawyer quit. That's just not the way it's done. You just move into the next case. As a lawyer you are very removed from the reality of it." Reflecting on his answer for a moment, I said, "I just can't believe that." "It's true," he assured me. I pushed him: "What would you do if it happened to you? What if you got a N.G. on a killer and he came around and killed again?" After a few moments he admitted that he "probably would move into another branch of law."

Most of the lawyers with whom I spoke said, as does Dershowitz, that it had not happened to them—and that while they hoped that it would not happen, they did not think that it would bother them. But one added: "As I say that, I am mindful of one public defender named____, I think one of the reasons he left was that he managed to get a guy acquitted on a murder and the guy went out and committed another murder. That really got to him. And I watched him suffer with that, and I wondered if I would suffer like that, and I came to no conclusion."

A few of the lawyers admitted that they had come close to winning cases that, deep down inside themselves, they had not wanted to win: "I've never felt bad about winning a case. The last jury trial I did I almost won, and I *was* worried about that. It really bothered me. But all of it has to do with the relationship you have with your client. He was a real asshole and hard to deal with, and he was a mean son of a bitch."

Often it seemed that one of the things that helps the lawyer not to feel too bad about winning is one of the things that makes it so hard to lose—that is, their relationship with the client. Most of the lawyers said that usually, especially when they go to trial, they end up liking their clients. In most cases, the lawyers spoke with some affection about their "guys."

> There is in any human being a soul you can reach. [Pause] Now I use language like this hesitantly, you know, people usually look at you like you're crazy when you talk like this. But if you are willing to take the risk and open up your heart and reach into their hearts, you will reach it.
>
> You need to do that for yourself. You need to do that too because if you are going to try the case for either a judge or a jury . . . you have to make that person human. They are not some black or brown face—or white face, for that matter. They are someone. And that is what costs. 'Cause everytime you do that you are giving something of yourself away. You get something sure, but you give away a lot.
>
> [At first] I was a little leery. You wonder, "Can I talk to a guy like this?" And you find out it's real easy [laugh], you find out that they are real people, just like you. Well [laugh], maybe not *just* like you, but real people. And you come to like most of your clients [laugh]. That surprised me, still does.
>
> A lot of criminals I have gotten to like. There are some real nice human beings even if they are in real serious trouble.
>
> [Recalling his first murder case] It was funny—I liked the shooter. He was a real nice guy.

The danger, of course, is in getting too involved with your client, getting to like him or her too much. That is when you lose your sense of proportion. As one lawyer told me, you "must always remember that he is a defendant, and you must treat him as a defendant."

Two of the lawyers with whom I spoke had experienced what one called the "defense lawyer's nightmare." One would not talk about it; one would:

> Once on a case with——, he came up with a brilliant idea about collateral evidence, and I wrote a brilliant brief. It persuaded the judge to dismiss the indictment—just unheard of.
>
> And three months later he killed three other people. He participated in a gang killing—didn't actually do the killing, but he was definitely part of it. That, of course, is the defense lawyer's nightmare.
>
> There are people who can—for example, my partner—who can say, "that's not my concern," but that is bullshit. That is why he is losing his hair and I'm not. You feel bad. You *have* to feel bad.
>
> *However*, the constitutional proposition was correct, and it made some important law in Illinois; and I would do it again. But I would not represent [that client] again. Because we could not wholeheartedly represent him zealously, we were let off representing him.

"How can you live with that?" I asked. "You either leave, stay and repress it, or you stay and cope. Sure you feel bad, but you deal with it by knowing that hopefully you are doing enough good to make you feel good about what you are doing."

At the time, that did not seem like much of an answer—but perhaps it is the only one.

Concluding Remarks: Public Defenders and Their Society

Justifying the public defender's rebellion against society is, in fact, a strict adherence to important social values. They believe that it is right to defend "those people" because of the principle that everyone is innocent until proved otherwise and so everyone is entitled to a defense. More important, they also believe that it is right to defend even the guilty because their clients *need* someone to defend them against police, prosecutorial, and judicial abuse. Because of what they see happen in the system every day, public defenders would be the last to claim that defense lawyers are unnecessary luxuries for defendants (guilty or innocent) in our criminal courts.

Beyond these rationales, public defenders are motivated by the desire to legitimize themselves as professionals, to act as professionals, and, as final proof of their right to professional status and respect, to win. Their desire to win makes them look very closely at each client's case: Where has the state failed to make its case? Did the state make an error? Did the police mess up the arrest? Public defenders want to find those cases, because those are the kinds of cases that make them look good. The closer they look, the more they find, and this, in turn, reinforces their view that their work is essential.

In an important sense, then, there is a synergistic relationship between the public defenders' egoistic and altruistic concerns, their desire to win, and their view that they are needed. It is that synergy that no doubt accounts for the combative tone of most of their remarks. In theory this could spiral into a process that is out of all proportion to realty. In truth, the lawyers—especially when they are on trial—do seem to get carried away with what they do. But what prevents them from losing all touch with reality is, I think, the fact that they are not totally enclosed in the cognitive ghetto of public defending. Each is still a member of a society that suspects the morality of what they do; this attachment to society is shown in a process that some public defenders call "honking." By honking each other, public defenders remind one another how the rest of their society regards their work:

> There is a term that I didn't know until I came to this office, a thing called honking, And that is needling or giving someone a hard time, ostensibly in a friendly manner—but it can be very pointed, very barbed. It goes on a great deal. People will get honked for their pretentiousness, for their actual performance on trial.
>
> And people will get honked *mercilessly* for things over which they have *absolutely no control*—the quality of the client, the heinousness of the act with which the person is charged. And people get honked for trying to defend people who really have hopeless legal positions.

Critical Thinking

Although this study was published nearly 25 years ago, the same issues the author discussed remain prevalent in courts to this day. In short, very little has actually changed in the working world of the public defender. However, McIntyre points out that maintaining their integrity was very important to them. "Being honest, ethical, and scrupled in a system that they may often believe is corrupt is very important to these lawyers with whom I spoke." How would you interpret the desire of public defenders to believe that it is morally correct to defend guilty clients because the accused need someone to defend them against police, prosecutorial, and judicial abuse? Would you be able to defend someone who you believe committed a heinous crime using such logic?

References

Blumberg, A. S. 1967. The practice of law as a confidence game: Organizational cooptation of a profession. *Law and Society Review* 1:15–39.

———. 1979. *Criminal justice; Issues and ironies*. New York: New Viewpoints.

Dershowitz, A. M. 1983. *The best defense*. New York: Vintage.

Eisenstein, J., and H. Jacob. 1977. *Felony justice. An organisational analysis of criminal courts*. Boston: Little, Brown and Co.

Friedman, L. M. 1973. *A history of American law*. New York: Simon & Schuster.

Greene, B. 1982. Lawyer closes the book on criminal defense. *Chicago Tribune*, 3 November, sec. 4.

Heumann, M. 1978. *Plea bargaining*. Chicago: University of Chicago Press.

Jackson, B. 1983. *Law and disorder; Criminal justice in America*. Urbana: University of Illinois Press.

Jacob, H. 1980. *Crime and justice in urban America*. Englewood Cliffs, New Jersey: Prentice-Hall.

Kalvin, H. and Zeisel, H. 1966. *The American jury*. Boston: Little, Brown and Co.

Nardulli, R. F. 1978. *The courtroom elite: An organizational perspective on criminal justice*. Cambridge, Massachusetts: Ballinger.

National Advisory Commission on Criminal Justice Standards and Goals. 1974. *Report*. Washington, DC: Government Printing Office.

Packer, H. L. 1964. Two models of the criminal process. *University of Pennsylvania Law Review* 113:1–68.

———. 1954. A sociologist looks at the legal profession. In *Essays in sociological theory*, 370–385. New York: Free Press.

Parsons, T. 1954. *Essays in sociological theory*. New York: Free Press.

Spencer, J. 1984. No glamour, no money: Public defenders still seek justice for all. *Chicago Tribune*, 8 January, sec. 2.

Sudnow, D. 1965. Normal crimes: Sociological features of the penal code in the public defender's office. *Social Problems* 12:235–277.

Weick, K. 1979. *The social psychology of organizing*. Reading, MA: Addison-Wesley.

Wishman, S. 1981. *Confessions of a criminal lawyer*. New York: Penguin.

Zemans, F. K., and V. C. Rosenblum. 1981. *The making of a public profession*, Chicago: American Bar Foundation.

15

Maintaining the Myth of Individualized Justice: Probation Presentence Reports

John Rosecrance

<u>Abstract</u>: *Probation presentence reports emphasize some offender characteristics more than others. John Rosecrance explains how a stereotyping process is used by probation officers who write these reports, and how their sentence recommendations to judges are determined on the use of a few relatively fixed factors (e.g., current offense and prior criminal history). Presentence reports are produced to provide the court with the illusion that each report is based on individual characteristics of the convicted person. However, Rosecrance questions whether probation agencies can really provide individualized justice as they claim to do.*

The Justice Department estimates that over one million probation presentence reports are submitted annually to criminal courts in the United States (Allen and Simonsen 1986:111). The role of probation officers in the presentence process traditionally has been considered important. After examining criminal courts in the United States, a panel of investigators concluded: "Probation officers are attached to most modern felony courts; presentence reports containing their recommendations are commonly provided and these recommendations are usually followed" (Blumstein, Martin, and Holt 1983). Judges view presentence reports as an integral part of sentencing, calling them "the best guide to intelligent sentencing" (Murrah 1963:67) and "one of the most important developments in criminal law during the 20th century" (Hogarth 1971:246).

Researchers agree that a strong correlation exists between probation recommendations (contained in presentence reports) and judicial sentencing. In a seminal study of judicial decision making, Carter and Wilkins (1967) found 95 percent agreement between probation recommendation and sentence disposition when the officer recommended probation and 88 percent agreement when the officer opposed probation. Hagan (1975), after controlling for related variables, reported a direct correlation of .72 between probation recommendation and sentencing. Walsh (1985) found a similar correlation of .807.

Although there is no controversy about the correlation between probation recommendation and judicial outcome, scholars disagree as to the actual influence of probation officers in the sentencing process. That is, there is no consensus regarding the importance of the presentence investigator in influencing sentencing outcomes. On the one hand, Myers (1979:538) contends that the "important role played by probation officer recommendation argues for greater theoretical and empirical attention to these officers." Walsh (1985:363) concludes that "judges lean heavily on the professional advice of probation." On the other hand, Kingsnorth and Rizzo (1979) report that probation recommendations have been supplanted by plea bargaining and that the probation officer is "largely superfluous." Hagan, Hewitt, and Alwin (1979), after reporting a direct correlation between recommendation and sentence, contend that the "influence of the probation officer in the presentence process is subordinate to that of the prosecutor" and that probation involvement is "often ceremonial."

My research builds on the latter perspective, and suggests that probation presentence reports do not influence judicial sentencing significantly but serve to maintain the myth that criminal courts dispense individualized justice. On the basis of an analysis of probation practices in California, I will demonstrate that the presentence report, long considered an instrument for the promotion of individualized sentencing by the court, actually deemphasizes individual characteristics and affirms the primacy of instant offense and prior criminal record as sentencing determinants. The present study was concerned with probation in California; whether its findings can be applied to other jurisdictions is not known. California's probation system is the nation's largest, however (Petersilia, Turner, Kahan, and Peterson 1985), and the experiences of that system could prove instructive to other jurisdictions.

In many California counties (as in other jurisdictions throughout the United States) crowded court calendars, determinate sentencing guidelines, and increasingly conservative philosophies have made it difficult for judges to consider individual offenders' characteristics thoroughly. Thus judges, working in tandem with district attorneys, emphasize the legal variables of offense and criminal record at sentencing (see, for example, Forer 1980; Lotz and Hewitt 1977; Tinker, Quiring, and Pimentel 1985). Probation officers function as employees of the court; generally they respond to judicial cues and emphasize similar variables in their presentence investigations. The probation officers' relationship to the court is ancillary; their status in relation to judges and other attorneys is subordinate. This does not mean that probation officers are completely passive; individual styles and personal philosophies influence their reports. Idiosyncratic approaches, however, usually are reserved for a few special cases. The vast majority of "normal" (Sudnow 1965) cases are handled in a manner that follows relatively uniform patterns.

Hughes's (1958) work provides a useful perspective for understanding the relationship between probation officers' status and their presentence duties. According to Hughes, occupational duties within institutions often serve to maintain symbiotic status relationships as those in higher-status positions pass on lesser duties to subordinates. Other researchers (Blumberg 1967; Neubauer 1974; Rosecrance 1985) have demonstrated that although judges may give lip service to the significance of presentence investigations, they remain suspicious of the probation officers' lack of legal training and the hearsay nature of the reports. Walker (1985) maintains that in highly visible cases judges tend to disregard the probation reports entirely. Thus the judiciary, by delegating the collection of routine information to probation officers, reaffirms its authority and legitimacy. In this context, the responsibility for compiling presentence reports can be considered a "dirty work" assignment

(Hagan 1975) that is devalued by the judiciary. Judges expect probation officers to submit noncontroversial reports that provide a facade of information, accompanied by bottom-line recommendations that do not deviate significantly from a consideration of offense and prior record. The research findings in this paper will show how probation officers work to achieve this goal.

The research findings emphasize the importance of *typing* in the compilation of public documents (presentence reports). In this paper "typing" refers to "the process by which one person (the agent) arrives at a private definition of another (the target)" (Prus 1975:81). A related activity, *designating*, occurs when "the typing agent reveals his attributions of the target to others" (Prus and Stratten 1976:48). In the case of presentence investigations, private typings become designations when they are made part of an official court report. I will show that presentence recommendations are developed through a typing process in which individual offenders are subsumed into general dispositional categories. This process is influenced largely by probation officers' perceptions of factors that judicial figures consider appropriate; probation officers are aware that the ultimate purpose of their reports is to please the court. These perceptions are based on prior experience and are reinforced through judicial feedback.

Methods

The major sources of data used in this study were drawn from interviews with probation officers. Prior experience facilitated my ability to interpret the data. Interviews were conducted in two three-week periods during 1984 and 1985 in two medium-sized California counties. Both jurisdictions were governed by state determinate sentencing policies; in each, the district attorney's office remained active during sentencing and generally offered specific recommendations. I did not conduct a random sample but tried instead to interview all those who compiled adult presentence reports. In the two counties in question, officers who compiled presentence reports did not supervise defendants.

Not all presentence writers agreed to talk with me; they cited busy schedules, lack of interest, or fear that I was a spy for the administration. Even so, I was able to interview 37 presentence investigators, approximately 75 percent of the total number of such employees in the two counties. The officers interviewed included eight women and 29 men with a median age of 38.5 years, whose probation experience ranged from one year to 27 years. Their educational background generally included a bachelor's degree in a liberal arts subject (four had degrees in criminal justice, one in social work). Typically the officers regarded probation work as a "job" rather than a profession. With only a few exceptions, they did not read professional journals or attend probation association conventions.

The respondents generally were supportive of my research, and frequently commented that probation work had never been described adequately. My status as a former probation officer enhanced the interview process greatly. Because I could identify with their experiences, officers were candid, and I was able to collect qualitative data that reflected accurately the participants' perspectives. During the interviews

I attempted to discover how probation officers conducted their presentence investigations. I wanted to know when a sentencing recommendation was decided, to ascertain which variables influenced a sentencing recommendation decision, and to learn how probation officers defined their role in the sentencing process.

Although the interviews were informal, I asked each of the probation officers the following questions:

1. What steps do you take in compiling a presentence report?
2. What is the first thing you do upon receiving a referral?
3. What do you learn from interviews with the defendant?
4. Which part of the process (in your opinion) is the most important?
5. Who reads your reports?
6. Which part of the report do the judges feel is most important?
7. How do your reports influence the judge?
8. What feedback do you get from the judge, the district attorney, the defense attorney, the defendant, your supervisor?

In addition to interviewing probation officers, I questioned six probation supervisors and seven judges on their views about how presentence reports were conducted.

Findings

In the great majority of presentence investigations, the variables of present offense and prior criminal record determine the probation officer's final sentencing recommendation. The influence of these variables is so dominant that other considerations have minimal influence on probation recommendations. The chief rationale for this approach is "That's the way the judges want it." There are other styles of investigation; some officers attempt to consider factors in the defendant's social history, to reserve sentencing judgment until their investigation is complete, or to interject personal opinions. Elsewhere (Rosecrance 1987), I have developed a typology of presentence investigators which describes individual styles; these types include self-explanatory categories such as hard-liners, bleeding-heart liberals, and team players as well as mossbacks (those who are merely putting in their time) and mavericks (those who strive continually for independence).

All types of probation officers, however, seek to develop credibility with the court. Such reputation building is similar to that reported by McCleary (1978) in his study of parole officers. In order to develop rapport with the court, probation officers must submit reports that facilitate a smooth work flow. Probation officers assume that in the great majority of cases they can accomplish this goal by emphasizing offense and criminal record. Once the officers have established reputations as "producers," they have "earned" the right to some degree of discretion in their reporting. One investigation officer described this process succinctly: "When you've paid your dues, you're allowed some slack." Such discretion, however, is limited to a minority of cases, and in these "deviant" cases probation officers frequently allow social variables to influence their recommendation. In one report an experienced officer recommended probation for a convicted felon with a long prior record because the defendant's father agreed to pay for an intensive drug treatment program. In another case a probation officer decided that a first-time shoplifter had a "very bad attitude" and therefore recommended a stiff jail sentence rather than probation. Although these variations from normal procedure are interesting and important, they should not detract from our examination of an investigation process that is used in most cases.

On the basis of the research data, I found that the following patterns occur with sufficient regularity to be considered "typical." After considering offense and criminal record, probation officers place defendants into categories that represent the eventual court recommendation. This typing process occurs early in the course of presentence inquiry; the balance of the investigation is used to reaffirm the private typings that later will become official designations. In order to clarify the decision-making processes used by probation officers I will delineate the three stages in a presentence investigation: 1) typing the defendant, 2) gathering further information, and 3) filing the report.

Typing the Defendant

A presentence investigation is initiated when the court orders the probation department to prepare a report on a criminal defendant. Usually the initial court referral contains such information as police reports, charges against the defendant, court proceedings, plea-bargaining agreements (if any), offenses in which the defendant has pleaded or has been found guilty, and the defendant's prior criminal record. Probation officers regard such information as relatively unambiguous and as part of the "official" record. The comment of a presentence investigator reflects the probation officer's perspective on the court referral:

> I consider the information in the court referral hard data. It tells me what I need to know about a case, without a lot of bullshit. I mean the guy has pled guilty to a certain offense—he can't get out of that. He has such and such a prior record—there's no changing that. So much of the stuff we put in these reports is subjective and open to interpretation. It's good to have some solid information.

Armed with information in the court referral, probation officers begin to type the defendants assigned for presentence investigation. Defendants are classified into general types based on possible sentence recommendations; a probation officer's statement indicates that this process begins early in a presentence investigation.

> Bottom line; it's the sentence recommendation that's important. That's what the judges and everybody wants to see. I start thinking about the recommendation as soon as I pick up the court referral. Why wait? The basic facts aren't going to change. Oh, I know some POs will tell you they weigh all the facts before coming up with a recommendation. But that's propaganda—we all start thinking recommendation right from the get-go.

At this stage in the investigation the factors known to probation officers are mainly legally relevant variables. The defendant's unique characteristics and special circumstances generally are unknown at this time. Although probation officers may know the offender's age, sex, and race, the relationship of these variables to the case is not yet apparent.

These initial typings are private definitions (Prus 1975) based on the officer's experience and knowledge of the court system. On occasion, officers discuss the case informally with their colleagues or supervisors when they are not sure of a particular typing. Until the report is complete, their typing remains a private designation. In most cases the probation officers type defendants by considering the known and relatively irrefutable variables of offense and prior record. Probation officers are convinced that judges and district attorneys are most concerned with that part of their reports. I heard the following comment (or versions thereof) on many occasions: "Judges read the offense section, glance at the prior record, and then flip to the back and see what we recommend." Officers indicated that during informal discussions with judges it was made clear that offense and prior record are the determinants of sentencing in most cases. In some instances judges consider extralegal variables, but the officers indicated that this occurs only in "unusual" cases with "special" circumstances. One such case involved a probation grant for a woman who killed her husband after she had been a victim of spouse battering.

Probation investigators are in regular contact with district attorneys, and frequently discuss their investigations with them. In addition, district attorneys seem to have no compunction about calling the probation administration to complain about what they consider an inappropriate recommendation. Investigators agreed unanimously that district attorneys typically dismiss a defendant's social history as "immaterial" and want probation officers to stick to the legal facts.

Using offense and prior record as criteria, probation officers place defendants into dispositional (based on recommendation) types. In describing these types I have retained the terms used by probation officers themselves in the typing process. The following typology is community (rather than researcher) designated (Emerson 1981; Spradley 1970): (1) deal case, (2) diversion case, (3) joint case, (4) probation case with some jail time, (5) straight probation case. Within each of these dispositional types, probation officers designate the severity of punishment by labeling the case either lightweight or heavy-duty.

A designation of "lightweight" means that the defendant will be accorded some measure of leniency because the offense was minor, because the offender had no prior criminal record, or because the criminal activity (regardless of the penal code violation) was relatively innocuous. Heavy-duty cases receive more severe penalties because the offense, the offender, or the circumstances of the offense are deemed particularly serious. Diversion and straight probation types generally are considered lightweight, while the majority of joint cases are considered heavy-duty. Cases involving personal violence invariably are designated as heavy-duty. Most misdemeanor cases in which the defendant has no prior criminal record or a relatively minor record are termed lightweight. If the defendant has an extensive criminal record, however, even misdemeanor cases can call for stiff penalties; therefore such cases are considered heavy-duty. Certain felony cases can be regarded as lightweight if there was no violence, if the victim's loss was minimal, or if the defendant had no prior convictions. On occasion, even an offense like armed robbery can be considered lightweight. The following example (taken from an actual report) is one such instance: a first-time offender with a simulated gun held up a Seven-Eleven store and then returned to the scene, gave back the money, and asked the store employees to call the police.

The typings are general recommendations; specifics such as terms and conditions of probation or diversion and length of incarceration are worked out later in the investigation. The following discussion will clarify some of the criteria for arriving at a typing.

Deal cases involve situations in which a plea bargain exists. In California, many plea bargains specify specific sentencing stipulations; probation officers rarely recommend dispositions contrary to those stipulated in plea-bargaining agreements. Although probation officers allegedly are free to recommend a sentence different from that contained in the plea bargain, they have learned that such an action is unrealistic (and often counter-productive to their own interests) because judges inevitably uphold the primacy of sentence agreements. The following observation represents the probation officers' view of plea-bargaining deals:

> It's stupid to try and bust a deal. What's the percentage? Who needs the hassle? The judge always honors the deal—after all, he was part of it. Everyone, including the defendant, has already agreed. It's all nice and neat, all wrapped up. We are supposed to rubber-stamp the package—and we do. Everyone is better off that way.

Diversion cases typically involve relatively minor offenses committed by those with no prior record, and are considered "a snap" by probation officers. In most cases, those referred for diversion have been screened already by the district attorney's office; the probation investigator merely agrees that they are eligible and therefore should be granted diversionary relief (and eventual dismissal of charges). In rare instances when there has been an oversight and the defendant is ineligible (because of prior criminal convictions), the probation officer informs the court, and criminal proceedings are resumed. Either situation involves minimal decision making by probation officers about what disposition to recommend. Presentence investigators approach diversion cases in a perfunctory, almost mechanical manner.

The last three typings generally refer to cases in which the sentencing recommendations are ambiguous and some decision making is required of probation officers. These types represent the major consequences of criminal sentencing; incarceration and/or probation. Those categorized as joint (prison) cases are denied probation; instead the investigator recommends an appropriate prison sentence. In certain instances the nature of the offense (e.g., rape, murder, or arson) renders defendants legally ineligible for probation. In other situations, the defendants' prior record (especially felony convictions) makes it impossible to grant probation (see, e.g., Neubauer 1974:240). In many cases the length of prison sentences has been set by legal statute and can be increased or decreased only marginally (depending on the aggravating or mitigating circumstances of the case).

In California, the majority of defendants sentenced to prison receive a middle term (between minimum and maximum); the length of time varies with the offense. Those cases that fall outside the middle term usually do so for reasons related to the offense (e.g., using a weapon) or to the criminal record (prior felony convictions or, conversely, no prior criminal record). Those typed originally as joint cases are treated differently from other probation applicants: concerns with rehabilitation or with the defendant's life situation are no longer relevant, and proper punishment becomes the focal point of inquiry. This perspective was described as follows by a probation officer respondent:

"Once I know so-and-so is a heavy-duty joint case I don't think in terms of rehabilitation or social planning. It becomes a matter of how long to salt the sucker away, and that's covered by the code."

For those who are typed as probation cases, the issue for the investigator becomes whether to recommend some time in jail as a condition of probation. This decision is made with reference to whether the case is lightweight or heavy-duty. Straight probation usually is reserved for those convicted of relatively innocuous offenses or for those without a prior criminal record (first-timers). Some probation officers admitted candidly that all things being equal, middle-class defendants are more likely than other social classes to receive straight probation. The split sentence (probation and jail time) has become popular and is a consideration in most misdemeanor and felony cases, especially when the defendant has a prior criminal record. In addition, there is a feeling that drug offenders should receive a jail sentence as part of probation to deter them from future drug use.

Once a probation officer has decided that "some jail time is in order," the ultimate recommendation includes that condition. Although the actual amount of time frequently is determined late in the case, the probation officer's opinion that a jail sentence should be imposed remains constant. The following comment typifies the sentiments of probation officers whom I have observed and also illustrates the imprecision of recommending a period of time in custody:

> It's not hard to figure out who needs some jail. The referral sheet can tell you that. What's hard to know is exactly how much time. Ninety days or six months—who knows what's fair? We put down some number but it is usually an arbitrary figure. No one has come up with a chart that correlates rehabilitation with jail time.

Compiling Further Information

Once an initial typing has been completed, the next investigative stage involves collecting further information about the defendant. During this stage most of the data to be collected consists of extralegal considerations. The defendant is interviewed and his or her social history is delineated. Probation officers frequently contact collateral sources such as school officials, victims, doctors, counselors, and relatives to learn more about the defendant's individual circumstances. This aspect of the presentence investigation involves considerable time and effort on the part of probation officers. Such information is gathered primarily to legitimate earlier probation officer typings or to satisfy judicial requirements; recommendations seldom are changed during this stage. A similar pattern was described by a presentence investigator:

> Interviewing these defendants and working up a social history takes time. In most cases it's really unnecessary since I've already decided what I am going to do. We all know that a recommendation is governed by the offense and prior record. All the rest is just stuffing to fill out the court report, to make the judge look like he's got all the facts.

Presentence interviews with defendants (a required part of the investigation) frequently are routine interactions that were described by a probation officer as "anticlimactic." These interviews invariably are conducted in settings familiar to probation officers, such as jail interviewing rooms or probation department offices. Because the participants lack trust in each other, discussions rarely are candid and open. Probation officers are afraid of being conned or manipulated because they assume that defendants "will say anything to save themselves." Defendants are trying to present themselves in a favorable light and are wary of divulging any information that might be used against them.

It is assumed implicitly in the interview process that probation officers act as interrogators and defendants as respondents. Because presentence investigators select the questions, they control the course of the interview and elicit the kind of responses that serve to substantiate their original defendant typings. A probationer described his presentence interview to me as follows:

> I knew what the P.O. wanted me to say. She had me pegged as a nice middle-class kid who had fallen in with a bad crowd. So that's how I came off. I was contrite, a real boy scout who had learned his lesson. What an acting job! I figured if I didn't act up I'd get probation.

On occasion, prospective probationers refuse to go along with structured presentence interviews. Some offenders either attempt to control the interview or are openly hostile to probation officers. Defendants who try to dominate interviews often can be dissuaded by reminders such as "I don't think you really appreciate the seriousness of your situation" or "I'm the one who asks the questions here." Some defendants, however, show blatant disrespect for the court process by flaunting a disregard for possible sanctions.

Most probation officers have interviewed some defendants who simply don't seem to care what happens to them. A defendant once informed an investigation officer: "I don't give a fuck what you motherfuckers try and do to me. I'm going to do what I fuckin' well please. Take your probation and stick it." Another defendant told her probation officer: "I'm going to shoot up every chance I get. I need my fix more than I need probation." Probation officers categorize belligerent defendants and those unwilling to "play the probation game" as dangerous or irrational (see, e.g., McCleary 1978). Frequently in these situations the investigator's initial typing is no longer valid, and probation either will be denied or will be structured stringently. Most interviews, however, proceed in a predictable manner as probation officers collect information that will be included in the section of the report termed "defendant's statement."

Although some defendants submit written comments, most of their statements actually are formulated by the probation officer. In a sociological sense, the defendant's statement can be considered an "account" (Scott and Lyman 1968). While conducting presentence interviews, probation officers typically attempt to shape the defendant's account to fit their own preconceived typing. Many probation officers believe that the defendant's attitude toward the offense and toward the future prospects for leading a law-abiding life are the most important parts of the statement. In most presentence investigations the probation investigator identifies and interprets the defendant's subjective attitudes and then incorporates them into the report. Using this procedure, probation officers look for and can report attitudes that "logically fit" with their final sentencing recommendation (see, for example, Davis 1983).

Defendants who have been typed as prison cases typically are portrayed as holding socially unacceptable attitudes about their criminal actions and unrealistic or negative attitudes about future prospects for living an upright life. Conversely, those who have been typed as probation material are described as having acceptable attitudes, such as contriteness about the present offense and optimism about their ability to lead a crime-free life. The structuring of accounts about defendant attitudes was described by a presentence investigator in the following manner:

> When POS talk about the defendant's attitude we really mean how that attitude relates to the case. Naturally I'm not going to write about what a wonderful attitude the guy has—how sincere he seems—and then recommend sending him to the joint. That wouldn't make sense. The judges want consistency. If a guy has a shitty attitude but is going to get probation anyway, there's no percentage in playing up his attitude problem.

In most cases the presentence interview is the only contact between the investigating officer and the defendant. The brevity of this contact and the lack of post-report interaction foster a legalistic perspective. Investigators are concerned mainly with "getting the case through court" rather than with special problems related to supervising probationers on a long-term basis. One-time-only interviews rarely allow probation officers to become emotionally involved with their cases; the personal and individual aspects of the defendant's personality generally are not manifested during a half-hour presentence interview. For many probation officers the emotional distance from offenders is one of the benefits of working in presentence units. Such an opinion was expressed by an investigation officer: "I really like the one-shot-only part of this job. I don't have time to get caught up with the clients. I can deal with facts and not worry about individual personalities."

The probation officer has wide discretion in the type of collateral information that is collected from sources other than the defendant or the official record. Although a defendant's social history must be sketched in the presentence report, the supplementation of that history is left to individual investigators. There are few established guidelines for the investigating officer to follow, except that the psychiatric or psychological reports should be submitted when there is compelling evidence that the offender is mentally disturbed. Informal guidelines, however, specify that in misdemeanor cases reports should be shorter and more concise than in felony cases. The officers indicated that reports for municipal court (all misdemeanor cases) should range from four to six pages in length, while superior court reports (felony cases) were expected to be six to nine pages long. In controversial cases (to which only the most experienced officers are assigned) presentence reports are expected to be longer and to include considerable social data. Reports in these cases have been as long as 30 pages.

Although probation officers learn what general types of information to include through experience and feedback from judges and supervisors, they are allowed considerable leeway in deciding exactly what to put in their reports (outside of the offense and prior record sections). Because investigators decide what collateral sources are germane to the case, they tend to include information that will reflect favorably on their sentencing recommendation. In this context the observation of one probation officer is understandable: "I pick from the mass of possible sources just which ones to

put in the report. Do you think I'm going to pick people who make my recommendation look weak? No way!"

Filing the Report

The final stage in the investigation includes dictating the report, having it approved by
a probation supervisor, and appearing in court. All three of these activities serve to
reinforce the importance of prior record and offense in sentencing recommendations.
At the time of dictation, probation officers determine what to include in the report
and how to phrase their remarks. For the first time in the investigation, they receive
formal feedback from official sources. Presentence reports are read by three groups
important to the probation officers: probation supervisors, district attorneys, and
judges. Probation officers recognize that for varying reasons, all these groups emphasize the legally relevant variables of offense and prior criminal record when considering an appropriate sentencing recommendation. Such considerations reaffirm the
probation officer's initial private typing.
    A probation investigator described this process:

> After I've talked to the defendants I think maybe some of them deserve to get special consid-
> eration. But then I remember who's going to look at the reports. My supervisor, the DA, the
> judge; they don't care about all the personal details. When all is said and done, what's really
> important to them is the offense and the defendant's prior record. I know that stuff from the
> start. It makes me wonder why we have to jack ourselves around to do long reports.

Probation officers assume that their credibility as presentence investigators will be
enhanced if their sentencing recommendations meet with the approval of probation
supervisors, district attorneys, and judges. On the other hand, officers whose recommendations are consistently "out of line" are subject to censure or transfer, or they
find themselves engaged in "running battles" (Shover 1974:357) with court officials.
During the last stage of the investigation probation officers must consider how to
ensure that their reports will go through court without "undue personal hassle." Most
investigation officers have learned that presentence recommendations based on a
consideration of prior record and offense can achieve that goal.
    Although occupational self-interest is an important component in deciding how to
conduct a presentence investigation, other factors also are involved. Many probation
officers agree with the idea of using legally relevant variables as determinants
of recommendations. These officers embrace the retributive value of this concept
and see it as an equitable method for framing their investigation. Other officers
reported that probation officers' discretion had been "short-circuited" by determinate
sentencing guidelines and that they were reduced to "merely going through the
motions" in conducting their investigations. Still other officers view the use of legal
variables to structure recommendations as an acceptable bureaucratic shortcut to
compensate partially for large case assignments. One probation officer stated, "If the
department wants us to keep pumping out presentence reports we can't consider
social factors—we just don't have time." Although probation officers are influenced by
various dynamics, there seems little doubt that in California, the social history which

once was considered the "heart and soul" of presentence probation reports (Reckless 1967:673) has been largely devalued.

Summary and Conclusions

In this study I provide a description and an analysis of the processes used by probation investigators in preparing presentence reports. The research findings based on interview data indicate that probation officers tend to de-emphasize individual defendants' characteristics and that their probation recommendations are not influenced directly by factors such as sex, age, race, socioeconomic status, or work record. Instead, probation officers emphasize the variables of instant offense and prior criminal record. The finding that offense and prior record are the main considerations of probation officers with regard to sentence recommendations agrees with a substantial body of research (Bankston 1983; Carter and Wilkins 1967; Dawson 1969; Lotz and Hewitt 1977; Robinson, Carter, and Wahl 1969; Wallace 1974; Walsh 1985).

My particular contribution has been to supply the ethnographic observations and the data that explain this phenomenon. I have identified the process whereby offense and prior record come to occupy the central role in decision making by probation officers. This identification underscores the significance of private typings in determining official designations. An analysis of probation practices suggests that the function of the presentence investigation is more ceremonial than instrumental (Hagan 1985).

I show that early in the investigation probation officers, using offense and prior record as guidelines, classify defendants into types; when the typing process is complete, probation officers essentially have decided on the sentence recommendation that will be recorded later in their official designation. The subsequent course of investigations is determined largely by this initial private typing. Further data collection is influenced by a sentence recommendation that already has been firmly established. This finding answers affirmatively the research question posed by Carter (1967:211):

> Do probation officers, after "deciding" on a recommendation early in the presentence investigation, seek further information which justifies the decision, rather than information which might lead to modification or rejection of that recommendation?

The type of information and observation contained in the final presentence report is generated to support the original recommendation decision. Probation officers do not regard defendant typings as tentative hypotheses to be disproved through inquiry but rather as firm conclusions to be justified in the body of the report.

Although the presentence interview has been considered an important part of the investigation (Spencer 1983), I demonstrate that it does not significantly alter probation officers' perceptions. In most cases probation officers dominate presentence interviews; interaction between the participants is guarded. The nature of interviews between defendants and probation officers is important in itself; further research is needed to identify the dynamics that prevail in these interactions.

Attitudes attributed to defendants often are structured by probation officers to reaffirm the recommendation already formulated. The defendant's social history, long considered an integral part of the presentence report, in reality has little bearing on sentencing considerations. In most cases the presentence is no longer a vehicle for social inquiry but rather a typing process which considers mainly the defendant's prior criminal record and the seriousness of the criminal offense. Private attorneys in growing numbers have become disenchanted with the quality of probation investigations and have commissioned presentence probation reports privately (Rodgers, Gitchoff, and Paur 1984). At present, however, such a practice is generally available only for wealthy defendants.

The presentence process that I have described is used in the great majority of cases; it is the "normal" procedure. Even so, probation officers are not entirely passive actors in this process. On occasion they will give serious consideration to social variables in arriving at a sentencing recommendation. In special circumstances officers will allow individual defendants' characteristics to influence their report. In addition, probation officers who have developed credibility with the court are allowed some discretion in compiling presentence reports. This discretion is not unlimited, however; it is based on a prior record of producing reports that meet the court's approval, and is contingent on continuing to do so. A presentence writer said, "You can only afford to go to bat for defendants in a few select cases; if you try to do it too much, you get a reputation as being 'out of step.' "

This research raises the issue of probation officers' autonomy. Although I depict presentence investigators as having limited autonomy, other researchers (Hagan 1975; Myers 1979; Walsh 1985) contend that probation officers have considerable leeway in recommendation. This contradictory evidence can be explained in large part by the type of sentencing structure, the professionalism of probation workers, and the role of the district attorney at sentencing. Walsh's study (1985), for example, which views probation officers as important actors in the presentence process, was conducted in a jurisdiction with indeterminate sentencing, where the probation officers demonstrated a high degree of professionalism and the prosecutors "rarely made sentencing recommendations." A very different situation existed in the California counties that I studied: determinate sentencing was enforced, probation officers were not organized professionally, and the district attorneys routinely made specific court recommendations. It seems apparent that probation officers' autonomy must be considered with reference to judicial jurisdiction.

In view of the primacy of offense and prior record in sentencing considerations, the efficacy of current presentence investigation practices is doubtful. It seems ineffective and wasteful to continue to collect a mass of social data of uncertain relevance. Yet an analysis of courtroom culture suggests that the presentence investigation helps maintain judicial mythology as well as probation officer legitimacy. Although judges generally do not have the time or the inclination to consider individual variables thoroughly, the performance of a presentence investigation perpetuates the myth of individualized sentences. Including a presentence report in the court file gives the appearance of individualization without influencing sentencing practices significantly.

Even in a state like California, where determinate sentencing allegedly has replaced individualized justice, the judicial system feels obligated to maintain the appearance of individualization. After observing the court system in California for several years I am convinced that a major reason for maintaining such a practice is to make it easier for criminal defendants to accept their sentences. The presentence report allows defendants to feel that their case at least has received a considered decision. One judge admitted candidly that the "real purpose" of the presentence investigation was to convince defendants that they were not getting "the fast shuffle." He observed further that if defendants were sentenced without such investigations, many would complain and would file "endless appeals" over what seems to them a hasty sentencing decision. Even though judges typically consider only offense and prior record in a sentencing decision, they want defendants to believe that their cases are being judged individually. The presentence investigation allows this assumption to be maintained. In addition, some judges use the probation officer's report as an excuse for a particular type of sentence. In some instances they deny responsibility for the sentence, implying that their "hands were tied" by the recommendation. Thus judges are taken "off the hook" for meting out an unpopular sentence. Further research is needed to substantiate the significance of these latent functions of the presentence investigation.

The presentence report is a major component in the legitimacy of the probation movement; several factors support the probation officers' stake in maintaining their role in these investigations. Historically, probation has been wedded to the concept of individualized treatment. In theory, the presentence report is suited ideally to reporting on defendants' individual circumstances. From a historical perspective (Rothman 1980) this ideal has always been more symbolic than substantive, but if the legitimacy of the presentence report is questioned, so then is the entire purpose of probation.

Regardless of its usefulness (or lack of usefulness), it is doubtful that probation officials would consider the diminution or abolition of presentence reports. The number of probation workers assigned to presentence investigations is substantial, and their numbers represent an obvious source of bureaucratic power. Conducting presentence investigations allows probation officers to remain visible with the court and the public. The media often report on controversial probation cases, and presentence writers generally have more contact and more association with judges than do others in the probation department.

As ancillary court workers, probation officers are assigned the dirty work of collecting largely irrelevant data on offenders (Hagan 1975; Hughes 1958). Investigation officers have learned that emphasizing offense and prior record in their reports will enhance relationships with judges and district attorneys, as well as improving their occupational standing within probation departments. Thus the presentence investigation serves to maintain the court's claim of individualized concern while preserving the probation officer's role, although a subordinate role, in the court system.

The myth of individualization serves various functions, but it also raises serious questions. In an era of severe budget restrictions (Schumacher 1985) should scarce resources be allocated to compiling predictable presentence reports of dubious value? If social variables are considered only in a few cases, should courts continue routinely to require presentence reports in all felony matters (as is the practice in California)? In summary, we should address the issue of whether the criminal justice system can afford the ceremony of a probation presentence investigation.

Critical Thinking

The stereotyping of convicted offenders is in direct contrast to our judicial system's claim that each person found guilty of a criminal offense has individual characteristics taken into consideration during the sentencing process. In reality, however, the vast majority of pre-sentence investigative reports for sentencing recommendations only perpetuate this illusion when the pre-sentence investigation is actually more ceremonial than instrumental. This raises the question, should justice be more individualized? Regardless of your answer to this first question, why do you think this "myth" of individualized justice is maintained?

References

Allen, Harry E. and Clifford E. Simonsen (1986) *Corrections in America*. New York: Macmillan.

Bankston, William B. (1983) "Legal and Extralegal Offender Traits and Decision-Making in the Criminal Justice System." *Sociological Spectrum* 3:1–18.

Blumberg, Abraham (1967) *Criminal Justice*. Chicago: Quadrangle.

Blumstein, Alfred J., S. Martin, and N. Holt (1983) *Research on Sentencing: The Search for Reform*. Washington, DC: National Academy Press.

Carter, Robert M. (1967) "The Presentence Report and The Decision-Making Process." *Journal of Research in Crime and Delinquency* 4:203–11.

Carter, Robert M. and Leslie T. Wilkins (1967) "Some Factors in Sentencing Policy." *Journal of Criminal Law, Criminology, and Police Science* 58:503–14.

Davis, James R. (1983) "Academic and Practical Aspects of Probation: A Comparison." *Federal Probation* 47:7–10.

Dawson, Robert (1969) *Sentencing*. Boston: Little, Brown.

Emerson, Robert M. (1981) "Ethnography and Understanding Members' Worlds." In Robert M. Emerson (ed.), *Contemporary Field Research*. Boston: Little, Brown, pp. 19–35.

Forer, Lois G. (1980) *Criminals and Victims*. New York: Norton.

Hagan, John (1975) "The Social and Legal Construction of Criminal Justice: A Study of the Presentence Process." *Social Problems* 22:620–37.

——. (1985) *Modern Criminology: Crime, Criminal Behavior, and Its Control*. New York: McGraw-Hill.

Hagan, John, John Hewitt, and Duane Alwin (1979) "Ceremonial Justice: Crime and Punishment in a Loosely Coupled System." *Social Forces* 58:506–25.

Hogarth, John (1971) *Sentencing As a Human Process*. Toronto: University of Toronto Press.

Hughes, Everett C. (1958) *Men and Their Work*. New York: Free Press.

Kingsnorth, Rodney and Louis Rizzo (1979) "Decision-Making in the Criminal Courts: Continuities and Discontinuities." *Criminology* 17:3–14.

Lotz, Ray and John Hewitt (1977) "The Influence of Legally Irrelevant Factors on Felony Sentencing." *Sociological Inquiry* 47:39–48.

McCleary, Richard (1978) *Dangerous Men*. Beverly Hills: Sage.

Murrah, A. (1963) "Prison or Probation?" In B. Kay and C. Vedder (eds.), *Probation and Parole*. Springfield, IL: Charles C. Thomas, pp. 63–78.

Myers, Martha A. (1979) "Offended Parties and Official Reactions: Victims and the Sentencing of Criminal Defendants." *Sociological Quarterly* 20:529–46.

Neubauer, David (1974) *Criminal Justice in Middle America*. Morristown, NJ: General Learning.

Petersilia, Joan, Susan Turner, James Kahan, and Joyce Peterson (1985) "Executive Summary of Rand's Study, Granting Felons Probation." *Crime and Delinquency* 31:379–92.

Prus, Robert (1975) "Labeling Theory: A Statement on Typing." *Sociological Focus* 8:79–96.

Prus, Robert and John Stratten (1976) "Factors in the Decision-Making of North Carolina Probation Officers." *Federal Probation* 40:48–53.

Reckless, Walter C. (1967) *The Crime Problem*. New York: Appleton.

Robinson, James, Robert Carter, and A. Wahl (1969) *The San Francisco Project*. Berkeley: University of California School of Criminology.

Rodgers, T.A., G.T. Gitchoff, and I. Paur (1984) "The Privately Commissioned Presentence Report." In Robert M. Carter, Deniel Glaser, and Leslie T. Wilkens (eds.), *Probation, Parole, and Community Corrections*. New York: Wiley, pp. 21–30.

Rosecrance, John (1985) "The Probation Officers' Search for Credibility: Ball Park Recommendations." *Crime and Delinquency* 31:539–54.

——. (1987) "A Typology of Presentence Probation Investigators." *International Journal of Offender Therapy and Comparative Criminology* 31:163–177.

Rothman, David (1980) *Conscience and Convenience: The Asylum and Its Alternatives in Progressive America*. Boston: Little, Brown.

Schumacher, Michael A. (1985) "Implementation of a Client Classification And Case Management System: A Practitioner's View." *Crime and Delinquency* 31:445–55.

Scott, Marvin and Stanford Lyman (1968) "Accounts." *American Sociological Review* 33:46–62.

Shover, Neal (1974) "Experts and Diagnosis in Correctional Agencies." *Crime and Delinquency* 20:347–58.

Spencer, Jack W. (1983) "Accounts, Attitudes and Solutions: Probation Officer-Defendant Negotiations of Subjective Orientations." *Social Problems* 30:570–81.

Spradley, Joseph P. (1970) *You Owe Yourself a Drunk: An Ethnography of Urban Nomads*. Boston: Little, Brown.

Sudnow, David (1965) "Normal Crimes: Sociological Features of the Penal Code." *Social Problems* 12:255–76.

Tinker, John N., John Quiring, and Yvonne Pimentel (1985) "Ethnic Bias in California Courts: A Case Study of Chicano and Anglo Felony Defendants." *Sociological Inquiry* 55:83–96.

Walker, Samuel (1985) *Sense and Nonsense About Crime*. Monterey, CA: Brooks/Cole.

Wallace, John (1974) "Probation Administration." In Daniel Glaser (ed.), *Handbook of Criminology*. Chicago: Rand-McNally, pp. 940–70.

Walsh, Anthony (1985) "The Role of the Probation Officer in the Sentencing Process." *Criminal Justice and Behavior* 12:289–303.

B Outsiders

ape Survivors Negotiating the
ss

Abstract: *Amanda Konradi explores the strategies that rape survivors undertake in prep-aration for court appearances and testimonies. She suggests that survivors' perceptions and expectations about various facets of the criminal justice process affect how victims prepare for the courtroom. Rape survivors typically employ one of six techniques when preparing for the courtroom. These techniques include adjusting their appearance to present an image of a respectable or moral woman, rehearsing testimonies in an attempt to sway judges, recruiting individuals to serve as credible witnesses or to provide emotional support, and educating themselves about their legal situation to strengthen their case. Overall, Konradi's findings indicate that many rape survivors become actively involved in the legal processes surrounding their cases.*

In trials and a variety of pretrial court events, including bond hearings, preliminary hearings, and motions, rape survivors come into the presence of their assailants and respond to direct- and cross-examination about the details of the assaults perpetrated against them. With few exceptions, the prosecution of rape would not be possible without the participation of survivors who are willing to attend court to testify. In spite of research that indicates women are not passive in the face of rape attempts (Bart and O'Brien 1985; Caignon and Groves 1987; Kleck and Sayles 1990) and selectively bring assaults to the attention of the legal system (Greenberg and Ruback 1992; Williams 1984), rape survivors' active involvement in the process of prosecuting their assailants has not been extensively examined.

This article explores what rape survivors report they have done to prepare themselves for upcoming court appearances. It is explicitly an effort to analytically separate the victimization of rape (the act of sexual assault) from women's responses to it. I examine how rape survivors approach the legal process as an instrument, as a means to accomplish justice, and how they take on and shape the organizational role of victim-witness available to them. This article considers the following questions: How do survivors' knowledge and beliefs about the law and the legal process shape the strategies that they use to prepare for court appearances? How do the cultural representations of rape with which survivors are familiar shape their self-preparation? How do survivors, as socially situated persons with ethnicity, age, class background, education level, friends, and families, draw on their various resources to negotiate the legal process? What other factors, including preparation received from prosecutors, shape survivors' preparation efforts?

I have chosen to focus on preparation because it falls between studies on reporting and ones on courtroom appearances. It is also behavior that takes place out of the physical space controlled by legal personnel. In addition, examining survivors' self-preparation allows me to examine their orientations to preliminary hearings, which they are far more likely to participate in than trials. Survivors' preliminary hearing performances figure importantly in district attorneys' decisions to pursue pleas or go to trial.

Rape Prosecution Research

Researchers concerned with the prosecution of rape have primarily focused on the *behavior* of legal actors. Existing studies provide compelling evidence that legal actors underenforce, rather than overenforce, rape statutes (Polk 1985). They show that, under pressure to conserve institutional resources, legal personnel rely on stereotypes in making decisions to prosecute rape and that a persistent bias remains against women whose rape experiences do not conform to the classic stranger stereotype (Martin and Powell 1994). LaFree (1989) and Kerstetter (1990) report that police officers make decisions about doing the work to bring rape cases to the attention of prosecutors based on the personal attributes of survivors and their relationships with their assailants. Similarly, studies have found that prosecutors refuse to file felony charges or pursue cases through to trial when victims know their assailants, the use or threat of force is unclear, or victims report assaults in questionable parts of town (Frohmann 1991; Stanko 1981). Furthermore, judges are found to minimize sentences when victims do not fit stereotypes (Schafran 1993).

With respect to the prosecution of rape, researchers have primarily focused on how the demands of the trial process affect rape survivors. Their research has focused primarily on the emotional and psychological impact of the common practices of legal personnel. The frequently cited chapter in Holmstrom and Burgess's (1983) book, "The Rape Victim's Reaction to Court," explicitly identifies this analytic perspective. Examining the prosecution of rape from this perspective, a number of researchers have documented that survivors are frustrated and distressed when their claims are not taken seriously by police or prosecutors as well as when they are grilled during cross-examination sequences of trials (Holmstrom and Burgess 1983; Madigan and Gambel 1989). The result of this direction in research is that rape survivors' legal experiences are represented as what happens *to* them. We know quite a bit about how legal personnel structure the survivors' legal "career," particularly the early stages, but we know little about how survivors understand the legal process and respond to its constraints.

It is no accident, I believe, that the authors investigating legal personnel and raped women's reactions to institutional treatment primarily use the term *victim* to conceptualize the women they discuss. It is a powerful term that places the responsibility for sexual assault/rape on the perpetrator and highlights the very real psychological and physical trauma that may result from a violent attack. Used with reference to the criminal justice process, *victim* can also imply an objective lack of decision-making power. Many researchers investigating women's experiences with the criminal justice process in the 1970s and early 1980s intended for their research to contribute to the reform of abusive investigative and prosecution policies and rape statutes that made prosecution difficult and painful for the women involved. Their use of *victim* was thus politically strategic. Current researchers appear to have adopted the term whether or not they share the feminist reform agenda, because its usage has become somewhat conventional. However, conceptualizing raped women as victims appears to have had a constraining effect on the scope of investigation of how rape is processed through the criminal justice system. Having assumed victimization, many researchers have apparently assumed passivity on the part of raped women.

The nature of research into the processing of rape also reflects the difficulty of obtaining relevant data about survivors. To examine rape survivors' participation in prosecution, researchers must either follow them through the justice process and contend with the lengthy time frame of cases (months or years) or find a substantial number of women (or men) who are, or have been, involved in prosecuting their assailants and are willing to talk about the matter. With the absence of a public directory of rape survivors and the confidentiality mandated of most counseling and legal agencies, it is difficult to reach potential research participants. The access Holmstrom and Burgess (1983) gained in 1972, to the Boston hospital in which they began their study of the institutional processing of rape victims, could be very difficult to obtain in the present! In addition, given the low percentage of cases that get processed through to trial, it is also difficult to find rape survivors with courtroom experience. Polk (1985) estimated that less than 15 percent of cases ever reach the court phase. Researching the processing of rape from the standpoint of rape survivors can be very time-consuming. By comparison, the schedules of police and prosecutors are much more predictable, and their offices produce mountains of paperwork that may be used for triangulation.

Methods

Data for this study were collected through intensive *life history* interviews with 32 women who survived rape and participated in the prosecution of their assailants to the point of testifying in court. Given the lack of a directory of rape survivors and the restrictions on institutional access coupled with my concerns over potentially producing a homogeneous sample by recruiting through therapists or advertising alone, I elected to recruit participants in a variety of ways.

Getting information about the study to women was one part of the recruitment problem. The other challenge was to encourage women with a range of experiences to feel that they could speak to me about a stigmatizing experience. One of my early methodological decisions was to use my own experience with prosecuting my rapists as the basis of recruitment (Konradi 1993).

I conducted face-to-face and telephone interviews with survivors. Survivors who were currently involved in the prosecution of their assailants were interviewed several times. The interviews feature survivors' recollections of their interactions and behavior; thus, save for my observations, I do not have an "objective" record of inter-action between survivors and legal actors. However, I gathered information that is not accessible through direct observation—reports of survivors' telephone conversations, reports of their behavior out of court, and reports of their thoughts off and on the witness stand. I also observed 12 court events and interviewed district attorneys and ancillary personnel to provide a context for my analysis.

The methods of recruitment I used were intended to produce a diversity of women in the study rather than to obtain a sample that would reflect the distribution of attributes that might be found among rape survivors involved in prosecuting their assailants in the general population. I was not successful in obtaining a racially diverse sample: 90 percent of the sample was White. Thus, the findings discussed below may omit culturally specific modes of preparation. I was more successful in obtaining socioeconomic diversity: 37 percent were employed in blue- or pink-collar work, 27 percent were professionals, and 3 participants were unemployed high school students. A total of 63 percent had more than a high school education, and 23 percent of those had completed college. The participants ranged in age from 16 to older than 50. This is consistent with the fact that women of all ages participate in prosecution. Of the survivors, 59 percent did not know their assailants, 16 percent were raped by past or present intimates, and 25 percent were raped by other nonintimates whom they knew. Of the rapes, 59 percent were intraracial; 41 percent were interracial. In comparison to what is known about the characteristics of rapes that occur, this sample has an overrepresentation of interracial rapes and stranger rapes. In comparison to the characteristics of cases that get prosecuted, the study percentages are more consistent and possibly overrepresent nonstranger rapes. According to the sampling frame, all of the 32 women in the study were English speakers and were raped vaginally and/or orally and/or rectally. I have used pseudonyms throughout this article to guarantee the confidentiality promised the participants.

Findings

In the interviews, I noted six kinds of purposeful activities that the survivors engaged in to prepare for their time on the witness stand: appearance work, rehearsal, emotion work, team building, role research, and case enhancement. In the remainder of this article, I will describe these modes of preparation and discuss why and how survivors believed that such activities would help them meet the demands of the courtroom.

Appearance Work

While all survivors must dress in the morning before they go to hearings for probable cause and trials, slightly more than half of the survivors in this sample described purposefully creating an image through their clothing and makeup. Survivors sought to dress in ways that demonstrated respect for the court and in ways that conformed with visual standards separating real victims from women "who asked for it." Survivors' criteria were consistent with classic cultural stereotypes of rape. I use the term *appearance work* (Goffman 1959) to refer to survivors' intentional efforts to meet the stereotypic expectations they perceived jurors and judges to have.

It is easy to presume that this type of preparation is always carried out. However, the comments made by Cindy, a White 37-year-old pink-collar worker, about knowing what to wear and her serious concern about the apparel of the "covictim" in her case underscore the fact that not all survivors engage in appearance work:

> No, she [the district attorney] didn't tell me what to wear, at all. You know, I mean, I knew. I knew that. I wish she had said something to the other victim. . . . They kept my case together with the attempted rape when he was caught. I wish the DA [district attorney] had said something to her and her family about how to dress in court, you know. I dressed conservatively, you know. Now she was coming in in tight pants, her brothers were there, and her brothers have long hair. Now I don't have anything against long hair, you know, but I mean, they looked like rock star wannabees, and then they got these girlfriends who look like, you know, rock star wannabees. These girlfriends that are in court with them, have like tight, short, skirts on [and] these little things that are exposing their midriffs, you know what I mean? So the jury is looking at this shit and thinking [about it] you know [laughs]. I mean, you know, that really affected things. I know it did, you know, it certainly affected the outcome [the jury was unable to reach a verdict].

While Cindy was intent on being perceived as a viable victim, the other victim-witness and her family did not seem to be concerned about the appearance-based attributions others might make.

The typical personas that survivors sought to project through appearance work were consistently conservative, businesslike, and nonsexual. Some survivors went to extra efforts to choose clothes that hid their bodies and to keep their makeup toned down. By the time Megan, an African American college student, finished dressing, only her head and hands were visible. She described her court attire as follows:

> A long, black floral dress, buttons down the front, about down to here [indicating her calf], and I wore boots. You couldn't see any of my body! [laughs] And not really, I don't usually wear makeup anyways, I just wear like a little lipstick, put my hair half up, I looked normal [laughing].

Connie and Theresa both viewed the court as business and dressed as they would for work. Theresa, a White 48-year-old woman, explained that a person who did not present herself in court in a businesslike way may not be believable:

> Well, I kind of had thought of what I wanted to wear, you know, something that was . . . something that I would normally just wear to work, you know, because I dress business-like when I go to work and so I thought you know, that that's the way it should be. I mean, you know, you're not gonna go to court in a miniskirt and be believable.

However, as Connie and Theresa drew on their respective wardrobes for executive and clerical work, they appeared for their assailant's preliminary hearing in quite different attire. Connie wore a business suit, while Theresa came to court in more casual attire: a light-pink short-sleeved blouse, a pair of black crop pants sprinkled with pink flowers, and flat shoes. Thus, while these two White women of comparable age have similar perceptions of what the court requires, the way they implement their understanding reflects their class position.

As these two women's use of their work wardrobes indicate, survivors often based their court personas on an existing role and aspect of their self-conception. However, survivors chose with care the aspects of their personalities that they would reveal in court. Connie recalled consciously avoiding being the aspect of herself that she associated with backpacking, which is a dimension of her persona that would, perhaps, appear to be too self-reliant. On the other hand, Arlene, also a White middle-class woman, created a court persona that bore little resemblance to who she believed she was because she thought that court personnel might question her character. She became in appearance and manner what she hoped was the cultural embodiment of a "real rape victim":

> I dressed in a . . . in a very uncharacteristic way for me. I wore, you know, a skirt and a blouse and a jacket and hose and heels and all that stuff, I mean I looked the part that I wanted the court to think I was. . . . I have always been the kind of person that runs around in jeans and T-shirts as much as I can, and that's essentially what I was dressed in when I was raped, and I was very clear that I wanted there to be no question on the part of the court about my character, that I was going to play every game that I thought that they expected me to play, and I'm very good at that, I had been an actress for a while, and I had a good idea of how to create a . . . that kind of space for myself. . . . I did very consciously create a persona, it was not about who I was or who he was or what could have happened, it was about my objective that this fucker was going to jail, that's what was on my mind.

Most survivors' attention to their appearance involved selecting clothes from their closets that conformed with their images of victim-witnesses. However, several spent their own money and extra time to create their court image. Julianne, a White college student, described shopping for an "appropriate outfit":

> I remember when I was home I went shopping to make sure I had an appropriate outfit for court. . . . Something, um, conservative, something, um, something very presentable, um, nice, a dress, a skirt, a blazer. . . . I remember even shopping and thinking . . . I have to get clothes just to present myself, you know, um, . . . [On the day of court I] definitely wore waterproof mascara, that was like necessity item, and I had two different outfits and put them both on to see which one my parents thought was better.

Spending money to appear appropriately cut across class lines. Thus, some poor and working-class women may take on a proportionally greater burden in preparing for trial than their middle- and upper-class peers.

Even in the absence of direct instruction from prosecutors, many survivors visually became "model victims" to make their cases stronger. Insofar as their actions were oriented to comply with cultural ideals of rape victims, they worked to support the prosecution effort. Other survivors reported that prosecutors led them to engage in appearance work because they told them how to dress for court. These women indicated that even when the attire requested was unpalatable to them, they followed the instructions they received. For example, 16-year-old Monica purchased a "silly dress" that the prosecutor requested she wear for her trial appearance after he decided that the dress shirt, blazer, and slacks she wore for the preliminary hearing made her look too old. Here, we see that Monica's perception of the businesslike nature of court is in contradiction with the district attorney's construction of her as the "victim" in the case.

In addition to appearing the part for others, appearance work may also make taking on the role of witness an easier task. Businesslike and modest clothing tends to restrict the wearer to businesslike and modest posture; thus, dress can be a small reminder to act the victim-witness part appropriately. Likewise, knowing that one is presenting oneself as a credible victim-witness can make it easier to put aside any doubts that one is not and to concentrate on the business of testifying.

Rehearsal

To convey their rape experiences convincingly to judges and juries, most survivors felt that they needed to give detailed accounts of their assaults. This was problematic for two reasons. For 29 percent of the survivors, the prospect of providing an adequately detailed account raised concerns about recall. They were unsure that they would be able to remember the specific details of the assault event, which usually transpired months or even years before. This made cross-examination, during which they expected to be held accountable for explaining their own as well as the assailant's actions, particularly worrisome. Other survivors were primarily concerned with adequately controlling their emotions during their potentially painful testimony. They knew that giving a detailed account would require them to get close to the experience of the rape. Many of the survivors thought such renewed closeness might bring forth strong feelings. They were anxious over the prospect of being overwhelmed with tears on the witness stand and being unable to complete their testimony. These two kinds of concerns prompted the preparation strategy of rehearsal.

Of the survivors, 25 percent reported rehearsing all or parts of their expected testimony to ensure an accurate portrayal of the assault event and to keep their emotions under control. Some survivors, like Natalie, a 26-year-old White Louisianan, prepared themselves by telling their stories to supportive friends and relatives. Unwilling to forget to include any details of her assailant's behavior, Natalie enlisted her husband to be an audience for her testimony the night before she was due in court. She explained,

> [W]hen I came home, you know, I knew that the next day that it was . . . it was my turn, it was my time, I would read over my [police] statement, and I would read over it and . . . I just wanted to know from my own self that I was ready. Everybody kept on tellin' me that I was ready, that I was gonna be such a good witness. . . . I have to know that I'm ready and that's how I was feelin'. I had to be certain that I could get up there and say everything that happened to me and I didn't want to forget anything, um, all these little details or whatever. [The DA] said, you know, it's okay if you forget this or that or whatever, but I didn't want to, I wanted to say everything that he [her assailant] . . . that he had did to me. 'Cause I wanted to make sure that I was ready . . . I said, "Sam," my husband, "I know this is hard, but what I really need instead of just readin' my statement is to say it, to say what happened, and for you [to listen]." And he did, and um, and Sam bein' the supportive husband that he was, he did. I could tell that he didn't like it, he didn't wanna really listen to this again, um, 'cause he had just gotten finished readin' over this statement and everything after a year, when he had gone with me to [the DA's] office. And just rehashing everything over again for him was painful, but um, but he did it, he sat there and he listened to me and I got through it all and I didn't forget anything and I felt better.

Natalie learned that she could rely on her memory and describe explicitly what transpired between her assailant and herself; thus, she resolved her questions about her ability to recall:

> When I went in to the courthouse Thursday, I mean I went up to [the DA], and I said, "NOW I'm ready," 'cause the day before I had told him, I'm not ready and I was scared and fallin' apart, but I told him that I was ready, I want to do it [testify] right now.

Other survivors rehearsed for their court appearances alone. One survivor who was troubled about conveying the sexual nature of her violation to a public court audience reported preparing statements. Prior to the court date, she selected the words to most comfortably describe how her assailant threatened and coerced her to orally copulate him. Alternatively, Arlene considered the account of the assault that she had given police from the perspective of the defense attorney. She composed answers to the hardest questions that she could imagine him asking her, and then she practiced reciting them. On the day she went to court, she said that she knew that she would not fall apart on the stand. She recalled,

> Well that thing about falling apart on the stand was [a problem]. I was very worried about it beforehand, but in the actual experience I had no question that I would do that. I had rehearsed it, I knew what I was going to say, and I had rehearsed the hard questions and how to say them. And [I] practiced it, and I knew that I wouldn't.

The last solo rehearsal effort involved visualization. To overcome her intense feelings and the tendency she had to cry when discussing the rape, one survivor explained that she would imagine herself successfully carrying out the role of witness, sitting on the witness stand testifying steadily with conviction.

Survivors who rehearsed their testimony in some fashion gained confidence that they could successfully talk about their assaults. They also entered court with a more complete sense of what they wanted to say, not just a general expectation that they would talk about the assault event. With the exception of a prosecutor's ability to object and temporarily stop interaction, survivors are alone in navigating cross-examination. One would expect that those survivors who are knowledgeable about their recall, who have identified language with which they are comfortable, and who have a clear sense of purpose would fare better in that interaction.

Emotion Work

I use the term *emotion work* to designate the efforts that survivors made to produce feelings and emotional displays that they deemed appropriate to the courtroom before they entered it (Hochschild 1979, 1983). Of the survivors in this study, 29 percent recalled actively seeking to prepare themselves to achieve courtroom demeanor that was consistent with idealized images of witnesses or victims. The feeling rules that accompanied the two ideal images and guided survivors' preparations were somewhat contradictory. The ideal witness was polite and composed, indicating honesty and an appropriate deference to the court's authority. Alternatively, the ideal victim was a woman overcome by tears brought on by recollection of the assault. Thus, while some survivors sought to repress displays of obvious anger or pain, which would result in loss of emotional control or make their truthfulness suspect, others prepared themselves to lose emotional control and to cry on the stand.

In the following series of comments, Donna, a White working-class woman who went to trial twice, explains how she went about achieving different emotional states as her analysis of what was required to convince a jury changed. Prior to the first trial, Donna sought to achieve an inner calm and to preclude any show of emotion.

DONNA: So I had gone to one of the elders in my church and I said I want a blessing
            before I go to court. . . . So, um, they got all together and they gave me a blessing,
            and it was like the day before, and I was totally calm when I went through that
            first trial.
AUTHOR: Because you thought you'd done what you could?
DONNA: Yeah, I felt that I had done everything that I was supposed to do and I was deter-
            mined I was not gonna cry.

After the first jury was unable to reach a verdict, Donna decided to become a "real" rape victim. She chose not to receive religious solace and turned away emotional supports. It had the desired effect; she fell apart on the witness stand. Her reconstruction of her thinking before the second trial follows:

> I had gone over the testimony that I knew I was gonna give, and I figured that I was . . . there was a part I was just gonna have to lose it on. And, I figured that was gonna be it and that's about the part that I did start to cry, and they called a recess and handed me some water and calmed me down, and then went on from there. But I figured that I was gonna have to, 'cause otherwise they weren't gonna believe anything. . . . Uh, CASA [a rape support service] offered to come and go with us to trial, but I said no, I didn't need anybody. I'd already made up my mind I was not gonna get a blessing this time, 'cause I was not gonna be calm, cool, and collected. If they [the jury] wanted somebody hysterical on the stand, they were gonna get one. And all I had to do was wait for [the DA] to push the right buttons 'cause I was sure he was gonna do that.

Other survivors' concerns about losing emotional control, which they believed would hamper their ability to complete their testimony in a rational, dispassionate way, led them to make preemptive emotive efforts. That is, they tried to work their feelings out before the court event. For example, Julianne tried to let herself cry freely as she went about her morning routine so she might use up her tears before the preliminary hearing. In spite of her efforts to be calm, she cried through much of her testimony. However, as Hochschild (1979) has theorized emotion work, it is the effort to achieve feelings or displays of feeling that are consistent with some social ideal that is important. In making an attempt to produce a tearless calm to comply with her belief that the courtroom called for such affect from witnesses, Julianne did emotion work.

Successful emotion work prior to court can assist the survivor in achieving a court-room demeanor that is consistent with her appearance and her story. Likewise, it can help her keep her mind on her testimony. In both of these ways, the survivor's emotion management efforts can assist a prosecutor's efforts. However, when a survivor feels that she must focus her energy on formulating and delivering her testimony, achieving a particular emotional display can be difficult. Constructing a particular courtroom demeanor is, thus, not a strategy that can be used by all survivors. For example, although 16-year-old Monica was told by the prosecuting attorney that a display of tears would be good during trial, she did not attempt to direct herself to achieve this emotional state. She explained to me that such an effort would have been wasted, because once she faced her assailant, she knew that she could not sustain a demeanor that was contrary to the way she really felt.

Team Building

The preparatory activity that survivors in the study most frequently reported (69 percent) was team building, recruiting specific people to attend court events with them. My use of the term *team* follows Goffman (1959), who identified persons who participated in maintaining individual's performances as team members. Survivors described carefully selecting from among those individuals who were available to enhance their ability to achieve credible performances as victim-witnesses. They sought both emotional and instrumental support from other persons. Some survivors had teams of one; others organized teams larger than six.

One of the more carefully considered support plans that I encountered was described by the White clerical worker named Theresa. Some time before the scheduled preliminary hearing, she evaluated her emotional and physical needs and asked two women to fill specific roles that she considered necessary to sustain a successful performance. One would sit by her on the stand and aid her ability to speak; the other would provide an audience for her testimony. She also recruited a third team member to ensure that her friend, who had been subpoenaed, would have company and support as well.

Many survivors felt that they needed others to emotionally support them on the days they were called to testify, to endure the seemingly endless waiting in hallways and usually windowless victim-witness rooms with them and to provide a friendly face in the courtroom during their testimony. While many persons may have been available to go to court with survivors, not all were chosen. Survivors constructed their emotional supports by weighing the investments of others against their own needs. They excluded from team membership those whose attention might be elsewhere, those who could not fully back them up, and those whose feelings might be hurt by hearing their testimony. The result was that persons who were close to the survivor, and may have been involved in reporting decisions, were occasionally ruled out as team members. For example, a 20-year-old White college student named Joanna asked her parents not to attend the preliminary hearing because they had not demonstrated unqualified support for her when she informed them that she was raped. She felt that it would be easier to describe the assault event in the courtroom without having to worry about what they were thinking and feeling:

> So right before trial time, we had . . . we kind of had it out. I said, well, I said, "I don't want you there. I don't want you there at all." In fact, I said, "I feel like I need to be strong on that day, and I don't need to feel like I'm hurting your feelings by anything I might be saying on the stand."

Arlene, a White 34-year-old, also cautiously constructed her team from among those who were available. She asked only her sister and a male friend who was "sympathetic" to go to the preliminary hearing with her. She chose not to involve several sympathetic women friends who she believed were triggered by her assault and another man whose inability to control his anger made her uncomfortable. A third woman, a 34-year-old White immigrant, Candace, recruited her 20-something daughter to be her main support through the preliminary hearing and the trial that followed. However, she did not tell her adult son the details of her assault or when the preliminary hearing would be held, fearing the pain and anger that hearing her describe the attack would produce in him. She explained,

> He'll get angry and angry and angry and angry, you know, because the way he was brought [up]. He doesn't believe in these kind of things [rape], and I don't want him to see how people could hurt me, you know, [how] somebody we don't know could hurt me. Because he might keep that as a grudge or something, you know, to himself, you know. And I don't want him to feel that way, you know?

Staff members from rape crisis centers and victim-witness advocacy programs were sometimes sought for emotional support, specifically, because survivors did not have to worry about their feelings and knew that they would provide unconditional sympathy. Of the 31 survivors in this sample, 10 reported requesting rape crisis or victim-witness personnel to attend court events with them. Anna, an African American working-class women in her 20s, chose a victim-witness advocate to be in court with her to protect her mother and her boyfriend from details of the assault that would be revealed through her testimony. If an advocate was not available, she had planned to go through the preliminary hearing alone. Candace explained that she recruited a victim-witness advocate to join her daughter and herself for the preliminary hearing and trial, because she felt that she could not risk involving her friends in the proceedings. She was unsure of her friends' beliefs about rape and feared that they might reject her after learning the extent of her degradation or possibly hold her accountable for being assaulted. She assumed that the advocate understood the nature of rape:

> I like [the victim-witness advocate] to be there because [she] understood, I think. You know, even though they are your friend, maybe they don't understand the whole thing. You know, maybe they might hear something or whatever, then maybe change their mind [about you] or whatever. But [the victim-witness advocate], she understands. Maybe my friend[s] understand too, but I, I don't know. It's hard for me to bring them there to see, to know that private part of me, you know? They know what happened really, sort of. But I don't want them to hear the whole thing.

Candace's concern about maintaining privacy in the midst of the public court performance was echoed by other survivors. Several gave would-be supporters limited roles that balanced their need for encouragement with their desire to protect their privacy. Megan, an African American college student, for example, took a number of people with her to the courthouse for moral support, but she asked them to leave before she testified. She explained that only people immediately connected with the prosecution needed to know the details of the assault.

When several survivors found that would-be supporters were unwilling to respect their standards for team membership, they experienced a difficult situation. At the least, they felt annoyed. Sandra, a White college student, fled the courthouse when her boyfriend, whom she had requested not come, appeared anyway:

> I was in a big fight with Peter, and I told him that he couldn't go, and he didn't understand why. I said, "Well, you're not going, I don't want you there." And I remember the [courthouse] elevator opening, and it was Peter, and he was standing there and I freaked. And I went into this, like, . . . I'm leaving [mode]. I actually got into the elevator and went down, and I was, like, leaving the courthouse because Peter was there.

Members of the support system that Sandra had assembled went after her and brought her back. Her boyfriend realized that he was jeopardizing her participation in the case and he left the courthouse.

Survivors also sought out team members who could increase their ability to affect the legal process. Some persons were selected for the knowledge they could impart to survivors. Others were included because they could be where the survivor could not. Survivors also recruited particular people in an effort to influence jurors.

Rape crisis counselors and victim-witness advocates were contacted for their knowledge of the legal process, as were friends who had prior experience with court events. In the absence of prosecutor contact, survivors believed that these team members could provide them with some idea of what to expect in the courtroom and the possible outcomes of the legal event. For example, Bernice asked an attorney friend who had previously worked for the district attorney's office to accompany her to court. Janice, who had no contact with the prosecuting attorney prior to the scheduled preliminary hearing, asked a coworker who had recently been involved in a criminal proceeding to attend the preliminary hearing with her. Janice explained,

> She had been through, um, not this type of court hearing, her son had died in a motorcycle accident about a year before. When I started working there she was going back and forth to court. Um, basically she told me what was gonna happen, how long it was gonna take, because she'd been through it before. Um, so, she offered to give me a ride [to court, and] I asked her if she would be there with me. And she said, fine, no problem. I asked her because she knew . . . she had been through this before, and she kinda knew what was coming.

Survivors indicated that crisis workers, who were trained primarily to help a person work through her/his immediate response to rape, made good moral supports but often had a minimal grasp of the legal process and criminal procedure. Those who relied on victim-witness advocates generally found them to be well informed. However, several survivors reported that victim-witness advocates were sometimes close with information. It is probable that they were cautious about saying things that could undermine the prosecutor, because victim-witness programs are often associated with the district attorney's office in some way.

Team members also sat in the courtroom and observed for several survivors who were legally excluded from the courtroom. These "eyes and ears" then reported back to the survivor, keeping her abreast of the proceedings. Survivors recalled that receiving reports on the progress of the prosecution and defense helped them to feel connected to the proceedings. In addition, they recognized that the information that team members relayed provided a context for them to construct testimony, if they were called back to the stand to testify.

Finally, several survivors reported that one of the reasons they encouraged other people to be present in the courtroom was to influence the jury. They indicated that they encouraged family members and friends to be present as a show of force—a visible representation that they were believed by a large number of people. Cindy's team-building effort was the most precisely focused toward influencing a jury. She reported that she sought out African American friends to be in the courtroom during the trial because they contradicted the race-bias argument she expected the defense attorney to make. It was her intent that the friends, along with the book by an African

American woman author that she openly carried about, would dispel any perception that she was a White bigot with a vendetta against African American men. She explained her strategy:

> The [trial was on the] Tuesday after the Saturday after the gubernatorial elections, so I . . . needless to say, things are a little strange between Blacks and Whites at this point because David Duke [former Grand Wizard of the Ku Klux Klan] is running [for governor], you know. I mean that whole thing was the topic of conversation in Louisiana for the previous month. And you know, it just . . . like I said, it made things very strange between Black people and White people. Um, and I, . . . you know, he [the Defense Attorney] was smart enough to kind of take advantage of all that. I think, he really set it up. So I found myself really consciously trying to, um, dispel that, you know. I had Black friends in the courtroom with me, I was reading a book by J. California Cooper, who is a Black woman writer, and I made sure that I was seen reading that book, you know what I mean? Um, you know, I did everything I could to try and dispel the whole kind of racial thing by manner and stuff.

Survivors' team building brings people into the legal process who can supply the survivor with orienting information in the absence of preparation from the prosecutorial staff. Team-building efforts also ensure that there will be people whom survivors trust and by whom they feel believed in the courtroom. Thus, survivors produce a sympathetic audience to whom they can direct their testimony. Finally, survivors may contribute to the prosecution effort by bringing into the courtroom people who symbolically underscore the validity of their claims to have been raped. Invested members of the court audience are an unexamined courtroom phenomenon worthy of additional investigation.

Role Research

Another way that survivors made an effort to manage the victim-witness role was to educate themselves about the parameters of the legal situation that they would be entering. In the absence of precourt preparation from legal personnel, six survivors in this sample sought the guidance of persons with legal knowledge and/or engaged in library research to better understand rape law, the legal process, and the possible interactions that they might have when appearing in court. By obtaining such information, they hoped that they would become better witnesses and be better able to convey their testimony. Unlike the activities of appearance work, emotion work, or case enhancement (described below), such role research was not directed toward meeting cultural expectations about rape victims. It was focused on obtaining the knowledge or skills that survivors perceived to be necessary to participate effectively in a foreign "legal" space and to produce legally appropriate responses to questions. Many survivors mentioned reading books about coping with the trauma of rape that included chapters on criminal prosecution, which suggests a possible continuum of research activity. However, the efforts that I have identified as role research stand out because the survivors were clearly intent on improving their grasp of the criminal justice process.

For example, Sandra and Joanna, both White and college students at the time that they were raped, described trying to find relevant information in their university libraries. They looked up legal terms and legal codes that defined rape as well as general court process information. Sandra recalled that although she put a lot of work into finding out information, she was not successful in obtaining all that she felt she needed:

> I was on this rampage of having this information, you know. [Sighs] So I got a lot of information just from reading. I went to the library and found out about laws, um, the laws and what the defense attorneys could do, I mean, I read it in the [California Penal Code].... I went to the library. It's like I felt I couldn't get any information [from court personnel]. Like, I had to go and read about it myself, and so that's what I did. I tried to read a lot about it, although it didn't [give me all I needed], you know, it's really not the same thing [as being talked to].

Joanna was more satisfied with the research effort she conducted and indicated that what she discovered guided her word choice while testifying. Specifically, Joanna reported that she learned that the state of Virginia differentiated between forced vaginal intercourse (rape) and sexual assault (forced sexual contact short of penetration) and that she needed to say the word *rape* while testifying rather than *sexual assault*, the term she used when reporting the incident to police. Megan, another college student, went to the university counsel's office for information. The four other survivors who researched their roles outside the college setting called therapists and lawyers for information about the law and legal procedure when it was not forthcoming from prosecutors and their assistants. The fact that all the college students undertook role research suggests that their presence in institutions for research and education shaped their response to the criminal justice system.

Role research helps a survivor gain information that she feels is necessary to successfully perform her role, and it is a productive way to become more involved in the legal process. The information obtained may ease her worry, thus boosting her confidence, and help her formulate her testimony in ways that support the prosecution effort. Furthermore, survivors who know more about the legal process and the way their testimony fits into a case constructed by the prosecutor may be better able to comprehend the logic of requests made by her or him. On the other hand, role research can be a frustrating experience for the survivor who comes to realize her ability to obtain knowledge falls short of gaining a complete picture of the witness role. This can undermine confidence, as it did for Sandra.

Case Enhancement

The final group of preparatory activities, carried out by survivors, was directed to enhance the strength of "their" case. Of their own volition, nine survivors brought documents that corroborated their version of the assault event to the attention of legal personnel or to court with them. Their behavior reflected an understanding that the courtroom is a place where proof is required and that their testimony alone was not, on its own, sufficient evidence that a rape took place. This type of preparation cut across class lines. The two working-class survivors quoted below brought corroborative documents with them to hearings for probable cause. Theresa supplied a telephone bill that supported her claim that she called a particular friend immediately after the defendant left her home. This provided evidence of a *fresh complaint*, although she did not report the assault to the police until several weeks later. Recognizing the telephone bill as important evidence, the prosecuting attorney asked Theresa to provide a copy when the hearing was over. This is how Theresa accounted for bringing the bill with her:

> I hadn't even thought about the phone bill, until the day of the pretrial. I keep my phone bills, and I dug it out, and there it was, 1:03 on that night, I was on the phone with her for over 20 minutes. . . . You know, it's like, anything I can do to prove my case. I know that any documentation is that much better for me. And just like telling them [the DA and the detective], I talked with the people at rape crisis and stuff, there's documentation there, too, you know, they have logs. So yeah, I just feel that anything I can do to make my case more sound makes it that much better for me. And like the footwork with getting the people for my support group for that day, um, I've been able to do what I consider footwork to get some of the things done that I need done that will help my case. At least I think [they] will help my case, or help me get through it.

Rachel, a White 26-year-old, brought her daily diary to the attention of the prosecuting attorney several weeks before the scheduled hearing for probable cause because she thought it might help the prosecutor understand the history of her relationship with her assailant, her ex-husband. At the hearing, Rachel used the materials for reference. She explained to me,

> Well, I thought that anybody who knew our relationship . . . all our friends know what our relationship was like, they know that he manipulated me. Even friends that were his best friend are no longer friends with him because they don't like the way he treated me, or the kids. I just felt it was important that she [the DA] kinda knew a little bit of the history. So, I gave her that and that was a big chunk of our history, that one diary, the black book that they kept referring to [during the preliminary]. That was a big chunk of our history.

Katherine, a White medical assistant, brought a similar document to court with her, a date book that documented an escalating pattern of abuse by her domestic partner that went back months from the day of the rape. She explained to me that her previous experience with family court demonstrated the need for such specific information. During the hearing, she limited her answers to the contents of the date book.

While physical evidence of rape is collected by hospital personnel and police investigators, information regarding a survivor's mental state that may account for her behavior during or after a sexual assault is not. The materials supplied by the survivors quoted above provided support for their claims that they did not consent to intercourse in spite of their decisions to be in the presence of their assailants. Their case-enhancement efforts, like appearance work and emotion work, indicate that they were aware of and were trying to accommodate cultural stereotypes of "real rape."

When prosecutors made defense strategies known to survivors, a few reported producing evidence to counter them. For example, Natalie, a White legal secretary, brought eight years of employment evaluations to the prosecuting attorney after learning that the defense was planning to argue that she had precipitated the assault during a drug deal. She recalled,

I knew that they didn't have anything to . . . to go on, they was gonna try to use drugs. His story was that he was my drug supplier and that, um, I had gotten upset because oh, he was gonna cut me off and I got mad and went crazy in the house, and that's how I got beaten up or whatever.

Natalie's provision of exculpatory evidence is particularly interesting because her case was one of the strongest that I came across. Most of its attributes were consistent with classic rape stereotypes. She had been severely beaten about the head, such that she was taken to the hospital in an ambulance and required stitches, and she contacted the police immediately. She also gave police an exceptionally detailed description of the defendant's tattoo. Despite all this, Natalie felt compelled to counter an argument that she recognized to be outrageous. Like the other women who provided evidence, she took personal responsibility for the successful outcome of prosecution.

The woman who took the greatest responsibility for the outcome of her case actually prepared it for prosecution. After the defendant was brought to trial once and the jury failed to reach a verdict, Donna and her husband gathered evidence, drew maps, photographed the area, insisted the prosecutor contact character witnesses for Donna, and constructed an argument for the prosecutor to use in a retrial.

In the cases that I have discussed thus far, survivors provided concrete pieces of evidence to back up their claims, and they found that their efforts were accepted and incorporated by the prosecuting attorneys. However, other survivors' efforts to shape prosecution strategy with their ideas were not as well received. Julianne's experience provides a straightforward example of this point. She learned specifics of the defense attorney's strategy from a mutual friend to whom her assailant had spoken several weeks before the scheduled preliminary hearing and communicated the information to the prosecutor, hoping that a rebuttal would be planned. Instead, he brushed her concerns off without addressing the validity of her information. Unfortunately, Julianne's information was accurate. The defense attorney asked her about previous occasions when she had initially resisted sexual intercourse and then acquiesced, and he introduced some Polaroid photographs that depicted her in provocative poses. The judge called the preliminary hearing to a halt and recommended an immediate resolution. A plea agreement to significantly lesser charges was quickly arranged.

Prosecutors' acceptance of evidence and their rejection of ideas speaks to a boundary issue. Provision of tangible corroborative evidence falls within the bounds of appropriate witness behavior from the standpoint of prosecution. Providing strategy appears to tread on prosecuting attorneys' toes as it challenges their right to determine whether and how prosecution will proceed. I suspect that Donna's efforts would have been dismissed as overly intrusive if the prosecutor had not failed to convict the defendant on his first attempt.

Case-enhancement efforts that bring to light documents that corroborate survivors' stories generally support prosecutors' efforts. Potentially, the information supplied by survivors can influence the way the prosecutor builds her/his case as well. If a survivor feels that her credibility is questionable, having something on paper to which she can refer during a hearing can build her confidence. Additionally, when a survivor brings documents to court, she can limit her testimony to their content. This, in turn, can support prosecutors' efforts to keep the scope of survivors' testimony within narrow bounds.

Discussion

The findings in this study indicate that it would be unwise to assume that all rape survivors are passive bystanders in the legal process, just as it would be unwise to assume that they are passive in the face of rape. Faced with a new witness role and a responsibility to testify in the public courtroom forum, many survivors in this study actively prepared themselves for scheduled court events.

Incentives to Prepare

Study participants' preparation efforts were inspired by three interrelated concerns: conforming to cultural stereotypes of rape victims, managing themselves in a situation that they explicitly recognized as legal, and dealing with the potential emotional impact of participating in the court events. Some of the survivors in the study had contact with prosecutors prior to their initial court event and received directions as well as information from them. These directions—to obtain specific attire, to sustain a particular demeanor in court, to read through police reports, to stay away from the courtroom— were usually followed, but survivors often went beyond what was asked of them. For example, the majority of survivors in the study built courtroom teams, but none were instructed to do so by a prosecutor. The survivors who had no contact with the prosecutor until 30 or 45 minutes before preliminary hearings conceived and carried out their preparation activities independently. Thus, rape survivors' preparation for court events cannot be conceptualized as solely determined by legal personnel (Konradi 1996).

Study participants' awareness of classic rape stereotypes encouraged their appearance work, emotion work, case enhancement, and instrumental team building. Through these preparation activities, they sought to present themselves as credible victims to judges and juries. Few of the survivors in the study knew what was legally required to establish rape, and many did not know the specific charges filed against their assailants before appearing to give their testimony at a hearing for probable cause. They did not know, for example, that to encourage a plea their assailants had initially been charged with attempted rape, and only if their testimony included a clear description of vaginal, oral, or rectal penetration would the charges be upgraded to rape. Thus, when they provided evidence, these women were not attempting to systematically establish penetration, specific force, or threat of force, some of the legal components of rape.

Some of the survivors in the study accepted the cultural stereotypes of rape as valid. Other study participants did not accept the cultural notions of rape as true but acknowledged that jury members and judges might well believe them. However, the strategies believers and nonbelievers used to prepare themselves were similar, because members of both groups were intent on proving during their courtroom appearances that they were legitimate victims. Thus, appearance work, emotion work, case enhancement, and team building did not contest common cultural categories for understanding rape. As a result, even survivors who identified as feminist and were ideologically oriented to resist being dominated in court were engaged in affirming the belief systems that oppressed them. This paradox occasionally was painfully acknowledged when survivors reflected back on their experiences.

Social Aspects of Preparation

The findings of this study suggest that how participants took on the victim-witness role was very much determined by their membership in particular social worlds. Other persons provided audiences for participants' rehearsal efforts, and they were consulted when participants conducted research and composed their courtroom personas. How survivors in the study managed interaction and the particular ways they sought to meet cultural expectations, therefore, emerged from their daily experiences and intimate contacts. Teams, which many participants constructed to provide themselves with emotional support and encouragement, were also largely drawn from their close contacts. Although some survivors in the study reported making efforts to exclude people who might be pained by their testimony, this was not universally attempted or universally successful. Consequently, at least three women felt compelled to construct their testimony so as not to harm or offend their supportive listeners. The preparatory activity of team building also laid the groundwork for an additional layer of interaction in the courtroom between the survivor and nonlegal personnel. Ultimately, it does not serve legal personnel well to approach the victim-witness role as an individual role and themselves, despite their special relationship with rape survivors, as the sole shapers of survivors' actions in court.

The small number of women of color in the sample made group comparisons between White women and women of color difficult. However, racial/ethnic background does not appear to limit the kind of preparation in which survivors engaged. In the study, women of color and White women carried out each of the six preparation strategies. Among the rape survivors quoted above, Janice, Megan, and Anna were women of color, and the remainder were White. Exploring whether women of color, as a group, embark on additional unique preparation strategies, prepare more or less than White women, or use particular strategies of preparation more frequently than White women must be the focus of additional investigation.

Understanding the role that race plays in survivors' involvement in the prosecution of rape is not, however, simply a matter of asking if White women and women of color do the same things. It also involves exploring how survivors' understanding of cultural stereotypes about rapists and their victims and race relations shape their behavior. This is particularly important in the case of interracial rapes. Some of the White women in this study who were raped by Black men described their awareness of stereotypes of the "Black rapist" at the time they entered the criminal justice system, and some expressed their belief that their assailants' race could make the prosecution's case more convincing to a jury. It is possible that such beliefs could translate into lack of self-preparation, although this was not explicitly stated by the survivors. However, such a supposition must not be casually generalized. Cindy's comments about building a courtroom team including Black friends, because she expected a predominately Black jury and was aware of heightened racial tension in her city, indicate that survivors of rape may respond to the race relations in their immediate geographic context. When rape survivors are knowledgeable that jury pools are drawn from specific geographic jurisdictions, this would seem likely.

Information provided by police or prosecutors can also make survivors attentive to their assailants' race or the expected race of jurors and shape their self-preparations.

For example, Monica and Janice reported that prior to trial prosecutors informed them that race would play a role in their case. The prosecutor told Monica that she should not appear to be vindictive when she testified because the defendant claimed she "cried rape" out of fear that she would have a Black baby. Janice was told that she would need to explain that she had previously frequented the predominately Black club where she met her rapist and address the fact that her children were biracial (Asian Black) to dispel jurors' concerns about racism. Interview questions focusing on this aspect of race would be a positive addition to future research about survivors' involvement in rape processing.

A greater variation in socioeconomic status and educational background existed in the study sample. The class differences among the women, as measured by these two indicators, also did not account for any substantial variation in preparatory behavior. Women who were highly educated and worked in professional capacities as well as women who were clerical workers with a high school education engaged in the full range of preparatory activities. Class status, however, did appear to contribute to the specific nature of team building and role research. Although women of all class backgrounds used rape crisis hot lines and drew victim-witness advocates onto their teams, it was several older, middle-class professional women who had lawyers as personal friends whom they could ask to accompany them to court. Young women attending college had access to extensive libraries and to the university counsel. Other role researchers relied on consulting experts by telephone. As with race, additional attention to the role of class in shaping survivors' preparation strategies would be worthwhile.

Like the civil plaintiffs studied by Merry (1990) and Conley and O'Barr (1990), many rape survivors in this study strategized and pursued their own agendas relative to their perceptions of courtrooms and the legal process more generally. To a great extent, their preparations supported the interests of the prosecution. However, some of the activities study participants carried out might not have the same effect. For example, women's efforts to prepare statements to defend their postrape actions might work against a prosecutor's plan that revolved around presenting the survivor as a dupe of the assailant. In addition, team members who provided information about courtroom activity to excluded survivors gave them information the prosecuting attorney did not know they had.

Critical Thinking

It is clear from Konradi's findings that the courtroom is a tremendous source of stress for victims of rape. In fact, the anxiety associated with the courtroom appearance is an explanation for why rape has a relatively low rate of reporting. How do you think anxiety and stress affect courtroom members' perceptions of the reliability or believability of rape victims' accounts and testimonies? Considering the article by Frohmann; how do you think defense attorneys exploit this feature of rape trials to help their clients? If you were a defense attorney would you exploit this feature in an attempt to get your client a favorable decision?

References

Bart, Pauline, and Patricia O'Brien. 1985. *Stopping rape: Successful survival strategies*. New York: Pergamon.

Caignon, Denise, and Gail Groves, eds. 1987. *Her wits about her: Self-defense success stories by women*. New York: Harper & Row.

Conley, John, and William O'Barr. 1990. *Rules versus relationships: The ethnography of legal discourse*. Chicago: University of Chicago Press.

Frohmann, Lisa. 1991. Discrediting victims' allegations of sexual assault: Prosecutorial accounts of case rejections. *Social Problems* 38:213–26.

Goffman, E. 1959. *The presentation of self in everyday life*. Garden City, NY: Doubleday.

Greenberg, Martin S., and R. Barry Ruback. 1992. *After the crime: Victim decision making*. New York: Plenum.

Hochschild, Arlie. 1979. Emotion work, feeling rules, and social structure. *American Journal of Sociology* 85:551–75.

———. 1983. *The managed heart: Commercialization of human feeling*. Berkeley: University of California Press.

Holmstrom, Lynda Lytle, and Ann Wolbert Burgess. 1983. *The victim of rape: Institutional reactions*. New Brunswick, NJ: Transaction.

Kerstetter, Wayne A. 1990. Gateway to justice: Police and prosecutorial response to sexual assaults against women. *Journal of Criminal Law and Criminology* 81:267–313.

Kleck, G., and S. Sayles. 1990. Rape and resistance. *Social Problems* 37:149–62.

Konradi, A. 1993. Discovering role modeling: An activist approach to the recruitment of rape survivors. Paper presented at the American Anthropology Meetings, 17 November, Washington, DC.

———. 1996. Understanding rape survivors' preparations for court: Accounting for the influence of legal knowledge, cultural stereotypes, personal efficacy and prosecutor contact. *Violence Against Women* 2:25–62.

LaFree, Gary. 1989. *Rape and criminal justice: The social construction of sexual assault*. Belmont, CA: Wadsworth.

Madigan, Lee, and Nancy Gambel. 1989. *The second rape: Society's continued betrayal of the victim*. New York: Lexington.

Martin, Patricia, and R. Powell. 1994. Accounting for the "second assault": Legal organizations' framing of rape victims. *Law and Social Inquiry* 19:853–90.

Merry, Sally Engle. 1990. *Getting justice and getting even: Legal consciousness among working-class Americans*. Chicago: University of Chicago Press.

Polk, Kenneth. 1985. Rape reform and criminal justice processing. *Crime and Delinquency* 31:191–205.

Schafran, Lynn Hecht. 1993. Maiming the soul: Judges, sentencing and the myth of the nonviolent rapist. *Fordham Urban Law Journal* 20:439–53.

Stanko, Elizabeth. 1981. The impact of victim assessment on prosecutor's screening decisions: The case of the New York district attorney's office. *Law and Society Review* 16:225–39.

Williams, L. 1984. The classic rape: When do victims report? *Social Problems* 31:459–67.

17

The Agencies of Abuse: Intimate Abusers' Experiences of Presumptive Arrest and Prosecution

Keith Guzik

Abstract: *Keith Guzik examines domestic abuse arrest policies, specifically those pertaining to presumptive arrest and prosecution. His goals are to gain insight into the power and effectiveness of these policies in initiating social change by exploring the experiences and perceptions of people convicted on such policies. Instead of encouraging personal reflection and change, an overwhelming majority of participants perceived the program as ineffective and described them as instigating only feelings of injustice. The participants suggest that the feelings of injustice are a product of substandard and discriminatory enforcement and implementation of programs. Guzik's findings indicate that the power and efficiency of such aggressive domestic violence policies may have been overestimated in previous research.*

Society's campaign against intimate partner abuse has generated a repertoire of innovative legal measures. Orders of protection bar abusers from contacting their victimized partners. Presumptive arrest policies encourage the police to arrest abusive partners. Presumptive prosecution policies commit state's attorney's offices to pursue charges against abusers, even if victims do not cooperate (Schneider 2000:92–5).

These legal measures represent a new regime of domestic violence "governmentality" (Merry 1995, 2002). For women who are primarily the victims of abusive relationships, the measures are intended to sever abusive relationships and push women to become individual subjects independent of their abusive partners (Merry 1995). For the men who are predominantly the offenders in abusive relationships, the measures are intended to change their behavior by sending "a clear social message that battering is impermissible" (Schneider 2000:94) and holding them accountable for their actions (Buzawa & Buzawa 1996:178; Herrell & Hofford 1990).

While these initiatives demonstrate the criminal legal system's responsiveness to the battered women's movement (see Mirchandani 2005), presumptive policies have proven controversial among advocates. Supporters contend that the policies provide women security by forcing the criminal justice system to respond to domestic violence (Flemming 2003; Hanna 1996) and relieve them of difficult decisions regarding the arrest and prosecution of their partners (Wanless 1996; Cahn & Lerman 1991). Critics argue that the policies further harm women by taking decisionmaking from them (Ford 2003; Mills 2003) and that they ignore the injustices that minority populations and the poor experience at the hands of the criminal justice system (Coker 2001; Ferraro & Pope 1993; Ferraro & Boychuk 1992).

This debate captures well the dilemmas that presumptive policies present to victims of abusive relationships. However, less attention has been given to the effects of these measures on abusers. A number of statistical analyses have examined how aggressive arrest and prosecution correlate to future reports of offending. But none have contacted batterers to understand how these policies affect them. In this article, I look to fill this gap. Informed by law and society research on the relational nature of legal power, and using interviews with 30 persons arrested and prosecuted under presumptive policies, this article describes how intimate abusers experience presumptive arrest and prosecution.

The study finds that intimate abusers anchor their experiences of presumptive arrest and prosecution in police investigations and plea bargaining. These events draw batterers into distinct arrangements of power. While police officers work to have domestic violence suspects pronounce their abuse during investigations, court officials press them to give up their right to address allegations of abuse during plea negotiations. Suspects respond to these operations of power by either complying with or defying legal authorities, stances that are shaped by their legal consciousness, the tactical force of authorities, and their own understandings of abuse. In the majority of cases, the police and courts are able to structure the outcomes of these encounters in their favor, leaving them with custodial authority over abusers. Regardless of substantive outcomes, however, nearly all the respondents in this study understand their punishments as unfair sanctions meted out by an unjust local legal system rather than as the consequences of their own actions. These injustice claims are most commonly based on group identities. In other instances, though, they are the echoes of legal authorities themselves, who use depictions of an unjust legal system as a tactic for realizing the compliance of criminal suspects.

Literature Review: The Efficacy of Arrest and Prosecution against Intimate Abusers and the Relational Nature of Legal Power

Research investigating the impact of aggressive arrest and prosecution policies on intimate abusers has primarily consisted of quantitative studies using quasi-experimental research designs. These experiments compare future reports of offending for abusers arrested and prosecuted under proactive policies with those of abusers experiencing other legal interventions, such as police mediation, issuance of citations, or traditional prosecution. Interesting to note, this research has found that the efficacy of arrest and prosecution against batterers differs.

These studies provide much-needed measures of intimate abusers' behavior following arrest and prosecution. But they are not designed to explain the operations of power that would account for such results. For instance, the studies do not identify which elements of arrest and prosecution affect abusers, which leaves them unable to explain the connection between criminal justice actions and offenders' behavioral outcomes (Dobash & Dobash 2000). In addition, because the studies do not consult abusers to determine how these sanctions affect them, researchers have begun to call for research that examines "how assailants experience the criminal legal system" (Fleury 2002:203; see also Maxwell et al. 2002:72–3). In this article, I look to provide a more comprehensive view of the power of presumptive arrest and prosecution by answering the following question: How do intimate abusers experience presumptive arrest and prosecution?

To approach this question, I take guidance from ethnographic sociolegal research that highlights the relational nature of legal power (Ewick & Silbey 2003; Sarat & Felstiner 1995). This scholarship emphasizes power not as "a thing that can be possessed," but as a "probabilistic social relationship whose consequences are contingent upon the contributions of ... those who turn out to be more powerful (superordinate) and those who turn out to have been less powerful (subordinate)" (Ewick & Silbey 2003:1333). Power, in this sense, is an "unstable and evanescent" phenomenon (Sarat & Felstiner 1995:vii).

Despite the contingent nature of power, patterns of social interaction do become entrenched over time. And those who exercise hegemony do so by "drawing upon the symbols, practices, statuses, and privileges that have become habitual in social structures" (Ewick & Silbey 2003:1334), such as the "rules" through which courts process cases and transform participants' voices (Conley & O'Barr 1990) and the "knowledge of, stature in, and connections to the local community" that court authorities possess (Yngvesson 1989). Still, the substantive outcomes and interpretive meanings of legal encounters are never fixed, and common people possess the capacity to exercise "resistance" in their encounters with legal authorities (Ewick & Silbey 1998, 2003; Merry 1995; Sarat 1990).

Abusers' experience of presumptive arrest and prosecution presents a particularly salient case for studying the power of law. Distinct from the contexts examined in the aforementioned studies, domestic violence law represents an effort to harness the force of the criminal legal system in order to counter the force of another set of hegemonic social relations, men's control over women. By examining abusers' interactions with legal authorities and the meanings that these legal encounters have for them, this study provides a look not only at the power of the law, but also at the potential of the law to serve as a force for progressive social change.

Data and Methods

The data presented in this article is drawn from 30 hour-long, semi-structured interviews I conducted with persons arrested and prosecuted for domestic violence in Centralia County, a Midwestern county home to a large state university and three small cities. Centralia County proved an ideal site for this study. Each of the county's major police departments follows a presumptive arrest policy, and the county state's attorney's office pursues a presumptive prosecution policy.

I completed the interviews as part of a larger research project on presumptive arrest and prosecution, which included ride-alongs with a local police department and observations and interviews with prosecutors and defense attorneys at the Centralia County criminal court. The timing of respondents' participation was a major consideration in this study. I sought to interview batterers before their enrollment in batterer intervention programs (BIPs)—the typical site for recruiting batterer research subjects (Ptacek 1988; Hearn 1998; Eisikovits & Buchbinder 2000; Dobash et al. 2000)—since these programs comprise a separate site of governmentality whose specific purpose is to change men by instilling "new forms of masculinity" (Merry 2001:16). In an effort to avoid "contaminating" my sample with persons who had been instructed on how to understand their violence in BIPs, I arranged to have the county jail provide invitation letters to arrestees following their release from jail. I also mailed invitation letters to suspects following the termination of their court cases. I initially paid participants $25 per interview. Given an initial low response rate, I increased the amount to $40.

Aside from sex, the respondents participating in this research were a heterogeneous group in terms of age, race, employment, marital status, and criminal history. To determine the severity of respondents' violence, I referenced the police reports associated with their cases, using Straus et al.'s (1996) Revised Conflict Tactics Scale (CTS2) as a basis for measurement. The physical violence reported by victims is predominantly severe (17 of 26 victims), with injuries reported by 14 victims.

The work of interviewing domestic batterers is challenging because they are evasive in discussing their violent pasts (Ptacek 1988; Anderson & Umberson 2001). In addition, masculine subjects may view an interview as threatening and react by minimizing their participation (Schwalbe & Wolkomir 2001). Anticipating this, I put respondents in charge of data production by having them construct narratives (Riessman 1993) describing their experiences with the criminal justice system. To investigate the question "How do intimate abusers experience presumptive arrest and prosecution?" I asked participants to narrate their encounters with legal authorities at different points in the criminal justice process and to offer their assessments of these encounters. More specifically, I followed a script containing the following questions: "What happens when the police arrive? What are they doing? What happens when you are brought to jail? What are the guards and other inmates doing? What happens at court? What has your defense attorney been doing with the case? How has the criminal justice system treated you?" When necessary, I used "probes" (Goodman 2001:314) to have respondents discuss elements of their legal encounters in greater detail.

Findings

Domestic violence arrests and prosecutions expose intimate abusers to a diverse range of power operations. During the typical arrest, law enforcement officers will enter a residence, separate suspected batterers from their victims, interrogate them to determine probable cause, and place them in state custody (Guzik 2003). During domestic violence prosecutions, suspects are made to appear before court to hear criminal charges read against them, have no-contact orders placed against them, are admonished by judges to abide by the orders, are offered plea bargains requiring partner abuse counseling, and are pushed by their defense attorneys to accept the plea bargains (Guzik 2007).

When asked to describe what happens in their interactions with the police and county court, however, the persons participating in this study neglected to mention many of these operations. The power operations that did register, meanwhile, tended to vary by individual respondent. In court, Carl recounted the challenge of abiding by his attorney's advice to remain silent while listening to what he believed was the state's misrepresentation of the facts of his case, while Walter remembered being admonished by a court peace officer after arriving late to a pretrial hearing.

Amongst this variability, common elements did appear in respondents' stories. When describing court, they tended to focus on the plea bargain agreements offered by the state. These elements and plea bargain agreements represent the core events of these respondents' legal experiences. In the following three subsections, I review suspects' accounts of these events, focusing on how they described these events unfolding and how they evaluated their experiences.

Intimate Abusers and Plea Bargain Agreements

The plea bargain represents a core feature of the modern criminal legal system that enables courts to process heavy caseloads (Alschuler 1968, 1975, 1976). In domestic violence cases, plea bargain can take on added importance. As Mirchandani (2005) explains in her observation of a specialized domestic violence court in Salt Lake City, by routinizing the court's processing of domestic violence cases, plea bargains allow judges the time to confront and challenge offenders' patriarchal beliefs in the court setting (2005:409). As such, the plea bargain serves as a linchpin in the domestic violence court's union of social control and social change functions.

Interestingly plea bargains have a different significance in Centralia County. Here, the state relies on them not only to process domestic violence cases efficiently, but also to secure convictions in the first place. As Matt, a state's attorney responsible for prosecuting domestic violence cases, explained to me, his office faces a conservative local community that produces juries disinclined to domestic violence convictions. "It's that attitude that it's the Midwest," he noted, "the attitude that family problems should stay in the family, until they get a certain point. If the jury believes it hasn't gotten to that point, then leave them [suspects] alone." To hold abusers accountable for their violence, then, the state's attorney's office believes it needs defendants to plead guilty.

To have suspects plea, the prosecutor's office attempts to make plea bargains more appealing to defendants than trials. In some situations, the attractiveness of plea bargains is inherent. As Matt explained. "If the defendant is sitting in jail, and he can't bond out, and you offer him a plea to misdemeanor domestic battery and he gets out of jail tomorrow, he's going to take it." In other instances, the state looks to heighten the appeal of plea bargains by "overcharging" its domestic violence cases both horizontally (by increasing the number of charges on a particular case) and vertically (by charging cases higher than circumstance would seem to warrant) (Alschuler 1968: 85–6). Matt revealed. "If there is the possibility of filing a felony, I will file a felony no matter what and then I will file a count two, misdemeanor domestic battery." The state then offers defendants a plea bargain to the misdemeanor domestic violence charge, which almost always includes partner abuse counseling as a condition of the sentence.

This framework for prosecuting domestic violence cases involves suspects in a power relation quite distinct from that of police investigations. While suspects are pressed during the police investigation to answer allegations of violence, they are here pressed to give up their right to answer the state's charges that they committed abuse. In this context of power, suspects again respond in one of two ways. They either *comply* with the court's push to have them accept plea bargains, or they *defy* the court by taking their cases to trial.

Defendants' reactions to plea bargains are influenced by both their legal conscious-ness and the tactical power of the state. With plea bargains, however, the degree to which legal consciousness is bound together with socioeconomic status becomes more pronounced. That is, for suspects who could not afford to bond out of jail, appraisals of plea bargain agreements were as straightforward as Matt described. Of the 13 respondents participating in this study who could not bond out of jail, only Ann did not sign a plea deal. Other study participants, meanwhile, based their responses to plea offers by considering the costs of conviction, whether the potential costs of trying their cases or the certain costs of a domestic violence conviction spelled out in the plea agreement. Ralph, for instance, who had had a few friends end up in jail on "domes-tics," said, "I don't want to end up in jail like them, so I'm just going to plea." Quinn, on the other hand, a former police officer arrested for a violation of an order of protec-tion against his wife, reflected on how a domestic violence conviction would affect his life. "Do you realize how bad this [a domestic violence conviction] makes you look?" he asked. "You can never own a firearm. Employers won't hire you. And when the cops pull you over, that V of OP is going to pop up. And that's going to affect how they handle you. I know, we used to do that all the time." With his past experience as a law enforcement officer on his mind, Quinn believed that he had to try his case in order to preserve the benefits that persons without criminal records enjoy in society.

In addition to weighing the costs of conviction, defendants also arrived at decisions on plea bargains by assessing the strength of their cases. In these instances, suspects most often appraised their cases based on the stance of their victimized partners. Suspects who believed that their victims would not cooperate with the state evaluated their cases strongly and rejected plea bargains. In his case, Mike was facing domestic violence charges that were four years old. Describing his thinking on his case, he asserted:

> Oh, I knew it was going to be dismissed, man. Some of that shit in there is three and four years old, you know what I mean? Mine is an old case, OK. I knew that Ayanna [ex-girlfriend] ain't living here. How you going to subpoena her? Her auntie stays in Texas, she's a low-life nobody. These are the people that were there that night. I knew they weren't going to get in touch with them.

Knowing that the state was unlikely to subpoena the main witnesses against him, Mike was confident about his case ("I knew it was going to be dismissed"). As a result, he decided to set it for trial and indeed had it dismissed.

While Mike acted on the basis of given circumstances (he said his ex-girlfriend had moved away), other suspects believed that the prospects of their cases could be swung in their favor if they could have their victims support them. Isaac, for instance, said that he knew "a lot of guys" whose "fiancée's been going up to the state's attorney [to] tell them that she ain't coming to court, she ain't testifying, and she ain't coming to no civil court, nothing. And she telling them that it was a mistake, they was mad and angry at each other." Thus while the state uses the law to disrupt abusers' relationships and push them to plead out their cases, these suspects saw their chances to defy the state contingent upon re-establishing influence over their partners and having them speak to the court on their behalf.

Respondents' ability to control their victimized partners was affected, however, by the web of power relations in which they found themselves during domestic violence prosecutions. In nearly every case it prosecutes, the Centralia County state's attorney's office has the court issue no-contact orders that forbid suspects from contacting their victims. According to their narratives, defendants seldom abided by these court orders. Nevertheless, most were aware that violating the orders could land them in further trouble with the law.

In these contexts of diminished power, abusers transformed rather than severed their forms of influence over their partners. Their narratives evidenced different strategies for effecting this end. One way they did this was by trying to be nice. Carl explained that he received this counsel from his attorney, an officer of the court whose formal responsibility it is to uphold the authority of the court. "He said," Carl remembered, "You're not supposed to have contact with her, but remain on good terms with her and, hopefully, I can get her to sign an affidavit saying that she doesn't want any further legal action. It was just all a misunderstanding."

A second tactic suspects used was attempting to generate or play upon feelings of regret from their partners about their arrests. Nic, for example, described violating the no-contact order with his wife:

> The last thing I wanted was for the cops to show up while I was at her apartment or she was at mine. I would remind her. I'm like, "Look, remember, you know you don't want to go and deal with these people. You don't want to have an interview with you know and have to deal with that. Part of that is that if the cops come here and I'm anywhere near you, you're not going to jail, I'm going to jail." You know, and she would calm down.

The strategy Nic described for violating the no-contact order clearly builds upon traditional gender roles and expectations. Assuming the role of patriarch, Nic felt it necessary to "remind" his spouse of her supposed uneasiness about legal authorities ("you don't want to go and deal with these people"). He then brought up the fact that he could get arrested for seeing her, which cast him as a potential victim ("you're not going to jail, I'm going to jail"). Implicit here is the expectation that she, rather than he, would have to sacrifice (both her voice and security) for the unity of the family. In doing so, he reported being able to control her during arguments ("she would calm down").

A third way in which the men in this study tried to exercise influence over their partners was through family members. For instance, respondents commonly related having mothers and sisters intervene on their behalf with their partners:

> Well, my girlfriend right now, we talk but it's through my mother. They basically put a no-contact on me, so I usually contact my mother to see if she can basically get a hold of her, because I know guys who have their girlfriends say, maybe it was something then, right there on the day it was happening, that made her call the police. Maybe she was scared or something, but it wasn't really that serious. So I've tried to get her to write letters or to get in touch with the state's attorney to tell him what happened, that it really wasn't as serious as she made it up to be.
>
> (John)

Such interactions represent a transformation of the gender politics at play in presumptive arrest and prosecution. While the state is using the police and courts to intervene in abusive intimate relationships to re-inscribe gender relations, these mothers, who embody localized notions of femininity in person, intervene to re-construct these relationships, John hoped that his mother would be able to have his partner realize that she "made [the violence] up" and contact the state's attorney.

Suspects' efforts to influence their victimized partners met with varying levels of success. Both Tom and Victor reported having their partners show up at court on their behalf, helping them to defy the state and eventually beat their cases. Women's efforts to terminate their relationships with abusive partners, however, sometimes disrupted men's efforts to control them. With his attorney out of town on vacation, Carl said he was delegated with the task of getting in touch with his ex-girlfriend to make sure that she had contacted the state's attorney's office and notified them of her unwillingness to testify. When meeting her, however, he got into another fight:

> Obviously, when someone throws you in jail, you don't want to be around them anymore. So, she had to schedule a meeting with the victim's coordinator. My attorney told me to call her and ask her if she could go and talk to the victim's coordinator. He was going to go on vacation, so it kind of fell on me. I said I would call her. So, we got into an argument, and she went and did everything against what she said she was going to do. She was just out to get me.

Unable to avoid getting into another argument with his ex-girlfriend, Carl lost what he thought would be her support on his case. As a result, he moved farther from trying his case and closer to accepting a plea bargain. And in the process, new meanings were constructed around the experience. His ex-girlfriend's refusal to do what he said and go to the state's attorney's office, a sign of her desire to be independent from him, was interpreted by Carl as a sign that "she was just out to get me."

Apart from the support of their victims, domestic violence suspects also molded their responses to plea bargains in relation to another base of power in the court setting: their defense attorneys. As past law and society research indicates, defense attorneys possess their own propensities for plea bargaining cases. While a minority of defense attorneys are "gamblers" (Skolnick 1974:95) or "mavericks" (Mather 1979:124) who maintain an adversarial stance with the prosecutor's office, most are "cooperative" attorneys (Skolnick 1974:97) willing to cooperate with the state's attorney's office by moving their defendants to plea-bargain.

For some respondents, consultations with defense attorneys moved them from defying the court to complying with it. Carl, who thought the state's case against him was ridiculous, noted that he nevertheless pled his case out. Asked why he would admit guilt to charges he thought were spurious, he explained:

> It was happening during the changeover of state's attorney—Nolan, who [was] on his way out, and the new girl was coming in. She was a female and she was going to crack down on domestic violence. My attorney just thought that maybe it was best for me to do this and get it over with.

Carl's attorney's depiction of the state's attorney's office is a tactic calculated to establish "client control" (Blumberg 1967). As Sarat and Felstiner's (1995) study of attorney–client relations in divorce cases reveals, attorneys rely on a repertoire of such tactics (defining "the legally possible," conjuring up a "parade of horribles," casting themselves as the "dean" of the bar) in order to move clients toward settling their cases (1995:26–52, 57). In the example above, Carl's attorney was able to move him to a plea deal by changing his perception of the fairness of the court process. Carl did not know that the outgoing state's attorney was an enthusiastic supporter of the presumptive prosecution policy. In this vacuum of knowledge about the local legal community, his attorney was able to sketch out a set of "circumstances," an outgoing male state's attorney and an incoming female state's attorney, that could be seen to increase the risk involved with trying the case.

Unlike Carl, other respondents were less susceptible to being influenced by client control tactics because they simply distrusted their defense attorneys. Some, based on past experiences, noted entering the court process skeptical of their attorneys' allegiance to them, while others explained that they came to distrust them over the course of their current case proceedings. Wise to the propensity of defense attorneys to plea-bargain, these defendants were nevertheless reliant on them to represent their cases at court. In response, defendants reported resorting to their own control tactics in order to direct the actions of attorneys whom they did not trust.

Walter, for example, was confident about his case because his ex-partner had called the police to drop the charges. His public defender, however, continued to seek a plea bargain for him:

> On one occasion, she actually made it seem like it [the plea offer] was some good news or something. "Good news for who? You or me? It would be good news for you, because you ain't got to deal with this case no more." You know what I'm saying? And I told her, "No. I'm not taking that. Take it to trial. And I mean that."

In this scene, Walter passed through the client control techniques of his attorney ("she actually made it seem like it was some good news") in order to assert control over his case.

Suspects' efforts at controlling their attorneys, like those aimed at their victims, met with different results. Tom, interestingly, claimed that he was only able to convince the public defender to set his case for trial upon proving to him that his partner would support him. "He was telling me, 'You don't want to go to trial if she with the attorneys.' . . . I told him, 'No, she out there [in the hallway] with me now. She said she going to tell them [the state] that she told the police that I didn't hit her' . . . So he went out there and he talked to her and he was like, 'OK.' "

Steve, in contrast, who wanted to try his case despite the objections of his defense attorney, recounted arriving late for a pretrial hearing in which the attorney was to announce the case ready for trial. From this error, the lawyer shifted her position on the case and began pushing a plea bargain on him in order to quash the arrest warrant the judge had just issued for his failure to appear in court.

> She [the public defender] just come over and whisper to me, she tell me, "You already got a warrant out for five thousand dollars," and she says, "You know in the past, he don't take them back." So, I took that plea because I was late for court and she had me thinking that he was going to lock me up. So, that's what happened to me. I made my decision to take that plea because I did not have $500 there.

In a position where he believed he had to plea in order to avoid arrest, Steve switched from defying to complying with the court's wishes to have him sign a plea bargain.

The substantive outcomes of respondents' court encounters varied more than those of their police encounters. Once again, the state was able to structure outcomes in its favor. Twenty-three of the respondents participating in this study pled guilty to domestic violence charges that required them to undergo counseling. Nonetheless, each of those suspects who refused to comply with the court's plea bargain arrangements experienced a favorable case outcome, either having their cases dismissed or winning verdicts in their favor at jury trials.

Respondents' plea bargain narratives depict the power of the law against intimate abusers as an interactive construction involving both legal authorities and suspects. Once again, suspects' compliance with and defiance of the law are layered phenomena, shaped by their legal consciousness (evaluations of the costs of convictions, assessments of their cases, familiarity with defense attorneys), the strategic force of the state (incarceration, overcharging, client control tactics), and their own abusive behavior (violation of no-contact orders, new forms of controlling behavior). Distinctly, however, the power of the law in the criminal court setting does not take shape through a single axis (e.g., the suspect–police officer axis), but through multiple axes involving suspects, the state's attorney office, defense attorneys, and victims. In this sense, power in the court setting is more dispersed.

The Meaning of Domestic Violence Arrests and Prosecution

In addition to giving the state custodial authority over intimate abusers, domestic violence arrests and prosecutions are intended to teach batterers that abuse is wrong. In discussing their experiences with the criminal justice system, a few respondents revealed connections between their criminal punishments and increased responsibility for violence. Mike, for example, explained that he realized "after all the shit I've been through" that, even though he just pulled his partner by her legs, "it's just something I shouldn't have did." In his quote, "all the shit" refers specifically to the long court process that he experienced before seeing the charges against him dismissed.

For most of the respondents, however, even those who recognized the wrongness of their actions, the lesson of punishment was different. Rather than triggering inward reflections by abusers on the wrongness of their behavior, arrests and prosecutions triggered outward reflections on the wrongness of legal authorities' actions. Overwhelmingly, the respondents in this study believed that they had been mistreated by the police and courts.

In terms of the court, most of the respondents cited elements of its case handling that struck them as unjust. Many interviewees complained that the court system, and by extension the legal system, was impersonal and insensitive to people's individual circumstances. In doing so, they identified elements of the criminal justice "process" that Feeley (1979) contends represent the true "punishment" for defendants. Walter, for instance, bemoaned that in court, "there's no consideration for the other person," and the money and time from work they lost by attending court dates. In addition, many respondents, similar to sociolegal scholars portraying the "practice of law as confidence game" (Blumberg 1967:15), described the court as a close-knit group of professionals who were uninterested in the lives of individual defendants. Frank noted, "I have to come to the conclusion that they all sit around in a bar and have nachos and chips and trade each other lives. 'I give you this guy for that guy, and you let him off, now I will give you this guy.'"

In addition to identifying *how* they believed legal authorities mistreated them, respondents also offered rationales for *why* they were treated this way. For instance, male respondents typically believed they were victims of gender bias at the hands of either individual officers or laws and policies designed to protect women. This is not completely unexpected. As Eisikovits and Buchbinder (2000) and Anderson and Umberson (2001) note in their studies of abusive men, abusers who are arrested view themselves as victims of either police officers or domestic violence laws that are biased against men. Participants in this study presented similar views. With regard to the former, men often noted that officers seemed to have "talked to the lady more and tried to get more information from her" (John). With regard to the latter, the participants described the law as "all just women's agenda" (Peter) and "strictly for a woman" (Walter).

Despite the primacy of gender as a framework for claiming injustice, respondents also interpreted their experiences through other, nonprivileged group identities. A wealth of sociolegal research has demonstrated that race plays a key role in how citizens perceive the criminal justice system, with African Americans consistently expressing greater distrust of legal authorities than whites (Weitzer 2000; Wortley et al. 1997; Hagan & Albonetti 1982).

Other respondents interpreted the criminal justice system's handling of their cases in terms of money. Quinn, the former cop, believed that domestic violence cases simply serve to enrich the state and lawyers. "It's all status and money," he noted, "I mean, there are guys out there who deserve to be arrested. But there's a lot of guys being arrested who don't deserve to be, couples who are trying to work things out. But it's about money. They want their money." Such comments express a certain class consciousness on the part of suspects, similar to that of people who stand "up against" the law (Ewick & Silbey 1998) and interpret their legal experiences in terms of resources. These respondents, for whom hiring a defense attorney, appearing in court, and abiding by their sentences represented significant financial costs, believed the criminal justice system punished them not to stop their abusive behavior, but to get their money.

Respondents' belief that their punishments were unfair arose not simply from group identities, but from the tactics of power used by the police and courts as well. That is, in describing aspects of their experiences with domestic violence law that struck them as unjust, respondents frequently echoed the statements that police officers, jail guards, and defense attorneys used to render them compliant with policing and court setting power:

> She [the public defender] said that they [the state] don't drop the charges, and most of the time they take the female side . . . she got to the point with, "Well, it's just how it goes. Well, how long you lived in Centralia County?"
>
> (Steve)

Each of these ideas is patently false. But each is calculated to effect a certain reaction from the suspect. Steve's case, meanwhile, is an example of "client control." Significant to note, the way in which both comments effect compliance is by sending the message to suspects that nothing they did was necessarily wrong, but that some aspect of the local legal system (departmental policy, state law, the state's attorney's office) is simply strict or unjust. In the process, the suspects came to see themselves as victims of the law.

Discussion

This study has highlighted the diverse operations of power defining domestic abusers' experience of prosecution. In the face of police requests to speak about their alleged violence and court pressure to give up their right to address allegations, domestic violence suspects respond through legal performances that fluctuate between compliance and defiance and are interactively shaped by their legal consciousness, legal authorities' tactics of power, and their own abusive behavior. As the substantive outcomes of respondents' legal encounters make clear, the police and courts are able to structure these interactions in their favor, leaving abusers under their administrative authority. Notably, domestic violence arrests and plea bargain convictions disrupt many abusers' attempts to explain away their violence during police investigations and to re-establish control over their victimized partners during plea negotiations. However, while these legal actions give the state a hold over batterers, they do not deliver strong messages about their abusive behavior. The majority of respondents in this study understand their arrests and court encounters as undeserved sanctions motivated by an unjust local legal system. These injustice claims emerge not only from abusers' group identities, but also from the very practices through which the police and courts gain authority over them.

The findings of this research offer important contributions to both law and society and domestic violence research. With regard to the former, a number of recent socio-legal studies highlight the expansion of the legal system from an institution primarily focusing on social control to one embracing social change as well. On the issues of drug abuse (Nolan 2003), juvenile delinquency (Kupchik 2004), mental health (Goldkamp & Irons-Guynn 2000), and domestic violence (Mirchandani 2005), justice is "reinventing" itself. Courts' traditional technocratic focus on procedural issues is giving way to a new therapeutic orientation emphasizing offender treatment and change, which is reflected in both the language of court officers and its interventions with deviant and criminal subjects (see Mirchandani 2005 and Nolan 2003 for somewhat contrasting appraisals of this process).

In the domestic violence context, judges, prosecutors, and defense attorneys adhere to a feminist perspective on the patriarchal nature of intimate partner violence and adapt their interactions with abusers in order to promote offender accountability. Judges admonish offenders in the court, while prosecutors and defense attorneys collaborate to have defendants plead guilty and get placed into counseling (Mirchandani 2005). Aspects of the court process that have traditionally been seen as "the punishment," the time and costs demanded for court appearances, take on a rehabilitative hue in this new setting (Mirchandani 2005:403). From these studies, one not only sees a new model of justice emerging, but a new potential for the law as a force for individual and social change.

Using the experiences of intimate abusers arrested and prosecuted under presumptive policies, this study finds that the power of the law as a force for social change may be more limited than some have claimed. In Centralia County, the state is able to gain custodial authority over intimate abusers. That is, it can detain them, impose no-contact orders against them, convict them, and sentence them to counseling. But it is unable to have them take responsibility for their actions.

One is reminded here of Foucault's (1979) distinction between "juridico-discursive" power, in which authorities inform subjects of what they can or cannot do (Foucault 1979:82–5), and "strategical" power, which operates through a "multiplicity of force relations" that shape and transform the subjectivities of those whom authorities target (Foucault 1979:92–3). In Centralia County, the state, within the framework of presumptive policies and through the various tactics it employs to condition suspects' compliance with authority, is able to gain and exercise juridical power over intimate abusers. Law enforcement and court officers can make suspects talk, place them in detention, have them appear before court, compel them to give up their right to contest charges and sign their guilt, and sentence them to therapy. But the state is unable to establish strategical power, or what post-structuralist theorists call *subjectifying power*, over them. That is, the same legal authorities cannot "govern the souls" (Rose 1991) of abusers in order to transform the abusive subjectivities from which their violence is thought to emerge.

In addition to sketching the boundaries of law's power, this article bears insight into the forces that oppose its subjectifying power. First, for instance, opposition to the meaning-making power of the law springs forth from intimate abusers' understanding of violence. Advocates of aggressive criminal justice interventions against domestic violence reason that punishments, by disrupting abusers' efforts to deny, minimize, excuse, and justify their behavior, will force them to face the truth of their actions. One reason this does not happen, however, may be that batterers actually believe their explanations of violence. As a result, it is perhaps not surprising that abusers resist the meanings that authorities look to impute to their punishments. Arrest and prosecutions provoke a certain crisis for these respondents. They do not believe they have done anything wrong, but they are nonetheless being punished. And from this incongruity injustice claims emerge.

Second, opposition to the law emerges from the diverse subject positions of domestic violence suspects as well. While the intimate abuser, domestic batterer, or wife-beater has emerged as a unified subject in the popular imagination, persons who commit intimate abuse occupy a variety of subject positions in the social world. And through these multiple positions, the respondents in this study defined their legal experiences of injustice. The injustices that African Americans and the working class (Brooks & Jeon-Slaughter 2001; Wortley et al. 1997; Hagan & Albonetti 1982) experience and perceive in the criminal justice system thus check the meaning-making power of the law.

Of course, the subject position from which most respondents based their injustice claims was gender. The majority of the male respondents believed that the police, courts, or laws were biased against men. Rather than reflecting the consciousness of traditionally disadvantaged groups and classes, these claims represent the disquietudes of a historically privileged group (i.e., men) as it witnesses the further dismantling of its architecture of advantage. In rearranging the boundaries between "private" and "public" space that have buttressed men's violence against women in intimate relationships, domestic violence law represents another instance of a larger "crisis of masculinity" through which men begin to perceive themselves as "the *real* victims in American society" (Kimmel 1996:305; emphasis in original). Regardless of its merit, the sense of victimization expressed by the abusers in this study is again important as it counters the subjectifying power of the law.

Third, community also plays a role in refracting the meaning of punishments. In recent work, Sampson and Bartusch (1998) and Weitzer (2000) highlight how neighborhoods can serve as "cognitive landscapes" shaping individuals' perception of deviance and trust in legal institutions. The legal narratives in this study suggest different ways in which community influences individuals' feelings of criminal injustice. On the one hand, communities carry or are imputed with a reputation that then colors people's legal experiences in those locales. Tom's mother, who lives in a major city, explained to him and his victimized partner "how those cops are down there" in more rural Centralia County. On the other hand, communities also serve as the stages upon which the events shaping people's collective experiences take place. And people tie their personal experiences with the law to these larger experiences in order to define their legal encounters. Carrie, for instance, explained to me why she felt her probation sentence was "all just about money":

> I know that it was in the paper they wanted to rebuild the clock of the courthouse or whatever. Ever since then the police are doing different stuff, you know, as far as trying to make more money. Like last week they stopped, oh, three hundred and something people on the corner of Columbia and Neal doing . . . I'm not sure what it's called, public safety search or something. *That's an African American neighborhood?* Yeah. And basically what they were doing was checking to see if you have your seat belt on, checking to see if you have a driver's license and insurance. And if you don't have it, they ended up arresting 60 people just that day.

In this cognitive landscape, where the courthouse is restoring its iconic clock tower and the police are stepping up a public order campaign specifically in a black neighborhood, Carrie's own experience with the law takes on a new meaning.

Finally, the power of law to serve as a force of social change is inhibited by itself. More specifically, the means by which the law is able to gain juridical power over domestic violence suspects are inimical to establishing subjectifying power over them. The control tactics that police officers and defense attorneys employ to have suspects cooperate with investigations and accept plea bargains ricochet to alter the meaning of punishment. Similarly, the strong-arm tactics (having suspects sit in jail, overcharging cases) that the state's attorney's office relies on to secure convictions become the substance of abusers' injustice claims.

These points are also important to the ongoing debate on the value of presumptive policies in the fight against domestic violence. In recent years, the voices of opponents who criticize the policies for disempowering victims (Mills 2003) and inflicting additional harm upon poor and minority communities (Maguigan 2003) have been increasing. These findings, based in the narratives of abusers, support these critical assessments of presumptive policies. Presumptive policies fail to fulfill their promise of increasing abusers' responsibility for violence. Significantly, this failure derives in large measure from abusers' experiences as members of traditionally disadvantaged groups and communities and the tactics of legal authorities. In addition, presumptive prosecution and no-contact orders fail to insulate victims from abusers' controlling behavior. Instead, abusers report using different tactics (playing nice, manipulating feelings of remorse, mobilizing female family members to pressure victims) during criminal prosecution in order to control their partners. The involvement of female family members in abusers' efforts to dissuade victims from supporting criminal sanctions against them is particularly worrisome. Further research is needed to identify the reasons female family members get involved (Do they not think violence against women is an important issue? Do they simply want to insulate sons and brothers from the police and state?) and the effects of their involvement on victims' future reporting (Are they dissuaded from calling the police in the future?).

But if this study offers a critical assessment of presumptive measures, the alternatives to mandatory interventions seem unclear. The most often-mentioned alternatives carry their own limitations. That is, while the clearest way to empower victims is through resources (financial and housing assistance) that would enable them to better manage their situations of violence (Schneider 2000; Coker 2001; Merry 1995), the political will to realize such a vision seems woefully absent. And while alternative adjudication procedures, such as restorative justice (Pennell & Burford 2002; Strang & Braithwaite 2002), would circumvent the court system and place the victim at the center of the justice process, allowing the victim to confront the abuser and pronounce the harm the abuser has caused, one wonders what outcomes would result from integrating communities and families unsympathetic to domestic violence victims more deeply in the justice process. In conclusion, then, what appears clear is that the promise for effective social change against domestic violence depends not on swinging the police and courts against this enduring social problem, but on building a base for more progressive change by continuing to convince communities across society that domestic violence is a serious problem.

Critical Thinking

According to Guzik, the primary goal of presumptive arrest policies is to teach offenders to recognize the immoral nature of their actions and to accept responsibility for such behavior. However, Guzik finds that despite participation and involvement in these aggressive domestic violence policies and programs, most offenders still do not take responsibility for their own violent behavior or report changes in their behavior. Based on your readings in the policing section and Guzik's article why do you think those convicted of domestic violence blame others and fail to take responsibility for their actions? Could this be a reflection of the social acceptability of domestic violence? Is it possible that there is truth to the claims of discriminatory enforcement by people convicted under these policies?

References

Alschuler, Albert (1968) "The Prosecutor's Role in Plea Bargaining," 36 *University of Chicago Law Rev.* 50–112.

—— (1975) "The Defense Attorney's Role in Plea Bargaining," 84 *The Yale Law J.* 1179–304.

—— (1976) "The Trial Judge's Role in Plea Bargaining, Part I," 76 *Columbia Law Rev.* 1059–154.

Anderson, Kristin, & Debra Umberson (2001) "Gendering Violence: Masculinity and Power in Men's Accounts of Domestic Violence," 15 *Gender and Society* 358–80.

Blumberg, Abraham (1967) "The Practice of Law as a Confidence Game," I *Law & Society Rev.* 15–39.

Brooks, Richard, & Haekyung Jeon-Slaughter (2001) "Race, Income, and Perceptions of the U.S. Court System," 19 *Behavioral Sciences and the Law* 249–64.

Buzawa, Eve, & Carl Buzawa (1996) *Domestic Violence.: The Criminal Justice Response*, 2d ed. Thousand Oaks, CA: Sage.

Cahn, Naomi, & Lisa Lerman (1991) "Prosecuting Woman Abuse," in M. Steinman, ed., *Woman Battering: Policy Responses*. Cincinnati: Anderson Publishing.

Coker, Donna (2001) "Crime Control and Feminist Law Reform in Domestic Violence Law," 4 *Buffalo Criminal Law Rev.* 801–60.

Conley, John, & William O'Barr (1990) *Rules Versus Relationships: The Ethnography of Legal Discourse*. Chicago: Univ. of Chicago Press.

Dobash, Rebecca, & Russell Dobash (2000) "Evaluating Criminal Justice Interventions for Domestic Violence," 46 *Crime and Delinquency* 252–70.

Dobash, R. Emerson, et al. (2000) *Changing Violent Men*. Thousand Oaks, CA: Sage.

Eisikovits, Zvi, & Eli Buchbinder (2000) *Locked in a Violent Embrace: Understanding and Intervening in Domestic Violence*. Thousand Oaks, CA: Sage.

Ewick, Patricia, & Susan Silbey (1998) *The Common Place of Law: Stories of Popular Legal Consciousness*. Chicago: Univ. of Chicago Press.

—— (2003) "Narrating Social Structure: Stories of Resistance to Legal Authority," 108 *American J. of Sociology* 1328–72.

Feeley, Malcom (1979) *The Process Is the Punishment: Handling Cases in a Lower Criminal Court*. New York: Russell Sage Foundation.

Ferraro, Kathleen, & Tascha Boychuk (1992) "The Court's Response to Interpersonal Violence: A Comparison of Intimate and Nonintimate Assault," in E. Buzawa, & C. Buzawa, eds., *Domestic Violence: The Changing Criminal Justice Response*. Westport, CT: Auburn House.

Ferraro, Kathleen, & Lucille Pope (1993) "Irreconcilable Differences: Battered Women, Police, and the Law," in N. Z. Hilton, ed., *Legal Responses to Wife Assault: Current Trends and Evaluation*. Newbury Park, CA: Sage.

Flemming, Barbara (2003) "Equal Protection for Victims of Domestic Violence," 18 *J. of Interpersonal Violence* 685–92.

Fleury, Ruth (2002) "Missing Voices: Patterns of Battered Women's Satisfaction with the Criminal Legal System," 8 *Violence Against Women* 181–205.

Ford, David (2003) "Coercing Victim Participation in Domestic Violence Prosecutions," 18 *J. of Interpersonal Violence* 669–84.

Foucault, Michel (1979) *The History of Sexuality*, Vol. 1. London: Allen Lane.

Goldkamp, John, & Cheryl Irons-Guynn (2000) *Emerging Judicial Strategies for the Mentally Ill in the Criminal Caseload: Mental Health Courts in Fort Lauderdale, Seattle, San Bernardino, and Anchorage*. Washington. DC: Bureau of Justice Assistance.

Goodman, Harriet (2001) "In-Depth Interviews," in B. Thyer, ed., *The Handbook of Social Work Research Methods*. Thousand Oaks, CA: Sage.

Guzik, Keith (2003) "Policing Domestic Violence: A Post-Structuralist Understanding of the Power, Practice, and Potential of Domestic Violence Arrests Against Domestic Batterers." Paper presented at the Law & Society Association Annual Meeting, Pittsburgh, PA, June.

—— (2007) "The Forces of Conviction: The Power and Practice of Mandatory Prosecution upon Misdemeanor Domestic Battery Suspects," 31 *Law and Social Inquiry* 41–74.

Hagan, John, & Celesta Albonetti (1982) "Race, Glass, and the Perception of Criminal Injustice in America," 88 *American J. of Sociology* 329–55.

Hanna, Cheryl (1996) "No Right to Choose: Mandated Victim Participation in Domestic Violence Prosecutions," 109 *Harvard Law Rev.* 1849–910.

Hearn, Jeff (1998) *The Violences of Men: How Men Talk about and How Agencies Respond to Men's Violence against Woman*. Thousand Oaks, CA: Sage.

Herrell, Stephen, & Meredith Hofford (1990) *Family Violence: Improving Court Practice*. Reno, NV: National Council of Juvenile and Family Court Judges.

Kimmel, Michael (1996) *Manhood in America: A Cultural History*. New York: The Free Press.

Kupchik, Aaron (2004) "Youthfulness, Responsibility and Punishment: Admonishing Adolescents in Criminal Court," 6 *Punishment and Society* 149–73.

Maguigan, Holly (2003) "Wading into Professor Schneider's 'Murky Middle Ground' Between Acceptance and Rejection of Criminal Justice Responses to Domestic Violence," II *The American University J. of Gender, Social Policy and the Law* 427.

Mather, Lynn (1979) *Plea Bargaining or Trial? The Process of Criminal-Case Disposition.* Lexington, MA: D. C. Heath and Company.

Maxwell, Christopher, et al. (2002) "The Preventive Effects of Arrest on Intimate Partner Violence: Research, Policy, and Theory," 2 *Criminology and Public Policy* 51–80.

Merry, Sally Engle (1995) "Wife Battering and the Ambiguities of Rights," in A. Sarat, & T. Kearns, eds., *Identities, Politics, and Rights.* Ann Arbor, MI: Univ. of Michigan Press.

—— (2001) "Spatial Governmentality and the New Urban Social Order: Controlling Gender Violence Through Law," 103 *American Anthropologist* 16–29.

—— (2002) "Governmentality and Gender Violence in Hawai'i in Historical Perspective," 11 *Social and Legal Studies* 81–111.

Mills, Linda (2003) *Insult to Injury: Rethinking our Responses to Intimate Abuse.* Princeton, NJ: Princeton Univ. Press.

Mirchandani, Rekha (2005) "What's So Special About Specialized Courts? The State and Social Change in Salt Lake City's Domestic Violence Court," 39 *Law & Society Rev.* 379–418.

Nolan, James (2003) *Reinventing Justice: The American Drug Court Movement.* Princeton, NJ: Princeton Univ. Press.

Pennell, Joan, & Gale Burford (2002) "Feminist Praxis: Making Family Group Conferencing Work," in H. Strang & J. Braithwaite, eds., *Restorative Justice and Family Violence.* Cambridge, United Kingdom: Cambridge Univ. Press.

Ptacek, James (1988) "Why Do Men Batter Their Wives?" in K. Yllo & M. Bograd, eds., *Feminist Perspectives on Wife Abuse.* Newbury Park, CA: Sage.

Riessman, Catherine Kohler (1993) *Narrative Analysis.* Newbury Park, CA: Sage.

Rose, Nikolas (1991) *Governing the Soul: The Shaping of the Private Self.* New York: Cambridge Univ. Press.

Sampson, Robert, & Dawn Jeglum Bartusch (1998) "Legal Cynicism and (Subcultural?) Tolerance of Deviance: The Neighborhood Context of Racial Differences," 32 *Law & Society Rev.* 777–804.

Sarat, Austin (1990) " 'The Law Is All Over': Power, Resistance, and the Legal Consciousness of the Welfare Poor," 2 *Yale. J. of Law and Humanities* 343–79.

Sarat, Austin, & William Felstiner (1995) *Divorce Lawyers and Their Clients: Power and Meaning in the Legal Process.* New York: Oxford Univ. Press.

Schneider, Elizabeth (2000) *Battered Women and Feminist Lawmaking.* New Haven, CT: Yale Univ. Press.

Schwalbe, Michael, & Michelle Wolkomir (2001) "The Masculine Self as Problem and Resource in Interview Studies of Men," 4 *Men and Masculinities* 90–103.

Skolnick, Jerome (1974) "Social Control in the Adversary System," in J. Robertson, ed., *Rough Justice: Perspectives on Lower Criminal Courts.* Boston: Little, Brown.

Strang, Heather, & John Braithwaite, eds. (2002) *Restorative Justice and Family Violence.* Cambridge, United Kingdom: Cambridge Univ. Press.

Straus, Murray, et al. (1996) "The Revised Conflict Tactics Scales (CTS2): Development and Preliminary Psychometric Data," 17 *J. of Family Issues* 283–316.

Wanless, Marion (1996) "Pro-Arrest: A Step Toward Eradicating Domestic Violence, but Is It Enough?" 2 *University of Illinois Law Rev.* 533–87.

Weitzer, Ronald (2000) "Racialized Policing: Residents' Perceptions in Three Neighborhoods," 34 *Law & Society Rev.* 129–55.

Wortley, Scot, et al. (1997) "'Just Des(s)erts?' The Racial Polarization of Perceptions of Criminal Injustice," 31 *Law & Society Rev.* 637–76.

Yngvesson, Barbara (1989) "Inventing Law in Local Settings: Rethinking Popular Legal Culture," 98 *Yale Law J.* 1689–1709.

18

Expecting an Ally and Getting a Prosecutor

Sarah Goodrum

Abstract: *Goodrum examines the experiences of the family members of murder victims, focusing particularly on interactions with prosecutors. The author describes two primary roles of prosecutors that are expected by grieving family members: the "key informant" and "sympathetic warrior." Participants expected prosecutors and other court personnel to act as key informants in that family members demanded detailed information regarding all aspects of their loved one's cases, including minute details of the investigation, prosecution, and the probable outcome of the case. The prosecutors' roles as sympathetic warrior was prompted by the participants' desires for court personnel to display empathy and compassion in dealing with the murder victims' cases and the participants expectation that the prosecutor and other personnel understand and share the families' grief and anger.*

Me and the DA got into it a few times, because I didn't like what she was telling me [about her plan to seek a 15-year sentence for the defendant] . . . That ain't your husband! . . . The DA needs to understand that when a life is taken, no matter what the circumstances may be, death is death . . . [T]hey need to work a little bit more closely [with the family].
                                                                    (Deidra Fiero, wife of 24-year-old man killed during a drug deal)

Since the 1970s, crime victims' rights advocates have fought to give victims a larger role in the criminal justice system with the belief that increased involvement would improve victims' satisfaction with the system and their recovery from the crime (see Kelly 1990; Kilpatrick and Otto 1987; Wiebe 1996). By 1995, all states in the United States had passed a victims' bill of rights, and in many states, the prosecution-related rights proved most substantive (e.g., right to be informed of all court dates in the case, right to give a victim impact statement). Empirical evidence indicates, however, that these rights have brought little to no improvement in victims' satisfaction and recovery (Davis and Smith 1994; Elias 1984; Erez 1994 and 2000; Erez, Roeger, and Morgan 1997; Kenney 1995), raising questions about what victims need from the criminal justice system. Recent survey research suggests that prosecutors may play a pivotal role in influencing victims' overall feelings about the criminal justice system (Carr, Logio, and Meier 2003), but few researchers have asked victims themselves what they want from prosecutors (for exceptions, see Erez and Belknap 1998; Hare 2006; Konradi 1996, 1997).

Understanding victims' expectations of prosecutors may help explain the reasons for the lack of improvement in the overall victim–criminal justice system relationship in the post-victims' rights era. Admittedly, victims' views of prosecutors may be unrealistic or incorrect. However, symbolic interactionists – who emphasize the significance of meaning in everyday social encounters – would point out that these views prove important to informing victims' expectations and shaping their experiences (see Blumer 1969). Blumer (1969:2) explains that people "act toward things [e.g., people, objects, or situations] on the basis of the meaning that things have for them." Thus, the meaning that victims attach to the prosecutor role (even if incorrect) guides their feelings about and behavior toward prosecutors, as well as their overall satisfaction with the criminal justice system and their recovery from the crime.

This study uses the symbolic interactionist perspective to examine victims' experiences with prosecutors and the criminal court system with a focus on people who have lost a loved one to murder ("bereaved victims"). The data come from in-depth interviews with thirty-two bereaved victims from Union County (pseudonym), nine criminal court workers (e.g., prosecutors, judges, and counselors) from Union County, and three crime victims' advocates based in Union County. Loss to murder proves a helpful focus for research on victims' experiences with prosecutors for three main reasons. First, a victimization to murder represents one of the most horrific types of criminal victimization, leaving victims with post-traumatic stress, anxiety, and depression (see Amick-McMullan, Kilpatrick, and Resnick 1991; Amick-McMullan, Kilpatrick, Veronen, and Smith 1989). The severity of the trauma exposes victims' and prosecutors' hidden assumptions about the prosecutor role and the victim–prosecutor relationship. Second, because of the seriousness of the crime, prosecutors tend to respond to murder cases with more intensity than other types of criminal cases. Thus, if bereaved victims are displeased with prosecutors' responses to their loved one's murder case, other victims are likely to be displeased with prosecutors' responses. Finally, the stark contrast between prosecutors' stoic demeanor and bereaved victims' emotional devastation accentuates the two groups' different investments in the case. For bereaved victims, the case represents a profoundly personal pursuit; for prosecutors, the case represents a professional responsibility. These different viewpoints can make for awkward encounters in victim–prosecutor interactions, and this awkwardness may help explain the lack of improvement in victims' experiences. This study examines the ways victims define the prosecutor role with the idea that this definition influences victims' experiences with and perceptions of prosecutors and the criminal justice system; the study compares victims' definitions to prosecutors', counselors', and others' definitions – to consider whether conflicts of meaning create conflicts in victims' experiences with the criminal justice system. The research has implications for research on victims, victims' rights, the criminal justice system, and symbolic interactionist theory. The research also offers insight into the effectiveness of rights-oriented legislation in bringing positive change.

Literature Review

Empirical research repeatedly suggests that victims want more information about their cases and more involvement in criminal justice proceedings (Carr, Logio, and Maier 2003; Erez 2000; Kenney 1995). Victims' rights legislation in the United States and elsewhere has tried to address these needs by guaranteeing victims the right to information on all of the court dates in their case and the right to make a victim impact statement to the court during the sentencing phase of the trial (Kelly 1990). The literature, however, offers mixed results on the ability of rights to improve victims' experiences with the criminal justice system. For example, in a study of the Australian criminal justice system, Erez, Roeger, and Morgan (1997) found that participation in a victim impact statement did not boost victims' satisfaction with the system, leading the authors to conclude that victim impact statements may not give victims the type of participation they want. Other research suggests that victims would rather have information about the case and interaction with criminal justice professionals than the opportunity to give a victim impact statement (Carr, Logio, and Maier 2003). Indeed, Riches and Dawson (1998) describe access to information as critical to bereaved victims' satisfaction with the criminal justice system.

For various reasons, however, access to information does not always help victims in the ways advocates and researchers expect. First, criminal justice workers often find that victims have difficulty understanding the legalities of the criminal justice system (Goodrum and Stafford 2003; Konradi 1997). Prosecutors working with rape survivors believed "it [did] not pay to put effort into explaining procedures thoroughly if the [survivor/witness did] not grasp the information" (Konradi 1997:38). Second, the current literature does not reveal what specific types of information victims want from prosecutors or other criminal justice workers, leaving the request to give victims information open to faulty interpretation.

Some research suggests that victims may want regular interaction with prosecutors, not just information from them. Carr, Logio, and Maier's (2003) survey of Philadelphia victims revealed that positive interaction with the prosecutor significantly related to overall satisfaction with the criminal justice system, feeling knowledgeable about the status of the case, *and* feeling connected to the prosecution of the case. The literature does not yet indicate how victims define a positive interaction with the prosecutor, although European countries offer some interesting possibilities. In Poland, victim–prosecutor interactions look like a partnership, because victims have the opportunity to serve as "subsidiary prosecutor" in the case (Erez and Bienkowska 1993). Using a national sample of victims, Erez and Bienkowska (1993) found that victims who served as a subsidiary prosecutor in their case reported higher levels of satisfaction with the criminal justice system and the defendant's sentence than victims who did not. In the United States, victims cannot serve as a subsidiary prosecutor, and the current literature does not even indicate whether American crime victims would want this type of interaction.

Victims' rights legislation may have a limited effect on victims' experience because of criminal justice workers' reluctance to welcome the victim's participation in the criminal justice process. Using in-depth interview data with rape victims and prosecutors, Konradi (1996) found that prosecutors welcomed victims' offers of case evidence but rejected victims' suggestions about case strategy. "Providing strategy appears to tread on prosecuting attorneys' toes, as it challenges their right to determine whether and how to proceed" (Konradi 1996:423). Many prosecutors view the victim's role as a symbolic one, not a substantive one (Erez and Laster 1999). Following in-depth interviews with legal professionals, Erez and Laster (1999:545) reported, "Victim participation reforms were understood by practitioners as only a minor or symbolic gesture that was not intended to modify court procedures and sentencing practices. The true intent of [victim impact statements], they maintained, was political." Frohmann (1998) concludes that rape reform legislation proves limited in its ability to empower victims, because to pursue a legal case, victims have to redefine their personal problem as a legal problem, omitting aspects of the victimization experience un-recognized by the law. In the United States, victims' rights legislation has been passed without asking victims themselves what they want from the criminal justice system (see Rock 1998). This study asks victims to describe in their own words what they expected of prosecutors following their loved one's murder with the idea that these words will give meaning to victims' experiences and inform victims' rights efforts.

Setting and Methods

Community and Legal Setting

Union County had a population of more than 700,000 people (U.S. Bureau of the Census 2001) and approximately 45 murders per year ([Omitted State Name] Department of Health 2000) at the time of this study. The Union police department, sheriff's department, and district attorney's office had victim services counselors on staff full-time and the police and sheriff's departments had an extensive network of volunteer victim services counselors. These counselors, victim-oriented programs, and a strong victims' advocacy group have given Union a national reputation for being an innovator in victim services, making it an ideal location for a study on victims' experiences. If victims are not having a good experience in this criminal justice system, they are unlikely to be having a good experience in others.

When a murder happened in Union County, law enforcement detectives collected evidence and interviewed witnesses, and they turned the case over to the District Attorney's Office for a grand jury indictment. After the indictment, a victim-witness counselor with the District Attorney's Office contacted the murder victim's family members, on behalf of the prosecutor, to notify them of the status of the case, give them information about criminal justice procedures, and invite them to meet with the prosecutor to talk about the case. Prosecutors and victim-witness counselors knew that most bereaved victims wanted a trial in their loved one's murder case, as opposed to a negotiated plea, and this knowledge shaped the direction and tone of their first few meetings. "[I]n almost all the homicide cases I've dealt with [the family] wants to go to trial. They think that a trial is a public airing of what happened, [and they think it] is going to fix them, and it doesn't fix them" (Prosecutor and Director of Trial Division). To prevent conflict over a trial versus a negotiated plea later in the case, Union County prosecutors and counselors tried to build rapport with bereaved victims in the very early stages of the process with the idea that the rapport would help them if they needed to deliver bad news about the strength of the case, their plans to dispose of it through a plea bargain, or their views on an appropriate sentence for the defendant. Union County prosecutors and counselors often honored bereaved victims' wishes for a trial but they reserved the right to reject their wishes if a trial seemed unlikely to bring a guilty verdict.

At the time of this study, the victims' rights laws in this state were very comprehensive and did not distinguish between various types of crime victims.[1] The prosecution related victims' rights included the right to the return of the victim's property when it is no longer needed by the criminal justice system, the right to information on the defendant's bail and criminal procedures and deadlines, and the right to give a victim impact statement during the sentencing phase of the defendant's trial.

Data Collection

The study included in-depth interviews with thirty-two bereaved victims whose loved ones were murdered between 1994 and 1999 in Union County and nine Union County criminal court professionals working on murder cases (e.g., prosecutors, judges, and counselors). The data also include interviews with three crime victim advocates (i.e., people who worked or volunteered for a non-profit victims' rights organization) in Union County. All interviews were conducted by the author and were tape recorded and transcribed. The study also include more than 144 hours of participant observation data, which the author collected while working as a volunteer victim services counselor for the Union Police Department and while observing Union County murder trials.

Bereaved Victim Interviews

Bereaved victims were recruited by contacting: (1) the next-of-kin listed on death certificate records for 1997–1999 Union County murder victims (n = 25), (2) the next-of-kin mentioned in newspapers' accounts of all 1995–1996 Union Country murder victims (n = 4), and (3) the family members of Union County murder victims referred by the Union County District Attorney's Office (n = 3). Each bereaved victim interview took approximately two and a half hours. The interviews contained questions about the criminal justice system, relationships with others, the meaning of the loss, demographic characteristics, and advice for others. The data presented here come from bereaved victims' responses to questions about their positive and negative encounters with prosecutors and the District Attorney's Office.[2]

Criminal Court Professional and Victim Advocate Interviews

The interviews with nine criminal court professionals (e.g., four prosecutors, three judges, and two counselors) working on murder cases in Union County and three crime victim advocates based in Union County took approximately one hour each. Participants were selected using judgment sampling, and all participants had two or more years of experience working on murder cases in Union County. The interviews continued until the saturation point (i.e., when additional respondents provided little new information). Criminal court professionals and advocates were asked open-ended questions about their work with bereaved victims and the positive and negative aspects of including bereaved people in the criminal justice process.

Bereaved Victim Sample Profile

Seventy-eight percent of the bereaved victims were female. Fifty-three percent were White, 31 percent Hispanic, and 16 percent Black. The mean age of bereaved victims was 49 years old. Six percent of bereaved victim respondents had not completed high school, 32 percent had completed high school, 39 percent had completed some college, 13 percent had completed college, and 10 percent had completed graduate school. The median household income was $40,000 to $59,999 (for additional information on the sample, see Goodrum 2007).

Although it is not ideal to use a population-to-sample comparison of murder victims to infer a population-to-sample comparison of bereaved victim respondents, the comparison sheds light on the possibility that the bereaved victims of some murder victims were more likely than the bereaved victims of other murder victims to participate in the study. The comparison indicates that the population and sample of murder victims look very similar in age and gender but less similar in race. The population of murder victims was 33 percent White, 24 percent Black, and 43 percent Hispanic, while the sample of murder victims was 50 percent White, 12 percent Black, and 38 percent Hispanic. Nineteen percent of the murder cases remained unsolved at the time of the interview.

Criminal Court Professional and Crime Victim Advocate Sample Profile

Five of the twelve court and advocate respondents were female. Nine of the twelve were White, one was Hispanic, and two were bi-racial (White and American

Table 18.1 Sociodemographic characteristics of bereaved victims in the sample*

Mean Age	Gender	Race	Marital Status	Level of Education	Next-of-Kin's Relationship to Victim[3]
49	22% Male 78% Female	53% White 16% Black 31% Hispanic	44% Married 41% Divorced[1] 9% Widowed 6% Never Married	6% Less than H.S. 32% High School 39% Some College 13% College 10% Grad School[2]	9% Child 6% Spouse 63% Parent 19% Sibling 3% Other

* *Source*: This information was obtained from in-depth interviews with bereaved victims.

[1] Divorced and Separated are combined under the label "Divorced."

[2] Grad School refers to people who either attended or completed Graduate School.

[3] Relationship to victim refers to the bereaved victim's relationship to the murder victim as listed on the death certificate. For example, if the mother is listed as the next-of-kin contact on the murder victim's death certificate, her relationship would be listed in this table as "parent."

Indian). These criminal justice professionals and advocates had an average of 10.9 years of experience on murder cases; the average number of murder cases dealt with was 115.

Findings

Defining the Prosecutor Role

Herbert Blumer's (1969:2) first premise of symbolic interactionism states that people act "toward things on the basis of the meaning that the things have for them." When people consciously think about a "thing" (e.g., object, person, or situation), they assign it meaning, and this meaning proves important in helping people decide how to behave in a given situation and around others. Knowing the meaning that victims assign to the prosecutor role provides insight into the ideas shaping their feelings about and responses to the criminal justice process. By examining the way bereaved victims describe their encounters with prosecutors, we begin to understand victims' expectations for the prosecutor in their loved one's murder case. The findings presented here reveal several small but important differences in how bereaved victims and others define the prosecutor role. In addition, the findings reveal several neglected areas of victims' needs in current victims' rights legislation in the United States. Bereaved victims' definitions of the prosecutor role included two main components: (1) key informant, and (2) sympathetic warrior. The central idea linking both components is ally; bereaved victims expected the prosecutor in their loved one's murder case to act as their intimate ally, a finding not discussed in previous research. While the data come from people who have lost a loved one to homicide, the findings could come from any group of victims – as the desire for information and compassion from prosecutors cuts across all types of victimization experiences.

Prosecutor as Key Informant

The first theme in bereaved victims' responses to questions about the prosecutor in their loved one's murder case indicates that they expected the prosecutor to give them detailed information about the prosecution process in general and their loved one's murder case in particular. Victims wanted specific information about: (1) the date and nature of upcoming court proceedings, (2) the status of the prosecutor's investigation, and (3) the most likely outcome of the case. Bereaved victims wanted as much information about every possible aspect of the prosecution as they could obtain, and their poignant responses suggest that having this information gave them emotional comfort. Riches and Dawson's (1998) in-depth study of six murder cases confirms that access to information is critical to bereaved victims' well-being, and Konradi (1997) found that knowledge specific to their case and general to the criminal justice system helped rape victims feel more control over the process. Social psychologists describe knowledge as critical to a sense of personal control, and a sense of personal control is positively associated with psychological well-being (Mirowsky and Ross 1989). Mirowsky and Ross write (1989:170), "Without knowledge, control is impossible." The findings presented below lend further support to the idea that information benefits psychological well-being, particularly following a criminal victimization.

The first type of information bereaved victims wanted from prosecutors related to the timing and purpose of the court proceedings in their loved one's murder case. Melissa Iker, the mother of a 24-year-old murder victim, lived out-of-state at the time of her son's murder and during the court proceedings that followed. She expressed tremendous appreciation for the time and effort the prosecutor and counselor spent in keeping her informed about the case. She said:

> They kept contact with us . . . and they . . . [let] me know about the indictment [of the defendant] and then when it was time . . . for him to go in front of the judge to plead guilty . . . They briefed us on what was going to go on [during the hearings] and what was going to happen, and there was always somebody with us during the day [during the court proceedings].

Bereaved victims wanted information on the dates for all of the court proceedings in the case, including the indictment, arrest, arraignment, preliminary hearing, and negotiated plea or trial. The victims' bill of rights in the state of study and in other states in the United States guarantees victims the right to information on the dates for all of the court proceedings in the case (see also Wiebe 1996). In fact, the President's Task Force on Victims of Crime (1982:114) recommended that, "[T]he victim, in every criminal prosecution shall have the right to be present . . . at all critical stages of judicial proceedings."

In addition to information on the court dates, Melissa and other participants also wanted the prosecutor to give them information on what to expect from those court proceedings, such as the purpose of the proceeding (e.g., defendant's arraignment), the difficult aspects of the proceeding (e.g., crime scene photos, coroner's testimony), and the likely outcome of it (e.g., defendant will enter a "not guilty" plea). Wendy Lawrence, the daughter of a 77-year-old murder victim, said that each day before they entered the courtroom, the prosecutors briefed her and her family on what to expect. She said:

> They would tell us . . . this is going to happen . . . [or during a court recess they would say] they're discussing whether we can do this or that . . . They explained the whole process to us as it was happening.

The second type of information bereaved victims wanted from prosecutors concerned the status of the prosecutor's investigation, including the content of witness testimony, the appearance of the crime scene, and the strengths and weaknesses of the evidence. Nora Harden, the mother of a 25-year-old son who was shot and killed during a party, wanted the prosecutor in her son's murder case to walk her through the crime scene and tell her about all of the evidence in the case, a practice not typically granted to victims. She said:

> I asked [the prosecutor] if [she] would come out [to the scene of the murder] and show me exactly where everything was; so I could picture everything in detail, exactly where the witnesses were standing [when my son was shot] and what they were saying . . . So, I feel [the prosecutor] really did wonders in the case. I mean, honestly, I think she just was wonderful.

Nora even expressed a desire to act as an investigator in the case. She explained:

> I don't know what you [would] call it, but I was kind of being my own investigator ... [I wanted] to have a handle on [the evidence in the case].

While many victims counted on the prosecutor to handle these details, several victims – like Nora – wanted to participate in the actual investigation, and they described this participation as helpful to their mental health. Wendy Lawrence (quoted earlier) felt frustrated when the prosecutors handling her elderly father's murder case neglected several pieces of evidence, including her 911 call, a towel from the crime scene, and her granddaughter's recorded testimony. She said:

> A week before we [went] to trial, I finally convinced [the DA] to listen to the 911 tape [where I described the crime scene] ... I thought that wasn't good [that I had to remind him of the tape and that] he didn't allow [the jury to hear] the 911 tape or my granddaughter's [taped interview].

A review of other participants' comments and previous research on victim–prosecutor interactions (see Konradi 1996, 1997) indicates that Wendy's interactions with the prosecutor are more typical than Nora's. Few victims get to walk the crime scene or learn about *all* of the evidence in the case from their prosecutor, and even fewer victims get to act as an assistant investigator in the case.

The third type of information bereaved victims wanted from prosecutors concerned the most likely outcome in the murder case – including the prosecutor's plan for resolving the case (e.g., negotiated plea or trial) and the anticipated length of the defendant's sentence. They wanted this type of information even when it brought bad news. Wanda Diaz, the mother of a 20-year-old murder victim, said:

> [I appreciated] the DA being up front and truthful [with me], even though the case was ruined [because of the inappropriately obtained confession]. I think [it helped me anticipate things] with them letting us know, "This is what might happen. If the [defendants] don't go for the plea bargain, then this is what will happen, and we'll have to let them go."

Wanda and other participants reported heartfelt appreciation for prosecutors who gave them the ugly truth about the problems with the evidence in the case, and while they disliked the idea of not getting their "day in court," they often eventually came to understand the need to settle the case with a negotiated plea. During prosecutors' filing interviews with rape victims, Frohmann (1998) found that prosecutors often described the likely outcome in a case to rape victims, but they did so in a way that ensured victims' compliance with their plan for the case – either to pursue a charge or drop the case. Thus, Frohmann (1998) found that prosecutors' primary motive for sharing information on the likely outcome of the case with rape victims was to ensure victims' cooperation, not to emotionally prepare them for the outcome.

It is important to note that several bereaved victims expressed a specific desire to deal directly with the prosecutor in the case, not the counselor. Nora Harden, the mother quoted earlier, explained:

> [The] Victims' Services [Counselors] were fine ... but I basically stuck straight with Christina [the prosecutor in my son's murder case]. Whenever I called [the DA's Office], I called for her specifically to ask how the case was going. It was just too personal to feel I could go through anybody else.

In the conclusion of her study on rape victims' encounters with prosecutors, Konradi (1997) warned that counselors may have trouble fully addressing victims' needs, because they do not always have access to the type of information victims want and they sometimes feel obligated to side with prosecutors and the criminal justice system instead of victims. As bereaved victims' responses suggest, almost all of the prosecutors, counselors, and advocates in Union Country recognized bereaved victims' need for information. A prosecutor with more than seven years of experience described:

> [O]ften [I meet with the family] after the case has already been through the grand jury process and [the defendant has] been indicted . . . I'll answer all their questions as best I can. Sometimes I can't tell them everything about the evidence . . . [but] I think it's very important that they know what actually happened, what the history of the people involved is, [and] I try to get them to understand what's going to happen [in the prosecution process].

As Wanda suggested earlier, prosecutors and counselors sometimes had to share bad news with victims, including unflattering aspects of the murder victim's history (e.g., drug use, domestic violence) or bad choices on the day of the murder (e.g., aggressor in altercation leading to murder). Prosecutors did not want victims to hear this bad news during the trial or from the media, and they viewed this type of "information sharing" as an important part of their role. Previous research on loss to murder indicates that part of prosecutors' motivation for sharing bad news is to prevent an emotional outburst from bereaved victims during the trial (Goodrum and Stafford 2003). A prosecutor explained:

> I have a case right now where it's going to be a battered wife syndrome defense, and the [murder victim's] family never had any idea that their brother or son was a batterer. They never saw that. So, it's very hard for them to believe that he [abused his wife]. So, you're breaking some news to them that they had no idea about.

For the most part, bereaved victim, prosecutor, counselor, and advocate participants defined the informant aspect of the prosecutor role similarly. Symbolic interactionists would argue that criminal justice workers' experiential knowledge and role-taking ability allowed them to imagine and anticipate victims' intense desire for detailed information about the case (see Blumer 1969). Current victims' rights legislation in the United States typically addresses crime victims' right to information about the court schedule in their case. This legislation, however, does not address the types of information victims want most from prosecutors – information on the status of the investigation and the most likely outcome in their loved one's murder case. The underlying message in the "key informant" component of victims' definitions of the prosecutor role suggests that bereaved victims wanted an ally in the prosecutor, not just a prosecutor.

Prosecutor as Sympathetic Warrior

The second theme in bereaved victims' responses to questions about the prosecutor in their loved one's murder case related to their desire for a sympathetic and emotionally connected prosecutor. Victims wanted the prosecutor to understand their profound grief over the loss and their tremendous anger toward the defendant. The frequency with which respondents mentioned the prosecutor's expression (or non-expression) of sympathy in the case suggests that they viewed compassion as a key component of the prosecutor role. In addition, this finding indicates that prosecutors (and other criminal justice workers) can enhance bereaved victims' experiences with the criminal justice system by expressing genuine sympathy for them and their deceased loved one. Nora, Donna, and Delia explained:

> [The prosecutor in my son's murder case] was very warm, always very warm.
> (Mother of 25-year-old murder victim)

> I could tell that it wasn't just any case to [the prosecutors]. They cared a lot about this case . . . They were very sensitive as to the way I would feel about things.
> (Sister of 20-year-old murder victim)

> [The prosecutor] did a very thorough job. [He] understood what was going on, [and he] was able to express some of our anger at the injustice of the murder. So, it wasn't like he was without passion once we got to trial.
> (Aunt of 24-year-old murder victim)

Nora described the prosecutor as "very warm," Donna described the prosecutors as "sensitive" to her feelings, and Delia said the prosecutor conveyed her family's "anger" to the jury during the trial. A careful examination of these (and other) responses reveals that bereaved victims valued having an emotional connection with the prosecutor in their case.

Norman Denzin (2007) describes emotional connections as the cornerstone to meaningful relationships. Shared emotions "lie at the core of what it means to understand and meaningfully enter into the emotional experience of another" (Denzin 2007:137). As this finding suggests and as Denzin (2007) might note, bereaved victims viewed "shared emotionality" with prosecutors as essential to the prosecutor role. To truly understand the devastating nature of the loss and the injustice of the murder, bereaved victims expected their prosecutor to move beyond an intellectual understanding of the case to an emotional understanding of the loss. Prosecutors' expressions of sympathy toward victims and statements of anger to the jury represented the best ways for prosecutors to convey that they had entered into their family's emotional experience of the victim, that they "got it." Entering into (as opposed to just observing) the emotional experience of another can improve a person's ability to understand another's situation, as well as their ability to offer emotional support. The literature on both crime victims and bereavement finds that social and emotional support aid recovery from trauma and loss (see Burgess 1975; Kelly 1990; Rando 1993). Thoits (1984) identifies socioemotional support as instrumental in counteracting the effect of difficult life events. For victims of crime, an emotional connection with the prosecutor handling the case may prove particularly important because they cannot wage their own legal battle against the defendant, they must rely on someone else – a stranger – to wage it for them.

Bereaved victims' desire to share emotions with the prosecutor in the case may relate to Clark's (1987) discussion of sympathy in social life. People expect sympathy in times of need; people who do not express sympathy to those in need are underinvestors whose "sin" is being "aloof and removed" (Clark 1987:313). An emotionally *un-invested* prosecutor signaled a lack of sincere interest in the case, and as the participant quoted at the opening of this chapter suggests when she exclaimed "That ain't your husband!" to the prosecutor, an unsympathetic prosecutor frustrated bereaved victims. Interestingly, only one of the four prosecutors (but both of the counselors) participating in the study defined the prosecutor role to include the sharing of victims' emotions.

> I think it's real important [that the murder victim's family] have a bond [with the prosecutor], and they trust [you as the prosecutor]. If you do go to trial, they need to trust that you really know what you're doing, that you really care [about the case], and that you're there to help them. If you're just some anonymous prosecutor . . . they're just not going to feel comfortable with what's going to happen to them.

The above prosecutor valued having an emotional connection with bereaved victims, but she was the exception. No other prosecutor participating in the study expressed an interest in emotionally connecting with victims. Counselors – the criminal court system's emotion managers – on the other hand, repeatedly mentioned the importance of "shared emotions" in their meetings with bereaved victims (see also Goodrum and Stafford 2003). A counselor and former victim advised prosecutors and counselors:

> Do not be afraid to tell [the murder victim's family] that you are really sorry that this happened to them . . . cause that's really what they need to hear; [they] need [you] to confirm with them the horror of what's happened in their life.

Including shared emotionality in the criminal justice system's and victims' rights legislation's definition of the prosecutor role presents a challenge for main two reasons. First, the culture of the criminal justice system does not typically encourage the sharing of emotions (Goodrum and Stafford 2003). Criminal justice professionals value unemotional objectivity (Erez and Rogers 1999; Stenross and Kleinman 1989). Second, prosecutors and other criminal justice workers may distance themselves from bereaved victims because they know there is little that will alleviate their grief and they dislike the emotional burden that comes with bereaved victim interactions (Goodrum and Stafford 2003). Requiring prosecutors to develop close personal relationships with crime victims on a daily basis may lead to emotional exhaustion and professional burnout (see Copp 1998).

Discussion and Conclusion

The bereaved victim quoted at the start of this chapter poignantly describes what she and many other bereaved victims expected from the prosecutor in their loved one's murder case – a close partnership. Bereaved victims wanted the prosecutor to openly and easily share both information and sympathy with them, and they viewed the exchange of information and emotion as critical components of the prosecutor role. Symbolic interactionist theory – which emphasizes the importance of meaning in social interaction (Blumer 1969) – helps to explain some of the reasons why victims' interactions with prosecutors prove so critical to their overall satisfaction with the criminal justice system (see Carr, Logio, and Maier 2003). In short, bereaved victims viewed the prosecutor as more than the state's representative in their loved one's murder case; they viewed the prosecutor as their intimate ally in their search for justice.

A challenge arises in how to incorporate all of victims' expectations for prosecutors into victims' rights legislation in the United States. The first change to victims' rights legislation implied by these findings concerns bereaved victims' access to information, a recurring theme in the larger literature on victims and the criminal justice system. When we carefully review the content of current victims' rights legislation, we see that victims are typically granted the right to be informed about and present at "all critical stages of judicial proceedings" (President's Task Force 1982:114). In the state of study, for example, victims have "the right to be informed of relevant court proceedings and to be informed if those court proceedings have been canceled or rescheduled prior to the event" (Goodrum 2007:732). This legislation, unfortunately, does not guarantee victims the right to information about the *content* or *purpose* of those court proceedings, nor does it guarantee victims the right to information about the investigation or the most likely outcome in the case (the second and third types of information bereaved victims requested). According to both bereaved victims' and criminal court workers' comments, however, many of the bereaved victims encountering Union County prosecutors received this type of information – without the stated right. Of course, some prosecutors withheld information on the evidence to help build a strong case, and the prosecutor's power to control the flow of information frustrated some bereaved victims and hindered their recovery from the crime. When prosecutors shared information on the investigation and bereaved victims understood that evidence, bereaved victims appreciated it when prosecutors and counselors related the evidence in their case to the evidence in other similar cases. The context gave them an idea of what to expect when their loved one's murder case went to trial and an idea of the possible outcomes.

To help address bereaved victims' concern about open access to all of the information in the investigation, state legislators in the United States could consider offering victims the opportunity to serve as a subsidiary prosecutor as in Germany or Poland (see Erez and Bienkowska 1993; Doak 2005). This position may give victims more information about criminal court procedure and a greater sense of closeness to the prosecutor. This type of change may facilitate an ideological and substantive change in the victim–prosecutor relationship (Frohmann 1998). The subsidiary prosecutor position for victims may usher in a new alliance with prosecutors, an alliance the bereaved victims in this study sought.

The second change to victims' rights legislation implied by these findings concerns prosecutors' emotional displays. Bereaved victims expected the prosecutor in their case to care about them and sympathize with their loss, an expectation that may prove difficult to guarantee through legislation. A question arises about whether it is practical or realistic to mandate sympathy for victims. Perhaps not. However, to help address victims' desire for some type of emotional connection with the prosecutor, the criminal justice system could encourage prosecutors to – at a minimum – recognize victims' emotions (e.g., It sounds like this has been very difficult for you, It sounds like you are in a great deal of pain over your son's death). In the ideal encounter, prosecutors would express sympathy for the bereaved victim (e.g., I'm very sorry for your loss). Norman

Denzin (2007) might suggest that a prosecutor's willingness to emotionally connect with bereaved victims – to engage in "shared emotionality" – over the death of their loved one and over their anger at the murderer may help to promote healing. Participants' responses suggest that shared emotionality, or "the intentional feelings of two or more persons [being] drawn together.... to produc[e] ... bonding" (Denzin 2007:152–53) represents the most intimate form of advocacy in the criminal justice system.

The criminal justice system could consider offering prosecutors training exercises that facilitate their taking the role of the victim to increase their compassion for and understanding of victims. Of course, a shift in the emotional culture of the criminal justice system – from stoic to compassionate – would need to accompany these types of exercises, because traditionally, the criminal justice system has promoted unemotional objectivity (Erez and Rogers 1999; Stenross and Kleinman 1989) and delegated emotion work to the system's victim service counselors (Goodrum and Stafford 2003). Bereaved victims' responses indicate that relegating all of the criminal justice system's emotion work to counselors compartmentalizes victims' intense feelings of sadness and anger to a therapeutic encounter, and they wanted the *prosecutor* (not the counselor) to convey all of those emotions to them as well as to the jury and the judge during the trial. As Konradi (1997) anticipated in her study of rape victims' encounters with prosecutors, bereaved victims wanted to share their feelings with and have them validated by the criminal justice professional championing their case, the prosecutor. For bereaved victims, the prosecutor embodied an intimate ally in their fight for justice.

Critical Thinking

Goodrum's findings suggest that the fulfillment of the roles by court personnel aids family members in continuing the grieving process and ultimately recovering from their loss. The findings also suggest that bereaved families and court personnel perceive the important roles of court workers in a similar manner. However, only one of four prosecutors interviewed described empathy with victims' grief as important. In light of this finding, do you think prosecutors should become emotionally involved in cases as the victims' families suggest? What would be the advantages and disadvantages of prosecutors becoming more emotionally involved in murder cases? Also, consider how expectations towards police differ from prosecutors. What occupational features of police and prosecutors may explain these differences?

Notes

1. The name of the state has been withheld to protect the identity of the study participants. Some of the details of bereaved victim respondents' experiences, as well as District Attorney's Office respondents' job titles and years of service, could make them identifiable if the name of the state were revealed.
2. These questions were asked only of the 19 bereaved victims whose loved ones' murder cases went to the District Attorney's Office, because the unsolved and murder-suicide bereaved victims had no contact with this part of the system at the time of the interview.

References

Amick-McMullan, Angelynne, Dean G. Kilpatrick, and Heidi S. Resnick. 1991. Homicide as a Risk Factor for PTSD among Surviving Family Members. *Behavior Modification* 15:545–59.

Amick-McMullan, Angelynne, Dean Kilpatrick, Lois J. Veronen, and Susan Smith. 1989. Family Survivors of Homicide Victims: Theoretical Perspectives and an Exploratory Study. *Journal of Traumatic Stress* 2(1): 21–35.

Blumer, Herbert. 1969. *Symbolic Interactionism: Perspective and Method*. Berkeley: University of California Press.

Burgess, Ann Wolbert. 1975. Family Reaction to Homicide. *American Journal of Orthopsychiatry* 45:391–98.

Carr, Patrick J., Kim A. Logio, and Shana Maier. 2003. Keep Me Informed: What Matters for Victims as They Navigate the Juvenile Criminal Justice System in Philadelphia. *International Review of Victimology* 10:117–36.

Clark, Candace. 1987. Sympathy Biography and Sympathy Margin. *American Journal of Sociology* 93:290–321.

Copp, Martha. 1998. When Emotion Work is Doomed to Fail: Ideological and Structural Constraints on Emotion Management. *Symbolic Interaction* 21:299–328.

Davis, Robert C. and Barbara E. Smith. 1994. Victim Impact Statements and Victim Satisfaction: An Unfulfilled Promise? *Journal of Criminal Justice* 22:1–12.

Denzin, Norman K. 2007. *On Understanding Emotion*. New Brunswick, NJ: Transaction Publishers.

Doak, Jonathan. 2005. Victims' Rights in Criminal Trials: Prospects for Participation. *Journal of Law and Society* 32(2): 294–316.

Elias, Robert. 1984. Alienating the Victim: Compensation and Victim Attitudes. *Journal of Social Issues* 40:103–16.

Erez, Edna. 1994. Victim Participation in Sentencing: And the Debate Goes On. *International Review of Victimology* 3:17–32.

———. 2000. Integrating the Victim Perspective in Criminal Justice through Victim Impact Statements. In *Integrating a Victim Perspective within Criminal Justice: International Debates*, eds. Adam Crawford and Jo Goodey. Burlington, VT: Ashgate.

Erez, Edna and Ewa Bienkowska. 1993. Victim Participation in Proceedings and Satisfaction with Justice in the Continental Systems: The Case of Poland. *Journal of Criminal Justice* 21:47–60.

Erez, Edna, and Joanne Belknap. 1998. Battered Women and the Criminal Justice System: The Service Providers' Perceptions. *The European Journal on Criminal Policy and Research* 6(1):37–57.

Erez, Edna and Kathy Laster. 1999. Neutralizing Victim Reform: Legal Professionals' Perspectives on Victims and Impact Statements. *Crime & Delinquency* 45(4):530–53.

Erez, Edna, Leigh Roeger, and Frank Morgan. 1997. Victim Harm, Impact Statements, and Victim Satisfaction with Justice: An Australian Experience. *International Review of Victimology* 5:37–60.

Erez, Edna and Linda Rogers. 1999. Victim Impact Statements and Sentencing Outcomes and Processes. *British Journal of Criminology* 39(2):216–39.

Frohmann, Lisa. 1998. Constituting Power in Sexual Assault Cases: Prosecutorial Strategies for Victim Management. *Social Problems* 45:393–407.

Goffman, Erving. 1959. *The Presentation of Self in Everyday Life*. Garden City, NY: Anchor Books.

Goodrum, Sarah. 2007. Victims' Rights, Victims' Expectations, and Law Enforcement Workers' Constraints in Cases of Murder. *Law and Social Inquiry: Journal of the American Bar Association* 32(2):725–68.

Goodrum, Sarah and Mark C. Stafford. 2003. The Management of Emotions in the Criminal Justice System. *Sociological Focus* 36(3):179–196.

Hare, Sara C. 2006. What Do Battered Women Want?: Victims' Opinions on Prosecution. *Violence and Victims* 21(5):611–28.

Kelly, Deborah. 1990. Victim Participation in the Criminal Justice System. In *Victims of Crime: Problems, Policies, and Programs*, eds. Arthur J. Lurigio, Wesley G. Skogan, and Robert C. Davis. Newbury Park, CA: Sage.

Kenney, J. Scott. 1995. Legal Institutions and Victims of Crime in Canada: An Historical and Contemporary Review. *Humanity and Society* 19(2):53–67.

———. 2004. Human Agency Revisited: The Paradoxical Experiences of Victims of Crime. *International Review of Victimology* 11:225–57.

Kilpatrick, Dean G. and Randy K. Otto. 1987. Constitutionally Guaranteed Participation in Criminal Proceeding for Victims: Potential Effects on Psychological Functioning. *Wayne Law Review* 34:17–28.

Konradi, Amanda. 1996. Preparing to Testify: Rape Survivors Negotiating the Criminal Justice Process. *Gender and Society* 10:404–32.

———. 1997. Too Little, Too Late: Prosecutors' Precourt Preparation of Rape Survivors. *Law & Social Inquiry* 22:1–54.

Mirowsky, John and Catherine E. Ross. 1989. *Social Causes of Psychological Distress*. Hawthorne, NY: Aldine de Gruyter.

[Omitted State Name] Department of Health. 2000. Homicide Data for [Omitted County Names], 1994–98 [MRDF]. [Omitted State Name] Department of Health, Bureau of Vital Statistics, Statistical Services Division [producer and distributor].

President's Task Force on Victims of Crime. 1982. *Final Report on President's Task Force on Victims of Crime*. http://www.ojp.usdoj.gov/ovc/publications/presdntstskforcrprt/front.pdf (accessed August 5, 2011).

Rando, Therese A. 1993. *Treatment of Complicated Mourning*. Champaign, IL: Research Press.

Riches, Gordon and Pam Dawson. 1998. Spoiled Memories: Problems of Grief Resolution in Families Bereaved through Murder. *Mortality* 3(2):143–59.

Rock, Paul. 1998. *After Homicide: Practical and Political Responses to Bereavement*. Oxford: Clarendon Press.

Stenross, Barbara and Sherryl Kleinman. 1989. The Highs and Lows of Emotional Labor: Detectives' Encounters with Criminals and Victims. *Journal of Contemporary Ethnography* 17:435–52.

Thoits, Peggy A. 1984. Explaining Distributions of Psychological Vulnerability: Lack of Social Support in the Face of Life Stress. *Social Forces* 53:2453–481.

U. S. Bureau of the Census. 2001. County Population Estimates for July 1, 1999 and Population Change for July 1, 1998 to July 1, 1999 (Population Estimates Program, Population Division). Washington, DC: U.S. Census Bureau. (http://www.census.gov/population/estimates/county/co-99-1/99C1_48.txt), (accessed October 2, 2001).

Wiebe, Richard P. 1996. The Mental Health Implications of Crime Victims' Rights. In *Law in a Therapeutic Key: Developments in Therapeutic Jurisprudence*, eds. David B. Wexler and Bruce J. Winick. Durham, NC: Carolina Academic Press.

19

Female Recidivists Speak about Their Experience in Drug Court while Engaging in Appreciative Inquiry

Michael Fischer, Brenda Geiger, and Mary Ellen Hughes

Abstract: *Fischer, Geiger, and Hughes address the way that female drug court participants assess the strengths and weaknesses of the program. The majority of participants
described the drug court program in a positive light, often comparing the program to
previous experiences in other drug programs. The participants described the intensive
structure, supervision, and rule enforcement as helpful in their recovery. However, the
participants also emphasized the importance of supportive staff members and court
personnel. The women's accounts indicated that although structure and supervision are
deemed helpful, these aspects of the program alone are not sufficient to encourage
compliance with rules and active participation in the program. Instead, the findings
indicate that a compassionate and supportive atmosphere is necessary to motivate the
women to succeed in the program and attempt to change their behavior.*

Arrests and convictions for drug abuse and drug-related crimes have become the
most frequent conviction offense for female offenders (Anglin & Perrochet, 1998;
Chesney-Lind & Pasko, 2004; Merlo, 1995). As indicated by the National Institute of
Justice (1998), between 33% and 82% of female offenders tested positive for drugs at
the time of their arrest. From 1995 until 2000, the number of women convicted of
federal methamphetamines charges increased by 133% (Chesney-Lind & Pasko,
2004). Additionally, about one quarter of all women in prison had some form of drug
treatment prior to imprisonment (Chesney-Lind & Pasko, 2004). Of those using
drugs, 41.8% participated in a treatment program the month before being arrested.
These figures suggest that most of the current interventions were not sufficient to
address women's underlying needs (National Institute of Justice, 1998). Female
offenders often share the same background characteristics of poverty and traumatic
childhood experiences (Geiger & Fischer, 2003, 2005). Most of these women are
mothers, oftentimes of minor children for whom there is no arrangement other than
adoption or foster care. More than 70% of the 869,000 women under criminal justice
surveillance have children under 18 years—1.3 million children (Chesney-Lind &
Pasko, 2004, p. 154). Loss of custody often shatters meaning and purpose in life and
provides additional reason to lose oneself in drugs (Chesney-Lind & Pasko, 2004;
Chesney-Lind & Shelden, 2004; Geiger & Fischer, 2003, 2005).

The nation's 1,400 drug courts seem to provide an answer to the ever-increasing
number of female recidivist felons with a desperate need for resources and
services. Based on the philosophy of Therapeutic Jurisprudence (Hora, Schma, &

Rosenthal, 1999), drug court provides its clients with intensive judicial supervision and community-based treatment alternatives without the stigma and dehumanizing effects of incarceration (Nolan, 2002). Suspended sentences are used to encourage offenders to participate in drug court and mandated mental-health and substance-abuse treatment. Graduated intensive supervision, monitoring for compliance with treatment, and graduated sanctions for noncompliance develop offenders' accountability and allow for gradual reintegration into the community (Berman & Feinblatt, 2005).

Drug courts are required, when receiving federal funding, to be evaluated every 6 months in their efforts to rehabilitate drug offenders (Goldkamp, 2000; Goldkamp, Weiland, & Moore, 2001; Gottfredson & Exum, 2002). These evaluations employ a variety of process and outcome measures including program-retention rates, urinalysis results, healthy babies, employment, and recidivism. Assessments show that by comparison to incarceration or standard rehabilitation programs, drug-court programs have lower recidivism rates and are more cost-effective (Goldkamp, 2000; Goldkamp et al., 2001; Gottfredson & Exum, 2002).

Despite regular formal quantitative evaluations, appreciation of the components and processes that give life to this unique program as perceived by the program participants themselves has not yet been explored, especially in reference to female participants. In agreement with Patton (2002), the researchers believe that to evaluate the effectiveness of a program one must listen to the voices and the stories of those about whom the statistics have been compounded. To compensate for this lack, this action research engaged Northern California drug-court female participants in an appreciative collaborative inquiry (Bushe, 1995, 1997).

The main tenets of appreciative inquiry are: (a) the focus on positive and effective programs and (b) amplification of what participants want more of, even if what they want more of exists only in a small quantity (Cooperrider, 1990; Cooperrider & Srivastva, 1987; Whitney & Cooperrider, 2000). Congruent with the tenets of appreciative inquiry, this study adopts a social and postmodernist perspective that views people as continuously reconstructing social reality (Gergen, 1990, 1994). Program participants have the ability to evaluate and create new and better programs simply by talking about their program and envisioning new realities (Barrett, Thomas, & Hocevar, 1995; Cooperrider & Srivastva, 1987).

Female drug-court participants were invited to talk about the characteristics of the people and processes that were conducive to their recovery. Engaged as core-searchers and change agents, these women were empowered to amplify those qualities and envision new potentials and possibilities for future drug-court programs.

Northern California Drug-Court Program Description

The Northern California drug-court program under study enrolled 119 felony-convicted offenders, of whom 30 were women. After individual assessment by the case manager, clients are provided with resources and referrals to various treatment facilities. Clients progress through three phases each lasting for 6 months, and after-care that lasts approximately 6 months. Participants are urine and Breathalyzer-tested twice a week, with the days of the test selected at random. Continuous graduated intensive supervision and monitoring for compliance with treatment are made possible by the joint collaboration of a judge, three probation officers, 12 treatment providers, two case managers, and two counselors. A mental-health specialist-court liaison plays the dual role of case manager and liaison, evaluating and reporting to the judge the client's progress. The client appears in court three times a week in phase one, twice a week in phase two, and once a week in phase three. Satisfactory progress is symbolized by advancement through the phases. Compliance with the program requirements leads to a decrease in the intensity of supervision and to greater autonomy and individual choice. Graduated sanctions for noncompliance range from explanation and planning, to being dropped to a previous stage or remaining longer in a phase, to being sent to jail.

Method

Participant Selection

Participant selection criteria for this research were (a) being female, (b) having repeat drug or drug-related offenses, (c) enrollment in drug-court program for at least 7 months, and (d) being in phases two or three of the program. In the opinions of the probation officers and case managers, these criteria would guarantee that only clients who had enough experience and knowledge of drug court would participate in this study. Eighteen of the 30 female Northern California drug-court participants satisfied these criteria. Of this eligible pool, 11 women consented to be interviewed. The age range of these 11 women was between 23 and 47 years, with a mean age of 34.1, and a median age of 32 years.

These women were felons convicted for drug-related offenses such as drug dealing and use, possession of drug paraphernalia, embezzlement, child endangerment, Driving Under the Influence, theft, possession of firearms, hit and run, forgery, possession of stolen property, and stolen credit cards. The reported average number of years of drug addiction was 13.4 years, with 64% of the women starting between ages 12 to 16. The drug of choice for 10 of these women was methamphetamine (meth). Five of these women had survived incest, rape, and/or had a family history of drug and alcohol abuse. The remaining 6 women did not report any family history of drug abuse or incest. In the words of Kim, "A lot of us are from the middle class, without a drug history."

All research participants were mothers of between one and five children, with a mean of 2.5. They all had experienced separation from their children, of whom they had either temporarily or permanently lost custody.

Procedure

A semistructured in-depth interview that included an interview guide was the main research tool of our appreciative collaborative inquiry. Aside from background information and a history of drug and sexual abuse, questions inquired about participants' experience in the criminal justice system, their experience in the present drug-court program, and the components that were conducive to their progress and recovery. Additional questions directed these women to envision innovative aspects of future drug-court programs. In order not to interfere with the flow of the narrative, the order of questions in the interview guide was not always adhered to (Brunner, 2004; Denzin, 1989; Patton, 2002; Plummer, 1995).

Before obtaining participants' consent, the two researchers conducting the interviews introduced themselves as a designated drug-court evaluator and coordinator from another state. The researchers wanted to hear the participants tell in their own words about the components, activities, and people in the program that had assisted them to succeed and change. It was also specified that participation was voluntary. The lack of therapeutic role of the interviewers and the informal nondirective style of the interview increased ease and facilitated rapport (Baron & Hartnagel, 1997; Hagan & McCarthy, 1992).

Results

Research participants were in awe of what drug court had offered them in their community. In the words of Paula, "Our drug court here is absolutely incredible. I never want them to retire. We are losing one gal due to budget cutbacks, and that will hurt us all."

In trying to comprehend what makes drug court so unique, these women often compared negative past experiences with positive present experiences. To them it was the staff that composed drug court that made this program so special and so different from previous experiences in the criminal justice system and, in a few cases, with other drug courts. Whether in drug court, in the treatment program, or in aftercare, these women felt supported by people who cared about them. The judge emerged in the foreground as one of the most if not the most important figure. He was described as fair, helpful, encouraging, and concerned about the client's progress. In the words of Arlene, "He is really nice, encouraging, doing something positive. He makes it much known to everybody. Actually, it makes you feel good."

Despite a rich past in the cogwheels of the criminal justice system, it seems that for the first time these women were treated with dignity. The judge was talking to them, not past them, or about them to someone else. He genuinely listened to what they had to say about their progress. In the words of Candy, "I think the judge is very fair and honest. He always treats me with respect. He does not talk to me as if I am some worthless addict. I think it is helpful to go in front of the judge." Similarly, Theresa explained while comparing past and present drug-court judges,

> There is a big difference. This time he actually wants you to talk to him. You get up in front of him and report how you are doing weekly, or how your program is going, and if you have a relapse, and if there is any trouble. You can tell him what the problem was and how you solved it. Before they called your name and you stood up and they have this piece of paper and the probation officer and drug court counselor would read it to the judge and say you are doing OK. Bye! It was the drug court staff talking.

The judge's uniqueness was related to a combination of empathy, professionalism, and knowledge about recovery. "He is very compassionate, very understanding, and very knowledgeable about recovery. He has our best interests and our welfare at heart" (Sharon). The drug-court probation officer and counselor were also appreciated for their concern and respect. To them, they no longer were a number, but people.

> You see them [probation officer and case manager] once a week. And they ask how are you doing, they want to know what's going on, and a regular probation officer isn't necessarily like that. They want to know everything, which is kind of nice because you know that they really care. You are not just a number.
>
> (Arlene)

> I go in and test on Tuesdays and Fridays. But it's just like, whenever I need to talk, I will go in and talk, and they will sit down and talk to me. They are always helpful.
>
> (Candy)

Sharon remembers how indifferent her other probation officers were: "The probation officer, before, she did not have any compassion. These guys even though they had to send me to jail, they are still smiling." Positive comments were also made in reference to the treatment providers and counselors. Attentive to these women's needs, they gave the women the feeling that they were there for them 24 hours a day.

> I couldn't say enough good things about this treatment staff. They are very conscientious about recovery. When I lost my last sister two months ago, they told me to go home, but I needed to be with people. They just gave me my space, whatever I needed, all I had to do was ask.
>
> (Paula)

Similarly, in aftercare and Narcotics Anonymous their sponsors were also always available.

> A counselor may not be available all the time, but somebody is always available from 12 Steps. The people in the meetings have been very supportive. I did not realize how much support there is around here.
>
> (Kim)

> On weekends you have sponsors you may call. Mine lives right up the street. I have had a sponsor for the last 10 months.
>
> (Paula)

Clear Rules and Consequences for Rule Transgression

For these women, intensive supervision, structure, and consequences for rule transgressions and delinquent behavior in the drug court and treatment program were judged helpful as long as they were not humiliating and the participants were treated with respect. In the words of these women,

> And the structure, having to be tested twice a week, forces you to be off of drugs. There are consequences. That helped me clean up long enough to get my bearings.
>
> (Kim)

New Beginnings is one of the most structured programs. But it's a neat program. They treat me very well.

(Theresa)

Testing positive—relapsing—could require remaining longer at a stage or being moved back to a prior stage, and, in serious cases, being sent to jail. In drug court participants knew they had to play by the rules. In the words of these women,

They don't take any crap off of you. If you are going to be defiant and are not going to follow the rules, you'll have a bracelet slapped on you in a heartbeat.

(Paula)

When you try to take advantage of the court you will get caught. They do not like it. You can only play games for so long. They will put you right in jail. Once you stop using, and stop playing games with them, you realize how good it is.

(Kathe)

Accurate Drug Testing

Participants' confidence in the drug-court system was increased because of accurate drug-testing procedures. Reliable laboratory results protected them from false positives. In the words of Theresa, "They sent it to the lab to break it down. They sent it to determine if it was drugs or a false positive. And they figured out that it was a false positive." Similarly, Thelma explains, while comparing past and present testing procedures,

Back in 1997 tests were not accurate. They accused me of using pot, and told me I was really in denial. "You had a dirty test, and you are going to jail." Today tests are very accurate. If you get a false positive they send it to the criminal lab and they test it, they break it down. It costs the client 45 dollars to send it to them, whereas it costs 6 dollars to do the regular test.

For these women, punishment and accurate testing were, however, still insufficient to prevent rule transgression and promote active participation in recovery. Piaget (1966) often mentioned in the context of moral development that it is the respect, firmness, and warmth of those who communicate the rules that motivate people to adopt and follow them. The women in this research expressed the same sentiment. In their own words,

You know not to mess up. You can feel the support. People in the front row, you can tell if they have screwed up or not.

(Kim)

He will pull a lot of people's collars and put them in jail. They are not serious about recovery. But for those of us who are, he has a lot of respect for us.

(Paula)

Realizing that drug court had their best interest at heart motivated these women to be honest. Being honest often meant communicating one's failure. It meant reporting drug use and alcohol consumption even when they were sure such use would not be detected by the test. Candy and Kathe recounted,

Around Mother's day, I used marijuana, I got sick to my stomach, I got dizzy, and I had to sit down. What do I do? Do I tell, or not? I drank a 32-ounce bottle of cranberry juice to clean my system out. I had to tell, it's not truthful and honest. I walked in there and told them. I just talked to them about it, and they made me write a little piece of paper about who I was with, and where I was. They tested me, and my test came back clean. It just set me back two months.

(Candy)

Alcohol gets out of your system really fast. I could drink on weekends and get away with it. Alcohol is the one thing you can get away in drug court. All the other drugs will show in your system even after three days.

(Kathe)

In drug court these women learned to assume responsibility and become active participants in their progress. In case of relapse, the judge would ask for the client's input and plans to prevent future drug and alcohol use. In the words of Thelma,

The judge asks you, "So what are you going to do next time? How can you stop it from happening again?" I answer, "I am going to do this and going to do that. I am not going to hang around with those people."

Assuming responsibility was also to accept the consequences of relapse, which at times meant returning to jail.

I did use; I did get a dirty test a couple of times. I told them I slipped up and used meth. I was sent to jail a couple of times. Now I am doing real good.

(Thelma)

I spent 68 days in jail, and I have done 90 days in jail, a week in jail, a couple of months. I know when I will have a dirty test, I have messed up. I will tell them about it, and they will arrest me right then and there.

(Sabina)

These women evoked the need to differentiate between drug and house-rule violations. Although the consequences for drug violation were accepted as fair, they requested more flexibility concerning treatment-program rule transgressions that were unrelated to drugs and supervision. To be sent to jail for technical violations such as smoking or drinking coffee was for them too extreme and unfair. In their own words,

Well, when I was in jail pregnant with my son I was not arrested for using; I was arrested for being kicked out of a program for smoking cigarettes and drinking coffee; and it was a nonsmoking program. So I had a really hard time with it, that was a violation, I hadn't used, but I had violated. Actually I did go to jail for 4 months. And they were going to send me to prison for 3 years. But the judge decided to give me another chance.

(Arlene)

I call it [treatment facility] boot camp: no coffee, no soda, or cigarettes, or chocolate. You get one cup of sugar. Nobody can know where you live, your phone number.

(Candy)

Personal Attitude and Motivaton to Mature Out of Crime

As they progressed in the interview, these women emphasized that client's personal attitude and motivation were conditions sine qua nons for successful recovery. The client must be ready to change and mature out of drugs. Kathe explained,

> And if you are not ready to change it, then you are not going to last long. And the turnover is like crazy. There have been over 100 people in this treatment facility in the six months I have been coming, and I have seen maybe six people graduate since I have been there.

Thelma explained that, "Drug court and New Beginnings. Everyone can say I have to quit all they want, but you have to do it."

These women understood that, no matter how much support they received from relatives, friends, or professionals, the desire to change had to come from within. If one is not ready to change, no change will occur. Kristine, who had been surrounded by many caring relatives, knew it best:

> If you want drugs, you will take drugs. I had everybody around me telling me to change; I had people trying to help me, my mother, my ex-husband, and everybody else. I did not want to hear it. I still went out to drink.

Being ready means "wanting off those chemicals" (Paula), whatever the reason one had for starting or continuing. The women in this study stated that to change one had to hit bottom. In the words of Paula,

> When I entered New Beginnings we had 11 people in the outpatient program. Now we have 4. That's how many have left to use drugs. They were not serious. I think you have to hit rock bottom . . . Each person's bottom is different.

For these women the phrase "hitting bottom" meant being tired of the vicious circle of drugs, prostitution, crime, and jail.

> The same vicious circle, the lies, the stealing, not knowing where I am going to sleep. I have slept on people's cars, bushes, porches. I have prostituted to get my drugs. I am not ashamed of what I did, just some of what I have gone though, you know, is crap. I am 24 years old and I have not accomplished anything but being a drug addict.
>
> (Candy)

"Hitting bottom" also meant coming close to losing it all, including oneself: "It devastated my life. I went from having everything in the world to having nothing. . . . Looking backward my relationship with my family, my sobriety are more important than any drug in the world" (Paula).

Only at the bottom could one reach a deeper level of understanding. Such an understanding was not related to their knowledge about the devastating effects of drugs. Rather, it came from the depth of one's being. In the words of Candy,

> Drug court is a big motivator and a big help, but you have to be ready, from in here [showing her chest]. Not just from your head, but from your heart too. You must really want to change from the inside. You must be ready to grow up.

To be successful one must want to mature, that is, to take personal responsibility for one's fate. Candy explained concerning her parents,

> Mom was also a heroine user, my father would dabble in alcohol, methamphetamine, heroine, marijuana, and I used meth and marijuana with my dad. I feel that they had something to do with how I started off my life; but the problems that I created for myself with the law were my own doing.

Research participants also searched for the components of community-based residential and aftercare treatment programs that were conducive to their progress and recovery.

Individualized Treatment Plan

All these women reported that only an individualized treatment plan could provide the services and supervision they needed. The intake interview with a case manager was, therefore, an essential step in this process. In the words of these women,

> He assesses, determines which program you should enter, whether you need to live in a residential facility. If there is a problem, he will ask you what's going on, etc. If you are doing well, you only have to test once a week, otherwise three times a week. Then both drug court and probation will test you if you need that much supervision.
>
> (Thelma)

Remembering past negative experiences, Kim spoke of a rigid counselor who was deaf to her wishes and excluded her from the decision-making process:

> My counselors in Prop 36 wanted me to go into a battered women's shelter with my 17 year old son, but he could not move in because he was too old. When I would have gotten out of there, I would have been homeless. It made absolutely no sense to me, so I did not sign their paper, and so I got a probation violation. I got kicked out of the program because I was being insubordinate. It frustrated me so much that I screwed up and used again.
>
> (Kim)

Learning from past experiences, these women stressed that decisions about treatment plans had to involve the client and take into consideration the client's concerns and preferences. Furthermore, assessments must be given periodically because the client changes and so do her needs for services and supervision.

> When you are originally assessed you may need more intensive treatment. However, going through the process of recovery, whether you are waiting to go to jail or waiting to get into that treatment facility, you have changed. You may no longer need an intensive treatment facility. Without being reassessed you may be sent to a place that does not fit you any longer.
>
> (Kim)

Treatment Facilities that Accept Children

Separation from their children and concern for their welfare remain major preoccupations. To these women, especially for those who did not have close relatives to assume custody, there was an eminent need for facilities that accepted children. Kathe was one of the lucky few with a helpful mother and treatment facility that accepted children. She recounts,

> My mom moved into my apartment to take care of the kids when I was in jail. Then they came with me to the residential center. I was extremely lucky, as this is one of the few programs that accept children over the age of four. So my son and daughter came to live with me.

By contrast, Theresa did not have such a choice. Her children were put up for adoption as a result of a lack of close relatives to take care of them and/or residential facilities to accept them. The loss embittered her. Theresa recounted,

> They put me in a program where I could not have my kids, knowing that I was running out of time. Knowing that if they put me in a program where I could not have my kids, I would lose my kids. I have a real problem with that. If they would have put me in a treatment facility with my children back then, maybe it would have made a big difference. But I wasn't in drug court yet, and it took me a few years to get to drug court. And even then they put me in a place where I could not have my children. That kind of screwed me and my children up.

Choice of Therapy

The women interviewed in this research generally found the intensive therapy and counseling instrumental to their recovery. It was helping them understand the source of their problems. In the words of Kim,

> It does make a difference to find the root. They may say it's because your parents drank or drug use, but a lot of it isn't. A lot of us are from the middle class, without a drug history. Now I understand myself more, and feel more confident with myself, not to let people push me around.

These women also mentioned the need to match therapy (group or/and individual) with the client's need. A mismatch often led to regression. Candy, who wanted individual therapy, complained about a treatment facility:

> It's always in a group. No one-on-one. They really don't work with you on an individual basis. They work with you in a group, and then they judge you individually.

Issues Addressed in Therapy

Group therapy had often helped these women confront past sexual abuse and unresolved anger. In the words of these women,

> We worked through a lot of underlying issues, a lot of anger that we had. That I did not know I had. If you learn to hide it at a younger age, drugs just mask it at an older age. With me it was incest.
>
>   (Thelma)

I had a lot of abuse in my past, and I get very anxious and angry, and so I have been in there and talked to people. I didn't really know where the anger was coming from, but they kind of helped me get down to the bottom of it, after I steamed off, like where is this anger coming from, which is really from abuse years ago. And that was really helpful. Because I had no idea as to why I was so angry, I was just mad at everything. And they helped me figure it out.

(Arlene)

Another Issue Confronted: Self-Blame and Guilt Consequent to the Separation From Children

Therapy was also needed to deal with separation and loss of the children. In the words of Thelma, who had lost custody of her children,

Separation from the children creates more issues of guilt and shame, issues that a woman cannot face, and it's going to hurt, and she just wants to use more. To heal the family would be to heal the person.

Candy, similarly, wondered whether there was some kind of therapy that could help her deal with the feeling of loss over her children.

I regret the loss of my children. I lost them for drugs. [Silence for 10 seconds.] I feel very messed up in the head over it. That I have lost them all. I lost them for drugs. It makes me sad, makes me think. Drug court does not really help with the feeling part.

Treatment Staff: Preference for Counselors Who Are Ex-Addicts

All the women interviewed mentioned the advantage of facilities that hired counselors who were ex-addicts. The reason for such preference was that only people who had gone through the same experience could understand and be compassionate.

It's hard to make a person understand what you are going through if they have not been there. If you have not been there, you have no idea what it's really like. You may be able to understand what they think and why, but unless you have been there, you really don't know.

(Arlene)

For these ex-addicts, counselors' judgment and insight as to what was best for them could be trusted. In their own words,

And that's a really big thing, to trust someone, especially in the system. And I have been in the system since I was 12 years old. If they do not think its right for you, they will give you another option. If they do not think it's right, they will tell you "This is what we're really thinking." And I really trust their judgment now.

(Theresa)

I do believe that they do have insight, and a lot of them have been through the process themselves, so they understand the problems we face as we go through the stages. I have been here for just over a year and I know that they know what they are doing. 1 trust them.

(Arienne)

Gender of the Counselor

Most of the participants mentioned that the gender of the counselor is important. In their opinion, female counselors were better able to help them deal with underlying "female" issues of separation of children, physical abuse, and sexual abuse. "It is nice to have a female counselor. It seems like everybody in the program had an abuse issue, sex, and incest" (Kim).

Paula formulated the golden rules for counselors: "(1) don't be judgmental with people; you don't know what they are going though, (2) have an open mind, (3) give that person the benefit of the doubt until they prove otherwise, (4) don't condemn an addict, because you are going to send that person right back out, (5) try being as positive as possible, and (6) maintain confidentiality."

Treatment Facilities' Comprehensive Set of Services

The treatment facilities that were considered superior were those that offered a comprehensive set of services. Project Innovation, which unfortunately closed because of lack of funding, was often cited as the prototype for such facility. In the words of these women,

> Project Innovation was from 8 until 4, with an hour for lunch, Monday through Friday. We had an hour of Alcohol and Other Drugs (AOD) program in group, and then a break, and then relapse recovery for an hour. . . . A speaker came in. It was a job thing and we learned how to do resumes. It was a really good program.
>
> (Arlene)

> It offered family recovery, women's issues, individual, group, parenting, anger management, art therapy, and relapse prevention. If you needed legal assistance, there was a counselor who would give it. If you needed medical assistance, they would provide it. If you needed a ride, they had a car. They would get you there and make sure you could get back.
>
> (Thelma)

Resources and Referrals

These women also appreciated resources and referrals at every phase, which enabled them to become independent. In the words of these women,

> They are hooked up with the EDD [Employment Development Department] place, and they should also be hooked up with Voc Rehab, which is different from the job place. It actually gets you started in something you want to do, hooks you up in school or finds you a job, or pays for tools if you do not have them, if you cannot get on your feet.
>
> (Theresa)

Sensitivity to the client's financial problems was also mentioned as an asset. If need be, drug court paid for drug rehabilitation, testing, counseling, transportation, and so on.

When you are in a residential program drug court helps you with your finances, when you can't pay for bus tickets, they will pay.

(Kathe)

They pay for my drug rehabilitation, my books [for drug rehabilitation] and stuff; they pay for my aftercare, 10 dollars every time I go. They pay for the one-on-one counseling, if that's what you need; people here in the office will help you get it.

(Arlene)

Skill Acquisition and Vocational Training

For these women, skill acquisition and vocational training were also crucial. The only way to leave welfare as a way of life is to acquire a job. In their own words,

There are women here who need help and training to get skills and stuff like that. To get them off of welfare, to feel better, stronger. But me, I am happy with what they have done for me.

(Paula)

People should be made to do something, where they get a skill, such as a welder. Then they could go to work when they get out rather than going back on the streets and drugs. Most of the people who end up incarcerated it's because they don't have a job, or a good job, a good paying job.

(Thelma)

To these women receiving wages during vocational training was an additional incentive to enroll. Kathe, who had enrolled in a vocational training project, explains, "They will pay your wages for up to three months; they will pay you for school if you need it."

Children as Anchor to Remain Clean and Sober

The prospect of being with or seeing their children renewed their hope and faith in life. When asked what would help them remain clean, Jasmine answered, "My daughter!" Similarly, Kathe explained, "For 17 years I was either doing meth, alcohol, or just getting high. And now I am sober, for me, and for them." Candy, who was about to receive 4-hr visitation rights, was very excited by the prospect: "I really only have contact with one of my children. I am excited. I am so happy. It starts on his birthday."

Several of these women wished to become productive and work. Kim enjoyed her work:

I am a waitress. I am getting ready to go back to work. I like work. It keeps me busy. I was stagnant then, it was a lot of wasted time, and I was not using my potential. I have been like this for too long.

Candy was very excited to have, for the first time, a paying job even if it is only on weekends and might result in her losing all governmental aid. "I really want to work; it's my first job ever. I have never had a job. And I just started two weeks ago and I really like it."

Another sign of complete recovery was to give back by helping other drug addicts. For Paula this was a way to express gratitude to all those who had helped her recover.

> I had wonderful people support me in my recovery, and it's important to give it back, to close the circle. I take them out shopping, or help them with reading, or take them to a movie. It's really important to get that support. These young people don't have the opportunity to get out. I have my freedom, my own space.

Discussion

This qualitative study engaged in an appreciative inquiry with female repeat felons participating in a drug-court program in Northern California. Eleven out of 18 females enrolled in phases two and three of the program consented to be interviewed. They were given a voice to talk about the strengths of the program and of the key persons who had helped them change. Empowered as change agents, these women looked at their past and present experiences in drug court and the criminal justice system and looked forward to envision future drug-court innovations. From these women's perspectives, the strongest component of the drug court they were enrolled in was being surrounded by many caring people who listened to them and who were genuinely concerned about their progress. These women did not mind the intensive supervision and graduated and immediate sanctions as long as they were imposed fairly by people who sought to educate rather than punish or humiliate them. Wraparound services, resources, and referral; treatment facilities that accepted children; and individualized treatment plans were essential components of a successful program. Group and individual therapy and counselors who were ex-addicts and preferably women helped these women get to the root of the drug problem and address women's issues of incest, anger, and guilt over the separation from the children. In drug court they were empowered to put the past behind and start a new life "without the rush of drugs." It is to be noted that not all these women were from disadvantaged social-economic strata, and not all of them had abusive parents. Remaining clean and sober as they moved through the three phases and aftercare, acquiring skills, finding a job, and visiting or regaining custody of their children, increased confidence in their ability to lead drug-free, meaningful lives.

Drug court assumes that reform can be achieved through coerced court and community intervention without requiring clients to obtain the highest levels of motivation (Prochaska, DiClemente, & Norcross, 1992). It furthermore assumes that motivation can be cultivated through suspended sentences and by having participants remain for longer periods of time than is customary in drug-rehabilitation programs (Satel, 1998, 2000). Our findings indicated that clients' participation in drug court increased motivation as they were supported and rewarded for progress through phases. The public announcement of such progress enhanced self-efficacy perception (Bandura, 1977) and motivation to complete recovery. Nevertheless, participants stressed that a condition sine qua non for drug-court program success was the participants' readiness to mature out of drugs, to stop being deceitful, and to be honest with themselves.

It is possible that the presently examined drug-court program was successful with the 11 women precisely because they were already in the process of maturing out on their own. Greater insight concerning the level of motivation and readiness of female drug-court participants could be obtained by conducting further research that would compare the subjective experience of female drug-court participants who did not go beyond phase one, that is, had failed the program, with those of female drug-court participants who progressed beyond phase one.

The women interviewed in this research repeatedly mentioned the human element of care, concern, and fairness of drug-court and treatment staff. What these persons gave them could not be compared with any other experience they had had in the criminal justice system, including in a few cases other drug courts. Given the unique personal characteristics of this drug court's personnel, it is recommended to replicate this appreciative inquiry with several drug courts located in the various counties of Northern California. Such a replication would allows us to find out whether the uniqueness of the drug-court team was related to the adoption of therapeutic jurisprudence philosophy or a single phenomenon related to the special mix of personal characteristics of drug-court staff and clients.

In conclusion, despite the small and selected sample of women who engaged in this appreciative inquiry in one drug court in Northern California, this research expands our knowledge in the field by showing the benefits of a drug-court program from female participants' perspective. The components of quality care of drug court and of the process of recovery go beyond traditional criteria of success—lack of recidivism and sobriety statistics so far compiled on drug courts. Terms such as caring drug-court staff concerned with the client's recovery, respect, honesty, bottoming out, wanting out of chemicals, relapsing and trying again, putting the past behind, having hope for the future, wanting therapy to deal with the roots of the drug problems and with the feeling of guilt consequent to separation with children, developing a sense of efficacy that increases motivation to take care of the children, work, and giving in return to other drug addicts are some of the many criteria of successful recovery that could only be comprehended through qualitative research. This study, therefore, shows the invaluable data obtained by conducting qualitative evaluations of drug-court programs.

Critical Thinking

Although the women evaluated the drug court program positively, they did provide some suggestions for improvement. The women expressed interest in gaining access to programs with vocational training and continuing education classes, residential programs that allow children, and counseling programs that included therapy for women separated from their children. The women also preferred programs where they could choose between secular or Christian based treatment and programs that primarily employed female counselors who were ex-addicts. Considering these women's suggestions, do you think these additions are feasible or important? In short, should evaluations of programs to deter or rehabilitate offenders take the perceptions of offenders into account?

References

Anglin, M. D., & Perrochet, B. (1998). Drug use and crime: An historical review of research conducted by the UCLA Drug Abuse Research Center. *Substance Use Misuse 33,* 1871–1914.

Bandura. A. (1977). *Social learning theory.* Englewood Cliffs, NJ: Prentice Hall.

Baron, S., & Hartnagel, T. (1997). Attributions, affect, and crime: Street youths' reactions to unemployment. *Criminology, 35,* 409–434.

Barrett, F. J., Thomas, G. F., & Hocevar, S. P. (1995). The central role of discourse in large-scale change: A social construction perspective. *The Journal of Applied Behavioral Science, 31,* 352–372.

Berman, G., & Feinblatt, J. (2005). *Good courts.* New York: The New Press.

Brunner, J. (2004). Life as narrative. *Social Research, 71,* 691–711.

Bushe, G. R. (1995). Advances in appreciative inquiry as an organization development intervention. *Organization Development Journal, 13*(3), 14–22.

Bushe, G. R. (1997). *Attending to others: Interviewing appreciatively.* Vancouver. BC: Discovery & Design Inc.

Chesney-Lind, M., & Pasko, L. (2004). *The female offender. Girls, women, and crime* (2nd ed.). Thousand Oaks, CA: Sage.

Chesney-Lind, M., & Shelden, M. (2004). *Girls, delinquency, and juvenile justice* (3rd ed.). Belmont, CA: Wadsworth.

Cooperrider, D. L. (1990). Positive image, positive action: The affirmative basis of organizing. In S. Srivastva & D. L. Cooperrider (Eds.), *Appreciative management and leadership* (pp. 91–125). San Francisco: Jossey-Bass.

Cooperrider, D. L., & Srivastva, S. (1987). Appreciative inquiry in organizational life. In R. Woodman & W. Pasmore (Eds.), *Research in organizational change and development.* (Vol. 1, pp. 129–169). Greenwich, CT: JAI.

Denzin, N. K. (1989). *Interpretive interactionism.* Newbury Park, CA: Sage.

Geiger, B., & Fischer, M. (2003). Female repeat offenders negotiating identity. *International Journal of Offender Therapy and Comparative Criminology, 47*(5), 496–515.

Geiger, B., & Fischer, M. (2005). Naming oneself criminal: Gender differences in offenders' identity negotiation. *International Journal of Offender Therapy and Comparative Criminology, 49*(2), 194–209. (Reproduced in *In her own words: Women offenders' views on crime and victimization,* pp. 45–54, by L. F. Alarid & P. Cromwell, Eds., 2006, Los Angeles, CA: Roxbury.)

Gergen, K. (1990). Affect and organization in postmodern society. In S. Srivastva & D. L. Cooperrider (Eds.). *Appreciative management and leadership* (pp. 153–174). San Francisco: Jossey-Bass.

Gergen, K. (1994). *Toward transformation in social knowledge* (2nd ed.). Thousand Oaks, CA: Sage.

Goldkamp, J. S. (2000, October). *What we know about the impact of drug courts: Moving research from "Do they work?" "When and how do they work?" Testimony before the Senate Judiciary Subcommittee on Youth Violence.* U.S. Department of Justice, Bureau of Justice Assistance.

Goldkamp, J. S., Weiland, D., & Moore, J. (2001). *The Philadelphia treatment court, its development and impact: The second phase (1998–2000).* Philadelphia: Crime and Justice Research Institute.

Gottfredson, D., & Exum, M. L. (2002). The Baltimore city drug treatment court: One year results from a randomized study. *Journal of Research in Crime & Delinquency, 39,* 227–356.

Hagan, J., & McCarthy, B. (1992). Streetlife and delinquency. *British Journal of Sociology, 43,* 533–561.

Hora, P. E, Schma, W. G., & Rosenthal, J. T. A. (1999). Therapeutic jurisprudence and the drug court movement: Revolutionizing the criminal justice system's response to drug abuse and crime in America. *Notre Dame Law Review, 74,* 439–538.

Merlo, A. (1995). Female criminality in the 1990s. In A. Merlo & J. M. Pollock (Eds.), *Women, law and social control* (pp. 119–134). Boston: Allyn & Bacon.

National Institute of Justice. (1998). *Women offenders programming needs and promising approaches.* Washington, DC: Office of Justice Programs.

Nolan, J., Jr. (2002). *Drug courts in theory and in practice.* New York: Walter de Gruyter.

Patton, M. Q. (2002). *Qualitative research and evaluation methods* (3rd ed.). Thousand Oaks, CA: Sage.

Piaget, J. (1966). *The moral judgment of the child* (M. Gabois, Trans.). New York: Free Press.

Plummer, K. (1995). Life story research. In J. N. Smith, R. Harre, & L. V. Langenhove (Eds.), *Rethinking methods in psychology* (pp. 50–63). London: Sage.

Prochaska, J. O., DiClemente, C. C, & Norcross, J. (1992). In search of how people change: Applications to addictive behavior. *American Psychologist, 47,* 1102–1114.

Satel, S. L. (1998). Observational study of courtroom dynamics in selected drug courts. *National Drug Court Institute Review, 1*(1), 56–87.

Satel, S. L. (2000). Drug treatment: The case for coercion. *National Drug Court Institute Review, 3*(1), 1–57.

Whitney, D., & Cooperrider, D. L. (2000). The appreciative inquiry summit: An emerging methodology for whole system positive change. *Journal of the Organization Development Network, 32,* 13–26.

20

Jurors' Views of Civil Lawyers: Implications for Courtroom Communication

Valerie P. Hans and Krista Sweigart

<u>Abstract</u>: *Valerie Hans and Krista Sweigart find that communication skills are necessary for lawyers to convey the merits of a case to jurors. Despite the significance of these exchanges, there have been surprisingly few studies on how jurors perceive attorneys. According to the authors, many attorneys overestimate the importance of their opening and closing statements. Although the opening and closing statements prove important as a means of structuring a logical argument, the majority of jurors remain neutral after the opening statement and claim that the closing statement did not overly affect their decision. The authors claim that the popular conception that attorneys do not have to be likeable to present an effective case is a myth. Instead, the authors find that demeanor and likeability was a key factor in the jurors' evaluations of the credibility and sincerity of the lawyer. Hans and Sweigart also determine that excessive use of emotional appeal and dramatics can hinder the credibility and sincerity of an attorney's case. Attorneys that employ overly aggressive interrogation tactics are also deemed less credible.*

I. Introduction

A. Conceptions and Misconceptions of Attorneys

In a recent address to a conference on communication in the courtroom sponsored by The Annenberg Washington Program, Robert Sayler, Chair-Elect of the Section of Litigation for the American Bar Association, asserted that many trial lawyers miscommunicate because they hold fundamental misconceptions about juries. The first misconception is that many attorneys believe that they should not be concerned about whether or not the jury likes them. Sayler claims that it does matter how jurors feel about attorneys because people accept a message more readily when they like the messenger. The second misconception is that jurors want to see a warrior or "Rambo" attorney. Sayler argues that warrior tactics reduce the attorney's credibility when it counts: An attorney who is constantly on the attack loses the opportunity to signal to the jury when he or she feels the witness really is lying. The idea that juries expect to be entertained is the third misconception that Sayler attributes to attorneys. He maintains that it is not bad to entertain, but cautions that entertaining can come to overshadow the evidence. The use of drama might cause juries to think that dramatics are necessary because the case is weak. Drama can also hurt the attorney's case if jurors do not like the theatrical presentation. Then, too, constant entertainment can become old and boring. The fourth misconception is that juries decide cases by the end of the opening statements. Sayler flatly rejects this premise, stating that although there used to be evidence supporting this view, more current work shows that jurors decide cases based on the evidence presented during trials. The idea that preparation can hurt an attorney's case because it produces nonspontaneous responses is the fifth misconception identified by Sayler. On the contrary, preparation is necessary and produces relaxed witnesses who are more credible. Finally, Sayler refutes the ideas that jurors respond to emotional rather than rational arguments, and that the trial judge does not matter. Sayler concludes that attorneys may miscommunicate with juries because attorneys simply do not know what factors jurors believe are important when making a decision. By relying on false assumptions, attorneys may not be defending their clients as effectively as they otherwise might.

Sayler appears to have based his assessment of attorney misconceptions about jurors on his own extensive experience and knowledge about the jury, but many of the observations he makes are supported by standard trial tactics handbooks and by social science data.

Several studies buttress Sayler's general point that attorneys have significant misconceptions about jurors' views of them. Opinion surveys conducted by Mindes and Adcock discovered divergence among (1) the public's view of lawyers, (2) lawyers' views of themselves, and (3) lawyers' views of how the public perceives them. These researchers polled 321 lay respondents and 305 lawyers to determine what images each group held about the occupation of the lawyer. Lawyers were also asked to estimate how the public viewed their occupation. There was a good deal of overlap across lay and lawyer samples in the characteristics ascribed to lawyers. However, lawyers believed that the public view of them was worse than it really was. Attorneys thought the public saw them as more likely to be greedy, tricky, evasive, manipulative, and overbearing than the public really did. They also thought the public saw them as less helpful, cooperative, understanding, and likable than the public actually did. Overall, the attorneys attributed to the public a view of lawyers that was high on "trickster" or "shyster" qualities and low on "helper" qualities. Attorneys apparently believe that their profession is viewed in a poor light, which may cause attorneys to act in the courtroom in a way more congruent with the way they think the public sees them rather than the way the public actually does.

When attorneys step into the courtroom, they may overestimate their own abilities as attorneys. In one inventive study conducted by Linz, Penrod, and McDonald, trained in-court observers watched the opening statements of fifty criminal trials and rated attorneys on factors such as friendliness, enthusiasm, and nervousness. The researchers compared the observers' ratings and jurors' evaluations of the attorneys with the attorneys' own self-perceptions. Although prosecutors showed no such difference, defense attorneys' ratings of their opening statements differed significantly from the evaluations of the courtroom observers along several dimensions. For both types of attorneys—prosecutors and defenders—there was no correlation between the number of trials in which they had participated or their years in practice and the observers' judgments of their rapport, enthusiasm, or articulateness. The researchers discovered that jurors' judgments and lawyers' self-evaluations correlated significantly for only some characteristics. The researchers also found that the greater the number of years an attorney was in practice, the greater the likelihood that the attorney would underestimate his or her level of nervousness, and overestimate his or her level of friendliness. Thus, although attorneys did not necessarily become more effective communicators as their careers progressed, they became more confident in their skills. It is not surprising to learn that lawyers hold misconceptions about effective trial tactics or even about their own abilities and performances. One of the key factors in promoting accurate self-perception is feedback. Frequent, specific feedback increases our chances of learning what others think of us. Yet the trial situation is one that precludes attorneys from learning what the key decision makers, the jurors, think about them and their actions. True, the jurors reach a verdict in each case, but that verdict reflects the multiple influences of the merits of the evidence, the strengths of the witnesses, the idiosyncrasies of the individual jurors, and the lawyers' impact. Litigators are often stymied in learning from experience because it is difficult to disentangle the different factors producing a favorable or unfavorable outcome in a case.

It would be valuable, then, to know what is in the minds of jurors as they observe attorneys' courtroom communications. A few studies have looked at the impact of lawyer characteristics on juror outcomes by examining actual jury trials and verdicts. In Kalven and Zeisel's landmark study of judge-jury agreement, the researchers asked trial judges presiding over criminal jury trials to indicate whether the attorneys were evenly balanced or whether the defense or the prosecution was superior. In 76% of the trials, the judges viewed the attorneys as evenly matched, and approximately the same percentage of defense and prosecuting attorneys were seen as superior (11% versus 13%, respectively). Additional analyses led Kalven and Zeisel to conclude that in only a little over 1% of all trials did the presence of superior defense counsel cause the jury to reach a verdict that was different from one that the judge would have reached had the judge been trying the same case without a jury.

While Kalven and Zeisel had to rely on global judicial evaluations of attorney behavior, another study conducted by Norbert Kerr correlated student observers' in-court ratings with the case outcomes in 113 criminal jury trials in San Diego. Kerr found that specific ratings of the defense and the prosecuting attorneys were in some instances significantly related to which side won the case. The greater the defense attorney's working knowledge of the evidence, the more convincing the arguments the defense advanced, and the more supportive the defense was toward the prosecutor, then the more likely the defense was to prevail. In a counterintuitive set of findings, the more supportive the prosecutor was toward the defense attorney and the more interested and respectful the prosecutor appeared to be, the *less* likely the prosecutor was to prevail.

Because many different factors varied, along with attorneys, in both the Kalven and Zeisel study and the Kerr study, it is difficult to make causal inferences about how the specific tactics or characteristics of an attorney influence case outcomes. Several mock-juror research studies, most using college students as subjects, have looked at aspects of attorney behavior or characteristics that appear to influence mock jurors. These studies have an advantage in that only one or a few characteristics are varied in a single study, making causal inferences possible. But, they are limited in that the evaluations are based upon hypothetical cases, and most use college students as subjects, representing a skewed group of respondents.

Although trial tactics manuals evidence great interest in juror perceptions, this brief summary of the available research shows that few studies, aside from the one conducted by Linz and his colleagues, have taken a systematic look at actual jurors' perceptions of attorneys and their communication strategies, indicating the value of the present project.

B. Summary

In light of the limited research in the area and the misconceptions that attorneys appear to hold about jurors, it is important to look more methodically at what qualities and actions impress jurors during actual cases. We attempt to identify some of these factors in our analyses of interviews with civil trial jurors.

II. Research Method

A. Cases and Participants

This study of jurors' views of civil lawyers, based on a total of ninety-nine tape-recorded interviews, is part of a larger interview study examining the reactions of 269 jurors to cases with business and corporate parties. During a one-year period in a state court of general jurisdiction, every civil jury trial that involved a business or corporate party was identified and included.

With the trial judges' permission, the names, addresses, and telephone numbers of jurors were obtained from the court files. Letters were sent to jurors on University of Delaware stationery requesting them to participate in an interview study about their experiences as jurors. Following the initial letter, a research assistant telephoned each juror. In an effort to contact the jurors, up to ten telephone calls and two additional letters were sent to the jurors. Only a small percentage of jurors could not be contacted by these methods.

The overall response rate of the jurors was sixty-four percent, with an average of seven out of twelve jurors on each case agreeing to participate. In total, there were 269 participants from thirty-six cases involving businesses and corporations. There were twenty-eight tort and eight contract cases. The subjects of the cases consisted of disputes over contracts, job-related injuries, consumer injuries, product liability, automobile accidents, and medical malpractice.

All quotes and data used in this article are from the tape-recorded interviews with ninety-nine jurors in these particular cases. In the fourteen cases that are being used, one or more plaintiffs sued business, corporate, or professional defendants. Nine of the cases dealt with personal or consumer injuries, four with contract disputes, and one with medical malpractice. The plaintiffs were successful in twelve of the fourteen cases, a success rate similar to that in the total sample of cases. The juror response rate for the cases used was comparable to the overall response rate for the entire project.

Forty-one attorneys were listed in court records as participating in the fourteen cases. Twenty-two represented defendants, and nineteen represented plaintiffs. One attorney represented a defendant in two cases. Using the *Martindale-Hubble* directory of lawyers, state bar directories, and telephone contacts, the law schools attended by thirty-six of these attorneys were identified. The remaining five attorneys could not be traced using any of these methods.

B. Procedure

Jurors were interviewed individually using a semi-structured interview format. In the interviews, jurors were asked to give their reaction to the parties, attorneys, and evidence in their case. The interviews were audio-taped and open-ended responses were allowed. A lengthy set of questions were used to determine the factors that jurors considered significant in reaching the verdict in their case.

III. Results

A. Influence of Opening Statements

In the interviews, the jurors were asked if they were drawn to either the plaintiff's or the defendant's side after the opening statements, or if they had remained neutral. While trial consultant Donald Vinson and others claim that most jurors' minds are made up after the opening statements, sixty-three percent of the jurors we interviewed maintained that they had remained neutral after the opening statements. In ten of the fourteen cases in our sample, the majority of jurors in those cases indicated that they were not drawn to either side after the opening statements. In two other cases, the majority of jurors interviewed reported being drawn to the plaintiff, while in the final two cases there was no clear majority position.

1. Why Jurors Said They Tried to Stay Neutral

In responding to the question about whether they had been drawn to one side or the other by the opening statements, jurors indicated a number of factors that led them to try to remain neutral. In their accounts, jurors cited the following factors: the judge's instructions, the lack of evidence at that point in the trial, the fact that they were genuinely undecided, or a desire to resist the impulse to be swayed by their emotions.

The main reason jurors said they were undecided after the opening statements was that they were following the judge's instructions to remain neutral. One juror who wanted to be careful to heed the judge's instructions stated: "[T]he whole idea that really stuck with my mind was that the opening [statements] were to be something you heard, but really didn't hear; you didn't base your decision on what was said in an opening [statement], but more what was going to come later." When maintaining that they were undecided after the opening statements, jurors often referred specifically to the instructions the judge had given them. A male juror explained, "The judge instructed us at the beginning not to take sides ... but to just ... soak up the information. Take your notes and think about it." Jurors who mentioned the judge's instructions regarding opening statements support the contention that most jurors strive to be responsible, to be "good jurors," and to follow the instructions they are given as closely as possible.

Other jurors who did not choose sides following the opening statements expressed a desire to be as neutral as possible. A forty-seven-year-old male juror showed a keen understanding of the nature of the adversarial process when he stated: "I was keeping an open mind throughout, because I know there's always two sides to a story, and sometimes you can be drawn [to one], and then later on see more evidence and sway to the other. . . ." A female juror with some college education wanted to wait to make a decision until she had heard from the plaintiff and the witnesses. She did not want to base her decision solely on the lawyers' opening statements: "I got an impression of both the lawyers themselves, but I kept on trying to repeat to myself that it's not those particular people that we were judging, and so I would have to say that that [was not] a deciding factor."

Lack of evidence was the second reason jurors commonly gave for remaining undecided after the opening statements. Without any proof to back up what the lawyers were saying, the jurors were unwilling to make even a tentative decision. One juror from an asbestos case said, "I had no feeling because I didn't have enough detailed information to really draw a conclusion one way or the other. . . ." The unwillingness of the jurors to take the lawyers' words at face value may be due to a distrust of lawyers. In the same asbestos case, another juror expressed some suspicion when he stated that he was not favoring one side over the other because "I wanted to hear the actual evidence . . . to see what was actually presented and whether they could back up their statements . . . [to see] if they were true or not."

Another rationale jurors gave for not being swayed by the opening statements was that the jurors understood the lawyer's job was to sway them, and they intended to resist being influenced so early in the case. When one male juror was asked if he had been "drawn to one side or the other," he responded, "That's what they wanted us to [do]. They were drawing us out, they were choosing sides, that's what the lawyers were trying to do." A sixty-year-old male juror with a high school diploma said that he did not want to make a premature decision:

> At that stage of the game, no. Not until I actually had in my hot little hands the documents that the lawyers were presenting, back and forth. Because they're great at picking up a piece of paper and reading off what they want you to read, and then . . . when it's time for rebuttal, they read what [the other lawyer] read, and then they read the rest of it. So, actually between lawyers, as far as I'm concerned, it's all a big act.

The juror saw that the attorneys were trying to sway him, and he wanted to wait for the actual evidence to make a decision.

Some jurors genuinely felt that they were not drawn to either side during the opening statements because both sides sounded so convincing. These jurors frequently mentioned that they felt both lawyers had brought out good points in their openings.

> [H]e made such a convincing introduction that before the other man got up, you would think, "Well, boy, I know I'm going to be on this guy's side." Or, "I know that this really sounds right."

> But, then when the other guy got up, he made such convincing statements, which were just the
> opposite, that you said, "Oh, well, I didn't think of that before."

With persuasive information from both the plaintiffs' and the defendants' attorneys, the jurors chose to remain undecided because, for them, there was no clear choice of who should win. A female juror explained, "I was half and half. There was a time I was gone for the plaintiff, and then there was a time I was gone for the defendant."

One element that some jurors felt was inappropriate in the opening statements was an exceptional amount of emotional appeal. This foreshadowed the jurors' negative reaction to excessive emotional appeals in later stages of the trial. Although most conceded that emotional appeal was an inevitable part of a case involving an injured plaintiff, they refused to make it their sole basis for being swayed by the opening statements in most cases. When one juror was asked if she favored one side or the other, she responded:

> No. I felt that the opening [statements] were a lot of sob stories, and they weren't that, espe-
> cially on the plaintiff's part, they wanted you to really feel sorry for these guys . . . [to] draw you
> into their personal lives, and I was determined I wasn't going to get drawn in, so no, I person-
> ally was not swayed by the opening [statements].

A young female juror discussed how her neighbor had suffered problems from asbestos similar to the ones the plaintiff had experienced in the case in which she was a juror. She felt an emotional urge to side immediately with the plaintiff, but she was firm when she stated, "I can't let my emotional feelings interfere with what . . . I'm supposed to be doing."

One can observe from these statements that jurors struggled to resist efforts to appeal to them emotionally. This resistance is reminiscent of some of the psychological research on how people react to one-sided persuasive communications in a two-sided communication context.

2. Why Jurors Said They Were Drawn to One Side after the Opening Statements

In a minority of instances, jurors reported being swayed by one side or the other by the opening statements. Overall, twenty percent of the individual jurors interviewed sided with the plaintiff following opening statements, and eight percent sided with the defendant.

In one case in which the majority of the jurors reported being drawn to the plaintiff's side after the opening statements, the defense attorney was trying his first case and was painfully nervous. Jurors cited this factor as the reason they were drawn to the other side. In another case where the jurors were drawn to the plaintiff's side, the defense attorney was viewed by many of the jurors as especially slovenly and obnoxious. The jurors were offended by his demeanor and chose early on to side with the plaintiff.

Other jurors reported that after the opening statements, it seemed clear that the side they had chosen was right. One juror favoring the plaintiff said that she had decided, right from the beginning: "I don't know why. I thought that it seemed reasonable, how the accident happened, and I didn't have any trouble with it. I sort of leaned right to his side from the very beginning." Thus the minority of jurors who admitted being drawn to one side or the other after the opening reported that either attorney demeanor or the merits of the case had influenced them. What is most striking, however, is how few jurors acknowledged that they were drawn to one side or the other by the opening statements.

B. Influence of Closing Arguments

Near the end of many of the interviews, jurors were asked if the closing arguments had an impact in convincing or changing their minds. In forty-four percent of the interviews, the question was either not asked or not answered. This was usually because, in the course of the interviews, many jurors stated their preference before the interviewer reached that question so the question was omitted. However, eighty percent of those jurors who were asked the question said that the closing arguments had not caused them to be drawn to one side or the other. In many cases, the jurors had already decided what side they were going to favor before the closing arguments.

Of the jurors asked about closing arguments, those who reported being drawn to the plaintiff's side and those who reported being drawn to the defendant's side by the closing arguments were nearly even. Eleven percent of the jurors said they were drawn to the plaintiff's side, while nine percent reported being drawn to the defendant's side. In none of the fourteen cases did a majority of the jurors report being drawn to either one side or the other by the closing arguments.

Some jurors reported not being swayed by the closing arguments because they saw them more as a summary of the case than an actual argument. They realized that the attorneys were trying to remind them of all that had transpired during the case. Some jurors expressed disappointment that the closing arguments were not as exciting as those they had seen on television or in the movies. One juror explained: "They weren't as strong as I thought they would be. Basically, it was just a brief summation from what went on. . . . [I]t was nothing glorifying, like you see on Perry Mason." Some jurors did feel that the attorneys were trying to sway them: "They were, at that point, both trying to leave their impression upon us, to convince us one way or the other. If the evidence didn't do it, possibly their last remarks would." These jurors often mentioned the fact that the plaintiffs attorney not only gave a closing argument, but also could rebut the defense attorney's closing argument. They felt it was unfair that the plaintiff had "two shots" at the jury:

> The [plaintiff] had the last word if I remember right, and I think he did. I think the last words said [are] what sticks in the jurors; minds the most; he's got the opportunity to contradict everything that [the defense attorney] said in his closing argument and I think that stuck with most people. I think he had a distinct advantage there.

Overall, the jurors expressed some disappointment in the closing arguments. They were frustrated that they were once again hearing what they had already heard in the opening statements and in the actual case. Some had envisioned climactic endings to their trials and were let down to realize the closing arguments were basically a summation of the facts. A retired female juror said, "Well, they were very much the same . . . rehashed over the same things. It was such a repetition." By the end of the trial some jurors also seemed disheartened by the adversarial nature of the cases. A juror complained that the closing arguments were "too long, too drawn out, too predictable. You knew what [the plaintiff] was going to say, you knew what [the defendant] was going to say, the complete opposite."

C. Creating a Framework

Although most jurors reported that their preference for one side or the other was not influenced exclusively by the opening statements and closing arguments, it would be a mistake to infer that the opening and closing had no impact. Further analysis of jurors' comments revealed that the opening and closing were critically important in providing a framework. Many jurors mentioned that the opening statements and closing arguments created a framework within which they viewed the case, and gave the case a clear structure that it might have otherwise lacked. By outlining in the opening statements the ideas that they were going to advance and later summing up the facts in the closing arguments, the attorneys gave the jurors a coherent idea of what to expect in the trial and of what they had delivered. This use of attorney communication is, of course, quite consistent with the story model of jury decision making described earlier.

The jurors used the opening statements to help them determine what they should be looking for in the case. After hearing the statements, the jurors felt they had a good idea of what was going to happen throughout the case. As a male college graduate explained:

> The plaintiff went first. He told the general overview of the case, and how he was going to try to prove his point. And the defense did the same thing. He gave a general overview of the case: and how he was going to prove his point, who he was going to call, [and] that we were going to have some taped testimony on videotape.

Similarly, a twenty-year-old juror felt that the opening statements were an attempt to "set the stage" of the case.

Many of the jurors thought the closing arguments were useful to clarify issues that had become confused during the trial. A female juror said the closing argument "was just summing things up to me and refreshing my memory. Kind of like making me go back to the beginning, to make me remember what was important down the road until this point for me."

Lawyers also had the opportunity in closing arguments to show the jurors the consistency of their arguments throughout the trial. A juror in a personal injury case said, "I believe the [plaintiff's attorney] put a lot of things back together as far as what he tried to do right from the start and how it paralleled his introduction." Without the closing arguments, jurors may not have been able to sift through the information the attorneys presented. Especially in long trials, jurors apparently began to confuse the arguments presented by the plaintiff and the defendant. One juror expressed the importance that the closing arguments held for her:

> I think it sort of just tied up some loose ends; it reiterated some stuff that was said in the begin-ning that I might have lost track of along the way. And it also led me to realize that they were boxing heads, solidified in my mind that they had actually two sides. Because when you get to hear all these plaintiffs and witnesses, and folks are up cross-examining each other, you begin to think, "Well, just who was for who, what was for what?" And you're taking down all the facts, but you have to go back and look over your notes to just really decide what you're going—you know, what your idea is, or what your thoughts are. However, in the closing arguments, it sort of brought it all back into perspective . . . [and made] you . . . remember that there are two sides.

Even if jurors reported that they stayed neutral during the opening statements and closing arguments, an attorney who clearly expressed the structure of the case appeared to have an advantage in encouraging jurors to focus on and recall the material that supported his or her client.

D. Jurors' General Views of Attorney Qualities

In addition to asking specific questions about opening statements and closing arguments, we also asked jurors to provide a general evaluation and ranking of the attorneys in their cases. Slightly more jurors reported favoring the plaintiff's attorney (thirty-seven percent) than the defendant's attorney (thirty-one percent). The remainder expressed no opinion or thought that the attorneys were evenly matched. Similarly, in five of the fourteen cases in the sample, a majority of jurors chose the plaintiffs representative as superior, compared to three cases in which jurors chose the defendant's attorney as the superior one. The small number of cases precluded us from conducting a statistical test to determine whether the perceived superiority of the attorney translated into a favorable case outcome.

1. What Made One Attorney Better

Issues that appeared to influence the way jurors evaluated attorneys were the credibility and demeanor of the attorneys, the emotionality of their arguments, and their organization of the case. Attorneys who were not credible, had poor demeanor, used excessive appeals to the jurors' sympathy, or were poorly organized tended to alienate the jurors.

It is interesting to note that jurors expressed ambivalence about emotionality in the arguments. They liked a small amount, but resented extreme appeals to their sympathy. In addition, the level of emotionality in argument was evaluated against the severity of injuries claimed in the case.

These points are best illustrated by specific examples from cases in which one attorney was considered to be better than the other. In one case involving a sports injury that left the plaintiff paralyzed, the majority of the jurors who favored the plaintiff's attorney referred to the level of the attorney's organization in explaining why they preferred him. Since he appeared to be better organized, the jurors concluded that he was a better attorney. Moreover, the defendant's lawyers did not seem to be as involved in the proceedings. A female juror explained:

> [The defense attorney] used the plaintiff's material so often, I felt that he was not as prepared as the other lawyer. He was forever leafing through, like he was confused, he wanted to find this, he wanted to find that. . . . And I felt that the lawyer from the company, as the time went on, he was not there a hundred percent of the time. But when he was there, he just didn't . . . seem to be interested.

The plaintiff's attorney came across as more likable. He used an amount of emotional appeal that the jurors felt was appropriate in this particular case. Although he tried to evoke the jurors' sympathy, his approach was not viewed as excessive given his severely injured client. None of the jurors felt he was exaggerating the injuries in order to play upon their emotions. A male juror said, "His was more of an emotional plea, whereas the other man was more of a legal correctness, who made a mistake and who didn't." This approach, focusing on the legal aspects of the case, tended to make the defense attorney appear unsympathetic to the plight of the severely injured victim. Throughout the interviews, the jurors described the defense attorney as "cold," "calculating," and "callous."

Even though no juror favored the defendant's lawyer over the plaintiff's, jurors did not believe that he was a bad attorney. The jurors simply tended to favor the approach of the plaintiff's attorney. A male juror explained the differences between the two lawyers:

> They were both good lawyers, and the thing of it was that they both have opposite personalities. One man was . . . a more story-type, personable, warm-type guy, and the other man was very legal and precision-minded, very dry, cut and dry, unemotional. . . . [The plaintiff's attorney], he was more positive and more flowery and descriptive and colorful and story-type. The other man was negative. He was . . . looking for everything that was wrong all the time, picking out all the dark, negative things, and enlarging on them deliberately. He seemed to be like one of these birds in the air that fly over, he never sees any beautiful scene, he just sees a dead cat on the ground or something like that. You know, always seeing the bad, the negative. So . . . those . . . were . . . their two different approaches.

In the case mentioned previously in which the defendant's attorney was trying his first case and was apparently very nervous, his nervous appearance put him at a disadvantage in the jurors' minds. The majority of jurors evaluated the plaintiff's attorney more positively. A male juror with graduate school experience explained:

> I thought that [the plaintiff's lawyer] had a better composure; I don't know that he displayed more skill or more insight or more intelligence about the case or the way to handle a case. Nor do I think that he displayed less. I thought in those respects they were equal, except [the defendant's lawyer] was a lot more nervous.

Throughout the interviews with jurors from this case, the main topic in the discussions of the quality of the attorneys was the defense lawyer's extreme nervousness. His nervousness was so intense that it made some jurors uncomfortable. A female juror said, "I felt embarrassed at the defendant's lawyer because he was new and he was making all these mistakes." The plaintiff's attorney may have looked better in relation to the defendant's attorney simply because he was more composed, but there are suggestions in some juror interviews that the nervousness also detrimentally influenced the organization of the case presentation. A thirty-five-year-old female compared the attorneys:

> There was a great difference. I mean, [the plaintiff's attorney] knew what he was doing or appeared to know what he was doing, and he was very cool and very collected and had all his facts together. I mean, he went through every witness and you could tell that his questions were

preplanned. And when he crossed he had everything written down and went right down in order. . . . [The defendant's attorney], on the other hand, had a very confusing way of addressing everything. He would put a chart up as to certain dates when the accident occurred, when she was released from the hospital, the first time she went to the doctor, and he would just put them up there in sort of a jumbled fashion. And he would bounce around, and it was very distracting at first, until you got used to him. And he was very, very disorganized all through the whole thing.

The defense attorney did help his situation somewhat by informing the jury that it was his first trial. A male juror reported:

I thought it was wise of him at a point in the trial to indicate to the jury that, "this is my first trial." But not come out and say, "I'm nervous because this is my first." [While examining a witness,] he very wisely pointed out that, "You're very nervous. Are you normally like this?" And she said, "No, I've never been on trial before." And he said "Well, I've never been on trial either, this is my first trial so we're both nervous." And they kind of kept going. But I thought it was excellent of him to point out to us, "I'm nervous because this is my first trial, not because of the case."

The lawyer's comments about his first trial let the jurors know that he was nervous for a reason other than the quality of his case. Otherwise, the jurors could have misread his nervousness to be an indication that he was not confident about the information he was presenting.

The preparedness of the lawyers was an important issue to the jurors in many of the cases. Not surprisingly, a well-prepared case tended to appear stronger. In a contract dispute case in which seventy-five percent of the jurors favored the plaintiff's attorney, the plaintiff presented a significantly greater amount of evidence than the defendant. Jurors saw this as an indication that the defense attorney was either too confident or had no case at all. A female juror said:

The plaintiff's attorney was definitely well-prepared. There's no doubt about it, he definitely had enough [evidence]. As a matter of fact he had too much information as it kept getting him into trouble. If he wouldn't drop it, he'd be looking for it, constantly fumbling through all pages looking for what he was looking for. He reminded you of the absent-minded professor, but he presented his case very well, needless to say. The defense attorney, I think they thought the case was out and dry, that they didn't have to present anything to us.

Although the plaintiff's attorney may have been a bit disorganized, his huge volume of material impressed the jurors enough to make up for it. The defense attorney's lack of material to present made him appear cocky or arrogant.

A female juror with some college experience also felt that the defense attorney was doing the minimum necessary to present the case:

All along I felt that the defense attorney just—really, I don't know, . . . he really was defending. I mean he was doing what he was supposed to do but, it was not like a proactive kind of an argument. It was just, "Well you said this, but . . . ." He wasn't as strong as [the plaintiff's attorney].

In another personal injury case, many of the jurors did not perceive the defendant's attorney as professional or credible. Four of the six jurors who chose the plaintiff as the superior lawyer mentioned that the appearance or demeanor of the defendant's attorney was inappropriate. A male juror stated: "The key issue had to be appearance, demeanor, credibility. [The defendant] or his attorney did not come across as professional, trustworthy, honest. We all said this in that courtroom. It was not very difficult to reach a decision." The difference between the two attorneys was clear to that juror:

> You had the clean-cut, professional-looking attorney, and you had this guy, [the defense attorney,] who certainly didn't appear—he did not have the credibility he should have [had, because of] his appearance. . . . I think his appearance took away from a lot of what he had to say . . .. His shirttails were hanging out, his shirt was wrinkled. He really did not have a professional [attitude].

The plaintiff's attorney, on the other hand, was well-respected by the jurors. A female juror said, "I thought he did an excellent job. He kept to the facts and didn't exaggerate anything and didn't make it emotional or anything."

An unusual aspect of this case was the fact that the defendant himself was an attorney. The defendant tended to get involved in the defense of his case, and two of the six jurors who sided with the plaintiff's attorney mentioned that his involvement had disturbed them. A male juror explained:

> I think [the defense attorney] was a puppet and he was doing what he was told to by [the defendant]. Because [the defendant] was at his side, and anything that the plaintiff would present, [the defendant] would go ahead and tell [the defense attorney] what it was, he would whisper in his ear a bunch of things. [The defendant] would write something down and would hand it to him and he would get up there and talk. It seems he was doing what he was told to by [the defendant].

These jurors felt that the defendant's attorney should have controlled the case, not the defendant. The defense attorney's lack of control in the case made him look weak in the jurors' eyes.

The final case in which the plaintiff's attorneys were viewed as better by a majority of jurors was an asbestos case. No single issue arose that marked the plaintiff's attorneys as superior; rather, the jurors generally felt they were better lawyers. Unlike another asbestos case in our study, the plaintiff's attorneys did not suffer in this instance because they specialized in a particular type of claim. In the other asbestos case, jurors were hostile to the idea that a lawyer would bring numerous asbestos claims. They saw this practice as attorneys "manufacturing" cases in order to make more money and described the plaintiffs' attorney as an "ambulance chaser." In contrast, in this case, jurors actually saw it as an advantage to specialize: "I know that there [are] lawyers that specialize in different fields—[prosecuting] murder[ers], suing, corporations, paperwork, and that kind of thing. I know there must be at least a half dozen categories or whatever it is. And when you specialize in that one field you become good at it . . . ." In this case, jurors did not seem at all disturbed by the idea that the lawyers were repeatedly bringing one type of claim. They rejected the notion put forth by the defense that this practice was unfair. A female juror said: "There was a little conjecture, and the defense tried to point out that there was a conspiracy of some sort. But as the trial progressed, we all came to the conclusion that there was damage that had been done to these people, and it really wasn't their fault." The defendants' attorney suffered because he did not appear as knowledgeable about cases involving asbestos injuries. A male high school graduate explained:

> This other fellow, [the defendant's attorney], he didn't know it that well. It just seemed like he took a crash course in it and got as much information pertaining to it and had to study it the night before to come in prepared. But the other guy, he knew his stuff.

There were three cases in which the defendant's attorney was considered the better attorney. In all three cases, calm defense attorneys opposed very emotional plaintiffs' attorneys. The defense attorneys seemed to have benefitted from the comparison.

The plaintiff in one case was injured as the result of a car accident. Her attorney used many arguments that jurors felt were designed to appeal to their emotions. Although jurors recognized the woman was hurt, they felt the plaintiff's attorney was exaggerating her injuries. It is useful to contrast jurors' negative reactions to emotionality in this case with their more neutral reactions to emotionality in the case involving the paralyzed plaintiff in the sports injury case. It appears to be important that attorneys carefully calibrate the amount of emotion they express in a case to the seriousness of the injury. Jurors did not automatically resent emotion, but instead resisted emotion that seemed out of proportion with the injury. Since the attorney in the car accident case made the plaintiff's injuries seem more serious than they appeared to be, he lost credibility. A male juror who works as a security officer explained:

> He was overly dramatic. You know what I'm talking about? Since it was about the case, he kept saying how perfect her body was before the accident . . . he made her almost seem like a cripple, but we could all look at her and see that there was no neck brace, no wheelchair, nothin', you know? And we're all just like . . . she looks fine to me.

It appears that jurors were annoyed by the constant emotional appeals in a case that they did not consider to be very serious. Also apparent is some suspicion on the part of the jurors about the plaintiff's claim of severe injury. Later in the interview the same juror said:

> [The plaintiff's lawyer] kept repeating: "This is our one shot. This lady has been calling for me for the last two years on the phone about this case, about her injuries, and her pain. And her pain will not go away, and this is our only shot, you people here. If we don't win, we can't come back. This is it." And we were all like, "So?"

The jurors were also confused in this case by the fact that the plaintiff's young son sat with her throughout the trial but did not testify. Six out of the eight jurors commented on this. They wanted to know why he was not in school. Many jurors saw this as a tactic to induce sympathy for the plaintiff and felt it was inappropriate. A female juror explained the reaction of the others involved in the case:

> We had one woman on the jury, she said "as soon as I walked in there and saw that boy sitting at the table I wondered why he wasn't at school." And they had said that he was having a civics lesson, the lawyer had said that he was there because this was a good civics lesson. [The jurors] didn't buy that, they weren't a bit sympathetic that the boy was there.

The son sitting with his mother seemed out of place to the jurors, and it became a major source of discussion during their deliberations. Most jurors assumed that it was a tactic or trick on the part of the plaintiff's attorney.

Throughout this personal injury case, few jurors referred to the defendant's attorney as a good attorney. It seemed that the jurors were rejecting the plaintiff's lawyer rather than commending the defendant's. The jurors seemed better able to respond to the calm, unemotional arguments that the defendant's attorney put forth, but this fact did not mean that they thought he was a superb attorney. A female juror described him: "He asked questions, he was very to the point, said what he had to say, that type." Another juror described him as "the lesser of two evils."

In another case pitting a calm defense attorney against a lawyer who was more emotional, one juror compared the attorneys:

> I guess [the defense attorney], you'd have to say, was a slicker. If you knew what a slick attorney was, that was a good definition of him. [The plaintiff's attorney] got a little more emotional sometimes. He'd get a little loud, scream and yell. [The defense attorney] would make his subtle theatrics: raise his eyebrows up in the air, look around the room. He'd sort of say "ha" without really saying it. He didn't really say it, but the jury could see him.

Jurors were more comfortable with the defense attorney's approach. He was thorough, but not excessive. The following juror explained, "[h]e was the best lawyer, because he was fighting for the case, but he wasn't going to an extreme." In contrast, the jurors distrusted the excessive emotional appeals of this plaintiff's lawyer, and felt he was exaggerating in his statements. As a result, the defense attorney and his client benefitted.

The final case where a defendant's attorney was favored by a majority of the jurors was another case in which the plaintiff's lawyer was very emotional (several of the jurors described him as a "showboat"), while the defendant's lawyer was calm and quiet. A male juror in his forties described the differences between the two attorneys:

> [The plaintiff's attorney] basically played on the emotional factor. Here's poor [plaintiff]: he's been damaged, he can't work, he can't bend, he can't walk, he can't stoop, he can't sit in a chair for more [than] ten minutes. Yet the guy sat in the chair for seven solid days and never moved. And he got to be quite flamboyant. And I had a little trouble with that. . . . [The defendant's] case was basically the facts. Here's what happened, here [are] the photographs, here's the testimony. Base your decision on what really happened in the case.

Jurors also felt that the plaintiff's attorney was exaggerating the plaintiff's injuries:

> I think his attorney was a little overzealous in trying to say [the plaintiff's] life had just come to an end and that if he didn't receive this settlement his life was going to be destroyed and he would never be able to take care of himself or his family and that . . . the thing that we as good citizens just had to do was award [the plaintiff] his six hundred thousand dollars. So I started to develop kind of a negative attitude about him probably around the third day of the case. The case went for seven days.

The emotionality of the plaintiff's attorney made him appear less believable to the jurors. They began to see him as a lawyer they could not trust. The defendant's attorney presented a straightforward argument; although the jurors did not feel she was exciting or especially talented, they did feel she was worthy of their trust. A male juror said, "I think I probably like [the defendant's attorney] a little better because she seemed to be playing it more legitimate than the [plaintiff's attorney] was."

2. Badgering the Witness

Jurors, especially female jurors, did not respond favorably to attorneys who attacked or badgered witnesses. It made the jurors feel uncomfortable and sometimes more sympathetic to the witness than they otherwise would have felt. In a knee injury case, the defense attorney badgered a female witness to the extent that a female juror began to identify with the witness and feel sorry for her:

> Another thing the plaintiff's attorney did at that point was to ask her if she had walked to the courtroom. She said, "Yes, I parked two blocks away." He said, "Do you have high heels on?," and she said, "No." And he, he frankly took her shoe off, and I would have been mortified if this were me, and showed it to the jury. And there was a small heel on there, but most working women do not wear flats. Even if you're in mortal pain, you're at least going to get a little bit of a heel out of it. And he really tried to rake, rake her over the coals over that. . . . So I really felt sorry for her there.

Being aggressive with a witness made the jurors dislike an attorney. A female juror described an especially forceful attorney:

> He was really cocky, and sometimes he'd be really mean and ugly to those people. [One witness] had a stutter, and as soon as he got up on the stand, it really came out. You couldn't understand him, and I thought [the attorney] was a little rude to him. I mean, I wanted to yell out, "Would you leave him alone!" But [I] didn't. I almost felt like you're in school. You didn't yell out, you didn't do any of that. You just kind of sat there, and it was like, "Urghh, leave, this guy alone!" . . . I wouldn't . . . like him at all if he came on to me that way.

Another juror acknowledged that she thought it was the role of the attorneys to try to upset and confuse witnesses, but she also understood that people cannot remember things perfectly—so witnesses are occasionally going to be inconsistent:

> I guess maybe . . . the [defendant's attorney] did a real good job of confusing him with dates and things like that which was annoying. He was kind of picking on him, but that's [his] job. And [the witness] was getting confused about some of the dates and the way that it had happened a long time ago. Anyone would be fuzzy about certain dates, when he had a doctor appointment and all that stuff.

In a case in which the defense attorney was reported by the jurors to have badgered a medical witness, the witness performed well under the circumstances and increased his credibility in the minds of many jurors. A male juror said:

> The lawyer kept baiting him, and baiting him, and baiting him. . . . He was getting pretty mad at the end. I think we all sympathized with the guy, so after a while the lawyer hurt himself more than anything because the doctor came with fixed straightforward answers, but he kept trying to bait the guy.

By constantly pressing the plaintiff's witness, the defendant's attorney made the jurors feel uncomfortable and sympathetic to the witness. Because the witness was consistently able to answer the attorney's questions during the cross-examination, the attorney actually increased the witness's credibility, instead of decreasing it.

Thus, in these cases the attorneys seemed to gain nothing from badgering a witness. The jurors were more likely to sympathize with roughly treated witnesses, and less likely to believe, when witnesses were badgered, that inconsistencies in their testimony were a result of weaknesses in the case.

3. Actors and Tricksters

Many of the jurors did not believe that the attorneys' actions were worthy of their trust. The word "actor" came up repeatedly throughout the interviews. Some jurors did not believe that the behaviors or the arguments of the attorneys were genuine; rather, they suspected the attorneys of playing a role in each case. Emotional displays by the attorneys were especially suspect. A male juror with some college experience said:

> When [the plaintiff] was on the witness stand, [the lawyer] started to break down in tears himself. Which I don't know if that . . . came natural, or whether that was part of the act. I don't know . . . when she started breaking down, he did too.

The juror had trouble believing that the lawyer might feel sympathy for the plight of his client. In the case with the nervous defense attorney, a female questioned his nervousness: "I just wondered, 'Is this a ploy to get our sympathy?,' because he was so nervous or 'Is he really like that?,' and that's the one thing that really stuck out in my mind, more than anything else." Instead of believing the attorney was nervous, the juror suspected the attorney of lying. Lawyers who showed excessive emotion—even nervousness—during the trial were considered by some jurors to be acting to elicit the jurors' sympathy.

Attorneys were also considered to be acting when they deviated from a straightforward approach while trying the case. Raised voices or abrupt actions were supposedly part of an act. A female juror said: "They were both very good at their theatrics, as far as hopping around, making faces. It was kind of funny. [The attorney] for the plaintiff—little guy—he'd get all fired up and hoot and holler. [The attorney] for the defense was very quiet." A male juror with college experience also saw these types of actions as part of an act:

> I enjoyed watching the lawyers go back and forth and some of the tactics that they would use. And, you know, the way they would roll their eyes. . . . I was really quite interested in the way the different attorneys played to the jury and played against each other. It was, it was very good. They must have been in drama class at one time.

Jurors seemed to neglect the possibility that the attorneys might actually get excited or frustrated during the progress of their case. Extreme displays of emotion appeared frequently to lower the attorney's credibility in the jurors' eyes.

Sometimes jurors suspected the attorneys of outright lying. They saw the lawyers as tricksters who would lie or try to manipulate the jury in order to sway them to their sides. A female homemaker said: "I think sometimes lawyers try to play games with your mind to try and make you, well, think their way. And I think it gets to the point where the jury has to decide who's lying." A juror from another case explained:

> [A]nd he was a lawyer, which was in the back of my mind too . . . because I kind of think . . . lawyers try to take you over. Maybe that was in the back of my mind too. [Lawyers] know the ins and outs to the whole thing, you know. While [the plaintiff] was just, a first time thing for him, he had an entirely different background.

Jurors also thought that attorneys might persuade plaintiffs to lie or to exaggerate their injuries. A juror who was a high school graduate thought the attorney had done this. "I think that [the plaintiff's] lawyer told her how to act and react. . . . She was very emotional and upset about it. I mean, she acted like it was yesterday when his hand got cut." The presentation of evidence by adversary attorneys thus appeared to alert jurors to be on guard for ways in which the evidence itself might be influenced by the attorneys.

IV. Discussion

A. Opening Statements and Closing Arguments

One of the most interesting sets of findings pertains to the jurors' estimates of how they were influenced by opening statements and closing arguments. Most jurors rejected the idea that they were strongly swayed by such arguments alone. They offered a variety of explanations for why they were not drawn to one side or the other after the opening statements. The most significant, of course, were judicial instructions to remain neutral. Closing arguments were similarly judged by jurors as not being particularly influential.

It is always difficult to evaluate the accuracy of people's responses to questions when strong cues indicate the socially desirable answer. The judge instructed the jurors that they must not allow themselves to be swayed by the opening statements, and thus it was clear what the court wanted them to do in order to fulfill their role as good jurors. Some jurors might well have been strongly influenced by the opening statements and closing arguments, but still attempted to maintain that they were not influenced—or reported to us that they were not—because of the judicial admonition. Yet the jurors' comments about trying to remain neutral have a compelling and realistic quality. Many jurors revealed some mistrust of the opening statements and expressed a desire to see whether or not the evidence would support these statements. This reported resistance to persuasion has also been found among subjects in studies of one-sided and two-sided communications.

Jurors remarked that the prime value of opening statements and closing arguments was that they provided a framework within which jurors could evaluate the cases. In this relatively subtle way, attorneys were able to affect jury decision making. By outlining the arguments they were going to advance, attorneys gave the jurors a way to order information in the case. The jurors' descriptions of the impact of opening statements in this study converge nicely with the findings of

Pyszczynski and his colleagues that opening statements create cognitive schemata that structure the jurors' processing and interpretation of evidence. In addition, the jurors' descriptions about the impact of opening statements correlate well with the theoretical arguments of other scholars about the importance of a story or script for ordering trial evidenced. Many jurors mentioned that the opening statements and closing arguments helped them to understand and recall information—but they did not consider this to constitute "influence." Attorneys, of course, might well disagree!

The comments by jurors showed that the summary statements were quite helpful to them in organizing the evidence. In this light, it is worthwhile to note that jury experts have recommended that, to enhance jury comprehension, attorneys should be permitted to make mini-summary statements throughout the trial in addition to their standard opening statements and closing arguments. The results of our study suggest that such statements would have maximum impact if they help to generate a strong framework within which jurors may organize the ongoing evidence.

Although jurors are affected by opening statements, in that they use them to create stories or frameworks to organize the evidence, the jurors' comments that they were not swayed by the opening statements strongly support Sayler's contention that jurors do not make up their minds right after the opening statements. In contrast to the claims of some trial consultants and attorneys, our study suggests that instructed jurors are aware of the adversary pressure during the openings and try to resist early persuasion attempts. The judge's forewarning about the opening statements appeared to alert jurors to attorneys' efforts to persuade them. This is an interesting finding in that many studies on the impact of judicial instructions upon jurors have shown them to have little effect on jury decision making. To test whether jurors who are admonished are actually more apt to resist persuasion attempts during the opening statements, or whether they are simply responding in a socially desirable way by reporting that they were not swayed by the openings, one could conduct a mock-juror experiment that includes or excludes a judicial instruction concerning opening statements and then observe whether jury decision making is affected thereby.

B. Qualities of Good Attorney Communication

Returning to Sayler's comments about how jurors respond to attorney communications, many of his points about jurors are confirmed by the juror interview results. The jurors in this project reported that the primary factors that influenced their opinions of an attorney were the attorney's credibility, organization, demeanor, emotionality, and treatment of witnesses. Jurors evaluated positively those attorneys who were credible, well-organized, and moderate in their use of emotion. Poorly prepared or extremely emotional attorneys, and attorneys who badgered witnesses, were all viewed negatively by jurors. This fits well with Sayler's recommendation to steer clear of "Rambo" lawyering, and to avoid relying exclusively on emotional—rather than rational, evidence-based—appeals.

In a related vein, our study reinforces one public opinion poll's findings that some people perceive attorneys as "tricksters." Jurors thought that many of the attorneys were behaving unnaturally, acting out a role specific to the case rather than behaving truthfully and naturally. Jurors were cognizant of the adversary nature of the trial and the opposing roles of the attorneys, and considered these roles in responding to lawyers' communications. The jurors' comments and reactions show the hazards of employing excessive or overly dramatic trial tactics, and the value of developing a highly credible courtroom style.

One interesting pattern in this study is that attorneys who expressed emotion were not universally disliked. The most important consideration in the jurors' evaluations of attorneys' emotional expression seemed to be the amount of emotionality that the attorneys used in proportion to the plaintiffs' injuries. It was necessary for an attorney to calibrate the emotionality of the argument to the level of injury or harm the plaintiff sustained. Thus, jurors viewed emotionality as appropriate when the plaintiff was severely or chronically injured, but not when the plaintiff had suffered a minor injury that could be corrected.

The peril of a defense attorney appearing cold and unsympathetic in a catastrophic injury case has been noted by the trial advocates who are members of the Federation of Insurance and Corporate Counsel. Recently, the Federation produced a videotape on handling sympathy in jury trials. In the video, they maintain that defense attorneys in severe personal injury cases should acknowledge to the jury the natural sympathy anyone feels for a badly injured person and should treat the injured plaintiff with dignity and respect. However, attorneys should caution the jury not to decide the case on the basis of sympathy alone.

On the other hand, it is clear that in cases where the plaintiff suffers relatively minor injuries, the plaintiff's attorney faces many suspicious jurors who are predisposed to believe that plaintiffs and their attorneys may, and are likely to, attempt to bring frivolous lawsuits and exaggerate the plaintiff's injuries. These predispositions were revealed in an analysis of tort-juror responses to a post-interview questionnaire from our larger study of jurors in business and corporate cases. A majority of the jurors in the study expressed disbelief and even hostility toward personal injury plaintiffs. Eight out of ten jurors believed that there are far too many frivolous lawsuits today; only about a third of the tort jurors in the entire sample agreed that "most people who sue others in court have legitimate grievances." The "litigation explosion" appears to exist in the minds of jurors, if not in reality, and is currently a factor that attorneys must consider in shaping their persuasive communications in the courtroom.

Critical Thinking

According to Hans and Sweigart, many popular opinions about attorneys and litigation are actually myths. For instance, the idea that many court cases are tried based on emotional appeal is debunked by these jurors. However, Hans and Sweigart's sample includes only corporate or business related cases. If the same study were applied to criminal cases and violent crimes, do you think the authors would have obtained similar results? Would emotional appeal become more important in a criminal case? Would aggressive interrogation tactics be deemed as ruthless when applied to suspected violent criminals?

References

Kalven, H., & Zeisel, H. (1966). The American jury. Boston, MA: Little, Brown & Co.

Kerr, N. (1982). Trial participants' behaviors and jury verdicts: An exploratory field study. In V. J. Konecni & E. B. Ebbeson (eds.), *The criminal justice system: A social-psychological analysis.* (Pp. 261–268) San Francisco: W. H. Freeman.

Linz, D., Penrod, S., & McDonald, E. (1986). Attorney communication and impression making in the courtroom: Views from the bench. *Law and Human Behavior,* 10, 281–302.

Mindes, M. W., & Adcock, A. C. (1982). Trickster, hero, helper: A report on the lawyer image. *American Bar Foundation Research Journal,* 7, 177–233.

Pyszczynski, T. A. (1981). Opening statements in a jury trial: the effect of promising more than the evidence can show. *Journal of Applied Social Psychology,* 11, 434–444.

Sayler, R. (1988). Rambo litigation: Why hardball tactics don't work. *ABA Journal,* March, 79–81.

Vinson, D. (1986). *Jury trials: The psychology of winning strategy.* Charlottesville, VA: Lexis Law Publishers.

III   Corrections

It is at the last stages of the criminal justice process that we find the lowest public visibility for organizational practices. Prisons, unlike police and judicial organizations, operate with very little scrutiny until something occurs that comes to the attention of the public. This is why field research is so important in these institutional settings. Although there have historically been numerous studies about the various aspects of prison life, the enormous growth of prison construction and heterogeneous inmate populations have changed the way these facilities operate. In addition, the past several decades has seen a dramatic change in the population of those who now occupy the positions of correctional officers. These two fundamental changes in the prison environment necessitate the need for a better understanding of the prison as a work world.

The five naturalistic oriented studies selected for the section on correctional practitioners explore some areas of our prison system that have not received a great deal of attention in recent years. The articles address such issues as the way correctional officers negotiate formal rules and regulations, how officers stereotype inmates and treat them accordingly, how gender influences the way correctional workers treat one another and those they supervise, and the impact of changing treatment models on those who work in probation and parole.

The experiences of those confined to prison and their families are often overlooked. Ignoring inmates' perspectives is likely due to their status. They are criminals after all. However, such a view does a great disservice to those interested in finding ways to deter and rehabilitate offenders. The five articles included in this section were chosen because they represent a broad overview of some of the issues inmates and their families face. These articles address such topics as how short term inmates cope with their incarceration, how inmates make sense of parole decisions, and what sex offenders think about registries. Inmates are not the only ones affected by their confinement. Thus, we have included two articles that address the difficulties families face due to their loved one's incarceration.

The articles in both sections should cause readers to consider how current corrections policies and practices directly affect the organizational operations of institutional corrections. Certainly there are numerous other issues that are of great importance to inmates and their families. If nothing else, we trust that these field studies will enlighten the readers to the realities and effects that the correctional environment has on both employees and prisoners.

A Practitioners

21

Accounts of Prison Work: Corrections Officers' Portrayals of Their Work Worlds

Stan Stojkovic

Abstract: *Stan Stojkovic examines correctional staff interactions with inmates in a maximum security prison to shed light on the gap between formal policies and the practices that officers actually carried out. His findings suggest that correctional officers portray their work worlds as filled with problems that stem from both correctional administrators and from inmates. According to officers, administration implements unrealistic rules that hinder their ability to do their jobs effectively. Correctional officers believe that they must overlook some of these formal rule violations otherwise their jobs would be too difficult and too dangerous.*

Sykes (1958) offers a sociological explanation for correctional officers' tendency to develop unapproved work routines, relationships, and orientations stating that the prison social system involves contradictions and pressures that undermine and, ultimately, "corrupt" correctional officers' authority. Although it is concerned with a variety of human service and social control organizations Lipsky's (1980) analysis of street-level bureaucracies also emphasizes how low level staff in prisons and similar organizations adapt to organizational problem and pressures over which they have little or no control. Lipsky focuses on the ways in which human service and social control professionals cope with such problems by approaching their work in officially disapproved, but functional ways in order to fulfill their professional obligations. He concludes that street level bureaucrats' coping strategies are realistic and necessary because organizational goals are seldom achievable in officially prescribed ways. Unauthorized procedures are often functional for organizational systems and the larger society.

This analysis offers a new way of understanding correctional officers and the work worlds. I consider many of the issues raised in the corrections literature but my focus is on how correctional officers explain and justify their development of officially disapproved work routines, relationships, and orientations Thus, I am not concerned with why correctional officers "really" modify organizational rules and expectations or the function of their actions for the prison system. Rather, I attempt to explicate correctional officers' *accounts* of the actions and relationships. As Scott and Lyman (1968, p. 46) state,

> An account is a linguistic device employed whenever an action is subjected to valuative inquiry. Such devices are a crucial element in the social world since they prevent conflicts from arising

by verbally bridging the gap between action and expectation. Moreover, accounts are "situated" according to the statuses of the interactants are standardized within cultures so that certain accounts are terminologically stabilized and routinely expected when activity falls outside the domain of expectations.

By taking accounts as its topic, the paper focuses on the ways that correction officers verbally bridge the gap between their work activities and relationship and official organizational expectations. Accounts are rhetorical; that is, they all expressed as rationales intended to anticipate and counter others' criticisms of persons' actions (Miller and Holstein 1989). Officers use these accounts to make sense of the actions that constitute their everyday work routines. Correctional officers' accounts of their work circumstances and relationships are thus both descriptions of their work world and features of it. The descriptions and rationales are available to, and used by, correctional officers to manage troublesome persons who may criticize them for acting in improper ways.

Setting and Organization of the Study

The study was conducted over a 12-month period in 1982–1983 and involved the observation of correctional staff interactions with prisoners in a maximum-security prison. The prison was built to house prisoners classified as especially dangerous to the public. During the research period, over 75% of the inmates were serving sentences of 20 years or more. Further, most of the inmates had records of violent and disruptive behavior in other prisons in the state. The correctional officer staff consisted of 150 persons, most of whom were new to correctional work. The inexperience of the correctional officer staff was intentional. The warden stated that he wished to put together a correctional officer staff that would bring new ideas, work habits, and attitudes to their work. He stated that hiring correctional officers with little or no experience was important because they would be unfamiliar with the "old ways of doing things," including the corrupt practices that flourish in many prisons.

I observed interactions in all areas of the prison, including its most restrictive segregation unit. Also, 20 correctional officers were interviewed about their work. The interviews were conducted at the officers' homes and/or in a local tavern. The questions asked of correctional officers were open-ended and intended to elicit portrayals of the purposes of the prison, the officers' work in it, and officers' relations with others, particularly inmates, administrators, and other correctional officers. The portrayals may be analyzed as accounts because they were responses to questions which asked the officers to evaluate aspects of their work world and explain disjunctures between officers' depictions of organizational ideals and their behavior. Put differently, the officers' responses are treated as culturally standardized explanations for bridging the gap between organizational expectations and practices.

Most correctional officers portrayed the primary purpose of the prison as maintaining institutional security and control over the prisoners. They expressed little concern for prisoners' rehabilitation. They stated that rehabilitation was not why the prison was built; rather, it was intended to make prisoners more manageable. As one officer stated, "We get all the fuck-ups from the other prisons that nobody else wants."

Although correctional officers stated that the security and control of prisoners was the prison's central purpose, they also stated that the accomplishment of this goal was made problematic by the prison's administrative structure and the conflicting demands placed on them by supervisors.

Thus, correctional officers' explanations and justifications of how they maintained a secure prison in an often hostile, uncertain, and contradictory environment is the primary topic of this paper. Officers stated that they maintained order by developing accommodative relationships with prisoners which violated officially prescribed rules and procedures, but which the officers portrayed as realistic and necessary adjustments to their work circumstances. In this way the officers described themselves as acting much as the street-level bureaucrats Lipsky (1980) analyzed. Central to both descriptions is the depiction of low-level organization members as competent and responsible persons trying to cope with difficult work circumstances.

The Prison as a Problematic Work World

For correctional officers, the prison world was organized in terms of routine activities and relationships. In the abstract, at least, the routines were interrelated ways that correctional officers' achieve the prison's organizational purposes. The officers stated, however, that the meaning of their everyday work activities and relationships was not so simple or clear-cut. They portrayed their work activities and relationships as adaptations to problematic circumstances. Specifically, the correctional officers stated that their work involved three major sources of uncertainty and problems: (1) prison system and correctional officers' place in it, (2) prison administrators' actions and interests, and (3) inmates. According to the officers, each of these aspects of the prison involved different practical problems which they sought to manage. The rest of this section is concerned with the way in which the correctional officers portrayed and oriented to aspects of the prison world as problems.

The Prison System as a Problem

The officers often portrayed themselves as forgotten people in a hostile social system made up of politicians, the public, prison administrators, and inmates. They stated that their problems and low social standing reflected politicians' and the public's negative attitudes toward prisons and correctional officers. The officers stated that members of each of these groups treated them as insignificant, largely incompetent, and expendable parts of the prison organization. Of most immediate importance to the officers, however, were prison administrators' orientations to them. They stated that prison administrators treated correctional officers as scapegoats; that is, administrators protected themselves by passing the blame for system problems from administrators to correctional officers. The officers portrayed prison administrators' and others' attitudes toward correctional officers as counterproductive and self-fulfilling prophecies because correctional officers partly adapt to the prison system by taking on the traits attributed to them by others.

Consider, for example, the following descriptions of the prison world. They are explanations of why correctional officers "have no togetherness" and eventually confirm others' negative evaluations of them. The portrayals center in treating correctional officers' work problems as system problems.

> We are Indians in the correctional system. Everyone shits on us. We have no togetherness in this place. . . . We are the screws no one really cares about. . . . we are shipwrecked in the society and are always labelled as the bad guys . . . they [administration] treat us like assholes and we will eventually become nothing but assholes.

> Who gives a fuck about corrections officers? We have to deal with all the assholes in the system and they expect us to like it. . . . It's this kind of attitude we have to live with . . . then they wonder why we are all alcoholics.

The correctional officers further explained that their problems and low standing in the prison were relatively recent developments. According to the officers, the problems were a result of changing prison policies which expanded prisoners' rights and reduced correctional officers' discretion, particularly their right to discipline prisoners as they saw fit. The officers explained that the changes were counterproductive restrictions on their abilities to effectively respond to troublesome prisoners. They stated that the ultimate effect of the changes was a reduction in correctional officers' authority and inmates' respect for officers. Consider, for example, the following discussions of how correctional officers' work circumstances had been adversely affected by changes in prison policies.

> It is not like in the old days when you could beat the shit out of an asshole. I wish they did still have this for some of these guys in this place. Some guys need a good ass kicking, then we wouldn't have that many problems at all in trying to keep them in line.

> There is no real punishment in this place. What would have happened in the old days is that the guy would have gotten his ass beat for about two weeks straight and the other inmates would have known it right away . . . the sad thing is that the inmates know that there is no real punishment and they flaunt it in our faces.

According to the correctional officers, a related problem with the prison system involved officers' inconsistent enforcement of prison rules. They stated that, while every correctional officer was supposed to strictly follow prison rules, they frequently deviated from them. Although the officers' comments might be taken as a call for the strict enforcement of prison rules, they were intended as critiques of the rules which the officers portrayed as unrealistic expectations and standards. Indeed, many officers stated that flexible rule enforcement was needed in the prison because officers could not effectively run their units under a policy of literal enforcement. In this way, the officers cast the enforcement of prison rules and their responsibility to effectively manage prisoners as contradictory aspects of the prison system. As one officer explained,

> If you [inmate] are doing time and you are decent, you will be alright in this place. Rules are meant to be bent in a place like this; you have to be flexible in how you deal with the inmates. If you are not flexible, then you will be in trouble.

However, while the officers portrayed flexible rule enforcement as a necessity, they also stated that it was a major source of work problems because too many officers were too flexible. Officers framed the issue as a practical dilemma. They stated that, on the one hand, the official prison rules to which they were accountable were unrealistic and inadequate because the rules did not take account of the practical contingencies faced by officers in managing inmates. Consequently, correctional officers engaged in selective enforcement to fulfill their larger obligation to maintain order in the prison. On the other hand, the officers stated that, although most of them agreed that they had to be flexible in enforcing prison rules, they did not agree on when and how to do so. According to the officers, the result was inconsistency and uncertainty among officers and inmates about appropriate inmate behavior.

Officers stated that this circumstance had practical consequences because inmates could get by with rule breaking by playing one officer against another much as children negotiate with, and get permission from, their parents by telling one parent that the other approves of their requests. Specifically, inmates responded to correctional officers who tried to strictly enforce prison rules by stating that other officers did not enforce them. The officers stated that such problems were most serious when supervisory officers were more lenient than the officers that they supervised. In this circumstance, officers could actually be punished for enforcing prison rules. Consider, for example, the following correctional officer's complaint about the inmates' practice of taking food from the prison kitchen. He portrays the practice as a practical dilemma and problem which focuses on how officers were sometimes punished for "doing their jobs."

> I am sick and tired of guys bringing all this shit from the kitchen into the housing units. It is something that just has to stop. But the problem is that so many officers allow it to happen and you can't get consistency . . . in rule enforcement. . . . remember one time when two officers stopped a guy with a whole coat full of stuff from the kitchen. The inmate responded that (another) officer allowed it to come to the unit. When they checked it out with the officer, who was their superior, he reprimanded them for enforcing the rules. All they were doing was their jobs. That type of shit is what really pisses me off about this job.

In sum, the correctional officers portrayed the prison system as fraught with problems, contradictions and dilemmas that made it difficult—if not impossible—for them to fulfill their organizational obligations. They further stated that in attempting to cope with the problems of the prison system, correctional officers sometimes produced new problems and injustices, making their work circumstances even more complex and difficult. The officers stated that these problems were exacerbated by problems in the correctional officer–prison administrator relationship. We turn to these problems next.

Prison Administrators as a Problem

The correctional officers portrayed the officer–administrator relationship as filled with tensions and distrust resulting from the prison administrators' lack of respect for correctional officers, over concern for protecting themselves from criticism and negative publicity, and willingness to use correctional officers as scape-goats. In other words, the officers described themselves as *victims* of the policies and practices of prison administrators in order to exonerate themselves from blame for their, and the prison's, failures (Holstein and Miller 1990). Specifically, the officers explained that the tensions and distrust underlying the officer–administrator relationship were based on three factors.

First, correctional officers expressed concern that prison administrators were changing the rules and regulations of the prison so rapidly that officers and inmates did not know what was expected of them. According to the officers, the changes created uncertainty among prisoners about organizational rules and expectations. As one officer stated,

> By fucking with the inmates' minds is where the problems begin. The inmates need to have rules and regulations consistently enforced. But the problem is that the administration always changes the rules of the game for both inmates and staff. Inconsistency pisses off a lot of inmates. Convicts want and need consistent rules. How can we expect them to follow the rules when the rules are always changing?

The officers explained the problem was a result of the prison administrators' unrealistic emphasis on controlling both inmate groups and the correctional officer's union. They stated that maintaining control over such groups was the administrators' highest priority. They further explained that frequent changes in prison policies created uncertainties and divisions between officers and inmates that served the administrators' interests. "All these different rules put inmates against officers and officers against themselves," stated one officer. According to the officers, the major results of the administrators' actions were that correctional officers learned to distrust prison administrators and to rely on their own judgment and methods in controlling inmates. As one correctional officer explained,

> You do what you think is right and you disregard anything the administration says. You are the one who is doing the job, and you do anything that you think will make your job more effective and easy in the long run.

A second issue raised by the officers in explaining their distrust of prison administrators was safety. Specifically, they stated that the administrators were unconcerned with the officers' safety. The officers further stated that the administrators' lack of concern increased the risks associated with their jobs. The officers cited a number of incidents in explaining and justifying their concerns about their personal safety and prison administrators' attitude toward it. One such incident involved an especially violent and disruptive inmate assault on a correctional officer in the cafeteria. The assault was done in the presence of over 30 correctional officers and 100 prisoners. Immediately following the incidents the inmate shouted "What can these assholes do to me anyway? I am serving double-life." The inmate was given segregation and punishment time, yet the officers stated that the assault warranted greater punishment and that the administration should have attempted to transfer the prisoner to another less "luxurious" prison in the state system.

The officers used such incidents to cast the prison as an unsafe place and prison administrators as unconcerned with officers' welfare. They also used the incidents to explain and justify a work orientation that involved avoiding actions that threatened their safety, including allowing inmates to flagrantly violate some prison rules. According to the officers, they had to take care of themselves first because prison administrators were unwilling to protect them. As one officer stated,

> Them administration types don't care about us or our jobs. So, why should I stick my neck out for them? I'll do anything to keep myself safe. . . . If that means letting them [inmates] burn down the place, that's fine with me.

Finally, correctional officers stated that prison administrators were too concerned with inmate lawsuits. According to the officers, the prison administrators' concern resulted in an improper emphasis on pleasing inmates. The effect of the emphasis was to reduce correctional officers' authority and discretion in dealing with inmates. The officers further stated that prison administrators responded to inmate lawsuits by allowing the officers to be blamed for the problems of the prison system. Consider, for example, the following officer's portrayal of the effect of prison administrators' concern for inmate lawsuits. Through his portrayal, the officer casts correctional officers as victims of prison administrators' over emphasis on inmate lawsuits. He also explains and justifies his interest in returning to law enforcement.

> The only reason I became a guard is because I was laid-off from my job as a sheriff. . . . As soon as that picks up, I am getting the fuck out of this place. . . . A lot of these administrators just care for the inmates. That's because inmates file lawsuits and the public thinks we are all assholes. . . . We can't even do our jobs without being thought of as bad by the public.

In sum, the officers stated that many of their problems with inmates were caused by prison administrators' policies. Specifically, prison administrators' policies and actions made it impossible for correctional officers to act as they preferred and/or as required by prison policies. We next consider the officers' descriptions of other sources of tension in the correctional officer–inmate relationship.

Prisoners as a Problem

Although we might expect inmates to resent and resist all rule enforcement by correctional officers, the officers stated that most inmates recognized the importance of prison rules. They stated that, although inmates expected the rules to be enforced in realistic and flexible ways, most inmates recognized that the rules were important to the maintenance of prison order. Officers added that flexibility in rule enforcement was especially important when it involved events which were the most relevant to the prisoners' ability to cope and adapt to the demands and constraints imposed by the prison environment. For example, the officers stated that telephone calls were very important to prisoners because they were the only way in which inmates could regularly interact with friends and relatives on the outside. Thus, for the officers, flexibility in enforcing rules about inmates' use of the telephone was an important way of maintaining stable relations with prisoners. As one officer stated,

> Phone calls are really important for guys in this place . . . you cut off their calls and they get pissed. So what I do is give them a little extra and they are good to me.

While flexibility in rule enforcement was important in interactions between correctional officers and prisoners, the officers stated that they selectively enforced the rules to achieve organizational goals. Put in the officers' language, they enforced the rules to "squeeze" inmates who were severely disruptive to the housing units or posed threats to other inmates. The officers stated that, in doing so, they solved problems for both themselves and inmates, both of whom had an interest in maintaining an orderly prison world. Consider, for example, the following correctional officers' explanations of the usefulness of selectively enforcing prison rules.

> I'll be easy on the rules if the guy is not causing trouble. . . . If he is into all those bullshit games, then I want his ass out of my unit. The problem is that nobody wants him . . . but if you are smart you can get the real troublemakers out of the place.

> For the inmate who doesn't force himself on anyone you got to give him a break. . . . I do that by giving him more dayroom [recreation] time and he respects that. . . . You know, you're not always on the guy and inmates admire that in an officer.

A related aspect of the correctional officer–inmate relationship centered in the officers' classification of inmates into those who "knew how to do time" and those who did not. The officers stated that it was the latter group of inmates who were most troublesome because they had no commitment to prison policies and procedures. Specifically, the officers stated that the younger inmates serving longer sentences had no understanding of what it meant to do time and that their adjustment to prison was, therefore, more difficult. Further, the officers stated that the presence of younger inmates in the prison made their jobs more difficult and problematic. They stated, for example, that although they warned younger inmates about the possible consequences of rule infractions, the warnings had no effect on their behavior.

> It's the bugs [young inmates] that cause all the problems. . . . They are the ones involved in spud juice [alcohol], dope, and sex . . . they don't give a shit about nothing and most have been state raised so they know nothing but prison.

The officers added that their concern for managing troublesome young inmates was shared with the older inmates who had been in prison for a number of years and viewed the prison as their homes. According to the officers, the older inmates also saw the younger inmates as troublemakers who were upsetting the established order developed and perpetuated by themselves and correctional staff.

> It seems to me that the older inmates understand the officer's job and buy into the system of rules and regulations. On the other hand, the younger inmates cause more problems because they don't buy the rules of the enforcers.

> Them older guys know what prison life is all about. They know that you're just doing your job and don't want any hassle. . . . You never have any problems with them.

Thus, although the correctional staff were officially obligated to enforce all prison rules all the time, they did not always do so. Rather, they selectively enforced prison rules to control troublesome prisoners and reward cooperative ones, always seeking to manage the practical contingencies associated with their jobs. The officers also used selective enforcement of prison rules to build alliances with inmates who could help them control troublesome inmates. Specifically, the officers depended on and used older inmates to control younger, more troublesome inmates. The older inmates aided the correctional officers by encouraging the younger inmates to cooperate with the officers. They did so by instructing the younger inmates on the practical advantages of cooperation. Thus, although it was not recognized in official prison policies and rules, the correctional officers stated that one way they fulfilled their professional responsibilities was by selectively enforcing rules in order to secure cooperation from older inmates.

The officers stated that it was one of several ways in which they adapted their relationship with inmates to the practical constraints and circumstances of their work. The adaptations were the basis for the accommodative relationships which prevailed in the housing units. We further consider how correctional officers portrayed and justified their relationships with inmates in the next section.

The Social Organization of Officer–Inmate Relations

Although all of the correctional officers did not agree that capitulation to inmates' desires and needs was appropriate, most of the officers who regularly interacted with inmates were accommodative, particularly those assigned to the housing units. The officers explained that accommodation was necessary because strictly enforcing prison rules did not produce inmate compliance; rather, it destabilized the prison environment and officer–inmate relationships. The officers gave two major reasons for this circumstance. Both reasons involved portraying accommodation with inmates' desires as a practical response to the constraints of correctional officers' work.

First, they stated that the strict enforcement was counterproductive because there was no real punishment attached to many of the violations. They stated that prison punishments were too soft and prison administrators did not support correctional officers in their disputes with inmates. For example, the correctional officers stated that officers who relied on ticket writing as their only way of controlling prisoners were doomed to failure. Ticket writing was the officially approved method of documenting inmates' misbehaviors and, according to the prison administrators, was the first step in taking formal action against troublesome inmates. The officers stated, however, that tickets were not taken seriously in the prison. As one officer stated,

> Your only formal authority is the tickets you write, but tickets are not written by a lot of officers because they do not really do anything in this place. A lot of tickets are thrown away by superiors anyway.

The officers also stated that writing tickets for many inmate rule violations did not make sense because many of the behaviors were "bullshit"; that is, they are minor offenses that did not warrant official responses. The officers stated that ticketing inmates was only appropriate when nothing else could be done with troublemakers. For example, I observed two prisoners pushing and shoving each other in one of the housing units. An officer broke up the disturbance and sent the inmates on their ways. Later, I asked him why he had not given them tickets for fighting. He replied,

What for? It only produces trouble between those two guys and myself. If someone got stabbed or seriously hurt, then I would have to write a ticket, but no one did.

Second, the officers stated that, although they could use physical force to gain short-term inmate cooperation, coercion was a last resort response to troublesome inmates because it involved unacceptable long-term costs. They stated that inmates resented such treatment and would respond by withholding future cooperation. Equally important, the officers stated that if they used physical force to manage inmates, it could lead to violent inmate responses, a circumstance that they wished to avoid. Thus, although the correctional officers had official access to resources which presumably allowed them to compel acquiescence from inmates, they did not emphasize them. Rather, they sought to build "noncoercive" relationships with inmates. According to officers, such relationships were realistic and necessary ways of dealing with inmates.

In so explaining and justifying their relationships with inmates, then, correctional officers cast accommodation to inmates' desires and behaviors as a rational response to the practical circumstances of prison life. They further stated that accommodation was good for both officers and inmates. The officers explained that accommodative relationships served the officers' interest in maintaining orderly and stable housing units and inmates' interest in reducing the insecurities of prison life. Although it was less emphasized by the officers, a related reason why accommodative officer–inmate relations prevailed in the housing units was because officers who sought to strictly enforce prison rules seldom remained in the housing units for long. Officers portrayed this approach as unrealistic because it was overly strict. Indeed, inmates referred to "strict" correctional officers as the "police," thereby highlighting their emphasis on rule enforcement.

The officers stated that many strict officers left the housing units and sometimes correctional work because they became frustrated by the selective rule enforcement of other correctional officers. According to the officers, strict officers were caught between their desire to enforce all prison rules and inmates' claims that they should ignore rule violations because other officers did so. In addition to strict officers' requests to leave, their time in the housing units was reduced by the intervention of prison administrators who frequently transferred them to jobs that did not involve regular contact with inmates. The administrators usually did so in response to inmates' and/or correctional officers' complaints portraying the strict officers as unreasonable and sources of problems in the housing units. In so responding to officer and inmate complaints, the prison administrators helped maintain and perpetuate accommodative officer–inmate relationships which centered in selected rule enforcement.

According to the officers, then, there were several practical reasons for the prevalence of accommodative officer–inmate relationships in the housing units. The officers further stated that, although the relationships involved violations of formal prison policies and rules, they were realistic, necessary, and served the interests of inmates, prison staff, and the public. The remainder of this section considers correctional officers' accounts of their accommodative orientation to inmates' desires and behaviors and treatment of some inmate rule violations as deviance. They were explanations and justifications of the correctional officers routine violation of official prison rules and policies. I discuss the issues in turn.

The Accommodative Orientation

Accommodative relationships between correctional officers and prisoners were rooted in three practices that may be stated as officers' claims:

1. Because correctional officers could not have total control over the inmates, negotiations were central to prisoner control.
2. Once an officer defined or negotiated a sct of informal rules with a prisoner or group of prisoners, the rules were to be respected by all parties.
3. Some rule violating behaviors in the prison setting were "normal" and, consequently, did not merit officer attention or sanctioning.

More specifically, the officers stated that proper accommodation to inmates' desires and interests involved "giving respect" to inmates and restricting officers' interactions with inmates. In doing so, correctional officers stated that they sought to effectively control and manage inmates while avoiding troublesome encounters with them.

> The officers stated that giving respect to inmates was a central aspect of building effective relationships with inmates. It involved enforcing only those prison rules that most inmates and correctional officers deemed important and realistic. For the officers, such selective rule enforcement allowed them to maintain an acceptable degree of control in the housing units while enabling inmates to "save face" by providing them with a sense of respect, dignity and self-control. As one officer stated, the importance of giving a man his respect is key to this place. I have found if you give respect you get respect in here. The inmates know it, and for the most part the good guards know it too.

The officers stated that a related and important aspect of giving respect to inmates was that in selectively enforcing prison rules they clearly defined the rules that mattered. That is, both correctional officers and veteran inmates knew and agreed on the types of behavior that called for official action by the officers. The officers stated that their selective enforcement of prison rules resulted in officer–inmate consensus about acceptable inmate behavior and, based on the consensus, a greater sense of predictability and order existed in officer–inmate interactions. The officers further stated that new correctional officers and inmates were partly a problem because they were unfamiliar with the working assumptions and rules of the prison. In learning the practical meaning of giving and getting respect, new officers learned how to properly do their jobs and new inmates learned to do their time.

The second aspect of the correctional officers' accommodative orientation to the officer–inmate relationship involved restricted interaction with inmates. Specifically, correctional officers tried to limit their interactions to those inmates who could help them control other inmates in the housing units. Thus, many inmates had limited and perfunctory dealings with correctional officers, such as fleeting contacts during count times or when inmates were leaving the housing units for jobs, school, or other institutional assignments. The officers explained that they did not interact with most inmates because it was not a necessary part of their jobs. One officer explained his orientation to interactions with inmates in the following way.

> Why should I get involved in something with a prisoner when I don't want to know him? I am
> not here to love him, only to watch him and make sure the housing unit is secured.

Nonetheless, the correctional officers did regularly interact with some inmates. They did so with inmates who were willing to help the officers fulfill their organizational responsibilities, the most important and cumbersome being the counting of inmates. The counts were conducted at 6:00 a.m. (right before many prisoners went to work), 11:00 a.m. (right before the staggered lunch times for prisoners), 4:00 p.m. (right after the shift changes of officers), and 10:00 p.m. (right before lights out in the prison). Counting inmates was a cumbersome task for the correctional officers because it required that prisoners be locked in their cells. To ensure this, correctional officers used "trusted" inmates to do their counts for them and help them move prisoners into their assigned cells. In return, the inmates were given privileges that other prisoners did not enjoy, such as extra phone time or dayroom time. They also had greater contact with the correctional officers, although their interactions were focused on the practical problems of counting inmates.

In sum, the correctional officers described their accommodative orientation to prison rules and inmate relationships as a pragmatic adaptation to their work circumstances. They gave respect to inmates because it was an effective way of gaining inmate cooperation and they restricted their interactions with inmates to those who could help them better manage their work problems. Put differently, the officers' portrayals of the accommodative orientation centered in avoiding trouble with inmates. A related way in which they managed inmates and avoided trouble was by treating some inmates' behaviors as normal deviance. The officers described normal deviance as rule violations that were not serious enough to warrant removing prisoners from their housing units or the normal daily activities of the prison. I next consider how the officers explained and justified their treatment of some inmate behaviors as normal deviance.

Avoiding Normal Deviance

According to the correctional officers, the two most important kinds of normal deviance engaged in by inmates were sexual relations and drug use. They were significant to the officers because the behaviors affected the correctional officers' orientation to their work and social control. Specifically, the correctional officers stated that although the behaviors were violations of prison rules, they were ongoing inmate activities which, at best, could only be partly controlled by the strict enforcement of prison rules. For the officers, then, a more realistic and productive orientation to the activities was to treat them as matters of negotiation and accommodation. Officers explained that in treating inmate sexual activities and drug use as negotiable, they were able to maintain a degree of control over them while not engendering the hostility associated with the strict enforcement of prison rules.

The officers stated that sexual relations between inmates was the most problematic kind of normal deviance. It was problematic because, although the correctional officers assumed that it was happening, they did not know when and where to be in the prison in order to avoid discovering it. The officers stated that avoiding the discovery of inmate sexual activities was important because the discovery of inmates having sexual relations was a threat to their safety. The officers explained that an inmate who is confronted by an officer with the fact that he is not a man, but a "sissy," "punk," or "fag" would resort to violence to ensure his respect among other inmates. They stated that no inmate wants to be viewed as being sexually weak, nor does he want other inmates to view him as a "woman" who can be exploited by other prisoners for sexual favors.

Thus, to avoid such confrontations the correctional officers watched for signs of inmate sexual activities and removed themselves from settings where signs of sexual activity were present. The officers explained and justified their actions as a realistic and necessary accommodation to the practical circumstances of prison life. As one officer stated,

> If I see three or four guys crowding around a guy's cell, I know something is going down, either they are getting high or someone is sucking or fucking. If I get in the middle of that shit, I would be crazy because I will either get seriously hurt or killed. I am not going to go down there and write tickets. It would be plain stupid.

This is not to suggest that the correctional officers tolerated all forms of inmate sexual activities. Specifically, they did not tolerate the public display of sexual behavior, inmates "squeezing off" other inmates into the "hole" (a segregation cell for those inmates who were afraid of being sexually assaulted), or coercing sexual relations from weaker inmates. The officers stated that, both they and inmates viewed these forms of sexual relations as intolerable and that they worked to control sexual exploitation. Finally, correctional officers justified their treatment of inmate sexual activities as normal by portraying the amount of such activity in the prison as less than that found in other prisons in the state. In doing so, they cast inmates' sexual activity as less of a problem than in other settings and, therefore, a tolerable form of rule breaking.

The correctional officers also portrayed their orientation to inmates' drug use as accommodative. They stated that, as in other prisons, narcotics were readily available to inmates in their prison and that they took account of it in their dealings with inmates. The officers further stated that so long as inmates were not causing trouble or exhibiting violent behavior, inmate drug use was a tolerable activity. Indeed, they stated that inmate drug use was a normal and expected part of the inmates' social world. As with inmate sexual activity, the correctional officers avoided confronting inmates about their drug use. The officers tried to anticipate occasions when inmates would being using drugs and avoid situations in which enforcement of prison rules forbidding drug use might be required. They explained that their orientation was realistic because the problems resulting from their enforcement of drug-related rules were more serious than those associated with inmates' drug use. As one correctional officer stated,

> One thing that you don't want to get involved in is the illegal bullshit between inmates. . . . If I know inmates are going to be smoking (marijuana), I'll let it slide if it isn't going to cause any problems. . . . Once you try to step in, then you got problems.

The correctional officers further justified their accommodative orientation to inmate drug use by stating that while drug use was common in the prison, it was not as problematic in this prison as in others in the state. They stated that the most serious danger stemming from inmates' drug use involved new dealers' efforts to move in on the markets of established dealers. According to the correctional officers, however, this problem could be controlled through proper negotiations with dealers, not the strict enforcement of prison rules.

Discussion and Conclusion

Looked at one way, the correctional officers' accounts discussed here are excuses intended to explain away the officers' selective enforcement of prison rules. Viewed this way, they are techniques of neutralization which the officers used to deny responsibility for failing to carry out their officially prescribed responsibilities (Sykes and Matza 1957). The officers partly did so by blaming others (particularly prison administrators) for their actions. In doing so, they cast themselves as victims both of others' actions and, more generally, of the prison system which the officers portrayed as organized to undermine their authority and efforts to fulfill their responsibilities in organizationally approved ways. The officers further described their selective enforcement of prison rules as realistic and necessary adaptations to the prison system.

Implicit in the analysis of the officers' accounts as excuses, however, is an assessment of their accuracy; that is, the accounts are treated as adequate or inadequate explanations of the officers' circumstances, actions, and motives. Further, such an analysis involves taking a side in the officers' disputes with others. By treating the accounts as accurate portrayals of their circumstances, actions and motives, persons align themselves with the officers in their disputes with inmates, prison administrators and others in their social world. On the other hand, emphasizing the inadequacy of the officers' accounts implicitly undermines their claims and the legitimacy of their positions in disputes with others.

There is, however, an alternative orientation to the officers' accounts that treats it as rhetoric—that is, as claims about reality intended to persuade others. Rhetoric is partisan discourse through which persons anticipate and/or counter others' criticisms of their actions and positions on practical issues (Perelman 1979). It is also an interactional procedure for assigning preferred identities to one's self and others. By formulating accounts of their activities that emphasize the practical constraints and injustices making up the prison system, correctional officers anticipated and countered others' criticisms of them as corrupt and uncaring functionaries. They also assigned preferred identities to themselves by portraying their actions as professionally responsible efforts to cope with difficult work circumstances. If we treat officers' accounts as *partisan* and *purposeful*—but not necessarily flawed—versions of reality, we can begin to analyze both how officers experience their work worlds and how they managed and made sense of those worlds through their accounting procedures. A rhetorical analysis can provide insight into how officers *produce* the social organization of their work lives. I conclude by discussing some of the implications of treating the officers' accounts as rhetoric.

First, rhetorical analysis does not involve assessing the truthfulness or accuracy of persons' accounts. Rather, it focuses on the practicalities of account-making; it considers how persons produce accounts to solve practical problems. Such problems include explaining why actions which might be seen as improper are "really" proper, as well as efforts to preserve a preferred image of self while acknowledging that one's actions might be taken as evidence of dispreferred motives. Equally important, rhetorical analysis of the officers' accounts highlights the multiperspectival nature of social relations in the prison. The officers' accounts are expressions and justifications of their orientations to aspects of the prison social world. We should expect that they will differ from prison administrators' and inmates' accounts of prison life.

The difference is not a matter of the truthfulness or accuracy of the officers' and others' accounts; rather it is a matter of orientation. We should expect diverse orientations to everyday prison life and partisan positions on correctional officers' work practices from officers, administrators, and inmates. Members of these groups bring different concerns and interests to their prison experiences, including their experiences with one another. Thus, the accounts of none of the groups are "better" than the accounts of the others, although they involve different reality claims and are used to pursue different practical interests.

A second and related implication of treating the officers' accounts as rhetoric involves the larger social and political context of prison life and relationships. To the extent that they are organized as conflicts of orientation and interest, we would anticipate that correctional officers', inmates', and prison administrators' accounts will involve differing, even opposed, reality claims. Indeed, the data reported here show that correctional officers also differ in their orientations to everyday life in the prison and their professional responsibilities. Although I have emphasized the ways in which the officers justified their accommodative orientation to inmate relationships, all of the correctional officers were not so oriented.

Some officers portrayed their jobs as involving the strict enforcement of prison rules. They justified the orientation by portraying selective rule enforcement as having long-term detrimental consequences for officer–inmate relations and the officers' authority. According to the strict officers, the most serious and detrimental consequence of the accommodative officer–inmate relationship was the encouragement of snitching among inmates. They stated that, although snitches served the short-term interest of correctional officers in maintaining control over the housing units, they created an atmosphere of distrust and increased inmates' sense of uncertainty in their dealings with officers and other inmates. Other officers countered this claim and justified their encouragement of snitching among inmates by stating that it was a necessary part of maintaining control over inmates and had no serious, detrimental consequences for prison life.

Thus, a third implication of analyzing the correctional officers' accounts as rhetoric is that it points to the variety of ways in which members of the same occupational and organizational group may orient to aspects of their work. But rhetoric and account-making are more than simple reflections of persons' orientations to practical issues; they are also interactional procedures for formulating orientations and perspectives. For example, the officers' responses to my interview questions were more than reports on their thoughts and feelings about their work. The questions were occasions for the officers to produce and justify a perspective on their work which they portrayed as based on enduring thoughts and feelings. Further, because the practical circumstances of correctional officers' account-making differ across situations, we should expect that their rhetoric will also vary situationally. For example, their positions on practical issues and justifications of them may differ when dealing with inmates, administrators, and correctional officers assessed as friendly and supportive versus those assessed as antagonistic.

Critical Thinking

In their role as social control agents, correctional officers are asked to maintain order among inmates while simultaneously carrying out administrative policies that pose a working dilemma for them. This conflict, between administrative demands for fair treatment of inmates and the actual realities of maintaining order, results in officers accommodating prisoner deviance on a daily basis. Do you think such discretion should exist? If, like those Stojkovic interviewed, you think that it should, do you think such discretion contributes to the inconsistencies in how inmates are treated by staff. Taking the role of an inmate, consider how you might interpret the distribution of this discretion.

References

Holstein, J. A. and G. Miller. 1990. "Rethinking Victimization: An Interactional Approach to Victimology." *Symbolic Interaction* 13(1): 101–120.

Lipsky, M. 1980. *Street-Level Bureaucracy*. New York: Russell Sage.

Miller, G. and J. A. Holstein. 1989. "On the Sociology of Social Problems." pp. 1–16 in *Perspectives on Social Problems*, Vol. 1 edited by J. A. Holstein and G. Miller. Greenwich CT: JAI Press.

Perelman, C. 1979. *The New Rhetoric and the Humanities*. Dordrecht, Holland: D. Reidel.

Scott, M. B. and S. M. Lyman. 1968. "Accounts." *American Sociological Review* 33: 46–62.

Sykes, G. M. and D. Matza. 1957. "Techniques of Neutralization." *American Sociological Review* 22: 664–670.

Sykes, G. M. 1958. *The Society of Captives*. Princeton: Princeton University Press.

22

Sensemaking in Prison: Inmate Identity as a Working Understanding

John Riley

Abstract: *John Riley examines the ways correctional officers who work in a maximum security prison formulate, communicate, and justify a shared understanding of how they construct identities for inmates. These shared inmate identities are then used by officers to stereotype the prisoners who come under their supervision. In short, sensemaking causes correctional staff to stereotype prisoners in order for them to get a working understanding of who the prisoners are. Riley suggests that this process of identifying inmates (what he calls "sensemaking") by officers allows for them to categorize (stereotype) inmates for the purpose of maintaining social control functions within the prison.*

Cultural studies of the justice system often direct our attention to activities through which actors construct the categories that structure collective action and promote cooperation in professional life (Bridges and Steen 1998). Sudnow (1965), for example, shows how courtroom workgroups use the category of "normal crimes" to promote collaboration and organize the efficient processing of cases. In the field of policing, Van Maanen (1978) describes "the asshole," a category used by street cops to distinguish between those who share an insider's view of the criminal justice process and citizens who bring naïve, unrealistic expectations to their encounters with police officers. Hunt's (1989) discussion of "normal force" focuses on related processes through which rookie police officers come to revise standards generated by academy training as they gain experience as street cops.

Although correctional officers do not share the long period of professional socialization common to members of courtroom work-groups, or the strong subcultural ties observed in policing, informal understandings about the nature of correctional work remain important (Farkas and Manning 1997; Klofas 1984; Klofas and Toch 1982; Philliber 1987). Crouch and Marquart (1980) increase the appreciation of these understandings by describing categories used by correctional officers when they encounter inmates. They suggest that these categories are similar to those described by Van Maanen in his work on policing, and include "good inmate" and "inmate troublemaker" types. Marquart (1986) describes "tune-ups," "attitude adjustments," and "ass whippings," unofficial categories of physical coercion observed in a Texas prison. And Guenther and Guenther (1980) discuss the "stick man," a term used to describe traditional correctional officers, and the "stick man ideology," a view of institutional life characterized by suspicion of inmates and by resistance to change.

In this paper I examine some of the ways in which correctional officers in a maximum-security prison construct, communicate, and defend a shared account of inmate identity. This process allows them to make sense of their work by making sense of the people they supervise. These efforts produce a generic categorization of inmates that is demeaning, derogatory, and often contradicted by firsthand experience (Goffman 1961; Jacobs and Restky 1975). Even so, it is central to the continuing reproduction of authority in the prison.

Members of most groups come to share operational understandings that define the typical people, places, and situations which demand their professional attention (McNulty 1994). These understandings are the building blocks of larger, socially constructed intersubjectivities that promote a sense of common identity and facilitate collective action. The identification and description of cultural categories that give structure and meaning to collective action in the justice system constitute an established tradition in the social sciences. Somewhat less, however, is known about the processes by which members maintain these understandings through time and in the face of criticism and experiential contradiction. In focusing on some of the ways in which correctional officers sustain a particular understanding of "the inmate," I examine strategies employed to preserve the functional integrity of a cultural category through which members construct accounts that make sense of their experience and coordinate collective action in the workplace.

Understanding Sensemaking

Much of what we know about the construction and maintenance of practical, working accounts of experience is captured by the literature on sensemaking. According to Weick (1995), sensemaking may be described as a continuous social process, which is retrospective, grounded in efforts at identity construction, and "enactive of sensible environments" (Weick 1995: 30; also see Turner 1987). Sensemaking links belief with action, as participants generate meaning in uncertain or ambiguous situations by searching for cues that allow them to connect past experiences with the challenges of the present. The accounts produced, and the processes that produce them, have important implications for the coordination of collective action, for the identity of the individual actors who contribute to their production, and even for the accomplishment of social change (Giddens 1984; Weick 1995). Sensemaking gives meaning to the activities of groups and their members. It turns events into accomplishments, converts problems into opportunities, and transforms individuals into leaders, team members, friends, and even enemies of the organization.

While sensemaking activities are grounded in "retrospective interpretation of past events" (Weick 1995:24), they also have important implications for future behavior. Sensemaking practices are a means by which participants may work to understand and actually influence change within the organization and in the larger society (Crank 1996; Weick 1995). Research on sensemaking suggests that relatively subtle interpretive practices, such as those embodied in tropes, play an important role in the social creation of meaning, in processes of occupational socialization, and particularly in shaping the course of change in complex organizations (Crank 1996; Shearing and Ericson 1991).

Tropes, which include metaphor, synecdoche, metonymy, and irony, are important to the study of occupational socialization and organizational change because they provide shorthand terms for the communication of professional sensibilities and so shape orientations toward collective action (Crank 1996). Like sensemaking in general, tropes may be used to create strategic links between past and present events. Metaphor, for example, may reduce uncertainty by demonstrating the essentially familiar nature of an apparently novel experience. In suggesting that a colleague will "meet his Waterloo" or that a candidate for a job might be "Borked," we communicate economically and precisely an evaluation of what may be fairly complex events.

The correctional officers studied here participate in a systematic and categorical devaluation of their prisoners that is grounded in a shared account of inmate identity. Their efforts generate a working understanding of the prisoner and help to sustain a sensibility that guides interaction in the prison. Like workers in other occupations, the correctional officers whose work is discussed in this paper engage in predictable conversational routines. Such sensemaking routines may be understood as ritual efforts to promote cooperation and solidarity. They also may be understood as efforts to preserve and defend the cultural categories that the officers use to understand their work and to structure collective action.

Research Design

The data discussed here were obtained between July 10, 1992 and February 17, 1993 at High Mountain Correctional Center (a pseudonym), a facility located in a small community in a western state. At that time High Mountain, a maximum-security prison for men, housed approximately 426 inmates who were supervised by 150 correctional officers. During the data collection period I was granted virtually unrestricted access to all areas of the prison, at any time during the day or night, with the exception of the institution's two armed posts: a watch tower and a roving perimeter vehicle. The data represent approximately 125 hours of on-site observation and an equal number of hours spent outside the institution, talking and socializing with members of the institutional staff.

I gathered the data through observation and unstructured interviews with correctional officers, administrators, and other staff members. Inevitably, researchers seeking to understand correctional officers' sensemaking practices face a number of difficult decisions about the collection and analysis of data. Understanding of sensemaking activities depends heavily on analysis and interpretation of conversational activities in natural settings. These conversations must be either electronically recorded or reconstructed from field notes taken during or shortly after the events observed. When used ethically, electronic recording devices have the potential to alter the events we want to study in significant and unpredictable ways.

Three Occasions for Sensemaking

In any group, sensemaking activities become most apparent, and thus most amenable to study, when circumstances call into question dominant assumptions about identity, behavior, and the nature of the environment in which members find themselves. Sensemaking activity is perhaps most obvious where routine patterns of activity are repeatedly called into question by events not easily reconciled with the understandings accepted and shared by members of a group. In most organizations, opportunities for sensemaking often present themselves in the form of new members or inquisitive visitors, who require additional socialization if they are to share the work-group's understanding of behavioral norms and occupational realities.

At High Mountain Correctional Center, one of the chief products of sensemaking is a working understanding of the inmate as an untrustworthy, manipulative, and dangerous individual. The inmate is understood by the staff to be unrestrained by a normal conscience and unwilling to take responsibility for his own behavior. Such failings are assumed to reflect serious faults that are essential, unchanging features of individual personality or character. Supported by the doctrine of "less eligibility" and consistent with the ideology of the "new penology," this view involves a conscious and collective effort to see the prisoner in disparaging and stereotypical terms (Feeley and Simon 1992). Correctional officers' common understanding of inmates can be described as a form of categorical devaluation. It is akin to a legal fiction, or one of the counterfactual safety maxims that we learn to accept for its utility even while maintaining reservations about its factual content. Correctional officers learn to regard all inmates as untrustworthy, manipulative, and dangerous for the same reason as firearms enthusiasts are taught to treat all guns as loaded, and dentists are taught to see all patients as potential carriers of infection. Therefore, this understanding of inmates' character expressed by correctional officers serves as a universal precaution. Like universal precautions in medicine and dentistry, it also serves as a touchstone of competent professional practice.

At High Mountain, three kinds of events routinely call into question the working sense of inmate identity that guides custodial staff members. This stereotypical view is challenged by favorable evaluations of individual inmates often voiced by newcomers to the institution, by instances in which the informal exercise of discretion in rule enforcement seems to favor the inmate, and by the formal requirements of due process associated with the institution's internal disciplinary procedures of the institution. Such events create dissonance by challenging the working assumptions about inmates and by raising important questions about the correctional officers' loyalty and character. In responding to the uncertainty reflected in each of these situations, correctional officers employ various sensemaking strategies to reconcile apparent inconsistencies and to communicate what they take to be an appropriate professional sensibility.

Reading the Record

Newcomers to the institution frequently question the custodial staffs blanket assessments of inmates' character and identity. In a well-managed institution, newcomers interact with inmates in a variety of settings. Finding that these interactions conform in predictable ways to the expectations that govern life outside the institution, visitors often conclude that inmates are essentially normal. Remarking favorably on a particular inmate's behavior, and so calling into question the working understanding of experienced correctional staff members, frequently gives rise to a form of sensemaking activity that may be called "reading the record."

Throughout the institution, officers have access to a thick computer printout called the Confidential Register, which provides selective biographical information on each inmate. Other than documenting institutional work assignments, these records contain no material that could be used to portray the inmate in a favorable way. They provide a succinct portrait of the inmate as an offender, describing his criminal history and his sentence, release date, security classification, and housing assignment. When treatment workers, visitors, or new staff members question an experienced correctional officer's categorical devaluation of inmates by referring to a particular inmate's success in program participation, his cooperative demeanor, or his strong work ethic, a reading of the record virtually guarantees that the working understanding of the custodial staff will be supported.

Reading the Confidential Register is a form of status degradation ceremony in absentia. Because High Mountain is a maximum-security prison, inmates' criminal histories generally involve extremely serious, often violent offenses. Institutional records show that in 1992, when data collection for this study began, 32 percent of the inmates were serving time for crimes involving homicide. Another 17 percent were serving sentences for sexual assault. But these "facts" have a compelling official quality. They portray a one-dimensional man, a man whose identity has been reconstructed to serve the needs of those who hold him captive. With this style of presentation, officers can confirm to skeptical outsiders, with apparent objectivity, the dominant view of an inmate's character and identity. Reading the record allows the custodial staff to participate in the social construction of inmate identity without committing themselves to a position that inexperienced outsiders might construe as unprofessional or inappropriately prejudicial. Claims about an inmate's identity thus become documented facts rather than subjective assertions. This form of sensemaking is compelling and influential in the prison. Like all such activities, reading the record links the past with the present so as to reinforce a particular set of dispositions.

Exercising Discretion

For those correctional officers who work most directly with inmates, the routine of a shift is typically punctuated by events requiring the exercise of individual discretion in enforcing institutional rules. These events, usually quite minor, challenge officers to find creative solutions to the many human relations problems associated with managing inmates. Like their law enforcement counterparts on the outside, correctional officers cannot respond to every instance of rule breaking with formal sanctions. To do so would be time-consuming, inefficient, and counterproductive.

A formal response to rule violation is a complicated process requiring the participation of perhaps four or five other officers, generating substantial paperwork, and often making demands on the institution's superintendent. An officer who places too much emphasis on formal sanctions imposes on others, creates doubt about his or her ability to manage inmates, and is viewed by inmates and staff as weak and ineffectual. For these reasons, officers at High Mountain often rely on informal strategies as they exercise their authority, overseeing the production of order through continuous negotiation with the individuals they encounter.

Because pressures to handle rule violation informally are strong, officers frequently must ignore, at least temporarily, obvious violations of relatively minor institutional rules. Sometimes they disregard such violations until an inmate can be isolated from potential sources of support and reprimanded in private, or until an inmate who is obviously very angry has a chance to "cool off." Although it is illegal to smoke in any building in the High Mountain compound, a prudent officer might ignore an inmate caught smoking in a doorway on a cold day if he or she is aware that the inmate just received news of a family member's death or the loss of an important appeal.

Such exercise of discretion may reflect the officer's perception that tolerance is an investment in cooperation. This perception is reflected in remarks recorded in the project field notes, though these remarks sometimes indicate ambivalence and uncertainty:

> Treat the inmates like human beings and they will treat you O.K. (Housing Unit Officer)

> [Officer Ryan] said he can never let himself see inmates as human beings. Then [he] said he could [treat an inmate like a human being] if he had to tell an inmate his father died. "I'm not going to go to him and say your dad just shit the bed."

Although tolerance sometimes makes good sense, and no officer would fault another for reluctance to turn a minor problem into a possible confrontation, the exercise of tolerance and understanding may be interpreted as inconsistent with the experienced correctional officers' understanding of inmates' character. Where it appears to involve tolerance, the exercise of discretion may seem to some to suggest, inappropriately, that an inmate deserves the special consideration we usually reserve for friends, neighbors, coworkers, and others who live law-abiding lives. Particularly when witnessed by a newcomer, a correctional officer's decision to tolerate an inmate's misconduct constitutes an important occasion for sensemaking.

When officers find themselves in situations where discretion may be interpreted contrary to their commonsense notions of inmate identity, they may choose among a variety of sensemaking options. Typically, discretion that might imply undeserved tolerance toward inmates is justified pragmatically with apparent acts of kindness reframed as maneuvers in the struggle to maintain control. Such pragmatic justification links the current minor infraction with previous experience demonstrating the wisdom of tolerance or delay. Storytelling about examples of institutional disturbances frequently focuses on the minor nature of confrontations that eventually escalated into major events. According to one accout, the 1971 Attica uprising was sparked when a guard tackled an inmate who refused to leave his cell for a disciplinary hearing. Simple requests for inmates' compliance take on new meaning when linked with historical accounts of prison violence.

The language of pragmatic justification may be used to recount stories of violence in abbreviated ways, using the shorthand of metaphor. As the following expressions suggest, the language of guarding offers a number of convenient ways to communicate danger and uncertainty:

> Inmates sometimes go off when you don't expect it, so you have to be careful about how you handle things.

> He's hot now because we just wrote him up this morning. We'll let him blow off a little steam now, but I'll talk to him later about this.

> Sometimes it pays to give them a little air. Screw the lid down too tight and you can make things worse. A tough attitude can come back to bite you.

Metaphors that bring to mind unvented boilers, explosions, and volcanic eruptions all succinctly communicate the need for caution; they may be used to justify correctional practices that seem inconsistent with a militant, oppositional approach to inmates.

Pragmatic justification is a strategy that allows custodial staff members to exercise discretion and show some tolerance toward inmates without undermining the understanding of inmates' character that informs their professional decision making. By linking minor infractions with serious trouble in the past, officers can demonstrate their commitment to control even while it might appear to some observers that they are failing to exercise complete control in the present.

Ritual Insubordination and Institutional Due Process

Institutional due process frequently provides occasions for sensemaking because it combines opportunities to exercise discretion with a process that forces officers to confront the inadequacy of their assumptions about inmates. Institutional due process highlights the contradictory role expectations that characterize correctional work. In the work of the institutional disciplinary committee, individual officers struggle to reconcile belief in fairness and the rule of law with commitment to a working conception of inmate identity that is ultimately demeaning and stereotypical. Disciplinary hearings may be understood as status degradation ceremonies, in which group activity focuses on the moral failings of deviant members in an effort that ultimately affirms moral boundaries and the social solidarity of members in good standing (Garfinkel 1956).

Although institutional due process at High Mountain involves important elements of status degradation, it would be a mistake to understand such events solely in these terms. These events have a double character: They are motivated as much by a rejection of efforts to impose an "official" view of the world on the correctional officer as by a rejection of the inmate's moral worth. In institutional due process, and perhaps in offensive speech more generally, we see both status degradation ceremony and ritual insubordination. At times it may be impossible to separate one from the other.

During the course of this study, institutional due process frequently elicited derogatory remarks that called into question the inmates' moral worth and the legal requirements associated with disciplinary proceedings. Although the unflattering language of the degradation ceremony sustains the inmate's unenviable position in the moral order of the institution, it also appears to have another, equally important quality.

Because the remarks made at these hearings both disparage inmates and show a lack of respect for institutional due process, they also distance the officers who make them from an official, administratively approved version of prison life that challenges the officers' understanding of inmate identity. In short, they constitute an instance of ritual insubordination.

The term *ritual insubordination* encompasses complaining, swearing, griping, or bitching, particularly when those forms of expression form a collective response to occupational stress. In contrast to more utilitarian versions of protest, the meaning of the term is partly captured in the commonsense notion of "blowing off steam." It applies when insubordinate behavior "is not realistically expected to bring about change" (Goffman 1961:315). Goffman chose to treat ritual insubordination as a largely expressive act, lacking in practical utility but important in the identity work of individuals experiencing conflict between institutional role expectations and conceptions of personal identity.

The "D-Board"

I routinely observed ritual insubordination during meetings of the institution's disciplinary committee, a group of correctional officers organized to hear charges of internal infractions brought against inmates. Known in the institution as the "D-Board," this committee provides inmates with the first elements of due process required by law when individuals are charged with consequential violations of institutional rules. Disciplinary hearings observed at High Mountain are conducted before a senior officer, who serves as chairperson, and three other officers. Service on the D-Board depends on availability, on shift assignments, and ultimately on the discretion of the officer in charge. The committee hears testimony from the accused inmate, from the officer making the charge, and from other officers, inmates, or staff members who might provide relevant testimony.

Although these hearings are roughly analogous to a courtroom trial, those who expect elaborate due process might be surprised by their organization. Because of the need to maintain institutional security, and particularly to protect witnesses from retaliation, prison inmates do not enjoy the right to confront witnesses or even to be present when testimony is offered against them. Disciplinary committees may elect to withhold information where security concerns are an issue. Both testimony and committee deliberations may take place in a room where only correctional officers are present. The routine of these hearings is such that the disciplinary committee is frequently alone: waiting for witnesses, deliberating the facts of the case, or considering punishment options in private. Although a tape recorder is used to produce an official record of each case, tape recording is routinely suspended when inmates are requested to leave the hearing room to facilitate private discussion.

When the D-Board is in session, a substantial amount of time is spent in waiting for cases to begin or for witnesses to arrive. Committee members typically view these "in-between" periods as opportunities for gossip, storytelling, jokes, and other forms of social activity. These relatively private moments frequently are characterized by the sort of griping or bitching that Goffman called ritual insubordination. Disciplinary committee members frequently comment on the character of both particular prisoners with whom they are called to interact and the "typical" prisoner incarcerated at High Mountain.

In the thirty-six cases that I observed during the study, I heard many derogatory remarks and stories about inmates, and numerous cynical remarks about the disciplinary process. Members commonly referred to the individual about to be heard by the board as "the next victim." Officers sometimes engaged in tongue-in-cheek discussion of punishment options before the facts of the case were heard. And in one typical instance, an officer inquiring about the charge at issue in a pending case asked "What's this one guilty of?" One inmate who refused to attend his hearing was said to have "PMS today," a particularly provocative remark in an environment where few things are considered more offensive than remarks that call into question another man's masculinity. Inmates were described as "stupid," were denigrated for their sexual preferences, and were compared to animals. Officers also complained about "ACLU lawyers," "liberal judges," and "out-of-touch" administrators.

These remarks are as much a rejection of the legitimacy of institutional due process and those who support it as they are a derogatory characterization of inmates. Equally important, they always were made off the record and out of the prisoners' hearing. Although these efforts may be regarded as status degradation in absentia, they lack the full force of ceremonies in which all parties meet face-to-face. They go beyond symbolic attack on the inmate. Officers explicitly criticize the due-process demands supported by "out-of-touch" administrators who spend too much time in their offices and by "liberal" judges who "think more of inmates than they do of guards." Those people do not seem to share the correctional officer's working understanding of the inmate. Hearings that involve inmates' testimony, after all, cannot make sense to those who share the operational assumption that inmates are dishonest and manipulative. And hearings in which an inmate can call into question an officer's account of a disciplinary write-up make even less sense in the partisan world of the prison.

In relation to the disciplinary hearing, ritual insubordination represents an effort to distance oneself not only from inmates but also from an official version of the situation which suggests that an inmate's version of events has value. This implied assumption of credibility cannot be reconciled with the officers' understanding of inmates' character. In the officers' view, those who impose demands for due process challenge that understanding and force the prison staff to support their effort. Ritual insubordination gives assembled officers an opportunity to verbally express allegiance to workgroup norms in circumstances in which the actions they are legally required to take may cast doubt on that loyalty.

Those seeking justification for moral outrage would find it easily if the informal conversation that accompanies disciplinary hearings were presented out of its larger context. Ultimately these exchanges are grounded in a generally derogatory conception of inmate identity. In the understanding that emerges and is reinforced in these conversations, inmates are characterized as immature, untrustworthy, unpredictable, weak, perverse, and a potential source of trouble for the staff.

Disciplinary boards are required to choose between the version of events offered by the officer who made the initial charge and the version offered by an inmate. In situations where the board finds that punishment of an inmate is unjustified, board members, in a sense, are breaking ranks. This is particularly clear to the officer in charge of the hearings. When interviewed, he described his role as leader of the disciplinary committee by saying "I'm here to make sure the officer doesn't get stepped on out there."

Correctional officers who show too great a concern for an inmate's rights are not only placed in a position in which they may seem, to some, to side with an inmate. They are also acting so as to call into question the working understanding of inmate identity, an important expression of group loyalty. Such action can be justified pragmatically, like any expression of discretion, but it creates high levels of cognitive dissonance for those involved. This is exactly the sort of situation in which one would expect conscientious correctional officers to suffer a great deal of stress, with a need to reaffirm their commitment to colleagues and to the central tenets of their occupational culture. In disciplinary hearings, offensive speech sometimes may serve as a way to affirm one's loyalty and professional identity under difficult and confusing circumstances.

Discussion

In reading the record, correctional officers respond to challenges to their working understanding of inmate identity by making an apparently objective biographical presentation from an official source. In the informal exercise of discretion, episodes that might be understood as suggesting sympathy for apparently deserving inmates are recast as strategic maneuvers in the struggle for control of the prison. In instances of ritual insubordination associated with due process, officers reaffirm commitment to the dominant assumptions of the group through symbolic protest, and work to elaborate a vision of occupational life that reconciles group loyalty with a commitment to the rule of law.

Working understandings, and the sensemaking activity that produces and maintains them, are inevitable features of collective action, and correctional officers' sensemaking activity inevitably may be somewhat oppositional. In view of their professional responsibilities, this is probably appropriate. A working definition of the inmate that discourages trust and encourages vigilance is necessary for correctional work in maximum-security facilities. Without such operational assumptions, it is hard to understand how the job could be done.

If conversational routines that disparage inmates are to be expected in corrections, problems will arise when the categorical devaluation of inmates is unchecked by competing elements of organizational culture, or when newcomers are exposed to these routines without first learning to appreciate their significance. New employees or prison visitors are unlikely to appreciate the difference between language that enthusiastically affirms unflattering working assumptions and language expressing a genuine contempt for prisoners' human rights. Demeaning and derogatory remarks may promote pluralistic ignorance, a condition that exists in institutions where many guards support legitimate institutional goals but feel that most others do not (Kauffman 1981; Philliber 1987). Even more important, they may create the impression that inmates are fair game for more serious forms of abuse.

Offensive speech associated with the categorical devaluation of inmates may create problems for some employees; certainly it does so for the inmates in their care. Regardless of the speaker's intention, language that denigrates others may encourage abusive and even violent behavior. Language gives license, whether we intend it or not. Therefore, it is as important to discourage offensive speech as to understand it. Because casual conversation may set the stage for violent behavior in the nature, and because we know that such behavior occurs regularly in American prisons, correctional supervisors must take casual conversation seriously.

In focusing on collective efforts to affirm and protect a working understanding of inmate identity, it is easy to forget the diversity that characterizes the workforce of correctional institutions (Klofas 1984). Officers may acknowledge the value of a shared definition of the inmate in connection with of collective action, but no officer is required to fully embrace this one-dimensional view, and many clearly do not. Officers approach the routines that express these understandings with varying levels of approval, enthusiasm, and commitment. Existing research suggests that many correctional officers hold attitudes favorable to inmates, and to the provision of services facilitating rehabilitation (Kauffman 1981; Klofas and Toch 1982; Logan 1996; Lombardo 1982). In addition, many observers of prison life indicate that correctional officers have more in common with the inmates they supervise than they might care to admit (Hassine 1999; Lombardo 1989; Owen 1988).

Conclusion

The sensemaking accomplishments of the correctional staff at High Mountain are frequently called into question by the people and events that constitute the routine of prison life. By focusing on ways in which officers respond to such challenges, I explore the processes through which members repair and maintain the categorical understandings produced through sensemaking activities. By participating in these processes, officers in one prison reproduce established patterns of social control.

Like police officers, correctional officers make sense of their world through conversational routines that often appear to take place when the real work of their profession does not require their full attention (McNulty 1994). In fact, informal conversational routines are the medium through which participants engage in work that is a fundamental precondition of effective collective action. As Gronn (1983:1) observes, "[T]alk is the work," and these efforts to fill the time are essential moments in the reproduction of occupational culture and social control in the justice system.

Social scientists have worked to identify and describe the activities through which actors construct and maintain the categories that structure collective action and promote cooperation in professional life. Such efforts are an important undertaking in the social sciences. Studies of the ways in which such categories contribute to the reproduction of social control in the prison offer opportunities to learn more about inmates and correctional workers, and to understand more clearly the strategies of social control that now shape the lives of millions of incarcerated Americans. Further research on sensemaking in correctional facilities, and particularly on the categories used by correctional officers to understand their work, would contribute to a more satisfactory account of workplace culture in the justice system, and to a fuller understanding of the dynamics of social control.

Critical Thinking

This article and the previous one by Stojkovic discuss the realities of prison work and the necessity for social control methods beyond formal policy. Yet, officers seem to justify their negative perceptions of inmates, often without cause, and consequently treat inmates as if they are all disciplinary problems. Further, officers consistently violate prison rules and policies by claiming such actions are necessary to maintain social control. Viewed with a critical eye, do you think that the informal social structure of the prison allows correctional officers to act in this way?

References

Bridges, G.S. and S. Steen. 1998. "Racial Disparities in Official Assessments of Juvenile Offenders: Attributional Stereotypes as Mediating Mechanisms." *American Sociological Review* 63:554–70.

Crank, J.P. 1996. "The Construction of Meaning During Training for Probation and Parole." *Justice Quarterly* 13:265–90.

Crouch, B.M. and J. W. Marquart. 1980. "On Becoming a Guard." Pp. 63–106 in *The Keepers: Prison Guards and Contemporary Corrections*, edited by B.M. Crouch. Springfield, IL: Thomas.

Feeley M.M. and J. Simon. 1992. "The New Penology: Notes on the Emerging Strategy of Corrections and Its Implications." *Criminology* 30: 449–74.

Farkas, M.A. and P.K. Manning. 1997. "The Occupational Culture of Corrections and Police Officers." *Journal of Crime and Justice* 20:51–68.

Garfinkel, H. 1956. "Conditions of Successful Degradation Ceremonies." *American Journal of Sociology* 61:420–24.

Giddens, A. 1984. *The Constitution of Society: An Introduction to the Theory of Structuration*. Berkeley, CA: University of California Press.

Goffman, I. 1961. *Asylums: Essays on the Social Situations of Mental Patients and Other Inmates*. New York: Anchor Books.

Gronn, P.C. 1983. "Talk as the Work: The Accomplishment of School Administration." *Administrative Science Quarterly* 28:1–21.

Guenther, A.L. and M.Q. Guenther. 1980. "Screws vs. Thugs." Pp. 162–82 in *The Keepers: Prison Guards and Contemporary Corrections*, edited by B.M. Crouch. Springfield, IL: Thomas.

Hassine, V. 1999. *Life Without Parole: Living in Prison Today*. 2nd edition. Los Angeles, CA: Roxbury Publishing.

Hunt, J. 1989. "Police Accounts of Normal Force." Pp. 345–63 in *Deviant Behavior*, edited by D. Kelly. New York: St. Martin's Press.

Jacobs, J.B. and G.R. Retsky. 1975. "Prison Guard." *Urban Life* 4:5–29.

Kauffman, K. 1981. "Prison Officers' Attitudes and Perceptions of Attitudes: A Case of Pluralistic Ignorance." *Journal of Research in Crime and Delinquency* 18:272–94.

Klofas, J. 1984. "Reconsidering Prison Personnel, New Views of the Correctional Officer Subculture." *International Journal of Offender Therapy and Comparative Criminology* 28:169–275.

Klofas, J. and H. Toch. 1982. "The Guard Subculture." *Journal of Research in Crime and Delinquency* 19:238–54.

Logan, C. H. 1996. "Public vs. Private Prison Management: A Case Comparison." *Criminal Justice Review* 21:62–85.

Lombardo, L.X. 1982. "Alleviating Inmate Stress: Contributions from Correctional Officers." Pp. 285–98 in *The Pains of Imprisonment*, edited by R. Johnson and H. Toch. Beverly Hills, CA: Sage.

——. 1989. *Guards Imprisoned: Correctional Officers at Work*. 2nd edition. Cincinnati, OH: Anderson Publishing.

Marquart, J.W. 1986. "Prison Guards and the Use of Physical Coercion as a Mechanism of Social Control." *Criminology* 24:347–66.

McNulty, E.W. 1994. "Generating Common Sense Knowledge Among Police Officers." *Symbolic Interaction* 17:281–94.

Owen, B. 1988. *The Reproduction of Social Control: A Study of Prison Workers at San Quentin*. New York: Praeger.

Philliber, S. 1987. "Thy Brother's Keeper: A Review of the Literature on Correctional Officers." *Justice Quarterly* 4:9–37.

Shearing, C.D. and R.V. Ericson. 1991. "Culture as Figurative Action." *British Journal of Sociology* 42:481–506.

Sudnow, D. 1965. "Normal Crimes: Sociological Features of the Penal Code in a Public Defender Office." *Social Problems* 12:255–76.

Turner, J.H. 1987. "Toward a Sociological Theory of Motivation." *American Sociological Review* 52:15–27.

Van Maanen, J. 1978. The Asshole." Pp. 221–38 in *Policing: A View from the Street* edited by P. Manning and J. Van Maanen. Santa Monica, CA: Goodyear.

Weick, K.E. 1995. *Sensemaking in Organizations*. Thousand Oaks, CA: Sage.

23

Gender and Occupational Culture Conflict: A Study of Women Jail Officers

Eric D. Poole and Mark R. Pogrebin

<u>Abstract</u>: *Offering a female perspective of custodial corrections work in county jails, Poole and Pogrebin consider the adjustment problems and work strategies of women deputy sheriffs. The authors discuss the issues of employment integration, sex role stereotyping, gender-based work strategies, and differential treatment within the organization. The authors find that in their role as jail officers, female deputies experience work integration difficulties predominantly imposed on them by their male co-workers. These difficulties increase gender stereotyping, role conflict, and differential performance expectations. Poole and Pogrebin also depict numerous obstacles that prevent women correctional deputies from being promoted to supervisory positions. They conclude with a discussion of the personal and occupational consequences of a system rife with institutionalized sexism, and they offer some possible means for addressing these occupational barriers that presently exist in the jail organizational culture.*

Since the early 1980s, the number of women working in state and federal jails has grown dramatically. According to the Bureau of Justice Statistics of the U.S. Department of Justice, the number of females employed as correctional officers rose from 16,545 in 1988 to 42,500 in 1999—an increase of 157 percent (Perkins, Stephan, & Beck, 1995; Stephan, 2001). Females now comprise 28 percent of the custodial/security staff in jails nationwide. The primary stimulus for the increased employment and utilization of female officers has been the need to comply with federal guidelines on hiring (Equal Opportunity Act of 1972 amending Title VII of the Civil Rights Act of 1964), as well as with various court orders to implement hiring quotas to increase female representation or to rewrite entrance exams and requirements to encourage the employment of women (see Camp, Steiger, Wright, Saylor, & Gilman, 1997). While the initial stimulus for increased hiring of women was prompted by legislative and judicial mandates, several administrative factors have also driven the need for more women employees. First, jails must house both male and female inmates, and women are needed to supervise the female residents. Second, female officers are needed to conduct searches of female visitors. Third, a rapid expansion of the jail work force has increased demand and opened job opportunities for qualified female applicants.

Despite women's increased presence in corrections work, the position of female jail officer is a unique form of non-traditional work for women; it is qualitatively different from other work in that violence is prevalent in the work environment and the job is perceived to be a highly sex-typed male one requiring qualities of dominance, aggressiveness, and authoritativeness (Hemmens, Stohr, Schoeler, & Miller, 2002). Female qualities of nurturing, sensitivity, and understanding are thought by many male jail officers not merely unnecessary, but potentially detrimental to job performance. Because female officers are expected to conform to masculine sex-typed work norms, it is likely that the integration problems faced by women entering this occupation are severe; however, little research attention has been focused on female officers working in local jails.

Based on studies of women working as guards in male correctional facilities, sexism and sexual harassment have emerged as persistent obstacles to workforce integration (Farnworth, 1992; Pogrebin & Poole, 1997). Women correctional officers experience a hostile work environment where they endure resentment, harassment, and discrimination. The research suggests that male officers seek to maintain male dominance and subordination of female co-workers by sexualizing the prison work environment (Pogrebin & Poole, 1997). What is lacking almost entirely from the research literature is a focus on the impact of the sexualized work environment on women jail officers. The present paper seeks to lay an initial qualitative research foundation upon which this area of concern may be addressed.

We will frame our study by focusing on gender as a normative system, a pervasive network of interrelated norms and sanctions through which female and male behavior is evaluated and controlled (West & Zimmerman, 1987). This conception of gender as a scheme of interpersonal evaluations is, of course, implicit in most critiques of the concepts of "femininity" and "masculinity." Guided by how workplace perceptions and practices bear a close relation to these sociocultural constructions of reality, we will stress what Padavic (1991) has described as the "re-creation of gender in the male workplace" (p. 279) and what Stockard and Johnson (1980) has termed "the reproduction of male dominance in everyday interactions" (p. 10).

Diverse studies of the gender system have irrefutably shown how the subordination of women is sustained through their being socialized for, and restricted to, limited aspirations, options, roles, and rewards. The weighty significance of such factors, along with the basic learning processes and major societal institutions that produce and perpetuate them, is unquestionable. Equally important is the role of interpersonal evaluation in ordinary life situations. In particular, informal social control must be recognized as a key mechanism that backs up and enforces many of the restrictions and limitations placed on women. There are various ways, then, in which gender—as a sociocultural complex of meanings, behaviors, and assessments—is instilled and maintained. Hochschild (1973) identifies four main perspectives adopted in studies of women and the gender system. One focuses on the nature of biological and psychological "sex differences"; a second emphasizes "sex roles and the norms which govern them"; a third treats "women as a minority group"; and the fourth—a "politics of caste" outlook—stresses power differentials and exploitation as a tool of control. As Hochschild notes, these alternative approaches reflect different disciplinary traditions, tend to favor different "conceptual vocabularies," and may carry different implications with respect to social change and public policy. In the present work, the first orientation ("sex differences") receives little attention. Each of the other three approaches, however, provides concepts and emphases that are useful for the analysis of women's work experiences. Our central concept of "gender norms" has close ties to the study of "sex roles," even if the focus here on reinforcement in daily interaction departs somewhat from the more usual stress on socialization. In exploring the basic perceptions and responses through which women are devalued, the analogy to deviance labeling and stigmatization will prove valuable. Finally, power and control differentials are going to be critical sensitizing concepts in examining the sexualization of the work setting, in general, and sexual harassment, in particular. In developing an overview of women working in jail it is unnecessary, therefore, and might even prove counterproductive, to attempt to adopt one of these orientations. The sociological penchant for identifying supposedly competing "schools" should not lead us to neglect points on which otherwise different approaches may converge or complement each other. Because the topic of women working in traditional male occupations is highly complex, to study it we may well need a varied arsenal of sociological concepts and outlooks.

Occupational Norms and Workplace Organization

Both early studies and the contemporary literature reveal that women who have entered a variety of traditionally male occupations have faced discriminatory hiring and assignment practices, resistance and opposition from male co-workers, and inadequate on-the-job training. The experiences of women entering the corrections field are illustrative of these organizational obstacles and challenges to changing occupational norms in a work setting undergoing integration (Britton, 2003; Carlson, Anson, & Thomas, 2003). To understand the persistence of an organizational climate of resentment, skepticism, and hostility toward women working in corrections, we must first examine the nature of the occupational norms that are at stake.

Occupational norms have traditionally been linked to work segregation by sex (Jacobs, 1989). For the most part, the sex typing of specific jobs is arbitrary and follows one basic rule: men and women are different and should be doing different things. Such stereotypical thinking has long sustained the stigmatization of those who violate such norms of occupational segregation, thus reinforcing sex-role typing in the workplace. Sex-role stereotypes function to keep women in ancillary and supportive roles rather than in positions of independence, authority, and leadership (Safilios-Rothschild, 1979). A consequence for women who challenge these sex-role stereotypes is the negative evaluation of their skills, capabilities, and competence. While women in corrections work may perform the job as well as men, they tend not to be seen as being men's equals (Belknap, 1996).

Negative reactions to or sanctioning of occupational "deviants" constitutes a powerful social control mechanism in maintaining a polarized male and female work force (Schur, 1984). Particularly when women enter what have traditionally been viewed as ultramasculine occupations (such as coal mining, steel manufacturing, firefighting, corrections, etc.), intense reactions are expected to occur. Several common responses are likely to be found in such situations of female occupational deviance (Schur, 1979). Consciousness of the deviant's femaleness will be heightened. Consciousness of the female's deviance also will be high, and she will be devalued, restricted and otherwise punished for it. Finally, male workers may convince themselves that a woman who commits such occupational deviance deserves whatever she gets. Women come to be viewed as "fair game" for whatever abuses—verbal, emotional, or physical—male co-workers decide to dispense. In such a work situation, then, a specific imputation of deviant identity to the woman is used to rationalize diverse forms of male untoward behavior directed toward her (Schur, 1984). This rationalization suggests that harassment may sometimes implicitly constitute punishment for women's perceived violation of specific gender norms

Some observers contend that a generalized perception of threat to male power and control on the part of male workers lies behind most harassment in the workplace (Erez & Tontodonato, 1992). It is important, however, to keep in mind that something besides occupational power and control is involved in the harassment phenomenon. As MacKinnon (1979) notes,

> The sense that emerges from incidents of sexual harassment is. . .[that men] want to know that they can go this far this way any time they wish and get away with it. . . .. The practice seems an extension of their desire and belief that the woman is there for them, however they may choose to define that.

(p. 162)

Harassment functions to sustain both male workplace power and male power to treat women as sexual objects (Zimmer, 1988). Workplace harassment, then, is not merely a result of women's violating occupational norms or their being vulnerable as tokens (i.e., being in the numerical minority). On the contrary, it also reflects the socialized and reinforced tendency of male co-workers to view women primarily as visual sexual objects (MacKinnon, 1979). From this standpoint, harassment of women workers has as much to do with the daily harassment they experience in many other contexts as it has to do with the specific features of women's work situations.

The sexualized work environment embodies the treatment of women as objects and a denial of personal autonomy (Farley, 1978). According to MacKinnon (1982), "Sexual objectification is the primary process of the subjection of women" (p. 541). This process is thus central to perceptions of female violations of occupational norms and gender roles, as individual women are submitted to standardized and stereotype-laden categorizations and responses. In this respect the sexualized work environment is the linchpin of occupational inequality (Martin, 1989). The research presented here seeks to explore the dimensions of the sexualized jail setting that women corrections officers face and to understand the significance of gender in their work experiences.

Method

Four county jails and three adult detention centers located in four counties in the Denver metropolitan area were selected for the present study. These facilities were managed and staffed by personnel from four sheriffs' departments. Utilizing personnel rosters of deputy sheriffs provided by the respective facilities, we drew a 50% systematic random sample (n = 135) of all female officers from each institution. We contacted sampled officers individually in order to inform them of the purpose of the study, request their participation, and obtain informed consent. A total of 119 women agreed to participate, and interview times were then scheduled. Because of conflicts related to vacation, sick leave, work assignment, transfer, etc., interviews with 11 women could not be conducted. Thus, the present study was based on interview data from 108 women deputies. Their ages ranged from 24 to 51 (median = 37), and their length of experience at their present facility ranged from one to fifteen years (median = 5).

Interviews were conducted at the respective facilities in private conference rooms, library carrels, or visitation rooms during off hours. Each interview lasted approximately ninety minutes and was tape recorded with the subject's consent. A semi-structured interview format was used, which relied on sequential probes to pursue leads provided by subjects. This allowed the deputies to identify and elaborate on important domains they perceived to characterize their experiences in jail work, rather than the researchers eliciting responses to structured questions.

Findings

Second-Class Status

According to Belknap (1991), the conflict between gender-role norms and occupational-role norms in jail work poses unique obstacles for female officers. The traditional male attitude about the inherent masculine nature of the job of jail guard makes the prospect of a female co-worker particularly offensive to some men officers. For example, corrections officers associate masculinity with physical ability and view the use of force as a defining feature of the job (Belknap, 1991). Jurik (1985) reports that male officers believe that women are incapable of exercising sufficient physical force to perform the social control tasks required to control incorrigible inmates; moreover, women are often seen as less reliable in back-up or cover roles when handling violent encounters with inmates. Implicit trust and reliance that an officer will come to another's aid and use any means necessary to protect a peer's life are vital components of the work expectations among corrections officers. Male staff are fearful that the presumed physical limitations of women will place officers at greater risk and make the environment potentially more threatening and dangerous because of the inmates' perception of diminished staff ability to maintain control. Women in line positions are thus regarded as second-class officers, unable to meet reliably job performance criteria of male officers.

Zimmer (1986) reports that female officers are afforded few opportunities to build skills or gain confidence in controlling prisoners in threatening situations. Since women are perceived as weak, indecisive, emotional, and timid, male officers tend to take charge in physical encounters between women deputies and inmates. This action, although necessary in aiding a fellow officer as back-up, reinforces male feelings of physical superiority over women and diminishes the status of female officers. One woman officer describes her experience:

> I've been on many codes [officer back-up] when there is a physical altercation going on and male officers have run in with me and I'm shoved aside so the guys can get in on the fight. . . . I don't know if it's ego. Some of it is patronizing, some protective, "We've got to take care of the little women."

The attitude that female officers need protection from aggressive inmates is also shared by supervisory staff. Instead of developing policy which is inclusive of women in these dangerous encounters, supervisory personnel tend to reinforce the stereotype of women's heightened vulnerability. A deputy illustrated this problem:

> We had a fight in the girls' pod day room, and there was all this concern all of a sudden that we can't have two female officers in the pod. . . . It's just not safe. The male supervisors think we can't handle it.

If women corrections officers are not afforded the opportunity to resolve inmate physical altercations, they are restricted in their repertoire of social control techniques. To the extent that supervisory personnel reinforce this subordinate position, women officers will have limited opportunities to demonstrate their physical abilities and gain experience and confidence in the skilled use of force. Such paternalistic treatment thus serves to undermine the authority of women officers and calls in question their ability to perform their job:

> A male deputy, in front of some inmates, put his arm around me and said, "Dear, I'm going to go to lunch. Can you handle this?"

The paternalistic treatment of women is in itself a denial of their basic role identity as agents of security and control. The notion that women officers can't take care of themselves subjugates them in their work relations with men, as well as imputing diminished capacities in their routine job performance. In her participant observer role as a coal handler in a power plant, Padavic (1991) reports that paternalistic treatment made her "unsure of [her] abilities, afraid of undertaking something new, doing it wrong, and thereby confirming a stereotype" (p. 286). Millett (1971) further notes that while paternalism is held as "a palliative to the injustice of women's social position, chivalry is also a technique for disguising it" (p. 37).

The irony of the self-fulfilling prophecy that operates in the jail setting is two-fold. First, women officers who are subjected to paternalistic protection and control are not given the opportunity to develop or prove their physical skills, which in turn tautologically confirms the male co-workers' stereotypes. Second, when women officers are treated as second class employees who are perceived in need of protection, they may experience heightened anxiety, exhibit less self-confidence, and even react in inappropriate or unsatisfactory ways. Thus the circle is complete—paternalistic actions serve to foster the stereotypical behavior that in turn confirms the original expectations.

Occupational Subculture

Pollock (1986) notes the guard subculture is an important component of work socialization. Yet male officers tend to adhere to a cult of masculinity that serves to isolate women co-workers as outsiders (Belknap, 1991). By excluding women staff from the informal organizational network of male deputies, the former are often forced to learn much of the job on their own. As a result of this purposive exclusion, women are denied occupational socialization opportunities and a sense of belonging associated with collegial relations. Because much of the job training is done on an informal basis as situations arise, the isolation of female officers undermines their ability to learn the particulars and peculiarities of the job from experienced male colleagues.

Zimmer (1986) reports that female officers are viewed by many of their male peers as being inferior and are therefore denied entree to the officer subculture. One deputy describes her experience of exclusion from informal work networks:

> The male officers go out for drinks after work. Nobody ever bothers to tell me until later on and I find out just in conversation. . . . I once asked a male deputy to let me know when the shift goes out and he said that he knows that some of the men bother me, so he didn't ask me along.

The social exclusion of women deputies makes them easy targets for jocular aggression and derogatory nicknames; moreover, male work group solidarity may be enhanced by directing humor at female officers. This "laughter of inclusion" (Dupreel, 1928) affirms the gender distinctions and relative male superiority. Innuendo, insinuation, and character assassination are effective strategies in maintaining social distance and social boundaries between the male in-group and the female out-group. As one deputy notes, "You're always mindful of your position here. You're at work doing your job, but you always feel somehow you don't really belong here." In short, women officers are often ostracized and belittled by their male co-workers. The male officers view women with a mixture of hostility and resentment, treating them with disdain or simply ignoring them.

According to Millett (1971), men have a vested interest in sustaining conventional sexual distinctions in role relationships, which reflect a recognition and acceptance of gender-based status and power differentials. In this point we can see a link between gender identity and work role dynamics. Gender norms and work relationships are concerned with maintaining boundaries—moral, social, and psychological. Imputed male work superiority and dominance require female devaluation and subordination. Thus Dworkin (1974) asserts: "The truth of it is that he is powerful . . . when contrasted with her" (p. 44).

Sustaining male workplace superiority dictates that women be isolated so that they cannot compete with males. In this way the strength of women's efforts to compete determines the force required by men to limit or restrict these attempts. Change on one side of the equation invariably affects the other side as well. It is the perception of a threat, regardless of whether that perception is well founded, that constitutes a central basis for resistance to change and triggers the systematic devaluation of women workers (Kanter, 1977).

When male workers' conceptions of their masculinity are closely linked to the nature and conditions of their work (particularly in what have traditionally been viewed as ultramasculine occupations), they are especially likely to feel threatened by female job entrants and resort to more overt subjugation (see Lutze & Murphy, 1999). Of course, if women are cowed into lowering their aspirations or limiting their efforts, it may not matter whether this happens because their workplace threats to men are real or imagined. Either way, the overall subjugation of females would again be taking its toll in lost work contributions and occupational achievements.

Emotion Work

Fox and Hesse-Biber (1984) suggest that certain forms of workplace harassment and abuse are so commonly tolerated that many women have come to regard such activity as inevitable and as virtually a condition of employment. These researchers report that women are reluctant to try to do anything about harassment out of fear of reprisals that may include being fired, demoted, passed over for promotion or a raise, transferred to an undesirable job, or given a poor performance evaluation. In hopes of protecting their job security, female officers often accept and endure the harassment as part of the work environment. Such stressful work conditions often produce feelings of anger, irritability, fear, anxiety, powerlessness, and depression. A female deputy described the types of emotional problems they have had to face:

> I became something of a zombie. I was emotionally numb. I didn't care about anything or anyone and as a result I was very lonely and isolated. Even at parties or at other social occasions I just didn't feel comfortable. . . . People like to talk about work, tell stories, you know. But I couldn't bring myself to talk about what I did at work.

Research in law enforcement agencies and correctional settings has shown that women and minority officers are especially vulnerable to the psychological and physiological disorders associated with sustained exposure to job-related stress. For example, Wexler and Logan's (1983) study of the sources of stress among women officers in a large metropolitan police department indicated that their greatest obstacle was in demonstrating that they could be effective officers without compromising their femininity:

> the most significant stressors seem to be ones in which others were denying them as officers, as women, or both. It is psychologically a very threatening and uncomfortable situation when one's self-perception is substantially different from the perception of others. This is particularly the case when such fundamental identities are at stake as one's gender and profession.
>
> (p. 53)

Individuals who feel or know they are deemed marginal employees experience anxiety and are more sensitive about their job performance, often assuming a defensive posture, attempting to overcompensate to prove others wrong in their attitudes, or otherwise reacting in ways that may be perceived as inappropriate or undesirable (Wright & Saylor, 1991). Two deputies relate their reactions:

> I found that I would lose my temper over the littlest of things. . . . Stupid little things would happen and I would start crying.

> I just stayed mad. I became defensive. I had a big chip on my shoulder. I hated the constant abuse and kept thinking that one day I would just kill someone.

The job stress experienced by women working in jails is further exacerbated by their lack of access to the peer-group support structure of fellow male deputies. The informal work subculture often functions to reduce stress, providing individual officers a forum within which they can vent safely. Women deputies' lack of acceptance in this traditional male fraternity thus denies them a critical organizational coping mechanism to mitigate the impact of work-related stress.

Female officers sometimes attempt to deal with their male co-workers by adopting a "give-and-take" approach, a sort of verbal jousting. This tactic, however, is risky, as shown by a women deputy:

> Bantering back and forth with the men takes a lot of stress out of the situation and kind of neutralizes the harassment we experience. But once it goes beyond or crosses the line, there seems to be no course of action for female officers.

Such inability on the part of female deputies to engage in verbal horseplay on an equal footing with male co-workers reflects their lack of acceptance in the work subculture. Pogrebin and Poole (1988) observe that "Joking relations among peers generate feelings of implicit understanding and camaraderie, thus strengthening group norms and bonds" (p. 184). The rub is that women deputies are not accepted as "peers" in the jail work setting; thus, women may find that their attempts to act like "one of the boys" via joking relations are met with "punitive" responses from male co-workers (Seckman & Couch, 1989).

Unequal Opportunity

Women in corrections routinely experience derision, hostility, and exclusion from male supervisors and co-workers. Their attitudes toward job commitment and aspirations to advance in the profession are adversely affected by such treatment (Belknap, 1991). Chapman and her colleagues (1983) report that female corrections officers perceive unequal opportunities and unequal treatment in promotion. Poole and Pogrebin (1988) uncover a similar perception among women police officers; specifically, after only three years on the job, policewomen view their chances of ever being promoted greatly diminished. A veteran officer who had many years working in the patrol side of the sheriff's department tells of her disappointment in not having an opportunity for advancement:

> I came off the street as a road deputy after 12 years on the front lines. I really did think I had the skills to come here and make some rank and do well, but that will never happen.

Jurik (1985) claims that supervisors who are biased against females working as corrections officers use performance evaluations to discourage them and keep them in subordinate positions. Since performance history is a critical criterion in advancement to supervisory ranks, women officers are viewed as less promotable. One deputy notes the nature of the inequality:

> There is one woman who really is an exceptional deputy and I like her a lot. She is really strong and stern and she knows her job very well. If she were a man, they would think she is the best deputy in the world, but because she is female they think she is a bitch. But if a male deputy would act like her, they would promote him real fast.

In those rare instances when a female officer receives a choice assignment or a promotion, she is perceived by male staff as not having earned it. For example, females are often teased about trading sexual favors for advancement:

> There are men on this job that think anytime a woman gets ahead the first thing out of their mouth is: "Oh, I wonder who she's sleeping with?" . . . That's their way of dealing with women who're better than them.

Such sexist attributions of female career advancement serve to impede the acceptance of women into the work subculture, which robs them of important training, peer support, sponsorship, and access to inside information for job assignments and promotional opportunities (Zimmer, 1986). If sexist attitudes and actions are allowed to prevail, women officers are unlikely to be seen as capable of becoming supervisors and joining the ranks of the management.

Among those women in our sample who had attained supervisory positions (n = 6), there was a consensus that they now experience more hostility and resistance than they had encountered when they were line officers. These women perceive greater resentment on the part of not only the male line staff but their fellow male supervisors as well:

> I finally realized after years on the job that I've been playing gin rummy and the men have been playing poker. . . . We are socialized to be a team player and sacrifice for the good of the group. . . . Men are like sharks. Play on a team with sharks, they'll eat you alive.

Supervisory work in many respects is associated with male role characteristics like independence, initiative, forcefulness, competitiveness, and tough-minded objectivity. Ironically, although the image of the supervisor is one that emphasizes masculine traits, the tasks that the supervisor actually performs are not exclusively those associated with maleness. Compassion, understanding, and interpersonal warmth, traits associated with the female role, have been shown to be just as important to supervisory success as the male qualities (Kim, DeValve, DeValve, & Johnson, 2003). Moreover, women in supervisory positions in jail are a new phenomenon, representing a complete reversal of the historically all-male management staff and directly challenging the traditional conceptions of the relationship between sex and power.

Given the greater exclusiveness of supervisory positions, especially the inner circles of upper management, the entry of women into positions of increased status and power may be seen as disruptive and detrimental to the intimacy, solidarity, and informality of the nearly all-male colleague group. And exclusion from this more powerful male management subculture again results in a lack of access to information, contacts, and informal participation, representing yet another barrier to career advancement.

Another source of resistance to women supervisors is the organizational perception that women simply do not make good managers. They are often viewed as overbearing and domineering, as well as inflexible and overly concerned with bureaucratic routines and details (Rosen & Jerdee, 1973; Schein, 1973). The women supervisors in our study do report sex differences in how they do their jobs. And these differences seem to originate in their performance as line officers. For example, Worden (1993) reports that women police officers emphasize rules and regulations more and exercise discretion less frequently than do their male counterparts. This is because the standard operating procedures define roles and evaluation criteria, establishing a level playing field with the men. Women jail officers similarly perceive "going by the book" as a safer method of operation, thus avoiding risky discretionary decision making which may lead to criticism.

> I've learned it's best to know the rules and stick to them in everything you do in here. Someone's always waiting for you to mess up...; so it's better to have rules you can rely on to do your job.... Because if a female officer messes up because she wasn't following the rules, then it's made ten times worse.

And most women in our sample also believe that adhering to rules and regulations is a function of their gender socialization:

> Women pay more attention to detail, more strict abidance to the rules. I mean, the rules are the rules, that's the way we've been socialized. We follow the rules or we lose our turn. And we follow the rules well. Even if some rules don't make sense, if it's a rule, we still follow it.

It is likely that women officers who have successfully survived and advanced in the jail organization still embrace these work strategies, tending to rely on what has worked for them in the past. The consequences of employing such a work strategy in the role of a manager, however, are deleterious, if not predictable, as three women supervisors observe:

> On my last [performance evaluation] I received several negative comments about how I handle officers.... I was criticized for how I write them up. They think I'm too picky and that I demand too much.

Kanter (1977) argues that negative perceptions of women in supervisory positions reflect sex differences in power and influence within organizations. In particular, performance ratings by supervisors are affected by the supervisor's power and influence; and more powerful supervisors generate higher morale, tend to be less rigid and authoritarian, and are generally better liked. Powerless supervisors, on the other hand, are more likely to be controlling in their relationships with subordinates, show favoritism, and generate lower morale. Since men are more likely to be in formal positions of power and authority and to be part of the informal networks of organizational influence, differences in the perception and behavior of female supervisors are more a function of the unequal distribution of organizational power than a reflection of sex differences in managerial or personal style.

Discussion

Women jail deputies find themselves in an occupational dilemma. Many male jail officers harbor negative attitudes toward competent women co-workers because they perceive women who can perform their job-related tasks satisfactorily as threatening. On the other hand, they view female officers who fail to perform the job adequately as confirming the stereotypical "unfitness" of female workers. Thus, the better officers women become, the greater their threat to the male establishment.

Several observers have noted that gender remains the defining or controlling (i.e., master) status in traditionally male occupations, with women treated first on the basis of their sex role and second on the basis of their work role (Williams, 1989). Hunt (1990) argues that gender-based norms support discriminatory practices and sexual harassment in the work setting, which in turn reinforce and maintain power differentials. The sexualized work environment is intended to keep a woman subservient by making her feel unwelcome, insecure, and fearful. The strategy is to exert control through intimidation and humiliation.

The consequences of institutional sexism may be such as to discourage aspirations and restrict opportunities, or to instill fear of being maligned or punished for even trying. In short, sexism may reduce the efforts of females to demonstrate their full potential. Systematic devaluation of women's work roles easily becomes self-fulfilling and self-perpetrating. It can create and maintain conditions that minimize the need for males to confront evidence contradicting their stereotypes, or to experience dissonance when they demean female coworkers (Schur, 1984).

Sexual harassment represents a violation of Title VII of the U.S. Civil Rights Act, which bans sex-based discrimination (Deitch, 1993). Any conduct which has the purpose or effect of substantially interfering with an individual's work performance or creating an intimidating, hostile or offensive working environment is prohibited; moreover, employers have an affirmative duty to take "all steps necessary" to prevent such conduct and to take remedial actions when it does occur. Yet, we find a great deal of misunderstanding as to what constitutes sex-based discriminatory practices. For example, Gutek and Morasch (1982) note that "men are more likely than women to project sexuality into ambiguous behavior between sexes at work, and to feel that such sexuality is appropriate in the work environment" (p. 59); consequently, what female workers perceive as unwelcome sexual advances may be viewed by male employees as innocent flattery. Konrad and Gutek (1986) further report that males employed in male-dominated jobs are less inclined than men working in gender-integrated jobs to define their gender-based behavior toward women co-workers as sexual harassment. It appears that gender-integrated work settings foster a greater congruence of definitions of acceptable behavior between the sexes, which may serve to reduce the nature and extent of gender-based behavioral misunderstandings.

A complicating factor in effecting change in the jail setting is the social pathology of a male-dominated work culture. The occupational culture of jail work is based on the values and eccentricities of a cult of masculinity, largely exemplified in behaviors such as aggression, taunting, horseplay, and sexually related conversation and innuendo (Belknap, 1991). Despite significant increases in the number of women in local corrections, the generally higher caliber (and more educated) people entering the field, better professional training, and implementation of policies to control sexual harassment and related misconduct, vestiges of the long-established characteristics of the occupational culture still persist. Since survival in the informal organization requires adherence to the subcultural norms, women must develop appropriate adjustment or coping strategies not only in doing their jobs but also in managing their work relations with male officers. Men tend to misinterpret culturally-related behaviors of women jail deputies—largely holding them to a double standard—and cannot understand why they are accused of harassment or conduct unbecoming an officer.

The sexualized work environment of the jail is thus grounded in and supported by a combination of structural factors (e.g., occupational segregation, tokenism, hierarchical power arrangements) and cultural themes and processes (e.g., occupational norms, gender-based stereotypes, status inequality) that become manifest in social interaction. Sex discrimination and job segregation regularly place working women under male supervision and control, heavily dependent on males for their economic security. Because of their subordinate economic and occupational situations, most women have neither autonomy nor authority in workplace relations (Kanter, 1977). These consequences of the sexualized work environment thus have implications that go beyond the job itself.

The prevailing opinion of female officers in all seven facilities was that the elimination of harassment in local corrections organizations was dependent on top administrators enforcing policies against sexual harassment. As long as sexist stereotypes are allowed to pervade the work setting, women officers will be viewed and treated as second class workers. Lovrich and Stohr (1993) further argue that managers and supervisors in corrections need to transform the work environment into one where women officers are recognized and appreciated as valuable resources and are fully integrated into both formal and informal organizational cultures, both of which are intolerant of sexual and gender harassment. Also, there must be a strong advocacy role adopted by jail administrators in order for female deputies to gain equal opportunities for career advancement (Zimmer, 1989).

In order to minimize harassing behavior in the jail setting, administrators need to invest in the career development of all employees, advance the ideals of professionalism, and establish closer linkages to line staff (Belknap, 1996; Zimmer, 1989). Such a work climate would help to lower the level of animosity and offensive behavior directed at women officers by male co-workers. The "affirmative duty" of jail management lies not simply in fostering a general atmosphere which will combat harassing behavior but also in implementing proactive mechanisms to monitor and prevent the conditions that give rise to such actions.

The organization of corrections work itself plays a role in producing and reinforcing workplace attitudes and behavior, and thus the extent to which sexism and sexual harassment may be institutionally tolerated. These discriminatory practices and subsequent difficulties faced by women officers can be affected significantly if the organization implements adequate administrative strategies to promote gender integration and institutionalize measures to provide equality of opportunity.

Conclusion

The presence of women in what has long been an exclusively male occupation creates a multitude of individual and organizational conflicts. The workplace functions as a complex occupational and organizational entity that shapes workers' perceptions of self and others. The relationship between gender and organizational status reveals that those work roles assigned to women are seen as appropriate extensions of their more diffuse social role of nurturance. These arrangements can act to reflect, magnify, or distort gender differences, which then confirm prevailing stereotypes and organizational norms. This situation has culminated in male co-workers' and super-visors' limited and often inaccurate appraisal of women officers' true potential and capabilities in the field.

To persist in this state of affairs is untenable because evaluating female officers on the basis of male sex-typed norms distracts from the organization's efforts to imple-ment competency-based standards and reduces its ability to analyze work problems and formulate solutions. The jail must demonstrate a philosophical commitment to the thorough integration of women within the formal and informal organizational structure. The more barriers women face in accessing informal channels of informa-tion and conflict resolution, the more they are compelled to respond formally with its associated implications of lesser control and power. Jail officers, whether male or female, are less likely to perform effectively if they are not perceived as exercising legitimate authority under conditions of equality.

The nature and scope of jail work continue to increase in complexity, presenting new job expectations and challenges for male and female officers alike. Given the need to adjust and respond to changing organizational demands, it becomes more critical that officers have the opportunity to hone their unique talents and utilize their special skills with greater latitude. Developing alternative or multiple work strategies would thus permit officers to maximize their effectiveness and accomplish tasks otherwise beyond their capacity. An important initiative in realizing such change in organiza-tional culture is to flatten the hierarchical control mechanisms and eliminate the administrative pressures for worker uniformity that have served to reinforce and maintain traditional job stereotypes in the jail setting. Finally, Wexler and Quinn (1985) report that the number of women present in an organization is a critical-mass variable in facilitating gender-integrated work groups. This finding would seem to encourage more aggressive recruitment and retention of women officers who by their sheer numbers may promote the development of an androgynous work culture where an individual officer's success is predicated on ability, rather than sexual physiology.

Critical Thinking

Institutionalized sexism is found in numerous professions and limits women's opportunities for employment and occupational advancement. This is espe-cially true in the criminal justice fields of law enforcement and institutional corrections, where males dominate in large numbers. Based on the readings on women police officers can you think of ways that women correctional officers adapt to the masculine norms of jails?

References

Belknap, J. (1991). Women in conflict: An analysis of women correctional officers. *Women & Criminal Justice*, 2, 89–115.

Belknap, J. (1996). *The invisible woman: Gender, crime, and justice*. Belmont, CA: Wadsworth.

Britton, D.M. (2003). *At work in the iron cage: The prison as gendered organization*. New York: New York University Press.

Camp, S.D., Steiger, T.L., Wright, K.N., Saylor, W.G., & Gilman, E. (1997). Affirmative action and the "level playing field": Comparing perceptions of own and minority job advancement opportunities. *Prison Journal, 77*, 313–334.

Carlson, J.R., Anson, R.H., & Thomas, G. (2003). Correctional officer burnout and stress: Does gender matter? *Prison Journal, 83*, 277–288.

Chapman, J.R., Minor, E.K., Rieker, P.P., Mills, T.R., & Bottum, M. (1983). *Women employed in corrections.* Washington, DC: U.S. Department of Justice, National Institute of Justice.

Deitch, C. (1993). Gender, race, and class politics and the inclusion of women in Title VII of the 1964 Civil Rights Act. *Gender and Society, 7*, 183–203.

Dupreel, E. (1928). Le problème sociologique du rise. *Revue Philosophique, 106*, 213–260.

Dworkin, A. (1974). *Woman hating.* New York: E.P. Dutton.

Erez, E., & Tontodonato, P. (1992). Sexual harassment in the criminal justice system. In I.L. Moyer (Ed.), *The changing roles of women in the criminal justice system: Offenders, victims, and professionals* (pp. 227–252). Prospect Heights, IL: Waveland Press.

Farley, L. (1978). *Sexual shakedown.* New York: McGraw Hill.

Farnworth, L. (1992). Women doing a man's job: Female prison officers working in a male prison. *Australian and New Zealand Journal of Criminology, 25*, 278–296.

Fox, M.F., & Hesse-Biber, S. (1984). *Women at work.* Palo Alto, CA: Mayfield.

Gutek, B.A., & Morasch, B. (1982). Sex-ratios, sex-role spillover, and sexual harassment of women at work. *Journal of Social Issues, 38*, 55–74.

Hemmens, C., Stohr, M.K., Schoeler, M., & Miller, B. (2002). One step up, two steps back: The progression of perceptions of women's work in prisons and jails. *Journal of Criminal Justice, 30*, 473–489.

Hochschild, A.R. (1973). A review of sex role research. In J. Huber (Ed.), *Changing women in a changing society* (pp. 249–267). Chicago: University of Chicago Press.

Hunt, J. (1990). The logic of sexism among police. *Women and Criminal Justice, 1*, 3–30.

Jacobs, J.A. (1989). *Revolving doors: Sex segregation and women's careers.* Stanford, CA: Stanford University Press.

Jurik, N.C. (1985). An officer and a lady: Organizational barriers to women working as correctional officers in men's prisons. *Social Problems, 32*, 375–388.

Kanter, R.M. (1977). *Men and women of the corporation.* New York: Basic Books.

Kim, A.S., DeValve, M., DeValve, E.Q., & Johnson, W.W. (2003). Female wardens: Results from a national survey of state correctional executives. *Prison Journal, 83*, 406–425.

Konrad, A.M., & Gutek, B.A. (1986). Impact of work experiences on attitudes toward sexual harassment. *Administrative Science Quarterly, 31*, 422–438.

Lovrich, N.P., & Stohr, M.K. (1993). Gender and jail work: Correctional policy implications of perceptual diversity in the work force. *Policy Studies Review, 12*, 66–84.

Lutze, F.E., & Murphy, D.W. (1999). Ultramasculine prison environments and inmates' adjustment: It's time to move beyond the "boys will be boys" paradigm. *Justice Quarterly, 16*, 709–734.

MacKinnon, C.A. (1979). *Sexual harassment of working women.* New Haven, CT: Yale University Press.

MacKinnon, C.A. (1982). Feminism, Marxism, method, and the state: An agenda for theory. *Signs, 7*, 515–544.

Martin, S.E. (1989). Sexual harassment: The link joining gender stratification, sexuality, and women's economic status. In J. Freeman (Ed.), *Women: A feminist perspective* (pp. 57–75). Mountain View, CA: Mayfield.

Millett, K. (1971). *Sexual politics.* New York: Avon Books.

Padavic, I. (1991). The re-creation of gender in a male workplace. *Symbolic Interaction, 14*, 279–294.

Perkins, C.A., Stephan, J.J., & Beck, A.J. (1995). *Jails and jail inmates 1993–94.* Washington, DC: U.S. Department of Justice, Bureau of Justice Statistics.

Pogrebin, M.R., & Poole, E.D. (1988). Humor in the briefing room: A study of the strategic uses of humor among police. *Journal of Contemporary Ethnography, 17*, 183–210.

Pogrebin, M.R., & Poole, E.D. (1997). The sexualized work environment: A look of women jail officers. *Prison Journal, 77*, 41–57.

Pollock, J.M. (1986). *Sex and supervision: Guarding male and female inmates.* New York: Greenwood.

Poole, E.D., & Pogrebin, M.R. (1988). Factors affecting the decision to remain in policing: A study of women officers. *Journal of Police Science and Administration, 16*, 49–55.

Rosen, B., & Jerdee, T.H. (1973). The influence of sex-role stereotypes on evaluation of male and female supervisory behavior. *Journal of Applied Psychology, 57*, 44–48.

Safilios-Rothschild, C. (1979). *Sex role stereotypes and sex discrimination: A synthesis and critique of the literature.* U.S. Department of Health, Education and Welfare, National Institute of Education. Washington, DC: U.S. Government Printers Office.

Schein, V.E. (1973). The relationship between sex stereotypes and requisite management characteristics. *Journal of Applied Psychology, 57*, 95–100.

Schur, E.M. (1979). *Interpreting deviance.* New York: Harper & Row.

Schur, E.M. (1984). *Labeling women deviant: Gender, stigma, and social control*. Philadelphia: Temple University Press.

Seckman, M.A., & Couch, C.J. (1989). Jocularity, sarcasm, and relationships. *Journal of Contemporary Ethnography*, *18*, 327–344.

Stephan, J.J. (2001). *Census of jails, 1999*. Washington, DC: U.S. Department of Justice, Bureau of Justice Statistics.

Stockard, J., & Johnson, M.M. (1980). *Sex roles*. Englewood Cliffs, NJ: Prentice-Hall.

West, C., & Zimmerman, D.H. (1987). Doing gender. *Gender and Society*, *1*, 125–151.

Wexler, J.G., & Logan, D.D. (1983). Sources of stress among women police officers. *Journal of Police Science and Administration*, *11*, 46–53.

Wexler, J.G., & Quinn, V. (1985). Considerations in the training and development of women sergeants. *Journal of Police Science and Administration*, *13*, 98–105.

Williams, C.L. (1989). *Gender differences at work: Women and men in nontraditional occupations*. Berkeley: University of California Press.

Worden, A.P. (1993). The attitudes of women and men in policing: Testing conventional and contemporary wisdom. *Criminology*, *31*, 203–237.

Wright, K.N., & Saylor, W.G. (1991). Male and female employees' perceptions of prison work: Is there a difference? *Justice Quarterly*, *8*, 505–524.

Zimmer, L.E. (1986). *Women guarding men*. Chicago: University of Chicago Press.

Zimmer, L.E. (1988). Tokenism and women in the workplace: The limits of gender-neutral theory. *Social Problems*, *35*, 64–73.

Zimmer, L.E. (1989). Solving women's employment problems in corrections: Shifting the burden to administrators. *Women & Criminal Justice*, *1*, 55–80.

24

Criers, Liars, and Manipulators: Probation Officers' Views of Girls

Emily Gaarder, Nancy Rodriguez, and Marjorie S. Zatz

Abstract: *Drawing on theories and research that focused on gender, race, ethnicity, and social class, Gaarder, Rodriguez, and Zatz study how democratic factors influence the perceptions of family court personnel's perceptions of juvenile girls as manipulative and more difficult to work with than boys. The authors focus on the repercussion of this image and address the issue of probation officers' understanding the need for gender and culturally specific programs for girls under their supervision. They find that as a result of scarce resources, gender and racial/ethnic stereotypes on the part of probation staff leave girls with few treatment options and services provided by the family court. In short, there is a lack of program options for girls under probation supervision. This frustrates some staff members who see the need to offer gender, ethnic, and culturally based treatment for juvenile girls who came under the court's jurisdiction.*

Feminist scholars and practitioners who work with girls in the juvenile justice system have long been searching for ways to raise awareness about girls' experiences and how their needs and issues might differ from boys' (Alexander, 1995; Belknap & Holsinger, 1998; Chesney-Lind, 1997; Chesney-Lind & Shelden, 2004; Kunzel, 1993; Odem, 1995; MacDonald & Chesney-Lind, 2001). A number of contemporary works by academics and practitioners alike call for an emphasis on gender, race, and class to fully understand girls' social and economic realities, and to provide programming appropriate to that context (Acoca, 1998b; Bloom, Owen, Deschenes, & Rosenbaum, 2002a; MacDonald & Chesney-Lind, 2001). Accordingly, we reviewed juvenile probation case files and interviewed juvenile probation officers in one metropolitan county in Arizona to better understand how girls are perceived, how their unique histories of abuse and related problems are interpreted, and how juvenile courts respond to these perceptions and interpretations in prescribing treatments for girls.

Drawing from theories and research on the social construction of gender, race, culture, and class, we observe how such constructions influence perceptions juvenile court personnel hold and how such perceptions sustain the "disconnect" between girls' images and their realities. How are ideas about "acceptable" behaviors and lifestyles embedded in notions of gender, culture, and class? To the extent that girls are seen as manipulative or "harder to work with," we ask: What are the repercussions of this image? Last, we address whether and how probation officers understand gender and culturally specific needs and programming, and the availability of such programming. One of the conundrums faced in this court, as elsewhere, is that these constructions are nested within an environment characterized by scarce resources. We end by discussing how attitudes of probation officers interact with the structure and priorities of juvenile probation, including especially treatment options (given scarce resources), and implications for girls in the system.

Review of the Literature

We still lack adequate knowledge of how probation officers and other court officials view girls' pathways to crime, personal attributes, and future possibilities (Miller, 1996). Such descriptions can tell us a great deal about how girls are perceived and socially constructed according to race, gender, and class. They also allow us to compare these perceptions with the reality of girls' lives, helping to discover whether common stereotypes permeate probation officers' analyses of girls and influence treatment or confinement decisions.

The Disconnect between Girls' Lives and Treatment Programs

We draw on the literature on the social construction of gender, race, and class to develop a more informed approach to effective programming for delinquent girls (e.g., Bloom et al., 2002b; Hoyt & Scherer, 1998; Miller, 1998; Messerschmidt, 1997; Chesney-Lind, 1999). Unfortunately, institutions and programs that house girls have often reinforced stereotypic gender norms such as femininity and passivity. These programs and institutions usually lack a more holistic approach to treatment, such as family involvement, drug/alcohol treatment, sexual/physical abuse counseling, and community involvement (Chesney-Lind, 1997).

What Do Gender- and Culturally-Responsive Programming Mean?

Given the importance that feminist scholars and practitioners place on the intersection of gender, class, race, and culture, the second part of our study explores how knowledgeable probation officers are with regard to gender- and culturally specific needs and programming. Defining gender and culturally appropriate programming is extremely important given the relatively few programs that address such needs. A national report by Girls Incorporated (1996, p. v) recommends that any program for juvenile female offenders "be gender specific, designed to meet the needs of young women as individuals, to take female development into account, and to avoid perpetuating limiting stereotypes based on gender, race, class, language, sexual orientation, disability, and other personal and cultural factors."

While there are few existing templates that demonstrate the above characteristics, some programs do exist that can help us identify and measure what kinds of programming work for girls. Nationally based organizations such as Girls Incorporated, and local programs such as P.A.C.E. Center for Girls can serve as examples of successful programming (Girls Incorporated, 1996). Such programs provide comprehensive evaluations of girls based on gender-specific education and therapeutic services in educational-based settings. In Canada, Toronto's Earlscourt Child and Family Centre has developed promising early interventions. Their Girls' Connection program is the first-known attempt in Canada to offer girls and their families a gender-specific, holistic intervention that provides long-term services and follow-up care (see Chesney-Lind, Artz, & Nicholson, 2001; Levene, 1997).

Data and Methods

To address whether and how gender, race/ethnicity, and class influence perceptions of girls held by juvenile court personnel and how such perceptions may contribute to the already limited treatment options for girls, we use two primary data sources. The first are official case file narratives from court records for a random sample of 174 girls referred to juvenile probation in Maricopa County, Arizona during 1999. These files include juvenile court petition information, disposition reports, progress reports, and psychological evaluations normally maintained by the juvenile court, both from the 1999 case and from any earlier referrals of these girls to juvenile probation.

Our intent with the girls' case files was threefold. First, we retrieved narrative statements about the girls and about juvenile court officials' presentations of their cases (i.e., perceptions of girls' behavior and situations). The majority of our data are these narratives written by probation officers, but we also include psychological reports. Although the latter are not written by probation officers, they contribute to the overall "image" of a girl that is created in a probation file. These psychological reports are used by probation and other court officers to assess a girl's background, behavior, and delinquency issues, and can influence the type of treatment or programming she receives. Second, in an effort to better assess girls' lives, we collected narrative information on the girls' parents/guardians, siblings, and extended family members. Third, given the well-documented need for gender appropriate treatment, we examined the treatment recommendations made by juvenile court staff and relate them to the experiences of girls (i.e., substance abuse, sexual abuse, pregnancy).

We supplemented the case file narratives with 14 semi-structured interviews conducted with juvenile probation officers. The women we interviewed included five Whites, two African Americans, one Asian American, one Hispanic, and one Middle Eastern. Of the four male probation officers, two were African American, one White, and one Hispanic. The probation officers averaged 11.2 years of experience, with a range from 1 to 24 years. Probation officers represented various units including standard probation, intensive probation, detention, a school safety program, treatment services, community services, a sex offender program, drug court, transfers, and program services. The semi-structured interviews lasted 45 to 90 minutes. All interviews were taped and transcribed by the interviewer.

The 174 girls in the sample were racially and ethnically diverse: 58% were White, 24% were Hispanic, 13% Black, 4% American Indian, and fewer than 1% Asian Pacific Islander. All were between 12 and 17 years old and had been referred to juvenile court for person, property, drug, and status offenses and for probation violations. To capture information on the structural dimensions of the girls in our sample, we linked their residential zip codes with 2000 census data (U.S. Bureau of the Census, 2000). While these data are aggregate, they provide insights into the demographic characteristics of the geographic areas where the girls lived. The median family income for census respondents within the girls' zip codes was $42,258 a year. Twenty-two percent reported having less than a high school education, 6% reported being unemployed, and 10% lived below the poverty level. The majority of the communities were occupied by Whites (61%) and Hispanics (28%). Twenty-two percent identified Spanish as their primary language.

Findings

Three dominant themes emerge from the case file narratives and interviews with probation officers. The first of these is the gap between probation officers' and other court officials' perceptions of the girls as whiny and manipulative and the realities of the girls' lives, including sexual abuse and teen motherhood. The second is the disconnect between official perceptions of the girls' families as "trashy" and irresponsible and the realities of the girls' family circumstances, including such structural dimensions as poverty as well as individual histories of abuse. The third is the lack of knowledge and understanding on the part of probation officers regarding culturally and gender appropriate treatments, as well as the reality of limited programming services for girls.

It is important to note that prevalence speaks not to how often girls in the sample were abused or how many mothers fit negative stereotypes, for example. Rather, prevalence refers to how often a juvenile court official noted a particular issue in the girls' files. Thus, the percentages that we present are underestimates if the court officials, for whatever reason, did not explore and/or comment on a particular theme (e.g., abuse that was part of the girls' family history and circumstances).

While the realities of girls' lives were consistently emphasized in case file narratives and interviews, we found that stereotypical images of girls outweighed any realities. We also found that girls were often referred to treatment services that did not appear to match their needs. Moreover, the juvenile court lacked the insight and capacity to meet their needs. That is, we found that probation officers, like other criminal justice officials, seem to inadvertently "blunder" when attempting to be sensitive to race, gender, and class (Zatz, 2000, p. 519). They also had little training and few resources at their disposal to match the gender and culturally specific needs of girls on their caseloads.

Perceptions of Girls: Criers, Liars, and Manipulators

Consistent with findings of Baines and Alder (1996), Belknap et al. (1997), and Bond-Maupin et al. (2002), common images in girls' probation files included fabricating reports of abuse, acting promiscuously, whining too much, and attempting to manipulate the court system. In our sample, about 20% of girls were depicted by probation officers and other court officials as sexually promiscuous and 16.5% as liars and manipulators. For example, girls were described in case files as: very manipulative, whining, pouting (#126—African American girl); not inhibited in any way. . . possesses loose morals (#39—Hispanic girl); and manipulative, unpredictable personality (#12—Hispanic girl).

Interviews with probation officers revealed similar images. Several probation officers used words like promiscuous, manipulative, liars, and criers in their descriptions. Girls were "harder to work with," "had too many issues," and were "too needy." The following responses convey these messages.

> They play the system real well. Girls play the system better than the boys do. They're manipulative. They, you know: "Pity poor me. I'm the innocent bystander and nobody's listening to me." They play the role as if they're so helpless . . . and the majority of the judges are male and they fall into that trap every single time.

> They're more like criers. Girls will do that. They'll break down and you'll be in the sympathy thing for awhile you know, but then you realize what they're doing.

Another officer who worked in the detention unit offered a different perspective.

> Oh yes, that's their survival sometimes. . . getting what they need by going around the back door, not giving the truth, or just flat out lying.

She recalled a recent incident where a girl had reported being raped at her residential treatment center. The girl wanted to speak to a counselor about it. The probation officer later discovered that the incident did happen, but more than 2 years ago. The girl had reported it as though it had just happened.

> What she wanted was some one-on-one attention with an adult staff. Girls get their needs met through attention, through their relationships with people.

When attempting to explain the cause of girls' delinquent behavior, Baines and Alder (1996) found that youth workers often relied on the abuse histories of girls to contextualize their path into delinquency. Consistent with their findings, 11 of the 14 probation officers we interviewed felt that most of the girls on their caseload had histories of sexual and/or physical abuse, emotional abuse, and neglect. Most made connections between the offending behaviors and past victimization. One remarked, "I hardly ever get a girl who hasn't been raped, sexually abused, or physically abused," noting an apparent direct correlation. Another indicated that girls have usually been victims and that "involvement in sexual activity, criminal activity, is increased after that."

Although most officers were sympathetic to the girls' histories, a few believed that the abuse stories that girls told were untrue or exaggerated, or that girls were partially responsible for being abused.

> They feel like they're the victim. They try from, "Mom kicked me out" to "Mom's boyfriend molested me" to "My brother was sexually assaulting me." They'll find all kinds of excuses to justify their actions. Because they feel if I say I was victimized at home that justifies me being out on the streets. . . Or while they were out there they got raped. Or, they were mistreated. Personally, I think 98% is false . . . 98% of the girls say the exact same story, so it's as if they just get together on the units and think up these things.
> [The interviewer asked about victimization/offending connections.] I think there is a connection but it starts before that. It started with their behavior, being out there on the streets, being out there with those people. You know, they end up in these situations. One of them— she was already incorrigible before this—took off with her boyfriend. She was raped and she refused to give his name because he was in a gang and she was afraid. She came home and did detention for a little while because she had run away, so yeah, because I don't think she's dealt

with these issues, she runs away from them. So they do have a correlation, but I don't know which one comes first. The behavior came first because she, you know, got in that situation.

As these probation officers and court psychologists indicate, girls are seen as being very difficult to work with. Whether the officers blame or sympathize, they perceive the girls as being troubled and troublesome. We turn next to the realities of the girls' lives, with particular attention to their histories of sexual abuse, substance abuse, and teen motherhood.

Reality of Girls' Lives: Sexual Abuse and Teen Motherhood

The direct and indirect relationships between girls' emotional, sexual, and physical abuse and delinquency have been substantially documented in prior work (Alexander, 1995; Belknap & Holsinger, 1998; Chesney-Lind & Shelden, 2004; McCormack, Janus, & Burgess, 1986; Rhodes & Fischer, 1993). Given the prevalence of sexual abuse histories reported in previous studies (e.g., Acoca, 1998a; Belknap & Holsinger, 1998), we were surprised to find that a relatively low percentage of girls in this study (18.8%) were identified as victims of sexual abuse. However, as previously noted, these data represent instances where a court official was informed of such abuse and actually reported it in the girl's file.

The depiction of girls' sexuality as "dirty" or inappropriate has led to an assumption that girls need to be protected from the dangers associated with their sexuality. Interestingly, we found minimal effort to protect or assist these girls. Girls' sexual activity, while documented in case files, was not dealt with in conjunction with other risk factors such as sexual abuse or mental health problems. In fact, even when these two girls had suffered extensive sexual abuse, they were still perceived *as* manipulators.

> [Girl's name] also claims a history of rape on two occasions, but according to her mother, she did not report it to anyone and did not mention it to anyone for over a year after it supposedly happened. She also was pregnant in [date omitted] and attempted suicide. The letter in the record is suggestive of a long and somewhat chronic history of mental health issues and it would appear that she has been somewhat manipulative in her behavior. There are indications to suggest that she has superficial lacerations on her forearms, suggestive of cutting herself subsequent to an argument with the parents. In the past, [Girl's name] was raped four different times. The first occurred when she was 7 years old; twice at age 13 [once by three boys] and another time at a party. She would not talk about the most recent incident, the fourth rape.
>
> (#82—White girl)

> She reports being sexually active and also reports having an abortion two months ago. She states that the father of her child is actually a 35-year-old man who has his own business. She reports being sexually active, as she prostituted herself on and off since she was 13. [Girl's name] reports for her evaluation in a very candid manner, yet she does appear to be somewhat manipulative. She likely, in fact, sexualizes many of her relationships when communicating with males. She states that she tried to commit suicide recently while in detention, reporting trying to tie a sheet around her neck.
>
> (#165—White girl)

We found these depictions of girls as manipulative thought provoking. On the one hand, it is not surprising that girls with a history of abuse might be seen as manipulative. For example, the mental health literature tells us that victims of incest might try to control or manipulate individuals (e.g., an abusive father) or situations to reduce the likelihood of further abuse. Manipulating others thus becomes a survival tactic.

Yet our reading of the case files and our reflections on the interviews with probation officers suggest that rather than simply describing a behavior as manipulative, the probation officers take the further step of ascribing a personality trait. There is a difference, we argue, between a recognition that girls may be manipulative in specific situations to achieve a desired end (e.g., not being abused) and the construction of the girl herself, and of all girls by extension, as manipulative by nature and therefore difficult to work with.

The key, we suggest, is whether the probation officers reflect on the girls' contexts and the underlying problems to which manipulative behaviors may be a reasonable response. If they do, we should expect to see them searching for appropriate programs that can adequately respond to the girls' problems and needs. Unfortunately, we do not find that to be the typical response. Rather, some probation officers simply assume that the girls are making up stories. Too many others recognize that girls have problems due to their histories of victimization but do not respond in sympathetic ways, instead writing the girls off through gendered stereotypes and treating the victimization and manipulative behaviors as independent realities.

Perceptions of Girls' Families: Trashy, Manipulative, and Sexually Irresponsible

Perceptions of girls' families were also examined. The majority of the probation officers interviewed felt that the family was crucial to the juvenile's success. In particular, they commented on how important it is that parents take responsibility for their children, seek help for their parenting problems, and be willing to work with probation officers.

Yet some of the same probation officers spoke of the girls' mothers in terms similar to those used to describe the girls themselves—"promiscuous" and "sluts." Indeed, in 6.1% of the case files, the probation officers made such notes. Again, we emphasize the particular language used to describe girls' mothers, and not on using such statements as an indicator of mothers' behavior.

> [From an interview] Her background is the classic. Her sister uses drugs. The other sister has a baby, has had two or three kids. Mom—she's a slut. Mom—she's on her third marriage.

> [From an interview] The daughters and sons are going through life with no supervision, no rules. All of the sudden the girl is 14, comes home with hickeys and dressed like a slut and Mom wants to give her rules. And Mom comes home at 3 a.m. with five different guys.

Interestingly, not a single probation officer commented on the fathers' marital status, physical attire, or sexual activities in the case files. We also found that 7.9% of mothers described in case files were presented as liars, or as manipulating the juvenile court system.

Class was an important factor in assessments of the girls' families, though this seemed to operate in several, perhaps contradictory, ways. The most extreme examples of economic disadvantage were cases where families were homeless. Three case files noted that girls living in homeless families were being punished for not attending treatment sessions regularly or missing appointments with their probation officers, both of which are considered probation violations. Probation officers sometimes noted that girls were being labeled delinquent simply because they were homeless. Some probation officers expressed sympathy for girls and families with economic challenges. One derogatory comment, however, targets the economic situation of a low-income, single-parent household.

> This officer has tried to work with this family in order for [Girl's name] to be successful on probation, since much of her problems appear to be related to the lifestyle which they choose to live. This officer was not raised in an environment where people chose to live around discarded items, even having disabled vehicles permanently placed in the driveway, but it is still this officer's opinion that it is a choice of lifestyle that [Girl's mother] chooses for herself and her family.
>
> (#6—White girl)

During interviews, some officers said that lower-income parents were easier to work with because they were uneducated, intimidated by the court, and not knowledgeable of court services. Another probation officer, however, identified these as barriers that poorer families face in seeking help for their children.

> Basic communication skills and having the confidence to interact with government and community agencies. A lot of lower-class/working-class parents are afraid to get the phone book out or go to the police station or their community center and start asking what they think are maybe awkward or silly questions. . . . Middle- and upper-class parents are more confident through their jobs and education and everything. They're more confident to interact with the bigger system.

This officer also noted that very poor and middle-class families receive more services than working poor families, because they either qualify for free services (in the case of poor families) or can afford to pay for treatment (in the case of middle-class families).

> The lower middle-class or working poor make $20,000 and don't qualify for welfare or have medical benefits. They can't pay $50 per hour for a counselor.

As a result, these girls are left with few options. If their families are working but do not qualify for federal assistance they do not receive services.

An African American probation officer noted that because his caseload was predominantly Hispanic and African American, it limited the types of services he was able to provide. He saw a relationship between race/ethnicity and class. Some services were located in geographic areas at a considerable distance from neighborhoods where economically disadvantaged minority families tended to live. Girls were frequently unable to travel to the locations where they could receive treatments. In essence, services were simply not an option for all.

Realities of Girls' Families: Abuse, Poverty, and Racism

Culture and class are central to the social construction of gender, including both what girls see as their available options and what others see as appropriate behaviors for girls. Portillos (1999) has shown how Chicanas and Mexicanas, in search of independence from the expectations of the family, may turn to gangs to alleviate experiences as marginalized women. Others have identified the traditional household duties of Hispanic girls (see Burgos-Ocasio, 2000) and the development of values such as strength and independence among African American girls to deal with the challenges of labor markets (Rice, 1990). We found that 12.3% of Hispanic women in our sample dealt with language barriers, poverty, discrimination, and familial and economic expectations associated with living close to the Mexican border.

> It is believed that this family is somewhat economically disadvantaged, which may influence the family, on occasions, to change their address. [Girl's name] parents are Spanish speaking only, but the juvenile seems to have a fairly good grasp of the English language.
>
> (#75—Hispanic girl)

Interestingly, and consistent with Bridges and Steen's (1998) findings regarding court officials' perceptions of intrinsic causes of African American delinquency and extrinsic causes of White delinquency, when Hispanics and/or their families contradict some of these cultural dimensions, their involvement in delinquent acts are viewed as mishaps. For example, a Hispanic girl's family is described as cooperative and functional because they speak English and are in the country legally.

Substance abuse plays a significant role in these girls' lives. Case file narrative data showed that 43% of girls were current drug users or had a history of drug use. For some, language barriers made treatment or assessment difficult given the probation officer's inability to communicate effectively with parents.

> There was no response from the family regarding my initial letter to them and the request to contact me. I was able to finally get a hold of the father at his work number. [Father's name] speaks mostly Spanish and therefore conversation with him was limited. He speaks some English but may not have fully understood some of my questions. Parents are divorced but are still living together. They both work long hours and [are] rarely home in the day. Both parents admitted that lack of supervision is contributing to the behaviors of their daughter. It was very clear that the parents know their children are using drugs but that there is little that they feel they can do to stop the behavior. This officer found their complacency about the activities in their home disturbing.
>
> (#59—Hispanic girl)

In 18.8% of cases, we found that extended family members served as guardians when biological parents were unable to raise their children.

> There are eight other children also living with grandparents. The grandparents are in their 70s and both are still working; they seem to be very responsible caring people. Both natural parents have histories of problems with the law. Mom has problems with alcohol and "rock" and dad also has alcohol problems.
>
> (#105—Hispanic girl)

Research has found that girls are much more influenced by family expectations and family conflict than boys (Hoyt & Scherer, 1998). These experiences vary by race/ethnicity. For example, Taylor, Biafora, Warheit, and Gail (1997) found that Hispanics are significantly influenced by family substance abuse, and African American youths by the levels of family communication. For some girls, substance abuse in combination with other family problems, including financial stability, domestic violence, and sexual abuse, compound their situations. Two narratives illustrate this clearly.

> [Girl's name] is currently a ward of the state and is living in a group home. She was brought to the interview by her CPS caseworker B. [Girl's name] mother is living somewhere on the streets in [city omitted] and reportedly is dying of AIDS while her father is incarcerated in Mexico for murder. The caseworker reported that [Girl's name] has had a lot of problems with anger but seems to be making some progress recently. She was kicked out of her grandmother's house for assaulting her and then kicked out of her foster mother's house for assaulting her also. She has run away, attempted suicide, been assaulted and abused, been involved with gangs, drugs, and marijuana and has been on probation previously. However, as I stated, it appears that there has been progress and [Girl's name] seems to have mellowed out some. According to her grandmother, [Girl's name] was sexually abused at 6 years of age.
>
> (#48—Hispanic girl)

> [Girl's name] is a 17-year-old American Indian youth who, at the present time, is doing quite well with her counseling and doing well at [school name]. She has had a very sad and rocky childhood, she had to watch her mother die in front of her eyes from drug and alcohol abuse and has been from foster home to youth home and in hospitals and numerous counseling sessions to deal with her depression, her anger, and some of the violent and abusive situations that she has been exposed to.
>
> (#58—American Indian girl)

Bond-Maupin et al. (2002) found that probation officers were often sympathetic to the conflicts Hispanic girls faced (i.e., having "traditional" parents and living as an "Americanized" girl). During our interviews with probation officers, we found they also identified with the struggles faced by Hispanics and commented on the valuable support system that extended families provide:

> Personally I think some of the girls, especially Hispanic girls, are brought up to believe that their purpose in life is to stay home and have kids and do nothing. But they're growing up in the 90s. . . . I think a lot of them feel really torn—well, am I supposed to go out and have kids or am I supposed to have a career?

Regarding family conflict, many probation officers expressed concern about domestic violence and noted that children were often punished for fights started by parents.

> The whole thing just burns a hole in me. . . . Say the police respond to a case of domestic violence. You have a 3-year-old girl, a 16-year-old girl, and the mother fighting. Say the mother grabbed that girl and started pounding her face into cement. They're not going to take Mom to jail when there is a 3-year-old daughter there. But they need to separate the two of them. So a lot of times it really is the parent's fault but the kid gets hauled away to jail for protection and they're not going to take Mom who has to support the 3-year-old and go to work the next morning.

Although some probation officers identified the conflicts at home, economic instability, and substance abuse as the root of the problems the girls faced, they were unable to provide the needed services. The lack of appropriate treatment options and services for girls is our third theme.

Gender-Specific Needs

Many scholars and practitioners recognize the need for more appropriate treatment for girls but the small number of girls relative to boys makes it difficult for court officials to justify specialized, often expensive, treatments that are culturally and gender appropriate (Alder, 1998; Bloom et al., 2002a; Freitas & Chesney-Lind, 2001; McDonald & Chesney-Lind, 2001).

In our interviews, we asked probation officers whether they believed girls had different problems or needs than boys. We also asked if they worked differently with the girls on their caseloads. The majority of probation officers noted immediately that girls were more likely to be referred for incorrigibility or domestic violence offenses. Other likely offenses included probation violations (usually running away), truancy, drugs, and prostitution. Half of the probation officers reported that girls were more likely to be arrested for status offenses. These officers said that parents tend to "keep a closer eye" on girls, or try to "over control" them. They also noted that boys were more likely to be rewarded for sexual behavior and girls punished. As one probation officer noted, "Girls get picked up for stuff that males don't." Another said, "Girls are involved with the court process more for their best interests, not necessarily because she is a danger to the community, but for her own safety." Yet not all officers saw this as positive. One commented, "Domestic violence and incorrigibility needs to be directed away from the courtroom and into specialized programs. We're turning a lot of these girls into criminals."

However, four of the 14 probation officers asserted that juveniles all had similar needs and should not be treated or approached any differently based on gender. They rejected the need for gender-specific programming, preferring to decide on treatment options based on individual characteristics or circumstances. When asked about the kinds of programs in which girls were successful, another officer replied,

> I don't feel like you can just say that this program works for girls or whatever—they're children. Some of them are ready and some of them aren't. Whether they be boys or girls.

Some of these officers believed that treating girls "differently" would be assuming that all girls had the same issues and problems. They alluded to the fact that some girls were not in fact acting normally.

> These days you can't do that. I have some young ladies on my caseload that are kind of like— they have a macho side, I guess.

> They're not your typical girls ... you know, the fingernails, the make-up, the Ms. Prissy. They're just like the boys. They're worse than some of the boys. They go out and they prove themselves like they're not feminine. You know they don't want anybody to think ... well, I'm helpless. I can take care of myself, so they play the role as portraying to be something that they're not.

When girls did not adhere to "feminine" behaviors or attitudes, there was often an assumption that they were "becoming more like boys," and should be treated as boys would be. Probation officers also relied on gender stereotypes to define specific issues facing girls. Several of the probation officers believed that the girls were promiscuous and needed sexual education programming. Early sexual activity, pregnancy, and sexually transmitted diseases were seen as feminine issues. As one officer commented,

> It would be good to have gender specific—all girls—for feminine problems or feminine-related issues—we have a lot of STDs transmitted.

Another suggested that sex education was needed, "definitely for the females because they . . . they produce the seed." Interestingly, one probation officer who earlier had called promiscuity a "girl problem," began to question herself after prompting from the interviewer.

> Probation officer: You know what? [long pause] I think there is . . . umm . . . you know I think there is, but maybe with the girls it's more noticeable. They're always getting STD's—but they must be getting them from the guys, so . . . [trails off]

In addition to labeling girls' sexuality as specifically problematic (as opposed to boys), probation officers also made reference to the "hormonal" issues underlying girls' tendency to be "difficult."

> Girls are much more difficult to case manage. Their affect is different—they will push you away when really they want to come closer. They will make your life miserable—whereas boys will just sort of go along with the program. . . . A lot of it, I think, in my opinion, is hormones. In fact, when I had a lot of girls on a caseload, you could almost watch the ebb and tide. When their hormones are on the move and they're ovulating, you couldn't stand to be around them.

Despite gender stereotyping, or conversely, the denial that any differences existed, nearly all the officers admitted that they "talked to girls more." Girls were more open than boys to sharing details about their lives and relationships. This was in spite of the fact that many of the probation officers felt uncomfortable "acting like counselors."

Research suggests that one of the most important factors in working with girls is establishing relationships (see Alder, 1998; Chesney-Lind & Sheldon, 1998; Taylor et al., 1995; Lindgren, 1996). For example, Belknap et al.'s (1997) data from focus groups with incarcerated girls outlined the importance of respectful and caring relationships between girls and adult staff. In general, girls did not feel respected by the staff in their agencies and institutions. They wanted to be listened to by caring adults, and desired one-on-one relationships in which they could discuss their feelings. In step with this, when asked what kind of problems the girls on her caseload faced, one officer had this to say:

> Girls face relationships. Their number one problem in my opinion is self-esteem issues, and how to relate to the world around them. . . . Girls are more interested in whether the relationship—you know, if they like you as a P.O. or whatever. You have to get through that barrier first.

Despite a few exceptions, which we have noted, most of the probation officers understood gender-specific needs and programming for girls as sex education (especially STD and pregnancy prevention), good parenting skills, and building self-esteem. Their interpretations are not surprising, given the attention to issues such as sexual activity, pregnancy, and victimization in case file narratives. When it came to dealing with these issues, however, the only resources that the probation officers offered the girls were Planned Parenthood and Parents Anonymous.

Gender-Specific Programming

Both the interviews and our review of case files revealed a severe lack of programming for girls. The majority of probation officers in our study could not name a single program designed specifically for girls. A persistent theme regarding treatment services for girls was the disconnect between the realities of the girls' lives and appropriate treatment options. As mentioned, a girl whose family was homeless and living on the streets had probation violations for not attending her drug treatment and for not staying in contact with her probation officer. Sadly, the only option the probation officer could suggest was counseling. In another case, a pregnant teen received sex education as part of her terms of probation.

> [Girl's name] is currently pregnant. She reports that she has used marijuana since being pregnant. She denies any other usage. [Girl's name] and her grandmother are hopeful that they can find an adoptive family for the baby. At her doctor's appointment on [date omitted], [Girl's name] admitted to having an abortion in [date omitted]. She is in need of life skills training and sex education.
>
> (#5—White girl)

Case file narrative data reveal that nearly 16% of girls were referred to detention or a state institution for treatment. Unfortunately, a lack of available and appropriate treatment programs made confinement the only option for some.

In some cases where girls were sexually active and suffered from histories of abuse, probation officers openly admitted to being "confused as to what is best for the child." For others, institutionalization was the only alternative given the "difficult" nature of girls' cases—often meaning that girls frequently ran away or did not succeed in existing programs. Many probation officers expressed frustration with the lack of funding for programming in general and for girls specifically. This attitude is consistent with Kempf-Leonard and Sample's (2000) survey of juvenile and family court judges and officers. The majority of those surveyed noted that females did not have adequate access to treatment, especially for mental health problems, status offending, chemical dependency, and sexual victimization.

Half the officers believed that gender-specific programming was a good idea. "Maybe it would be good to have a gender-specific program for girls—just to see how they'd react," one officer said, adding, "I don't know if any are available." Different reasons were given, however, for why gender-specific programming might be needed. Some reasoned that girls and boys become distracted by each other when they are together. Others recognized that girls may be reluctant to talk about their situations when boys are present.

Attempts to address girls' needs all too often result in ill-fitting programs and frustration regarding the limited options available. Most programs that were all girl were in locked institutions. There were even fewer options for early intervention programming or chemical dependency issues. Once a psychological evaluation was conducted and mental health issues were identified, girls were usually placed on medication and sent to counseling.

Culturally Specific Needs

The cultural differences identified in prior works have stressed the importance of addressing the cultural dimensions of girls' lives (e.g., Fishman, 1998; Miller, 1998; Chesney-Lind, 1999). Recognizing the relationship between gender, culture, and class is a first step toward providing girls with the services they need. Some officers spoke at length about cultural differences and needs of the girls on their caseloads. One response was particularly representative.

> Girls of color have a double whammy pretty much. They are minorities from ethnic standing. They are female from gender standing. There are different psychodynamics when you talk about different ethnic females. If you have Hispanic females—the males the machismo. If you have African American—African American females tend to be the backbone of the Black culture. It's just different. It's different all the way down the line.

Other officers tried to incorporate culturally sensitive methods in their work, but lacked training and resources. Racial stereotypes and misunderstandings regarding cultural differences can persist if probation officers are not adequately trained. False assumptions about cultures can lead to inappropriate assessments of girls' needs. For example, a probation officer told the story of a Hispanic boy molesting a cousin, and of their therapist not being aware that cousins do marry in some Hispanic cultures. The officer suggested that therapists should better understand the cultures of those they work with.

Culturally Specific Programming

When asked about culturally sensitive programs we found that, again, probation officers could not name even one program that was culturally aware. Many officers reported that they referred kids to programs based on the gender and race of the counselor, not on what the program itself offered. The growing and varying racial/ethnic make-up of juveniles on probation seems to only compound the problems associated with providing proper programs for juveniles. Probation officers mentioned that there were no culturally appropriate resources available to deal with the growing Asian American population.

> We don't have anything within the probation department that focuses on Asian American issues. Right now, I'm seeing more kids of Asian parents . . . the parents may be first or second generation in the U.S. They don't know the language. They're more easily manipulated by their kids. And the kids are more quickly sucked into the drugs and alcohol and partying and rebellious stuff . . . that's happening a lot with Asian American families. I got a bunch of Filipino families . . . They do not know how to be a parent in the U.S. with all these problems. They're just desperate. They're begging for help. [But] they're not real receptive once we start making suggestions, because it is totally foreign to them.

When asked if there were differences in terms of race/ethnicity that needed to be considered in programs or counseling, one probation officer remarked:

> The only time I'll typically look for ethnicity is when I have a Spanish-only speaking kid and I need a counselor who speaks Spanish. . . . I don't like making big issues about that. I have major issues with people saying a lot of rights are broken because of the color they are, when a lot of rights for White people are as well. My perspective is, if they're a good counselor, they can work with any of them. It's only an issue if it's a language barrier or an ethnic issue in it. Like Indians—they do their sweat lodges and they do all that. I can't do one of those. So in essence, they need to have an Indian do that.

On the other hand, another probation officer saw her race/ethnicity (Asian American) as a helpful attribute in working with girls of color:

> I went with another probation officer to see the girls on our caseload. She had an American Indian girl on her caseload and the girl would not talk to her. She made some kind of comment about "just another White agency person coming to see me." But she would talk to me.

Discussion of the Findings

The social construction of gender, race/ethnicity, and class has a profound impact on girls in the juvenile justice system. In this study, we found that juvenile court staff often act based more on the perceptions they have of girls and their families than on the realities the girls face, including both individual and societal factors. Our findings suggest that gender and racial/ethnic stereotypes leave girls few options for treatment and services in juvenile courts.

There is still much discussion and debate around the meaning of "gender-specific" needs and programming. Not surprisingly, the lack of clarity regarding the concept of gender or cultural needs/programming (along with the relative "newness" of the terminology) leads to confusion among practitioners about how to implement such ideas. In step with our findings, Belknap et al. (1997) found that practitioner awareness of gender differences and appropriate services varied widely. One of their recommendations includes the coordination of "regional gender-specific sensitivity training and information sharing sessions for juvenile justice and youth serving professionals" (1997, p. 33). They also note that "few individuals have developed the ability to identify appropriate and effective programs for delinquent girls" (1997, p. 33). They urge the development of assessment tools to measure the effectiveness of girls' programs, as well as periodic program evaluations. While we recognize that additional resources are needed to better serve all juvenile offenders in the juvenile court system, risk/needs tools that focus on mental health (e.g., depression, which is more often internalized by girls than boys) and victimization would more appropriately address female delinquency than current efforts. Programming that highlights relationship building and incorporates an understanding of how culture directly influences girls' delinquent and nondeliquent behavior is also needed. Last, family-based treatment can provide girls with an important support system, one that is often lacking in girls' lives.

Conclusion

The juvenile justice system has long been criticized for inadequate attention to the situations and needs of girls. We suggest that framing the problem theoretically as the social construction of gender, race, and class in juvenile probation helps us to better understand the disjunctures between court actors' perceptions of girls and what they see as culturally appropriate gendered behaviors. Probation officers expect one set of behaviors and attitudes from the girls and their families, but due to economic and social forces (e.g., homelessness, immigration restrictions, histories of sexual abuse) as well as individual factors (e.g., mental health problems), the girls do not manifest these hegemonic expectations. This results in disappointment on both parts—girls are not treated according to the reality of their lives, and probation officers continue to express frustration and even hostility towards girls who are not responding favorably to the programming being offered.

As Chesney-Lind and Shelden (2004, p. 6) remind us, "An appreciation of a young women's experience of girlhood, particularly one that attends to the special problems of girls at the margins, is long overdue." We urge the continued development and implementation of gender and culturally responsive approaches and programming that can help confront the social and economic realities of girls. More detailed information and rigorous evaluation of programming for girls is needed. Without these analyses, probation officers and other court officials will continue to rely on stereotypical images of "proper girl behavior" and psychological assessments of their conduct, while discounting the power that oppressive structures and institutions hold over people. As contemporary feminist research begins to solidify its definition and understanding of "what works for girls," we face the equally enormous task of communicating this information to practitioners, administrators, and other decision makers. It is apparent from this study that the message has not yet been heard.

Critical Thinking

Similar to the gender issues discussed previously by Poole and Pogrebin, it appears that juvenile females on probation are perceived by some probation staff as more difficult to work with than juvenile males, and they receive less program treatment resources for gender specific and cultural needs. One critical issue raised by this article is should court and probation staff incorporate gender, class, and cultural perspectives in their treatment of juvenile girls in their supervision practices?

References

Acoca, L. (1998a). Outside/inside: The violation of American girls at home, on the street, and in the juvenile justice system. *Crime & Delinquency, 44,* 561–589.

Acoca, L. (1998b). Defusing the time bomb: Understanding and meeting the growing health care need of incarcerated women in America. *Crime & Delinquency, 44,* 49–69.

Alexander, R. (1995). *The "girl problem": Female sexual delinquency in New York, 1900–1930.* London: Cornell University Press.

Alder, C. M. (1998). "Passionate and willful" girls: Confronting practices. *Women and Criminal Justice, 9*, 81–101.

Baines, M., & Alder, C. (1996). Are girls more difficult to work with?: Youth workers' perspectives in juvenile justice related areas. *Crime & Delinquency, 42*, 467–485.

Belknap, J., & Holsinger, K. (1998). An overview of delinquent girls: How theory and practice have failed and the need for innovative changes. In R. Zaplin (Ed.), *Female crime and delinquency: Critical perspectives and effective interventions* (pp. 13–64). Gaithersburg, MD: Aspen.

Belknap, J., Holsinger K., & Dunn, M. (1997). Understanding incarcerated girls: The results of a focus group study. *The Prison Journal, 77*, 381–404.

Bloom, B., Owen, B., Deschenes, E., & Rosenbaum, J. (2002a). Moving toward justice for female juvenile offenders in the new millennium: Modeling gender specific policies and programs. *Journal of Contemporary Criminal Justice, 18*, 37–56.

Bloom, B., Owen, B., Deschenes, E., & Rosenbaum, J. (2002b). Improving juvenile justice for females: A statewide assessment in California. *Crime & Delinquency, 48*, 526–552.

Bond-Maupin, L., Maupin, J., & Leisenring, A. (2002). Girls' delinquency and the justice implications of intake workers' perspectives. *Women and Criminal Justice, 13*, 51–77.

Bridges, G. S., & Steen, S. (1998). Racial disparities in official assessments of juvenile offenders: Attributional stereotypes as mediating mechanisms. *American Sociological Review, 63*, 554–570.

Burgos-Ocasio, H. (2000). Hispanic women. In M. Julia (Ed.), *Constructing gender: Multicultural perspectives in working with women* (pp. 109–137). Belmont, CA: Brooks/Cole.

Chesney-Lind, M. (1997). *The female offender: Girls, women, and crime.* Thousand Oaks, CA: Sage Publications.

Chesney-Lind, M. (1999). Girls, gangs, and violence: Reinventing the liberated female crook. In M. Chesney-Lind and J. M. Hagedorn (Eds.), *Female gangs in America: Essays on girls, gangs and gender* (pp. 295–310). Chicago: Lake View Press.

Chesney-Lind, M., Artz, S., & Nicholson, D. (2001). *Making the case for gender-responsive programming.* Paper presented at the Annual Meeting of the American Society of Criminology, Atlanta.

Chesney-Lind, M., & Shelden, R. G. (2004). *Girls, delinquency, and juvenile justice.* Los Angeles, CA: West/Wadsworth.

Fishman, L. (1998). Images of crime and punishment: The black bogeyman and white self-righteousness. In C. R. Mann and M. S. Zatz (Eds.), *Images of Color, Images of Crime* (pp. 109–125). Los Angeles: Roxbury.

Freitas, K., & Chesney-Lind, M. (2001). Difference doesn't mean difficult: Practitioners talk about working with girls. *Women, Girls and Criminal Justice, 2*, 65–79.

Girls Incorporated. (1996). *Prevention and parity: Girls in juvenile justice.* Washington, DC: Office of Juvenile Justice and Delinquency Prevention.

Hoyt, S., & Scherer; D. (1998). Female juvenile delinquency: Misunderstood by juvenile justice system, neglected by social science. *Law and Human Behavior, 22*, 81–107.

Kempf-Leonard, K., & Sample, L. (2000). Disparity based on sex. Is gender specific treatment warranted? *Justice Quarterly, 7*, 89–128.

Kunzel, R. (1993). *Fallen woman, problem girls: Unmarried mothers and the professionalization of social work.* London: Yale University Press.

Lindgren, S. J. (1996). Gender specific programming for female adolescents. Unpublished Master's Thesis. Minneapolis, MN: Augsburg College.

Levene, K. (1997). The Earlcourt girls connection: A model intervention. *Canada's Children, 4*, 14–17.

MacDonald, J., & Chesney-Lind, M. (2001). Gender bias and juvenile justice revisited: A multiyear analysis. *Crime & Delinquency, 47*, 173–195.

McCormack, A., Janus, M., & Burgess, A. W. (1986). Runaway youth and sexual victimization: Gender differences in an adolescent runaway population. *Child Abuse and Neglect, 10*, 387–395.

Messerschmidt, J. W. (1997). *Crime as structured action: Gender, race, class, and crime in the making.* Thousand Oaks, CA: Sage Publications.

Miller, J. (1996). An examination of disposition decision making for delinquent girls. In M. D. Schwartz and D. Milovanovic (Eds.), *Race, gender, and class in criminology: The intersection* (pp. 219–245). New York: Garland Publishing.

Miller, J. (1998). Up it up: Gender and the accomplishment of street robbery. *Criminology, 36*, 37–65.

Odem, M. E. (1995). *Delinquent daughters: Protecting and policing adolescent female sexuality in United States.* Chapel Hill: University of North Carolina Press.

Portillos, E. L. (1999). Women, men and gangs: The social construction of gender in the barrio. In M. Chesney-Lind and J. Hagedorn (Eds.), *Female gangs in America: Essays on girls, gangs, and gender* (pp. 232–244). Chicago: Lake View Press.

Rhodes, J. E., & Fischer, K. (1993). Spanning the gender gap: Gender differences in delinquency among inner city adolescents. *Adolescence, 28*, 879–889.

Rice, M. (1990). Challenging orthodoxies in feminist theory: a black feminist critique. In L. Gelsthorpe and A. Morris (Eds.), *Feminist Perspectives in Criminology* (pp. 57–69) Bristol, PA: Open University Press.

Taylor, D. L., Biafora, F. A., Warheit, G., & Gail, E. (1997). Family factors, theft, vandalism, and major deviance among
   a multiracial multiethnic sample of adolescent girls. *Journal of Social Distress and the Homeless, 6,* 71–87.
United States Census Bureau, (2000). Summary File 3. [Online]. Available: http://www2.census.gov/census_2000/
   datasets/Summary_File_3/Arizona/
Zatz, M. S. (2000). Convergence of race, ethnicity, gender, and class on court decision making: Looking toward the
   21st century. In J. Homey (Ed.), *Policies processes, and decisions of the criminal justice system* (pp. 503–552).
   Washington, DC: U.S. Department of Justice, Office of Justice Programs, National Institute of Justice.

25

The Construction of Meaning during Training for Probation and Parole

John P. Crank

Abstract: *John Crank assesses the ideological changes in the training environment of probation and parole officers. He illustrates how the organizational culture of a Peace Officer Training division reflects a changing correctional philosophy that has moved from a treatment model to a more punitive one. Crank shows how the shift toward a crime control and surveillance model changed the method of teaching probation and parole personnel new values, practices, and beliefs that fit in with the mandated, public safety oriented policies that currently exist. This punitive change in probation and parole functions was instituted on a national level and is best characterized as favoring a public safety emphasis for probation and parole staff at the expense of an offender rehabilitative model.*

According to conventional wisdom on organizational reform in criminal justice, local agency culture will blunt efforts to institute meaningful change. Efforts for change have had only a limited impact on the day-to-day activities of criminal justice practitioners, as has been cited widely (Fogelson 1977; Guyot 1986; Kerner Commission 1967). Among courtroom actors, the resistance of courtroom work groups to change has been described in terms of the influence of local legal culture (Church 1982). Among the police, occupational resistance to change has been characterized in terms of organizational culture and described in terms of police insularity, the blue curtain, and the code of secrecy (Manning 1970; Pollock-Byrne 1988; Stoddard 1968; Westley 1956). In the field of corrections, the guard subculture, sometimes with the support of charismatic administrators, has been associated with widespread resistance to the expansion of prisoner rehabilitation programs (Jacobs 1977) and with the use of violence to maintain social control (Marquart and Crouch 1984, 1990).

This literature has frequently described resistance to organizational change in terms of individual or group self-interest—the idea that the agent of resistance to change lies in purposeful individual or group behavior. From this perspective, advocates seeking reform through organizational change have failed because changes are perceived to be inconsistent with the self-interest of members of the particular organizational culture or subculture. For example, a factor in the failure of team policing reforms in the 1970s has been described as the resistance of mid-management personnel who feared losing their jobs in the wake of command decentralization (Skolnick and Bayley 1986; Walker 1992). Similarly, resistance to change from local legal cultures has been attributed to courtroom actors' vested interest in maintaining established relations (Walker 1985).

While acknowledging the powerful influence of self-interest as a source of resistance to change (DiMaggio and Powell 1991), I argue here that change efforts may encounter local customs regarding how action should be organized in particular organizational cultures (Jepperson 1991). Organization members' response to change may not be resistance for reasons of self-interest, but assimilation of that which is new into customary ways of doing and thinking about things (Meyer and Rowan 1977). In other words, how an organizational culture responds to change will depend on the meanings and values carried by its members. This point suggests that the study of the impact of change on organizational culture requires three steps: first, the identification of the changes bearing on the organization; second, an assessment of the values and meanings embedded in a particular organizational culture; and third, an analysis of how those changes are perceived in terms of prevailing patterns of cultural meaning. In this paper I perform these three steps in order to understand how a particular parole and probation organization is affected by contemporary changes in parole and probation.

POST and the Diffusion of Institutional Knowledge

Three broad areas of change affect the field of parole and probation today: the shift toward crime control and surveillance, accountability to the rule of law, and the rationalization of the work environment (Feeley and Simon 1992; Fogel 1984; Simon 1993).

Over the past 60 years, Peace Officer State Training (POST) has evolved as a carrier of formal training across the institutional environment of criminal justice. As an institutional form, POST legitimates individuals as "sworn" officers: it prepares recruits who will occupy positions in corrections, parole and probation, and policing for duties associated with the status of professional peace officer with the license to carry a weapon. POST training emerged relatively recently as an institutional form for the transmission of training and education. In the 1920s and 1930s, August Vollmer and two of his proteges, William Wiltberger and O.W. Wilson, emerged as advocates of educational reform in California and in Wichita; all three made use of facilities available at institutions of higher education for providing peace officer training (Morn 1984). In 1959 California founded a commission on POST to establish minimum standards for hiring and training peace officers. By 1969 there were 45 police academies in California; 17 of these were housed in colleges, and 14 others were affiliated with colleges.

Areas of Institutional Change

POST, a means for transmitting knowledge across the institutional environment of parole and probation, also transmits changes that occur within that environment. That is, changes in values, practices, and beliefs will be reflected in the selection and content of topics and classes provided by the POST curriculum (Meyer and Rowan 1977). In the current era, these changes can be organized into three categories, discussed below: those which emphasize the role of surveillance and crime fighting, those which involve officers' accountability to the rule of law, and those which emphasize the rationalization of administrative process.

The first area of institutional change is the reconstruction of the work of parole and probation officers around ideas of law enforcement and surveillance. With the decline of the rehabilitative ideal in the 1980s, probation has shifted its emphasis from traditional ideas of offender counseling to a public safety enterprise oriented around ideas of surveillance and enforcement (Fogel 1984; Rothman 1980). This shift, occurred simultaneously with the federal government's divestment of funding for community-based rehabilitation for offenders during the Reagan era (Duffee 1990). At the same time, a deinstitutionalization process has increased the population of probationers and parolees. Legislators have responded by trying to make parole and probation look "tough" (Gordon 1991). The continuing intensification of peace officers' law enforcement role has been noted in current research on community corrections (Feeley and Simon 1992; Petersilia 1989).

Many elements of the curriculum and topics of POST reveal the emphasis of parole and probation on enforcement and surveillance. Peace officer skills, an area that includes topics such as range safety, firearms handling, and handcuffing, is the single largest block, accounting for 66 of the 240 hours of instruction. Topics such as survival skills, aimed at preparing recruits mentally for work in a hazardous environment, promote a perception of parole and probation as dangerous work dealing with lawbreakers. To illustrate the extent to which parole and probation focus on crime control, the instructors of defensive tactics, two parole and probation officers, also teach defensive tactics to the city-county police department.

The second area of institutional change is peace officers' accountability to the rule of law. Though parole and probation historically have been perceived as correctional functions, accountability concerns are increasingly comparable to those confronted by police rather than those addressed by correctional agents, whose authority is limited by the confines of a correctional institution. The traditional tasks of reintegrating offenders are being delegated to community organizations, while officers focus on control (Harris, Clear, and Baird 1988). Consequently issues of accountability increasingly parallel those of municipal police officers.

Accountability is a topic of sustained interest in POST, as indicated by the large numbers of classes on aspects of that subject. In this context, accountability aims to upgrade individual officers. Many of the POST courses, which focus on procedures regarding arrest and detention, paperwork preparation and timeliness, and community relations, instruct recruits in the nature and limits of their authority. Other courses related to accountability include Professional Ethics, Legal Liability, Undercover Activity, and Search and Seizure. The class titled Strategies of Case Supervision, for example, includes the topic of legal and illegal officer behavior in a practicum. The Bill of Rights is disseminated to students and discussed. In short, accountability to the rule of law is a topic of continual discussion in POST classes.

The third area of change is the rationalization of the administrative process in parole and probation work (Feeley and Simon 1992). This rationalization also has been noted in criminal justice institutions including police (Crank and Langworthy 1992) and the courts (Heyderbrand and Seron 1990). Feeley and Simon (1992), discussing the "new penology," distinguish this process from the rightward shift in penal thinking that characterized the 1980s. The new penology, they suggest, is marked by the development of bureaucratic strategies that focus on the management of risk groups and dangerous populations (Cohen 1985). Community-based sanctions become risk-management strategies whose purpose is to maintain control and surveillance over offenders (Feeley and Simon 1992:461, 450). System goals have shifted from the reintegration of offenders to the efficient control of internal system processes—for example, the use of urine testing to determine whether offenders are using drugs.

Occupational Culture, Common Sense, and Tropic Knowledge

Information transmitted by POST across the institutional environment of parole and probation is not accepted unconditionally, but is subjected to evaluation by local organizational cultures. In this process of evaluation, institutional information is weighed against standards of "common sense."

Common sense is the lifeblood of occupational culture. Occupational cultures embody "accepted practices, rules, and principles of conduct that are situationally applied" (Manning 1989:360). These practices and rules are recipes for behavior, and are codified loosely into organizing themes that participants perceive as common sense. The use of commonsense judgments in assessing justice has been noted at all stages of the criminal justice process (Walker 1985).

The presence of commonsense knowledge is indicated by the use of linguistic devices called tropes (Shearing and Ericson 1991). A trope is essentially something described in terms of something else. In occupational cultures, this something else is often a story, an irony, a metaphor, or some combination of these, constituted from everyday experience. The accumulation of tropes makes each organizational culture unique, depending on its work circumstances and its members' collective experiences.

Tropes are processes of "analogous reasoning" or "cultural repertoires" that "allow action to be both orderly and improvisational" (Shearing and Ericson 1991:482). They provide culturally acceptable ways for organizing knowledge under common-sense ideas. The craft of policing, for example, can be characterized as an extensive repertoire of tropes that enable officers to move easily from one ambiguous situation to the next, practicing their craft according to commonly held ideas, embodied in a story-based vocabulary, of what policing is (McNulty 1994).

Four types of tropes are frequently cited (Eco 1984). Metaphor, defined as a "way of seeing something as if it were something else" (Manning 1979:661), has been called the master trope in that other types of tropes are special types of metaphors. Stories are metaphors in that they explain something in terms of personal, concrete experience, although the stories themselves may be constructed of strings of tropes. The other tropes are special cases of metaphors. Synecdoche refers to seeing a part for the whole. Burke (1969) defined synecdoche as representation—that is, the presentation of one thing to represent another. Metonymy takes a whole and reduces it to its constituent parts (Turner 1974). Ironies convey meaning through their opposites.

Tropes are often carried by stories about what peace officers do. Story telling among peace officers to depict their work is recognized widely (Harris 1973; VanMaanen 1979). That these stories might be the object of research, however, has been noted only recently (McNulty 1994; Shearing and Ericson 1991). Stories are not merely glosses that arise from peace officers' inability to articulate why they do what they do; rather, they represent a "narration that is the quintessential form of customary knowledge" (Shearing and Ericson 1991:488–89). Put another way, stories provide a vocabulary of precedents that construct an appropriate cultural, or intersubjective, way of seeing the world (Mills 1940). A member of an organizational culture learns not how to act, but "rather the sensibility out of which she or he ought to act" (Shearing and Ericson 1991:493). McNulty (1994) describes an interactive training scenario in which police recruits are taught the "problematic quality of the truth" (Ericson 1982:62).

Because stories use the intersubjective world of occupational activity as their referent, culture is transmitted as knowledge about the natural order of things (McNulty 1994). Thus recruits, when taught the lore of police work, simultaneously receive a vocabulary of police culture whenever tropes are used to convey information. When training occurs in a classroom provided for POST academies, the use of stories imparts a lexicon of organizational culture masquerading as commonsense knowledge.

POST instructors, by virtue of their occupational position, span the boundaries between the institutional environment and the local organizational culture. As members of the organizational culture, they participate in its commonsense language. Their natural language for organizing action is metaphoric and story-based (McNulty 1994). These individuals are also responsible for providing rational instruction as it is embodied in the content of the curriculum and the topics selected for POST. Thus they are ideological boundary spanners: as instructors they are expected to provide the rational discourse of institutional change, while as members of the local organization they participate in a culturally created common sense worldview communicated by tropes.

Boundaries between areas of institutional change and local organizational culture emerge when instructors are asked a question or when they feel compelled to explain something during a class. Explanations based on the instructors' lore will be drawn from their commonsense worldview, and consequently will be expressed as a trope. These explanations thus convey organizational or cultural perspective presented as commonsense knowledge (Shearing and Ericson 1991). In this way, instructors convey cultural tools that enable trainees to organize the knowledge presented in POST (Kappeler, Sluder, and Alpert 1994). Because these tools are conveyed in regard to particular topics, trainees learn, to use Shearing and Ericson's (1991) phrase, "the sensibility out of which" to think about whatever material is being taught. When topics involve changes in the institutional environment of parole and probation, recruits are taught how to think about those changes.

This tool kit—the stories and tropes used by instructors to convey local culture—is the object of the present analysis. Because tropes emerge frequently in discussions involving institutional change, an assessment of tropes helps us to consider how local organizational culture responds to those changes.

Research Design

In the summer of 1992 I conducted research as a nonparticipant observer of a POST session offered by the Nevada Department of Probation and Parole. The session lasted six weeks, from June 15 to July 27. The academy employed 35 POST-certified instructors during this period; all but three were members of the Department of Probation and Parole. All instructors were sworn peace officers and were employed by the Department of Probation and Parole.

The integration of training into organizational structure, process, and culture was indicated by the organization of the regional Department of Probation and Parole. This department consisted of five units. Three units supervised offenders; one provided court services. The fifth, the POST unit, was housed in the same building complex as the three supervisory units. The unit manager and both supervisors of operations carried offender caseloads, as did the district trainer, the rangemaster, and the program coordinator. These individuals also were instructors in the POST academy. The other instructors also typically carried caseloads. Consequently, the instructors' values and beliefs complemented the occupational perspectives of the members of the organization, among both administrators and line officers.

During the session, I gathered data primarily from classroom observation and conducted follow-up interviews with training staff members and students. POST instructors were informed of my presence before class. I took the role of a nonpartici-pant observer to minimize the impact of my presence on the conduct of the class. With the passage of time, however, I was increasingly accepted as a member of the group, and occasionally was invited to participate in class activities. In this way my nonparticipant status was breached on several occasions. This breaching probably aided in the collection of valid data: at the outset, I suspected that information was filtered in that students and instructors, distrustful of academic outsiders, were guarding their conversations and discussions. With the relaxing of the nonparticipant barrier, however, I sensed that instructors, particularly those who appeared before the class on multiple occasions, were more "open"—that is, likely to lecture, speak, or reveal their sentiments as they would if I were not present.

Findings

Findings are presented here by domain. Tropes in each domain are presented below as vignettes and are organized into themes of cultural meaning.

Crime Fighting

The first domain, crime fighting, was marked by tropes that emphasized the role of the parole and probation agent as a crime fighter. Instructors' crime-fighting stories dominated the tropic landscape. The tropes were organized into two themes.

The first theme cast probationers or parolees as lawbreakers or, in the metaphorical parlance of probation and parole officers, "the bad guys," and emphasized the need to control their behavior and surveil their activities. Tropes with this theme underscored the importance of labeling probationers or parolees as offenders and as persons probably engaged in continuous wrongdoing. The following synecdoche, in which the appropriate term *parolee* or *probationer* was replaced by the figurative term *offender*, was stated several times in academy classes:

> Keep in mind: we do not service clients. We supervise offenders.

This dictum carried the weight of administrative authority:

> The district administrator is very adamant about that. They are offenders, not clients.

The following trope, from a class on home visits, emphasized the idea that offenders were engaged in continuous wrongdoing:

> A fella just got out of jail, and I gave him one of my cards. The next day Metro called, and asked me about my cards, they had found a card at the scene of a burglary. I asked them to read it to me, and they did, and it was this guy. We went to his place, and the police checked for the stolen items. When he came home we arrested him. He was out only one day.

The labeling process was reinforced with interrogative interviewing strategies. The following example and associated trope refer to "wedging the alibi with a minor admission" to uncover wrongdoing during interviews.

> Most offenders will not admit all at one time, they will admit by hints and pieces at a time. Any time you can get the offender to admit a little bit of it, you've opened the door.

An instructor told a long story of an individual who would not admit to a crime. The agent, however, by gaining admission of small units, one at a time, was able to obtain evidence that this individual had committed the crime. In the same class, this was another principle of interviewing:

> They forget to cover up their closest associations. You can get a lot of information from loved ones.

This statement was followed by a story about an offender who had thoroughly alibied his offense but had failed to provide the alibi to his sister. These tropes characterized an ordinary component of probation and parole activity—interviewing the probationer or parolee—in terms of strategies which, when followed correctly, would uncover law-breaking. The tropes revealed the extent to which interviewing has shifted from rehabilitative counseling to interrogation aimed at uncovering wrongdoing (Cohen 1985).

The second theme concerns tropes that describe the potential danger of routine activities. These were the most common of the crime-fighting tropes. In a class on lethal force, the following advice emphasized the potential for danger in a home visit:

> If someone says "I can kill you six ways before you hit the ground," well, maybe they can. Get an extra one or three people before you go in. Most of the time they are bluffing, but don't take any chances.

This theme was echoed in a class on operations. Students were provided with a vocabulary list of terms used by the agency. Two of these terms were tropes which, according to the instructor, provided direction for home visits. The first was "JDLR," defined as "Just don't look right. Refer to GTHO, p. 5." The definition of GTHO was "Get the hell out." These two tropes were ironies by which a keen observer transformed apparently safe circumstances into perilous ones.

The following story, from a class on the return of violators, emphasized the danger-ousness of offenders and the need to search carefully, however repugnant the process might be. The instructor was discussing body searches and was referring to the area around the groin:

> This is the place where people hide all kinds of stuff. There was a case in California where a guy was up for parole. He went before the board, and they turned him down. He bent over and pulled a stabbing tool out of his anal cavity. He jumped over the desk and stabbed a parole board member that he didn't like in the shoulder a couple of times.

Tropes can be chillingly persuasive. The following tropes were taken from a class on officer survival. The class opened with a two-minute film in which an officer was talking against the backdrop of a city street (a visual metaphor of the street as a place where the work takes place). This example illustrates the metaphorical richness of tropes that can imbue even a brief statement with meaning. In this instance, tropes (in bold type in the following quote) emphasized the crime-control aspect of the work.

> I'm not going to let any **son-of-a-bitch** (depraved animal: metaphor for violator) get me **out there** (the street: metaphor for work). No **animal** (animal: metaphor for client) **out there** (the street: metaphor for work) is going to **beat me** (physical confrontation: metaphor for doing one's job). You'll have to **cut my head off** (cutting one's head off: metaphor for keeping from doing one's job) to **stop me** (stop me: metaphor of physical resistance obstructing someone's work).

The instructor presented this statement as an example of a healthy attitude that would enable a recruit to survive in a hostile environment. It was followed by a heuristic trope, a film story of unpredictability and danger during a routine activity. The film was taken by a videocam mounted on an officer's car. The officer was engaged in a routine traffic stop of a car when he was suddenly and violently assaulted by the occupants. The footage showed the officer being beaten and murdered at the side of a dark road. In the last few minutes of the film, the officer was shown lying dead on the pavement behind the patrol car, enveloped in the somber Texas night. This story served as a powerful irony; it transformed a traffic stop into an activity with peril, in which the greatest peril was to take things as they appeared to be.

The theme of unpredictability as a basis for story telling has been noted by other scholars (Harris 1973; VanMaanen 1979). The following story, from a class on prob-able cause, uses the irony of difficulty in gaining entry to convey unpredictability.

> A door can *hurt* you. I've got a big foot [points at his foot]. We were over at a fellow's place, and we could see him on the bed. I kicked the door, and that door it kicked back. I kicked that door nine times. When it finally broke open, there was a great big piece of the door around the deadlock still stuck to the wall. When I pulled it out, there was a deadbolt that long (gestures about nine inches) in concrete reinforced wall. It was specially reinforced.

The Morality of Personal Responsibility

Many tropes identified a precept of personal responsibility for both offenders and officers: responsibility for one's own actions morally imbued probation and parole work at all levels. Whether such responsibility involved the behavior of a probation and parole officer in the courtroom or when making house calls, or whether it involved an offender's ability to maintain personal cleanliness or conform to terms of probation or parole, these tropes emphasized the morality of responsibility for one's own behavior.

Among officers, personal responsibility involved personal demeanor, emotions, and case preparation. In a class on courtroom procedure, accountability for probation and parole officers was linked to their demeanor and case preparation, as indicated by the following tropes:

> Don't read a paper. I was in reviewing a case, leafing through the pages, and the judge stopped, pointed at me, pointed to the bailiff, and the bailiff made a big circle around the courtroom, a big show, and came up to me and said "Please don't rustle your paper,"

> If a judge asks you a question, and you don't know the answer, he'll ask "Who knows?" He'll call for a new date for the hearing, and instruct you to bring in everyone who has that information.

In these examples, responsibility was an immediate, concrete issue of demeanor and preparation. Responsibility, however, also involved the control of emotions. The following story, stated in a class on lethal force, provided local cultural perspective on personal emotions:

> A PR24 [baton] is a deadly weapon. A few years ago an LASD officer saw a fellow he knew standing on a corner, a guy he knew was a burglar. He told him to leave. He drove around the block, and when he came back the guy was still there. He executed a power takeout with a PR24 and hit the guy across the skull, and literally knocked his brains out the side of his head. So be careful. You may be tempted to strike someone, but you'll end up in the trick bag.

The message here was to avoid being overcome by anger; this was viewed as a loss of emotional integrity.

The extent to which moral responsibility was perceived as an issue of personal integrity was underscored in a class titled "Hazardous attitudes." Such attitudes were detrimental to the use of common sense. The five hazardous attitudes—anti-authority, impulsiveness, macho, apathy, and invulnerability—were presented ironically as exemplars of the absence of common sense.

After the instructor's opening presentation, the class divided into five groups, each charged with acting out one of the hazardous attitudes. These skits were heuristic dramas on the ironies. Thus recruits were taught to think tropically by constructing and enacting tragic dramas that demonstrated how a hazardous attitude could conflict with the application of common sense to daily work. Inevitably each drama ended in mock tragedy, affirming the trainees' understandings of local cultural values. The instructor's concluding trope, "Don't drive faster than your guardian angel can fly," conveyed the sentiment that agents should not let their emotions get the best of them.

Among offenders, personal responsibility was presented the-matically in terms of "taking responsibility for [the offender's] life." The director of the training unit emphasized this theme in cited discussions with offenders. She stated the following trope many times:

> I had an offender accuse me of building a case against him. "Are you building the case?" No sir. I told him he was building his own case. Am I writing it down? You betcha!

This theme was echoed in the following statement that made use of a correctional metaphor: doing time for someone else.

> You've got to avoid doing time for them. They'll have a million excuses. They have to be responsible for themselves.

The morality of offenders' responsibility justified retribution. An instructor in a class on probable cause defined the probable cause standard for probation and parole: a crime has been committed, or is about to be committed, or a condition of probation or parole has been violated. The instructor then stated:

> Suppose you have a guy that is usually clean, starts dressing dirtier, makes payments late, but doesn't show drugs in his urine. Is this basis for a search? Yes. Behavioral change. This is probable cause.

In this hypothetical story, behavioral changes indicating untidiness in demeanor, even in the absence of legal or technical violations, become grounds for reinvoking the intervention of the criminal justice system.

Bureaucracy

Many classes dealt with issues salient to participants in bureaucracies, and tropes frequently were bureaucratic in reference. These tropes were organized into two themes. First, they provided guidance for organizing action in terms of local values on topics made complex by a proliferation of legal or organizational structure. Second, they allowed recruits to consider ways to offset some of the more dehumanizing aspects of the crescive rationality of the organizational and legal bureaucracy.

The following metaphorical trope I obtained in a class on case supervision that presents the offender as a construction of the record-keeping system:

> Until Central receives the Initial Risk and Needs Assessment form, the person does not *live*. They do not *die* until Central gets the Termination Data form. The computer says this person lives and dies, and no logic prevails.

In regard to the first theme, several tropes acted as cultural guideposts for action to simplify bureaucratic complexity in order to act more directly and sometimes more retributively against offenders. Drug use is one such topic for which these tropes come into play. This offense classification is highly rationalized by the state legal code. Drugs are categorized by type in five schedules; each contains several different drugs. For example, Schedule 2 includes amphetamines, methaqualone, morphine, thebaine, and hydrocordane. Moreover, three quantities differentiate the charges of trafficking; each charge carries different recommended sentences and fines. Each offense in turn is compounded by previous offenses. From this mass of legal complexity emerged cultural bases for organizing retributive action for drug violators:

> I had a woman, I work over at Gersham Park, that just wouldn't quit [using drugs]. I just couldn't get her to quit. So we went in, took her kid away. Stopped her welfare, told her she couldn't get her kid back until she cleaned up her act. She was in a program in three days.

Another way to organize retribution was provided in a class on filing new charges. This example also reveals how local organizational culture was presented as common-sense knowledge. Here a trainee was told to use common sense, and then was provided with a cultural recipe to organize commonsense action:

> Basically, the rule of thumb is that if you have a lot of stuff on them, go ahead. Just use common sense. We had a bad guy that was causing a lot of trouble. He was picked up, searched, and a small piece of a roach was found. They found him guilty of a gross misdemeanor, and he pled it way down to introducing a controlled substance into interstate commerce. That's the lowest of the low. They'll use that when they really want to get someone.

The following story reveals how organizational culture was masked as organizational process by adding new charges for drug violators:

INSTRUCTOR: We rarely do these [file new charges]. I did three over the past year, and that's a lot. For example, you might have a pregnant mother using drugs.
TRAINEE: Is that a case where we don't do this?
INSTRUCTOR: No, that's the kind of case where we usually make an arrest.

These tropes revealed how violators, particularly individuals who use drugs, were legally chastised. In these stories, tropic language simplified organizational complexity with rule-of-thumb guides for delivering sanctions to drug-using offenders.

This simplification of procedure occurred around important local values—for example, assisting one's partner. I witnessed this in a class on radio communications. Communications have become highly rationalized, and agents are expected to learn a complex array of procedures to communicate by radio. Recruits were introduced to the five types of radios used in the district, details of radio panels, basic radio functions, and the 400 code; officers were advised to memorize this code. Heuristic dramas introduced officers to the complexities of the communications system and emphasized Code 444—assisting another officer.

Dramas were scripted from known events involving officers in the department. The first drama was about a traffic accident that changed to a Code 444 when an officer received gunfire and an armed suspect was chased on foot. The second concerned an aborted holdup that changed into a siege situation when the offender escaped to the roof of a building and shot a medical officer. Both of these skits were about officers in trouble. Through the administrative and technical complexity of police communications emerged one fundamental cultural precept: always respond to officers' calls for assistance.

The second theme was that of balancing bureaucratic excess against offenders' particular needs. The first trope reveals a sympathy for individuals whose circumstances make it difficult to deal with conditions of probation or parole.

> We have a bad situation in our country. A lot of times it is impossible to find work for an unemployed mother. There's no way minimum wage can provide the support [she can get] from unemployment and ADC. However, a condition of parole is employment. You may have to talk to your supervisor. A low-skill offender with three children, her children will literally starve if she has to take a minimum-wage job. They can't afford child care. You can write it up so that they have to work, but you can write it up so that they can take care of their children at home.

The theme of balancing bureaucracy against offenders' needs was revealed particularly by the "success story" tropes, which described how offenders had overcome particular problems in dealing with the bureaucratic apparatus of the criminal justice system. The following story was told in a class on offender services:

> There is essentially no public transportation in the city. When classes are over, people may be dumped at the terminal and be stuck. There is no bus service when classes are over at 9:15. Also, transportation is a significant problem for many of them. One woman started catching buses at 3 to be at class at 7. One kid took a skateboard every morning to get from Henderson to the Bonanza office. He always managed to get there on time.

Another story was told in a class on case supervision:

> The judge ordered a high school completion [a needs form] for a woman with an IQ of 70. What I did was put my woman into Rancho High School classes. She wrote a book report she was exceptionally proud of. I sent a report to the judge telling him what she had accomplished. The judge liked it.

These tropes suggest that probationers or parolees who have displayed the ability to overcome personal hardships become "success stories," a valued commodity in the story-telling language of the organizational culture.

Discussion

Domains are a cognitive map of the organization of common sense in the local culture. Because common sense is produced in POST, these domains become a cultural interface with the institutional environment and, by implication, with areas of institutional change. Here I discuss domains in the light of contemporary changes in the institutional environment of parole and probations.

The first domain, crime fighting, revealed local accommodation to surveillance and crime-control trends in contemporary probation and parole (Duffee 1990; Gordon 1991; Simon 1993). Themes of tropes in the crime-fighting domain— labeling the probationer or parolee as an offender, and the danger and unpredictability of routine activities—suggested that the role of crime fighter was integrated fully into the organizational culture. The commonsense worldview, with its emphasis on crime fighting, danger, and unpredictability, is similar to the worldview of occupational activity frequently attributed to police officers (Manning 1970; McNulty 1994).

Tropes favorable to crime control appear to be matched by a corresponding devaluation of rehabilitative concerns. Probationers and parolees were labeled offenders rather than clients, a label from which there was no escape as long as an offender remained under the department's administrative authority, yet if formal terms of probation or parole and informal norms of personal responsibility were honored, offenders were not subjected to further status degradation. The awkward accommodation between the supportive nature of rehabilitation and the adversarial nature of surveillance was revealed in an incident related by the director of the training unit. A prisoner said "You don't trust us, do you?" She responded "You're right, I don't trust you, but I care."

The second domain, the morality of personal responsibility, is particularly relevant to officers' accountability to the rule of law. Accountability issues are more complex for probation and parole officers than for other sworn officers in criminal justice. Probation and parole officers have broader search and arrest authority than do police officers. Although probation and parole officers are subject to the same due process constraints as police officers regarding revocation of probation or parole, the due process standard for the former is more lenient. Evidence seized in violation of the Fourth Amendment, for example, cannot be entered into evidence for any new crime, but it can be used as a basis for revocation of probation or parole. Searches of a probationer's residence do not require probable cause. Also, violation of contractual terms of probation or parole is a basis for the rearrest of offenders for existing charges, but it has no legal bearing on new charges. These examples reveal that issues of accountability vary according to the legal situation encountered by the officer.

Throughout the six-week period, not a single trope disdained due process concerns. Tropes suggested that these issues were interpreted in terms of preexisting cultural meanings— specifically, the morality of individual responsibility. These criteria were behavioral: how an individual dresses, courtroom demeanor, and the following of technical procedures for arrest. Thus, contrary to the often-cited resistance of policing cultures to accountability, probation and parole instructors provided tropes favoring such accountability. The officer's personal integrity and, by application, the integrity of the organization were of utmost importance.

The third domain, bureaucracy, revealed how the local organizational culture accommodated the contemporary process of rationalizing the administrative environment of parole and probation (Feeley and Simon 1992). Rationalization was revealed in the elaboration of record-keeping systems. The increasing emphasis on surveillance facilitates the rationalization and centralization of the record-keeping and information-collecting systems used by criminal justice agencies; officers were taught detailed procedures when dealing with interstate compacts, for returning violators, and in court services. As one student noted, "P and P stands for paperwork and more paperwork."

Tropes emerged to facilitate problem solving in bureaucratically complex areas. I noted simplifying strategies in the sanctioning of offenders in areas that were organizationally or legally complex, and also in limited efforts to counter the bureaucratic rigor of particularly stringent probation contracts or parole conditions. In institutional terms, tropes instructed how officers could "loosely couple" their behavior to areas of administrative or legal complexity by using local cultural recipes for action.

Conclusions

> One must pick one's root metaphors carefully (Turner 1974:25).

A POST class, viewed through the lens of culture, is a practical theory of action grounded in the experiential world, steeped in rational knowledge, and based on powerful metaphorical imagery. Its metaphors are consequential. The above quote by Turner (1974), with its suggestion that foundational metaphors may have far-reaching implications, is accepted here as an invitation to illuminate some of those implications.

First, the "crime fighting" metaphor has sweeping implications for the organization and activity of parole and probation. That crime fighting is accomplished by individual officers with superior skills was made evident in tropes that labeled probationers or parolees as offenders, and in the use of investigative skills to uncover possible wrongdoing, this metaphorical imagery is similar to Manning's (1991) description of the master detective as the organizing principle for much of police work, in which the ability to ferret out and control offenders' crime stems from the skill of the individual peace officer. Tropes also scripted surveillance and enforcement with stories of the danger and unpredictability of enforcement activity. In a national climate of intense crime control activity and in the face of cultural expectations of controlling crime among offenders, temptations to circumvent due process may become strong, particularly in view of the already relaxed due process protections for probation and parole officers. Organizational pressures to make arrests have strongly influenced the corruption of undercover police officers (Manning and Redlinger 1978). Probation and parole officers, facing increased pressures to convert to a crime-control mode, may find it difficult to avoid similar problems with due process, particularly in view of their expanded enforcement authority.

Second, personal responsibility infuses cultural morality; this finding supports Simon's (1993) important work on the history of parole. Simon (1993:105) conceptualizes parole officers' perceptions of their work in terms of controlling "poor discipline." Parole provides an ideological corrective; it seeks to ensure that offenders are returned to a condition of social normality (also see Garland 1985). I observed this ideological corrective in the current research in the use of streamlined disciplinary tactics to sanction drug offenders. The diverse accounts of organizational shortcuts for penalizing drug violators suggests that normalization of offenders is pursued with a moral vengeance. On the other hand, offenders who displayed moral responsibility in the face of administrative adversity become "success stories." These stories consequently may serve as a moral counterweight to the legal degradation of offenders who violate precepts of morality, and thus, in an ironic logic, may justify retribution for offenders who violate the local culture's moral sensibility.

Third, bureaucratic tropes provide organizational shortcuts for dealing with areas swathed in technicality to facilitate control of offenders. Put another way, the bureaucratization of probation and parole appears to be accompanied by the development of informal processes to facilitate the organization of officers' day-to-day routines. This was particularly evident in the development of shortcuts for dealing with problem cases in areas dense with legal complexity. If, as Feeley and Simon (1992) suggest, the process of system rationalization continues to accelerate for probation and parole, one might anticipate the increasing decoupling of probation and parole officers' work from the administrative processes of the organization, and the increasing isolation of line-level probation and parole officers from administrative process.

In the aggregate, findings suggest that rather than resisting change, as suggested by common wisdom, the local organizational culture absorbed changes in terms of existing areas of meaning, such as offenders' and agents' morality. In doing so, however, the culture itself changed: it adapted to increased legal complexity, for example, by developing rules of thumb for dealing with particular types of offenders. The organizational culture apparently responded to the content of POST by incorporating areas of change into a continual redefinition of itself. Organizational culture thus is passed on to each new cohort in ever-changing form, providing the flexibility to adapt and survive regardless of changes imposed externally on the organization.

The finding that stories are integral to the language of motive. Stories are not simply illustrative fillers that ground a technical lecture empirically, they imbue an account with cultural meaning and value. By the tropes an instructor uses, he or she adds organizational "spin," or cultural interpretation and value, to an area of instruction. This point has a powerful policy implication: a class is a transmitter of organizational culture. POST leaders at the agency level should not only monitor the technical quality of classes, as they do currently through an assessment of testing materials, instructor evaluations, and evaluations of performance, they also should be sensitive to the tropic devices used by instructors to convey information. The transmission of information through tropes will affect recruits' loyalties and the meanings they acquire about their work as powerfully as the technical knowledge will affect their skills and abilities. POST leaders who fail to recognize the power of tropes for instilling cultural knowledge may find that all of their efforts to instill change or knowledge in a particular area are circumvented by offsetting cultural precepts and values.

Both cultural and institutional perspectives rely heavily on case-study methods of observing and presenting information. The usual call to develop quantifiable measures for future research will not be issued here. I believe that additional and more elaborate case-study research can contribute most to these perspectives. We need to assess the wellsprings of organizational meaning and to learn how meanings are modulated through cultural and institutional contexts.

I have examined here only one source of organizational change. Actors have sought to change the administration and behavior of criminal justice organizations in many ways: through the efforts of the chief executive, college education, civilian review boards, media supervision, and policy-oriented research. The central thesis of this paper, however—that organizational culture will influence how particular changes are perceived, and ultimately will determine the success or failure of those changes—should apply to those sources of change as well.

Critical Thinking

The 1990s were the era of the incapacitation model for corrections. Longer sentences for offenders, fewer treatment programs, and a tremendous increase in the correctional population occurred on a national level. Only recently have state legislators begun to question the expense and failure of our correctional institutions to transform prisoners into law-abiding citizens. They emphasized concern for public safety at the expense of treatment programs, which also directly affected the operations of probation and parole departments throughout the country. Why do you think these changes in penal philosophy (i.e., massive incarceration) occurred during the 1990s? Do you think the rise in incarceration rates is responsible for the drop in crime rates across the United States? What do you think are some of the unintended consequences of this trend towards incarceration?

References

Burke, K. 1969. *A Grammar of Motives*. Berkeley: University of California Press.

Church, T. 1982. *Examining Local Legal Culture: Practitioner Attitudes in Four Criminal Courts*. Washington, DC: National Institute of Justice.

Cohen, S. 1985. *Visions of Social Control: Crime, Punishment and Classification*. Oxford: Polity Press.

Crank, J.P. and R. Langworthy. 1991. "An Institutional Perspective of Policing." *Journal of Criminal Law and Criminology* 83:338–63.

DiMaggio, P.J. and W.W. Powell. 1983. "Institutional Isomorphism and Collective Rationality: The Iron Cage Revisited." *American Journal of Sociology* 48:147—60.

Duffee, D. 1990. *Explaining Criminal Justice: Community Theory and Criminal Justice Reform*. Prospect Heights, IL: Waveland Press.

Eco, U. 1984, *Semiotics and the Philosophy of Language*. Bloomington: Indiana University Press.

Ericson, R. 1982. *Reproducing Order: A Study of Police Patrol Work*. Toronto: University of Toronto Press.

Feeley, M.M. and J. Simon. 1992. "The New Penology: Notes on the Emerging Strategy of Corrections and Its Implications." *Criminology* 30:449–74.

Fogel, D. 1984. "The Emergence of Probation as a Profession in the Service of Public Safety: The Next Ten Years." Pp. 65–99 in *Probation and Justice: Reconsideration of Mission*, edited by P. McAnany, D. Thompson, and D. Fogel. Cambridge, MA: Oelgeschlager, Gunn and Hain.

Fogelson, D. 1977. *Big-City Police*. Cambridge, MA: Harvard University Press.

Garland, D. 1985. *Punishment and Welfare*. Brookfield, VT: Gower.

Gordon, D.K. 1991. *The Justice Juggernaut: Fighting Street Crime, Controlling Citizens*. London: Rutgers University Press.

Guyot, D. 1986. "Bending Granite: Attempts to Change the Rank Structure of American Police Departments." Pp. 43–68 in *Police Administrative Issues*, edited by M. Pogrebin and R. Regoli. Millwood, NY: Associated University Press.

Harris, P., T. Clear, and S.C. Baird. 1989. "Have Community Supervision Officers Changed Their Attitudes toward Their Work?" *Justice Quarterly* 6:233–46.

Harris, R.N. 1973. *The Police Academy: An Inside View*. New York: Wiley.

Heyderbrand, W. and C. Seron. 1990. *Rationalizing Justice: The Political Economy of Federal District Courts*. New York: SUNY Press.

Jacobs, J. 1977. *Stateville: The Prison in Mass Society*. Chicago: University of Chicago Press.

Jepperson, R.L. 1991. "Institutions, Institutional Effects, and Institutionalism." Pp. 143–64 in *The New Institutionalism in Organizational Analysis*, edited by W. Powell and P. DiMaggio. Chicago: University of Chicago Press.

Kappeler, V.E., R.D. Sluder, and G.P. Alpert. 1994. *Forces of Deviance: Understanding the Dark Side of Policing*. Prospect Heights, IL: Waveland Press.

Kerner, O. and the National Advisory Commission on Civil Disorders. 1967. *Report of the National Advisory Commission on Civil Disorder*. Washington, DC: U.S. Government Printing Office.

Manning, P. 1970. *Police Work*. Cambridge, MA: MIT Press.

———. 1979. "Metaphors of the Field: Varieties of Organizational Discourse." *Administrative Science Quarterly* 24:660–71.

———. 1989. "Occupational Culture." Pp. 360–64 in *The Encyclopedia of Police Science*, edited by W. Bayley. New York: Garfield.

Manning, P. and L.J. Redlinger. 1978. "The Invitational Edges of Corruption: Some Consequences of Narcotic Law Enforcement." Pp. 147–66 in *Policing: A View from the Street*, edited by P.K. Manning and J. VanMaanen. Santa Monica: Goodyear.

Marquart, J. and B. Crouch. 1984. "Coopting the Kept: Using Inmates for Social Control in a Southern Prison." *Justice Quarterly* 1:491–509.

McNulty, E.W. 1994. "Common-Sense Making among Police Officers: The Social Construction of Working Knowledge." *Symbolic Interaction* 17:281–94.

Meyer, J. and B. Rowan. 1977. "Institutionalized Organizations: Formal Structure as Myth and Ceremony." *American Journal of Sociology* 83:430–63.

Mills, C.W. 1940. "Situated Actions and Vocabularies of Motive." *American Sociological Review* 5:904–13.

Morn, F. 1984. "The Academy of Criminal Justice Sciences and the Criminal Justice Education Movement: Some History." Unpublished manuscript.

Petersilia, J. 1989, "The Influence of Research on Policing." Pp. 230–48 in *Critical Issues in Policing*, edited by R. Dunham and G. Alpert. Prospect Heights, IL: Waveland Press.

Pollock-Byrne, J. 1988. "Ethics and Criminal Justice." *Justice Quarterly* 5:475–85.

Rothman, D. 1980. *Conscience and Convenience*. Boston: Little, Brown.

Shearing, C.D. and R.V. Ericson. 1991. "Culture as Figurative Action." *British Journal of Sociology* 42:481–506.

Simon, J. 1993. *Poor Discipline: Parole and the Social Control of the Underclass, 1890–1990*. Chicago: University of Chicago Press.

Skolnick, J. and D. Bayley. 1986. *The New Blue Line: Police Innovation in Six American Cities*. New York: Free Press.

Spradley, J.P. 1979. *The Ethnographic Interview*. New York: Holt, Rinehart and Winston.

———. 1980. *Participant Observation*. New York: Holt, Rinehart and Winston.

Stoddard, E.R. 1968. "The Informal Code of Police Deviancy: A Group Approach to Blue-Collar Crime." *Journal of Criminal Law, Criminology, and Police Science* 59:201–13:

Turner, V. 1974. *Dramas, Fields, and Metaphors: Symbolic Action in Human Society*. Ithaca: Cornell University Press.

VanMaanen, J. 1979. "Observations on the Making of Policemen." Pp. 292–308 in *Policing: A View from the Street*, edited by P. Manning and J. VanMaanen. Santa Monica: Goodyear.

Walker, S. 1985. *Sense and Nonsense about Crime*. Belmont, CA: Wadsworth.

———. 1992. *The Police in America*. 2nd ed. New York: McGraw-Hill.

Westley, W.A. 1956. "Secrecy and the Police." *Social Forces* 34:254–57.

B Outsiders

26

Ambivalent Actions: Prison Adaptation Strategies of First-Time, Short-Term Inmates

Thomas J. Schmid and Richard S. Jones

Abstract: *Thomas Schmid and Richard Jones examine the ways that short-term inmates adapt to their incarceration and the social world of prison. Using data from participant observations and focused interviews with inmates they show that short-term inmates seldom achieve a significant prison status because participation in the prison world is inhibited by their continued identification with the outside world. Although these prisoners soon learn to define their experiences through a shared subcultural belief system, short-term prisoners never completely abandon their outsiders' perspective or their marginal status. Despite, or perhaps because of their marginalized status, the authors find that these inmates go through several stages of coping and adaptation during their incarceration.*

"Doing time" in a maximum security prison is not simply a matter of being in prison. It is, rather, a creative process through which inmates must invent or learn a repertoire of adaptation tactics that address the varying problems they confront during particular phases of their prison careers.

There is an extensive literature on the informal organization of prison life and the socialization processes through which inmates come to participate in this informal organization. Clemmer (1958) defines prisonization as "the taking on in greater or lesser degree of the folkways, customs, and general culture of the penitentiary" (p. 279). Prisonization is thus fundamentally a process of cultural accommodation through which inmates are first initiated into and then made a part of the prison social and cultural system. Neither of the two theoretical models developed to account for inmate adaptations to imprisonment—the "deprivation model" (Goffman 1961; Sykes [1959] 1971; Sykes and Messinger 1960) or the "importation model" (Thomas 1973; Thomas and Peterson 1977)—adequately represent the multiple ambiguities faced by the sociologically distinctive category of inmates who have no prior experience with the prison world and whose imprisonment is relatively brief.

When first-time inmates are sentenced to prison they have already lost their status as free adults but have not yet achieved any meaningful status within the prison world; they are, to older inmates, "fish" (see Cardozo-Freeman 1984; Irwin 1980). They can shed this label through their increasing participation in prison life, but if they are short-term inmates as well as first-timers they are unlikely to ever achieve a significant prison status. Their participation in the prison world will continue to be inhibited by their ties to, and identification with, the outside world. Their social marginality, grounded both in place and in time, is thus parallel to that experienced by immigrants who expect to return to their country of origin within a few years' time (see Morawska 1987; Shokeid 1988) or who otherwise manage to maintain a "sojourner orientation" (Gibson 1988). Immigrant sojourners, however, can typically draw on shared symbols or institutions in their transient adaptations to a new culture. New inmates, in contrast, have little in common with one another except their conventionality (Schmid and Jones 1991) and consequently have fewer collective resources available to resist assimilation into the prison culture.

In this article, we examine how first-time, short-term inmates in a maximum security prison make use of their social marginality, and the sociological ambivalence that results from it, to forge highly delimited adaptation strategies to the prison culture.

Method

Our study originated, when one of the authors (R. Jones) was serving a year-and-a-day sentence in a maximum security prison for men in the upper midwestern region of the United States. Through negotiations with prison officials, Jones was permitted to enroll in a graduate sociology course in field methods. What began as a directed studies course between professor and former student rapidly evolved, at Jones's suggestion, into a more comprehensive project conducted by co-researchers. At the same time, it evolved from a general observational study of prison life to an analysis of the prison experiences of first-time, short-term inmates.

Jones's prison sentence, our decision to conduct the study together, and our focus on first-time, short-term inmates offered us an unusual strategy for balancing the participant observer's needs for both objective and intimate knowledge about the group or culture being studied (see Davis 1973). This balance can be particularly difficult to achieve in prison research, where suspicions about academic roles often lead researchers to cultivate alternative roles that are more acceptable or better defined (Giallombardo 1966; Jacobs 1977). The circumstances of our study enabled us to examine the prison world for a period of 10 months from the combined viewpoints of both a "complete participant" and a "complete observer" (Gold 1958).

As the "inside observer," Jones had a number of specific advantages. In his interactions with other inmates and with guards, he was not viewed as a sociologist or a student or any other kind of outsider: He was viewed as a prisoner. Moreover, he was not merely assuming the role of a prisoner to learn about the prison world—he *was* a prisoner. He literally shared the experiences of other first-time, short-term inmates, enabling him to contextualize his observations of others with a full measure of sociological introspection (Ellis 1991). Because of his prior training, which included an undergraduate degree in sociology, a university course in participant observation, and a supervised field research project, he was also prepared to document his own experiences and those of his fellow inmates.

Any researcher role closes as well as opens lines of information, and Jones's role had certain limitations as well. As a new inmate, he did not have immediate access to the entire prison world, a limitation that directly influenced our decision to focus on the experiences of first-time inmates. He was also constrained by prison interaction norms, especially those governing relations between members of different racial or ethnic groups. At the prison we studied, these norms were not entirely rigid, but they were sufficiently strong to suggest that Jones's initial observations primarily depicted the experiences of White inmates. (We were able to compensate for this racial selectivity to some extent through a second phase of our fieldwork.) Finally, the most critical question about any "auto-ethnography" (Hayano 1979, 1982) is whether researchers will be able to examine their own social world objectively. Jones expressed concerns about his objectivity early in the directed studies course; it was in response to this problem that we agreed to conduct the research together.

Our analysis of the prison experiences of first-time, short-term inmates thus draws on three primary sources of data. Our principal source is the field notes, representing 10 months of participant observation by a "complete participant" in collaboration with a "complete observer." Included in these notes are specific events and interactions, quotations from Jones's fellow inmates, and general observations of the prison world. A second source is Jones's prison journals in which he recorded his own prison experiences. We used these journals throughout our project as a form of research development, and we draw on them to illustrate portions of our analytic model. Our subsequent interviews with other inmates constitute our third source of data; these interviews allowed us to pursue a number of topics in greater depth and provided us with an independent source of data to test our initial findings.

Marginality, Prison Imagery, and Prison Adaptations

Our earlier analysis of experiential orientations to prison (Schmid and Jones 1990) demonstrated that, at the beginning of their sentences, first-time, short-term inmates defined prison from the perspective of an outsider, drawing on the shared public meanings that exist in our society about prison. By the midpoint of their sentences they had not lost their outsiders' perspective completely and still had only a marginal status within the prison world, but they nonetheless defined prison principally in terms of shared subcultural meanings learned from other inmates. This "insider's perspective," however, subsequently gave way to concluding images that again expressed an outsider's point of view. (More precisely, their concluding imagery was a reflection of their marginal involvement in both worlds; it was a synthesis of their anticipatory and midcareer images and hence a synthesis of their outsider's and insider's perspectives.) These changes in prison imagery are summarized in Table 26.1.

Inmates' subjective understandings of the prison world are important because they provide a basis for action (Blumer 1969). Our earlier analysis also demonstrated, in a general way, how inmates' adaptation strategies followed their shifting prison imagery (as summarized in Figure 26.1). For example, in response to the violence of their initial outsider's imagery, their earliest survival tactics were protective and defensive in nature. As cultural outsiders, however, new inmates also recognized their need for more information about the prison world, and virtually all of their early survival tactics served as information seeking as well as protective measures. Thus territorial caution, impression management, and their partnerships (a friendship with another prisoner recognized by other inmates and guards) guided their ventures into

Table 26.1 Orientation and prison imagery

	Preprison	*Prison*	*Postprison*
Inmate perspective	Outside looking in	Inside looking in	Inside looking out
Central concerns	Violence/uncertainty	Boredom	Uncertainty
Specific problems	Survival	Endurance	Re-integration
Orientation to space	Prison as separate world	Prison as familiar territory	Prison as separate world
Orientation to time	Sentence as lost time	Killing time/time as measure of success	Sentence as lost time/using time
Supportive others	Family and friends	Partners	"Real" family and friends
Perception of sentence	Justified and unfortunate	Arbitrary and unjust	Arbitrary and unjust (intensified)
Predominant emotion	Fear	Detachment	Apprehension (about outside)

ANTICIPATORY IMAGE ⟶ **ANTICIPATORY SURVIVAL STRATEGY**

Outsider's perspective: violence; uncertainty; fear

Protective resolutions: to avoid unnecessary contacts with inmates; to avoid unnecessary contacts with guards; not to be changed in prison; to disregard questionable information; to avoid all hostilities; to engage in self-defense if hostilities arise

↓

SURVIVAL STRATEGY

Territorial caution
Selective interaction with inmates
Impression management with inmates
Partnership with another inmate
Redefinition of prison violence as "explained" rather than random events

↓

MIDCAREER IMAGE ⟶ **ADAPTATION STRATEGY**

Insider's perspective: boredom

Legal and illegal diversions
Suppression of thoughts about outside world
Minimization of outside contacts
Impression management with inmates and outsiders
Partnership

↓

CONCLUDING IMAGE ⟶ **DISSIPATION OF ADAPTATION STRATEGY**

Synthetic perspective: revision of prison image and reformulation of outside image

Continued diversions
Decreasing impression management
Decreasing suppression of outside thoughts
Disassociation with partner
Formulation of outside plan

Figure 26.1 Prison images and strategies.

the cafeteria, the yard, the gym, and other unexplored areas of the prison. Selective interaction with other inmates, impression management, and their partnerships helped them confront such prison experiences as parole board hearings, cell transfers, legal and illegal recreational activities, and participation in the prison economy. The barrage of often conflicting information they received through these tactics was the raw material out of which they continuously revised their prison images. Although they continued to view prison with essentially an outsider's perspective, their survival tactics allowed them gradually to acquire an insider's knowledge of the prison and to modify their adaptation tactics accordingly.

A common form of prison adaptation is the creation of a survival "niche" (Seymour 1977) that allows inmates some measure of activity, privacy, safety, emotional feedback, structure, and freedom within the larger, hostile environment of the maximum security prison (Johnson 1987; Toch 1977). Because of their inexperience, first-time inmates were particularly ill-equipped for finding such niches (Johnson 1987, 114), and new short-term inmates were further handicapped by their continuing marginality in the prison world, which restricted their ability to exert personal control (Goodstein, MacKenzie, and Shotland 1984) and inhibited their acceptance by other inmates. But short-term inmates, in contrast to those facing years of imprisonment, needed only to develop a *transient* niche in prison. The problems they faced were similar—understanding the prison status hierarchy and recognizing their place in it, learning whom to trust and whom to avoid, and determining how to evade trouble in a trouble-filled environment—but their solutions did not need to be as enduring. The men we studied were able to achieve such transient "accommodation without assimilation" (Gibson 1988) within a few months' time. To a casual observer, moreover, they soon became indistinguishable from long-term inmates, relying on such adaptive tactics as legal and illegal diversions and conscious efforts to control their thoughts about the outside world. Their relative integration into the prison world was short-lived, however, and their marginality within this world again became evident as they prepared for their departure from prison. Like more experienced inmates, their preparatory concerns included both practical problems, such as finding a job and a place to live, and existential concerns about how the outside world had changed and how the inmates themselves had changed during their time in prison (see Irwin 1970). Faced with these problems, it became increasingly apparent to inmates that most (though not all) of the adaptation tactics associated with their prison orientation were inadequate for dealing with the outside world.

Based on this general pattern, it is tempting to infer that inmates' adaptations strategies change simply because their reference group changes. In this explanation, suggested by Wheeler's (1961) finding of a curvilinear relationship between institutional career phase and conformity to staff expectations, inmates come to abandon the beliefs, values, and norms of the outside world as they acquire more information about and eventually achieve membership in the prison world. In similar fashion, they abandon the beliefs, values, and norms of the prison world when they are about to regain membership in the outside world. Our earlier analysis (Schmid and Jones 1990) challenged this explanation by focusing on inmates' continuous and active work to *interpret* the prison world. This explanation becomes even more unsatisfactory when we introduce into our analysis the ambivalence that inmates experience throughout their entire prison careers.

Ambivalence and Prison Strategies

In its most general sense, ambivalence refers to the experience of being pulled in psychologically different directions; because prison inmates *share* this experience, it becomes sociologically as well as psychologically significant. The ambivalence of first-time, short-term inmates flows directly from their transitional status between the outside social world and the prison's: It is an ambivalence grounded in the marginality of "people who have lived in two or more societies and so have become oriented to differing sets of cultural values . . . [or] of people who accept certain values held by groups of which they are not members" (Merton and Barber 1976, 11–12). Although inmates' ambivalence affects their prison imagery and strategies in various ways, its principal effect is to limit behavioral changes by inhibiting new inmates from becoming fully assimilated into prison culture.

Feelings of ambivalence characterized the thoughts, emotions, and, sometimes, the actions of the inmates throughout their entire prison careers. Their adaptations to prison expressed both the outsider's perspective they preferred and the insider's perspective they provisionally accepted. Because their strategies were guided by their imagery, their outsider's perspective was most apparent in their behavior at the beginning of their sentences, whereas their insider's perspective was most apparent during the middle part of their sentences. Their behavior during the final months of their sentences was a mixture of nonprison forms of interaction and prison adaptive tactics because their concluding imagery was a synthesis of outsider's and insider's perspectives. Yet a closer inspection of inmates' evolving strategies reveals that the simultaneous influence of the outside and inside worlds was not restricted to the end of their sentences. At every stage of their prison careers, their actions were influenced by the underlying ambivalence that resulted from their marginal position in both the outside and prison social worlds. Table 26.2 presents the various manifestations of this ambivalence that occurred throughout the prison career.

Preprison and Early Career Experiences

Inmates' ambivalence began before they arrived at prison. Like most outsiders, they viewed prison as a world quite different from their own and had difficulty picturing themselves within that world. In the final days of their freedom, they were faced with conflicting desires: They wanted desperately to avoid their sentences—to escape or be forgotten about—but they also wanted their sentences to proceed because they knew this was inevitable. They retained an outsider's perspective but knew that they were no longer full members of the outside world.

Their ambivalent feelings continued throughout their sentences, although the form and emphasis of their ambivalence changed as they progressed through their prison careers. But even in their earliest days in prison, the dominant form of their ambivalence emerged: Their desire to insulate themselves from the surrounding prison world was countered by their desire for human sociability (see Glaser 1969, 18–21). Throughout their careers, but especially during the first half of their sentences, both sides of this fundamental conflict between an outsider's detachment and an insider's

Table 26.2 Experiences of ambivalence during prison career

	Career Experiences	Reported Ambivalence
Preprison	Conviction and sentencing Detention in county jail Transportation to prison	Desire to postpone sentence versus desire to proceed with sentence
Early months of sentence	Holding cell In-processing First night in cell	Desire to insulate self versus desire for sociability
	Orientation classes (first week) Initial correspondence and visits with outsiders	Desire to proceed with new experiences versus relief at security of close supervision during first weeks of sentence
	Transfer to another cell Assignment to caseworker First contacts with general inmate population Job or program assignment Cellblock transfer	Desire for greater mobility within prison versus fear of greater contact with inmates
Middle portion of sentence	Work/program participation Legal and illegal diversions Correspondence and visits with outsiders	Desire to discontinue outside contacts and "do your own time" versus desire to maintain outside contacts
Conclusion of sentence	Application for transfer to minimum security Transfer to minimum security Outside passes Home furloughs Transfer to reentry program Release from prison	Desire for greater freedom versus willingness to complete sentence in maximum security Desire to put prison in past and return to free world versus desire to avoid existential concerns about return to free world

participation in the prison world influenced their behavior. Of importance here is that inmates began to *act*, albeit cautiously, on their desire for contact with others during the first week of their sentences. Their initial contacts with others were quite limited, and they did not appreciably alter their images or strategies, but these contacts did indicate that their isolation did not need to be as extreme as they had anticipated. A 23-year-old inmate, convicted of narcotics sales, described his earliest encounter with another inmate:

> There was one guy that they brought in with me, and we sort of talked off and on. He was sort of scared too, and it was his first time too. He was talking to a guard; I overheard him talking to a guard. I heard him say that he was just basically scared as hell. The guard was trying to calm him down. We were all together in a group; we eat at the same table and everything, and I got talking to him. So I had somebody to talk to.
>
> (Interview)

During their first week in prison, in which they were housed together with other incoming inmates but segregated from the general inmate population, they were able to express their desire for contact with others through limited interaction with both guards and inmates. They learned that not all guards fit their initial stereotypes, and many new inmates encountered one or more fellow inmates with backgrounds similar to their own. They were still intimidated by the prison, particularly by those aspects of prison life that they had not yet experienced, but they began to reduce their isolation and expand their knowledge of the prison world.

The first week thus enabled new inmates, through passive observations and direct interaction, to modify (but not radically transform) both their images and their strategies. Their segregation during this week also led to yet another variant of their ambivalence: They were relieved at the protection of close supervision, but because they knew that they could not avoid facing the general inmate population indefinitely they were anxious to move on to the next phase of their sentences. Similar feelings of ambivalence resurfaced with each new experience. When they learned that they would be transferred to a different cell, and later to another cellblock entirely, they looked forward to the greater mobility these moves offered, but they feared the increased inmate contact the moves would necessitate:

> After only 2 days they moved me [to another cell]. . . . With this move came more freedom. . . . I could go out in the yard and to the dining hall for meals. I was a little apprehensive about getting out. I had made friends with one guy, so we went into the yard together. We were out for about an hour when we were approached by a black dude. He wanted to get us high. I'm sure that's not all he wanted. . . . It helps to find a friend or two; you feel safer in a crowd.
>
> (Field notes)

Their fear mirrored the violence of their prison imagery, whereas their desire to proceed reflected their acceptance that they were now prison inmates.

The evolution of inmates' prison perspectives continued and accelerated through the early months of their sentences. The survival strategies they formulated during these months, like their anticipatory survival strategies, were based on their images of prison. But increasingly their strategies led to modification of these images. This happened because their strategies continued to be influenced by the same motivational factors: (a) their concern for safety but also their recognition that their prison imagery was incomplete and (b) their ambivalence, especially their desire to proceed with new and inevitable prison experiences. The same tactics that gave them new information also reflected the opposing directions of their ambivalence. Their practice of territorial caution and their rudimentary impression management skills expressed their apprehension over contact with other prisoners and their desire for self-insulation, but these tactics also allowed them to initiate or accept limited interaction with others. Their selective interaction with other inmates and their partnership with one other inmate directly expressed their desire for sociability while providing them with a means of maintaining social and emotional distance from the majority of the inmate population.

Midcareer Experiences

Inmates' midcareer adaptation strategies, like their earlier survival strategies, were based on their prison imagery and their ambivalence. Their adaptation strategies differed from their survival strategies because their images changed and because the form and emphasis of their ambivalence changed. Their survival strategies were intended to insulate them from the violence of their anticipatory images but also to allow them to confront new prison experiences and to provide them with new information about the prison world. By midcareer their imagery was dominated by the theme of boredom rather than violence, and they no longer saw a need for more information. But boredom was only one of the problems associated with "doing time" at midcareer: Their relationships with the outside world presented them with other difficulties. As they approached an insider's perspective on the prison world, they came to share the long-term inmate's belief that preoccupation with the outside world could make their sentences more difficult:

> I was talking with [a long-term inmate] and he was telling me that he doesn't usually hang around short-timers because they are so preoccupied with time. He said it took him a long time to get over counting the days, weeks, and months, and that he doesn't really like to be reminded about it.
>
> (Field notes: conversation with middle-aged inmate convicted of murder)

Intimate relationships were likely to be questioned and might even be curtailed (see Cordilia 1983). As expressed by a 37-year-old convicted thief,

> I think it would be almost impossible to carry on a relationship, a real close relationship, being here for 2 years or a year and a half. It's literally impossible. I think that the best thing to do is to just forget about it, and if the relationship can be picked up again once you get out, that's fine. And if it can't, you have to accept that.
>
> (Interview)

Similar concerns were raised regarding all outside contacts. A 26-year-old inmate, convicted of the possession and sale of marijuana, told us,

> When they [the inmate's visitors] left I felt depressed . . . . It's a high when they come, and you get depressed when they leave. I was wondering if that's good. Maybe I should just forget that there is an outside world—at times I thought that, maybe as a survival mechanism to forget that there are good people in the world.
>
> (Interview)

Within a few months' time, inmates' adoption of an insider's perspective thus resulted in yet another manifestation of their ambivalence: Their desire to maintain their involvement in the outside world was countered by a temptation to discontinue all outside contacts so that they could do their own time without the infringement of a world to which they no longer actively belonged.

In a matter of months, then, inmates' perspectives underwent a substantial transformation: They were now viewing the outside world from the perspective of the prison world rather than the reverse, and their adaptation strategies, accordingly, were designed to help them cope with their insider's problems of "doing time" rather than their outsider's fears. Their viewpoints were only an *approximation* of an insider's perspective, however, and their insider's tactics were equivocal because they never achieved more than a marginal status within the prison world. During the middle portion of their sentences they may have been tempted to sever all outside contacts to make their time pass more easily, but they did not actually follow through on this temptation. And although the relationships they established in prison, especially their partnerships, might have seemed more important than their outside relationships, they knew that they would not have freely chosen to associate with most of these people on the outside, and they knew that they would not continue most of these relationships once they were released from prison. In this respect, the prison relationships of the men we studied were more cautious than those typically formed by long-term inmates (Cordilia 1983, 13–29; Johnson 1987, 62–63): They acknowledged that they did not fully belong to the prison world in the same sense that long-term or multiple-term inmates do, and they recognized that these other inmates did not fully accept them as members of their world. First-time, short-term inmates, in other words, never completely relinquished their outsider's perspective, even in the middle stage of their prison careers when they were most alienated from the outside world.

Concluding Experiences

Inmates' continuing ambivalence was a motivating factor in their decision to apply for a transfer to the minimum security unit in the concluding months of their sentences. Their behavior, once again, embodied both directions of their ambivalence: Their outsider's perspective was apparent in the application itself, which indicated a desire for the greater privileges and outside contacts available in minimum security, whereas their insider's perspective was reflected in their emotional caution about their chances that the transfer would be approved:

> As much as I try to, it is very difficult to keep [minimum security] off my mind. I figure that if I don't think about it, it won't be as agonizing waiting for it to happen. It would be much easier if they would give a date to go, but they won't.
>
> (Journal)

If their applications were approved, their ambivalence also influenced their response to the transfer itself:

> I am looking at this transfer a little bit differently from my coming to prison and my transfer to "B" Hall. I don't want to expect too much from [minimum security] because then I won't be disappointed. Also, there is one big difference; if I don't like it out there I can always come back here.
>
> (Journal)

They were aware that their transfer marked the final phase of their prison sentences and a first step toward rejoining the outside world, but they were equally aware that they would still be in prison for some time and that they could be returned to maximum security at the whim of prison officials. Consequently, they were reluctant to admit—to themselves or others—that their transfers held great symbolic importance. They armed themselves with an insider's rationalization: If they didn't like minimum security, they could always come back. And if they should be sent back involuntarily, they were now confident of their capabilities to survive the remainder of their sentences in maximum security.

Once inmates were transferred to minimum security, they experienced yet another manifestation of their ambivalence, similar to that reported by long-term inmates after they have been placed in halfway houses (Cordilia 1983, 99–100): They wanted to put their prison experiences behind them and prepare for their return to the free world, but they also wanted to avoid the existential concerns raised by this preparation and to complete their sentences by "doing their own time," just as they did when they were in maximum security:

> Doing time is not as easy as it may sound; actually, it is a rather complicated business. For one thing, you must try to keep yourself busy even though there is very little for you to do . . . . You would like to plan for the future, but it seems so far away that it doesn't really seem like it is worth thinking about. Also, thinking about the future tends to make the time drag. You also don't want to think about the past, because eventually you get around to the dumb mistake that got you in here. So, I guess it must be best to think about the present but that is so boring . . . that it can lead to depression. You don't want to think too much about the outside because it makes you realize all that you are missing, which can be somewhat depressing. But then, you don't really want to just think about the prison, because there isn't anything more depressing at all.
>
> (Journal)

In the final months and weeks of their sentences they vacillated between directly confronting questions about their futures and avoiding these questions through their continuing tactics of thought control and diversionary activities.

Each of the manifestations of ambivalence itemized in Table 26.2 reflects inmates' marginality because each involved a conflict between an outsider's and an insider's point of view. At various stages in their careers, inmates might place more emphasis on one or the other viewpoint but they never fully resolved their feelings of ambivalence. During the middle portion of their sentences, for example, they might believe that thoughts about the outside world made their sentences more difficult (an insider's belief) and hence might consciously suppress these thoughts (an insider's tactic), but they did not generally terminate outside contacts and would be severely disappointed if their visitors or letters had ceased to arrive. Thus, even when inmates placed greatest emphasis on an insider's viewpoint, their perspectives (that is, the interdependent relationship between their images and their strategies) expressed their marginality. Similarly, when they placed most emphasis on an outsider's viewpoint, namely, at the beginning and end of their sentences, closer inspection of their perspective again reveals their marginality. Our analysis thus suggests that inmates' changing imagery and strategies did not represent a total conversion to an insider's point of view and a subsequent reversion to a more conventional point of view, as suggested in Wheeler's (1961) cyclical model of prison socialization. Rather, the inmates we studied experienced a subtler transformation in which their movement toward either an insider's or an outsider's perspective was circumscribed by their ambivalence.

Discussion

Using ambivalence in any explanatory scheme can place social scientists in a precarious position. Psychological ambivalence is such a universal condition, and one that can result from such myriad causes and situations, that its use in sociological analysis inevitably leads to charges of reductionism. Moreover, as Room's (1976) critique of this concept in the alcoholism literature has demonstrated, pervasive ambivalence resulting from ambiguous cultural norms is a seductively easy but not very useful causal explanation for deviant (and other forms of) behavior. And yet the very pervasiveness of ambivalence in social life also suggests that its interactional significance cannot be ignored.

The ambivalence experienced by the inmates we studied was derived from a very specific set of circumstances: involuntary but relatively brief confinement in a total institution that was both entirely unknown and absolutely feared. Similar, if less extreme, feelings of ambivalence can emerge whenever human beings become fully immersed in highly demanding but time-limited social worlds or social situations. For example, we would expect ambivalence to characterize the behavioral adaptations of new mental patients, military recruits, ethnographic researchers, or students entering college or graduate school. The nature and effects of ambivalence will obviously be influenced by a host of other considerations: how the individuals involved define and evaluate the social world in question, whether their participation is voluntary or involuntary, whether participants share a previous culture, the extent to which they desire to maintain that culture, and so on. Although acknowledging the importance of such situational variations, we nonetheless believe that our analysis of inmates' prison adaptations may help interpret the experiences of others whose ambivalence results from social marginality.

In his critique, Room (1976) specifically points to three connotations of the term "ambivalence" that result in theoretical difficulties: that it "draws attention away from the content of norms or values and places the emphasis on the fact of a conflict in values," that it implies a continuous state rather than an occasional condition, and that it suggests "an especially excited and explosive state, where irrational behavior is to be expected" (p. 1053). Although we are using ambivalence in a holistic rather than a causal model (Deising 1971), Room's comments are nonetheless helpful for our specification of how sociological ambivalence operates in the prison world.

First, for a new inmate the conflict of value systems was as important, or more important, than the content. The first-time inmates we studied were socially heterogeneous; one of the few characteristics they had in common was their belief that they were different from other inmates and hence did not "belong" in the prison world (Schmid and Jones 1991). To differing degrees they learned (but did not fully accept) the norms and values of the prison world. The prison strategies of new inmates had to acknowledge and deal with the content of prison norms and values, but it was the conflict between this value system and their outside values that resulted in their marginality.

The second connotation noted by Room (1976)—that ambivalence refers to a pervasive social condition—is a temporal one. But time itself was central to the marginality of the inmates we studied: They knew that they would be in prison for a year or two but they hoped (and later expected) to return to the outside world. Although ambivalence pervaded their entire prison careers, their role in prison, as defined by themselves and other inmates, was primarily determined by their status as short-timers. Their ambivalence was thus situational, imposed by the specific circumstances of their imprisonment.

It is the connotation of an excited, explosive state that makes ambivalence such an attractive variable in causal explanation. Yet this connotation, which derives from the use of ambivalence in the psychotherapeutic literature, is not inherent in the concept itself; citing *Hamlet*, Room (1976) notes that the term has traditionally suggested paralysis more than action (p. 1058). In our analysis, inmates' feelings of ambivalence served sometimes to motivate action (for example, to break through their initial isolation or later to apply for transfer to minimum security) and sometimes to inhibit action (not to break off ties to the outside world during the middle portion of their sentences despite a temptation to do so). At some career points, the inmates' ambivalence offered them no real choice in behavior (after orientation, inmates were transferred to another cellblock regardless of how they felt about it); at other points, they did face choices (decisions about continuing outside contacts). The principal effect of their ambivalence, however, was to circumscribe their behavior, keeping it somewhere between the more extreme perspectives of the prison outsider and the long-term inmate.

The traditional model of prison socialization suggests that inmates enter prison with conventional values, become socialized to the values of an inmate culture, and then subsequently become resocialized to the values of the outside world. Our research suggests an alternative model of the prison experiences of first-time, short-term inmates, in which their social marginality continuously shapes both their subjective understanding of the prison world and their adaptations to it. Specifically, we argue that the ambivalence that results from these inmates' transitional status limits the behavioral adaptations they make in prison and inhibits their assimilation into prison culture.

The importance of ambivalence in the prison experiences of the men we studied extended beyond its effect on their prison behavior: It also affected their identities. As we have shown elsewhere (Schmid and Jones 1991), these inmates drew a distinction between their "true" identities (i.e., their preprison identities) and the artificial "prison identities" they created and presented through impression management. This self-bifurcation was itself an expression of both directions of the inmates' ambivalence. Because their prison interactions were based almost exclusively on their shared prison role, conditions existed for a "role-person merger" (Turner 1978). Actual identity change was moderated, however, by the inmates' marginality within the prison world and their consequent ambivalence toward their temporary prison role. In this respect, ambivalence helped to shape not only inmates' adaptations to the prison world but their subsequent adaptations to the outside world. By extension, if the final measure of cultural assimilation is whether a new cultural identity emerges, understanding cultural ambivalence in specific, time-limited social worlds may have larger theoretical implications as well.

Critical Thinking

According to the authors, inmates' ambivalence serves to prevent them from a full assimilation into the prison culture. This often leads them to creating a "prison identity" that differs from their "true identity." If short-time inmates make distinctions between their real selves and their prison selves do you think this will limit rehabilitation and behavioral changes? In light of this study, do you think short-term sentencing is less effective as a deterrent? If so, should policy makers force short-term prisoners to identify more as a prisoner and less as an outsider?

References

Blumer, H. 1969. *Symbolic interactionism: Perspective and method*. Englewood Cliffs. NJ: Prentice-Hall.

Cardozo-Freeman, I. 1984. *The joint: Language and culture in a maximum security prison*. Springfield, IL: Charles C Thomas.

Clemmer, D. 1958. *The prison community*. New York: Holt, Rinehart & Winston.

Cordilia, A. 1983. *The making of an inmate: Prison as a way of life*. Cambridge, MA: Schenkman.

Davis, F. 1973. The Martian and the convert: Ontological polarities in social research. *Urban Life* 2:333–43.

Deising, P. 1971. *Patterns of discovery in the social sciences*. Chicago: Aldine-Atherton.

Ellis, C. 1991. Sociological introspection and emotional experience. *Symbolic Interaction* 14:23–50.

Giallombardo, R. 1966. *Society of women: A study of a women's prison*. New York: Wiley.

Gibson, M. A. 1988. *Accommodation without assimilation: Sikh immigrants in an American high school*. Ithaca, NY: Cornell University Press.

Glaser, D. 1969. *The effectiveness of a prison and parole system*. New York: Bobbs-Merrill.

Gold, R. 1958. Roles in sociological field observations. *Social Forces* 36:217–23.

Goffman, E. 1961. *Asylums: Essays on the social situation of mental patients and other inmates*. Garden City, NY: Doubleday.

Goodstein, L., D. L. MacKenzie, and R. L. Shotland. 1984. Personal control and inmate adjustment to prison. *Criminology* 22:343–69.

Hayano, D. 1979. Auto-ethnography: Paradigms, problems, and prospects. *Human Organization* 38:99–104.

———. 1982. *Poker faces: The life and work of professional card players*. Berkeley: University of California Press.

Irwin, J. 1970. The *felon*. Englewood Cliffs, NJ: Prentice-Hall.

———. 1980. *Prisons in turmoil*. Boston: Little, Brown.

Jacobs, J. 1977. *Stateville: The penitentiary in mass society*. Chicago: University of Chicago Press.

Johnson, R. 1987. *Hard time: Understanding and reforming the prison*. Monterey, CA: Brooks/Cole.

Merton, R. K., and E. Barber. 1976. Sociological ambivalence. In *Sociological ambivalence and other essays*, by R. K. Merton, 3–31. New York: Free Press.

Morawska, E. 1987. Sociological ambivalence: Peasant immigrant workers in America, 1880s–1930s. *Qualitative Sociology* 10:225–50.

Room, R. 1976. Ambivalence as a sociological explanation: The case of cultural explanations of alcohol problems. *American Sociological Review* 41:1047–65.

Schmid, T. J., and R. S. Jones. 1990. Experiential orientations to the prison experience: The case of first-time, short-term inmates. In *Perspectives on social problems*, edited by G. Miller and J. A. Holstein, vol. 2, 189–210. Greenwich, CT: JAI.

———. 1991. Suspended identity: Identity transformation in a maximum security prison. *Symbolic Interaction* 14:415–32.

Seymour, J. 1977. Niches in prison. In *Living in prison: The ecology of survival*, by H. Toch, 179–205. New York: Free Press.

Shokeid, M. 1988. *Children of circumstances: Israeli emigrants in New York*. Ithaca, NY: Cornell University Press.

Sykes, G. [1959] 1971. *The society of captives: A study of a maximum security prison*. Reprint. Princeton, NJ: Princeton University Press.

Sykes, G., and S. Messinger. 1960. Inmate social system. In *Theoretical studies in social organization of the prison*, by R. A. Cloward, D. R. Cressey, G. H. Grosser, R. McCleery, L. E. Ohlin, G. M. Sykes, and S. L. Messinger, 5–19. New York: Social Science Research Council.

Thomas, C. C. 1973. Prisonization or resocialization? A study of external factors associated with the impact of imprisonment. *Journal of Research in Crime and Delinquency* 10:13–21.

Thomas, C. C., and D. M. Peterson. 1977. *Prison organization and inmate subcultures*. Indianapolis: Bobbs-Merrill.

Toch, H. 1977. *Living in prison: The ecology of survival*. New York: Free Press.

Turner, R. H. 1978. The role and the person. *American Journal of Sociology* 84:1–23.

Wheeler, S. 1961. Socialization in correctional communities. *American Sociological Review* 26:697–712.

27

Denial of Parole: An Inmate Perspective

Mary West-Smith, Mark R. Pogrebin, and Eric D. Poole

Abstract: *West-Smith, Pogrebin, and Poole examine inmates' perceptions of being denied parole. Inmates find it difficult to understand the rationale of the board and believe that board members were searching for any reason to deny their parole. Many of these complaints are based on various other aspects of their hearing such as: composition of the board, behavior and attitude of members, setbacks due to previous parole violations, denial despite family needs, unhelpful case managers, retroactive application of laws, general denial of all inmates on that particular day, and unfair hearings due to lack of individual consideration.*

Like many other discretionary decisions made about inmates (e.g., classification, housing, treatment, discipline, etc.), those involving parole are rather complex. Parole board members typically review an extensive array of information sources in arriving at their decisions, and empirical research has shown a wide variation in the decision-making process. The bulk of research on parole decision-making dates from the mid 1960s to the mid 1980s (e.g., Gottfredson & Ballard, 1966; Rogers & Hayner, 1968; Hoffman, 1972; Wilkins & Gottfredson, 1973; Scott, 1974; Carroll & Mondrick, 1976; Heinz et al., 1976; Talarico, 1976; Garber & Maslach, 1977; Sacks, 1977; Carroll et al., 1982; Conley & Zimmerman, 1982; Lombardi, 1984). Virtually all of this research focuses on the discretion exercised by parole board members and the factors that affect their decisions to grant or deny parole. Surprisingly, only one study, conducted over 20 years ago, has examined the inmate's perspective on the parole decision-making process (Cole & Logan, 1977). The present study seeks to advance the work on parole decision-making from the point of view of those inmates who have had their release on parole denied.

Inmates denied parole have often been dissatisfied with what they consider arbitrary and inequitable features of the parole hearing process. While those denied parole are naturally likely to disagree with that decision, much of the lack of acceptance for parole decisions may well relate to lack of understanding. Even inmates who have an opportunity to present their case through a personal interview are sent out of the room while discussions of the case take place (being recalled only to hear the ultimate decision and a summary of the reasons for it). This common practice protects the confidentiality of individual board members' actions; however, it precludes the inmate from hearing the discussions of the case, evaluations of strengths and weaknesses, or prognosis for success or failure. More importantly, this practice fails to provide guidance in terms of how to improve subsequent chances for successful parole consideration. A common criticism of parole hearings has been that they produce little information relevant to an inmate's parole readiness (Morris, 1974; Fogel, 1975; Cole & Logan, 1977); thus, it is unlikely that those denied parole understand the basis for the decision or attach a sense of justice to it.

Parole Boards

The 1973 Supreme Court decision in *Scarpa v. United States Board of Parole* established the foundation for parole as an "act of grace." Parole is legally considered a privilege rather than a right; therefore, the decision to grant or deny it is "almost unreviewable" (Hier, 1973, p. 435). In fact, when federal courts have been petitioned to intervene and challenge parole board actions, the decisions of parole boards have prevailed (see *Menechino v, Oswald*, 1970; *Tarlton v. Clark*, 1971). While subsequent Court rulings have established minimal due process rights in prison disciplinary proceedings (*Wolff v. McDonnell*, 1974) and in parole revocation hearings (*Morrissey v. Brewer*, 1972), the parole hearing itself is still exempt from due process rights. Yet in *Greenholtz v. Nebraska* (1979) and *Board of Pardons v. Allen* (1987), the Supreme Court held that, although there is no constitutional right to parole, state statutes may create a protected liberty interest where a state's parole system entitles inmates to parole if they meet certain conditions. Under such circumstances, the state has created a presumption that inmates who meet specific requirements will be granted parole. Although the existence of a parole system does not by itself give rise to an expectation of parole, states may create that expectation or presumption by the wording of their statutes. For example, in both *Greenholtz* and *Allen*, the Supreme Court emphasized that the statutory language—the use of the word "shall" rather than "may"—creates the presumption that parole will be granted if certain conditions are met. However, if the statute is general, giving broad discretion to the parole board, no liberty interest is created and due process is not required. In Colorado, as in most other states with parole systems, the decision to grant parole before the inmate's mandatory release date is vested entirely within the discretion of the parole board. The legislatively set broad guidelines for parole decision-making allow maximum exercise of discretion with minimal oversight.

Normalization and Routinization

Sudnow's (1965) classic study of the processes of normalization and routinization in the public defender's office offers insights into the decision-making processes in parole board hearings. Like Sudnow's public defender, who works as an employee of the court system with the judge and prosecutor and whose interests include the smooth functioning of the court system, the parole board member in Colorado works with the prison administration, caseworkers, and other prison personnel. Public defenders must represent all defendants assigned to them and attempt to give the defendants the impression they are receiving individualized representation. However, public defenders often determine the plea bargain acceptable to the prosecutor and judge, based on the defendant's prior and current criminal activities, prior to the first meeting with the defendant (Sudnow, 1965).

The parole board theoretically offers individual consideration of the inmate's rehabilitation and the likelihood of future offending when deciding whether or not to release an inmate. However, the parole board, like the public defender, places a great deal of emphasis on the inmate's prior and current criminal record. The tremendous volume of cases handled by the public defender necessitates the establishment of "normal crime" categories, defined by type and location of crime and characteristics of the defendant and victim, which permit the public defender to quickly and easily determine an appropriate and acceptable sentence. Such normalization and routinization facilitate the rapid flow of cases and the smooth functioning of the court system. Similarly, a two-year study of 5,000 parole decisions in Colorado in the early 1980s demonstrated that the parole board heard far too many cases to allow for individualized judgments (Pogrebin et al., 1986, p. 149).

Observations of parole hearings illustrate the rapid flow of cases and collaboration with other prison personnel. Typically, the case manager, in a brief meeting with the parole board member, discusses the inmate, his prior criminal history, current offense, institutional behavior, compliance with treatment programs, progress and current attitude, and makes a release or deferral recommendation to the parole board member prior to the inmate interview. The inmate and family members, if present, are then brought into the hearing room. The parole board member asks the inmate to describe his prior and current crimes, his motivation for those crimes, and the circumstances that led to the current offense. Typical inmate responses are that he was "stupid," "drunk," or "not thinking right." Inquiries by the parole board about the programs the inmate has completed are not the norm; however, the inmate is often asked how he thinks the victim would view his release. The inmate typically tries to bring up the progress he has made by explaining how much he has learned while institutionalized and talks about the programs he completed and what he learned from them. A final statement by the inmate allows him to express remorse for the pain he has caused others and to vow he will not get into another situation where he will be tempted to commit crimes. Family members are then given time to make a statement, after which the inmate and family leave the hearing room. A brief discussion between the parole board member and the case manager is followed by the recommendation to grant or defer parole. A common reason given for a deferral is "not enough time served." If parole is granted, the parole board member sets the conditions for parole.

"Normal" cases are disposed of very quickly. The time from the case manager's initial presentation of the case to the start of the next case is typically ten to fifteen minutes. Atypical cases require a longer discussion with the case manager before and after the inmate interview. Atypical cases also can involve input from other prison personnel (e.g., a therapist), rather than just the case manager. Those inmates who do not fit the norm, either through their background or the nature of their crime, are given special attention. The parole board member does not need to question the inmate to discover if the case is atypical since the case manager will inform him if there is anything unusual about the inmate or his situation.

During the hearing, the board member asks first about the prior and current crimes and what the inmate thinks were the causal factors that led to the commission of the crimes. Based on his observations of public defenders, Sudnow (1965) concludes, "It is not the particular offenses for which he is charged that are crucial, but the constellation of prior offenses and the sequential pattern they take" (p. 264). Like the public defender who attempts to classify the case into a familiar type of crime by looking at the circumstances of prior and current offenses, the parole board member also considers the criminal offense history and concentrates on causal factors that led the inmate to commit the crimes. It is also important for the board member that the inmate recognize the patterns of his behavior, state the reasons why he committed his prior and current crimes, and accept responsibility for them. The inmate, in contrast, generally wants to describe what he has learned while incarcerated and talk about the classes and programs he has completed. The interview exchange thus reveals two divergent perceptions of what factors should be emphasized in the decision-making process. In Sudnow's (1965) description of a jury trial involving a public defender, "the onlooker comes away with the sense of having witnessed not a trial at all, but a set of motions, a perfunctorily carried off event" (p. 274). In a similar manner, the observer at a parole board hearing has the impression of having witnessed a scripted, staged performance.

As a result of their journey through the criminal justice system, individual inmates in a prison have been typed and classified by a series of criminal justice professionals. The compilation of prior decisions forms the parole board member's framework for his or her perception of the inmate. The parole board member, with the help of previous decision-makers and through normalization and routinization, "knows" what type of person the inmate is. As Heinz et al. (1976) point out, "a system premised on the individualization of justice unavoidably conflicts with a caseload that demands simple decision rules. . . . To process their caseloads, parole boards find it necessary to develop a routine, to look for one or two or a few factors that will decide their cases for them" (p. 18). With or without the aid of parole prediction tools to help in their decision, parole board members feel confident they understand the inmate and his situation; therefore, their decisions are more often based on personal intuition than structured guidelines.

Theoretical Framework

Based on a combination of both formal and informal sources of information they acquire while in prison, inmates believe that satisfactory institutional behavior and completion of required treatment and educational programs, when combined with adequate time served, will result in their release on parole. They also believe that passing their parole eligibility date denotes sufficient institutional time. Denial of parole, when the stated prerequisites for parole have been met, leads to inmate anger and frustration. As stories of parole denials spread throughout the DOC population, inmates are convinced that the parole board is abusing its discretion to continue confinement when it is no longer mandated.

Control of Institutional Behavior

The majority of inmates appearing before the parole board have a fairly good record of institutional behavior (Dawson, 1978). Inmates are led to believe that reduction in sentence length is possible through good behavior (Emshoff & Davidson, 1987). Adjustment to prison rules and regulations is not sufficient reason for release on parole; however, it comprises a minimum requirement for parole and poor adjustment is a reason to deny parole (Dawson, 1978). Preparation for a parole hearing would be a waste of both the prisoner's and the case manager's time and effort if the inmate's behavior were not adequate to justify release.

Research suggests that good behavior while incarcerated does not necessarily mean that an inmate will successfully adapt to the community and be law-abiding following a favorable early-release decision (Haesler, 1992; Metchik, 1992). In addition, Emshoff and Davidson (1987) note that good time credit is not an effective deterrent for disruptive behavior. Inmates who are most immature may be those most successful at adjusting to the abnormal environment of prison; inmates who resist conformity to rules may be those best suited for survival on the outside (Talarico, 1976). However, institutional control of inmate behavior is a crucial factor for the maintenance of order and security among large and diverse prison populations, and the use of good time credit has traditionally been viewed as an effective behavioral control mechanism (Dawson, 1978). Inmates are led to believe that good institutional behavior is an important criterion for release, but it is secondary to the background characteristics of the inmate. Rather than good behavior being a major consideration for release, as inmates are told, only misbehavior is taken into account and serves as a reason to deny parole.

Inmates are also told by their case manager and other prison personnel that they must complete certain programs to be paroled. Colorado's statutory parole guidelines list an inmate's progress in self-improvement and treatment programs as a component to be assessed in the release decision (Colorado Department of Public Safety, 1994). However, the completion of educational or treatment programs by the inmate is more often considered a factor in judging the inmate's institutional adjustment, i.e., his ability to conform to program rules and regimen. Requiring inmates to participate in prison programs may be more important for institutional control than for the rehabilitation of the inmate. Observations of federal parole hearings suggest that the inmate's institutional behavior and program participation are given little importance in release decisions (Heinz et al., 1976). Noncompliance with required treatment programs or poor institutional behavior may be reasons to deny parole, but completion of treatment programs and good institutional behavior are not sufficient reasons to grant parole.

Release Decision Variables

Parole board members and inmates use contrasting sets of variables each group considers fundamental to the release decision. Inmates believe that completion of treatment requirements and good institutional behavior are primary criteria the parole board considers when making a release decision. Inmates also feel strongly that an adequate parole plan and demonstration that their families need their financial and emotional support should contribute to a decision to release on parole.

In contrast, the parole board first considers the inmate's current and prior offenses and incarcerations. Parole board members also determine if the inmate's time served is commensurate with what they perceive as adequate punishment. If it is not, the inmate's institutional behavior, progress in treatment, family circumstances and parole plan will not outweigh the perceived need for punishment. Inmates, believing they understand how the system works, become angry and frustrated when parole is denied after they have met ail the stated conditions for release.

Unwritten norms and individualized discretion govern parole board decision-making; thus, the resulting decisions become predictable only in retrospect as patterns in granting or denying parole emerge over time. For example, one of the difficulties Pogrebin et al. (1986) encountered in their study of parole board hearings in Colorado was developing a written policy based on previous case decisions:

> This method requires that a parole board be convinced that there exists a hidden policy in its individual decisions. . . . [M]ost parole board members initially will deny that they use any parole policy as such . . . [and] will claim that each case is treated on its own merits. . . . [However] parole decisions begin to fit a pattern in which decisions are based on what has been decided previously in similar situations.

> (p. 149)

Method

In October of 1997, Colorado-CURE (Citizens United for Rehabilitation of Errants), a Colorado non-profit prisoner advocacy group, solicited information through its quarterly newsletter from inmates (who were members of the organization) regarding parole board hearings that resulted in a "set-back," i.e., parole deferral. Inmates were asked to send copies of their appeals and the response they received from the parole board to Colorado-CURE. One hundred and eighty inmates responded to the request for information with letters ranging in length from very brief one- or two-paragraph descriptions of parole board hearings to multiple page diatribes listing not only parole board issues, but complaints about prison conditions, prison staff, and the criminal justice system in general. Fifty-two letters were eliminated from the study because they did not directly address the individual inmate's own parole hearing. One hundred and twenty-eight inmate letters were analyzed; one hundred and twenty-five from male and three from female inmates. Some letters contained one specific complaint about the parole board, but most inmates listed at least two complaints. Several appeals also contained letters written to the parole board by family members on the inmate's behalf. Two hundred and eighty-five complaints were identified and classified into thirteen categories utilizing content analysis, which "translates frequency of occurrence of certain symbols into summary judgments and comparisons of content of the discourse" (Starosta, 1984, p. 185). Content analytical techniques provide the means to document, classify, and interpret the communication of meaning, allowing for inferential judgments from objective identification of the characteristics of messages (Holsti, 1969). In addition, parole board hearings, including the preliminary presentation by the case manager and the discussion after the inmate interview, were observed over a three-month period in 1998. These observations were made to provide a context for understanding the nature of the hearing process from the inmate's perspective and to document the substantive matter of parole deliberations.

The purpose of the present study is not to explore the method the parole board uses to reach its release decisions; rather, our interest is to examine the content of the written complaints of inmates in response to their being denied parole.

Findings

Those complaints relating to parole hearings following a return to prison for a parole violation and those complaints regarding sex offender laws will not be addressed in the following discussion. Parole revocation hearings are governed by different administrative rules and are subject to more rigorous due process requirements and are thus beyond the scope of the current study. In addition, sex offender sentencing laws in Colorado have evolved through dramatic changes in legislation over the past several years and a great deal of confusion exists regarding which inmates are eligible for parole, when they are eligible, and what conditions can be imposed when inmates are paroled. We now turn to an examination of the remaining categories of inmate complaints concerning parole denial.

Inadequate Time Served

Forty-eight percent of the inmates reported "inadequate time served" as a reason given for parole deferment. Their attempt to understand the "time served" component in the board's decision is exemplified by the following accounts:

> [I]f you don't meet their [the parole board's] time criteria you are "not" eligible. Their time criteria is way more severe than statute. . . . [The risk assessment] also says, if you meet their time amounts and score 14 or less on the assessment you "shall" receive parole. This does not happen. The board is an entity with entirely too much power. . . .

> If the court wanted me to have more time, it could have aggravated my case with as much as eight years. Now the parole board is making itself a court!

> [Enclosed] is a copy of my recent deferral for parole, citing the infamous "Not enough time served" excuse. This is the third time they've used this reason to set me back, lacking a viable one.

These responses of the inmates to the "inadequate time served" reason for parole deferral demonstrate that they believe the parole board uses a different set of criteria than the official ones for release decisions. Inmates do not understand that the "time served" justification for parole deferment relates directly to the perception by the parole board member of what is an acceptable punishment for their crime. They believe the parole board is looking for a reason to deny parole and uses "time served" when no other legitimate reason can be found.

Completed Required Programs

Thirty-five percent of the inmates complained that their parole was deferred despite completing all required treatment and educational programs. Related complaints, expressed by 9 percent of the inmates, were the lack of mandatory classes and the long waiting lists for required classes. The following excerpts from inmate letters reflect this complaint:

> When I first met with them [the parole board] I received a 10 month setback to complete the classes I was taking (at my own request). But was told once I completed it and again met the board I was assured of a release. . . . Upon finishing these classes I met the board again [a year later]. . . . I noticed that none of my 7 certificates to date were in the file and only a partial section of the court file was in view. I tried to speak up that I was only the 5th or 6th person to complete the 64 week class and tell about the fact that I carry a 4.0 in work plus have never had a COPD conviction or a write-up. He silenced me and said that meant nothing. . . . I later was told I had been given another one year setback!!!

> They gave me a six month setback because they want me to take another A.R.P. class. . . . [I]t was my first time down [first parole hearing], and I have taken A.R.P. already twice. . . . I have also taken . . . Independent Living Skills, Job Search, Alternatives to Violence, workshops and training in nonviolence, Advanced Training for Alternatives to Violence Project, mental health classes conducted by addiction recovery programs. I also chair the camp's A.A. meetings every week and just received my two year coin. I have also completed cognitive behavioral core curriculum. . . .

Inmates view completion of required programs as proof that they have made an effort to rehabilitate themselves and express frustration when the parole board does not recognize their efforts. The completion of classes was usually listed with other criteria the inmates viewed as important for their release on parole.

Parole Denied despite Parole Plan

Deferral of parole even though a parole plan had been submitted was a complaint listed by 27 percent of inmates. It is interesting to note that this complaint never appeared as a solo concern, but was always linked to other issues. These inmates seem to believe that a strong parole plan alone will not be sufficient to gain release and that the parole plan must be combined with good institutional behavior and the completion of required classes. Even when all required criteria are met, parole was often deferred. The frustration of accomplishing all of the requirements yet still being deferred is expressed in the following excerpts:

> I was denied for the third time by the D.O.C. parole board even though I have completed all recommended classes (Alcohol Ed. I and II, Relapse Prevention, Cognitive Skills and Basic Mental Health). I have a place to parole to [mother's house], a good job and a very strong support group consisting of family and friends. . . . To the present date I have served 75% of my 3-year sentence.

> [After having problems with a previous address for the parole plan] . . . my parents and family . . . were assured . . . that all I needed to do is put together an alternative address. I managed to qualify for and arrange to lease a new low-income apartment at a new complex. . . . My family was helping with this. I also saw to it that I was preapproved at [a shelter in Denver], a parole office approved address, so that I could go there for a night or two if needed while I rented and

had my own apartment approved by the parole office. My family expected me home, and I had hoped to be home and assisting them, too. I arranged employment from here, and looked forward to again being a supportive father and son. . . . I received a one-year setback! I was devastated, and my family is too. We are still trying to understand all of this. . . . I am . . . angry at seeing so many sources of support, employment, and other opportunities that I worked so hard at putting together now be lost.

Preparing an adequate parole plan requires effort on the part of both the inmate and the case manager. When a parole plan is coupled with completion of all required treatment and educational programs and good institutional behavior, the inmate is at a loss to understand how the parole board can deny parole. Inmates often expressed frustration that the plans they made for parole might not be available the next time they are eligible for parole. "Inadequate time served" is often the stated reason for parole deferment in these cases and does not indicate to the inmate changes he needs to make in order to be paroled in the future.

Parole Board Composition and Behavior

Twenty-one percent of the inmates complained about the composition of the parole board or about the attitude parole board members displayed toward the inmate and his or her family. Several inmates expressed concern that at the majority of hearings, only one parole board member is present and the outcome of an inmate's case might depend on the background of the parole board member hearing the case:

The man [parole board member] usually comes alone, and he talks to the women worse than any verbal abuser I have ever heard. He says horrible things to them about how bad they are and usually reduces them to tears. Then he says they are "too emotionally unstable to be paroled!" If they stand up for themselves, they have "an attitude that he can't parole." If they refuse to react to his cruel proddings, they are "too cold and unfeeling." No way to win!! Why in the *world* do we have ex-policemen on the parole board? Cops always want to throw away the key on all criminals, no matter what. Surely that could be argued . . . as conflict of interest!

My hearing was more of an inquisition than a hearing for parole. All of the questions asked of me were asked with the intent to set me back and not the intent of finding reasons to parole me. It was my belief that when a person became parole eligible the purpose was to put them out, if possible. My hearing officer did nothing but look for reasons to set me back.

Inmates often expressed the view that the parole board members conducting their hearings did not want to listen to their stories. However, if parole board members have generally reached a decision prior to interviewing the inmate, as indicated by the routinization of the hearing process, it is logical that the board member would attempt to limit the inmate's presentation. In addition, if board members have already determined that parole will be deferred, one would expect the questions to focus on reasons to deny parole. One inmate stated, "I believe that the parole board member that held my hearing abused his discretion. I had the distinct feeling that he had already decided to set me back before I even stepped into the room."

Family's Need for Inmate's Support

Many inmates criticized the parole board for failing to take into account their families' financial, physical, and emotional needs. Seventeen percent of the inmates expressed this concern, and several included copies of letters written by family members asking the board to grant parole. The primary concerns were support for elderly parents and dependent young children:

> My mom has Lou Gehrig's disease.... [S]he can't walk and it has spread to her arms and shoulders.... [No] one will be there during the day to care for her. The disease is fast moving.... My mom is trying to get me home to care for her.... I am a non-violent first time offender. I have served 8 years on a 15. I have been before the parole board 5 times and denied each time.... (I got 6, 6, 9, 6, 12 month setbacks in that order). Why I'm being denied I'm unsure. I've asked the board and wasn't told much. I've completed all my programs, college, have a job out there, therapy all set up, and a good parole plan.

> [My 85-year-old mother] has no one. Her doctor also wrote [to the chair of the parole board] as well as other family members, including my son. All begging for my release. She *needs* me!! I wish you could [see] ... how hard I have worked since I have been in prison.... Being good and trying hard does not count for much in here.... This is my 5th year on an 8 year sentence.

The parole board does not consider a dependant family as a primary reason to release an inmate on parole; however, inmates regard their families' needs as very important and are upset that such highly personal and emotionally charged circumstances are given short shrift during their parole hearing. And if they believe they have met the conditions established for release, inmates do not understand why the parole board would not allow them to return home to help support a family.

Case Manager Not Helpful

Thirteen percent of the inmates expressed frustration with their case manager, with a few accusing the case manager of actually hurting their chances to make parole. Although the inmate was not present during the case manager's presentation to the board member, many inmates declared satisfaction with their case manager and felt that the board did not listen to the case manager's recommendation. Since the present study focuses on inmate complaints, the following excerpts document the nature of the dissatisfaction inmates expressed concerning their case managers:

> [The case manager] has a habit of ordering inmates to waive their parole hearings. Many inmates are angry and do not know where to turn because they feel it is their right to attend their parole hearings.... [He] forces most all of his caseload to waive their parole hearing. That is not right! ... How and why is this man allowed to do this? I would not like my name mentioned because I fear the consequences I will pay.... [T]his man is my case manager and I have not seen the parole board yet.

> I have not had any writeups whatsoever and I have been taking some drug and alcohol classes since I have been back [parole revoked for a dirty U.A.]. I had a real strong parole plan that I thought that my case manager submitted but he never bothered to. I was planning on going to live with my father who I never asked for anything in my life and he was willing to help me with

a good job and a good place to live. My father had also wrote to [the chair of the parole board] and asked if I could be paroled to him so he can help me change my life around.

[Some] case managers are not trained properly and do not know what they are doing. Paperwork is seldom done properly or on time. Others are downright mean and work *against* the very people they are to help. Our liberty depends on these people, and we have no one else to turn to when they turn against us.

Inmates realize they must at least have a favorable recommendation by the case manager if they are to have any chance for parole. Yet they generally view the case manager as a "marginal advocate," often going through the motions of representing their interests but not really supporting or believing in them. Case managers after all are employees of the Department of Corrections, and their primary loyalties are seen by inmates to attach to their employer and "the system."

Few Inmates Paroled the Same Day

Five percent of the inmates related in their letters that very few inmates were paroled on a given hearing day, leading them to suspect that the parole board typically denies release to the vast majority of inmates who come up for a hearing.

I just received a letter ... and she told me that 2 out of 24 made parole from [a Colorado women's facility]. ... [Also] out of 27 guys on the ISP non-res program from [a community corrections facility] only 4 made parole!! ... What is going on here?!! These guys [on ISP] are already on parole for all intents and purposes.

Went [before parole board] in June '97. 89 went. 2 made it (mandatory).

I realize they're not letting very many people go on parole or to community. It's not politically correct to parole anyone. Now that Walsenburg is opening, I'm sure they will parole even less people. I have talked to 14 people that seen the Board this week. 2 setbacks. ...

Inmates circulate such stories and cite them as evidence that the parole board is only interested in keeping prisoners locked up. Many inmates express their belief that the parole board is trying to guarantee that all the prisons are filled to capacity.

Appeals Not Considered on an Individual Basis

Although Colorado-CURE asked inmates to send copies of their appeal and the response to the appeal, the majority of inmates mailed copies of their appeal before they received the response. Thus, it is not surprising that only four percent of the inmates discussed the apparent uniformity of appeal decisions. The standard form letter from the chair of the parole board, included by those who stated this complaint, reads as follows:

I have reviewed your letter ..., along with your file, and find the Board acted within its statutory discretion. Consequently, the decision of the Board stands.

Word of the appeals circulates among the general prison population and between prisons via letters to other inmates. Inmates suggest that the form letters are evidence that the parole board is not willing to review cases and reconsider decisions made by individual board members.

> I finally got their response. They are basically sending everyone the same form letter. I was told by someone else that it [is] what they were doing and sure enough that is what they are doing.

> After receiving the denial of my appeal, I spoke with a fellow convict about his dilemma, which prompted him to show me a copy of his girlfriend's denial of her appeal. . . . It seems that [she] was given an unethical three (3) year setback, even though she has now completed 3/4 of her sentence. And she too received a carbon copy response from the [chair of the parole board's] office. It should be crystal clear that these files are *not* being reviewed as is stated in [the] responses, because if they had been, these decisions would surely seem questionable at best.

Conclusion

The nature of the written complaints reflects the belief among many inmates that the parole board in Colorado is using criteria for release decisions that are hidden from inmates and their families. A parole board decision, made without public scrutiny by members who have no personal knowledge of the inmate, depends on the evaluation of the likelihood of recidivism by others in the criminal justice system. While guidelines and assessment tools have been developed to help with the decision-making process in Colorado, it is unclear the extent to which they are used. Release decisions by the parole board appear to be largely subjective and to follow latent norms that emerge over time. The emphasis on past and current crimes indicates that inmates—regardless of their institutional adjustment or progress in treatment, vocational, or educational programs—will continue to be denied parole until they have been sufficiently punished for their crimes. As one inmate lamented in his letter of complaint,

> When the inmate has an approved parole plan, a job waiting and high expectations for the future and then is set back a year . . ., he begins to die a slow death. They *very often* use the reason: *Not enough time served* to set people back. If I don't have enough time served, why am I seeing the parole board? Or they will say: *Needs Continued Correctional Treatment.* If I have maintained a perfect disciplinary record and conformed to the rules, what more correctional treatment do I need. . . . I had a parole plan and a job in May when I seen the Board. I was set back one year. I will see them in March. . . . I will have no job and nowhere to live. . . . The Colorado Dept. of Corrections does not rehabilitate inmates. That is solely up to the inmate. What they do is cause hate and bitterness and discontent.

Findings of this study indicate that the factors inmates believe affect release decisions are different from the factors the parole board considers and thus suggest why inmates fail to understand why their parole is deferred despite compliance with the pre-requisites imposed upon them. As evidenced by the above examples, inmates are not only confused and angry when they believe parole should be granted, they begin to question whether or not it is worth the effort if they are only going to "kill their numbers" (i.e., serve the full sentence). The prison grapevine and the flow of information among the entire Department of Corrections inmate population allow such stories and theories to spread. Prison officials should be concerned that if inmates feel compliance with prison rules and regulations is pointless, they will be less likely to conform to the administration's requirements for institutional control. Currently, inmates who are turned down for parole see themselves as victims, unfairly denied what they perceive they have earned and deserve. Each parole eligible case that is deferred or set back becomes another story, duly embellished, that makes its rounds throughout the prison population, fueling suspicion, resentment, and fear of an unbridled discretionary system of power, control, and punishment.

Inmates denied parole are entitled to a subsequent hearing usually within one calendar year. But the uncertainty of never knowing precisely when one will be released can create considerable tension and frustration in prison. While discretionary release leaves them in limbo, it is the unpredictability of release decisions that is demoralizing. As we have found, this process has resulted in bitter complaints from inmates. Perhaps the late Justice Hugo Black of the U.S. Supreme Court best summarized the view of many inmates toward the parole board:

> In the course of my reading—by no means confined to law—I have reviewed many of the world's religions. The tenets of many faiths hold the deity to be a trinity. Seemingly, the parole boards by whatever names designated in the various states have in too many instances sought to enlarge this to include themselves as members.
>
> (Quoted in Mitford, 1973, p. 216)

Critical Thinking

It is common for members of parole boards to want inmates to accept full responsibility for their crimes. When inmates present excuses or justifications for their acts parole board members interpret this as evidence they will likely go back to crime. In short, parole board members expect inmates to accept "criminal" as an identity status. Think about some of the improper things that you have done. Were there "legitimate" excuses for why you did them? Should your identity be tied solely to these acts? Think about some excuses that you would accept from inmates if you were on a parole board and ones you would not?

References

Board of Pardons v. Allen, 482 U.S. 369 (1987).

Carroll, J.S., Wiener, R.L., Coates, D., Galegher, J., & Alirio, J.J. (1982). Evaluation, diagnosis, and prediction in parole decision making. *Law and Society Review, 17*, 199–228.

Carroll, L, & Mondrick, M.E. (1976). Racial bias in the decision to grant parole. *Law and Society Review, 11*, 93–107.

Cole, G.F., & Logan, C.H. (1977). Parole: The consumer's perspective. *Criminal Justice Review, 2*, 71–80.

Colorado Department of Public Safety (1994). *Parole guidelines handbook*. Denver, CO: Division of Criminal Justice.

Conley, J.A., & Zimmerman, S.E. (1982). Decision making by a part-time parole board: An observational and empirical study. *Criminal Justice and Behavior, 9*, 396–431.

Dawson, R. (1978). The decision to grant or deny parole. In B. Atkins and M. Pogrebin (Eds.), *The invisible justice system: Discretion and the law* (pp. 360–389). Cincinnati: Anderson.

Emshoff, J.G., & Davidson, W.S. (1987). The effect of "good time" credit on inmate behavior: A quasi-experiment. *Criminal Justice and Behavior, 14*, 335–351.

Fogel, D. (1975). . . . *We are the living proof: The justice model for corrections*. Cincinnati: Anderson.

Garber, R.M., & Maslach, C. (1977). The parole hearing: Decision or justification? *Law and Human Behavior, 1*, 261–281.

Gottfredson, D.M., & Ballard, K.B. (1966). Differences in parole decisions associated with decision-makers. *Journal of Research in Crime and Delinquency, 3*, 112–119.

Greenholtz v. Nebraska Penal Inmates, 442 U.S. 1 (1979).

Haesler, W.T. (1992). The released prisoner and his difficulties to be accepted again as a "normal" citizen. *Euro-Criminology*, *4*, 61–68.

Heinz, A.M., Heinz, J.P., Senderowitz, S.J., & Vance, M.A. (1976). Sentencing by parole board: An evaluation. *Journal of Criminal Law and Criminology*, *67*, 1–31.

Hier, A.P. (1973). Curbing abuse in the decision to grant or deny parole. *Harvard Civil Rights-Civil Rights Law Review*, *8*, 419–468.

Hoffman, P.B. (1972). Parole policy. *Journal of Research in Crime and Delinquency*, *9*, 112–133.

Holsti, O.R. (1969). *Content analysis for the social sciences and humanities*. Reading, MA: Addison-Wesley.

Lombardi, J.H. (1984). The impact of correctional education on length of incarceration: Non-support for new paroling policy motivation. *Journal of Correctional Education*, *35*, 54–57.

Menechino v. Oswald, 430 F.2d 402 (2nd Cir. 1970).

Metchik, E. (1992). Judicial views of parole decision processes: A social science perspective. *Journal of Offender Rehabilitation*, *18*, 135–157.

Mitford, J. (1973). *Kind and unusual punishment: The prison business*. New York: Knopf.

Morris, N. (1974). *The future of imprisonment*. Chicago: University of Chicago Press.

Morrissey v. Brewer, 408 U.S. 471 (1972).

Pogrebin, M.R., Poole, E.D., & Regoli, R.M. (1986). Parole decision making in Colorado. *Journal of Criminal Justice*, *14*, 147–155.

Rogers, J., & Hayner, N.S. (1968). Optimism and accuracy in perceptions of selected parole prediction items. *Social Forces*, *46*, 388–400.

Sacks, H.R. (1977). Promises, performance, and principles: An empirical study of parole decision making in Connecticut. *Connecticut Law Review*, 9, 347–423.

Scarpa v. U.S. Board of Parole, 414 U.S. 934 (1973).

Scott, J.E. (1974). The use of discretion in determining the severity of punishment for incarcerated offenders. *Journal of Criminal Law and Criminology*, *65*, 214–224.

Starosta, W.J. (1984). Qualitative content analysis: A Burkean perspective. In W. Gudykunst & Y.Y. Kim (Eds.), *Methods for intercultural communication research* (pp. 185–194). Beverly Hills, CA: Sage.

Sudnow, D. (1965). Normal crimes: Sociological features of the penal code in a public defender's office. *Social Problems*, *12*, 255–276.

Talarico, S.M. (1976). The dilemma of parole decision making. In G.F. Cole (Ed.), *Criminal justice: Law and politics*, 2nd edition (pp. 447–456). North Scituate, MA: Duxbury.

Tarlton v. Clark, 441 F.2d 384 (5th Cir. 1971), *cert, denied*, 403 U.S. 934 (1971).

Wilkins, L.T., & Gottfredson, D.M. (1973). *Information selection and use in parole decision-making: Supplemental report V*. Davis, CA: National Council on Crime and Delinquency.

Wolff v. McDonnell, 418 U.S. 539 (1974).

28

How Registered Sex Offenders View Registries

Richard Tewksbury

Abstract: *Richard Tewksbury assesses the perceptions of registrants about the value of sex offender registries as a tool to enhance community awareness and promote public safety. In addition, he examines offenders' perceptions of the strengths and weaknesses of the registry format and structure. Results show that registrants see significant potential for registries but seriously question the efficacy and efficiency of how registries are currently constructed and used.*

Sex offenders are considered by many in society as the "worst of the worst" among criminal offenders. Sex offenders are subjected to increasingly stringent sentences and post-sentence restrictions on where they may live and work and with whom they may spend their time. These are not entirely new issues, however. Historically, sex offenders have been subject to severe sentencing laws and harsh treatment (Quinn, Forsyth, & Mullen-Quinn, 2004). The recent enhancements of sentences and restrictions, including sex offender registries and community notification, are premised on the idea of deterrence. The idea is that known sex offenders can be more closely monitored and potential sex offenders will recognize that sanctions are extreme, thus, offending will not be in his or her best interest. Sex offender registries and community notification are also designed to "shame" the offender and further deter future unlawful behavior. However, little research has been devoted to examining the way in which sex offenders perceive their sanctions (do they experience shame?), and if and how sex offender registration may be related to such perceptions.

The aim of the present study is to assess the perceptions of registered sex offenders about the use of sex offender registries as a means of enhancing public safety and reducing sex offender recidivism. Obtaining such insights from sex offenders may therefore allow both policymakers and criminal justice practitioners to better understand how the sanction of sex offender registration may or may not have an effect on offenders.

Research on Sex Offender Registries

Research regarding sex offender registries and community notification comes in four general types: statistical profiles of registrants (Adams, 2002; Szymokowiak

& Fraser, 2002), assessments of recidivism (Adkins, Huff, & Stageberg, 2000; Pawson, 2002), evaluations of the accuracy of registry information (Levenson & Cotter, 2005; Tewksbury, 2002), and assessments of collateral consequences of registration (Tewksbury, 2004, 2005; Zevitz & Farkas, 2000a, 2000b, 2000c). The most of important of these foci for the present study is the last focus, assessment of if and how sex offender registration provides additional punishments and consequences for offenders.

Collateral Consequences

Research on sex offender registries and community notification has clearly shown that there are numerous collateral consequences that accompany sex offender registration. Researchers have identified numerous legal consequences that accompany criminal convictions of any variety. These collateral consequences include disenfranchisement, loss of the ability to own or possess a firearm, and numerous employment restrictions. Social consequences such as stigmatization, relationship difficulties, employment problems, and feelings of shame and diminished self-worth have also been found to accompany felony convictions (Dodge & Pogrebin, 2001; Pogrebin, Dodge, & Katsampes, 2001). Such consequences can create a very difficult reintegration into society for the offender (Harding, 2003).

Collateral consequences specific to sex offender registration include all of the above, as well as additional consequences arising from registration and community notification. Interestingly, research has also suggested that the nature and extent of these consequences may be much greater for sex offenders than for other felons. For instance, beginning in 2005 numerous communities across the nation began to pass ordinances establishing residential buffer zones around locations known to be frequented by children – including schools, day care centers, churches, libraries, public parks, and bus stops. Evaluations of the effects of these restrictions suggest both that many offenders live in violation of such buffer zones (Tewksbury & Mustaine, 2006) and that these have little, if any, effect on rates of sex offender recidivism (Duwe, Donnay, & Tewksbury, 2008). Also, numerous studies (Levenson & Cotter, 2005; Mustaine & Tewksbury, 2008; Tewksbury, 2004, 2005; Zevitz & Farkas, 2000a) have documented stigmatization, damaged relationships, and harassment, as well as housing and employment difficulties for registered sex offenders in Kentucky and Indiana.

Collateral consequences of sex offender registration also affect people other than the convicted offender. Included among those who suffer from restrictions imposed on sex offenders are their family members and criminal justice officials. Tewksbury and Levenson (2009; also see Levenson & Tewksbury, 2009) have shown that spouses, children, and parents of registered sex offenders suffer socially, financially, and emotionally from legal restrictions placed on their loved ones. In regards to criminal justice officials, probation and parole officers in Wisconsin reported a loss of personnel, time, and budgetary resources as a result of a recent community notification program (Zevitz & Farkas, 2000b). Negative consequences have even been experienced by the very people that sex offender registration was designed to help. Zevitz and Farkas (2000c) report increased levels of anxiety for citizens attending community notification meetings in Wisconsin. Zevitz and Farkas (2000a) also explain that citizens who are notified of sex offenders' presence in the community can be held at least partly responsible for preventing successful reintegration of the offender into society.

Offenders' Perceptions of Sanctions

Research findings consistently identify a strong relationship between offenders' perceptions of the legitimacy of the criminal sanctions imposed on them and recidivism (see Makkai & Braithwaite, 1994). As Sherman (1993, p. 452) explains, "People obey the law more when they believe it is administered fairly than when they don't." Studies have linked positive offender perception of sanctions to increased compliance with the law (Williams & Hawkins, 1992). Conversely, offenders who do not believe sanctions are fair, effective, or appropriately administered have been reported to commit crime as a result of such beliefs (Sherman & Berk, 1984; Sherman, 1993; Petersilia & Deschenes, 1994).

Research has not only looked at perceived legitimacy of received sanctions, but also offenders' perceptions of the severity of sanctions. If a penalty is seen by an offender as too severe, it may be viewed as too hard to overcome, which may in turn lead to the offender repeating their crime(s). Strong evidence of this comes from Sherman and Berk's (1984) classic study of the effects of mandatory arrest for domestic violence cases in Minnesota. They concluded that only for certain types of individuals did the arrest effectively deter future crime. The authors noted that men with "high interdependencies," such as married and employed offenders, were likely to be deterred by mandatory arrest policies. However, the authors also reported that a majority of individuals (who were unemployed and unmarried) showed a counter-deterrent effect and rather than seeing mandatory arrest as reducing their likelihood of re-offending, it led to additional, sometimes more extreme, violent behavior.

Taking this idea a step further, Williams and Hawkins (1992) have suggested that collateral consequences of sanctions may be seen as especially punishing and consequently serve an important role in deterring re-offending. In short, offenders who perceived their punishment as severe yet fair and appropriate were less likely to anticipate re-offending, and those who did not perceive their sanctions as such may be likely to act out against those they felt were as responsible for their situations.

As a result of this line of research, Sherman (1993) argued that the ways offenders view the sanctions they receive are important for understanding the likelihood of recidivism. When an offender believes that a punishment holds a fair and reasonable level of severity, deterrence is likely to occur. Punishments that are most likely to be viewed as fair are those which are perceived to be proportional to the offenses committed (Petersilia & Deschenes, 1994). This perception of fairness is consequently seen in whether offenders' future behavior is criminal or not.

The Present Study

The goal of the present study is to identify perceptions registered sex offenders have about the sex offender registry as a tool for public safety. The existing literature on offenders' perceptions of sanctions has shown that perceptions of sanctions may influence behavior. However, this line of inquiry has yet to be extended to sex offender registration. The views sex offenders hold of their received sanctions, as well as their suggestions for where sanctions can be improved or enhanced, may enable law makers, correctional administrators, and the public to re-evaluate the current structure and practice of sanction imposition.

Methods

Data for this study are all qualitative and were collected by way of one-on-one, personal interviews conducted with a sample of offenders listed on the Kentucky Sex Offender Registry (http://kspsor.state.ky.us) at the time of data collection. The Human Studies Protection Program office at the author's university reviewed all materials. Data collection was conducted in February and March, 2005.

Sample

A total of 22 sex offenders participated in the study. These individuals were randomly selected from Kentucky's sex offender registry, and all lived in the city of Louisville. The sample of interviewees is almost exclusively male (95 percent), primarily white (86 percent) and has a mean age of 48. In terms of their registration characteristics the sample is evenly distributed between lifetime and 10 year registrants. Also, the sample has a mean length of time on the registry of just over 3 years. In regards to their conviction offenses, 27 percent have been convicted of rape, 59 percent have a sexual abuse conviction, 45 percent have a conviction for sodomy and 5 percent have a conviction for some other sexual offense.

Procedure

All data are from one-on-one, in-person, semi-structured interviews. Interview length ranged from 30 to 90 minutes. Interviews included a range of topics including registrant's knowledge of the sex offender registry, perceptions of reactions from family members, friends, acquaintances, and coworkers, perceptions of strengths and weaknesses of the registry as a tool for public safety, general social/work/educational experiences as a known, convicted, registered sex offender, whether or not (and to whom) the registrant had disclosed their registration status and demographics. No questions were asked about the offenses or criminal justice processing of the registrant's case, although a large majority of interviewees did discuss their offenses, victims, and case processing.

Findings

Analysis of the interviews shows that registered sex offenders do perceive the sex offender registry as a good and valuable entity, believe the existence of the registry can and does make positive contributions to society, but also believe there are a number of problems and difficulties in the structure, form, and uses of the registry. Although registered sex offenders (RSOs) have a generally positive view about the existence and use of sex offender registries, registrants question whether or not the registry in its current form can be and is effective in enhancing community awareness of sex offenders and public safety. Also, there is widespread belief among registrants that while use of a sex offender registry for some types of offenders may be valuable and important, there needs to be more differentiation, classification, and/or distinction between which offenders are subject to registration and what information is provided on the registration about registrants.

Registrants' Perceptions of the Value of Sex Offender Registration

When viewing sex offender registration as a concept, and while attempting to remove themselves from the picture, registrants universally recognize the value and potential contributions to community awareness and public safety that registries offer. The value of having a listing of known sex offenders, along with their residences and descriptions is seen as something that makes sense and is perceived to be a possible contributor to public safety. Almost without exception RSOs expressed an understanding of why society would want to have a sex offender registry. However, there is also widespread dissatisfaction with having oneself listed.

As a concept and tool for both the public and law enforcement, sex offender registries are perceived in mixed ways. Two questions are central to RSOs' perceptions about the practical value of sex offender registries. First, there are mixed views expressed by registrants about whether registries can raise community members' awareness of dangers and potential predators in their neighborhoods. Second, RSOs also are of varying mindsets regarding whether being listed on the registry is likely to influence the likelihood of offenders recidivating.

Among those registrants who believe that the registry may be an important tool for enhancing community awareness, this belief appears to be largely based on their assumptions that registries are regularly consulted by community members. As other research has shown, RSOs generally believe that sex offender registries are checked by many (if not most) community members. Because of this assumption, RSOs also commonly believe that these community members who consult the registry will be vigilant about both watching registrants in their neighborhoods, and informing other neighborhood residents about RSOs. This sentiment is expressed clearly by Preston, a child molester and lifetime registrant:

> I think it's a good thing. If my being there and the other people being there will help cut down on the child sex abuse and all that, then it's a damn good thing.

Or, in the more concise statement, Andy, who has been on the registry for 9 months for conviction for more than a dozen counts of sodomy with a 14-year-old boy, "I think people should be knowledgeable."

However, not all RSOs share this view. Many also question whether a registry, especially in its present form, can realistically be expected to promote widespread community awareness. These registrants recognize that the registry is quite large and that locating specific individuals, especially by chance, is not a very likely event. Also, those who question the efficacy of the registry for promoting community awareness point out that for it to be effective, community members need to regularly go to the Internet site and search for registrants. Many registrants recognize this is also not very likely to occur. Arthur, a 53-year-old, 3-time divorced registrant who has had no contact with his siblings or adult children for nearly a decade, explained:

> I don't see that it would prevent a lot of sexual abuse occurring. One, I don't see where a large enough segment of the public is aware of the registry to take advantage of it. I don't see where it – it's too broad for all the people it has on it. . . . I just don't see where it has a major impact on the public or on the prevention of sexual abuse.

Or, in the words of Jon a lifetime registrant who has been on the registry for only a year and a half:

> By literally taking 95% of the people who come out and putting us all on the list for life – and they put how many more thousand people on there every year. At some point there will be so damn many people on that list that, to some extent, you're just another face in the crowd. I think that lessens the impact of it to the public. When they look at it and there is 400 people on there – you say, "Hell, it's everywhere, what can you do?"

Just as the population of RSOs is split in their beliefs about whether sex offender registries may or may not be effective for raising community awareness of the presence of sex offenders in a neighborhood, so too are they split in their beliefs about registries' abilities to reduce recidivism. A minority of registrants do believe that RSOs are less likely to re-offend, primarily because they believe registrants are under careful and constant watch by community members. Additionally, this assumption is complemented by the view that registrants' knowledge of their existing label will deter them from re-offending, since they are likely to be suspects and investigated in any future reported instances of sexual offenses.

More common, however, is the view that having a sex offender registry is a highly inefficient and ineffective means of deterring offenders and reducing recidivism. As Jon very bluntly puts it, "If I'm going to re-offend, that registry is not going to keep me from it." Explaining this common view a bit more, Mike, a 10 year registrant convicted of molesting his stepson suggested that:

> There has to be a deterrent so if people know about the registry before they offend, maybe they won't offend again. It might act as a good deterrent, but I doubt it. The electric chair doesn't keep people from killing people.

Questions about the abilities of sex offender registries to achieve their stated purposes – raising community awareness and reducing recidivism – lead RSOs to point out that a number of changes to the structure, format, and process of registries and the registration process are needed. Changes, whether in who is registered, what information is listed about registrants, or how determinations about who is listed and for how long, are perceived by registrants as critical to the success of the registry, and vitally important for both community safety and "fairness" for offenders.

Remembering that RSOs universally believe in the concept and idea of sex offender registries, their near-universal call for (varying) changes to the registry reinforce their expressions of support for the concept. No registrant interviewed for this project called for the end of the registry or registration process, but nearly all advocated for at least some types of modifications so that the registry would be more likely to achieve its stated goal(s).

As discussed below, a number of specific changes are suggested by RSOs, typically focusing on providing some degree of categorization or differentiation between types of registrants. It is important to be able to differentiate between "true sex offenders, those that are actually a danger" and those not seen as dangerous (i.e. themselves). Without such distinctions users of the registry may not be able to effectively distinguish RSOs that they should and should not fear. As one registrant summed up what he sees as the problem with the lack of differentiation in registrants' listings, "It's one size fits all . . . So, in its present form, it's a waste of time."

The failure to distinguish between RSOs based on degrees of dangerousness, whether registrants have or have not completed a treatment program, and those that target children sits at the core of registrants' frustrations with the registration experience. More than any other issue, registrants decry being equated with predators, "real pedophiles" and offenders they themselves define as "dangerous," "heinous," and " a real threat to others." Commenting on his frustrations at being registered in the same way and virtually indistinguishable from more serious sex offenders, Tyler, a 29-year-old lifetime registrant reflected that:

> I don't think it's really appropriate for me. I'm sure there are some people who it is appropriate
> for. I think it should go more into repeat offenses with different victims, different dates – more
> into people who are deemed more predatory. . . . I think there's a place for it, but I don't think
> they took a lot of time to think about the effective way to use it. I think they've done it like
> running cattle through fields, it's just massively done.

For many registrants, their frustration and dissatisfaction with the registry and their experiences with it could be significantly diminished if only they believed that the information provided to the public about them and their offense(s) allowed others to "see that I'm not like those others."

"I Don't Associate with Those Kinds of People"

A near-universal theme expressed by RSOs is the belief that they are different from "those kinds of people" who are – and are generally believed should be – on the sex offender registry. RSOs express a strong desire to distinguish themselves from those whom they see as the "real criminals" and sex offenders that they believe are "dangerous," "vicious," or "sexual predators."

Almost without exception, the RSOs interviewed for this project explained, sometimes in lengthy detail, that they did not believe themselves to be dangerous or "as extreme" as other RSOs. Scott, a lifetime registrant with convictions on 11 counts of molesting 12- and 13-year-old boys, explained his frustration at being listed alongside, and not distinguished from other sex offenders, saying:

> To read some of the things on there, you can't make a distinction between the monsters and the people that are in there for lesser evils. The wording on there is so brief and simple. My own charge – if I read that and I was John Q. Citizen, I would say, "Lord, that's a dangerous guy right there!"

The belief that one is different from other sex offenders is not only pervasive, but also seen as a major contributor to both strong social stigmas experienced by RSOs and negative interactions experienced with others who know of one's status as an RSO. Registrants generally believe that they are widely perceived and defined simply by the status as a "sex offender" and not as individuals. Arthur lamented what he perceived as his being inaccurately perceived by others saying:

> Just being on the registry and being called a sex offender. People have visions of the most extreme cases. They don't think, "Oh, I wonder if Arthur put his hand on an underage female's breast through her clothing while he thought she was asleep?" They think, "I wonder if Arthur dragged some 6-year-old out into the woods and repeatedly raped her and then left her to die on the side of the road?" That's what people think of when they hear "sex offender."

One of the most bothersome parts of being seen "just like all those others" for RSOs is the belief that when the public thinks of a registered sex offender they assume all such persons are child molesters or pedophiles. Frustrations at being perceived as such are present across the sample and expressed in often very strong and sometimes harsh language. When comparing themselves with other RSOs it is common for interviewees to explain that although their victims may have been legally too young to consent to sexual activity of any form, they did not victimize "children." Charlie, convicted for sexually abusing his pre-adolescent stepdaughter complained that:

> They don't differentiate between the guy that goes out and goes to a party and runs across a 16-year-old girl and has oral sex with her, or the guy that drags a 5-year-old off the playground and rapes and kills here. It's still a sex offender.

Or, Andrei, a 64-year-old convicted child molester who was not sure if he was a 10 year or lifetime registrant, argued that he was not a pedophile and strongly disliked having others (presumably) assume he was such. Explaining his view, he stated:

> If a guy goes out here and stalks a kid at a school yard or a young kid – I think he ought to be (on the registry) . . . But this girl . . . she was 13 years old and, in my opinion, old enough to have said "no." I basically didn't have sex with her – it was oral sex. . . . I never was exposed to her, I had my clothes on, fully dressed – it was here in this house. And I kissed her vagina and put my finger in it.

In his mind, Andrei did not have sex with a child since he believed she was "old enough to have said 'no.'" Therefore, he reported being extremely frustrated that his sex offender registry listing might lead others to assume he was a pedophile.

Across the sample of interviewed RSOs there was an expressed sentiment that to be considered one and the same as "those kinds of people" (i.e. pedophiles, sexual predators, and "real" sex offenders) was both insulting and perhaps the worst aspect of registration. Jordan, who was 51 years old and convicted of molesting his daughter, explained this experience:

> I hate to be categorized and monitored with all these people who are serial, re-offender or vicious child predators. I don't put myself in that category with them. I hate to be looked upon as that kind of person because I don't feel I am that kind of person. . . . It's degrading and dehumanizing to know that people can pull my picture up and compare me to the guy under me or the guy they saw before me.

Related to the frustration regarding being seen "just like all of those other guys" is RSOs' questioning of why only sex offenders are subject to placement on a publicly accessible registry. For many RSOs there is a belief that the existence of the sex offender registry serves only to reinforce stereotypes and stigmas of sex offenders as the "worst kind of criminal." However, in the minds of RSOs there are a number of other varieties of offender that are "much worse, and much more of a danger than we are." One of the most common sentiments expressed by RSOs was that having a registry for only sex offenders was unfair, illogical, and an inefficient use of resources.

Having a sex offender registry, but not a registry for all (other) violent offenders, or as suggested by a few RSOs, any criminal offenders, serves only to exacerbate stereotypes and stigmas, and fails to provide much additional safety for society. Frequent mention was made in interviews of the efficacy of sex offender treatment programs; many RSOs recited statistics about the low recidivism rates of sex offenders (especially those who complete treatment programs), followed by questioning about why such "low risk" types of offenders are subject to registration, but "truly violent" and "the more dangerous types" of criminal offenders are not.

Many RSOs offered suggestions along with their questioning and criticism for how a more valuable registry might be structured and operated. Primary suggestions centered on requiring registration for offenders convicted of all forms of violent offenses, registering offenders who victimize children (but not adults) and registering only repeat offenders.

Questions persisted across the sample of RSOs. Questions regarding why only sex offenders were subject to registration, questions about whether the registry could be effective, and questions about what registering only sex offenders says about society and common values in society emerged from all of the interviews. Preston, a 63-year-old convicted of multiple counts for fondling and performing oral sex on a 12-year-old girl expressed his belief that the sex offender registry shows that society may have misplaced values. In his words:

> I wish we could do the same thing for burglars and drunk drivers and some of the others. My problem is that it seems like I committed the crime du jour. I mean had I got drunk and run over the same 12-year-old girl and killed her I probably would have got 3 years (in prison) and it all would have been over with. But, to use a vulgar term, her ass was worth more than her life.

Sex offenders see registration in its current form as particularly frustrating and the source of many problems in their lives. Registrants call into question the consistency and proportionality of registries when compared to other criminal justice policies and practices. Changes in the process and form of registration would seem to placate offenders and increase their perceptions of registries as a fair and just tool for society.

Registrants' Suggestions for Improving the Sex Offender Registry

As indicated above, nearly all registrants identified and advocated changes to the structure and form of the registry or the registration process. Although numerous suggestions for change were offered, three main modifications were commonly expressed. First and most frequently and strongly articulated, RSOs desired to see the registry distinguish between types of sex offenders. Second, the process by which individuals are assigned to registration for either 10 years or lifetime was questioned, and based on their assumptions about how this determination is made, suggestions for alterations were offered. And third, restrictions on who would be provided access, and under what conditions or circumstances were voiced by a number of RSOs.

The strong, collective call for better differentiation between types of offenders listed on the registry is a direct outgrowth of registrants' frustrations at being equated with and listed alongside offenders they define as more serious and more distained than they perceive themselves. Nearly all RSOs offered explanations of how and why they believed they were different from other RSOs. And, again reinforcing their general support for the concept of a sex offender registry, almost all registrants acknowledged the value of having "those other kinds of sex offenders" on a registry. But, they also desperately wanted to be able to point to something on their own registry listing to show they were "not nearly as bad as some of those others on there."

Matt, a 28-year-old convicted of multiple counts of sodomy with his 15-year-old stepdaughter expressed his desire to see distinctions between listed registrants saying:

> I just wish that they would categorize it. There's guys that are there – a guy rapes a 15-year-old girl, cuts her clothes off, then cuts her throat – yeah, put them on there. They need to be on there. Like myself, it was non-violent, consensual – it was wrong – but put me on there in a different category. Like the guy who was 18 and his girlfriend (was underage) – they was going together. He got charged with rape just because they broke up. That's wrong – he didn't hit her or beat her or nothing and he's in that category too – and there's no getting off of it.

Or, as Jordan suggested, "I can understand these repeat offenders and killers. We've got to do something with them."

In a related issue, a majority of RSOs also call for having an objective assessment or evaluation of registrants completed and used to determine dangerousness and registration status. It is at this point in the registration process that RSOs believe clinicians need to be included. Those who suggest that registries should have clinicians – most often mentioning psychiatrists, psychologists, or those who run sex offender treatment programs – involved in the decision also expressed a belief that presently the decisions about who is listed and whether registration is for a period of 10 years or lifetime seemed random or based on little objective evidence. Whether an individual is included on the registry is not really a decision, but based on one's conviction offenses. Determinations about length of registration are based on a risk evaluation, although many registrants believed "the people who made this decision . . . weren't more qualified that I am to do so." Or, as another RSO stated, "the psychiatrists know who's likely to re-offend."

Having some type of evaluation completed is believed by registrants to be the first step toward limiting which convicted sex offenders are included on the registry. It is the belief of these individuals that if objective, clinically-based evaluations were completed on sex offenders, those deemed to be low (or "no") risk would be unlikely to be listed. As Chris, a 67-year-old convicted 8 years earlier for molestation of his granddaughter, explained:

> I don't think they should have it for people who are not a threat, not violent folks. I don't think they should have it for exhibitionists. I think some of those people are not harmful but just got screwed up somewhere along the way and need some counseling. I think the therapists who have them could sign off and say they should be or shouldn't be [on the registry]. I don't think that the courts should be, I think that the therapists and doctors should be the ones to sign off. In other words, if they make that positive move to sign off that they wouldn't have to be on it.

Registrants not only call for having objective, clinical assessments completed as a tool for determining if particular individuals should be listed on the sex offender registry, but so too is there a belief that completing a risk evaluation during the time that a registrant is on the registry would be productive. The idea here is to identify registrants that could be removed from the registry, or having their listing reflect a diminished threat level. Again, the belief is that this needs to be done by qualified, specially trained clinicians. The idea of reviewing registrants with an eye toward identifying those who need to remain on the registry and those who could be removed was thoughtfully presented by Tyler.

> I think there needs to be a way that after X amount of time people can be reviewed or interviewed again, tested, psychology-wise, to see if it's really efficient leaving these people on there for lifetime. I think after a while it's kind of not necessary. . . . It needs to be more about how we deal with these guys after they've been on there for a period of time. Instead of just saying they're on there and to hell with them. There needs to be like a committee to review the people on it after a certain amount of time to see if it's really serving a purpose by still listing these people on here after X amount of years.

For some registrants, having a risk evaluation completed while on the registry is perceived as providing an incentive and motivation for RSOs to pursue treatment, to avoid problematic situations, and simply provide yet another reason for maintaining a crime-free lifestyle. However, this is not a possibility at the present time (although several registrants thought it was the case). Jordan also put forth the idea of an evaluation of registrants at some point following their listing. As he suggested,

> I've paid the price and I feel that enough should be enough. There should be some way that I could be able to cut the leash from this program, and I am not being given this opportunity and I don't think it's fair. . . . If I'm ever given the opportunity where I could have my name taken off the sex offender registry, I would like to see, in the future, about maybe some way a

person could earn a way to get off it. Even a life sentence in prison is 20 years. A life sentence on this is until death.

Some RSOs had their biggest problem with the registry center on the fact that anyone, anywhere, at any time can access the registry and find their name, description, home address, and photograph. For these registrants they desired to see strict limits placed on who could access the registry. In essence, although claiming to support the idea of a sex offender registry in concept, these registrants believed the registry should be used primarily/exclusively by law enforcement and other "officials," not the general public. Paul, a 52-year-old lifetime registrant who transferred his registration from another state following a rape conviction summed up this argument and well represents the views of this set of registrants.

> I would probably change the fact that it's too easy for people to have access to a sex offender registry and then form their own opinion about the person on the registry just by the information they are looking at. If I could change anything about the registry, I wouldn't even allow people to know that person is on there unless it directly affects them personally.

An additional suggestion, although offered by only a few of the RSOs is to remove registrants' pictures from their listings. The issue of including registrants' photographs is perceived by those calling for their removal as "an invasion of my privacy" and "just going too far, having your name and address on there should be enough." Others, however, while not necessarily liking the fact that their picture is included recognize the reasons they are included. The suggestions for modifications to the sex offender registry offered by RSOs directly arise from their experiences, and frustrations, with how registration has affected RSOs on a personal level. Stemming from their beliefs that "not all sex offenders are the same," these registrants believe that there should be more detailed and careful review and classification of offenders, and these distinctions should be reflected in individual listings. Suggestions are also related to registrants' desires to be able to more carefully manage who knows of their status, and what information others are able to access about them and their offenses. This is not to imply that the suggestions RSOs offer are without merit. Implementation of some of the approaches and structural changes that are presented in fact could be beneficial, for both registrants and the wider community.

Conclusion

The purpose of this study was to identify and understand the perceptions of registered sex offenders regarding sex offender registration as a tool for public safety. Overall, this study suggests that sex offenders generally believe that the concept of a sex offender registry is a valuable and worthwhile tool. Although they may believe that registries are a generally "good thing," most still dislike being included on the registry. Additionally, while seeing registration as good in concept, there is disagreement among registrants regarding the practicality of sex offender registries. Some offenders believe that goals of community awareness and increased safety are unlikely to be achieved since the registry contains a large number of offenders and requires community members to actively seek out information. Individuals holding this view simply doubt the effectiveness of registries since they feel it is unlikely that very many citizens actually check the registry and would be able to locate a specific individual out of thousands of listed names. Conversely, many offenders are under the assumption that citizens look at the registry often and are keenly aware of who is on the registry. For those who hold this belief, there is significant impact on the offender's lifestyle and interactions with others. This also means that for these sex offenders, the experience of collateral consequences is greater.

Sex offenders interviewed in this study also expressed mixed views in the way that being listed as a sex offender may affect recidivism. A small portion of offenders believe that registries are able to prevent re-offending. Among those believing this, most offenders believe that registered sex offenders are more carefully watched and monitored by society and would be likely suspects when sexual offenses do occur. However, the majority of sex offenders hold the cynical view that registries are highly inefficient and ineffective for reducing recidivism.

Commonly, sex offenders expressed a belief that registries could deter future sex crimes if changes were made in the format, structure, and process of sex offender registration. Overwhelmingly, the main flaw that offenders saw in the current system was the failure to distinguish between different types of sex offenders and the "one size fits all" mentality displayed in the current form of the registry. This sentiment was typically coupled with the belief that they individually were not the same as the "other" registrants, perceiving themselves as neither dangerous nor predatory.

A second frustration held by many offenders was the process by which registrants were assigned to lifetime or 10 year registration. Most offenders did not feel that this process was well thought out and failed to show uniformity. They also expressed discontent for the fact that they were "trapped" with being listed on the registry for a predetermined period of time. Here it is important to recall that other studies have shown that offenders viewing punishment as too severe or inescapable may be more likely to re-offend (Sherman & Berk, 1984; Petersilia & Deschenes, 1994). In the eyes of many registrants, the use of lifetime registration may be an overly strict and restrictive sanction. This may be especially damaging for registrants convicted as teenagers or during their early 20s.

A final suggestion for improvement mentioned by a number of sex offenders was the accessibility of the registry. Some offenders were frustrated with the fact that any person can access the registry for any reason, at any time. Most registrants did not question whether law enforcement officials should have access, but they did not understand the rationale for allowing registries to be accessible for others. In the minds of many offenders this simply invites harassment, stigmatization, and increased collateral consequences.

In the end, this study both identifies how sex offenders subject to registration and community notification perceive their sanctions and identifies suggested possible improvements to the format, process, and structure of sex offender registries. While the perspective of offenders is often of minimal concern to those who oversee and implement sex offender registry programs, the insights provided by offenders may offer opportunities for modifications which could lead to a more efficient and effective system. In order for the goals of decreased recidivism and community awareness to be achieved, changes may need to be made to meet the needs of both offenders and society.

Critical Thinking

Tewksbury finds varied opinions as to whether the registry serves as an effective deterrent. The minority of participants who claim that community members regularly consulted the registry think that the policy was an effective deterrent. However, most participants claim that the registry does not serve as a deterrent or reduce recidivism and is not consulted regularly by community members. Though the participants describe many issues with the current implementation of the policy and provide several suggestions for improvement, no participants suggest complete eradication of the policy. How effective do you think the sex offender registry is in reducing recidivism? If you were given the task of improving the effectiveness of sex offender registries how would you change them based on the findings of this study?

References

Adams, D. B. (2002). *Summary of state sex offender registries, 2001*. Washington, DC: U.S. Department of Justice.

Adkins, G., Huff, D., & Stageberg, P. (2000). *The Iowa sex offender registry and recidivism*. Des Moines: Iowa Department of Human Rights.

Charmaz, K. (1983). The grounded theory method: An explication and interpretation. In Robert Emerson (Ed.), *Contemporary Field Research* (pp. 109–126). Boston: Little and Brown.

Dodge, M., & Pogrebin, M. R. (2001). Collateral costs of imprisonment for women: Complications of reintegration. *Prison Journal, 81*(1), 42–54.

Duwe, G., Donnay, W., & Tewksbury, R.. (2008). Does residential proximity matter? A geographic analysis of sex offense recidivism. *Criminal Justice and Behavior, 35*, 484–504.

Harding, D. (2003). Jean Valjean's dilemma: The management of ex-convict identity in the search for employment. *Deviant Behavior, 24*(6), 571–596.

Levenson, J. S., & Cotter, L. P. (2005). The effects of Megan's Law on sex offender reintegration. *Journal of Contemporary Criminal Justice, 21*(1), 49–66.

Levenson, J. S., & Tewksbury, R.. (2009). Collateral damage: Family members of registered sex offenders. *American Journal of Criminal Justice 34*, 54–68.

Makkai, T., & Braithwaite, J. (1994). Reintegrative shaming and compliance with regulatory standards. *Criminology, 32*(3), 361–386.

Mustaine, E. E., & Tewksbury, R.. (2008). Registered sex offenders, residence, and the influence of race. *Journal of Ethnicity in Criminal Justice 6*, 65–82.

Pawson, R. (2002). *Does Megan's Law work? A theory-driven systematic review*. ESRC UK Centre for Evidence Based Policy and Practice: Working Paper 8. London: University of London. (Available at http://www.evidencenetwork. org, retrieved August 5, 2011.)

Petersilia, J., & Deschenes, E. P. (1994). What punishes? Inmates rank the severity of prison vs. intermediate sanctions. *Federal Probation, 58*(1), 3–8.

Pogrebin, M., Dodge, M., & Katsampes, P. (2001). The collateral costs of short-term jail incarceration: The long-term social and economic disruptions. *Corrections Management Quarterly, 5*(4), 64–69.

Quinn, J., Forsyth, C., & Mullen-Quinn, C. (2004). Societal reaction to sex offenders: A review of the origins and results of the myths surrounding their crimes and treatment amenability. *Deviant Behavior, 25*(3), 215–233.

Sherman, L. W. (1993). Defiance, deterrence, and irrelevance: A theory of the criminal sanction. *Journal of Research in Crime and Delinquency, 30*(4), 445–473.

Sherman, L. W., & Berk, R. A. (1984) The specific deterrent effects of arrest for domestic assault. *American Sociological Review, 49*(1), 261–272.

Szymkowiak, K., & Fraser, T. (2002). *Registered sex offenders in Hawaii*. Honolulu, HI: Department of the Attorney General.

Tewksbury, R. (2002). Validity and utility of the Kentucky sex offender registry. *Federal Probation, 66*(1), 21–26.

Tewksbury, R. (2004). Experiences and attitudes of registered female sex offenders. *Federal Probation, 68* (3), 30–33.

Tewksbury, R. (2005). Collateral consequences of sex offender registration. *Journal of Contemporary Criminal Justice*, *21*(1), 67–81.

Tewksbury, R., & Levenson, J. S. (2009). Stress experiences of family members of registered sex offenders. *Behavioral Sciences and the Law, 27*, 611–626.

Tewksbury, R., & Mustaine, E. E. (2006). Where to find sex offenders: An examination of residential locations and neighborhood conditions. *Criminal Justice Studies, 19*, 61–75.

Williams, K. R., & Hawkins, R. (1992). Wife assault, costs of arrest, and the deterrence process. *The Journal of Research in Crime and Delinquency, 29*(3), 292–310.

Zevitz, R. G., & Farkas, M. (2000a). Sex offender community notification: Managing high risk criminals or exacting further vengeance? *Behavioral Sciences and the Law, 18*(2–3), 375–391.

Zevitz, R. G., & Farkas, M. (2000b). *Sex offender community notification: Assessing the impact in Wisconsin*. Washington, DC: National Institute of Justice

Zevitz, R. G., & Farkas, M. (2000c). Sex offender community notification: Examining the importance of neighborhood meetings. *Behavioral Sciences and the Law, 18*(2–3), 393–408.

Zhang, L., Messner, S. F., & Lu, Z. (1999). Public legal education and inmates' perceptions of the legitimacy of official punishment in China. *The British Journal of Criminology, 39*(3), 433–450.

29

Riding the Bus: Barriers to Prison Visitation and Family Management Strategies

Johnna Christian

Abstract: *Johnna Christian investigates the process of and barriers to visiting family members incarcerated in New York prisons. According to Christian, maintaining contact with an incarcerated family member is often very challenging and involves copious amounts of time, resources, and effort. The family members who continue to visit prisoners despite the extensive complications of the trip provide various rationales for doing so. Many believe that visiting allows them to monitor the prison system and ensure the protection, health, and livelihood of their loved one. Many participants describe a duty to protect the prisoner and provide him moral support and basic necessities. Findings suggest that family members often find this process difficult, tiring, and emotionally demanding and eventually fail to maintain ties with prisoners. The difficulties associated with visiting prisoners often lead to infrequent visitation and breaking off contact altogether.*

As the nation's incarceration rates rise, researchers and policy makers have begun to highlight several gaps in our understanding of and approach to studying incarceration. A growing body of research considers that incarceration has unintended consequences (Clear, 1996) or collateral consequences (Hagan & Dinovitzer, 1999) that reach far beyond the prisoner and in fact extend to families and communities. The role of prisoners' families has taken on added significance as scholars have highlighted the geographic concentration of incarceration and release, making some neighborhoods and communities particularly vulnerable to the collateral consequences of incarceration and the subsequent challenges of reintegrating large numbers of former prisoners (Travis & Waul, 2003). Little, however, is known about what it is like for families to bridge the gap between their lives outside and the life of their incarcerated loved one. Examining potential barriers to family connections and bonds with prisoners is one contribution to our understanding of the broader effects of incarceration.

This article draws from an ethnographic study of how families' lives are affected by incarceration to look at some barriers to prisoner ties to family that stem from the challenges of visiting at prisons. Data come from observation on bus rides families take from New York City to prisons throughout New York to visit incarcerated male family members and in depth, open-ended interviews with prisoners' family members. The study illustrates that staying connected to a prisoner is a time, resource, and labor intensive process, which may create barriers to prisoners' maintenance of family ties.

In addition to describing what the process of getting to a prison visit is like, high-lighting the barriers to visiting and ways that families manage this process are the foci of the article.

Literature about Family Ties to Prisoners

Connectedness to Family

Surveys of prison inmates show that 55% of state and 63% of federal prison inmates have children younger than age 18, and 46% of those parents were living with their children at the time they were admitted to prison (Mumola, 2000). When fathers are incarcerated, in 90% of cases the children's mother is the primary caregiver. In addition, Mumola found that 57% of male, state prison inmates had never had a personal visit with their children since their admission to prison. Of the prisoners who did have contact with their children in 1997, 42% had phone contact, 50% mail contact, and 21% visits. These figures indicate that the majority of male prisoners are not connected to their children at the most basic level. Such contact could be the starting point for the development of deeper bonds and attachments that facilitate the prisoner's integration into the family unit while incarcerated, which provides the basis for a strong support system fostering successful reentry into the family and community upon release (Casey-Acevedo & Bakken, 2002; Petersilia, 2003).

A recent report issued by the National Institute of Corrections (2002) detailed the types of services that departments of correction in various states provide to facilitate family contact with prisoners. Slightly more than half of the responding departments of correction reported that proximity to family is one criterion for facility assignment. Of the 54 department of corrections that responded to the survey, 37% reported providing some type of visitation assistance, such as transportation services, to families in at least one facility in their jurisdiction. Moreover, 78% of the departments had some type of policy or program to encourage prisoners to maintain family contacts. This type of study provides a strong basis for shaping institutional policy that may make it easier for families to maintain contact with prisoners, and it speaks to recognition of the importance of family contacts and relationships.

Incarceration's Effect on Families

Carlson and Cervera (1992) found that wives of incarcerated men experience a great deal of strain, including feelings of guilt and stress because of pressure to fulfill the multiple roles of the incarcerated man. Some of the problems children face, related to parents' incarceration, include behavioral problems at home and in school, difficulty sleeping, mistrust, and fear of abandonment (Carlson & Cervera, 1992; Lowenstein, 1986; Shaw, 1987, 1992). In addition, children without family members to take care of them are placed in foster care, further disrupting their lives.

Raising children alone and dealing with financial problems are two of the most prominent problems. In addition to the hardships related to incarceration, planning for visits to the prison and trying to maintain a relationship with the incarcerated individual become an integral part of life and coping mechanisms are often developed (Fishman, 1990; Girshick, 1996). Prison visits may bring feelings of excitement, anticipation, joy, and yet sadness (Carlson & Cervera, 1992; Fishman, 1990; Girshick, 1996). The literature suggests that the prison experience becomes an integral part of life for the wives and girlfriends of prisoners and that incarceration affects the family at many levels.

This literature, however, provides inconsistent findings about specific effects of incarceration on families (Hagan & Dinovitzer, 1999). If an inmate has been abusive to his partner or children, incarceration is likely to be beneficial. Substance abusers may significantly drain already limited family resources. Dominant themes in the family literature, however, highlight substantial negative effects on the family unit when a member is incarcerated (Carlson & Cervera, 1992; Fishman, 1990; Girshick, 1996; Hagan & Dinovitzer, 1999; Shaw, 1987) and that more research in this area is warranted (Travis, Solomon, & Waul, 2001).

For example, Braman and Wood (2003) conclude that incarceration's negative consequences reach far beyond the prisoner and that their family members suffer as much as, if not more, than the incarcerated individual. They discovered that the stigma related to incarceration was so great that many family members isolated themselves from the people in their lives who could help form a support system. Another recent addition to the research is Comfort's (2003) ethnographic study of the "secondary prisonization" of women visiting inmates at San Quentin State Prison in California. She makes a compelling argument that "women, whose loved ones and close acquaintances are caught in the revolving door of 'corrections' experience restricted rights, diminished resources, social marginalization, and other consequences of penal confinement, even though they are legally innocent and reside outside of the prison's boundaries" (p. 79). Her work contributes greatly to the understanding of what it is like for family members to go through the process of visiting an incarcerated individual, and she critiques the degradation ceremonies visitors are subjected to.

This literature highlights potential benefits to prisoners maintaining contact with families, broader ways family life may be affected by incarceration, as well as family experiences visiting at prisons. Drawing from these findings in the existing literature, the article will focus on barriers to families visiting at prisons and the ways families manage these barriers.

Method

Sample and Data

According to New York Department of Corrections data, of the 71,466 inmates under custody on January 1, 2000, 66% were committed from New York City counties. Fifty-one percent of the inmates are African American and 31% are Hispanic (Bernstein & Davis, 2000). There is a small cluster of facilities relatively close to New York City, with the closest maximum-security prison, Sing Sing, only 34 miles away—about a 50-minute drive. There is, in fact, a commuter train that goes from New York to the city of Ossining. Some of the other closer facilities are Woodbourne, a medium-security prison 100 miles from New York—a 2-hour drive. Attica is 350 miles from New York, a 6½-hour drive, and Upstate prison, located near the Canadian border in Malone, New York, is 383 miles from New York. The distance of the prisons makes visiting a very costly and time-consuming process.

Data come from a qualitative study of how social capital development in families and communities is affected by incarceration. The family-focused portion of the study included 200 hours of observation at prison family support group meetings, attendance at activities aimed at prison families, and observation on five bus rides, each covering a 24-hour period, to two upstate New York prisons. In addition, open-ended in depth interviews were conducted with 19 family members of prisoners such as wives, girlfriends, mothers, and one brother. The race and ethnicity of the sample was African American and Latino, 18 females and 1 male, with an age range from the early 20s to mid-60s. These demographic characteristics of the sample closely parallel the demographic composition of the riders on the buses.

Before observation bus rides began, community sponsors were used to introduce the researcher into the setting. Permission was obtained from the owner of the bus company Operation Prison Gap to ride buses taking families for visits to prisons in upstate New York. Two prisons were chosen because they include a population representative of prisoners throughout the state, and they were located between 250 and 300 miles from New York City. The families of male inmates were chosen for this study, recognizing that the processes highlighted would likely be different when studying the experiences of women's families (Casey-Acevedo & Bakken, 2002). During the bus rides, the researcher approached family members and explained the study, and any willing person was interviewed. Eventually, participants were chosen to include individuals residing in two high-incarceration neighborhoods in New York.

The Prison Visit

Describing the Journey

One component of understanding the family perspective of incarceration is examining what the process of getting to a prison visit is like. The main bus company in New York, which transports families to visits, is Operation Prison Gap, a privately operated bus service started in 1973 by a former prisoner. On a typical weekend, approximately 800 people use the service to get to a prison visit (Schlosser, 1998), with buses leaving throughout the night. In addition to Operation Prison Gap, there are many smaller bus and van services that transport people to prisons from New York City, some only leaving from specific neighborhoods. The companies compete for business, handing out discount coupons at visiting centers and mailing them to inmates to pass along to family members.

The majority of the individuals on the buses are women traveling alone. Some have children with them, ranging from infants to teenagers. There are also some men on the bus, but they are usually traveling with a woman. The people on the bus are prisoners' wives, girlfriends, mothers, sisters, fathers, brothers, and friends. Most of the riders I spoke with came from neighborhoods in New York already identified as having high concentrations of incarceration, and riders must take the subway or cabs into Manhattan to get the bus.

Cost and Timeline

The cost of bus tickets averages $40, more or less depending on the distance of the facility. Tickets for children are half price. There are other costs in addition to the price of the bus ticket. A low estimate of additional costs is $20 for food and drinks during the 24-hour period of the trip and $20 for food from the vending machines inside of the prison (visitors are not allowed to bring food into the visiting room). In addition, many families bring packaged food and snacks, clothing items, and cash. These additional items can easily cost $50 or more. On one visit, a woman had $40 worth of candy with her. Another said her husband ate $50 worth of food during the visit because he was so hungry. The costs associated with one visit are a minimum of $80 and could easily be twice that amount. This is assuming that there is only one family member visiting and does not include other expenses such as child-care. In addition to these monetary costs, the journey to a visit is extremely tiring and time consuming. The process involves a tremendous amount of waiting. The timeline of a visit varies, depending on which facility an individual is going to. Buses to the farthest facilities leave New York around 9:00 PM to arrive in time for visiting hours at 9:00 AM the next morning. The timeline was generated from the rides the researcher took to a maximum-security prison 263 miles from New York City.

The timeline illustrates that the first potential barrier to visiting is the amount of time, energy, and money required merely to get to the visit. As families engage in this process, other aspects of their lives, such as spending time with and supervising children, or involvement with community or neighborhood organizations necessarily suffer. Maintaining a connection with a prisoner at the most basic level of going on a visit could jeopardize the family well-being in areas outside of the involvement with the incarcerated individual. Families recognize that they must make choices about the resources they devote to the prisoner. The following sections illustrate that only a portion of the time devoted to the process is actually spent with the prisoner, and one consequence of this is that families going on visits form relationships with each other.

Waiting for the Visit

Some facilities have hospitality or visitor centers that are a resource for families when visiting at the prison. One prison I went to had a center that was on state property but operated by a nonprofit organization. The center provides a comfortable place for families to wait for the visit, as well as a coordinator who has very good rapport with family members. The center coordinator helps visitors fill out the paperwork necessary to get into the prison and drop off packages. She also helps explain the prison rules, sometimes counseling people about the likelihood that they will be refused entrance to the prison because of the clothes they are wearing. For example, the prison rules at one facility specify that clothing cannot be skimpy, including no short skirts or low cut tops, shirts cannot show more than half of the back, and sleeveless tops are not allowed. The hospitality center coordinator also helps people who have a problem getting into the prison, sometimes calling the prison to speak to someone on their behalf.

The center provides a supportive environment for families and tries to mitigate some of the hardships created by visiting. There is coffee for families when they arrive in the morning. The center is set up like a small house with a dining area; a living room area with a TV and VCR, a coffee table with a basket of magazines on it, a sofa, love seat, and a couple of soft chairs; a children's area, which has a small table and chairs, books, and toys; and a kitchen with a fridge, microwave, and toaster. It also has restrooms, an iron and ironing board, and two small changing rooms. The hospitality center coordinator said that the families are "spending money from the time they leave their homes," so the center attempts to cut some of their expenses by providing coffee, snacks, and sometimes meals.

Based on what people who had been to other prisons said, as well as my observation at another prison, this center was one of the best as far as what it offered family members. Some prisons had no center, requiring families to wait outside until the visit starts, and others are less comfortable and provide fewer amenities. Winter presents a special challenge when families visit at a prison without a waiting area.

A number of the women are regular riders who have been coming to the prison together for some time and interact with each other throughout the journey. They buy each other coffee, sit together, watch over their belongings, and just spend time chatting. Part of the bond between the bus riders centers around commiseration about the difficulties of making the visit, such as the cost, and the amount of time and energy required. In some instances, they complain about the excess demands the incarcerated man places on them and they discuss things that occurred between them and their partners during the visit. The shared experiences are one means of managing the barriers to maintaining family contact.

The hours at the hospitality center before the visit starts bring out the sense of community among the women. Grooming for the prison visit is the primary focus of the hours before the visit starts. Children's faces are washed, their hair is brushed, and their clothes changed. The women paint their fingernails and fix their hair. They also sign up for turns to use the iron and ironing board and the changing rooms in the visiting center. Some of them have favorite diners and coffee shops in town where they go for breakfast. Many stand outside smoking and talking. Before one visit, a few women discussed a local store back in their neighborhood where they could buy items for prisoners, which the store shipped to the facilities directly. They were very happy with the convenience, eliminating the step of having to take items home to box them and then wait in line at the post office.

There is a motel a few blocks from the prison that allows the women to pay $10 each to take a shower in a room. I once went and inquired about the cost of renting the room for a few hours (thinking it would be a private and comfortable place to conduct interviews) and was told I would have to pay the full daily rate. Each woman using the room for a shower is required to pay $10 with the expectation that they will be out of the room within about an hour. Three or four women sometimes go together to use one room.

During the hours before the visit, the women sometimes share their concerns about news they may be getting during the visit, especially about parole hearing outcomes. They wish each other luck, offer encouragement based on successful hearings they have heard about, and share their own anticipation about pending hearings, even if they are several months to a year away.

On at least two of the visits I have been on, family members have made the trip to the prison to discover that they cannot get in to the facility, which means that their wait is prolonged until the bus returns to New York. After September 11, the prison instituted a policy that photo identification was necessary to get in to the prison. One woman brought her 14-year-old sister with her to visit their brother. Because the older sister did not have identification and was denied access to the prison, the younger sister could not get in either. In the other instance, a woman had been told by one prison official that she could visit her brother, even though it was not on the regularly designated day. In both of these cases, the family members were disappointed that they had made the long and costly trip for no reason, but they were even more distressed that their brothers had been expecting them and would not receive a visit they had depended on.

Barriers to Visiting and Maintenance of Connections

Several explanations exist for why families fail to stay connected with prisoners. These include the financial difficulties of visiting and accepting collect phone calls, the emotional demands, and the other demands of life that prevent visiting (Hairston, 2003). In some instances, families are tired of the prisoner's cycling in and out of the system and essentially experience a last straw incident that leads them to cut the person off. When substance abuse or mental illness has been a factor, families may be particularly weary of such patterns. In addition, prisoners sometimes tell their families not to visit them in order to spare them the hardship and trouble. When families do visit, it is in the face of significant obstacles and barriers that they must navigate and manage.

Several themes emerged with regard to the families' rationale for visiting despite these problems. Paradoxically, many express an attitude of, I don't like it, but I do it anyway. During an interview with a woman waiting to go on a bus ride, she said that she didn't want to go on the 8-hour ride, pointing out that she could be going on a vacation to Virginia Beach in that period of time. Families realize that they must make tradeoffs to stay connected to a prisoner. The following field note excerpt describes part of a telephone conversation overhead on a bus:

> While the bus was still in Manhattan a young African American female in her late teens to early twenties with a headscarf on made a phone call. She was talking to someone and said I don't know what it's like on your bus, but I just want to know how you do this. I hate this. I can't stand it. How do you do it? She said that the bus was so crowded you would think it was Easter or something. She said that when she gets to the visit she's so tired and mad they just fight. She said, "I do o.k. when I'm on my own. But I just can't take this." She sounded very annoyed and kind of desperate. She told the person that she just called because she needed someone to talk to.
> (March 22, 2002)

Other women talked about the fact that they were so tired from the process of getting to the visit, once they met with the prisoner they could not truly enjoy the visit, and the quality of the time with the prisoner suffered. The following sections discuss reasons families give for visiting despite the sentiment that the visits present hardships.

Watching the System

A prominent feeling among families is that visiting provides them a means of monitoring the prison system. They believe that when a prisoner does not receive visits, it is a sign that no one cares about him, which gives prison personnel free license to treat him however they wish. Further, when no one visits a prisoner, no one knows what is happening to him, and the system is not accountable to anyone. The following quote illustrates this perspective:

> I mean the person could die today or tomorrow, you would never know. These prison officers ain't gonna tell you. They'll tell you like a year later. Oh we couldn't get in contact with nobody. And when that person don't have no mail, or they don't have no contact with the outside world, they say well they don't have a family. So they meaningless to them, so we gonna do whatever we want to do to them. And they do. And they do. You sit here for a whole year and have not seen one letter for him. You have not had one visit, so we gonna do whatever we want to you. You know, and that's bad, that's really, really bad.
>
> (Family 2)

Families may see themselves as protectors of their incarcerated relatives and feel they at least have a chance of generating a response from the system if they have stayed involved in the prisoner's life. One mother whose son has mental health problems, requiring injections of an antipsychotic drug prior to his incarceration, expressed concern that he was not receiving medication in prison. She tried to visit monthly to determine whether he was getting the medication and to "keep an eye on things." She called his counselor and asked her son directly if he was getting his medication. In addition, family members knew of prisoners who did not receive visits and had stories about abuse that went unchecked and prisoners with no recourse because they had no family to defend them.

Watching the system also entails making up for some of the deficits in the level of care the prison provides the inmate. One family member described his brother as one of the fortunate inmates because he provided some of the "basic necessities" the prison allows inmates to receive from family members. He made sure his brother had books, underwear, and money for commissary, which allowed him to cook his own food rather than rely on the facility's meals. He explained,

> They give you the basic necessities of food and what not, but there's a lot of things that you don't get unless you have someone to provide for you. And for those who are less fortunate, it's really tough, you know because they have to settle for whatever meals they have. [Brother's name] on the other hand has the opportunity to cook his meals. He has his own cell, and with the money I give him he goes food shopping in the commissary, and he cooks his meals. Makes rice and chicken. So he has options. He doesn't have to settle for the food that, the facility gives him. And so I know that gives him a totally different feeling as opposed to. You know, he has an option. It's not like others that are less fortunate, we're not. He can go to commissary and buy a bag of chips, or soda, or any little munchies, whereas others may not be able to do so.
>
> (Family 19)

Providing food also extends beyond a mere preference for better food, as when prisoners have been in solitary confinement and received "the loaf," they are ravenous during visits with family members and eat a great deal.

Moral Support

Families also see a role in providing moral support for the prisoner to counter some of the psychological damage resulting from the incarceration. One wife counseled her husband about how to deal with challenges brought on by other prisoners and corrections officers. She explained,

> I mean these people put them through so much. And, if they don't have nobody there, that's the main reason they lose self-control, and they start to do things. Because nobody's behind them. And they feel well I don't have no family behind me, and I'm dealing with this all by myself. But that's why I let my husband see, you're not going through this alone, and you never forget that. You've been in here and I've, I mean I may be out in the world, but I'm still here with you.
>
> (Family 2)

There is a feeling that the family is also serving the sentence as a show of support to the inmate. Similarly, another family member summarized the different kinds of support he offers his brother by visiting him regularly, and why he is so strongly compelled to do so.

> I just felt the need to give him that companionship, you know? To be honest with you, I've never been incarcerated, and this is the first time I've ever set foot in a correctional facility, but I can imagine how terrible it must be to be locked up in four walls and not have any companionship. Even though I'm in the free world, I know what it's like to go without. I can only imagine what it must feel like for them, you know.
>
> (Family 19)

The need to monitor the prison system and provide support for the offender may foster a sense of devotion that overrides other demands in the family's life. One wife who has several children, one of them severely disabled, visited her husband every other week. There was a chance he would be transferred to a facility even farther away than the one he was already in. When I asked if she would maintain the same visiting schedule even if he were so far away, she replied, "I have to, he's my life." She also expressed a belief that if someone is committed to their marriage, they will stick by that person and visit them regardless of the personal sacrifices. This suggests that the people who go on the visits may be the ones who are already tightly bonded to the prisoner. As stated in the Method, section, the families who visit are not representative of prisoners' families, and the individuals who do maintain bonds through visiting may have stronger motivation to overcome the barriers presented by visiting.

Hope/Parole

One way that families seem to keep themselves going on visits, assisting the prisoner with legal matters, and sending money and packages is their hope for a different future. This hope is expressed through the chance that there will be a legal change in the prisoner's status through an appeal or parole release. Most common is that when a prisoner is going up for parole, families are very hopeful it will be granted. Visitors tend to be apprehensive when they know they will be hearing news about a parole-hearing outcome. They share stories about people they know who were successful at their parole hearing and hope the person they are visiting will have similar fortune. There is always an assumption on their part that there is at least a chance of success. When a parole hearing was not successful, family members find themselves playing a supportive role for the prisoner and then experiencing their own frustration and sadness after the visit is over. Other family members often provide consolation at this point, understanding why someone may hide her disappointment from the prisoner. One prisoner's wife said that she would cry on the ride back home because she had to be strong for her husband during the visit.

Visiting Cycles and the Fluid Nature of Connections to Prisoners

Despite the sense of devotion that compels some family members to make the visit, families also describe cycles in which the frequency of visiting changes for a number of reasons. This article has illustrated that going on one visit entails a major expenditure in time, money, and energy. We may be quick to assume that the relatively low levels of family contact with prisoners are because families do not want to maintain contact or visit, but evidence indicates that the maintenance of familial relationships is more complex. Whether a family visits may have nothing to do with a desire to maintain connections with the inmate but rather the difficulties of getting to the visit, as recorded in the following field note:

> I stood next to a short Latina female about 50 years old, who was wearing a skimpy tank top and tight, short black pants. She had a lot of exposed skin, showing tattoos on her neck, upper arms, and legs. Her black hair was pinned up with bobby pins all over her head. There was a bus in front of us being loaded with people. I ask her where she's going, and when she says [prison name] I'm excited and say me too. She doesn't say anything at first, but somehow we start talking. I think I asked if she has been taking the bus for a long time and she nods and says four years. She said that she goes to the facility every two weeks to visit her husband. She says that [prison name] is a short ride, and when I ask how long she says four or five hours. At one point her husband was in [prison name], which is an 11-hour ride, and it was really hard to visit. She says that her husband is in the box right now, so he can't have phone calls, only letters and visits every 7 days. He'll be there 18 months, and might get transferred. She says that she hopes he doesn't get sent somewhere far away because "that will kill me." She says the rides are so tiring, once you get to the visit you don't want to talk. You just sit there and let him do all the talking.
>
> (August 17, 2001)

Families may go through cycles of visiting that are partly determined by the strain that visiting puts on the family's economic and emotional resources. One interview participant explained,

> And a lot of people can not afford to come up here on these buses. . . . And I don't blame them for charging. That's a long ride. But you know. A lot of people can not afford it. And a lot of people just forget about 'em. Because you know that's money coming out they pocket. They kids gotta eat. That $50 break people's back. That's bill money.
>
> (Family 1)

One result of the strain of visiting is that family members are forced to make choices about how scarce resources will be spent. One wife described how her mother's and sisters' criticism led to her decision to sever contact with her incarcerated husband for a 3-year period. She said,

> And then they got to the point where that three-year gap they kept jumpin' on me because it was like oh, the kids, they had no shoes at one point because I was runnin' up there, spending my money to go and see him, commissary things he needed, cause, you know, it's cold in the jails, he needed blankets, you know, all kinda things. I mean, when you get to a point you just forget that you have children. You forget you have kids, you forget you have another life, you know, you have to take care of the kids just as well. My whole life was just focused on him. I didn't even realize that my daughters needed shoes, you know, cause I was so much worrying about him, you know, is he all right. And then also, he was callin' me, oh I need you to go to the courts, I need you to do this, I need you to get that, I need you to go to Albany. So, I was like I was like, I felt I was like just losin' my mind. And then there was a time that I just shut down and I was like I can't do it no more. And that was that three-year gap.
>
> (Family 14)

This woman had recently resumed contact with her husband, including letters, phone calls, and visits. She was concerned that the old patterns would repeat themselves and was trying to make an extra effort to prevent that. Her situation was not unique, as the frequency of family members' visiting varied considerably, from weekly to every 6 months. Moreover, families reported changes in patterns that varied because of other factors in the family's life. Findings suggest that research using cross-sectional data about familial contact with prisoners may miss some of the long-term trends in the maintenance of relationships and could therefore underestimate families' willingness to be involved with prisoners depending on their life circumstances.

Families may vary on several dimensions, including the frequency of visits, the intensity of the connection to the incarcerated individual, the stage of visiting and connection, as well as the different family members' histories of relationships to the incarcerated individual. Whereas some families set clear boundaries with the prisoner (i.e., refusing to accept collect telephone calls or limiting the number of visits), others become completely engrossed in caring for and sustaining the prisoner as other aspects of their lives suffer. These relationships are complex, changing for reasons both directly and indirectly related to the incarceration. Families must make decisions about the extent of energies to devote to the person who is incarcerated. They realize that the family's welfare may suffer in other ways as they give more time to the incarcerated person. This may lead to periods of time when the family doesn't visit the prisoner at all or completely severs communication including by phone and mail.

Considering the previous review of research about the potential benefits of family ties to prisoners, more research exploring the fluid nature of prisoner ties to family is called for. The findings in this article suggest that families face a number of barriers in attempting to maintain contact with prisoners despite the myriad of reasons they desire to visit and have connections. The process of managing ties with prisoners may place families in a position in which they are forced to make decisions about the extent of ties they can afford to have with the prisoner.

Discussion

This research indicates that prisoners' relationships with family are complex, fluid, and dynamic, in part because of the demands of visiting at prisons and maintaining contact with prisoners. This study highlights the collateral consequences of incarceration, especially what is required for families to maintain contact with prisoners. Some families may deliberately sever their ties with a prisoner. At the same time, many families who wish to maintain bonds with prisoners may be deterred from doing so because of the demands of visiting.

Whereas traditionally, family connections to prisoners have been studied with cross-sectional data, this study proposes that there is a great deal of fluidity in family/prisoner relationships and that a variety of factors may explain the degree of connectedness and the reasons that relationships change over time. The changing nature of these relationships may in part be due to the demands of visiting at prisons and maintaining contact with prisoners. Further research in this area may apply the life history approach to prisoners' relationships with family, including both the period before the incarceration and the period after. Five specific domains that could be relevant in understanding how and why families stay connected to prisoners over time are (a) the prisoner's relationship with the family prior to the incarceration, (b) the prisoner's efforts to improve or rehabilitate himself while incarcerated, (c) the strain (emotional, economic, stigma) the incarceration has placed on the family, (d) the economic resources available to the family to maintain the prisoner, and (e) the family's social support system.

Although the existing body of scholarship examines different ways that prisoners' families are affected by their incarceration, as well as the importance of prisoner ties to family, further empirical investigation of the collateral consequences of incarceration related to prisoners' families is needed. Such information is crucial from a policy standpoint, particularly with increasing attention to prisoner reentry. Families may be caught in a double bind as they prepare to be the primary avenue for successful prisoner reentry. Maintaining close ties with prisoners necessarily takes away from their abilities to connect with the social networks and resources they need to have a strong foundation of support for the prisoner upon his release. Research focused on understanding the life course of a prisoner's connection to family, and the role the barriers to visiting play in the trajectory of that life course, is needed.

Critical Thinking

It is clear that incarceration can be detrimental to families. In fact, many inmates prefer to distance themselves from their family while incarcerated to reduce the burden on their families. In light of this study, how could the hardships suffered by family members affect an inmate's chance for successful rehabilitation? If you could change policies on visiting inmates what specific practices would you implement to facilitate successful reintegration once released?

References

Bernstein, D., & Davis, L. (2000). *The HUB system: Profile of inmates under custody on January 1, 2000*. Albany: State of New York, Department of Correctional Services.

Braman, D., & Wood, J. (2003). From one generation to the next: How criminal sanctions are reshaping life in urban America. In J. Travis & M. Waul (Eds.), *Prisoners once removed: The impact of incarceration and reentry on children, families, and communities* (pp. 157–188). Washington, DC: Urban Institute.

Carlson, B., & Cervera, N. (1992). *Inmates and their wives: Incarceration and family life*. Westport. CT: Greenwood.

Casey-Acevedo, K., & Bakken, T. (2002). Visiting women in prison: Who visits and who cares? *Journal of Offender Rehabilitation, 34*(3), 67–86.

Clear, T. R. (1996). Backfire: When incarceration increases crime. In *The unintended consequences of incarceration* (pp. 1–20). New York: Vera Institute of Justice.

Comfort, M. (2003). In the tube at San Quentin: The "secondary prisonization" of women visiting inmates. *Journal of Contemporary Ethnography, 32*(1), 77–107.

Fishman, L. T. (1990). *Women at the wall: A study of prisoner's wives doing time on the outside*. Albany: State University of New York Press.

Girshick, L. B. (1996). *Soledad women: Wives of prisoners speak out*. Westport, CT: Praeger.

Hagan, J., & Dinovitzer, R. (1999). Collateral consequences of imprisonment for children, communities, and prisoners. In M. Tonry & J. Petersilia (Eds.), *Prisons* (pp. 121–162). Chicago: University of Chicago Press.

Hairston, C. (2003). Prisoners and their families: Parenting issues during incarceration. In J. Travis & M. Waul (Eds.), *Prisoners once removed: The impact of incarceration and reentry on children, families, and communities* (pp. 259–282). Washington, DC: Urban Institute.

Lowenstein. A. (1986). Temporary single parenthood—The case of prisoners' families. *Family Relations, 35*, 79–85.

Mumola, C. J. (2000). *Incarcerated patents and their children. Bureau of Justice Statistics special report*. Washington, DC: Bureau of Justice Statistics.

National Institute of Corrections. (2002). *Services for families of prison inmates*. Longmont, CO: National Institute of Corrections Information Center.

Petersilia, J. (2003). *When prisoners come home: Parole and prisoner reentry*. New York: Oxford University Press.

Schlosser. E. (1998, December). The prison-industrial complex. *The Atlantic Monthly*, pp. 51–77.

Shaw, R. (1987). *Children of imprisoned fathers*. London: Hodder and Stoughton.

Shaw, R. (1992). *Prisoners' children: What are the issues?* London: Routledge.

Travis, J., Solomon, A. L., & Waul, M. (2001). *From prison to home: The dimensions and consequences of prisoner reentry*. Washington, DC: Urban Institute.

Travis, J., & Waul, M. (2003). *Prisoners once removed: The impact of incarceration and reentry on children, families, and communities*. Washington, DC: Urban Institute.

30

Keeping Families Together: The Importance of Maintaining Mother–Child Contact for Incarcerated Women

Zoann K. Snyder

Abstract: *Snyder examines the effectiveness of special visitation programs designed to keep imprisoned mothers and children connected. Using semi-structured interviews with incarcerated mothers she discusses their perspectives about how their children are coping with the separation, their concerns for their children, their views of their roles as mothers, and their post-release needs. Snyder suggests that keeping mothers and children connected may produce positive behavioral and emotional outcomes for both the mothers and their children that could possibly reduce correctional costs and increase community safety.*

Contemporary U.S. crime control policy stresses individual responsibility for crime, with an emphasis on such retributive penalties as mandatory minimum sentences, determinate sentencing structures, habitual offender statutes, and truth-in-sentencing policies. Such policies do not take into account the social, political, and economic factors that may contribute to an individual's criminality. This focus also fails to take into account the social connections damaged or severed by state intervention. Failure to consider the personal situation of the offender when punishing can have devastating consequences for the family of the offender. This devastation can be particularly severe for women offenders and their children.

Women prisoners carry the burden of a criminal conviction and the violation of societal norms about what good women and mothers are supposed to be. Although state penal codes do not explicitly state that women with criminal convictions are bad mothers and should be denied contact with their children, contemporary correctional practices often result in the loss of family contact and control for incarcerated mothers. More recent studies (cf. Hagan & Coleman, 2001; Radosh, 2002) have proposed that punishing incarcerated mothers with separation from and loss of contact with children may be more deliberate than has been previously acknowledged.

Although many readers may presume that children are better off separated from their criminal mothers, I discuss why that assumption is not necessarily true and may be a greater threat to the well-being of affected children and mothers and to the safety of the larger community. The popular argument "Why should I pay for criminals to have family privileges?" prompts a critical and overlooked question: "What will be the harm if incarcerated mothers and their children are not kept together?"

Greene, Haney, and Hurtado (2000) called for the need to listen to the voice of incarcerated women to better understand the issues for mothers and their children.

They suggested that one can learn from the women themselves their needs and, hopefully, provide better, more relevant services to women and children at risk. Toward that end, the current research addresses how incarcerated women and their children are affected by the forcible separation of incarceration. Through the use of interviews, incarcerated mothers were encouraged to share their perceptions of how incarceration has impacted their children, their relationships with their children, their perceptions of themselves as mothers, and the needs they see for themselves and their children post-release. A demographic overview places the women interviewed within the larger frame of offenders and prisoners in the United States.

Demographics

The separation of children from their families due to a parent's incarceration is a large and growing problem. The U.S. Bureau of Justice Statistics (BJS; 2000) estimated that nearly 1.5 million children had at least one parent in prison in 1999. This number represents an increase of more than 33% since 1991. In state institutions, 65% of incarcerated women and 55% of imprisoned men had at least one minor child (younger than age 18). Of these minor children, 22% were younger than age 5 (BJS, 2000). Nearly two thirds of women housed in state prisons reported living with their minor children prior to their incarceration as compared to 44% of men (BJS, 2000). Proportionately more mothers (46%) than fathers (15%) were the sole care provider for their children prior to arrest. The majority of incarcerated fathers' children (90%) were reportedly living with the child's mother, whereas only 28% of the children of imprisoned mothers were with the child's father (BJS, 2000).

Between 1990 and 2000, the women's prison population increased 108% while the men's population grew by 77% (BJS, 2001). Although men remain the numerical majority of the incarcerated population, the incarceration of women has the potential for greater impact on minor children. When a father goes to prison, a child is more likely to live with his or her mother, whereas the children of incarcerated mothers are more likely to be passed along to other family members (BJS, 2000).

The growing number of incarcerated women increases the proportion of minor children who will be impacted by family separation. The disruption caused by the mother's incarceration is impacting more children and for potentially longer periods as mandatory minimum sentences and truth-in-sentencing guidelines increase the length of confinement. The majority of these young children will not be living with their fathers. Consequently, these children may be at risk of placement in foster care and/or permanent loss of their mothers as their primary guardians.

Punishment versus Rehabilitation

The majority of incarcerated women are serving sentences for nonviolent crimes and drug offenses (Belknap, 2001; Pollock, 1999). Radosh (2002, p. 310) argued that the current get-tough-on-crime approach "does not fit either the crime or the offender," when it comes to women:

> Women's crime commonly reflects prior life experiences with men who clearly perpetrated serious criminal acts, such as childhood sexual molestation, rape, incest, and domestic violence. The fact that such offenders frequently were not prosecuted or punished cannot frame the defense of women in their current offense. Yet the underlying injustice inherent in societal tolerance of suffering on one level, while overreacting to less crime on another level, frames a basic violation of human rights.
>
> (p. 310)

Although all criminal offenders are to be subject to state penalties, the impact of women's punishment extends beyond the individual offender. Two thirds of incarcerated women are mothers to minor children and were living with these children immediately prior to their incarceration (BJS, 2000). Crime control efforts do not recognize the harm being extended to children when state officials punish mothers with forcible removal from their children (Radosh, 2002). The physical separation of incarcerated mothers from their children may rightfully be addressed as a crisis for the family members involved. This particular occurrence needs to be viewed within the context of families that already may be at risk due to physical, emotional, and sexual abuse; addiction to drugs and alcohol; mental illness; unemployment; or poverty (Adalist-Estrin, 1986; Gabel, 1992; Greene et al., 2000; Myers, Smarsh, Amlund-Hagen, & Kennon, 1999; Sharp & Marcus-Mendoza, 2001). Many young children will face changes in caregivers and possibly their home environments (Koban, 1983; Myers et al., 1999; Phillips & Harm, 1997; Schafer & Dellinger, 1999; Sharp & Marcus-Mendoza, 2001). Most children will be placed with family members which may include the same individuals who reportedly abused the incarcerated mothers (Greene et al., 2000; Sharp & Marcus-Mendoza, 2001).

These life changes often extract a sizable toll on the emotional and behavioral well-being of the children. Researchers have noted that children are harmed when separated from their mothers (Bloom & Steinhart, 1993; Clark, 1995; Gabel, 1992; Greene et al., 2000; Hairston, 1991; Johnston, 1995; Kampfner, 1995; LaPoint, Pickett, & Harris, 1985; Martin, 1997; Myers et al., 1999; Schafer & Dellinger, 1999; Schoenbauer, 1986; Sharp & Marcus-Mendoza, 2001; Young & Smith, 2000). Children experience a gamut of emotions: anger, fear, depression, anxiety, and frustration. Behavioral problems may also occur, such as truancy, poor school performance, expulsion from school, running away, fighting and aggression toward others, and conflict with caregivers (Gaudin, 1984; Henriques, 1982; Johnston, 1995; Kampfner, 1995; McGowan & Blumenthal, 1976; Myers et al., 1999; Sach, Siedler, & Thomas, 1976; Sharp & Marcus-Mendoza, 2001; Stanton, 1980).

Children who witness their mother's arrest may suffer from posttraumatic stress disorder and fear of state agents such as the police and court officials (Hannon, Martin, & Martin, 1984; Kampfner, 1995; LaPoint et al., 1985; Myers et al., 1999). Although none of these authors suggest that state officials actively intend to punish or harm the children of adult offenders, the failure to provide for the needs of children to be with their mothers penalizes the children for their parent's behavior.

The extant literature has also noted the connection between a child having an incarcerated parent and ending up in the criminal justice system (Bloom, 1993, 1995; Gabel, 1992; Greene et al., 2000; Henriques, 1982; Johnston, 1995; Light, 1993; Moore

& Clement, 1998; Muse, 1994; Thompson & Harm, 1995). The estimates of how many children with a family history of incarceration end up in the justice system are varied. About half of all incarcerated women have at least one family member who has been incarcerated (BJS, 1994). Muse estimated that about one third of incarcerated juveniles have had at least one parent who has been incarcerated. Regardless of the actual numbers, there is evidence to suggest that an intergenerational link exists between parental incarceration and children entering the criminal justice system as defendants. More attention is needed to examine the connection between parents' imprisonment and children engaging in juvenile and/or adult criminal behavior.

The temporary separation caused by prison may become permanent for some incarcerated women and their children. Hagan and Coleman's (2001) critical analysis of the 1997 Adoption and Safe Families Act (ASFA; Public Law 105–89) indicated that efforts to shorten children's stays in foster care may impede or prevent family reunification post-release. Under ASFA, the state may initiate termination of parental rights when children have been in foster care for 15 of the preceding 22 months. With an average sentence length of 18 months, incarcerated women may lose custody of their children if there are no other caregivers and the children are placed in foster care. Although intended to prevent children from being housed long term in the foster care system, ASFA may be used as a "second sanction" for mothers in prison who are viewed as not fulfilling their parenting roles as required by the state (Hagan & Coleman, 2001, p. 359).

Hagan and Coleman (2001) noted ASFA presumes that foster care is not safe-keeping for children. Its supervision should be limited and children placed with permanent caregivers as soon as possible. But state action creates the need for foster care. State officials claim that children should not spend too long in foster care. The language of the law creates a presumption of parental failure when mothers are incarcerated and unable to provide for the daily living needs of their children. The policy fails to take into account the state's responsibility for the forcible separation rather than child neglect or abandonment by the mothers.

Incarcerated mothers who seek to parent from prison encounter numerous obstacles. Institutional policies in place to control the conduct of prisoners may hinder efforts at communication and contact between incarcerated mothers and their children. Incarcerated mothers face such communication barriers as limits on number and length of phone calls, restrictions on days and times of visitation, and geographical distance between the institution and the location of families (Bloom, 1995; Clement, 1993; Hairston, 1991; Snyder, Carlo, & Mullins, 2001; Young & Smith, 2000). Institutions with restrictive visitation policies or limited parenting services may further erode mothers' efforts to maintain their roles as parents (Beckerman, 1991; Coll et al., 1997; Young & Smith, 2000).

Incarcerated mothers no longer have their children in their custodial care. They have concerns for the emotional and physical safety and well-being of their children (Browne, 1989; Hairston, 1991; Koban, 1983; LaPoint et al., 1985; Moore & Clement, 1998; Sharp & Marcus-Mendoza, 2001; Snyder et al., 2001; Thompson & Harm, 1995; Weilerstein, 1995; Young & Smith, 2000). The mothers also experience guilt about failing their children, anxiety about their parenting abilities, and remorse for being removed from their children (Baunach, 1985; Browne, 1989; Clark, 1995; Moore & Clement, 1998; Young & Smith, 2000).

Release back into the community will not be the end of mothers' concerns and needs. The transition to life in the community and with their children has many pressures for women. There will be multiple demands on their time as they attempt to satisfy the requirements of parole, such as establishing a permanent residence, seeking and securing employment, caring for children, and possibly attending substance abuse treatment and counseling. Harm and Phillips (2001) noted a complex relationship between substance abuse, familial relationships, and employment for women post-release. Anxiety about meeting the needs of their children while attempting to fulfill requirements of supervision may overwhelm some women. Although children may be seen as positive motivators for women, they can also be stressors that trigger substance use/abuse to cope. It will be difficult for women to meet all of the technical requirements of parole and still fulfill societal expectations of mothers (Richie, 2001; Young & Smith, 2000).

Research Setting

Given the issues of concern for incarcerated mothers and their children, the current research examines if and/or how women and children remain connected during incarceration and the impact that such contact has on their relationships. The Nebraska Correctional Center for Women (NCCW) in York, Nebraska, was the research site. The research participants were women with one or more minor children who were incarcerated at NCCW in 2000. The targeted participants included women who were participating in the Mother Offspring Life Development (MOLD) program. MOLD provides classes in parenting, child development, and personal development, and onsite overnight and day visits for women prisoners and their children. The MOLD program has been in place since 1974 and is the first and oldest continuously operating mother–child visitation program offered in any U.S. prison. MOLD requires that women who want to take part in the program enroll in and complete a portion of the parenting classes prior to having special visitations with their children. These women must also maintain a good institutional conduct record to begin and retain the specialized visits. These visits take place at the prison but in an atmosphere very different from that of the standard visitors' room. Through MOLD, mothers are permitted to meet with their children in a more neutral environment where guards are not present. During these visits, the women and children are permitted to have close contact and play games, build crafts, read, and so on.

Methods

The current research was designed with the intent of enabling and empowering incarcerated women to identify and discuss the issues of concern central to them and their families. Through personal interviews, the incarcerated mothers were invited to engage in a dialogue about their roles as mothers and their interaction with their children. The interview questions and format were developed using feminist standpoint epistemology (cf. Harding, 1991; Stanley & Wise, 1993) and emphasized the importance of understanding incarcerated mothers' concerns from their position and not according to socially defined perspectives of mothering.

Efforts were made to reduce the hierarchical structure often found in traditional interviews (cf. Finch, 1981; Oakley, 1981). Interviews were completed with only myself and one woman present at a time. Questions were offered as prompts for conversation, and the women were encouraged to expand on issues as they chose. Topical areas of interest were grouped together, but the numbering of questions was not rigidly adhered to in order to facilitate a more normal conversation.

The sample was limited to the first 50 participants who met the research criteria. A total of 25 mothers active in the MOLD program and a comparison group of 25 mothers not in MOLD participated. The women in the comparison group were not receiving visits through the MOLD program but were not prohibited from doing so by NCCW, the Nebraska Department of Correctional Services, or any other legal restrictions. Women could not receive visits if they had not completed the required parenting classes. Lack of space availability, children living out of state or too far from the institution to make regular visits, or caregivers for the children who could not or would not bring the children to the prison may have prevented participation.

The women were asked a series of open-ended questions focusing on their experiences as mothers and their separation from their children. Central to the inquiry were their observations about their relationship with their children, how incarceration has impacted them and their children, and their plans for after release. Text from the interviews is used throughout this article to give voice to the women's observations. It is important to note that the names of mothers and their children have been changed to protect their privacy.

Findings

Maintaining Contact with Children

The women at NCCW have a variety of media for maintaining contact with their children, including cards and letters, telephone calls, audio- and videotapes, messages communicated through friends and family members, and regular visitation in the standard visitors' room. MOLD program participants also have the opportunity for on-grounds visits and overnight stays for younger children. Most mothers have nearly the same opportunities for contact with their children with few institutional restrictions. Whether women are able to access these opportunities, however, is affected by social and financial considerations. Some women reported that family members have placed phone blocks or refuse incoming collect calls. Lynelle (not in the MOLD program) spoke to this issue:

> My ex has no kind of long distance, so collect calls are out of the question. My fiancé told me that he'd call my ex and offer to bring my daughter to my house where I could call and talk to her, but as of yet I don't know whether that's gonna happen.

Geographical distance, time constraints, or lack of money necessary for onsite visits may preclude regular family contact for some women. Other mothers noted that their children are in juvenile facilities, jail, or treatment programs and are unable to visit. Caregivers for children may refuse visits in the best interests of the child. Laura (non-MOLD) addressed why she does not have visits with her preschool-age son: "Yeah, they [her family] thought that if he came up here, it would damage him in some way and so they chose not to have him come up."

With regard to the frequency of written or phone contact, a greater proportion of MOLD mothers (88%) reported writing several times per month in comparison to non-MOLD mothers (75%). MOLD and non-MOLD mothers are equally likely (48%) to receive several letters per month from their children. MOLD mothers (84%) are more likely to have several phone conversations per month with children in comparison to non-MOLD mothers (64%). A greater proportion of non-MOLD mothers (36%) than MOLD mothers (24%) communicate with their children through family members.

Family members can provide a vital link that otherwise may be missing between mothers and children. Laura was able to have some contact with her son through her mother and brother:

> My brother will tell him that "your mom called and she loves you" and "she called and she was asking about you." I get lots of pictures and he sees pictures of me and they talk about me every day. My mother said on the phone that she missed me and wanted a picture of me and so I sent a picture and he pointed to me and said "mommy," so he knows. I haven't seen him for 342 days.

Bonnie, a MOLD participant, reflected on the importance of letters in her relationship with her children:

> Being in communication through correspondence has opened up a different facet of our relationship because we've really never been apart and the written word is something I think that you can hold onto and look back on and read over and over again. It's not something like a phone call or even a conversation that is just gone. It's there in black and white, so I think in that way it's been helpful.

There is a significant difference between the MOLD and non-MOLD mothers with regard to regular visits and the frequency of such contact. The majority of MOLD program participants (92%) reported visits from their children in the standard visitors' room, whereas less than half of the non-MOLD women (48%) have face-to-face contact with their children. For the mothers receiving visits with children, 65% of the MOLD mothers have at least monthly contact as compared to 33% of the women not participating in MOLD.

Although the frequency of contact other than visitation is comparable for the two groups of mothers, there is a significant distinction when physical contact is addressed. MOLD mothers and their children have more regular contact in comparison to mothers not in the MOLD program. Mothers in MOLD suggested that their contact visits form the basis for phone calls and letters. The women and their children discuss their recent time together or plan future visits. It is very likely that phone calls, cards, and letters are the links that strengthen the connection between mothers and children. Regular communication may help mothers and children to feel less awkward when they come together for visits. Extra-visitation exchanges may provide greater continuity in relationships than can be achieved through traditional visitation alone. Regular contact may also account for why MOLD mothers do not have significantly greater extra-visitation communication in comparison to non-MOLD mothers. Frequent visits may take the place of additional phone calls, cards, and letters.

Mothers' Observations about Their Children

Another essential component of inquiry was the mother–child relationship. The women were asked questions regarding how they view their relationships with their children and their perceptions of how their incarceration has affected their children.

The variable for mother's assessment of her relationship with her child/ children was coded into dichotomous categories of "fair to good" and "poor to none." More MOLD mothers (92%) than non-MOLD mothers (80%) reported that their relationships with their children are positive, but these assessments are tempered with the reality of families divided by incarceration.

One MOLD mother, Celine, spoke with candor of her relationship with children:

> It's a good relationship, but there's a lot of room for improvement. They're mad that I came here. Well, I was incarcerated from '95 to '98 and I got out on parole, and then in 1999 I came back, so that really angered them that I didn't do good and had to come back.

Monica (MOLD) addressed the difficulties she is experiencing with her children:

> My relationship with my children is not where I want it to be at this point in their lives. There's a lot of damage. My youngest daughter, they're getting ready to terminate my rights as a parent, and I'm trying to just soak her in as much as I can. I'll probably lose her before I get out of here. My oldest daughter I'm struggling with because I know she's going through a lot and I know that there are some problems at her dad's house. I feel frustrated. I have no control, and I think that's got to be one of the worst things about being incarcerated is that you don't have any control and you know that your children are hurting and there's nothing you can do about it. It's almost like just holding my breath and pray that they can hold on.

Janine (non-MOLD) provided insight about what is needed to improve her relationship with her children:

> I think it's as good as it can be for the moment. I think on the phone they're reassuring that they love me and I reassure them. We talk about different things and we try to give them a lot of positive reinforcement. I think that their trust was broken by my parole violation.

When asked how their incarceration has impacted their children, MOLD mothers were more likely than non-MOLD mothers to suggest that their children are having difficulty dealing with the incarceration. A greater proportion of non-MOLD mothers (23%) than MOLD mothers (4%) felt that their children are coping with their incarceration.

The concern that children are having difficulties dealing with their separation from their mothers was expressed by Tamica, a MOLD program participant:

> My kids get counsel. They counsel once a week and that's good because they have a lady that comes and talks to them. They also work with the counselors at their school. I don't know. When I see my children, I almost feel like it's weird because I get this sense that they are desensitized somehow. Just like with my son, some children at that age it would've happened to them, they would've been crying. My son didn't even do that. He didn't share a tear. I'm not trying to read too much into that, but it almost makes me wonder if they are not used to [the separation] already, that, okay, this is what might happen sometimes. I might be taken from mom. Mom might be taken from me. Dad might be taken. So we're just going to numb ourselves to not show any emotion. I'm just so scared that that's happening with them.

Tamica reported having twice-monthly contact in the traditional visitors' room with her son, who is too old for on-grounds visits. Her younger children see her weekly, either in the regular visits or in the MOLD area.

Rose, another MOLD mother, discussed her preschool-age daughter:

> Well, when I first got here, she was—I could tell that she had anger towards me from the way she acted out, and as I'm getting closer to going home, her attitude changes when she comes to visit. It's easier for her to leave. She doesn't cry anymore. When we talk on the phone, you know, it's just simple conversation. So she's understanding now that I'm where I'm at. My mom felt that there was probably a little bit of abandonment, thinking she was abandoned by me. That's basically why my parents keep bringing her up every week, and I'm allowed to call home every day to keep us close to reassure her that I did not abandon her. She's like me where when we're hurt, we express it more in anger.

Maria (non-MOLD) has contact visits with her children about twice a year, though she indicated weekly phone conversations. She feels her children have benefited from her incarceration:

> I think [her incarceration has] affected them in a positive way. In the beginning they were very angry. It was tough at first because they were very angry at me, but I think as I explained to them how I've changed and how things are gonna change when I get home, I think they've let go of that anger. They're starting to regain that trust.

There are several things to consider from these responses. Regular visits provide mothers with the opportunity to see their children and to talk about what is happening in their lives. The reality of incarceration is clear and perhaps less frightening when children can visually confirm that their mothers are okay. Deeper communication into thoughts and feelings may be more difficult to express or address in letters and relatively brief phone calls. Younger children do not have the language skills to express their feelings, and body language cannot be intuited from phone calls or letters. MOLD mothers' participation in parenting classes may also provide them with more skills with which to observe and communicate with their children. Mothers with more contact time with their children may have a more balanced and realistic view of their children and their children's emotions.

It is important to note that although children's health and well-being may be intact, this does not preclude the possibility that children are negatively impacted by separation from the mother. The positive aspects of visitation and contact do not completely offset the trauma and pain of living apart. Rather, the mothers with more stable connections to their family may have a broader and more informed perspective on their children and their children's lives.

Mothers' Views of Their Roles as Parents

The mothers were also asked to discuss their roles as parents. The women reflected on how incarceration affects them as mothers. The question was divided into categories of "coping" and "difficult and painful." MOLD mothers were slightly more likely to indicate that they are coping with their incarceration than were non-MOLD mothers. In all, 72% of the MOLD mothers and 76% of the mothers not in the program were candid about the pain and anxiety associated with being separated from their children. Although MOLD participants may have more opportunities to explore their roles as mothers through parenting classes and other related activities, they are still apart from their children. Contact visits and communication cannot completely offset the loss and pain incurred through incarceration.

Women not in the MOLD program shared their experiences:

> It's hard. It hurts a lot. I had to put my trust in God because I can't do much until I get out. I don't really feel like a mother anymore in here.
>
> (Jaycee)

> I think for me the hardest thing was my fear. The first time I didn't fear it. I don't know why. The first time here was good. It really was. It was not fun but it was not hard either. This time it's been miserable from the day I got here and I don't want to come back. I don't want my children to have this. It's hard knowing that they may not want me to be a part of their life. They may not want me around.
>
> (Janine, reflecting on her second incarceration)

Mothers who participate in MOLD noted similar feelings about how incarceration has affected them as mothers:

> It's tore me down. I've spent the past seven years . . . I've spent all this time being a mother and nothing else. That was my main thing in life. That was my career. I guess you could say it's damaged me, the fact that I'm gonna have to try to get over the fact that I wasn't there for my kids for two years.
>
> (Josie)

> At times I feel guilty. I feel like I should be there with them and helping to take care of them. I feel like I abandoned them. A mother should be there. My mother was there to raise me and I should be there with them.
>
> (Meg)

> It's been a huge kick in the ass, a lot of guilt, a lot of shame.
>
> (Monica)

The anxiety, guilt, shame, and fear for their children during their separation add to the pain of incarceration experienced by many of the women in NCCW. These issues are compounded for the mothers who do not have regular contact with their children. The enforced estrangement from their children causes anguish during the mothers' incarceration and flavors how they think about their lives post-release. With an aware-ness of how incarceration has affected their roles as mothers, the women were asked to discuss their future needs.

Needs and Plans for the Future

The final question put to the women was what types of services could be offered to help the mothers and children after release. The four categories of the question were "shelter and subsistence needs," "counseling and therapy," "more parenting classes and support groups," and "nothing more is needed." Significant differences were expressed by the two groups of mothers regarding their post-release needs. The primary concern expressed by the majority of mothers is the need for ongoing counseling and therapy for themselves and for their children. In all, 68% of the non-MOLD and 48% of the MOLD mothers identified counseling and therapy as an important need. In addition, 12% of the non-MOLD women said subsistence concerns, such as shelter, food, and employment, are their primary needs. Additional parenting classes and support groups were viewed as necessary by 20% of the women in MOLD and 12% of the women not in the program. Nearly one third of the MOLD mothers indicated that no further services are necessary after release as it is up to them to make their own way in the community.

The women's concerns for after their release were summed up by two of the mothers:

> I think that they should have some kind of housing for women that stay in Nebraska with their children because a lot of times when they get out and they don't have anywhere to go to so they leave their children with their mother, and then they get stressed out and go to drugs or drinking or whatever problem that come the first time. If they had a halfway house or some kind of organization out there that would benefit the mother and the child, it would give the mother some responsibility because they don't give them any responsibility when they're in prison. The only thing they do is give them $100 and 99% of these women don't have nowhere to go, so they go back to what they know best.
>
> (Rowena—non-MOLD)

> I'm gonna need more parenting classes. I know that for a fact. When I had my oldest, when I got pregnant, my case workers let me in . . . a program for teenage mothers . . . I really feel like I'm gonna need a visiting nurse just to get me back into things with my kids, or a family support worker. I had one of those when I was in foster care. Something like that to get you back into the swing of being with my children and the things they like to do and did want to do . . . It's just that I'm gonna need somebody to support me through—my bond with my kids is really strong—but through reuniting after being gone for so long. I'm gonna need a support person.
>
> (Randi—MOLD)

There are differences in the women's views of post-release needs. Mothers partici-pating in the MOLD program identified with the need for both counseling/therapy and a parenting support group after their release. Women not in the MOLD program expressed the most concern for counseling and therapy services. The mothers' recog-nition of needs and the resources to provide these services are very much at odds with one another. Community-based programs for drug and alcohol abuse counseling are limited primarily to Narcotics Anonymous and Alcoholics Anonymous or programs for a fee. Community mental health programs do exist but are often stretched for financial support and/or human resources to meet the demands for services. Most of the women expressed concerns about their financial status post-release and will likely not have the resources necessary for private counseling services. The findings leave the paradox of those most in need of services being least likely to receive them.

Criticisms of MOLD and NCCW

Although many of the women spoke favorably of the MOLD program and its staff, parenting classes, and institutional staff, there were criticisms aimed at institutional personnel and programs. A total of 28% of the women interviewed noted that they do not the have the opportunity to speak about their concerns as parents. The lack of opportunity was attributed to several different sources.

Some women reported that the prison administrator in place at that time did not support the MOLD program or parenting initiatives. Carrie, a MOLD participant, expressed her feelings about MOLD and its place in the prison:

> The program is great because that's what keeps us in touch with our kids and that's what makes—the warden, she's trying to cut it out. She just don't want it here and the institution, they're not fighting for us to keep it. You have inmates that aren't fighting for us to keep it because they don't have any children, so they don't care if we have the program or not. It's the institution that will eventually make the program fall.

Kaylee (MOLD) voiced a similar concern:

> Now since Warden Wayne is gone, it's like nobody cares. There's talk that they should get rid of the MOLD program. If people do, like the TV people come, the staff people come and talk to them, but the real people that has real concerns, they're afraid to let it all come out. They just hush it up like it's really wrong.

Staff indifference was cited as a barrier to talking about family concerns: "I don't think the staff really care about your, kids, but other women will listen to you, yeah. The staff, you're just a number to them. They're just doing their job," said Brenna (non-MOLD). "These people don't give a darn. They have parenting classes but they're a joke, so you're pretty much kind of on your own," said Carrie (MOLD).

Janine, not in the MOLD program, did not talk about her parenting concerns due to lack of confidentiality: "I don't really share much with the other women. I have people I talk to, but I stay to myself. The minute you tell somebody something or share something, it's everywhere. I don't like that."

For other women, institutional programming is tailored more toward women in crisis or for mothers with marginal parenting skills:

> We take classes and stuff, but it's really more surface. There's too many for us to be a one-on-one kind of thing . . . To be quite honest, I don't think it has [affected her relationship with her children] because this is stuff that I already know because even if you're the worst parent, these are things that maybe strengthen you or things that I already knew and did.
>
> (Celine—MOLD)

If you're not a drug addict or an alcoholic or not an habitual offender or something like that, you really don't get much.

(Naomi—non-MOLD)

As with most programs, MOLD is not able to meet all of the needs of all of the women incarcerated in NCCW. Although it is unlikely that any one project could provide complete user satisfaction, the women provided insights into their needs and expectations that could be integrated into institutional or community-based parenting services.

Summary

Mothers in the MOLD program have more regular visitation with their children and a higher frequency of visits than do mothers not in the program. These visits can form the foundation for understanding and caring for their children. The parenting classes combined with visitation may enable the women to identify their needs during and after incarceration. Empowering and privileging the voices of mothers in prison can provide the knowledge necessary to better serve women and families impacted by incarceration. Their needs must be central to and addressed by community-based and institutional programs.

Institutional programs designed to help incarcerated mothers meet post-release demands are crucial for mothers' successful transition back into society. Incarcerated women do not stop being mothers despite their geographical separation from their children. Martin (1997) found that imprisonment did not break the family ties for all women. She noted the existence of *connected mothers*, defined as women who had "not only legal custody, they also had an emotional connection with their children and a mature grasp of their needs" (p. 3). Although she noted that not all women can become connected mothers, institutional programs and services can provide a valuable support structure for mother–child relationships.

Contact visits can comfort both mothers and children. Speaking face-to-face and visually confirming one another's well-being can reduce anxiety and fear for both mothers and children. Although onsite visitation cannot reproduce the normalcy of daily living for families, it can provide a means for mothers and children to build or retain relationships. Such bonds may help facilitate post-release reunification.

Critical Thinking

In light of Snyder's findings, how do you think the pain and loss the women describe hampers their recovery? How do you think the pain and loss of their children affects their current behavior and future behavior? Why do you think the non-program mothers believe their children are coping better even though they enjoy less contact with their children than the other mothers?

References

Adalist-Estrin, A. (1986). *Parenting from behind bars* (Family Resource Coalition Report No. 1). Jenkintown, PA: Parent Resource Association.

Baunach, P. J. (1985). *Mothers in prison*. New Brunswick, NJ: Transaction Books.

Beckerman, A. (1991). Women in prison: The conflict between confinement and parental rights. *Social Justice, 18*(3), 171–183.

Belknap, J. (2001). *The invisible woman* (2nd ed.). Belmont, CA: Wadsworth/Thomson Learning.

Bloom, B. (1993). Incarcerated mothers and their children: Maintaining family ties. In *Female offenders: Meeting the needs of a neglected population* (pp. 60–68). Laurel, MD: American Correctional Association.

Bloom, B. (1995). Imprisoned mothers. In K. Gabel & D. Johnston (Eds.), *Children of incarcerated parents* (pp. 21–30). New York: Lexington Books.

Bloom, B., & Steinhart, D. (1993). *Why punish the children? A reappraisal of the children of incarcerated mothers in America*. San Francisco, CA: National Council on Crime and Delinquency.

Browne, D. C. H. (1989). Incarcerated mothers and parenting. *Journal of Family Violence, 4*(2), 211–221.

Clark, J. (1995). The impact of the prison environment on mothers. *Prison Journal, 75*(3), 306–329.

Clement. M. J. (1993). Parenting in prison: A national survey of programs for incarcerated women. *Journal of Offender Rehabilitation, 19*(1/2), 89–100.

Coll, C. G., Miller, J. B., Fields, J. P., & Mathews, B. (1997). The experiences of women in prison: Implications for services and prevention. *Women & Therapy, 20*(4), 11–28.

Finch, J. (1981). "It's great to have someone to talk to": The ethics and politics of interviewing women. In H. Roberts (Ed.), *Doing feminist research* (pp. 70–87). London: Routledge & Kegan Paul.

Gabel, S. (1992). Behavioral problems in sons of incarcerated or otherwise absent fathers: The issue of separation. *Family Process, 31*, 303–314.

Gaudin, J. M., Jr. (1984). Social work roles and tasks with incarcerated mothers. *Social Casework, 65*, 279–286.

Greene. S., Haney, C., & Hurtado, A. (2000). Cycles of pain: Risk factors in the lives of incarcerated mothers and their children. *Prison Journal, 80*(1), 3–23.

Hagan, J., & Coleman, J. P. (2001). Returning captives of the American war on drugs: Issues of community and family reentry. *Crime & Delinquency, 47*, 352–367.

Hairston, C. F. (1991). Mothers in jail: Parent-child separation and jail visitation. *Affilia, 6*(2), 9–27.

Hannon, G., Martin, D., & Martin, M. (1984). Incarceration in the family: Adjustment to change. *Family Therapy, 11*(3), 253–260.

Harding, S. (1991). *Whose science? Whose knowledge?* Ithaca, NY: Cornell University Press.

Harm, N. J., & Phillips, S. D. (2001). You can't go home again: Women and criminal recidivism. *Journal of Offender Rehabilitation, 32*(3), 3–21.

Henriques, Z. W. (1982). *Imprisoned mothers and their children*. Washington, DC: University Press of America.

Johnston, D. (1995). Effects of parental incarceration. In K. Gabel & D. Johnston (Eds.), *Children of incarcerated parents* (pp. 59–88). New York: Lexington Books.

Kampfner, C. J. (1995). Posttraumatic stress reactions in children of imprisoned mothers. In K. Gabel & D. Johnston (Eds.), *Children of incarcerated parents* (pp. 89–100). New York: Lexington Books.

Koban, L. A. (1983). Parents in prison: A comparative analysis of the effects of incarceration on the families of men and women. *Research in Law, Deviance and Social Control, 5*, 171–183.

LaPoint, V., Pickett, M. O., & Harris, B. F. (1985). Enforced family separation: A descriptive analysis of some experiences of children of Black imprisoned mothers. In M. B. Spencer, G. K. Brookins, & W. R. Allen (Eds.), *Beginnings: The social and affective development of Black children* (pp. 239–255). Hillsdale, NJ: Erlbaum.

Light, R. (1993). Why support prisoners' family-tie groups? *Howard Journal, 32*(4), 322–329.

Martin, M. (1997). Connected mothers: A follow-up study of incarcerated women and their children. *Women & Criminal Justice, 8*(4), 1–23.

McGowan, B. G., & Blumenthal, K. L. (1976). Children of women prisoners: A forgotten minority. In L. Crites (Ed.), *The female offender* (pp. 121–135). Lexington, MA: Lexington Books.

Moore, A. R., & Clement, M. J. (1998). Effects of parenting training for incarcerated mothers. *Journal of Offender Rehabilitation, 27*(1–2), 57–72.

Muse, D. (1994, Fall). Parenting from prison. *Mothering, 72*, 98–105.

Myers. J. M., Smarsh, T. M., Amlund-Hagen, K., & Kennon, S. (1999). Children of incarcerated mothers. *Journal of Child and Family Studies, 8*, 11–25.

Oakley, A. (1981). Interviewing women: A contradiction in terms. In H. Roberts (Ed.), *Doing feminist research* (pp. 30–61). London: Routledge & Kegan Paul.

Phillips, S. D., & Harm, N. J. (1997). Women prisoners: A contextual framework. *Women & Therapy, 20*(4), 1–9.

Pollock, J. M. (1999). *Criminal women*. Cincinnati, OH: Anderson.

Radosh, P. F. (2002). Reflections on women's crime and mothers in prison: A peacemaking approach. *Crime & Delinquency, 48*, 300–315.

Richie, B. E. (2001). Challenges incarcerated women face as they return to their communities: Findings from life history interviews. *Crime & Delinquency, 47*, 368–389.

Sach, W. H., Siedler, J., & Thomas, S. (1976). The children of imprisoned parents: A psychological exploration. *American Journal of Orthopsychiatry, 46*, 618–628.

Schafer, N. E., & Dellinger, A. B. (1999). Jailed parents: An assessment. *Women & Criminal Justice, 10*(4), 73–91.

Schoenbauer, L. J. (1986). Incarcerated parents and their children—Forgotten families. *Law & Inequality, 4*, 579–601.

Sharp, S. F., & Marcus-Mendoza, S. T. (2001). It's a family affair: Incarcerated women and their families. *Women & Criminal Justice, 12*(4), 21–49.

Snyder, Z. K., Carlo, T. A., & Mullins, M. M. C. (2001). Parenting from prison: An examination of a children's visitation program at a women's correctional facility. *Marriage & Family Review, 32*(3–4), 33–62.

Stanley, L., & Wise, S. (1993). *Breaking out again.* London: Routledge.

Stanton, A. M. (1980). *When mothers go to jail.* Lexington, MA: Lexington Books.

Thompson, P. J., & Harm, N. J. (1995). Parent education for mothers in prison. *Pediatric Nursing, 21*, 552–555.

U.S. Bureau of Justice Statistics. (1994). *Women in prison.* Washington, DC: Author.

U.S. Bureau of Justice Statistics. (2000). *Incarcerated parents and their children.* Washington, DC: Author.

U.S. Bureau of Justice Statistics. (2001). *Prisoners in 2000.* Washington, DC: Author.

Weilerstein, R. (1995). The prison M.A.T.C.H. program. In K. Gabel & D. Johnston (Eds.), *Children of incarcerated parents* (pp. 255–264). New York: Lexington Books.

Young, D. S., & Smith, C. J. (2000). When mothers are incarcerated: The needs of children, mothers, and caregivers. *Families in Society, 81*, 130–141.

Credit Lines

Norman Conti
Norman Conti. 2009. "A Visigoth System: Shame, Honor, and Police Socialization," *Journal of Contemporary Ethnography*, 38: 409–432. Used by permission of Sage Publications.

Claudio G. Vera Sanchez, and Dennis P. Rosenbaum
Claudio G. Vera Sanchez and Dennis P. Rosenbaum. 2011. "Racialized Policing: Officers' Voices on Policing Latino and African American Neighborhoods." *Journal of Ethnicity in Criminal Justice*, 9: 152–178.

Barbara Stenross and Sherryl Kleinman
Barbara Stenross and Sherryl Kleinman. 1989. "The Highs and Lows of Emotional Labor: Detectives' Encounters with Criminals and Victims." *Journal of Contemporary Ethnography*, 17: 435–452. Used by permission of Sage Publications.

Mark R. Pogrebin and Eric D. Poole
Mark R. Pogrebin and Eric D. Poole. 1993. "Vice Isn't Nice: A Look at the Effects of Working Undercover." *Journal of Criminal Justice*, 21: 383–394. Used by permission of Elsevier Ltd.

Mark R. Pogrebin, Mary Dodge, and Harold Chatman
Mark R. Pogrebin, Mary Dodge, and Harold Chatman. 2000. "Reflections of African-American Women on their Careers in Urban Policing: Their Experiences of Racial and Sexual Discrimination." *International Journal of the Sociology of Law*, 28: 311–326. Used by permission of Elsevier Ltd.

Jacinta M. Gau and Rod K. Brunson
Jacinta M. Gau and Rod K. Brunson. (2010). "Procedural Justice and Order Maintenance Policing: A Study of Inner-City Young Men's Perceptions of Police Legitimacy." *Justice Quarterly*, 27: 255–279. Used by permission of Taylor & Francis.

Robert Durán
Robert Durán. 2010. "Urban Youth Encounters with Legitimately Oppressive Gang Enforcement." Original contribution to book.

Paul Stretesky, Tara O'Connor-Shelley, Michael J. Hogan, and N. Prabha Unnithan
Paul Stretesky, Tara O'Connor-Shelley, Michael J. Hogan, and N. Prabha Unnithan. 2010. "Sensemaking and Secondary Victimization." Original contribution to book.

B. Joyce Stephens and Peter G. Sinden
B. Joyce Stephens and Peter G. Sinden. (2000). "Victims' Voices: Domestic Assault Victims' Perceptions of Police Demeanor." *Journal of Interpersonal Violence*, 15: 534–547. Used by permission of Sage Publications.

Eli Buchbinder and Zvi Eisikovits
Eli Buchbinder and Zvi Eisikovits. (2004). "Between Normality and Deviance: The Breakdown of Batterers' Identity Following Police Intervention." *Journal of Interpersonal Violence*, 19: 443–467. Used by permission of Sage Publications.

Deidre M. Bowen
Deidre M. Bowen (2009). "Calling Your Bluff: How Prosecutors and Defense Attorneys Adapt Plea Bargaining Strategies to Increased Formalization." *Justice Quarterly*, 26: 2–29. Used by permission of Taylor & Francis.

Alexes Harris
Alexes Harris. 2008. "The Social Construction of 'Sophisticated' Adolescents: How Judges Integrate Juvenile and Criminal Justice Decision-Making Models." *Journal of Contemporary Ethnography*, 37: 469–506. Used by permission of Sage Publications.

Lisa Frohmann
Lisa Frohmann. 1991. "Discrediting Victims' Allegations of Sexual Assault: Prosecutorial Accounts of Case Rejections." *Social Problems*, 38: 213–226. Used by permission of University of California Press.

Lisa J. McIntyre
Lisa J. McIntyre. 1997. "But How Can You Sleep Nights?" In McIntyre, Lisa J. *The Public Defender: The Practice of Law in the Shadows of Repute* (pp. 139–170). Used by permission of University of Chicago Press and Lisa J. McIntyre.

John Rosecrance
John Rosecrance. (1988). "Maintaining the Myth of Individualized Justice: Probation Presentence Reports." *Justice Quarterly*, 5: 235–256. Used by permission of Taylor & Francis.

Amanda Konradi
Amanda Konradi. 1996. "Preparing to Testify: Rape Survivors Negotiating the Criminal Justice Process." *Gender and Society*, 10: 404–432. Used by permission of Sage Publications.

Keith Guzik
Keith Guzik. 2008. "The Agencies of Abuse: Intimate Abusers' Experiences of Presumptive Arrest and Prosecution." *Law & Society Review*, 42: 111–143. Used by permission of John Wiley & Sons, Inc.

Sarah Goodrum
Sarah Goodrum. 2010. "Expecting an Ally and Getting a Prosecutor." Original contribution to book.

Michael Fischer, Brenda Geiger, and Mary Ellen Hughes

Michael Fischer, Brenda Geiger, and Mary Ellen Hughes. 2007. "Female Recidivists Speak about Their Experience in Drug Courts while Engaging in Appreciative Inquiry." *International Journal of Offender Therapy and Comparative Criminology*, 51: 703–722. Used by permission of Sage Publications.

Valerie P. Hans and Krista Sweigart

Valerie P. Hans and Krista Sweigart. (1993). "Jurors' Views of Civil Lawyers: Implications for Courtroom Communication." *Indiana Law Journal*, 68: 1297–1332. Indiana University.

Stan Stojkovic

Stan Stojkovic. 1990. "Accounts of Prison Work: Corrections Officers' Portrayals of Their Work Worlds." *Perspectives on Social Problems*, Vol. 2, pp. 211–230. Used by permission of Emerald Publishing.

John Riley

John Riley. 2000. "Sensemaking in Prison: Inmate Identity as a Working Understanding." *Justice Quarterly*, 17: 359–376. Used by permission of Taylor & Francis.

Eric D. Poole and Mark R. Pogrebin

Eric D. Poole and Mark R. Pogrebin. 2009. "Gender and Occupational Culture Conflict: A Study of Women Jail Officers." Pp. 423–443 in R. Tewksbury and D. Dabney (Eds.) *Prisons and Jails: A Reader*. New York: McGraw Hill.

Emily Gaarder, Nancy Rodriguez, and Marjorie S. Zatz

Emily Gaarder, Nancy Rodriguez, and Marjorie S. Zatz (2004). "Criers, Liars, and Manipulators: Probation Officers' Views of Girls." *Justice Quarterly*, 21: 547–578. Used by permission of Taylor & Francis.

John P. Crank

John P. Crank. 1996. "Construction of Meaning during Training for Probation and Parole." *Justice Quarterly*, 13: 265–290. Used by permission of Taylor & Francis.

Thomas J. Schmid and Richard S. Jones

Thomas J. Schmid and Richard S. Jones. 1992. "Ambivalent Actions: Prison Adaptation Strategies of First-Time, Short-Term Inmates." *Journal of Contemporary Ethnography*, 21: 439–461. Used by permission of Sage Publications.

Mary West-Smith, Mark R. Pogrebin, and Eric D. Poole

Mary West-Smith, Mark R. Pogrebin, and Eric D. Poole. 2000. "Denial of Parole: An Inmate Perspective." *Federal Probation*, 64: 3–10.

Richard Tewksbury

Richard Tewksbury. 2010. "How Registered Sex Offenders View Registries." Original contribution to book.

Johnna Christian

Johnna Christian. 2005. "Riding the Bus: Barriers to Prison Victimization and Family Management Strategies." *Journal of Contemporary Criminal Justice*, 21: 31–48. Used by permission of Sage Publications.

Zoann K. Snyder
Zoann K. Snyder. 2009. "Keeping Families Together: The Importance of Maintaining Mother–Child Contact for Incarcerated Women." *Women and Criminal Justice*, 19: 37–59. Used by permission of Taylor & Francis.

Index